The Civil War Veterans of San Diego California

Including Citations to
Genealogical Research Sources in
San Diego, California

Barbara Palmer, Ph.D.

HERITAGE BOOKS
2006

HERITAGE BOOKS
AN IMPRINT OF HERITAGE BOOKS, INC.

Books, CDs, and more—Worldwide

For our listing of thousands of titles see our website
at
www.HeritageBooks.com

Published 2006 by
HERITAGE BOOKS, INC.
Publishing Division
65 East Main Street
Westminster, Maryland 21157-5026

Copyright © 1998 Barbara Palmer, Ph.D.

Other books by the author:
Family History Research in San Diego, California

All rights reserved. No part of this book may be reproduced or transmitted in any form or by any means, electronic or mechanical, including photocopying, recording or by any information storage and retrieval system without written permission from the author, except for the inclusion of brief quotations in a review.

International Standard Book Number: 978-0-7884-3580-9

"Now is the Stately Column Broke;

The Beacon Light is Quenched in Smoke;

The Trumpets' Silver Sound is Still;

The Warder Silent on the Hill."

                        Sir Walter Scott
                        From "Marmion"

THE PAST MEETS THE PRESENT
A. E. Vest, 91, commander of Datus E. Coon post, G. A. R., displays a photograph of himself at the age of 18 taken shortly before his hat was shot off in battle. He served in the Civil war with Co. F., 57th Indiana infantry, for four years and 10 days.

Table of Contents

Table of Contents / v

Acknowledgements / ix

Introduction / xi

Chapter One: California and San Diego in the Civil War

    California in the Civil War / 1

    San Diego in the Civil War / 2

    Outline of Chapters / 6

Chapter Two: Research Design and Sources

    Purpose of the Research / 7

    Research Design/G.A.R. Records / 7

    The Cemeteries Studied / 8

        Presidio Hill Cemetery / 8
        El Campo Santo (Old Town) / 9
        Old Town Cemeteries No Longer in Existence / 9
        Calvary Cemetery (Mission Hills Cemetery) / 10
        Mount Hope Cemetery / 12
        Cypress View Mausoleum / 15
        Greenwood Memorial Park and Mortuary / 16
        Holy Cross Catholic Cemetery and Mausoleum / 18
        Home of Peace Cemetery / 18
        Fort Rosecrans National Cemetery / 19
        Los Angeles National Cemetery--Sawtelle / 20

    Other Cemeteries In or Near San Diego / 22

        Glen Abbey Cemetery, Bonita, CA / 22
        La Vista Memorial Park, National City, CA / 22
        El Cajon Cemetery, El Cajon, CA / 22
        El Camino Memorial Park and Mortuary, San Diego, CA / 23

Additional Research Sources / 23

    San Diego Historical Society / 23
    San Diego Public Library / 24
    San Diego Family History Center / 25
    San Diego County Historian / 26
    San Diego Genealogical Society / 26
    San Diego County / 27
    National Archives / 28
    Congress of History of San Diego / 28
    San Diego County Law Library / 28
    Carlsbad Library / 29
    Genealogy Upcoming Events/Classes/Opportunities / 29

Specific Genealogical Records Available in San Diego / 29

    Military Records / 29
    Death Records / 33
    Probate Records/Wills / 34
    Coroner/Mortuary Records / 35
    Cemetery Records / 36
    Census Records / 38
    Biographical and Vertical Files / 39
    Pedigree Charts / 39
    City/County/General Histories / 39
    Photos / 41
    City Directories / 41
    Newspapers / 42
    Oral History Interviews / 43
    Voter Registers / 43
    Property Records / 44
    Tax Records / 45
    Marriage Records / 46
    Birth Records / 47
    Divorce Records / 47
    Civil/Criminal Records / 47
    Church Records / 48
    Naturalization Records / 50
    Maps / 50
    Historical Site Board Records / 50
    State of California Vital Records / 52

Chapter Three: General Findings

        Numbers / 53
        Nativity/Enlistment of Native Born Veterans / 53
        Nativity/Enlistment of Foreign Born Veterans / 54
        Union/Confederate Affiliation / 55
        Date of Arrival in San Diego / 56
        Proportion of San Diego Population / 56
        Race / 57
        Marital Status / 58
        Year/Age of Death of Wives / 59
        Occupation of Veterans / 61
        G.A.R. Membership / 63
        The Encampment / 67
        Prominence / 69
        Building the City/San Diego Soldiers' Home / 70
        The Die-Off / 78
        Age at Death / 80
        Burial / 81
        The Mortar / 82

Chapter Four: Civil War Veterans Buried in San Diego / 83

Chapter Five: Civil War Veterans With Burial Locations Unknown / 197

Chapter Six: State of First Enlistment of Civil War Veterans / 265

Chapter Seven: Source Notes / 305

Chapter Eight: Index of Civil War Veterans and Their Wives / 313

ACKNOWLEDGEMENTS

I wish to gratefully acknowledge the help of Marianne Fitzgerald, Eleanor Peterson, Mary Rigdon, Anne Ogden Beinert, Charlie Johnson, Karna Webster, Michael S. Evans, Vanessa Evans, Joan Campbell, Dave Jackson, Dr. Ray Brandes, and Rick Crawford and Sally West of the San Diego Historical Society for all of their help and guidance.

For valuable additional help, I wish to thank Emily Palmer Jenkins, Bertha Palmer Wohlers, Paula-Jo Cahoon, Helen Halmay, Karen O'Connor, Jonathan and Mary Parker, Carol Kiva Petty, Wayne Chilstrom, Tony Alexander, Bob Rynerson, Michael Kaye and Pat Lopez of the San Diego County Law Library, Judith Bond of the Hotel del Coronado, and Jane Selvar and staff of the California Room and Newspaper Room of the San Diego Public Library.

I also wish to acknowledge the following sources for their assistance: John Montoya, Ray Snider, Mario Sierra, Karen Baker, Sue Shackelton, Katina Turgeon, Linda Trejo, Maria Castillo, Jackie Beavers, Norman Ferguson, and Eddie Nolan of Mount Hope Cemetery, Shawn Aylesworth and Myrna Flores of Greenwood Cemetery, Dean A. White and John L. Sullivan of Cypress View Mausoleum, Mario De Blasio of Holy Cross Cemetery, and Cynthia DF. Nunez and Delia Fernandez of Fort Rosecrans National Cemetery.

Also, Ed Scott, Laurie Bissell, Elizabeth MacPhail, John Rojas and the Chula Vista Historical Society, Judy A. Deeter, Stuart McConnell and Vickie Wells of University of North Carolina Press, Jerry Thompson and George Ward of Texas State Historical Association, Gina Lubrano of San Diego Union-Tribune, Russell Stockwell and Eldonna P. Lay of El Cajon Historical Society, and Patti Rebello and staff of Master Productions Printing and Graphics.

Finally, I would like to acknowledge all San Diego historians and genealogists who have toiled to keep the field alive, but particularly Penny Feike, the late Lois Meier, Joan Lowrey, Kathleen Lund, June Hanson, Jackie Bohan, Diana Sampsel, Mary Russell, Ellie Naliboff, members of BIGRA, Ray Brookhart, Doris Greeson, Bob Holland, Tom Adema, Alex Bevil, Jim and Kathleen Kelly-Markam, the late Mary Ward, Charlie Best and Helen Halmay of the Congress of History, members of Save Our Heritage Organization (SOHO), and archeologists Therese Adams Muranaka and Jack Williams.

Also Ergo Majors, a descendant of a founder of the Pony Express, Betty Mary Majors, Gretchen Majors Hills, Phil Rader, Sarah Rader, Rebecca Rader, fellow members of Linares Chapter D.A.R. and Colonial Dames XVIIth Century, the patient and kind workers at the San Diego Family History Center, members of San Diego Genealogical Society, North County Genealogical Society, and other genealogical groups in San Diego, my cousins Doris Palmer Buys and Elmer Hall Palmer, and the inspiring people of Self Realization Fellowship.

Also to be acknowledged are individuals or organizations who provided images for this book. Permission to use map images came from the following sources: Mount Hope Cemetery and Calvary Cemetery, Ray Snider, Cemetery Manager; Greenwood Cemetery, Shawn Aylesworth, General Manager; Cypress View Mausoleum (two maps), Dean A. White, General Manager; Holy Cross Cemetery, Mario DiBasio, Cemetery Manager; Fort Rosecrans Cemetery, Cynthia Nunez, Director; and Los Angeles National Cemetery/Sawtelle, from the cemetery staff.

Thanks also to Rick Crawford, archivist of the San Diego Historical Society Research Archives, for permission to publish the following: image of Arthur Vest (p. iv) from the Biographical Files; image of Datus Coon (p. 65) from G.A.R. letterhead in the Datus Coon Post G.A.R. records, MS 365; images of Matthew and Augusta Sherman (p. 65) and of Alonzo Horton, William Wallace Bowers and Lucy Horton Bowers and the Hotel Florence (p. 71) from the Biographical Files; and images of the Henry Bentzel family from *San Diego County Pioneer Families*, a publication of the San Diego Historical Society. Permission was also granted by Rick Crawford to quote excerpts from his publication *A Guide to the San Diego Historical Society Public Records Collection* and intake information from the Heintzelman Post and Datus Coon Post of the G.A.R. files, MSS 365.

Images of Amaziah Knox and Illa Birdseye Knox (p. 60) are used with the permission of Russell Stockwell and Eldonna P. Lay of the El Cajon Historical Society.

Heintzelman Post and Datus Coon Post G.A.R. advertisements from city directories (p. 65), image of the Hotel del Coronado (p. 74) from the "Hotel del Coronado" vertical file, and map of "Campus and Soldier's Home" (p. 77) from "Back to the Boom-Bust 1880's," *Navajo News*, April 18, 1994, p. 9 from the "Grantville" vertical file, are all used courtesy of the San Diego Public Library.

Image of Elisha Babcock (p. 74) is from William Smythe's *History of San Diego*, (San Diego: The History Company, 1908).

Image of Hampton Story (p. 74) is from *The Golden Era*, Vol. XXXIV, No. 9, (October, 1890).

Image of Col. H. H. Holabird (p. 77) is from *The City and County of San Diego, Illustrated*, published by Leberthon and Taylor in 1888.

Permission to quote excerpts from various publications was also granted for use of the following: Dr. Ray Brandes, for excerpts from *Coronado: The Enchanted Island*; Judy Deeter, for an excerpt from *Veterans Who Applied For Land in Southern California*; Gina Lubrano, for permission to quote articles or obituaries from the *San Diego Union-Tribune*; George Ward, for an excerpt from *Fifty Miles and a Fight: Major Samuel Peter Heintzelman's Journal of Texas & the Cortina War*; and Vickie Wells of the University of North Carolina Press, for permission to quote several passages from Stuart McConnell's book *Glorious Contentment: The Grand Army of the Republic, 1865-1900*.

INTRODUCTION

It is a great honor to provide information about Civil War Veterans who came to the City of San Diego. The Civil War was a war fought at close quarters--a deadly, bloody war in which many were lost forever in battle. Others were separated from their families by time and distance, having moved "West" to seek their fortunes. It is my hope that those who undertook the westward journey may be found again within the confines of this book.

This study is of obvious importance for the genealogical information it transmits. It will help San Diegans identify their ancestors, and persons "back East" to find long lost relatives. Some individuals with an interest in joining patriotic groups might be aided by tracing back through their San Diego Civil War ancestors. This book will help others to break through to ancestors from Colonial times.

Above and beyond genealogy, this is an important study because no one has yet done a study of this depth on individual Civil War Veterans in a particular location. It is of importance from a military standpoint because service records of the veterans are included. It is of importance to students of migration because the veterans took part in the vast westward migration of people from 1840 on. It is also important to local history because of low population levels in San Diego from 1860 to 1900. The Civil War veterans of this study were a vital part of the population base, and contributed to city growth and development. One, in fact, became mayor of San Diego for a short time.

That they came to San Diego and stayed is the story here, but the bigger story is that they came in such numbers. This study includes nearly 2,000 veterans who eventually settled in San Diego, and burial records were obtained for nearly half of them. The odd thing about the veterans was that they were virtually ignored by local historians. One wonders why such a large group was neglected, especially when many of the veterans had served full enlistments, and participated in some of the most famous battles of the war. It is probably because of this treatment that the veterans banded together into affinity groups when they arrived in San Diego, and did so in large numbers.

In *Glorious Contentment: The Grand Army of the Republic, 1865-1900*, Stuart McConnell described veterans returning from the Civil War. The Grand Review was taking place in Washington, where:

> "...in the American experience up to 1865, nothing like the Grand Review had been seen. The sheer size of the armies involved was new, as was their concentration in a single city."[1] ..."The massing for parade of all the troops in service at the end of a war was unprecedented, and it gave the spectators at Washington some sense of the size of the force about which they had been reading in the newspapers for four years."[2]

> "An Associated Press reporter thought the mass of uniformed men presented 'a grand appearance.... Looking up the broad Pennsylvania avenue, there was continuous moving line as far as the eye could reach of National, State, division, brigade, regiment and other flags.'"[3] "All observers routinely complimented the uniform appearance and marching style of the troops. The unprecedented spectacle of thousands of soldiers from all parts of the country--or, to be more precise, all parts of the North--marching as one well-oiled machine was breathtaking. It was more than a collection of local militias; it was, as more than one newspaper put it, 'the grand national pageant.' The Grand Review was the visual embodiment of a reunified nation."[4]

Then the soldiers went home, or migrated to where the sight and smell of war and its desolation were not constant reminders of what they had been through.

"In smaller and more distant cities, the soldiers were welcomed back with even less fanfare."[5] ... "Instead, the townspeople--many of whom, in such unsettled territory, were strangers to the returning veterans--watched the discharged soldiers slip back into town in ones and twos. They were, the [Eau Claire, Wisconsin] *Free Press* editor said, 'quiet, unobtrusive men.... They are, 'tis true, stern looking men, and pass along our streets, with a gloomy melancholy, particularly the disciplined soldiers, claiming no immunity, asking no applause, and seemingly unconscious of the great service they have rendered.'"[6]

Some of the Civil War Veterans of San Diego took part in the Grand Review. Then they migrated here. They came to this city in large numbers, and contributed to it in ways that were sometimes unseen, but contributed to it nonetheless. They helped build the city. They helped feed and clothe the population. They ministered to the people. They were attorneys and doctors and ordinary men who had lived through a ghastly and yet historic time. They need to be remembered. They are remembered here.

CHAPTER ONE: CALIFORNIA AND SAN DIEGO IN THE CIVIL WAR

CALIFORNIA IN THE CIVIL WAR
"When the last gun was fired at Fort Sumpter, S.C., April 13, 1861, two-thirds of the United States Army was garrisoning the frontier posts scattered over the country west of the Mississippi River. One-fourth [of the force] was on the Pacific slope...."[1]

"Southern California was an open powder keg. All that was needed was an able leader to ignite the fuse which would rend the state asunder and bring the Civil War to the Pacific coast. There were many Southerners and their sympathizers in California, especially in Southern California, in the San Joaquin Valley, and in the mining camps of California and Nevada. A number of officers of the army who were Southerners resigned their commissions to join the Confederate Army.... Los Angeles, San Bernardino, El Monte and Visalia were hotbeds of succession rumors, and loyal Unionists appealed to the military authorities for help. They feared an open outbreak within the state and invasion from Lower California."[2]

Help came in the form of Brigadier General Edwin V. Sumner. "Operating under confidential orders of the War Department, General ... Sumner ... arrived at San Francisco on April 24, 1861, and assumed command of the Department of the Pacific, relieving Brevet Brigadier General Albert S. Johnston ... [who] resigned his commission"[3], fled across Southern California, joined the Confederacy with the rank of General, and was subsequently killed while in command at the battle of Shiloh.

General Sumner's first act "...was to order the regular Army garrisons in Oregon and Washington Territory moved to San Francisco; the troops at Fort Mojave, on the Colorado River, to New San Diego and those at Fort Tejon to Los Angeles. Two companies were at Fort Yuma, and one at San Diego." [4]

"During the Civil War, the state of California supporting the Union cause, 'is credited with having furnished 15,725 volunteers' [which] represented a composition of two regiments of cavalry, a battalion of native cavalry, eight regiments of infantry, one battalion of veteran infantry, and the First Battalion of Mountaineers."[5] "... these units were recruited and organized in the northern part of the state, around the Bay region and the mining camps. During the four years of the war close to seventeen thousand joined one or another branch of the service; all volunteered, there was no draft. However, very few recruits were obtained from the southern part of the state. The volunteers replaced the regular troops, nearly all of whom were transferred to the eastern theater before the year 1861 ended."[6]

"Many young men from California wished to go East and join the Army. Though the War Department would not accept volunteers from the Pacific Coast for fighting in the East, it did not oppose the authorized arrangement by which the state of Massachusetts was able to raise troops in California, take them East, and have them credited to the state's quota. These California troops were the only soldiers from California to engage in major battles of the Civil War, [and] in the two and a half years of hard service in the field, [the California Cavalry Battalion] had participated in over 50 engagements."[7]

"California troops, except for those assigned to Massachusetts, remained on the western frontiers. They fought in no major battles of the war. Rather their military engagements were with small forces of Confederate troops in New Mexico and with Indians throughout the West. Of their many functions, three stand out as being extremely significant: First, to prevent the Confederacy from gaining a foothold in the West; second, to relieve United States regular soldiers stationed in outlying posts on the western frontiers and thus enable them to be returned to the East for military duty; third, to prevent the Indians from their depredations (destroying government property, stealing, raiding, plundering, etc)."[8]

"The records of the regiments of California troops serving outside of California show frequent encounters with Indians in their areas of assignment. Moreover, one battalion, the Mountaineers, was raised in 1863-1864 exclusively for service against the Indians in Humboldt County and in the northwestern portions of California. As one authority has said--the California volunteers in doing their duty 'preserved peace in these western States and Territories, and the flag of rebellion was soon driven beyond the Rio Grande.'"[9] Men in the California volunteer regiments saw service in California, Arizona, New Mexico, Texas, Utah, Nevada, Oregon, and Washington.

"It was a constant source of regret among [the California] troops that they were never ordered East, and the question was continually asked: 'When are we to be ordered to the seat of war?' The Government deemed it wisest to keep them on the Pacific Coast and in the Territories. They occupied nearly all the posts from Puget Sound to San Elizario, Texas, and they did their duty faithfully, notwithstanding their disappointment. By their loyalty, they preserved peace in these western States and Territories...."[10]

In so doing, however, the "... fatalities for California troops were not high in comparison with the total Union casualties. George W. Adams stated that 300,000 Union soldiers lost their lives from 1861-1865. This would approximate a twenty percent loss. Of the total number of troops assigned to duty during the war, from California, seven officers and 494 enlisted men, exclusive of the casualties in the Massachusetts quota, died in the service of the United States ... a fatality figure of less than three and one-half percent."[11]

Fifty veterans included in this study served in California volunteer units, at least one serving in each of the California units active in the Civil War (see Chapter Six for details.) Of those, 21 are buried at Mount Hope Cemetery, seven at Calvary Cemetery, one at Greenwood Cemetery, and one at Fort Rosecrans National Cemetery. Of the remaining veterans, 20 were buried outside of the City of San Diego, or in undetermined burial locations.

SAN DIEGO IN THE CIVIL WAR
San Diego did not have much of a presence in the Civil War. The location prohibited active involvement; military commanders would not allow California men to go East to fight; and there were few people in San Diego at the time of the war (the population of San Diego in 1860 was only 731). Those who lived in San Diego were indigenous Indians, the founding Hispanic families, and a few American families, most of whom lived at "Old Town." There were also soldiers who stayed after participation in the Mexican War, and soldiers who arrived later to guard the population and the Boundary Commission that was to chart the new boundary between Mexico and California.

San Diego's early history spanned four eras: The Kumeyaay/Luiseno Indian Period; the Spanish Mission Period (1769-1820); the Mexican Rancho Period (1820 to 1846); and the American Empire Period (1846-1900). Early explorers touched down in what was to become San Diego, but none stayed for an extended period. When the area later known as "California" was a vast, open space, several countries were interested in conquering it. Spain, having developed a population base in Mexico, considered colonization of "Alta California". A group accompanied by Father Junipero Serra set out in 1769 to do this, and arrived in San Diego the same year.

What they saw when they arrived here was a wonderful natural harbor surrounded by land and by an island later called the "Peninsula," or "Coronado." Among those who arrived with Father Serra were military men who quickly sought the high ground for protection. "From its inception in 1769, San Diego was garrisoned by a military force. When [a] Mission [established on the same high ground] was relocated [to "Mission Valley"] in 1774, the military continued to occupy the former mission site today embraced by Presidio Park...."[12] When the Spanish Mission Period ended, the former solders who had guarded the Presidio began to move down the hill to found Old Town. Then, for the next 50 years or so, settlement in San Diego centered around the Mission in Mission Valley and Old Town. There were also hide and tallow facilities located across the bay from Old Town at "La Playa."

A period of slow population growth occurred after 1821, but growth was internal, not from the outside. The reason was location. San Diego was surrounded on the west by the Pacific Ocean; on the east by an almost impassible mountain range; on the south by Mexico, from which the local population had split; and on the north by Los Angeles and San Francisco. For a long time, San Diego was very isolated and for the most part forgotten.

By the time of the Mexican War, a westward expansion movement was growing in the eastern states. Through the eyes of explorers who traveled here, people in the east saw a land which held great promise. The Mexican War was launched as an expansion scheme, and California, New Mexico, and whatever parts of Mexico that the easterners could capture became the primary targets.

After the fall of California to the Americans and the Treaty of Guadelupe Hildago, the military began to occupy San Diego in some numbers. "Military camps of the United States Army first appeared in Southern California with the advent at San Diego of Brig. Gen. S.W. Kearney's 'Army of the West,' December 12, 1846. The Mormon Battalion, under command of Lt. Col. Philip St. G. Cooke made camp at San Diego Mission January 29, 1847...."[13]

"The Mission San Diego, which had been secularized in 1835 and was badly run down, now became the principal military station. It was not intended that any significant construction be undertaken in San Diego at this time because the army had not decided upon the proper location for permanent fortifications and because of the difficulty and high cost of obtaining building materials in California. The Mission was occupied because it was available and, despite its poor condition, offered some facilities, thus providing an economical answer until other arrangements could be made. It continued to function as a military post until 1858."[14]

Some soldiers who arrived in San Diego after the Mexican War later went back to serve in the Civil War. One such soldier was Major General Samuel P. Heintzelman, U.S. Army. He is of interest because in 1881, Matthew Sherman organized a GAR Post in San Diego which was named after him.

"S.P. Heintzelman, the commanding officer at Mission San Diego and Fort Yuma from 1849-1856, served with the 1st Regiment after leaving Fort Yuma until the [Civil War] began. [He] became a Brigadier-General on May 17, 1861, and commanded a division in the Battle of Bull Run in July. He was wounded in that engagement, before retreating along with the entire Union command under General McDowell."[15]

"The following spring he was given command of 3rd Corps, and promoted to Major-General. [He] was a brave man under fire and a capable field commander, but by some quirk of fate ... was caught in poor position ... during the Peninsular Campaign.... He directed Union units in ... battles from Yorktown to Malvern Hill in 1862. ... [and] spent the last half of the war at a desk."[16] ... "Following the war, he had command of the 17th Regiment in Texas until his retirement in 1869, after forty-three years of dedicated service. Congress made Heintzelman a Major-General by a special act soon after he retired. The old soldier lived in Washington among his old friends until his death in 1880."[17]

Surveyors for the Boundary Commission arrived, and proceeded to lay out the boundary between Mexico and California. "In 1850, William Heath Davis and Andrew B. Gray, surveyor for the Boundary Commission, with their associates, formed a partnership for the purpose of developing a townsite which became known as New San Diego,"[18] an area several miles south of Old Town. "...[T]hey gave land to the government on which a sub-depot for commissary and quartermaster supplies was erected. Almost immediately...the new installation was separated from the command of the Mission. As a sub-depot it was not garrisoned but was the station for a few officers of the quartermaster, commissary and pay departments...[with] no troops nor population."[19]

"The first building was erected on the 'barrack block' in 1850 and later was used for enlisted men's barracks. ... Capt. Nathaniel Lyon, 2nd Infantry, was constructing quartermaster in charge of the erection of the depot buildings. He became celebrated during the Civil War, rising to the rank of brigadier general. ... General Lyon was killed August 10, 1861, at the Battle of Wilson' Creek (Springfield), Missouri [and] for their gallantry and distinguished services at this victory, he and his command received the Thanks of Congress."[20]

"On December 6, 1858, Company G, 6th Infantry, Capt. W.S. Ketchum commanding, moved into New San Diego Depot, which now became a garrisoned post. ... Upon the promotion of Captain Ketchum to major in June, 1860, command of the post devolved upon Brevet Maj. Lewis A. Armistead of Gettysburg fame, who was killed at the head of his brigade on Cemetery Ridge during Pickett's charge."[21] When the Civil War broke out, "...Major Armistead wrote his letter of resignation from the United States Army at New San Diego on May 26, 1861. ... Command of G Company, U.S. 6th Infantry evolved to Lt. Orlando H. Moore, whose Captaincy was dated on the day Armistead resigned."[22]

"A plea went to California in July for volunteers.... After this call Californians responded quickly. Within a matter of weeks California Volunteer Regiments were formed, and as Regulars departed for the war, California Vol[unteers] moved into the vacated posts."[23] Several units of men arrived to man the San Diego Barracks. One unit in particular, during a winter season of heavy rain, took down a wharf that William Heath Davis had constructed and several other New Town buildings for firewood, making New San Diego look like a ghost town.

"When Company G, 4th Cal. Infantry, commanded by Captain Alfred S. Grant, relieved D Company in November of 1862 at New San Diego Barracks, the post presented a desolate picture. There were now five civilian buildings besides a big drab yellow barracks, [and the] ruined wharf.... Grant had a big company totaling 152 men ... [a] fine company of responsible men. ... Captain Alfred S. Grant and his Company executive officer, 1st Lt. Matthew Sherman, spent all of their Civil War service in San Diego County, and returned when the war ended to play leading roles in starting the city of today...."[24]

"Conditions in Old Town remained static during the Civil War. Since there was no newspaper, we have no contemporary picture of public feeling of San Diegans during the war, no reports on the weekly happenings in town, no list of ship arrivals, and no advertisements of business activity. Most San Diegans were staunch Unionists and Republicans, but ... there were some Confederate sympathizers."[25]

"Captain Grant's G Company, 4th California Infantry, soldiered quietly at New Town until August of 1865 when Grant received orders to proceed to La Paz, Arizona Territory. He posted a small detail at the New San Diego Barracks and marched eastward. The Post Returns of Fort Yuma noted the arrival of Grant's Company on 13 August, and its' departure two days later. The report stated Company G was headed for Fort Rock, but official records reveal the company went to La Paz, where martial law was needed."[26]

"In June of 1866, after all stores and gear were shipped out, the guard detail from Company G, 4th California Volunteer Infantry, locked the big faded yellow barracks and departed. New San Diego was totally deserted, prey to pilfering Gringos, animals, birds and 'ould Injuns', which the soldiers called the older Indians who slept in the vacant houses. There were four houses, the Quartermasters house nearby built by General Lyon, the big barracks, some naked wharf pilings, bush-covered, gullied streets, and nothing more."[27]

"New San Diego subdivision remained deserted only eleven months after the guard detail of Company G, 4th California Infantry, vacated the barracks in June, 1866. In May, 1867, Captain Matthew Sherman, and his bride, Old Town's young schoolmarm, lovely Augusta Jane Barrett, moved into either the big barracks building or the nearby cottage built by Captain Nathaniel Lyon in 1851. ... [Sherman] left the volunteer Army in 1865 with the rank of Captain and returned to San Diego as a deputy Customs Collector in the (southern) San Francisco district. As a government official, he had his office at the New San Diego Army installation. Lyon's house was considered a part of the barracks, so the Shermans would have lived there rather than the big barracks itself."[28]

"On May 10, 1867, the date of the Sherman wedding in Old Town, a newcomer named Alonzo E. Horton bought 960 acres of pueblo land from the San Diego Board of Trustees for $265,"[29] and the development of New Town began in earnest. "Horton's Addition was not [the former] New San Diego, but people started calling it New Town in 1868, and the name stuck."[30]

"The tract Horton purchased covered the area east of New San Diego and Middletown subdivisions from [the] Front Street of today east to 15th Street, from the bay northward to Upas, excluding an area from A to Upas between 6th and 15th. A number of old-timer tales of Horton have been told and retold again and again, until several myths are called fact. In 1867, San Diego's pueblo lands totaled over forty-eight thousand virgin acres, available to land developers like a huge melon in a sunny field. Alonzo E. Horton received the juiciest slice from the heart of the melon by reaching San Diego ahead of the post Civil War land developers."[31]

Thus was San Diego in the Civil War. For more information on the growth and development of San Diego through the early periods down to 1900, there is a series of books by Richard F. Pourade that discuss the various stages of growth of San Diego which are available at the San Diego Public Library and many of its branches. [See in particular *The Glory Years: The booms and busts in the Land of the Sundown Sea* (San Diego: Union-Tribune Publishing Company, 1966) for a description of San Diego from 1865-1900.]

For a wonderful explanation of the military presence in San Diego from the time of the start of the American Period to about 1870, read Ed Scott's *San Diego County Soldier-Pioneers 1846-1866*, available at the San Diego Public Library, San Diego Historical Society and Family History Center. For a description of the San Diego Barracks in 1852, see Robert W. Frazer's "Military Posts in San Diego" in *The Journal of San Diego History* XX (July, 1974), 44-52. For a description of the New Town Barracks, a map showing their location and buildings therein, and the people who manned them, see "San Diego Barracks" by Col. George Ruhlen in *The Journal of San Diego History* XIII (April, 1967), 7-15.

For the development of New Town from the time of Andrew Gray through the Alonzo E. Horton years, read Elizabeth MacPhail's highly detailed and interesting book, *The Story of Early San Diego and of its Founder Alonzo E. Horton*, available at the San Diego Historical Society and San Diego Public Library. For a description of the development of Coronado Island and Hotel del Coronado by Elisha S. Babcock and Hampton L. Story, with promotional efforts on their behalf taken by Robert J. Pennell and W.H. Holabird, all Civil War veterans featured herein, see *Coronado: The Enchanted Island*, co-authored by Dr. Ray Brandes and Katherine Eitzen Carlin.

===

Who, then, are the Civil War veterans of this study? None of them, save Captain Matthew Sherman and possibly a few others who may have come to San Diego as part of a California Civil War unit, took part in the activities discussed above. All of the veterans of this study migrated to San Diego from somewhere else. They had certain characteristics which will be discussed more fully in Chapter Three. But their most outstanding characteristic was that all but one (James J. Chard) were survivors of the war. They may have been wounded in battle. They may have been in prison camps, may have seen some cruel fighting and the slaughter of their friends. But they had made it through the war, and were now poised to go on with their lives. Some trickled into San Diego immediately after the war. But then they came in a flood, and contributed to the city.

OUTLINE OF CHAPTERS
The following is an outline of what will appear in the chapters and lists of the remaining book:

CHAPTER TWO--Research Design and Sources
Chapter Two discusses the purpose of the study, the research design, and an explanation of how to conduct further research at local cemeteries. The cemeteries studied included Mount Hope, Greenwood, Calvary, Fort Rosecrans, and Holy Cross, plus Cypress View Mausoleum and the Los Angeles National Cemetery (Sawtelle). Other cemeteries are mentioned in passing, and an extensive list of research sources is discussed. Maps and photos of the cemeteries are included at the end of this chapter.

CHAPTER THREE--General Findings
In Chapter Three, the Civil War veterans are described in a general way. Charts depict certain broad findings such as state or country of birth, state of first enlistment, Union/Confederate affiliation, time of arrival in San Diego, race, marital status, occupations, Grand Army of the Republic (G.A.R.) memberships, the Coronado Encampment of 1890, the prominence of the veterans, their year and age of death, and their burial patterns. There is also burial information about wives of the veterans, where available. Images of some of the Civil War veterans and their wives are included at the end of this chapter.

CHAPTER FOUR--Civil War Veterans Buried in San Diego
Chapter Four features "List 1"--burial information about veterans who were buried within the city limits of San Diego. Information obtained about individual veterans includes government and family tombstone inscriptions, death and burial dates, burial location within a cemetery, a G.A.R. record, where available, and burial information about their wives, if available. Most of the wives included in this study are on List 1; the few who appear on List 2 are generally those named in an individual veteran's obituary, or those who were found on brief visits to three cemeteries in communities near San Diego.

CHAPTER FIVE--Civil War Veterans With Burial Locations Unknown
Chapter Five features "List 2"--G.A.R. records for those veterans for whom no death or burial information was available. The records come from two sources: Heintzelman Post #33, and Datus E. Coon Post #172. These records are described more fully in Chapter Two, "Research Design and Sources." At times, a G.A.R. record noted the veteran was buried at "Soldier's Home," and burial information from Sawtelle Soldier's Home in Los Angeles is presented for veterans who were buried there. Additionally, citations to a few burials at La Vista Cemetery in National City, CA, two burials at Glen Abbey Cemetery in Bonita, CA, and one at El Cajon Cemetery in El Cajon, CA (communities south and east of San Diego) are also included.

CHAPTER SIX--State of Enlistment of Civil War Veterans
Chapter Six features the state of enlistment of the veterans, and an alphabetical list of all veterans who served from each state. Grouping the veterans by state allows one to discover possible family relationships, and to determine who the veteran fought with during the war. Some veterans enlisted from more than one state. Look at the full record for the veteran in Chapter Four or Chapter Five to determine which states these veterans served from, and then consult Chapter Six for more details.

CHAPTER SEVEN--Source Notes
Chapter Seven contains citations to sources in the first three chapters of the book.

CHAPTER EIGHT--Index
Chapter Eight contains an alphabetical index of the veterans and wives included in Chapters Four and Five, plus their state or country of nativity and state of first enlistment, where available, so that individual migration patterns can be seen.

CHAPTER TWO: RESEARCH DESIGN AND SOURCES

PURPOSE OF THE RESEARCH
The purpose of the study was to identify Civil War veterans who migrated to the City of San Diego and who lived and died here. The task seemed an easy one; low numbers were expected. To the contrary, the research seemed to build and grow until nearly 2,000 veterans were identified. This number is very surprising considering an initial assumption that San Diego was so far west that few veterans would have traveled here.

RESEARCH DESIGN
The best way to start the research seemed to be to visit older cemeteries in San Diego to see whether tombstone inscriptions might reveal individuals with a Civil War presence. Walk-throughs were thus conducted of the earlier sections of five cemeteries: Mount Hope, Greenwood, Calvary (also known as Mission Hills or Pioneer Cemetery), Holy Cross, and the old Post Section of Fort Rosecrans National Cemetery. Tombstone inscriptions were transcribed for all Civil War veteran burials. At the end of this chapter is a map showing the location of the cemeteries visited, individual maps for all of the cemeteries, and some cemetery photos. Each cemetery had its own best methods for research, and these will be discussed below. Information about several additional cemeteries will be mentioned in passing to make the discussion of the cemeteries of San Diego complete.

About a month after starting the cemetery walk-throughs, Grand Army of the Republic (G.A.R.) post rosters were located at the San Diego Historical Society. The Heintzelman Post had two rosters in oversize ledger books, with some overlap of names between the first and second roster. The rosters were not in alphabetical order; names were entered into the rosters by the date a veteran joined the Post. All names from the Heintzelman Post rosters were entered onto a computer along with the page number that each individual name appeared on. The names were sorted alphabetically, duplicate names were removed, and a list of all who were members of this Post was thus created. Later, information for each veteran listed on these rosters was also entered into the computer.

The roster for the Datus Coon Post was in a large ledger book, with post members listed in alphabetical order. This record was transcribed, and entered into the computer.

Both Heintzelman and Datus Coon rosters were then combined, and an alphabetical "Master List of G.A.R. Members" was created. This list was compared to the list that was being developed from the cemetary walk-throughs, and after several months of sorting and comparing, a "Master List of Civil War Veterans in San Diego" was created.

Not knowing where some of the veterans on the "Master List" were buried, a search of the records in the card file at Mount Hope Cemetery was conducted, for this was the cemetery where many of the veterans of this study were buried. An additional number of veterans were found to have been buried at Mount Hope. A further walk-through of Mount Hope was conducted to transcribe tombstone inscriptions for these veterans, where such stones existed.

Records of Calvary Cemetery were researched via the R. Clinton Griffin Collection (see below). Records of Greenwood and Holy Cross Cemeteries were not open to the public, but staff at both facilities provided date of death and burial information for veterans who were found buried there from the cemetery walk-throughs. Records at Fort Rosecrans could be searched on a computer located in a kiosk outside the cemetery office, and tombstone inscriptions were also noted for the small number of veterans found at this cemetery. A site survey was not done at Cypress View Mausoleum as the G.A.R. rosters indicated only two veterans were buried there. Dates of death were obtained for these veterans from the staff at this facility.

Researchers interested in locating possible burials for veterans listed in Chapter Five should contact these cemeteries for additional information because many of the veterans in Chapter Five may indeed be buried in San Diego. Addresses, phone numbers, and hours of operation for all cemeteries featured in this study are provided below.

When the above research was completed, the "Master List of Civil War Veterans" was split into the two major lists of this study: **List 1:** Veterans for whom burial information was available, featured in Chapter Four; and **List 2:** Veterans with burial location unknown, featured in Chapter Five.

The study led to the assembling of a list of San Diego Civil War veterans who were buried at Los Angeles National Cemetery. Formerly known as the "Sawtelle Soldier's Home", this cemetery is located near the UCLA campus in Los Angeles. The Sawtelle list was given to Dave Jackson of Sherman Oaks to research. My personal thanks go out to Dave for the excellent work he did of transcribing date of death and burial information for San Diego Civil War veterans buried at Sawtelle, and for sending me citations to newspaper or journal articles about this facility which are discussed later in this chapter.

The study took shape using the above resources. There are other sources which can be accessed if one wants to do more in-depth research on an individual veteran. These are discussed below under the headings "Additional Research Sources" and "Specific Genealogical Records Available in San Diego."

THE CEMETERIES STUDIED

In discussing the cemeteries of San Diego (and the Sawtelle Soldier's Home in Los Angeles), I relied on and am very grateful for several excellent research sources, particularly the following: an article in *The Journal of San Diego History* by Laurie Bissell (published in the fall of 1982); the R. Clinton Griffin Collection of Catholic burial records at the San Diego Historical Society, a manuscript on the cemeteries of San Diego by Fred Jay Rimbach (located at the California Room of the San Diego Public Library), newspaper articles, and other sources which will be cited below.

Presidio Hill Cemetery

Laurie Bissell writes: "Of the three hundred men who set out to colonize Upper California in 1769...as well as to found San Diego...more than one-third died, mainly of scurvy and dysentery. ... On July 1, 1769, soon after the arrival of [Father Junipero] Serra, burials began in consecrated ground on Presidio Hill. ... Even though people [later] began moving off Presidio Hill and settled in Old Town, burials still took place within the Presidio walls. These burials included early settlers as well as Mission Indians. The last recorded burial in this location was Henry Delano Fitch who died in 1849, the same year as the first burial at El Campo Santo in Old Town. ... Although it was no longer used by Europeans, the Indians continued burying their dead on Presidio Hill through the 1870s."[1]

This cemetery includes well known San Diego historical figures. "Jose R. Carrillo and Jose Maria Estudillo were buried on Presidio Hill; Carrillo on November 10, 1809 and Estudillo on April 9, 1830. Henry D. Fitch, born May 7, 1799, died January 13, 1849 at 4:00 o'clock and 20 minutes in the afternoon [and] was buried on Presidio Hill.

Sylvester Patti, pathfinder, leader of the first party of Americans into Alta California over the Southern trails, arrived at San Diego Presidio [on] March 27, 1828. [He] ...died near the present Serra Museum on Presidio Hill, April 24, 1828. He was the first American buried in California soil."[2]

Others were buried here: Henry Fitch's younger daughter, Natalia Fitch; Fitch's associate Joseph Francis Snook, Jose Arroyo, and several young children. There is an excellent article by the late Dr. Paul Ezell entitled "The Excavation Program at the San Diego Presidio", *The Journal of San Diego History* XXII (Fall 1976), which discusses the excavation of the Fitch and other graves. The article contains citations to additional journal articles on this subject.

As the last European burial at the Presidio was the Fitch burial in 1849, as far as can be determined, no Civil War veterans are buried at this cemetery.

El Campo Santo (Old Town)
When the Presidio settlers moved off the hill to found Old Town, El Campo Santo, the second oldest cemetery in San Diego, was created. Burials here dated "...back to 1849 with the burial of Juan Adams. Burials continued through 1880, consisting of early San Diegans from varied backgrounds,"[3] and included members of the Bandini, Osuna, Pedrorena, Estudillo and Aguirre families.

Burials at El Campo Santo were documented by Lawrence Riveroll and Orion M. Zink (see "Cemetery Records", p. 34) for more information on these two sources. The R. Clinton Griffin Collection contains indexed records for burials at El Campo Santo from 1849-1880 (see p. 11 for more information on this collection). As far as can be determined, no Civil War veterans were buried at El Campo Santo.

Old Town Cemeteries No Longer in Existence
According to John H. Sneed, compiler of burial records of Johnson-Saum and Knobel mortuary for the San Diego Genealogical Society (see "Death Records", p. 33), there was a Protestant Cemetery in or near Old Town, as well as an Odd Fellows and Masonic Cemetery.

The earliest burial entries in the Johnson-Saum and Knobel records contain citations to several individuals who were buried at Protestent Cemetery, including a "U.S. Soldier" who died February 11, 1870 (p. 2), and Capt. George A. Pendleton, an early resident and leader of Old Town, who died March 5, 1871 (p. 3). The final burial at Protestent Cemetery appears to be Henrietta Huick (p. 16), who died in 1876.[4] There are also burial entries in the Johnson-Saum and Knobel records to burials at the "Odd Fellows" and "Masonic" Cemeteries at Old Town.

Regarding Protestent Cemetery, Laurie Bissell writes that "Alcalde Joshua H. Bean deeded land to Adolphis Savin on February 18, 1850. Savin sold it to Juan Bandini and William Heath Davis a month later. Soon after, San Diego Protestants began to bury their dead there. As San Diego's population moved away from Old Town, relatives of those buried on this land in 'Protestant Cemetery' began to transfer their dead to other cemeteries."[5]

At least four burials were documented there by Laurie Bissell: Tommie Whaley (infant son of Thomas Whaley of Old Town), Jack Hinton, Frank Ames, and Francis Steele, all of whom were reinterred at Mount Hope Cemetery. The Johnson-Saum and Knobel burial records, however, list more names of people who are interred at Protestent Cemetery.

The location of Protestent Cemetery was acquired by the state of California to build Interstate 5, and the site is now buried under a freeway. (See p. 51 for more on the Historical Site Board and the records from this agency.)

Because the Protestent, Odd Fellows and Masonic Cemeteries of Old Town no longer exist, it would be difficult to prove that a Civil War veteran was buried in any of them. Additionally, regarding the Odd Fellows and Masonic Cemeteries in Old Town, listings in the Johnson-Saum records and Knobel do not distinguish the Old Town burials from later burials in the Odd Fellows (IOOF) and Masonic sections of Mount Hope Cemetery. Also, and it is uncertain whether anyone knows where the Odd Fellows and Masonic Cemeteries of Old Town were located.

Please note, however, that Civil War veterans are named in the Johnson-Saum and Knobel burial records. This information will be included for those veterans in Chapter Four where such information is available. The information will be flagged by a "J/S" symbol, indicating a Johnson-Saum and Knobel citation.

Calvary Cemetery (Mission Hills Cemetery)
Laurie Bissell writes: "In 1870, the City of San Diego set aside ten acres of land, bought from Joseph Mannasse, for a cemetery. Half of the cemetery would be for Protestant burials, the other half for Catholics. The Protestants never used their plot. The Catholic section, said to have been laid out by Father Antonio Ubach, became known as 'Calvary Cemetery.' Many early San Diegans such as the Bandinis and Couts, the Ames, and Father Ubach were amongst the 1,650 buried at Calvary."[6] The count of those buried there varies from 1,600 to 2,000, and many have Irish, Italian and Hispanic surnames.

"The period of greatest activity at this cemetery was 1880-1920. After that, usage fell off sharply. By the 1940s, the only people being buried there were relatives of those already interred at Calvary."[7] Another factor in the abandoment of Calvary as a burying ground was the establishment of Holy Cross Cemetery. "With the opening of 'Holy Cross' a new Catholic cemetery in 1919, Calvary fell to disuse. Burials continued through 1960, but were rare. The Catholic Parish of the Immaculate Conception continued to maintain Calvary through 1939, when the City took on the responsibilitiy to provide employment under the W.P.A. Just before the City took over, a fire in the caretaker's shack, located on Calvary grounds, destroyed all the burial records except one book which dated back to 1899. Unmarked graves lost their identity."[8]

Calvary Cemetery has an interesting history. If you go there today, you will see a park. The cemetery was only a little over a half century old when it started falling into ruin. Albert V. Mayrhofer worked to restore the cemetery using funds from the W.P.A. to build an adobe wall around it. However, vandals kept pushing over tombstones, and the cemetery was a community eyesore. Several groups tried to clean it up, but the vandalism and destruction continued.

In September, 1968, the City Council authorized an architectural firm to convert the cemetery into a passive recreation park. Conversions such as this could be carried out under a state law which provided that abandoned cemeteries could be turned into pioneer memorial parks with a single central memorial. Plans for the cemetery indicated that the area surrounding the central memorial would be landscaped.

During early 1970, the cemetery conversion to passive recreation park took place. "Persons having valid claims to headstones [and supposedly to those interred at the cemetery could] remove them. ... This was done in some cases; however, so many buried there were the last of their line or relatives [had] moved elsewhere, that a majority of the bodies are still there. The graves [were] sodded over after a record [was] made of [the exact whereabouts of the bodies]."[9]

Over 300 unclaimed tombstones were taken from Calvary Cemetery to Mount Hope Cemetery, and subsequently buried there after discussions occurred about what to do with them. Suggestions included dumping them at sea or removing them to another location, but the stones were judged to be too heavy to move, and too many man hours would be required to do the work. A few Calvary tombstones remain above ground at Mount Hope as a memorial, but they are in an isolated, undeveloped area near the San Diego trolley tracks, and it is not safe to view them.

Tombstones which remained at Calvary were relocated to an area at the southeast corner of the cemetery next to Grant Elementary School. It is here that we find most of the tombstones of Civil War veterans buried at Calvary, for tombstones of historic value were preserved prior to the cemetery's conversion into the park. There is also a memorial plaque nearby which lists most of those buried at this cemetery.

What does one do to research a cemetery when tombstones are missing, no exact count of how many are buried at the cemetery is available, and no information is available about whether Civil War veterans were buried there? The answer: Read on! The following points will help those who wish to research burials at Calvary Cemetery:

1. Tombstone Research: Because the tombstones of historical interest were for the most part preserved at this cemetery, it is a simple matter to go view them. One can find most of the Civil War veterans buried at Calvary by this method. The cemetery is not fenced, so access to the tombstones is assured, although no records of burials are available at the cemetery location.

2. Pioneer Memorial: To create the passive recreation park, the City had to provide a memorial listing all known burials at Calvary cemetery, and this they have done. Again, because the cemetery is not fenced, the plaque listing those interred at Calvary is accessible. The names are presented in alphabetical order.

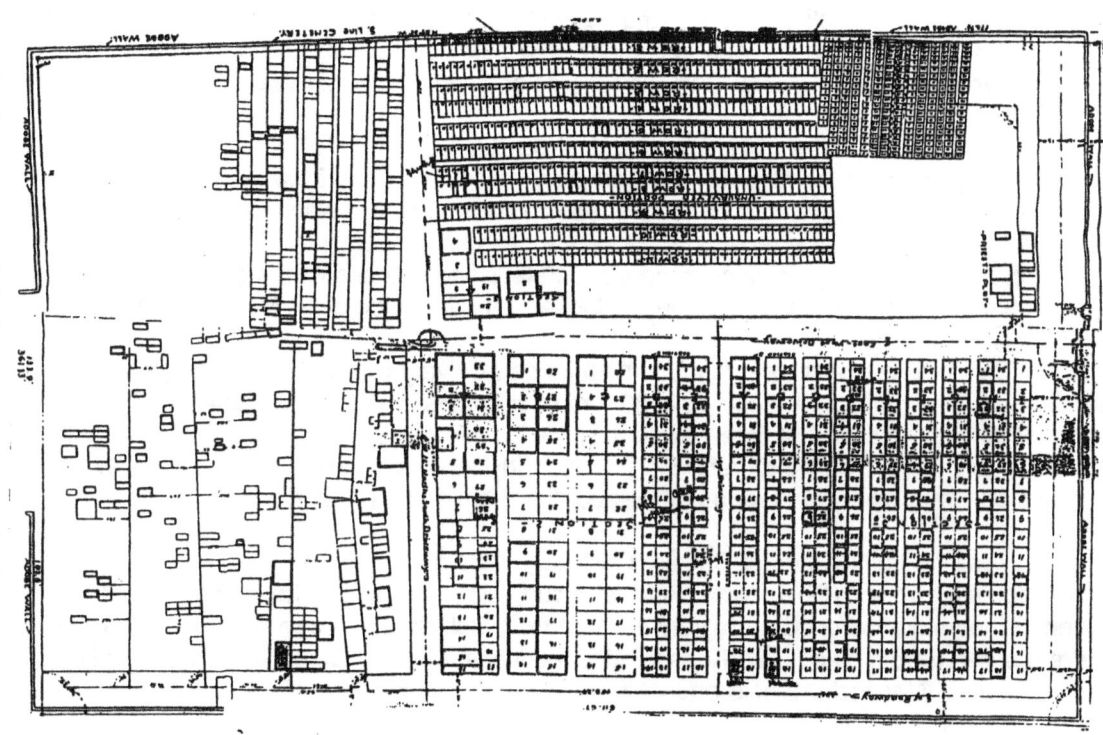

Note: Map, reversed to show street side at bottom, causes grave numbers and map lettering to be upside down

CALVARY (MISSION HILLS) CEMETERY

3. Photographs of Calvary Tombstones: Photos of most of the tombstones that were at Calvary Cemetery can be found at the Photo Archives of the San Diego Historical Society. The photos are grouped into jackets, and notations on the jackets indicate the section of the cemetery in which the photographs were taken. A researcher can thus locate individual graves within this cemetery from the photo jacket notations.

4. The Griffin Collection of Catholic Records
The R. Clinton Griffin Collection of Catholic records is located at the San Diego Historical Society Archives in Balboa Park. R. Clinton Griffin, with the assistance of Sister Catherine Louise LaCosta, CSJ, Karna Webster of the San Diego Genealogical Society, Sally West of the San Diego Historical Society, and Georgia L. Callian of the Descendants of Old Town San Diego, worked many years to compile records of burials at all the older Catholic cemeteries in San Diego.

In the Griffin collection is an indexed volume entitled *Mission San Diego De Alcala: Burials for Mission & Presidio 1775-1831; El Campo Santo 1849-1880; and Mission Hills Catholic Cemetery (Old Calvary) 1875-1969*.[10] This volume contains information about burials at Calvary Cemetery. Look in the index for an individual's name, and see whether children's burials are listed. Marital information can be obtained by checking the children's burial citations, for the citations also list the names of a child's parents. Death dates and in some cases place of death, cause of death, dates of internment and at times spouses of deceased adults might also be found. Additionally, there are also death records from church sources plus mortuary records which are included in this collection.

The Griffin Collection is large and valuable group of records for early Catholic burials in San Diego. The collection was just made available to the San Diego Historical Society in 1998. Anyone researching early Catholic records should consult this valuable collection!

5. Calvary Cemetery Maps and Index Cards: Maps for Calvary Cemetery are located in the storage room at the Mount Hope Cemetery office, and one of these maps (entitled "Mission Hills Cemetery") is reproduced on the preceeding page. There is also a drawer of index cards at Mount Hope which contains records of some of those buried at Calvary Cemetery. However, the Griffin collection probably contains a more accurate listing of those who are buried at Calvary Cemetery than either the "Pioneer Memorial" plaque or the index cards at Mount Hope.

In all, 33 Civil War veterans were found to be buried at Calvary Cemetery, including Dr. David B. Hoffman and Colonel Elmer Otis. Of these, only 20 had exact dates of death (see Chapter Four). Ten had died before 1900, and 10 after that date. All died by 1917, which indicates that the group at Calvary Cemetery were probably older than other veterans in this study for whom death information was available. The veterans buried in other San Diego cemeteries died from 1869 to 1943.

The Civil War veterans buried at Calvary Cemetery were also more likely to be from Ireland or from the more populated states (Ohio, New York, Missouri, Massachusetts) than other veterans in this study. Seven of the veterans buried at Calvary enlisted from California; 14 were in the U.S. regular troops, and the rest enlisted from places like Kansas, Massachusetts, Pennsylvania, Indiana, New Hampshire, New York, Missouri, Wisconsin, Illinois and Ohio. The veterans were:

Bryant, Richard	Hayes, Thomas	New, Edward
Buckley, Michael	Healey, Bernard	O'Neill, Patrick
Camacho, Lorenzo	Henneberry, Garrett J.	Otis, Elmer
Connell, Cornelius	Hoffman, David B.	Parsons, Benjamin F.
Courtney, James	Johnson, Peder	Salazar, Jose Maria
Duffy, W.E.	Loomis, M.S.	Shay, William
Flinn, Daniel L.	McCarty, John	Singleton, J.A.
Gallagher, John	McConville, Patrick H.	Smith, Henry
Giddings, J.R.B.	McGirl, Barney	Sweeney, Henry
Gray, J.S.	McKenna, Augustine P.	Welsh, James
Greenleaf, William C.	Minor, August	Williams, James

Mount Hope Cemetery

Mount Hope Cemetery is currently operated as a City-owned cemetery. It was established in 1869 by Alonzo E. Horton, founder of New Town, and others. Mount Hope was named by Augusta Sherman, wife of Matthew Sherman, the veteran who served in San Diego during the war.

Civil War veteran burials at Mount Hope most often occurred on G.A.R. Hill (G.A.R. Div.1) or in G.A.R. Divisions 2 and 3; the Odd Fellows (IOOF) and Masonic sections; and scattered throughout Divisions 1 through 6 of the older portion of the cemetery. Division 3 was the location of the first burials at Mount Hope, although Civil War veteran A.B. Morey was buried in "Div. 1 + 2" near the old cemetery office. His was the cornerstone or earliest burial at Mount Hope. Under current mapping, his burial would be in the northwest corner of Division 1, not far from the burial location of city father Alonzo E. Horton.

A meeting was called to plan Mount Hope Cemetery on October 23, 1869 at 7:00 p.m. "A.E. Horton, Esq., was elected chairman of the meeting. ... [It was decided that] ...sanitary considerations require that such cemetery should be distant, not more than four, nor less than three miles from the shores of San Diego Bay",[11] according to the minutes of a meeting (which Civil War veteran William W. Bowers of this study attended), "Original prices per lot ranged from five to twenty dollars, depending on the size and location."[12]

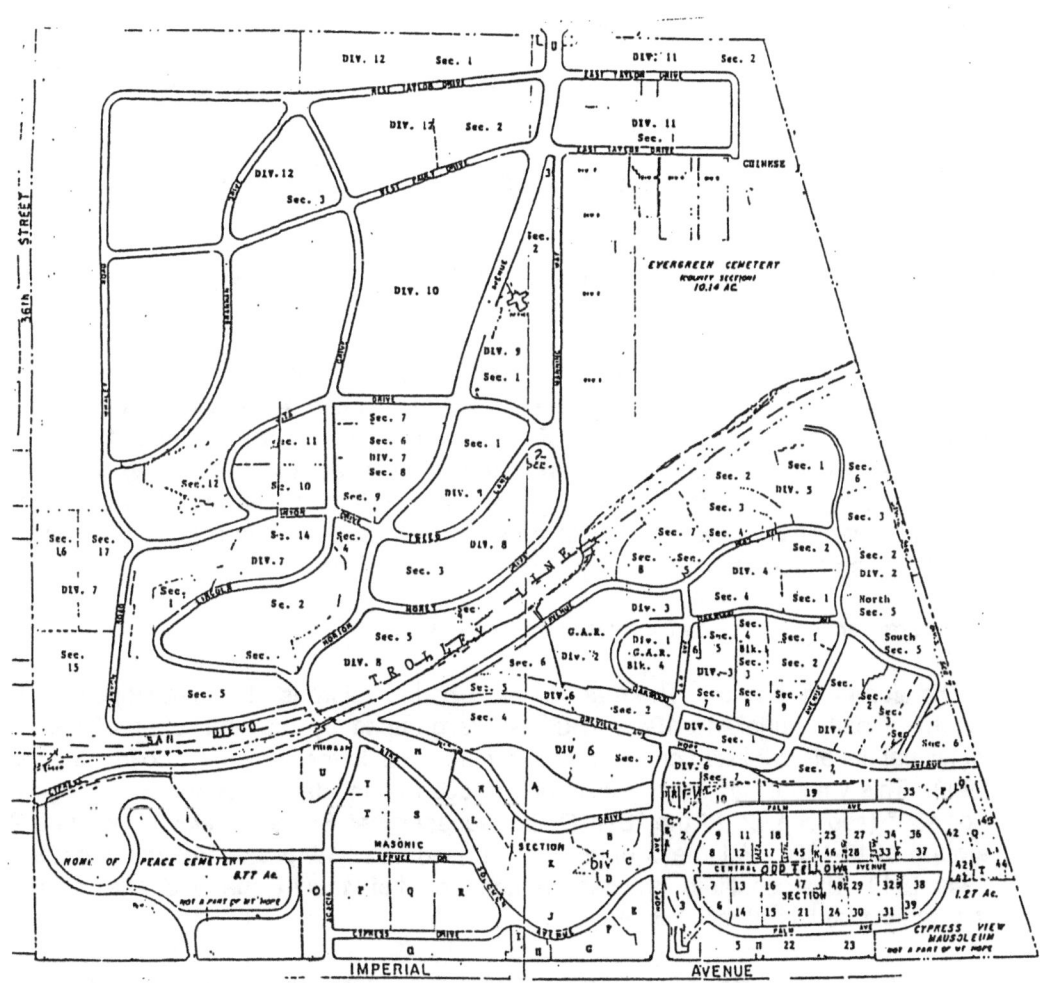

MOUNT HOPE CEMETERY

According to Fred Jay Rimbach's report, plans were made in 1870 to fence the cemetery, and a portion of the cemetery was laid off in 1871 to avoid confusion in the digging of graves thereafter. By January 4, 1872, a map was accepted and declared the official map by the Board of City Trustees. By November 3, 1872, lots were ready for sale.

A report on September 12, 1873 stated: "Since the first of June of this year, there have been but five internments at Mount Hope in this city--four children and one adult."[13] Looking at the old record books at Mount Hope, however, a more accurate count would be 34 people buried at Mount Hope Cemetery by 1873.)

Mount Hope was started as a city cemetery, but surrounding it were cemeteries owned and operated by other groups. Odd Fellows had a cemetery. There was a Masonic cemetery as well as the Jewish Home of Peace Cemetery (which is now a separate facility with separate gate.) Civil War veterans of Heinzleman Post G.A.R. had their own cemetery in G.A.R. Divisions 1, 2, and 3.

One by one, all but the Jewish Cemetery were taken over by Mount Hope. The following additional information was available about these earlier cemeteries:

> 1. "January 29, 1874, the Legislature granted the City of San Diego authority to give a tract of Pueblo Land for a Masonic Cemetery."
>
> 2. "June 30, 1916, the Grand Army of the Republic requested that the city take over the G.A.R. plot in Mt. Hope Cemetery."
>
> 3. "The Cemetery Board took over the control of the Odd Fellows Cemetery on February 15, 1932, in Mt. Hope Cemetery."[14]

In a Park and Recreation Department annual report dated June 30, 1948, Randall L. Taylor, cemetery manager, reported:

> "A large project in the office consists of setting up the control of all records in a system of lot books. The unreliable, un-uniform, obscure and incomplete records which the City inherited from former operators of various sections of the cemetery, have been a constant source of trouble in operations. These old records are being searched, verified and checked against corrected maps. A complete individual record of every grave with the date of sale, name of deed holder, number of deed, date of burial and name of deceased will appear in the Lot Book, and it will be an authoritative source of information for all future operations."[15]

There are several record sources at Mount Hope, as follows:

> **1. Old cemetery books:** There are four old bound volumes at Mount Hope which constitute a record of early burials to 1948. Burials are grouped by the first letter of the surname, and individual burials are listed chronologically under each letter. Volume 1 covers the period of 1869-1909. This volume has been transcribed (though is unindexed) by the San Diego Genealogical Society[16] (see citation to the "San Diego Genealogical Society" below). Volume 2 dates from around 1910-1926; Volume 3 dates from around 1927-1940 and Volume 4 dates from around 1941-1948. This constitutes the early written record of Mount Hope, and reflects internments from the earliest burials at this cemetery.
>
> The information in these books varies. The first two books contain more genealogical information, including a decedent's name, date of death, date of burial, race, age at death, sex, marital status, nativity, and location of burial within the cemetery. Some of the nativity listings contain the word "American", but many citations mention a state of birth. The last two books only contain basic burial information, i.e., date of death, date of burial, and location of burial within the cemetery.
>
> **2. Burial cards:** There are about 30 drawers of index cards currently in use at Mount Hope which provide information on burials. At times (but not often), the information in the above volumes conflicts with the information on the cards. Additionally, the "nativity" line from Books 1 and 2 was not copied onto the cards, so the researcher must use the first two bound volumes to determine nativity.

3. Lot cards: These 8 1/2 x 11 cards show the lot owner and who is buried in a particular lot. It was through the lot cards that a determination could be made in a number of instances of the name of a veteran's wife, although the woman listed might be his sister or daughter. To research whether the woman was indeed the veteran's wife, check city directories around the time of the veteran's death, obituaries, church records, and other sources listed below.

4. Maps: Maps at Mount Hope are valuable because they show who is buried next to or near a veteran. Some Mount Hope maps, particularly those for G.A.R. Divisions 1, 2, and 3, show existing tombstones, a valuable clue about whether there is a tombstone which may yield inscription information. However, for the most part, there are no tombstones drawn on maps for the other older sections of Mount Hope. A walk-through of the areas was necessary, using a photocopy of map grave locations, to see if there were Civil War veteran tombstones in these areas.

Hopefully, the tombstones will not be buried, overturned, or otherwise damaged. However, during the length of time it took to conduct this research, several tombstones were overturned on their inscription face, making it impossible to record what was on the stones. In two instances, the tombstones had been seen and transcribed prior to the vandalism; in several other instances, they had not been seen. The information on these overturned tombstones is lost to research until the stones are restored to their proper positions.

Please note: The G.A.R. section of Mount Hope contains burials of people who are not Civil War Veterans. Sometimes, the veteran's children were buried there. At times, women with different last names were buried there (perhaps remarried wives and/or married daughters.) Sons of veterans are also buried there, and must be distinguished from their fathers. People who have no connection whatsoever to the Civil War were buried there in later years. Finally, some grave sites in G.A.R. Divisions 1, 2 and 3 are empty.

Even if someone is buried on in the G.A.R. section of Mount Hope, do not assume the burial represents a Civil War Veteran or his wife. One of the goals of this study was to distinguish between veteran burials and non-veteran burials. The rosters from the two G.A.R. Posts were extremely helpful in this regard.

If you believe that a veteran or relative may be buried at Mount Hope Cemetery, contact their office at (619) 527-3400 for additional information. Their address is 3751 Market Street, San Diego, CA. 92102. The office is open from 8 a.m. until around 3:30 p.m. M-F, and not open on weekends. The grounds are fenced and open every day, but only from 8 a.m to 4 p.m. (not until dusk, like some other San Diego cemeteries). The gates at Mount Hope close at 4:00 p.m. daily.

Cypress View Mausoleum
At the southeast corner of Mount Hope Cemetery (originally near the first entrance to Mount Hope; see the Mount Hope map for details) is a large structure called Cypress View Mausoleum. It faces away from Mount Hope Cemetery toward Imperial Avenue and is not enclosed by the Mount Hope fence. The cemetery office is directly across Imperial Avenue, and additional mausoleum crypts are located there.

"State law [did] not allow above-ground graves in public cemeteries, but this was not always the case. In 1927, after years of discussion and debate, the city contracted with a private company to build a mausoleum at Mount Hope. The city was to receive royalties from its operation, and retain ultimate authority. Later, it was sold to the funeral firm that built it.

Cypress View Mausoleum, as it came to be called, once contained a grand piano and bird cages with canaries. Recitals were sometimes held."[17] Cypress View Mausoleum is currently owned by Bonham Brothers Mortuary. It is one of the nation's largest mausoleums, composed of sanctuaries with burial crypts built above the ground.

Only two Civil War veteran burials were identified at Cypress View, Arthur E. Vest and Barton Neer. Doubtless, there are others. At the office, there is a file of index cards with the names of all persons buried at the mausoleum. The cards contain date of death, location of burial and possibly other information such as name of spouse, date the burial crypt was sold, who it was sold to, and the mortician handling the burial.

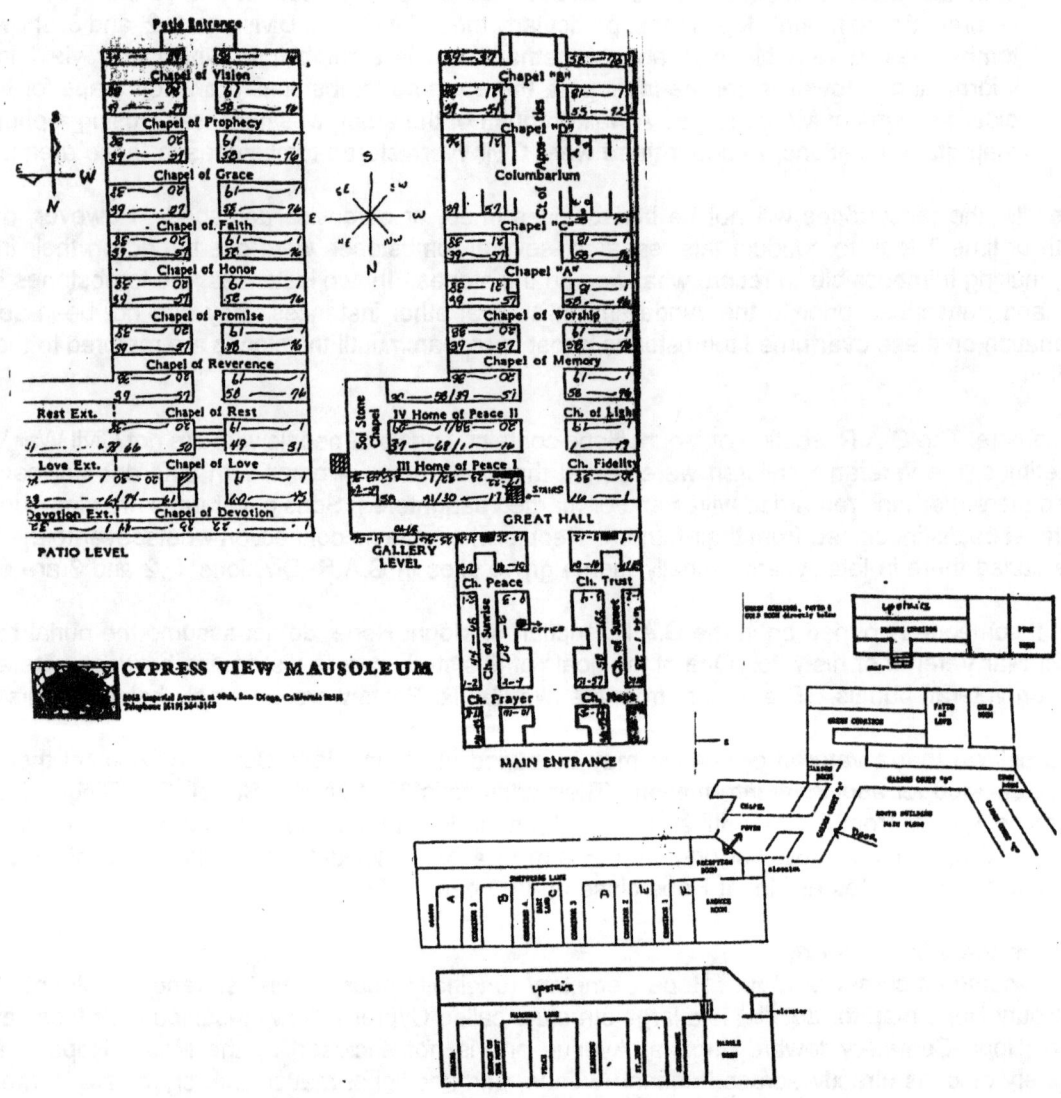

If you believe that a veteran is buried at Cypress View Mausoleum, contact them at (619) 264-3168, and they will search their card file for the individuals you request information about. The address of the mausoleum is 3953 Imperial Avenue, San Diego, CA 92113. They are open 8 a.m. to 5 p.m., seven days a week.

Greenwood Memorial Park and Mortuary
"When San Diego was showing early efforts of what was later to be a phenomenal growth, a group of progressive business men organized Greenwood Memorial Park. ... The first burial took place on December 17, 1907 ... in Laurel Place."[18] Greenwood Memorial Park and Mortuary is adjacent to Mount

Hope on the east, and is one of the more beautiful cemeteries in San Diego. As the cemetery expanded, its office was removed to the eastern end of the cemetery, where it is located today. The old office stood inside and to the left of a now-locked entrance gate just adjacent to Cypress View Mausoleum.

Because this was the first entrance to the cemetery, it was in sections near here where Civil War veterans were buried. The sections where most of their burials are found include: Laurel Place, Hawthorne, Palm Terrace, Arbor Vitale, Magnolia Place, and Olive. Because access to cemetery office records at this cemetery was not permitted, it was not possible to tell if Civil War veterans were buried in any other locations here.

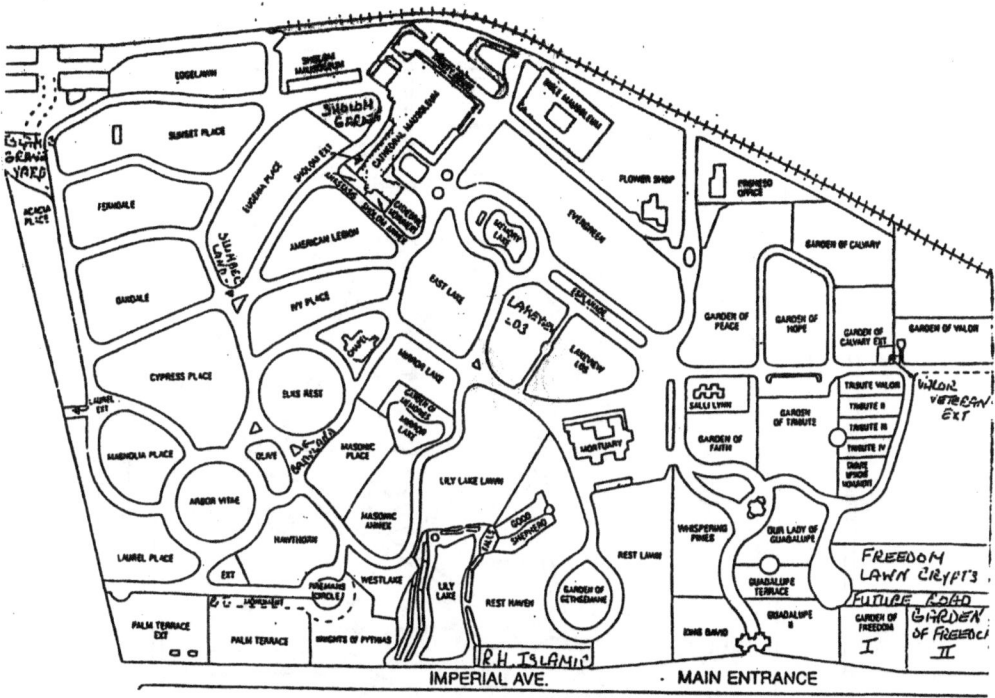

GREENWOOD MEMORIAL PARK AND MORTUARY

The cemetery is pleasant to walk around in. Most of the tombstones are similar in appearance because "...for uniformity, Greenwood has regulations for plantings and monuments."[19] "Over the years, development of Greenwood included several chapels, a mortuary, crematory, three mausoleums, a collection of international and rare vegetation, a flower shop, and statuary.

Judging by the names of some of the people resting in Greenwood, it must have been attractive from the start. A few of the prominent burials include the Seftons, Scripps, ... Putnams, Kettners, Frosts, and Timkens."[20] Ulysses S. Grant, Jr, and family are buried here, as is Moses A. Luce, Civil War Medal of Honor Winner.

Many of the Civil War veterans listed in Chapter Five of this study may be buried at Greenwood Cemetery. The veteran's death would have had to occur after 1907, when the cemetery was opened. If you believe that a veteran might be buried at Greenwood, call the cemetery office for additional information. Their phone number is (619) 264-3131, and their mailing address is 4300 Imperial Avenue, San Diego, CA 92102. The grounds are fenced. Grounds hours are 8:00 a.m. to dusk, but the records department is only open from 8:00 to around 4:00 p.m.

Holy Cross Catholic Cemetery and Mausoleum
Holy Cross Cemetery was dedicated in 1919. It is the only Catholic cemetery currently in operation in San Diego. "Holy Cross covers 40 acres. In 1939...the Holy Cross Chapel Mausoleum was built. On May 31, 1948, the latest addition to the mausoleum was added, which includes about 2,000 more crypts, making a total of 3,600 crypts."[21]

Extensive work was not done at Holy Cross Cemetery because my walk-through of the older portions of this cemetery (the St Bernards, St Pauls, St Josephs and St Francis sections) revealed very few government (soldier) tombstones. Additionally, the tombstones erected by the families did not, for the most part, have Civil War citations on them.

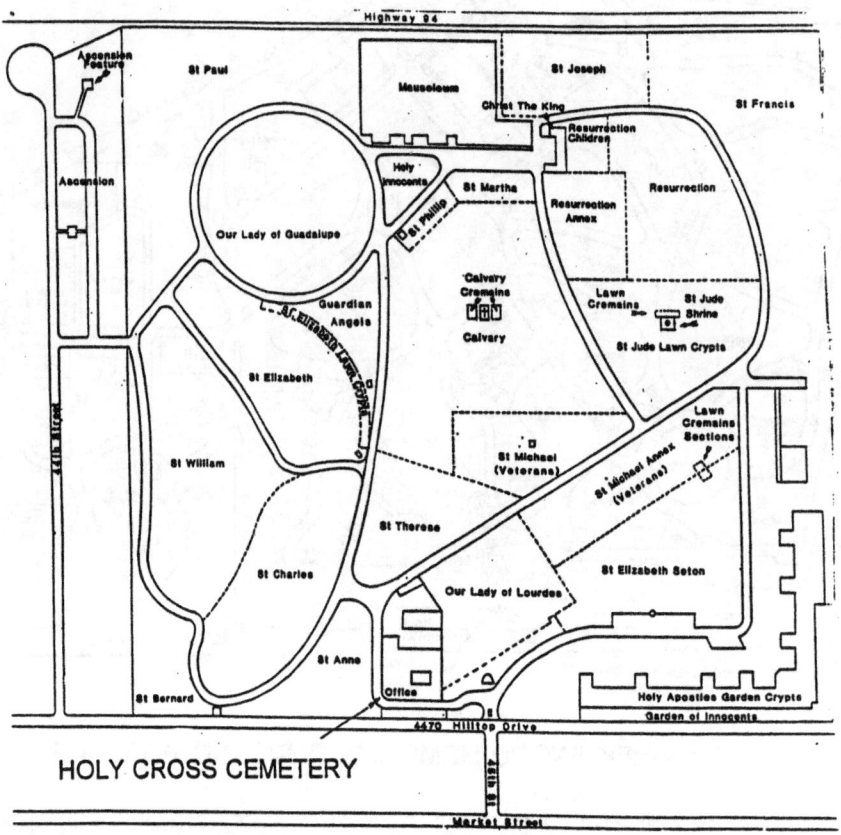

HOLY CROSS CEMETERY

Only three Civil War veterans were found to be buried at Holy Cross: Patrick Callaghan and Patrick Fogarty in St. Bernards, and William F. Hunt in St. Pauls. Holy Cross is an important cemetery, however, because most Catholic burials after 1919 took place here.

If you believe that a veteran is buried at Holy Cross Cemetery, contact their office for further information. The address is 4470 Hilltop Drive, San Diego, CA 92102. The phone number is (619) 264-3127. Office hours are M-F, 8 a.m. to 4:30 p.m., and Saturday from 9 a.m. to 1 p.m. The grounds are fenced, and are only open from 8 a.m. to 4:30 p.m. The mausoleum is open until 4:00 p.m. daily.

Home of Peace Cemetery
Laurie Bissell writes: "Louis Rose arrived [in San Diego] in 1850. Immediately he began to purchase land, eventually developing 'Roseville'. Soon more Jews settled in San Diego. ... Top priority would be acquiring land for a Jewish Cemetery. Louis Rose answered the need by deeding Adath Joshurun five acres in Roseville. Both [Louis] Rose and [Jacob] Mannasse were among those buried in the cemetery."[22]

"Population shifted with time leaving Roseville and the cemetery inconveniently far from town. Congregation Beth Israel petitioned the City for land in Mount Hope Cemetery for a Jewish burial ground. They received the land in 1892, establishing the 'Home of Peace' cemetery.

"With Home of Peace available, the Jewish community discontinued use of the old cemetery. In 1937, they reinterred those buried at the Old Jewish Cemetery into Home of Peace, but retained ownership of the land. During World War II they leased the old cemetery land to the Federal Government for a housing project, those homes eventually being replaced by Doctor's (now Sharp Cabrillo) Hospital."[23]

A survey has been done of Home of Peace Cemetery, and the information has been computerized. Contact the cemetery office below for additional information. There is also a tombstone book containing Home of Peace tombstone inscriptions (see p. 36 below for information on a book entitled *"Tombstone Inscriptions for San Diego, CA"*, located at the Family History Center.) The book contains 30 pages of inscriptions for this cemetery, but the recent survey of the cemetery will probably be more complete.

A spokesperson for Home of Peace Cemetery said there were no Civil War veterans buried there. The cemetery gates are open often, but the site is unstaffed. For further information about burials and hours of operation, contact Home of Peace, 6363 El Cajon Boulevard, San Diego, CA. Their phone number is (619) 286-1867. This fenced cemetery is located at the southwest corner of Mount Hope cemetery, with an entrance off Imperial Avenue. The cemetery address is 3668 Imperial Avenue, San Diego, CA 92102.

Fort Rosecrans National Cemetery
The Post Cemetery at Ft. Rosecrans is "...popularly known as the 'Bennington Cemetery'. [It marks] the last resting place of those killed when the American gunboat of that name blew up in San Diego Harbor, July [21], 1905, killing 60 men. It also contains the bodies of 18 officers and men killed in the Battle of San Pasqual. Rosecrans was established as a post cemetery in June, 1883."[24]

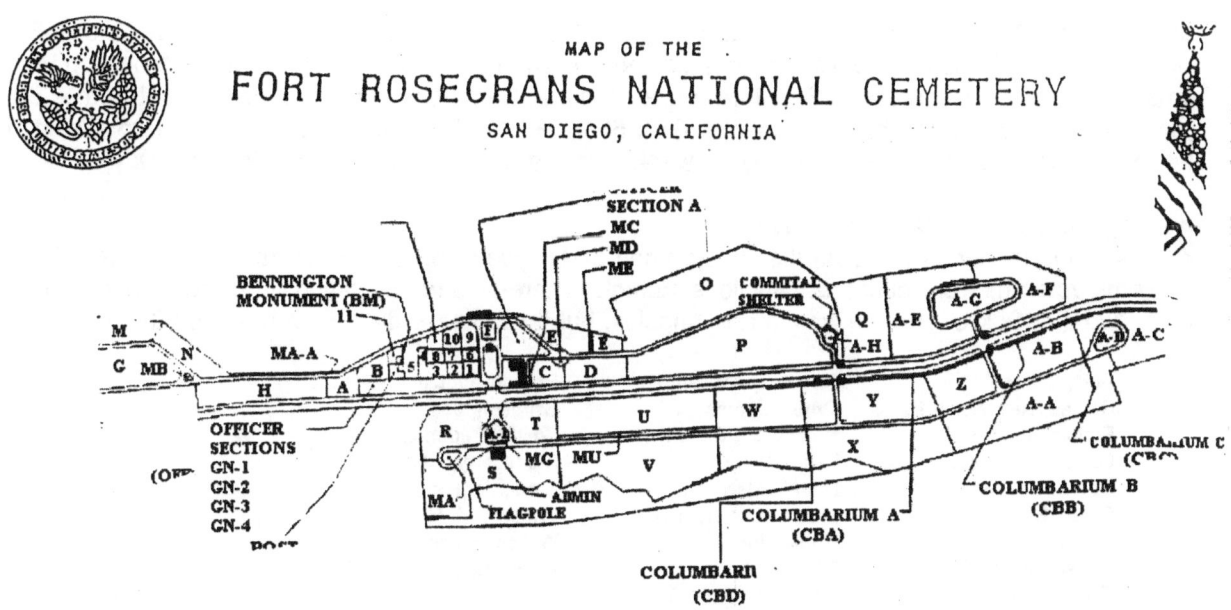

This cemetery is "...located on Point Loma in an area with a spectacular view of the ocean and San Diego. Fort Rosecrans Cemetery began as part of 1,000 acres set aside for military purposes in 1852. Although Ballast Point is believed to be the location of burials from 1542 and 1602, the first recorded burials in the area began in 1856. Later, a one-acre plot was designated for use as a burial ground for the Army's San Diego Barracks."

"The cemetery expanded to 10 acres with the [1899] dedication of the fort named after General William Starke Rosecrans who died the previous year. His contribution to the United States included military service in the Civil War, as U.S. Minister to Mexico, and as U.S. Congressman from California. ... Servicemen from as far back as the Civil War rest in Fort Rosecrans, including seven Medal of Honor winners, the government's highest award for bravery."[25]

A brief tombstone search in the "Post" section and Section A of this cemetery was undertaken. Both sections are near the Bennington monument. Two veterans listed in the G.A.R. rosters were buried here (John E. Shattuck in Section A, Grave 203, and John A. Young in Post Section 5, Grave 67). Additionally, two Civil War veterans were located from tombstone inscriptions (James J. Chard, who died on January 25, 1863 during the Civil War, and was buried in Post Section 4, Grave 1); and Patrick Dooley, buried in Post Section 5, Grave 76).

While there are a few non-government tombstones in the Post section, most tombstones are of the standard government variety seen in National Cemeteries, and it is impossible to determine from their inscriptions which burials represent Civil War Veterans. The government tombstones do not give date of death or burial, nor do they indicate the war the veteran served in, except in some instances for Spanish American War Veterans.

As in all National Cemeteries, there are records for burials. A computer screen housed in a kiosk outside the cemetery office can be used to determine if a particular veteran is buried at this cemetery. Also in the kiosk are about 12 ring binders containing alphabetical lists of all veterans buried at Fort Rosecrans, giving the date of internment, rank, and section of the cemetery where the veterans are buried. Many tombstones have numbers on the back, and by going to a section and looking at the tombstone numbers, a researcher can find particular tombstones. At times, the veteran's wife is named on the back of the tombstone, along with her date of death.

Fort Rosecrans National Cemetery is listed in the San Diego phone book under "National Cemetery--Fort Rosecrans". This cemetery is physically located one mile short of the Cabrillo National Monument on Point Loma. Their mailing address is Fort Rosecrans National Cemetery, P.O. Box 6237 Point Loma, San Diego, CA 92106. Their phone number is (619) 553-2084. Office hours are M-F, 8 a.m. to 4:30 p.m. The fenced grounds are open seven days a week from 8 a.m. to 5 p.m. (8-7 on Memorial Day).

Los Angeles National Cemetery--Sawtelle
While studying the records of both the Heintzleman and Datus Coon G.A.R. posts, notations were found that some veterans were buried at "Soldier's Home". There was no indication in the records except for one or two that Soldier's Home was in Los Angeles, but those below died or were buried there:

Auld, George	Ganoung, William H.	Rumpf, August
Barnes, Rev. Henry B.	Green, James	Simpson, Joseph
Brooks, John H.	Herrington, Beverly A.	Smith, Frederick P.
Connor, Samuel P.	Lane, Ansel S.	Stansberry, Charles H.
Cook, Augustus	Lowell, Marcus L.	Stout, James
Dakin, Horace E.	Moore, Augustus H.	Wattles, M. Richard
Dana, William	Noble, John	Wilson, Frank
Duvall, William H.	O'Brien, James	Witter, Charles
Ewing, Edward	Paull, Benjamin B.	
Field, William B.	Rapeleye, A.W.	

In 1887, a board was convened to decide where to locate a Soldier's Home in California. After much discussion, the Los Angeles site was selected. The criteria for entrance into such a home was that "...the applicant be 1. an honorably discharged soldier or sailor of the Union Army in either the War of 1812, the Mexican War, or the War of the Rebellion; and 2. without means of support; 3. physically unable to maintain himself by his own labor."[26]

An article in the Los Angeles Times described the Sawtelle facility as having four large barracks standing with their backs against the mountains; a 12-pound mortar in the central courtyard by a flagstaff; a bakery, kitchen, storehouse and laundry, a hospital in one of the barracks, and natural red-shingled roofs that stood out boldly against the blue mountains in the background. Plans at that time were for eight or ten barracks to be built, each calculated to accommodate 98 men. "However, at present, 650 inmates are housed in them, and that without serious crowding."[27]

As these veterans were not buried in San Diego, they are included in Chapter Five of this study (those with burial locations unknown, or those who were buried outside the City of San Diego). A map of this facility is below. Civil War veterans are buried in the sections containing street names of the various battles of that war. Again, thanks to Dave Jackson of Sherman Oaks for all the assistance he gave in collecting information about the San Diego Civil War veterans who were buried at the Sawtelle facility. His information came from kiosk computer records and from tombstone inscriptions.

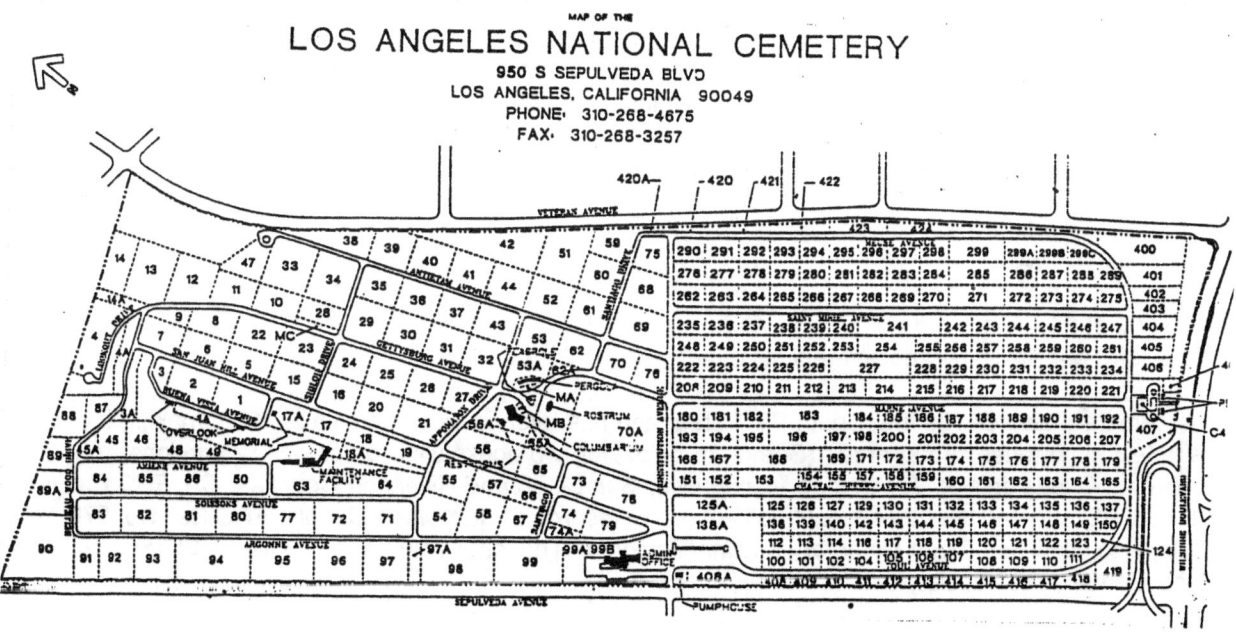

The address of the Sawtelle facility is: Los Angeles National Cemetery, 950 South Sepulveda Boulevard, Los Angeles, CA 90049. Their phone number is (310) 268-4675, and fax number is (310) 268-3257. They are open 8 a.m. to 5 p.m. every day. Office hours are Monday through Friday, 8 a.m. to 4:30 p.m.

The Family History Center (see "Military Records" below) has a microfilm available for burials at the Sawtelle facility. The film number is US/CAN 1577617, and the film can be ordered from Salt Lake City through the Family History Centers. This film provides information about burials at the Sawtelle facility prior to around 1940.

The film entries are cataloged by surname, county of death, the veteran's company and regiment in the Civil War, the barracks the veteran stayed at while at Sawtelle, their registration number, furlough date (the date when the veteran left the Sawtelle facility), the number of days at Sawtelle, and destination. For those who died at Sawtelle, the destination is "Died" with no further information concerning the veteran's death. See also a microfilm at the National Archives entitled "Registers for the Pacific Branch, SAWTELLE, Home for Disabled Veterans, 1882-1936.

OTHER CEMETERIES IN OR NEAR SAN DIEGO

Civil War veterans appearing in Chapter Five may be buried in the following cemeteries. One, El Camino Memorial Park and Cemetery, is within the San Diego city limits, and the others are in communities adjacent to the city of San Diego. These cemeteries were not researched in depth, and are listed here for reference purposes, as follows:

Glen Abbey Cemetery
3838 Bonita Road
Bonita, CA 91902
(619) 498-4600
Office: M-F, 8-5; S-S, 8-4:30; Grounds: 7 a.m. to dusk.

This cemetery is located south of the San Diego city limits, and serves the "South Bay" area (National City, Chula Vista, Bonita, Imperial Beach, etc.).

There is a list of persons buried at Glen Abbey at the Family History Center (see p. 36) entitled *"Glen Abbey Cemetery, Chula Vista, California--Tombstone Inscriptions to 1968,"* compiled by the LDS (Call No. 979.498/C4 V22s). This large volume contains at least 324 pages of tombstone inscriptions from this cemetery, and a 70 page index by surname. Samuel B. Rowley and William H. Holderness are buried at Glen Abbey, and their tombstone information is included with their individual citations in Chapter Five. Many tombstone inscriptions dating from the late 1800s appear in the Glen Abbey book.

La Vista Memorial Park
3191 Orange Street
National City, CA
(619) 262-1225
Office: 8-5, M-F; S-S, by appointment Grounds: 8-5, M-F; S-S, 9-4

This cemetery also serves the "South Bay" area, and has been in existence since 1868, making it one of the oldest cemeteries in that area. (See p. 36 below for two books with tombstone inscriptions from this cemetery. One is entitled *Tombstone Inscriptions: San Diego and Riverside Counties, CA*, FHC Call No. 979.498 V22sdr, and the other is entitled *Cemetery Records of San Diego County*, FHC Call No. 979.498 V22ls, also titled *San Diego Cemetery & Burial Records*. The latter volume is for sale for $5 from the San Diego Genealogical Society.)

A visit to La Vista reveals a fenced, hilly cemetery with a number of tombstones dating from the 1870's. The "Non-Endowment" section of the cemetery contains some of the oldest graves. Frank A. Kimball, founder of National City, CA, is buried here. The following Civil War veterans of this study were found buried at La Vista, and their tombstone inscription information will be featured in Chapter Five of this study, as they were not buried within the city limits of San Diego. The veterans buried at La Vista include:

G.W. Ainsley, J.M. Davidson, Leonard F. Davis and wife Sarah (Trimble) Davis, brothers Charles Warren Diamond, Ira Kimball Diamond, and Levi Woodbury Diamond (sons of Ira & Lucy Diamond & nephews of Frank Kimball), Nathan H. Downs and wife "Mother Downs", B.F. Fletcher, David Palmanteer, T.R. Palmer and Madison Traylor. Not included in Chapter Five: Veterans Hiram Dillon and Ira Mullen, noted in *San Diego Cemetery and Burial Records*, as their tombstones were not seen on a walk-through of La Vista.

El Cajon Cemetery
1270 Pepper Drive
El Cajon, CA 92021
(619) 442-0052 (Cemetery Office)
Office: M-F, 9-3:30; Grounds--every day: 8 a.m to dusk (5:00 p.m. in winter; 7:30 p.m. in summer)

El Cajon Cemetery serves the East County area of San Diego, including primarily El Cajon, but possibly also Lakeside, La Mesa, and the Mt. Helix areas. Some of the Civil War veterans of this study--Enoch Birdseye, Levi Chase, Matthew Sherman and Uzzial Stevens--lived for a time in the El Cajon area, although they are not buried in this cemetery. Others may have lived in El Cajon valley, and this would be a worthwhile cemetery to investigate further for Civil War burials. On a recent visit, one government tombstone was found of Martin B. Battroff, Civil War veteran of this study. He is listed in Chapter Five.

A three page listing of some individuals buried at El Cajon Cemetery appears in a book mentioned on p. 36, entitled *"Tombstone Inscriptions, San Diego and Riverside Counties, CA* (FHC Call No. 979.498 V22sdr), located at the Family History Center. Additionally, a group from San Diego Genealogical Society is hoping to transcribe tombstone inscriptions at this cemetery in the near future.

El Camino Memorial Park and Mortuary
5600 Carroll Canyon Road
San Diego, CA 92121
(619) 453-2121
Office: M-F, 8-5; Grounds: 7:30 a.m. to dusk

This cemetery serves the northern areas of the City of San Diego, and is one of the newer cemeteries in the area. It is unlikely that Civil War veterans would be buried there.

There are other cemeteries in the outlying areas of San Diego County which I will not name here. If you wish further information on these cemeteries, check the listings below on pp. 36-38, where several additional cemetery books containing tombstone inscriptions are discussed. Also contact the San Diego Historical Society and California Room of the San Diego Public library, plus historical societies in the location you are interested in for further information.

ADDITIONAL RESEARCH SOURCES
The study of genealogy is "alive and well" in San Diego. The following is a list of libraries, historical societies, government offices, etc. having records, books, or manuscripts of genealogical interest:

San Diego Historical Society (SDHS)
P.O. Box 81825
San Diego, CA 92138
(619) 232-6203
Archives Director (to be named shortly), Ext 124
Greg Williams, Photo Curator, Ext 127
Hours: Thurs-Sat, 10-4 (closed in August)

The Archives of the San Diego Historical Society (SDHS) are physically located in the Casa de Balboa in Balboa Park, near downtown San Diego. The SDHS has genealogical resources which are discussed below under "Specific Genealogical Records Available in San Diego", and many, many additional resources too numerous to mention.

Card Catalogs/Computerized Catalog: There are two card catalogs at SDHS: one available to researchers, and an older card catalog which is not accessible to patrons. There is also a computerized catalog which patrons can use. These catalogs contain many citations to individuals, county histories, journal articles, oral history interviews, and other source materials of use to researchers.

San Diego Journal of History: The main publication of SDHS is *The Journal of San Diego History*, which contains many articles of local interest. In 1975, the Historical Society published an *Index to the Journal* *of San Diego History* and *San Diego Historical Society Quarterly, Volumes I to XX*, 1955-1974, compiled by Thomas Lance Scharf and Iris Wilson Engstrand, which can be purchased for $4.00 at the SDHS bookstore. (An index to later volumes has not been published, but is available for researchers to use at the SDHS Archives.)

Additional guide books or articles available at SDHS include:

Guide to Public Records: Richard W. Crawford and others wrote *A Guide to the San Diego Historical Society Public Records Collection* (San Diego: San Diego Historical Society, 1987). This publication is available from the San Diego Historical Society bookstore for $1.00, and selected verbatim citations will be made to this book in the "Specific Genealogical Records Available in San Diego" section below, using a "SDHS/PRC" code to identify these citations. I wish to acknowledge and thank Rick Crawford and his staff for work on this publication. The publication is also available at the Family History Center library in Salt Lake City. The call number for this book is US/CAN Book Area 979.498 A3c.

List of Master's Theses and Doctoral Dissertations: The Historical Society is maintaining a list of Master's Theses and Doctoral Dissertations in history, anthropology, and various other disciplines from local colleges, and a number of titles relate to early San Diego pioneers. The list was originally compiled by James D. Newland in an article entitled: "A Preliminary Checklist of Master's Theses and Doctoral Dissertations on the History of San Diego", *The Journal of San Diego History* 39 (Summer 1993) 201-216.

The article notes all theses and dissertations completed up to 1993 at San Diego's four local colleges (University of California San Diego: Central Library, San Diego State University: Love Library, University of San Diego: Copley Library, United States International University: Walter Library), plus some from Los Angeles (primarily UCLA) and one or two from other locations.

The staff at SDHS is continuing to update the list of theses and dissertations, although only six have been added to the list for 1994, ten for 1995, and six for 1996 as of October, 1998. There are probably additional theses and dissertations available at the above-named schools for the years 1994-1998.

There is an article authored by Richard W. Crawford, Susan A. Painter, and Sarah B. West, entitled "Local History Materials in the Research Archives of the San Diego Historical Society," *Journal of San Diego History* 37 (Spring 1991) 129-148. This article can be obtained at the following SDHS Internet address:

http://edweb.sdsu.edu/sdhs/journal/91spring/archives.htm

SDHS Internet Access: SDHS also has a main Internet address that can used to obtain more information about the collection, hours of operation, etc. The address is: http://edweb.sdsu.edu/sdhs/

San Diego Public Library (SDPL)
820 "E" Street
San Diego, CA 92101
(619) 236-5834 (California Room/Genealogy Room)
(619) 236-5835 (Newspaper Room)
(619) 236-5820 (History Department)
Hours: M-Th, 10-9 F-S, 9:30-5:30 and Sun 1-5

San Diego Public Library (SDPL) Special Collections: The Newspaper Room, California Room, and Genealogy Room are all located adjacent to each other on the second floor of the San Diego Public Library in downtown San Diego. Information will be presented about the holdings of these collections below, under the heading "Specific Genealogical Resources in San Diego". An "RCC" designation indicates a book in the California Room; an "RGY" number indicates a book in the Genealogy Room. Rick Crawford, former head archivist of the San Diego Historical Society, is now working with special collections at SDPL.

The History Room at the library (1st Floor) contains books on California and San Diego history, accounts of individuals, diaries of Civil War soldiers, maps of and books about war sites, regimental histories, local histories of communities surrounding San Diego (El Cajon, Ocean Beach, La Jolla, Spring Valley, Chula Vista, to name a few), and so on. Once the veteran has been placed in San Diego, local sources provide information about the community in which he lived. Obtain the veteran's place of residence from city directories, and go from there.

Mary Allely, former librarian for the California Room, wrote an article describing its holdings entitled: "Local History Materials in the California Room of the San Diego Public Library", *The Journal of San Diego History* 37 (Summer 1991), 215-229, which will be helpful to researchers unfamiliar with the holdings in this collection.

SDPL Library Card: You may register for a SDPL library card. The general rules: Show up in person at the main library or a branch library; bring a picture ID, and proof of your address. These rules apply to both California and non-California residents.

If you live in the state of California, you may obtain a lifetime card which must be updated every two years. There is no fee for California residents. If you live out of state, you may obtain a yearly card with no lifetime privileges. The fee for obtaining the yearly card is $15 per year. For more information, contact the SDPL at (619) 236-5826.

On-Line Service: SDPL's card catalog can be accessed on-line. Call the library for more information about this service.

==

San Diego Family History Center (FHC)
4195 Camino Del Rio South
San Diego, CA 92108
(619) 584-7668
Hours: M-S, 10-5; open W-Th nights until 9 p.m.

There are Family History Centers throughout the United States, and all tap into the large collection of genealogical materials at the main FHC library in Salt Lake City, compiled by the Church of Jesus Christ of Latter Day Saints (LDS). Use of the computers at local FHC's is free; printouts of information are at a nominal cost (5 cents a page for computer printouts; 25 cents a page for reader/printer printouts of microfilm or microfiche pages). To locate a Family History Center in your area, call 1 (800) 346-6044, or visit the FHC Web site:

www.kbyu.byu.edu/ancestors.htmlwww.lds.org

The following indexes or library catalogs are available on FHC computers:

Ancestral File Computerized Index: By typing in a surname you are researching, you may be able to tap into another person's research, pull up an entire pedigree chart for the individual, and go several generations or more up your family tree. This is a simple system to use, and you can print out the charts for 5 cents a page. There is a small instruction book to this computer search program called *FamilySearch: Using Ancestral File*, available from the FHC for a minimal charge.

International Genealogical Index (IGI) Computerized Index: This is a computer list of several hundred million names of deceased persons, and again you can request information about particular individuals. Pedigree charts cannot be printed out from this source. If that is needed, re-enter the name in the Ancestral File (see above). A small instruction book to this index is called: *FamilySearch: International Genealogical Index*, which can be purchased from the FHC for a minimal charge.

Family History Library Catalog: This data base lists and describes microfilms and microfiche containing vital records, books, family and local histories, maps, etc. that are available at the main FHC library in Salt Lake City (and/or locally if someone has ordered the materials at your local FHC). The file can be searched by locality or surname. Obtaining a film or fiche number, you can order the microfilm or microfiche from Salt Lake City for a small charge. An instruction book on this index is: *FamilySearch: Family History Library Catalog*, which can be purchased from the FHC for a minimal charge.

===

San Diego County Historian (SDCH)
4370 Sweetwater Road
Bonita, CA 91902
(619) 472-7575

Lynne Christenson, the County Historian, can also be reached at lchrispk@co.san-diego.ca.us. This office has many records available on local history (particularly records concerning county parks), and vertical files on subjects and individuals. Call the County Parks information number for an update on what the future office hours of this facility will be. Their phone number is (619) 694-3049.

===

San Diego Genealogical Society (SDGS)
1050 Pioneer Way, Suite E
El Cajon, CA
(619) 588-0065 (ans machine)
Internet Addr: http://www.genealogy.org/~sdgs

This group is very active in San Diego. Examples of the types of research done by this group can be seen below, under "Special Genealogical Records Available in San Diego," <u>many of which can be viewed at the Family History Center (FHC).</u> This organization has its own library collection in El Cajon, located just east of the City of San Diego. Additionally, the group puts on an annual family history fair in the Fall of each year, with speakers, book vendors, etc.

Meetings of the SDGS are held on the second Saturday of the month from around 11:30 a.m. to 2:30 p.m. (except for the months of January, when the group holds its annual luncheon, and December). The monthly meeting is at St. Dunstan's Episcopal Church, 6556 Park Ridge Boulevard, in the San Carlos area just east of San Diego. Many SDGS publications are available for sale at these meetings.

The group publishes *Leaves and Saplings*, which presents information month after month that is important to local researchers. (Examples of the research projects published in *Leaves and Saplings* appear in "Special Genealogical Sources in San Diego", below.) An *Index to San Diego Leaves and Saplings, 1974-1985* is available at the Family History Center (FHC Call No. 979.498 X2Is/Index). Additionally, about 20 volumes of *Leaves and Saplings* dating from Winter of 1973 to January/March of 1989 are available at the FHC.

San Diego County (SDC) (Birth/Death/Marriage/Property Records)
Recorder/County Clerk
County Administration Building
1600 Pacific Highway
San Diego, CA 92101
(619) 237-0502--Records below are in Room 260
    Birth Records--Ext.22
    Death Records--Ext. 20
    Marriage Records--Ext. 24
(619) 236-3771, Ext. 0--Property records information, Room 103
Hours: M-F, 8-5; closed holidays

San Diego County Superior Court (SDC) (Civil/Criminal Records)
220 West Broadway
San Diego, CA 92101
(619) 531-3244 (Superior Court, Older Records)
Hours: M-F, 9-4:30

San Diego County Superior Court (SDC) (Probate/Divorce Records)
220 West Broadway
San Diego, CA 92101
(619) 531-3244 (Superior Court, Older Records)
Hours: M-F, 9-4:30

Note: Recently, Californians voted to combine both Municipal and Superior Courts into a "Superior Court" system. The records of Municipal Court will be moved shortly, and housed in new areas. However, these records are not of interest to those studying Civil War veterans, for they are purged when they are ten years old. Thus, no "Older Records" department exists for Municipal Court records.

San Diego County has birth, death, marriage, divorce, property, civil and criminal indexes and other records, most of which are available for public viewing. One of the more important records for research on Civil War veterans are death certificates. The County began keeping records of death from 1850 on. See details about death records under "Specific Genealogical Records Available in San Diego", below.

Information regarding the office of Assessor, Recorder or County Clerk can be obtained at the County's Internet site. The following information is now available: General information about the department, office locations and telephone numbers, various programs administered by the department, and on-line services. Future on-line services will include Assessors Parcel Maps, Grantor/Grantee Indexes of Recorded Documents, Fictitious Business Names, and Property Ownership and Assessed Valuation. The County's Internet address is:

    http://www.co.san-diego.ca.us/cnty/cntydepts/general/assessor

Questions concerning the Internet or services provided on the Web site can be sent directly to the County Assessor/Recorder/Clerk's E-Mail Coordinator at the following address:

    fsharias@co.san-diego.ca.us

==

National Archives (NA)
24000 Avila Road, 1st Floor
East Laguna Niguel, CA 92677-3497
Phone: (949) 360-2641
Hours: 8-4:30, M-F; 8-8:30, first Tuesdays of the
month (except Federal holidays)
E-Mail address is: archives@laguna.nara.gov
Internet address is: www.nara.gov
Note: This facility is a two hour drive north of San Diego.

Ordering a Veteran's Civil War Records: You may call this facility to obtain at least two copies (per phone call) of NATF Form 80 ("Order for Copies of Veterans Records"). This form can be used to order copies of a Civil War veteran's pension, military or bounty land warrant applications, but only one type of record can be ordered on each form. The forms will be sent to you free of charge.

Next, order the records from the National Archives in Washington, D.C., for the National Archives at Laguna Niguel does not process these requests. However, the NA does have census records, naturalization records and other information which can be viewed at the address above. See "Specific Records Available in San Diego" below for information about microfilms available for viewing at the Laguna Niguel facility.

==

Congress of History of San Diego
Charlie Best, President
854 Rosecrans Street
San Diego, CA 92106
Ph: (619) 223-3418

The Congress of History was formed in 1964 as a networking organization to bring together representatives of all of the major historical groups in San Diego and Imperial Counties. Their meetings are held at various locations throughout the county, and are noticed in their publication, *Adelante*. The group hosts an annual history convention in the Spring, and is attempting to document and have computer access to all of the historical collections in San Diego County; Imperial County and Baja California will also be included. Please contact Charlie Best for additional information.

==

San Diego County Law Library
1105 Front Street
San Diego, CA 92101
Ph: (619) 685-6553
E-mail: www.sdcll.org
Pat Lopez, Curator of Historical Collection
Hours: M-Th: 8 a.m. to 9:00 p.m.; Friday: 8-5; and Saturday, 10-5

The County Law Library has the following information of historical interest: Biographies and folders of newspaper clippings/photos) of local attorneys, judges, etc., Grand Jury and Justice Court files, files on the Colorado River water litigation, the San Diego Daily Transcript newspaper, old appellate court briefs from San Diego and California, a "Pioneer Room" which contains book collections of local attorneys, and books with bios of local attorneys. Contact Pat Lopez for further information on this collection.

Carlsbad Library (about 30 miles north of San Diego)
1250 Carlsbad Village Drive (just east of I-5)
Carlsbad, CA 92008
Ph: (760) 434-2931
Hrs: M-Th, 9 a.m. to 9 p.m., F-S, 9 a.m. to 5 p.m.

This library has ten or more drawers of <u>microfiche</u> containing family histories, local histories, vital records, etc., and also the largest collection of U.S. census indexes in the area, making a trip there a must if searching migration patterns of individuals and families through census indexes. The library catalog can be accessed on-line. Contact Mary Van Orsdol or Harold Williams for further information about this library.

===

Genealogy Upcoming Events/Classes/Opportunities
Joan Lowrey
7371 Rue Michael
La Jolla, CA 92037
(619) 454-7046 Web: http://www.cgssd.org; e-mail: jlowrey@connectnet.com

This is a listing of all genealogy libraries, classes and groups in the San Diego area, published monthly by Joan Lowrey. Charge: $6.00 per year. Contact Joan Lowrey for additional information.

SPECIFIC GENEALOGICAL RECORDS AVAILABLE IN SAN DIEGO
The following specific records (books, etc.) are available in San Diego. Each record (book, etc.) has a code which identifies where the record (book, etc.) is housed. (See above for addresses and phone numbers of these facilities). The codes used for some of these facilities are as follows:

SDHS: San Diego Historical Society
SDPL: San Diego Public Library (RCC indicates the California Room; RGY the Genealogy Room)
FHC: San Diego Family History Center
SDCH: San Diego County Historian
SDGS: San Diego Genealogical Society (Many publications of this organization are at the FHC.)
SDC: San Diego County
NA: National Archives

MILITARY RECORDS

SDPL: A major source for research on the Union forces in the Civil War (although the work does contain much information on the Confederacy as well) is Frederick H. Dyer's *A Compendium of the War of the Rebellion* (New York: Thomas Yoseloff, 1959) (SDPL Call No. R 973.7, History Department, first floor). This exhaustive work originally consisted of 4,025 typed sheets, and when published contained three parts:

> Part 1: Summarizes enlistments and losses, gives all national cemeteries and their locations, lists (by state) 2,494 regiments, 126 battalions and 939 batteries and independant companies. It also lists 900 Federal regiments that lost 50 or more men in combat (grouped by state and numbers killed and wounded). Additionally, it contains an alphabetical list of 7,800 persons who commanded brigades and larger organizations, and all of the Union's departments, armies, corps, divisions and brigades.

> Part 2: Contains a record of all Civil War engagements and losses, arranged chronologically and by state. This listing comprises 10,455 military events.

Part 3: Contains 3,550 Regimental Histories, including where each unit was organized, when it was mustered into the Federal service, the higher headquarters to which it was assigned, the areas and actions in which it served in, changes in its designations and status, the date it was mustered out, and the number of officers and men who died from battle causes or diseases.

The *Compendium* is a primary tool for researching both individual soldiers, the regiments in which they served, and the broader scope of the war, its engagements and campaigns.

SDPL: *Records of California Men in the War of the Rebellion, 1861-1867*, by Brig.Gen. Richard H. Orton, Adjutant General of California (Sacramento: State Printing Office, 1890.) (SDPL Call No. RGY 973.741). This book documents the various infantry and calvary units (including native Hispanic units) that were assembled in the State of California during the time periods described in the title. This work is also available at the FHC's Salt Lake City library. (FHC Call No. US/CAN Book Area 979.4 m2a 1979). Check the FHC computer to see if there is a microfilm that can be ordered to your local FHC of this work.

SDPL: *Personal Name Index to Orton's "Records of California Men..."* J. Carlyle Parker has done an index to the Orton book cited above which is entitled *"Personal Name Index to Orton's Records of California Men in the War of the Rebellion"*. It is located at SDPL Call No. RGY 973.741/Parker.

SDPL: *Consolidated Index to Compiled Service Records for Confederate Soldiers, Cavinah-Chambers* The SDPL has an isolated microfilm (which was probably donated to them) with the above title at SDPL Call No. RGY 973.742, Reel #81. This film would be valuable to use for researchers having Confederate ancestors with surnames that fall within this alphabetical range.

SDPL: National Archives Military Records: A book available in the Genealogy Room entitled *Military Service Records: A Select Catalog of National Archives Microfilm Publications* (SDPL Call No. RGY 355.6016/National), lists film numbers of films containing military service records which are available from the National Archives.

NA: National Archives Microfilms The following microfilms are available at the National Archives in Laguna Niguel. The list below is only a partial list of the microfilms available. To obtain a copy of their "Index to Microfilms in the Research Room," call the National Archives in Laguna Niguel at (949) 360-2641, or contact your regional National Archives for a similar listing of their microfilm holdings.

Index to Compiled Service Records of Confederate Soldiers	M253	V9
Index to Compiled Service Records of Volunteer Union Soldiers	Various	V9-11
Index to Compiled Service Records of Union Colored Troops	M589	V11
Special Census Enumerating Veterans & Widows of the Civil War, 1890	M123	11
Burial registers for Military Posts, Camps, and Stations, 1768-1921	M2014	V12
Army Post Returns for CA & AZ, 1800-1916	M617	V12

**Headstone Records for Civil War Union and some
1812 Veterans, 1879-1903**   M1845 V12

**Registers for the Pacific Branch, SAWTELLE, Home
for Disabled Soldiers, 1882-1938**   M1749 V12

SDHS: Military records pertaining to San Diego Civil War veterans are in a set of six boxes at Call No. MS 365, "Military Records". These boxes contain G.A.R. records, one of the primary records used in this study. There are three ledger books, two for Heintzelman Post (in Box 3) and a third for Datus Coon Post (in Box 6). (See "Research Design," earlier in this chapter, for more information on how these ledger books were used in this study.) The ledger books for Datus Coon Post contained obituaries (and possibly obituary photos) for some of the veterans. The boxes additionally contained other smaller Heintzelman Post address and ledger books not used in this study, as well as minutes of meetings of this Post, which give an insight into the operation of the group and its activities.

SDHS: [County Assessor] "Militia Rolls 1853-1894" (SDHS/PRC Call No. R2.82 14, p. 25) (2 boxes) "Annual rolls show the names of all men eligible for local military service. After 1880, the records also indicate residence. There are several missing years. Arranged chronologically."

FHC: The Family History Center publishes a number of "Research Outlines" about a variety of topics. A "Military Records" guide called *"Research Outline: U.S. Military Records"* will be helpful in organizing research about Civil War sources. The guide is currently 39 pages long, and the Civil War section of this publication is 11 pages. That section contains "General Reference Sources"; "Union Sources" and "Confederate Sources", with the following topic headings for each: Service records of soldiers, sailors and officers, pension records, draft records (for Union veterans), POW records (for Confederate veterans), unit histories, census records, cemetery records, and veteran and lineage organizations. This booklet is available at the San Diego FHC at a cost of around $1.50, and is well worth the price.

If there is no FHC located in your area, write for a copy of this outline to: Publications Coordinator, Family History Library, 35 North West Temple Street, Salt Lake City, Utah 83150.

FHC: United States Military Records--Pension Index File--1861-1934 You can obtain pension papers pertaining to your Civil War veteran; the papers may contain valuable genealogical information. But in order to obtain the pension papers and to expedite the search for the veteran's record at the National Archives, it is good to have the veteran's pension file number.

At the FHC, there is a ring binder (FHC Call No. is: Ref Military Records - Civil War) which lists microfilms containing pension file numbers for individual veterans, arranged by "Union Troops", "Confederate Troops" and "Civil War Colored Troops" in listings like the following:

Name	**Film No.**
Aab-Ackerman	540,757
Ackerman-Adams	540,758
Adams-Ahh	540,759
Etc.	

Scan the lists for the microfilm which contains the alphabetical range for the surname that you are researching. The actual microfilm may or may not be available at your local FHC. If not, order it from Salt Lake City. If the film is in, obtain your Civil War veteran's pension number from the film (being aware that if the veteran's name is missing, he might not have obtained a pension). To order copies of your veteran's pension file, call your nearest National Archives regional center and have them send you NAFT Form 80.

(For more information on obtaining this form, see the heading "National Archives/Pacific Region" on p. 28.)

Fill out the form and send it to the Washington, D.C. address on the form [NOT the St. Louis address], and you will obtain a photocopy of the pension file for the veteran you are researching from the National Archives. There is a charge for this service. To obtain the records faster (after you have received an estimate of costs which the National Archives will send you once it determines that the veteran's file is available for photocopying), you can charge the copies to your credit card.

FHC: Index to Historical Register of Soldier's Home, Sawtelle, Pacific Branch, Los Angeles, CA (US/CAN, Film No. 1577617) This Register, located on Roll 188, comprises records of the Pacific Branch, Sawtelle, CA, Indexes. The information in this index relates to those veterans who were disabled, unable to care for themselves, and who sought care from the Sawtelle Soldier's Home in Los Angeles. The record entries are by surname, county, regiment and company of service in the Civil War, barracks the veteran stayed in at Sawtelle, their "Registration Number", their furlough date (the date they left the Sawtelle facility), the number of days they were there, and their "Destination". For some, the destination was "Died," and no further information is available for those veterans. This film can be ordered from Salt Lake City through your local FHC.

FHC: 1890 Census of Union Veterans and Widows of Union Veterans of the Civil War. This series of microfilms represents a special census of Union Civil War veterans and their widows taken in 1890, for selected states. (Records for Alabama through Kansas, and the first half of the Kentucky records were apparently lost in a fire). The films can be ordered from the FHC Library in Salt Lake City, and film call numbers can be obtained by using the FHC computers and accessing the "Family History Library Catalog" mentioned above. Once into that data base, get to the information using the following prompts: "United States Census Office 11th Census 1890." The films are organized like the following example, if you were looking for census returns for "Blue Earth County, Minnesota":

Minnesota: Blue Earth, Brown, Cottonwood, Dodge, Faribault...(etc.)   Film No. 0338181

Obtain the film number of the town or city, county and state where the veteran resided in 1890, and order the film from Salt Lake City through your local FHC. Note: California is not represented in this film series, but as most of the Civil War veterans who lived in California were from somewhere else, this resource might prove useful to research all veterans who are named in this study, save those who served from states where the records were destroyed, or those who moved to California before 1890.

FHC: California Civil War Veteran Burial Listings (FHC Film No. 1,000,138, Item 4). This is a compilation of burial locations for many veterans who served in California volunteer units in the Civil War. Most of the burials listed herein occurred in the Los Angeles area; some occurred in Arizona and other locations. The records were compiled by Sherman L. Pompey from cemeteries, DAR records, Government records and other sources. His goal was to list the burial locations of all men who served in the Civil War from west of the Rocky Mountains. The eight page work, containing nearly 700 names, carries a 1965 copyright, and was published by the Southern California Genealogical Society. Their address (then) was P.O. Box 8295, Long Beach, CA 90808. No veterans in this compilation were buried in San Diego.

FHC: California Military Records/Pension List 1883 (Film No. 1,035, 781, Item 3). This is a listing of veterans living in California who were pension recipients in 1883. Only a few of the Civil War veterans of this study were in San Diego County at that time, but the list might be a valuable resource to search for those with ancestors from other California counties, as the work includes pension recipients from all over the state for 1883. The list for San Diego County includes the following veterans (and in some instances, veteran's wives or parents.) Veterans from this study are highlighted in bold:

California 1883 Military Pension List

No.of Certif	Name of Pensioner	P.O. Address	Reason for Pension	Monthly Rate	Date of Original Allowance
31,053	Willard Whitney	Bernardo	GSW in face	$5.00*	Feb 1877
13,177	Ed A. Foss	El Cajon	GSW l. leg	$2.00	Jan 1863
51,671	Eli T.Blackmer	National City	Chron.diarr	$3.50*	Oct 1865
131,772	Robt.E.Haywood	National City	GSW l. shoul	$4.00	Dec 1876
105,410	Jacob Bergman	Oak Grove	GSW l. shoul	$12.00*	Jan 1877
62,594	Levi H. Utt	Pala	Unstated	$20.00	Aug 1866
13,218	Chas.C.Watson	Poway	Loss rt arm	$24.00	Aug 1874
104,222	Delarau Craft	Poway	GSW rt thigh	$2.66*	Jul 1870
144,194	Chas.M.Burks	San Diego	GSW l. arm	$4.00	Mar 1877
33,213	Sampson Ward	San Diego	Wd face	$18.00	Not stated
180,451	Walter Parker	San Diego	Malaria	$18.00	Not stated
187,729	John F. Miles	San Diego	GSW l arm	$17.00	Apr 1881
39,301	Alexander Smith	San Diego	Frac patella	$4.00	Mar 1865
106,792	Hiram Harrell	San Diego	Wd l thigh	$2.00	Nov 1870
9,142	Hiram S. Hall	San Diego	Aneurism/aorta	$24.00	Not stated
159,622	John Allen	San Diego	Dis lungs	$18.00	May 1879
179,994	Wm.J.England	San Diego	Dis lungs	$18.00	Dec 1880
154,395	Henry V.Richil	San Diego	GSW r chest	$8.00	Jul 1878
68,150	Martin Hamilton	San Diego	Amput r arm	$24.00	Oct 1874
102,617	Albert Gore	San Diego	Chron.diarr	$17.00	Not stated
164,730	Martin Telleu	San Diego	Chron rheu	$12.00	Feb 1880
142,161	Maria Burton	San Diego	Widow	$30.00	Apr 1870
15,773	Eliz.Brewster	San Diego	Widow 1812	$8.00	Jan 1879
193,453	Lyman Roberts	San Diego	Father	$8.00	Oct 1881
123,591*	Curtis Johnson	San Dieguito	GSW l arm	$15.00	Jun 1873
218,208	Alfred Confer	Temecula	GSW l thigh	$6.00	Sep 1882

* Some numbers hard to read on the microfilm

DEATH RECORDS

SDC: Death Certificates: San Diego County has records of deaths from 1905 on in a computerized system, and a file number leads to a Death Certificate which can be purchased for $8.00. There are also older index books containing death information which are not out in the open, and a request must be made to view them. These books date from 1850, when the county was created. Death information is grouped alphabetically and then chronologically by individual names as individuals died. The dates at which the recording of death information began in these books <u>varied by letter of the alphabet.</u> For example, if the surname being searched starts with "D", deaths were recorded from 1851 on. If the surname being searched starts with "K", deaths were recorded from 1871 on. So, there is a good deal of variation, as the chart below indicates:

A--Deaths from 1877 on
B--1854 on
C--1850 on
D--1851 on
E--1851 on
F--1863 on
G--1853 on
H--1868 on
I--1854 on
J--1853 on
K--1871 on
L--1850 on
M--1851 on
Mc-1890 on
N--1852 on
O--1851 on
P--1850 on
Q--1870 on
R--1850 on
S--1852 on
T--1868 on
U--1880 on
V--1854 on
W--1853 on
X--No listings in early book
Y--1851 on
Z--1851 on

The ledger books list death information as follows: Date of death, name of decedent, race, age at death, sex, marital status, nativity, cause of death, coroner/doctor attending, and occupation. There is a good deal of information in these old ledger books, particularly information on nativity. San Diego County death records can be viewed in Room 260 at the County Administration Building, 1600 Pacific Highway. Their phone number is (619) 237-0502, Ext. 20.

According to an instruction sheet which the staff uses, the following was stated: "Death records are open to the public. Anyone may purchase copies and/or view these records free of charge. Death: 1873-1904, old books in the vault; and from 1905-present, on the computer and on microfiche." But consult the chart above, because death records go back further in time than 1873, in many instances.

FHC: California Death Index, 1905-1929 and 1930-1939 (Film No.s 1,686,044 through 1,686,048 for the earlier years, and Film No.s 1,686,048 through 1,686,050 for the later years.) This is a compilation of death records from the State of California Department of Public Health, Bureau of Vital Statistics and Data Processing. Information on this index is listed alphabetically by name of decedent, initials of spouse, age at death, county the which the death was filed, date of death, and a number such as the following: 19-030543. The "19" stands for 1919, the year the death certificate was filed in the county of death; the "030543" is the state number under which the decedent's record is filed.

Original death certificates are on file at the Office of the State Registrar of Vital Statistics. Copies of the death certificates are on file at the County Recorder's office in the county of death. Note: While state records start in 1905, San Diego County has records which start much earlier (See "SDC Death Records" above). This record was not consulted for purposes of this study, but is available for those who wish to check death dates and locations, particularly those researching veterans for whom burial locations were unascertained in this study (veterans listed in Chapter Five).

SDHS: The Griffin Collection of Catholic Death Records: The R. Clinton Griffin Collection of Catholic records (SDHS Call No: "Ves & Misc No. 685", "Griffin Collection, Burials, Mission Records, 1 box--16f3") was compiled by R. Clinton Griffin, with assistance from Sister Catherine Louise LaCosta, CSJ, Karna Webster of the SDGS, Sally West of SDHS, and Georgia L. Callian of Descendants of Old Town San Diego. In the collection are records of Catholic burials at all of the older Catholic cemeteries in San Diego (except Holy Cross, where records can be easily accessed at the cemetery office). In the Griffin collection is a bound and indexed volume entitled *Mission San Diego De Alcala: Burials for Mission & Presidio 1775-1831; El Campo Santo 1849-1880; and Mission Hills Catholic Cemetery (Old Calvary) 1875-1969*. Also in the collection are Catholic diocese records and possibly records of internment plus some mortuary records.

SDHS: [County Recorder] Certificate of Death, 1873-1876: (SDHS/PRC Call No: R2.80 14, p. 37) (1 box) "Death certificates show the name, age, marital status, sex, occupation, and birthplace of deceased; names of medical attendant, person making report, and undertaker; location of burial; location, date and cause of death. Arranged chronologically by date of death and indexed by name."

PROBATE RECORDS/WILLS

SDC: Probate Records 1850-Present: Probate records are located in the "Older Records" office at the County of San Diego, and they can be reached at (619) 531-3244. The records start with the beginning of county formation in 1850 and go to a recent cutoff date. After that, the records are kept in the "Newer Records" area. As all included in this study died by 1955, their probate records would be housed in "Older Records. Be aware that old probate ledger books must be searched (filed by letter of the alphabet and chronologically as individuals died), as indexes are not available for probates filed before 1960.

FHC: San Diego County Probate Index 1850-1922 (Call No. 979.498 S2Is) "All information contained in these books was taken from the index of the San Diego County Superior Court Probate Records, located in the San Diego County Court House, County Clerk's Office, Third Floor", and cover the dates July 1, 1850-Janury 14, 1922. The listings are alphabetical (re-arranged as such by the authors from the earlier chronological listing), followed by the Probate Court file number assigned to the case. In some instances, guardianships for those who were incompetent and for minors are also reported.

SDHS: The following probate records and wills are available at this facility:

> **SDHS: [Superior Court] "Probate Court Case Files, 1891-1920"** (SDHS/PRC Call No. R3.53 14, p. 60) (11 ft of material) "Case files contain vouchers, dispositions, and bills submitted to estates by creditors. Court testimony is found in some files. Arranged chronologically by year and indexed by name of estate."
>
> **SDHS: [Superior Court] "Probate Orders and Decrees, 1886-1940"** (SDHS/PRC Call No. R3.4 S-6, p. 60) (125 vols) "Record contains court minutes, orders and decrees showing name of estate, case number, and date of hearing; names of testator, attorneys, judge, witnesses, and legatees. Arranged chronologically by court date and indexed by name of estate."
>
> **SDHS: [Superior Court] "Record of Wills, 1880-1927"** (SDHS/PRC Call No. R3.5 7, p. 60) (17 vols) "Record of wills probated in San Diego shows names of deceased (testator), heirs, and witnesses; dates of death and recording of will; and transcript of will. Arranged chronologically by recording date and indexed by name of testator."
>
> **SDHS: [Office of the Treasurer] "Estates of Deceased Persons, 1876-1886, 1923-1924"** (SDHS/PRC Call No. R2.38 6, p. 42) (2 vols) "Record of receipt and disposition of monies from estates shows name of deceased, date of entry, source and amount of receipts, date of disbursements and to whom disbursed, and names of heirs. Arranged chronologically by date of entry and partially indexed by name of deceased."

CORONER/MORTUARY RECORDS

SDHS: [San Diego County Clerk] "Coroner's Inquest Papers, 1853-1904" (SDHS/PRC Call No. R2.69 1, p. 33) (22 boxes) "Coroner's jury papers contain transcripts of testimony from inquests and certificates of death. Certificates show name, age, occupation, marital status, place of birth, length of residence in San Diego County, and previous residence of deceased; and date, cause, and location of death. Arranged chronologically by date of death and indexed by name, cause, and location."

Several veterans in this study were mentioned in these rolls, namely, Peter Elford, Arthur H.M. Haddock, Miles Hughes, Horace Hull, George Hurd, Henry Lamb, J.W. Langdon, Erasmus Payne, Ludlow Pruden, and Simeon Skinner. Information about these individuals from the Coroner's files is flagged with a "Coroner's Inquest File" designation in each individual's death records in Chapter Four.

SDGS: Coroner's Inquest Records of San Diego County 1871-1896 (FHC Call No. 979.498 V27Is). This volume was copied by Thelma L. Faircloth; typed by Norman W. Reed, and states: "The information contained in these pages 1-12 was obtained from Serra Museum, located in Presidio Park, San Diego County (file now transferred to the San Diego Historical Society Archives in Balboa Park). This record dates from 4/18/1871 to 1/5/1896, and contains the name of the deceased, date of death and location, age at death, nativity, and occupation, where available, the names of coroner, witnesses, and jurors who heard the case, and a case number citation.

SDGS: Johnson/Saum and Knobel Mortuary Records, Various Dates (FHC Call No. 979.498 V27ls) Compiled by John H. Sneed, this collection of mortuary records covers the period of 1869-1888 (giving year, name, date of death, age at death, place of birth, sex, marital status, and disposition ("shipped East", "bur Catholic Cem Old Town", etc). Additionally, there are some records from 1907-8 that are more complete (giving date of death, name, age at death, race, nativity, sex, marital status, cause of death, physician, where buried, and place of death).

FHC: Goodbody Funeral Home: Permits for Burial and Removal 1913-1919, and Funeral Home Records from 1914-1921 (US/CAN Film Area, Film No. 1598078) This film can be ordered from the main FHC library at Salt Lake City. These microfilmed records were in the possession of Bernard Goodbody and may be an excellent research source for Catholic burials in San Diego, for Goodbody's Funeral Home was in operation in San Diego for many years, and served the Catholic community. These records include the following: Name, age, sex, residence, name and birthplace of parents, spouse, dates of birth and death, etc. of the deceased as well as county burial permits. The "Author" citation for this microfilm is "San Diego County (California) Registrar".

CEMETERY RECORDS

FHC: The following tombstone or cemetery books are available at the FHC, the best collection of this type of work in the city; however, most of the books feature cemeteries in outlying areas of San Diego, primary in north and east San Diego County. The available books are the following:

Tombstone Inscriptions for San Diego, CA (FHC Call No. 979.498 V22sd) This is a listing of tombstone inscriptions for Mount Hope (29 pp only, partial listing of what appears to be the Masonic Section only), Home of Peace (Jewish), (approx. 30 pp), Holy Cross (several pages), and Calvary Cemetery (approx. 30 pages).

Tombstone Inscriptions: San Diego and Riverside Counties, CA (FHC Call No. 979.498 V22sdr), compiled by the LDS. This volume contains tombstone inscriptions from El Camino Memorial Park (9 pp), Jamul Cemetery (2 pp), Miramar Cemetery (2 pp), La Vista Cemetery, partial (12 pp), Mt. Olivet Cemetery in Nestor (5 pp), El Cajon Cemetery (3 pp), Temecula Cemetery (9 pp), Alpine Cemetery (12 pp), and several small cemeteries (Kolb Cemetery, Higgins Family Cemetery, and a small private cemetery), each with 2 pp. There is also a ten page index to this publication.

Cemetery Records of San Diego County (FHC Call No. 979.498 V22ls) Compiled by SDGS, this volume contains tombstone information from Rancho de la Nacion and Vista Cemeteries (1870-1888), San Pasqual Cemetery tombstone inscriptions compiled in 1981; records for La Vista Cemetery in National City (1881 to the-1890s), Escondido Cemetery records containing birth and death information (1883-1960) and Mount Hope Cemetery records ("B" and "C" surname listings only, probably from Volume I of the Mount Hope Cemetery office records--1869-1909). All these cemetery records were published in <u>Leaves and Saplings</u> magazine. Note: This book was re-named *San Diego Cemetery & Burial Records*, and is available for $5 from SDGS.

Glen Abbey Cemetery, Chula Vista, California: Tombstone Inscriptions to 1968 (FHC Call No. 979.498/C4 V22s) This 393 pp. book contains 324 pp. of inscriptions from the late 1800s to around 1940, and a 70 pp. index.

Evergreen Park Cemetery (FHC Call No. 979.498/L3 V22c) This group of miscellaneous records of La Mesa, CA burials (La Mesa is just east of San Diego) includes burials and an index of burials for Evergreen Park Cemetery, La Mesa, plus internment records from Stokes Funeral Parlor (1911-21) and Erickson Funeral Parlor (1921-1930). It was complied by Thomas Cox in 1992.

Escondido Cemetery Records 1883-1960 (FHC Call No. 979.498/E3 V22c) This SDGS volume contains about 40 pages of records filed by name, plus birth and death dates.

San Diego County Cemeteries, CA (FHC Call No. 979.498 V22s) This information was compiled by the LDS in 1969, and includes Oceanview (37 pp.), Brodie (1 p.) and Hays Cemeteries (1 p.) in Oceanside, and San Luis Rey (13 pp.), Episcopal All Saints (3 pp.) and Freeman Cemeteries (2 pp.) at San Luis Rey.

Oceanview Memorial Park Cemetery Records, Oceanside, CA (FHC Call No. 979.498 V22m) Data from this cemetery was copied by Mary McCann and Velva Mansir in 1965)

Eternal Hills Cemetery, Oceanside, CA--Tombstone Inscriptions (FHC Call No. 979.498/01 V22s) This volume, compiled by the LDS, contains 177 pp. of inscriptions and a 40 pp. index.

Inscriptions and Records of Oceanview Cemetery (FHC Call No. 979.498/01 V22DAR) This group of records was compiled by the DAR, and contains around 100 pages of inscriptions, with a 39 page index.

Olivenhain County Cemetery: A Written Record (FHC Call No. 979.498/02 V22h) Compiled by Chip Haddock as an Eagle Scout Project, this document contains 14 pages of inscriptions.

Two San Diego Cemeteries--Julian [at Julian, CA] and Dearborn Memorial Park [at Poway, CA] (FHC Call No. 979.498 V22f) This volume was compiled in 1980 by an unknown author.

Flynn Springs Cemetery, Lakeside, CA (FHC Call No. 979.498/L2 V22g) Compiled by Joshua Godfrey as an Eagle Scout Project, this document contains two pages of names.

Evergreen Cemetery, El Centro, CA (FHC Call No. 979.499 V22e) Completed by the LDS in 1982, this volume is nearly 1,000 pages long, and contains tombstone inscriptions from El Centro in Imperial County, the county to the east of San Diego County.

SDGS: Mount Hope Cemetery Volume I--1869-1909: This organization has transcribed Volume I of the Mount Hope Cemetery records from the old ledger books at Mount Hope. It is a chronological presentation by letter of the alphabet, and unindexed. The publication is available from the SDGS (see address above). It is not presently available at the FHC.

SDPL: The following cemetery books or articles are available:

Inventory List of El Campo Santo Cemetery, by the late Lawrence Riveroll (SDPL Call No. RCC 979.498/Riveroll)

Confederate Veterans Buried in the United Daughters of the Confederacy Plot at Mt. Hope Cemetery, San Diego, CA, by the United Daughters of the Confederacy (SDPL Call No. RGY 929.5/Confederate)

A History of the Cemeteries in the City of San Diego, California, by Fred Jay Rimbach (SDPL Call No. RCC 393/Rimbach)

Burying Grounds at Old Town San Diego and Mission Hills, by Orion M. Zink (SDPL Call No. RCC 979.498/Zink)

California Cemetery Lots Sold 1889-1915, by Johnson (SDPL Call No. RCC 614.6/Johnson)

Vital Records From Cemeteries in California (SDPL Call No. RGY 929.5/Microfilm--Vol. 11 covers San Diego)

CENSUS RECORDS

FHC: San Diego census records <u>printed in book form</u> are available for the years 1850-1880 (FHC Call No. prefix 979.498 X2Is, followed by the year designation--1850, 1860, 1870, or 1880.) Additionally, there is a printed 1850 census index for California at FHC Call No. C 979.4 X2p 1850)

Regarding microfilmed census records, the California state census index is available on microfilm for 1860; Soundex microfilms are available for California for 1880, 1900 and 1910; and Enumeration District microfilms for California for 1900, 1910, and 1920. The 1910 Enumeration District information is also available on microfiche.

SDPL: Census records <u>printed in book form</u> at SDPL include:

    1850 California Census (AIS) (SDPL Call No. RGY 929.3/Jackson)

    1850 Federal Census of San Diego (SDPL Call No. RGY 929.3794/San)

    1870 Census of San Diego County (SDPL Call No. RGY 929.3974/Census)

    1900 Census Index: Federal Census for San Diego County, compiled by the North San Diego County Genealogical Society (SDPL Call No. RGY 929.3794/SD)

Regarding the 1900 census index, this is the only index of that census available to residents in San Diego proper, as it was compiled by a genealogical organization in North San Diego County. A circulating copy is available at Carlsbad Library in North County. It is an alphabetical listing of heads of households and any other surnames found within the house. The citations read like the following:

Abbey, Eunice-----202-1
Abbott, Mrs. E.---197-6
Abbott, Ephrahim--187-16

The first column names individuals. The second lists the Enumeration District, followed by the page number within that district. The authors explain: "San Diego County Census for 1900 is on two rolls of microfilm prepared by the National Archives and Records Service. Roll T623-99 includes Enumeration Districts No. 172 through 199, and Sheets 1-4 of Enumeration District No. 200. Roll T623-100 continues the rest of the census for the county. Fort Rosecrans is not assigned an Enumeration District number, and appears in the index as 'Fort Rosecrans.' At the time of the 1900 census, San Diego County included what is now Imperial County." This census contains a wealth of information on individuals and family members, and an index to it helps to enable the researcher to go directly to the persons being researched.

SDPL also has census records for San Diego County on microfilm from 1850-1920. Additionally, the 1860 California Census Index is on 8 microfiche at SDPL Call No.s RCC 929.3794/Microfiche (California Room) and RGY 929.3794/Microfiche (Genealogy Room).

SDHS: [Federal Records] "U.S. Census-Manuscript, 1850, 1860, 1870, 1880, 1900, 1910": (SDHS/PRC Call No: R4.4 13, p. 63) "Transcripts of decennial census schedules may include the following information for San Diego County individuals: Name, age, sex, color, occupation, value of real and personal property, place of birth, marital status, and education. Schedules for 1880, 1900 and 1910 on microfilm only."

NA: The National Archives has all the census information for California. However, these are all available locally, as noted above.

BIOGRAPHICAL AND VERTICAL FILES

SDHS: Biographical & Vertical Files: The "Biographical Files" contain over 260 notebooks of newspaper clippings for individuals, arranged alphabetically by surname. The "Vertical Files" contain 1,300 folders of clippings arranged alphabetically for over 700 topics. Both collections are continually being updated by the SDHS archives staff.

SDPL: Biographical & Vertical Files: There are at least ten 3-drawer file cabinets in the California Room which contain newspaper clippings, excerpts from magazines or journals, and possible citations to individuals, locations, historic sites, or events.

SDPL: Personal Name Index: A book is available entitled: *Personal Name Index to 1856 City Directories of California*, by Nathan C. Parker, (SDPL Call No. RGY 929.3794/Parker) although this book predates most of the Civil War veterans of this study, who arrived in San Diego primarily after 1870.

PEDIGREE CHARTS

FHC: Early San Diego, CA Families, Vols I and II (Call No. 979.498 D2F) These two volumes contain pedigree charts for members of the following families: Altamirano, Alvarado, Ames, Arguello, Connors, Cota, Couts, Dominguez, Estudillo (in Vol I), and Horton, Lopez, Machado, Pico, Pio Pico and Serrano (in Vol. 2.) Additional information about early San Diego families can be obtained from members of the "Old Town Descendants" group which meets on a somewhat regular basis. They can be contacted through Old Town State Park in San Diego, at (619) 694-3049.

FHC: San Diego Pedigrees (Call No. 979.498 D3s) This is a compilation of donated pedigrees of San Diegans, including a 26 pp. index and about 500 pages of pedigree charts.

CITY/COUNTY/GENERAL HISTORIES

SDHS: This facility has the best collection of city and county histories, although many are duplicated at the California Room of the SDPL: These books often contain bios of the more prominent Civil War Veterans. Some of the veterans included in this study are mentioned in these sources. They are discussed in the "Prominence" section, Chapter Three.

SDPL/FHC: At the SDPL, some city and county histories are stored in locked storage in the California Room (RCC designation); in open stacks in the Genealogy Room (RGY designation), in the History Department, or in storage (go to the storage books desk near the History Department on the first floor).

The following city or county histories are at SDPL and/or FHC (see Chapter Seven "Source Notes" for full citations to these texts): (Note--some public library books may also be located at branch libraries; check your local branch for details.)

> Adema, Thomas Joseph, *Our Hills and Valleys: A History of the Helix-Spring Valley Region*, (SDPL Call No. 979.498/Adema), a copy in the History Department.

Black, Samuel F., *San Diego County, California: A Record of Settlement, Organization, Progress and Achievement*, Vol. 1; and _____, *San Diego County, California: A Record of Settlement, Organization, Progress and Achievement*, Vol. 2. There are three copies of Vol.s 1 and 2 in the California Room (at SDPL Call No. RCC 979.498/Black). There is at least one copy of both volumes in the History Department and in Storage, at 979.498/Black. Note: Samuel F. Black is the author of only the first of the two volumes of this book.

Bigger, Richard, et al, *Metropolitan Coast*, one copy in the California Room at SDPL Call No. RCC 979.49/Bigger, and one copy in the History Department at 979.49/Bigger.

_____, *The City and County of San Diego, Illustrated*, published by Leberthon and Taylor. At least six copies in the California Room at SDPL Call No. RCC 979.49807, and one copy in the Genealogy Room at RGY 979.49807. This book is also at the FHC Salt Lake City library (FHC Call No. US/CAN Book Area 979.498 H2t).

City of Chula Vista, *Chula Vista Heritage, 1911-1986*, (SDPL Call No. 979.498/Chula), a copy in the History Department.

Heilbron, Carl H., *History of San Diego County*, one copy in the California Room at SDPL Call No. RCC 979.498/Heilbron, and two copies in storage at 979.498/Heilbron.

Heintzelman, Samuel Peter, *Fifty Miles and a Fight: Major Samuel Peter Heintzelman's Journal of Texas and the Cortina War*, (SDPL Call No. 972.014/Heintzelman), one copy, located in the History Department).

Lay, Eldonna P., *Valley of Opportunity: The History of El Cajon*, (SDPL Call No. 979.498/Lay), a copy in the History Department.

Lewis Publishing Company, *Illustrated History of Southern California*, two copies in the California Room at SDPL Call No. RCC 979.49/Illustrated; one copy in the Genealogy Room at RGY 979.49/Illustrated, and one copy in Storage at 979.49/Illustrated.

MacPhail, Elizabeth Reinbold, *The Influence of German Immigrants on the Growth of San Diego*, one copy in the California Room at SDPL Call No. RCC 325.79498/MacPhail. The FHC also has a copy of this book (FHC Call No. 979.498 H2mp). It doesn't appear that any Civil War veterans of this study are mentioned in it, however.

MacPhail, Elizabeth, *The Story of New San Diego and of its Founder Alonzo E. Horton*. One copy in the California Room at SDPL Call No. RCC 979.498/MacPhail, and two copies in the History Department at 979.498/MacPhail.

McConnell, Stuart, *Glorious Contentment: The Grand Army of the Republic 1865-1900*. (SDPL Call No. 973.74/McConnell), one copy in the History Department.

McGrew, Clarence, *City of San Diego and San Diego County*, two sets of two volumes in the California Room at SDPL Call No. RCC 979.498/McGrew; and one set of two volumes in the Genealogy Room at RGY 979.498/McGrew. These volumes are also at the FHC Salt Lake City library (FHC Call No. US/CAN Book Area 979.498 H2m).

Parker, J. Carlyle, *Index to Biographees in 19th Century California County Histories*, one copy in the California Room at SDPL Call No. RGY 979.404/Parker. The listings are by surname and reference particular county histories. All of the county histories for San Diego which are listed in this book are available in the SDPL California Room.

Parker, Nathan C., *Personal Name Index to the 1856 City Directories of California*, one copy in the Genealogy Room at RGY 929.3794/Parker.

San Diego Historical Society, *San Diego County Pioneer Families*, one copy in the California Room at SDPL Call No. RCC 920/San, and one copy in the History Department at 920/San. The FHC also has this book at FHC Call No. 979.498.

Scott, Ed, *San Diego County Soldier Pioneers 1846-1866*, one copy in the California Room at SDPL Call No. RCC 979.49806/Scott, with an additional copy in the History Department and in storage, both at 979.49806/Scott) This book is also available at the Family History Center (FHC Call No. 979.498 M2s).

Smythe, William E., *History of San Diego 1542-1907*, eight copies in the California Room at SDPL Call No. RCC 979.498/Smythe, one in the History Department at 979.498/Smythe, plus a two volume set is available: Vol. 1--Old Town; Vol. 2--The Modern City, in storage at SDPL Call No. 979.498/Smythe. (These duplicate, as far as can be determined, the one volume Smythe books.)

San Diego Public Library, *Index to [William E. Smythe's] History of San Diego*, three copies in the California Room at SDPL Call No. RCC 979.498/San Diego; one copy in the Genealogy Room at RGY 979.498/San Diego, and a reference copy in the History Department at R979.498/San Diego.

Stanford, Leland Ghent, *San Diego's LLB: Legal Lore and the Bar* is available at the FHC (FHC Call No. 979.498 H2st).

Stewart, Don, *Frontier Port*, one copy in the California Room at SDPL Call No. RCC 979.498/Stewart, and two copies in the Wangenheim Special Collection.

Wohlers, Bertha Palmer, *Follow the Light: The Palmer Family and the Savoy Theater*, one copy in the California Room at SDPL Call No. CC RCC 929.20973/Palmer, and a copy in the History Department at 929.20973/Palmer.

PHOTOS

SDHS: The Photo collection at the San Diego Historical Society is the largest collection of its kind in the city. It dates from 1870 to the present, and now totals approximately 2.5 million images of San Diego. SDHS obtained the photographs of the Title Insurance & Trust collection and those of many commercial and amateur photographers. SDHS has built the collection into a strong one over the years.

Included in the collection are photographs of individuals, landmarks, architecture, and historic events, plus negatives of photos which appeared in San Diego newspapers. The collection has just been described in a special edition of *The San Diego Journal of History* entitled "Guide to the Photograph Collection of the San Diego Historical Society" by Greg Williams, Photo Curator. It can be purchased from SGHS at a cost of around $14.95. The photo archives are open for research Thursday through Saturday from 10:00 a.m. to 4:00 p.m., and their phone number is: (619) 232-6203, ext. 127.

CITY DIRECTORIES

SDPL: City Directories: This facility has directories from 1886-1950 on 25 reels of microfilm (SDPL Call No. RCC 910). There are also printed directories on the shelves in the California Room from 1900 to the present. Printed directories from the late 1800s are kept in a locked area near the California Room.

The early city directories listed wives, wives as widows, and deaths of individuals. An example of the latter is: "Dr. Gilbert P. Bennett died 10/19/1910, aged 75." This listing was printed in the city directory for 1911, a year after Dr. Bennett's death. Scan the directories in five year increments to see when an individual arrived in San Diego or in outlying communities, and when he or she dropped out of the listings. Check movement around the city by addresses, and notice occupations, which are often listed. City directories rank right up with tax rolls in placing an individual at a location within a specific time period.

SDHS: City Directories: The date range for city directories at SDHS is from the late 1850s (several early directories), to the Pacific Coast Directories of 1882-1885, followed by city directories from 1886-1984.

FHC: The FHC has San Diego city directories for the following years: 1924, 1926, 1940, and 1958-1974.

NEWSPAPERS

SDPL: Newspaper Room: One of the best resources at this library is the collection of early newspapers on microfilm, and enough readers to spend time reading them on. There are also three reader printers. The most important microfilm holdings in the Newspaper Room are:

   San Diego Union: October 10, 1868-February 1, 1992

   San Diego Evening Tribune: December 1895-February 1, 1992

   San Diego Union-Tribune: February 2, 1992 to the present

   San Diego Herald: 1851-1860 (incomplete); 1914-1946

   San Diego Sun: July 1881-November 1939 (Incomplete)

SDPL: Index to San Diego Newspapers: 1851-1903; 1930-1983 In the California Room, there is a very important set of microfiche containing photos of index cards with references to subjects, individuals, organizations and events reported in San Diego newspapers within the date ranges above. Please note that the index has a gap in years when newspapers were NOT indexed.

Find a citation in this index to a newspaper article about a subject, individual, organization, event, etc. and go next door to the Newspaper Room to view the microfilm for the year and date you need. Be aware that at times an article will appear in a newspaper other than the San Diego Union or Tribune, and if it does, the index cards note that fact. Otherwise, you might be viewing a San Diego Union newspaper microfilm, and really need a microfilm for the San Diego Herald, for example.

SDPL: Newspaper Records 1851-1860: The Genealogy Room has a publication by the SDGS entitled "Newspaper Records" (SDPL Call No. RGY 929.3794/Newspaper), which contains transcriptions of vital records from the San Diego Herald from May 29, 1851 to April 7, 1860, copied by Ruth T. Dryden and Jeanette K. Nelson.

Several obituaries from this volume are cited in Chapter Four of this study for the following individuals who died during the earliest years that Civil War veterans and their wives were in San Diego: Henry M. Bentzel, Enoch Birdseye, Lucy Knowles, Maria Leonard, James D. Mantania, Jennie P. Paine, Josiah Rowe, and Charles Whipple.

SDHS: Newspapers: The SDHS has a 70+ page printout of all of its newspaper holdings, which are extensive. It has the same microfiche index to newspapers as the San Diego Public Library does, but only one film reader. Contact the SDHS at (619) 232-6203 for more information on this collection.

FHC: Newspapers--Various Dates: A SDGS publication entitled "Newspapers" (FHC Call No. 979.4) has the following: Several pages of births, deaths, and marriages from the San Diego Herald, 1851-1854; about 80 pages of vital records from the San Diego Union for 1868-1885; three pages of unknown content from the San Diego Bulletin for 1869-1871; a two page list of letters left at the Post Office at San Diego from the San Diego Herald on 5/29/1851; and three pages from the Otay Press dated 3/28/1889.

FHC: Union List of Newspapers for San Diego and Imperial County (FHC Call No. 979.498 N2s. Compiled by San Diego State University, 1976.) On pp. 12-18 of this publication are listed all of the newspapers that were published in the San Diego region, and the library which has copies or microfilms of each of them; however, the list is outdated.

ORAL HISTORY INTERVIEWS

SDHS: Oral History Interviews: There is a large collection of oral history interviews at SDHS (SDHS Call No. "OH" and filed by surname) which contain accounts of people, lifestyles, and events. The collection consists of over 550 taped and transcribed interviews. An example: The grandson of veteran Moses A. Luce was interviewed about his grandfather and the beginning of the Luce Forward law firm, etc. SDHS also has many books, artifacts, diaries, etc. donated by families that are wonderful to use to enhance a research project.

VOTER REGISTERS

SDPL: Great Register of Voters SDPL has the Great Register of Voters for the years 1866 through 1909.

SDHS: [County Clerk] "Great Register of Voters, 1877-1898" (SDHS/PRC Call No. R2.119 1-3, p. 33) (8 vols) "Published voter registration lists show name of voter, age, nativity, occupation, local residence (township), whether naturalized, and date registered. Volumes after 1892 also indicate height, complexion, color of eyes and hair, visible marks and scars, and post office address. Arranged alphabetically by name of voter."

SDHS: [County Clerk] "Registrations, 1902, 1906" (SDHS/PRC Call No. R2.53 6 12, p. 34) (3 Vols) "Record indexes the Great Register of San Diego County, listing name, address, and age of voters in city and outside precincts. Arranged alphabetically by name of voter."

FHC: Great Register of Voters 1866-1873, 1866-1879, and 1880-1887 (FHC Call No. 979.498 X31s) Describing the first date range of 1866-1873, the SDGS authors state: "All information contained in this document was taken from the Great Register of San Diego County, CA covering the years of 1866 through 1873 and is accurate to the best of our ability to transcribe the handwritten records contained therein."

An example of an earlier 1866 record in the SDGS Great Register is that of a merchant named Cajetan Anchner, below. This earlier Register is alphabetical by surname, and uses the following key: (1)--Age (2)--Country of Nativity (3)--Occupation (4)--Local Residence (5)--Naturalized (6)--Locality (7)--Date of Voting Registration. Later Great Register entries added the following additional information in category (8)--D: No longer in country or deceased; R: Removed; or C: Cancelled. The Cajetan Anchner cite reads:

    Anchner, Cajetan (1) 29 (2) Austria (3) Merchant (4) San Diego (5) 102172 (6) San Diego County Court House (7) 102172

The ease of use of the Great Register makes it a valuable tool for genealogical purposes. Follow up research in the Great Register with census and other sources to fully establish that an individual ancestor was indeed in San Diego at an early date.

PROPERTY RECORDS

SDC: Land Records: Property records are housed at the County Assessor's Office, Room 130, 1600 Pacific Highway in San Diego. At the county, the earliest grantor/grantee indexes are on microfilm, not in book form, unlike death and marriage records. The early records were very difficult to read. Thus, they were not researched to determine the date the county first started recording information for each letter of the alphabet, as was done in this section for marriage and death records. Deed Information was gathered by the county from 1850 to the present. Early grantor/grantee indexes are alphabetical by surname, and give deed numbers. Go to other microfilms containing the deed number you wish to research. You can print out deeds and other property records from reader/printers for $2 per page.

More recent deed indexes are available on the county's computer. but only for the years 1982-Present for alpha or numeric searches, and 1970-1989 for alpha searches (an additional index). In the computer, deeds are registered by either surname or deed number. Once a reference number to a particular deed is obtained, then the deed microfilm can be viewed, and a copy printed out for $2 per page.

SDPL: Grantee/Grantor Index: There is a citation to "Land Records, San Diego County, California-- Grantor Index--Deed Books A-25" at the California Room, SDPL Call No. RGY 929.3794/Land.

SDHS: This source has the following information on deeds:

> **[County Recorder] "Index to deeds, 1850-1886":** (SDHS/PRC Call No. R2.57 6, p. 37) (5 vols) "Index shows names of grantors and grantees, date of deed, and book and page of recording. Arranged alphabetically by name of grantor and grantee."
>
> **[County Recorder] "Deeds, Miscellaneous 1850-1919"** (SDHS/PRC Call No. R2.118, p. 37) (2 boxes) "Deed instruments show names of grantor and grantee, legal description of property, amount of consideration, book and page of recording, and date filed. Arranged chronologically by date of filing and indexed alphabetically by names of grantor and grantee."
>
> **[City Clerk] "Deeds (Deed Record) 1850-1947":** (SDHS/PRC Call No. R1.10, p. 21) (12 Vols) "Transcripts of legal deeds show real property and property rights obtained by the City of San Diego. Entries include the date and type of deed, location, names of owners, amounts of compensation paid, and purpose of city acquisition. Arranged chronologically by date of deed."

FHC: Deeds of San Diego County, 1850-1876 (FHC Call No. 979.498 R2L) Compiled by the SDGS, the information is listed by Grantor, Grantee, Deed Date and Page (in deed book). According to the text, "The first deed recorded in San Diego County was Feb. 6, 1850. Deed Index Book One commences with this date, ending in 1876, providing the index for Deed Books A through E and 1 through 28."

FHC: Preemptions from San Diego County, CA (FHC Call No. 979.498 R2Is) According to the text, [Preemption] "...declarations read as follows: I, _____, county of San Diego, a citizen of the U.S., ... conformity to an Act prescribing the mode of maintaining, defending, possessory actions on public lands ... State of California, passed April 20, 1852, has claimed occupied and settled for (grazing, or whatever purpose), 160 acres public land (gives location of land and boundaries). The oath says boundaries ordained in the preemption are correct and does not contain more than 160 acres and he has not taken up any other land and same is not under any existing title. Name of recorder and deputy."

The data in this volume are keyed to Page (the preemption found on), Name, Date Filed, Recorded, and Abandoned, as the following examples show:

Page	Name	Filed	Recorded	Abandoned
135	R.M. Barton	April 18, 1868	July 8, 1868	Received for filing June 27, 1868
160	William Cant	July 20, 1868	July 21, 1868	May 22, 1869
163	Edward Burr	July 21, 1868	July 22, 1868	August 10, 1868

"Veteran's Who Applied for Land in Southern California"

Judy A. Deeter transcribed a series of entries in the above-named book of veterans who sought to secure land from the Federal Government. The information is at the National Archives Laguna Niguel facility (address on p. 24), and can be located using the following citation: Record Group 49, titled "Bureau of Land Management Records at the National Archives Pacific Southwest Region, Laguna Niguel, California". The files in that record group are: "Records of Entries Filed Pursuant to Soldiers and Sailors Act: ca 1872-1896", and Military Warrant Index Books for the Acts of 1847, 28 Sept. 1850, and 3 March 1855.

Some of the Civil War veterans of this study are included in the book, namely: James L. Dryden, a Henry W. Fletcher, William H. Francis, Thomas B. Hartzell, William P. Henderson, William H. Holabird, William F.C. James, Alymer Keith, Samuel W. Kroff, William E. Miller, Joseph C. Milliron, James G.B. Nichols, Samuel J. Nickens, John Noble, Patrick Noble, George W. Parker, Winfield Scott, Jonathan R. Spencer, William P. Stone, Melvin D. Sunnocks, Thomas M. Tartt, Samuel Waugh, Calvin M. Wood, Horace P. Woodward, and a William D. Woodward.

To order this book, contact Judy A. Deeter at 4 Altezza Drive, Mission Viejo, CA 92692-5107.

TAX RECORDS

SDC: San Diego County has tax and assessment records dating from the beginning of the county in 1850, and they are available at the County Administration Building, Room 103, 1600 Pacific Highway, San Diego. For property records information, call (619) 236-3771, Ext. 0.

SDHS has the following assessor's records:

[County Assessor] "Assessment Lists, 1853-1873." (SDHS/PRC Call No. R2.102 14, p. 25) (8 boxes) "Lists of property, real and personal, show name of property owner, legal description of property, nature and value of taxable personal property (farm animals, financial instruments, etc.) and date filed. Arranged chronologically and indexed by name of property owner."

[County Assessor] "Reports of the County Assessor, 1875-1894." (SDHS/PRC Call No. R2.11 15, p. 25) (1 Vol) "Annual summaries of county taxable property--real and personal--show description of property or item, values, and totals. Arranged chronologically."

[County Assessor] "Assessment Roll (Tax Books). 1850-1854, 1859, 1869, 1871-1876." (SDHS/PRC Call No. R2.20 12, p. 26) (9 Vols) "Rolls of real property and secured personal property show owner's name, residence, legal description of property, number of acres, value of property and improvements, value of personal property, total taxes due, and date paid. Arranged alphabetically by name of taxpayer."

FHC: Taxpayers of San Diego County, Book II--1851 (FHC Call No. 979.498 X2I) This SDGS publication copied by Virginia Rodefer lists tax assessment rolls for the early 1850s, but is probably too early in time for most Civil War veterans who came to San Diego. The author notes: "This 1851 Tax Assessment Roll was found in the collections of the San Diego Historical Society, Junipero Serra Museum, (now the SDHS Archives), and represents only a partial list. Most of the entries are for ranches, with only a few in the town."

MARRIAGE RECORDS

SDC: Marriage records: Some Civil War veterans of this study were married after arriving in San Diego, and would perhaps be listed in the San Diego County marriage indexes. These are available for viewing in Room 260 of the County Administration Building. There are old marriage record books, and they have been indexed either by name of groom or name of bride. The first groom's ledger book, for example, gives the following date ranges when the first names were entered for various letters of the alphabet. For example, groom surnames starting with "A" were being listed from 1850 on; for "L" from 1859 on, etc., as seen below:

A: 1850 on	N: 1874 on
B: 1858 on	O: 1859 on
C: 1859 on	P: 1850 on
D: 1851 on	Q: 1876 on
E: 1857 on	R: 1859 on
F: 1854 on	S: 1859 on
G: 1859 on	T: 1864 on
H: 1856 on	U: 1876 on
I: 1872 on	V: 1866 on
J: 1851 on	W: 1857 on
K: 1864 on	X: No dates in early book
L: 1859 on	Y: 1877 on
M: 1859 on	Z: 1874 on
Mc:1865 on	

Dr. David Hoffman, Civil War veteran of this study, was listed under "H" in the marriage index book. He was married on July 3, 1857 to Maria Wilder in San Diego, and the citation in the index is to Book 1, p. 5 of the marriage records. The old marriage records were microfilmed, and can be viewed on a microfilm reader. The actual marriage records are not in ledger books but in fragile books that are not available for public viewing. A certified copy of a marriage record can be purchased for $12.

According to the information sheet that the staff uses, the following was stated: "Public marriage records are open to the public. Anyone may purchase copies and/or view these records free of charge. Confidential marriage records are not open to the public, and may be purchased only by the bride or groom. They must show ID."

The information sheet also states that public marriage records are available for the following date ranges: "Public marriages from 1856-1904 (old books in vault); 1905-1972 (on microfiche under overhead in Vital area); 1973 to the present (on computer and on microfiche)." There are also "Confidential Marriage Records: 1973-1976 (on microfilm in the copy area; order by the computer); or from 1976-present (on computer and microfiche) Confidential marriages began in 1973. Note: please compare these date ranges with the actual date ranges of records in the "Grooms First Ledger Book chart, above, as marriage records began at an earlier time than is printed on the staff information sheet. Contact the County of San Diego for additional information on marriage records at (619) 237-0502, ext. 24.

SDHS: [County Recorder] "Marriage Certificates 1880-1881" (SDHS/PRC Call No. R2.87 14, p. 37) (2 files) "Certificates show the names of bride, groom, and witnesses; name and title of person officiating;

nativity of bride, groom, and parents; and dates of marriage and recording. Arranged chronologically and indexed by name."

SDHS: [County Recorder] "Quarterly Returns of Marriages and Births 1858-1860" (SDHS/PRC Call No. R2.86 14, p. 38) (2 files) "Returns of marriage show names, age, color, residence, and nativity for bride and groom; date and location of marriage; name, residence, and position of person officiating; and date of recording.

BIRTH RECORDS

SDC: Birth Records: Some Civil War veterans of this study had children after arriving in San Diego. Birth records are available from 1873 to 1904 (old books in vault), and from 1905-present on computer and on microfiche. The staff information sheet states: "Birth records are not open to the public. They may be purchased only. Customers must have information necessary to locate the record. If the customer does not have the full name and birth date of birth record being requested, a supervisor must be contacted by the counter staff." Call the County for additional information on birth records at (619) 237-0502, Ext. 22.

SDHS: [County Recorder] "Quarterly Returns of Marriages and Births 1858-1860" (SDHS/PRC Call No. R2.86 14, p. 38) (2 files) Returns of birth show name, sex and color of newborn; date and location of birth; names, residence, color and nativity of parents, and date of recordation. Arranged chronologically and indexed by name."

SDHS: [County Recorder] "Return of Birth 1874-1876" (SDHS/PRC Call No. R2.79 14, p. 38) (1 box) "Birth notices show the name, sex, and race of the newborn; date and place of birth; name and residence of parents; names of medical attendant and person making report. Arranged chronologically by date of birth and indexed by name."

SDGS: Newspapers, 1871-1884 (FHC Call No. 979.498 V21s) This SDGS list contains birth information from the San Diego Herald, published from May 29, 1851 to April 7, 1860.

SDPL: Parish Register, Mission San Diego de Alcala The SDPL has a set of baptismal records entitled *Baptisms for the Mission and Vicinity, 1769-1850* (SDPL Call No. RCC 979.403, Vol. 1 and Vol. 2--two reels). These may be early records of baptisms; the records were submitted by R. Clinton Griffin. While these records are too early for the Civil War veterans, they are of historic value in the study of early inhabitants of the Mission and its surrounding areas.

DIVORCE RECORDS

SDC: Divorce Records Divorce records are found in the Superior Court Older Records office at 220 Broadway, San Diego, Ph: (619) 531-3244. Records before 1960 are not indexed, and are in old ledger books divided into 10 year periods. The 1940-49 book (for example) had names filed by letter of the alphabet, and then chronologically as each divorce was filed. When searching the "H" surnames recently, it was found that listings in the 1940-1949 ledger book would run from 1940-1949 for a few pages, and then start over with 1940 and go to 1949 again. This happened several times in the "H" alphabet being researched. Additionally, divorce records were mixed with civil case filings. Thus, research in divorce records could prove to be a tedious process unless an exact date a divorce was filed is known.

CIVIL/CRIMINAL RECORDS

SDC: Civil/Criminal Records: Superior Court civil and criminal records are also located in Older Records at 220 Broadway, San Diego, CA 92101. (See above discussion of the older ledger books at this facility.)

Contact Older Records at (619) 531-3244 for additional information on these files.

SDHS: SDHS has the following Civil/Criminal case files:

[County Court] "Case Files--Civil and Criminal 1850-1880" (SDHS/PRC Call No. R3.55 14, p. 49) (7 boxes) "Case files contain the official documents of the court including complaint, subpoenas, arrest warrants, transcripts of testimony, jury verdicts, court actions and judgments. Arranged chronologically by court date and indexed by names of plaintiffs and defendants, and cause."

[Court of Sessions] "Case Files--Civil and Criminal 1850-1860" (SDHS/PRC Call No. R3.54 14, p. 50) (2 boxes) "Case files contain the official documents of the court including complaint, subpoenas, arrest warrants, transcripts of testimony, jury verdicts, court actions and judgments. Arranged chronologically by court date and indexed by names of plaintiffs and defendants, and cause."

[District Court] "Case Files--Civil and Criminal 1850-1880" (SDHS/PRC Call No. R3.38 S-6, p. 50) (56 boxes) "Case files of civil and criminal proceedings show names of plaintiffs, defendants, and judge; court dates and actions. Papers contained in typical case files include: Complaints, subpoenas, affidavits of witnesses, receipts, arrest warrants, testimony, verdicts, and other documents. Arranged numerically by case number and indexed by names of plaintiffs and defendants."

[Grand Jury] "Grand Jury Reports 1906-1928" (SDHS/PRC Call No. R3.40 14, p. 51) (2 boxes) "Record contains official transcripts of preliminary and final reports of investigations conducted in San Diego County, including supplemental reports and audits of county departments. Arranged chronologically by year."

[Justice Court] "Case Files--Civil and Criminal 1870-1918" (SDHS/PRC Call No. R3.37 1, p. 52) (9 boxes) "Justice court case files show names of plaintiff, defendant, and justice; court dates and actions. Papers contained in the files may include: complaint, subpoena, affidavits of witnesses, receipts, arrest warrants, verdict and testimony. Arranged alphabetically by name of township and chronologically thereunder by court date. Indexed by names of plaintiff and defendant, subject, and township."

[Superior Court] "Case Files--Civil and Criminal 1879-1921" (SDHS/PRC Call No. R3.39 7, p. 58) (630 ft of materials) "Case files contain the official documents of the court, including complaint, subpoenas, arrest warrants, transcripts of testimony, jury verdicts, court actions and judgments. Arranged chronologically and indexed by names of plaintiffs and defendants."

[Superior Court] "Judgements--Civil 1886-1947" (SDHS/PRC Call No. R3.3 5, p. 59) (113 Vols) "Judgement books show the case number, names of plaintiffs, defendants and judge; and all judgments and orders. Arranged chronologically by date of judgment and indexed (vols. 19-119) by name of plaintiff."

CHURCH RECORDS

FHC: Episcopal Church Records (FHC Call No. 979.498 V26I) This SDGS study contains early parish register records for Holy Trinity Episcopal Church (1872-1887) which became St. Paul's Episcopal Church on January 22, 1887. The records contain the following:

Parish Register at Holy Trinity Church for 1872. This register lists the following Civil War veterans or their wives: Mrs. Birdseye, William Wallace Bowers and family, David Bancroft Hoffman, Joseph Leonard and Maria Caroline Leonard (the latter was deceased), Matthew and Augusta Sherman, a William Wallace Stewart and family, and Erastus Weegar and family.

Record of Baptisms at Holy Trinity Church from October 1872 to February 1887. This register lists the following veterans: Josiah Lemuel Rowe, Augusta Sherman, two Sherman children, Lucy Horton Bowers, two Bowers children, Ackley child, three Remondino children, and James Mylon Nosler, who was baptized as an adult and died the same evening, with the respective family members of these individuals also listed.

Record of Marriages at Holy Trinity Church from April 1873 to June, 1887. This register lists the marriages of the following veterans (Note: because marriage records are important, a complete citation to each marriage is given below):

Utt, Lee H. & Gunn, Sarah M., at home of Dr. Gunn. 29 Apr 1876. Wit: Charles S. Hamilton and J. Gordon.

Remondino, Peter C. & Earle, Sophie, at res. of Mr. Earle. 27 Sep 1877. Wit: Father & brother of bride and B. Etcheverry. [Note: an earlier citation read: Etchevery, Bernard & Earle, Louise at home of Mr. Earle. 2 Apr 1877.] Minister: Rev. Hobart Chetwood.

Paine, J.O.W. & Crofts(?), Anna B. at res of A. Kooken. 22 June 1886. Wit: J.A. Kooken and C. Paine. Minister: H.B. Restarick. Minister: Rev. Hobart Chetwood.

Brabazon, George Philip Augustus & Nugent, Rhoda Jane, at house on D St., 11 Aug 1886. Wit: J.G. Nugent & Marion Nugent.

Record of Burials for Holy Trinity Church from January 1873 to March, 1887 This register lists deaths for the following veterans or their wives: _____ Birdseye, Maria Leonard, R.V. Dodge, and Joseph Leonard. Note: See death information for these individuals in Chapter Four.

Various Church Registers (church unstated) from 1873-1881. These list the following veterans or their wives: Joseph and Maria Leonard, Augusta Sherman, Lucy Horton Bowers, and Mrs. Weegar.

There are also several **Registers of St. Paul's Communicants for 1887-1894**, which list the following names: Lucy Horton Bowers, Matthew and Augusta Sherman, George and A. Puterbaugh, George and Rhoda Jane Brabazon, William and Adaline Bailhache, Frank and Harriet Earle, and Mrs. Van Arman.

FHC: Presbyterian Church Records (FHC Call No. 979.498 V26ls) This volume (also available at the SDPL Call No. RGY979.498) contains records spanning the time period of 1880-1930, with most records dating from 1910-1930. The Presbyterian Church was started in San Diego with 12 members on June 7, 1869. A church building was built in 1887, and a second one in 1912. Citations are given alphabetically by surname and year of entry into the church.

The Civil War veterans that were Presbyterian Church members included George M. Dannals and his wife Lucy L. Dannals (who joined this church in 1887 or before), and Isaac A. Esleek (who joined on 3/1/1891 from Fall River, MA.)

NATURALIZATION RECORDS

A study was not done on naturalization records for purposes of this book. The following is a brief survey of the types of records that are available.

NA: The National Archives naturalization records for San Diego are the following:

Index to San Diego Superior Court Naturalizations, 1929-1956	M1526 VI
Index to Citizens Naturalized, San Diego Superior Court, 1853-1956	M1609 VI
San Diego Superior Court Records, 1883-1940	M1613 VI
Index to San Diego Superior Court Declarations, 1853-1956	M1612 VI
Declarations of Intent to the San Diego Superior Court, 1871-1941	9L-RA-1 VI

SDPL: There is an **Index to Declaration of Intention in the Superior Court of San Diego County, California**, 1853-1956 (original and duplicate, 2 identical reels) in the California Room at SDPL Call No. RGY 929.3794; and **Naturalization Index Cards from the Superior Court of San Diego County, CA**, 1920-1956 from 1920-1956 (five reels, also in the California Room at SDPL Call No. RGY 929.3794.)

FHC: The FHC has many records on naturalization because this is a primary genealogical tool. These records are too numerous to mention here. Visit the FHC (address on p. 25) for additional information on naturalization records. Also, search the FHC Library Catalog for naturalization records available from the Salt Lake City library.

MAPS

SDHS: Sanborn Maps There is an extensive collection of maps at SDHS, which also includes Sanborn Company Maps. These maps show individual city blocks and the buildings that were built on them.

SDPL: Sanborn Maps Sanborn maps are also available at SDPL, on both microfilm (1884-1970--the City of San Diego being on Reels 53,54 and 76) and printed Sanborn maps which are available in the California Room. Often on the printed maps, the individual plots of land will have overlays of paper showing subsequent ownerships. The Sanborn maps at the California Room are too fragile to photocopy, but a microfilm version is available in the Newspaper Room for that purpose. The History Department of SDPL also has many atlas books containing maps of current and historic interest.

FHC: There is a map drawer at the FHC with a collection of maps sorted by state and country. The FHC card catalog gives references to the maps in these drawers.

HISTORICAL SITE BOARD RECORDS

SDHS: San Diego Historical Site Board Reports: This set of reports describes the various buildings, sites and locations that have attained "historic site" status through the San Diego Historical Site Board. For example, Calvary Cemetery is Historic Site No. 5; El Campo Santo is Site No. 26; the San Diego Barracks is Site No. 30; and Old Town's Protestant Cemetery is Site No. 47.

The descriptive data in the Historical Site Board Reports includes the name of the site, its location, its current and original ownership, original use and period (such as "Early American Period"); other comments, physical details of the property, a summary of its historic significance, a map showing site location, and photographs of the property, along with other supplemental information where available. Originals are housed with the Historic Site Board at the City Administration Building in downtown San Diego.

A call to the City Planning Department will access the Historical Site Board; their phone number is: (619) 235-5200. Because Historical Site Board records are often overlooked, an example of a such a record is presented below:

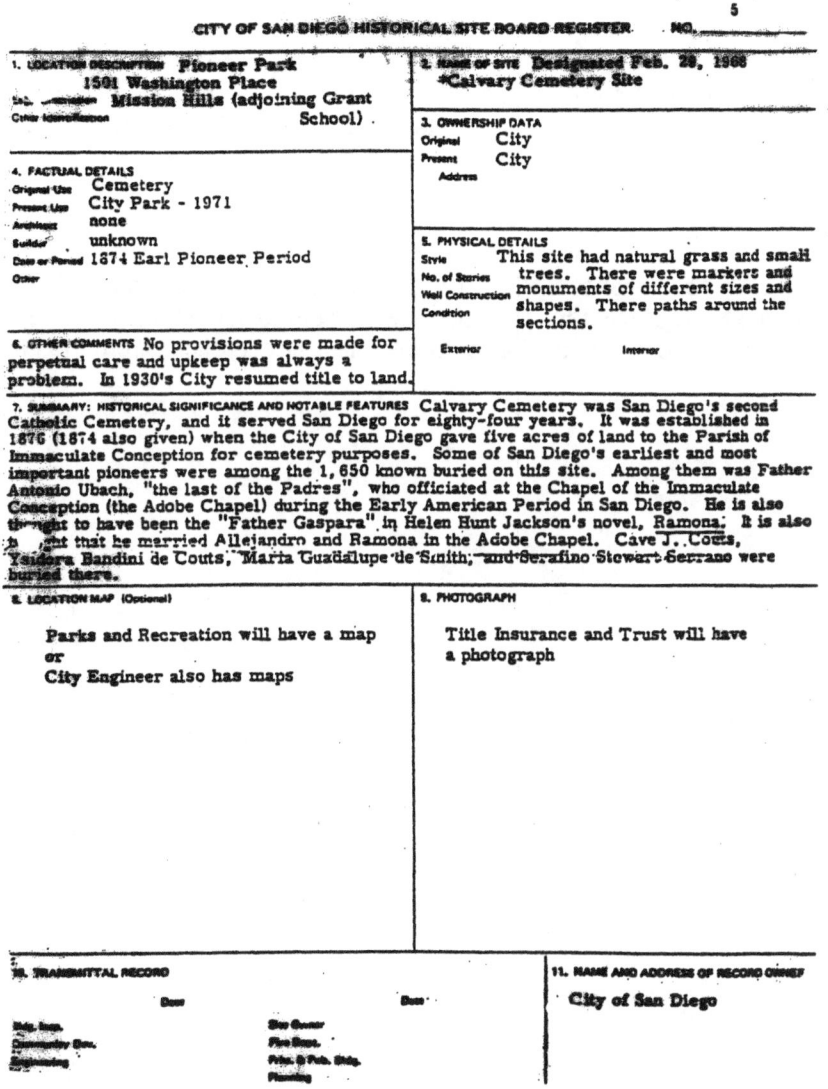

There are countless other records in San Diego which the reader might research. A veteran's address found in a city directory could lead to an old house, possible relatives, photos, nearby church going activities, club memberships, school activities of children, etc.

Histories of various neighborhoods could include a discussion of the veteran, and small local historical societies could be contacted to get additional informaion once it has been determined where the veteran lived within the city. For information about local historical societies, contact the Congress of History (see cite on p. 28.)

STATE OF CALIFORNIA VITAL RECORDS

Office of the State Registrar of Vital Statistics
Department of Health Services
304 S Street
P.O. Box 730241
Sacramento, CA 94244-0241
Ph: (916) 445-2684
Fx: (800) 858-5553

The Office of the State Registrar has birth, marriage and death records from July 1, 1905 to the present, and certificates of record for divorces from 1962 to June 1984. Copies of records can be obtained for a fee from this office. (Fees change over time--contact this office for fee information.) Fees as of April 1997 were $15 for a certified birth certificate; $12 for a certified marriage or divorce certificate, and $8 for a certified death certificate.

If a request is urgent, the State Registrar's Office can be contacted at their fax number, and copies ordered by fax for a $5 additional fee. Check with your local FHC to obtain forms that can be used to order records from the State Registrar. Also check with them to see what date ranges for State Registrar birth, marriage, or death records are available on microfilm or microfiche from the FHC in Salt Lake City.

CHAPTER THREE: GENERAL FINDINGS

The following is a presentation of some research findings about the veterans memorialized in this study. It is hoped that the information will place the veterans in context with San Diego history from the late 19th to the early 20th Centuries.

NUMBERS

The first major finding is that 1,952 Civil War veterans lived in San Diego from about 1867, when Matthew Sherman came back to San Diego after serving in "New Town" for a large part of the war, to 1943, when Horace Bly Day, the longest lived veteran in time died at age 93.

One wonders why the veterans came in such large numbers. Judge Moses A. Luce, Civil War Medal of Honor winner, gave what are probably the most often cited answers: climate and better health. "I came here ... because I had developed a weak throat. It troubled me so much that I could not well deliver an address to a jury, and I thought that it was time that I was coming to a gentler climate. I had subscribed to the San Diego Union in the fall of 1872, and what I read in that newspaper about San Diego proved so satisfactory that I started here, arriving in May, 1873."[1]

Elizabeth MacPhail's book, *The Story of New San Diego and of its Founder Alonzo E. Horton*, confirms the health hypothesis.[2] This book documents the arrival to San Diego of successive waves of migration in the early years of interest to us here (1867-1909). MacPhail discusses the beginning of what is now "downtown" San Diego by Alonzo E. Horton, who began the second, successful attempt to establish a city at "New Town." Horton had a vision of what the future city would look like, and with the help of his family (among them brother-in-law William Wallace Bowers, Civil War veteran of this study) helped pull together the origins of the San Diego we know today.

"When Horton came west, it was for his health. While living in Oswego, NY, he developed a cough, and '...it was thought he might have consumption ... [which] came as a great shock not only to Horton but to his family and friends.'"[3] But Horton, along with others, stayed in San Diego for climate and health reasons, even during the bust periods.

From 1874-1879, for example, "Those who were retired or who had come for their health were content to live on climate and savings they had brought with them. The boomers and speculators left. Others who remained stayed because they liked it here and, like Horton, were confident that because of its climate and bay San Diego would one day be a great city."[4] So climate and health had a lot to do with why people came here.

NATIVITY/ENLISTMENT OF NATIVE BORN VETERANS

Of the 1,952 Civil War veterans in this study, 1,421 (73%) were native-born, 254 (13%) were foreign born, and nativity was not available for 277 (14%) of the veterans. Of the 1,421 native-born veterans, state of birth was available for 1,363 (96%) of them (the remaining being "American" born). Nativity information comes from G.A.R. records, tombstone inscriptions, city and county histories, and from information on burial cards at Mount Hope cemetery.

Chart 1 shows that many of the native born veterans represented in this study were born in the more populous states. Compare that figure with the next column--state of first enlistment of native born veterans, and distinct patterns of migration begin to appear. Index One in Chapter Eight also lists veterans by nativity and state of first enlistment, so patterns of individual migration can be seen. Note: State of first enlistment figures in Chart 1 include an additional 92 veterans from the "American" born group mentioned above.

Chart I: Native Born Veterans: State of Birth/State of First Enlistment

State	Births	Enl.	State	Births	Enl.
NY	281	133	NJ	16	13
OH	257	164	WI	14	99
PA	172	97	MD	14	7
IN	112	134	TN	13	9
IL	106	229	RI	8	7
ME	80	43	WV	6	8
MA	71	58	MS	3	3
MI	39	62	KS	1	31
KY	30	11	MN	1	35
VT	29	18	CA	0	40
MO	27	58	CO	0	12
CT	23	20	NE	0	6
NH	20	14	OR	0	4
VA	20	8	WA	0	1
IA	20	131			

NATIVITY/ENLISTMENT OF FOREIGN BORN VETERANS
254 (13%) of the veterans of this study were foreign born. Many of these veterans came from the following eleven countries:

Chart 2: Birthplace of Foreign Born Veterans

Country	Number
Germany	57
England	50
Ireland	43
Canada	32
Scotland	10
France	8
Norway	7
Nova Scotia	6
Switzerland	6
Denmark	5
Sweden	5

Additionally, four veterans came from Prussia and Wales, three came from Poland; two came from Austria, Bavaria, Belgium and Holland, and one each came from Bohemia, Hungary, Italy, Mexico, Newfoundland and Russia.

Chart 3 is a sort by country of origin and state of first enlistment of foreign born individuals in this study. Note: States with low veteran counts are not included in this chart:

Chart 3: Foreign Birthplace by State of First Enlistment

Country	IL	NY	OH	IA	WI	IN	PA	MA	MI	MO
Germany	6	10	6	1	3	2	2	2	3	4
England	8	5	3	3	9	0	1	2	2	1
Ireland	2	8	1	2	2	1	3	3	1	0
Canada	6	5	1	1	3	2	0	1	3	0
Scotland	1	1	2	1	0	0	0	0	0	0
France	1	1	2	0	0	1	1	0	0	1
Norway	2	0	0	0	2	0	0	0	0	0
Nova Scotia	0	0	0	0	0	1	0	2	1	0
Denmark	0	3	0	0	1	0	0	0	0	0
Sweden	2	1	0	0	0	0	0	0	1	0
Wales	0	0	0	2	1	0	1	0	0	0
Switzerland	3	0	1	0	1	0	0	0	0	0

Thus, the veterans of this study a migrating group. As far as can be determined, all of the 1,952 veterans of this study were from somewhere else. Some started their migration as children of families who were going west. Many traveled long distances while fighting in the Civil War. After the war, they continued to move on, and were probably more used to moving than their fathers were, for they had either walked or rode a good portion of the American landscape during the war.

The Civil War veterans studied here were all immigrants to San Diego, and kept their immigrant identity intact by associating with each other. Many also married back East prior to moving here, for the maiden names of the wives who were identified in this study have a distinct "Anglo" sound.

Birthplaces of the wives for whom such information is available indicates they were born in places like Ohio, New York, Maine, Massachusetts, Pennsylvania, Vermont, Missouri, Indiana, Iowa, Maryland, Rhode Island, Virginia and North Carolina, although five were born in California. Or they were foreign-born, from Canada, England, France, Germany, Ireland, Scotland, Sweden, and most unlikely of all, from Tahiti. Thus the veterans appear to have maintained their eastern connection via marriage when arriving in San Diego.

UNION/CONFEDERATE AFFILIATION
Only 27 (1%) of the veterans of this study were identified as Confederate veterans. Those for whom nativity was determined (21) were born in the following states or countries: Five from Virginia, three from Mississippi, two from Tennessee, two from England, and one each from Canada, Germany, Georgia, Ohio, Arkansas, North Carolina, Texas and Vermont; additionally, one was "American" born. The nativity of the remaining six could not be determined.

Five Confederate veterans enlisted in the states they were born in (two from Tennessee, and one each from Virginia, Texas, and Mississippi). The remaining veterans for whom both factors of nativity and state of enlistment could be determined had the following patterns: A veteran from Virginia enlisted in Mississippi; one from Mississippi enlisted in Alabama; one from Ohio enlisted in Texas; one from Arkansas enlisted in Texas; and one from Vermont enlisted in Alabama.

For those buried at Mount Hope's Confederate Plot, an identification as a Confederate veteran was assured by one's burial at this location. A few placed their Confederate affiliation on their tombstones. Confederate Major Hugh G. Gwyn organized a parade of G.A.R. groups from California and Nevada who met in San Diego in 1895. Confederate veteran John M. Riddle accompanied several Union veterans to a Gettysburg assembly in 1938, as discussed in the San Diego Union. But few other Confederate veterans were identified, and no records on them were available at the San Diego Historical Society.

It may be difficult to discover who the Confederate veterans of San Diego really were, unless National Archives information or United Daughters of the Confederacy records were accessed to determine this. Perhaps these veterans did not want to be identified, or for it to be known that they fought for the South. Perhaps they lived in rural San Diego, South Bay, East County or North County. Further study is needed, using National Archives microfilms and resources discussed in the FHC "Research Outline--Military Records" (see p. 31 for both references) to determine who the Confederate veterans of San Diego were.

DATE OF ARRIVAL IN SAN DIEGO
The date of arrival of the veterans to San Diego can only be determined approximately. In August of 1890, there was an Encampment that attracted some veterans from around the country. Veterans from other states converged on Coronado where a tent city was set up, numerous activities were scheduled, and a mock battle held. However, San Diego's Heintzelman Post #33 was already nine years old by then. San Diego suffered boom and bust periods from 1880 to 1900, and these are reflected in the dates of arrival of earlier veterans to this area (See Chart 4 below). A great impetus for local settlement in 1885 was railroad service which connected San Diego to the East. This was a dream come true for local developers, for prior to that people arrived by boat, stagecoach or wagon. Civil War veteran migration to San Diego slowed in the 1890s, and then steadily increased until 1927, when it started dropping off again.

The only way approximate time of arrival could be determined was to use G.A.R. records for individual veterans. Most of these records listed a date which veterans entered the G.A.R.--thus giving a clue about the approximate time of their arrival in San Diego. Using that information, the following arrival dates were extracted. Such information was available for 1,438 (74%) of the veterans of this study:

Chart 4: Date of Approximate Veteran Arrival in San Diego

Date G.A.R. Joined	Number Joining in Date Range
1868-1880*	4
1881-1884	137
1885-1889	217
1890-1894	101
1895-1899	77
1900-1904	131
1905-1909	159
1910-1914	174
1915-1919	154
1920-1924	188
1925-1929	90
1930-1934	6

* For veterans with G.A.R. memberships in these early years, the memberships were in G.A.R. Posts outside of San Diego. The first G.A.R. Post started here was Heintzelman Post, organized in 1881; the second was Datus Coon Post, organized in 1894.

PROPORTION OF SAN DIEGO POPULATION
It would be difficult if not impossible to determine what proportion the veterans were of the population in the City of San Diego for two reasons:

1. Most veterans arrived in San Diego over a 53 year period from 1881-1934, and while the Chart 4 figures are available, they are only rough estimates of time of arrival because a veteran may have arrived long before he joined the G.A.R.

2. For 26% of the veterans, there is no date of arrival information. However, a good way to determine date of arrival for those veterans would be to check death certificates, for they often list the length of time a veteran lived in San Diego. Check Great Register of Voters and census records to pinpoint arrival dates.

Additionally, one could check city directories, but this is not the best way to determine date of arrival, for a veteran might not have been listed in city directories until years after they came to San Diego. Also, early city directories were divided into several sections based on the area of town in which a veteran lived (San Diego proper or outlying areas like National City, Chula Vista, etc.) So, all separate directories would have to be searched. The task is simple, however, if only one or several veterans are being studied.

For reference purposes, Chart 5 presents population figures for the City and County of San Diego from 1850-1940. As the authors of *Metropolitan Coast: San Diego and Orange Counties, California* point out:

> "Transition from Mexican to American rule between 1846 and 1850 did not change modes of life in San Diego County as quickly and as thoroughly as it did in Los Angeles. Title to most of the great ranchos granted by the Mexican government, into which much of the area was divided, passed from Mexican to American hands through purchase, marriage, or lawsuit, but the pattern of feudal-like landholdings remained. ... The first United States census in 1850 counted 798 persons in the county (not including Indians). Ten years later, the number had risen to 4,324; by 1870, to only 4,951. The city of San Diego contained most of this population, and there was no other town in the county. ... Development of rail transportation and of local water resources, and fervent promotion by land speculators combined to bring the first major influx of settlers to San Diego's back country. The decade of the eighties increased the county's population by almost fourfold, particularly during a great real estate boom which lasted from 1886 to 1888."[5]

Chart 5: Population Figures 1850-1940 for the City/County of San Diego

Date	City	County
1850	650	798
1860	731	4,324
1870	2,300	4,951
1880	2,637	8,618
1890	16,159	34,987
1900	17,700	35,090
1910	39,578	61,665
1920	74,683	112,248
1930	147,995	209,659
1940	203,341	289,348

RACE

There were nine African American soldiers (Walker Davis, Amos E. Hudgins, Thomas M. Jackson, William H. Laws, James L. Lilley, Alexander Luckett, Edmund Marshall, Samuel I. Nickens and Robert Tillman, all buried at Mount Hope), and two Hispanic veterans (Lorenzo Camacho/Comacho and Jose Maria Salazar, both buried at Calvary) identified by race in burial records or G.A.R. information. There may be African American or Hispanic veterans listed in Chapter Five, but race was not identified for veterans on that list. A number of soldiers of this study also commanded various Colored Troop units in the U.S. Service. As those units were with the regular army, the names of the commanders of those troops are listed in Chapter Six under the "US Regulars" section, and their commands would be listed for U.S.C.T. (U.S. Colored Troops) or a similar listing. Further study is needed to determine whether more African American and Hispanic veterans were in San Diego, using National Archives microfilms and Orton's *Records of California Men in the War of the Rebellion* (see p. 30).

MARITAL STATUS

Finding the wives of the Civil War veterans of San Diego proved to be a difficult undertaking. Some veterans were identified as "widowed" in the burial records. A look at Mount Hope lot cards revealed that some wives were not buried near their husbands. Additionally, many veterans were buried side-by-side with other veterans at Mount Hope, where the greatest number of veterans were buried. No wives intruded into these "patterned" burials. So, often the wives of the Civil War veterans were difficult to find.

However, 523 "wives" are included in this study, 503 in Chapter Four, and 20 in Chapter Five. If wives were located, they were found by tombstone inscriptions, on a cemetery map, or on the lot cards for the veterans at Mount Hope and incidentally at other cemeteries. It is hoped that these are truly wives of the veterans, although at times their ages suggest that they might be sisters or daughters. As Civil War veterans arrived home after the war, many women were already married, and the veterans had to marry either younger or older women if they were to marry at all.

The place of origin of the wives was available only for 102 wives: 17 were from Ohio; 14 from New York; 7 from England; 5 from California, Maine, and Vermont; 4 from Germany, Indiana, Massachusetts, Missouri, and Pennsylvania; 3 from Iowa and Maryland; 3 from Canada, North Carolina, Rhode Island, and Virginia; and one each from Connecticut, Delaware, France, Illinois, Ireland, Kentucky, Louisiana, Minnesota, New Hampshire, Scotland, South Carolina, Sweden, and Wisconsin. Most improbable of all, one was from Tahiti!

Some of the veterans married after they came to San Diego, and local marriage records could be checked. (See Chapter 2, "Specific Genealogical Resources in San Diego--Marriage Records" (pp. 46-47) to find sources for marital information. There are marriage records at the county which could be researched, for example).

Another good place to check for marital information would be a veteran's death certificate (See "Death Records", pp. 33-34) where a wife is often named, or the California Death Index (see p. 34) where a spouse's initials are given. Another source would be census records, particularly those that have been indexed (See "Census Records", pp. 38-39) City directories could also be checked (See "City Directories", p. 41-42). To determine the date of a veteran's arrival in San Diego for use of the city directories, find his G.A.R. record (if available) in Chapters Four or Five, and look at the "G.A.R." citation listed in that record, for the year the veteran joined the G.A.R. might coincide with the year he entered the city directories.

I found several wives other than Augusta Barrett Sherman (mentioned earlier and later herein) who were included in San Diego city and county histories and other records. One was Cella Boucher Slocum, wife of Confederate Colonel Milton L. Slocum.

As indicated in McGrew's *City of San Diego and San Diego County*[6], Mrs. Slocum was born and educated in Randolph County, Missouri, married ex-Confederate officer Slocum in 1882 at Cowan, Tennessee, and later moved to National City, CA (an area south of San Diego's city limits), where she started a kindergarden. She became an avid student of philosophic thought, and opened her home to teachers and lecturers of advanced philosophy.

The Slocums later moved to Front Street in San Diego in 1915, where Mrs. Slocum started a metaphysical library. In 1916, they moved to 1024 Broadway, and after Col. Slocum died in 1919, Mrs. Slocum moved to 1023 Seventh Street (Avenue), where she had a large lecture hall and a library which had grown to several hundred volumes. Mrs. Slocum died in 1944.

Col. Slocum was one of the leading bridge construction engineers in the United States, associating with the Spreckels interests for over 20 years. He later worked on Morena Dam and other parts of the water system. Col. Slocum and Mrs. Slocum are both buried in the Confederate Plot at Mount Hope Cemetery.

Another wife included in a printed history and in other records was Illa Birdseye, wife of veteran Enoch Birdseye. A "Mrs. Birdseye" was mentioned on the list of parishioners of Holy Trinity Episcopal Church in 1872. Her residence was "Cajon" (today's El Cajon, east of San Diego). By 1875, Illa Birdseye's husband Enoch Birdseye had died. The San Diego Herald reported this fact: At his residence near Cahon Valley, Nov. 27, E.L. Birdseye, native of Norwalk Co, OH, aged 34 years. Funeral from Episcopal Church.

After burying her young husband at Mount Hope, Illa Birdseye returned to El Cajon, and in the 1880 census for Cajon Judicial Township is listed as having married Amaziah L. Knox, "Hotel Keeper." Her two children by Enoch Birdseye and a child by Amaziah Knox were all listed in the same household. Illa Birdseye was a young widow who became an important figure in El Cajon history. Her story appears on p. 12 of Eldonna P. Lay's book, *The History of El Cajon: Valley of Opportunity*. A similar fate befell Carrie Bentzel, who lost her husband Henry Bentzel at age 35. Both of these couples appear on the next page of this book.

A third wife mentioned in a printed history was Marcella Rolph Darling, wife of Charles W. Darling. Marcella Darling and her husband lived in Chula Vista, an area south of San Diego's city limits. As noted in the book *Chula Vista Heritage, 1911-1986*, Mrs. Darling was a prominent resident of Chula Vista, and first president of the Chula Vista Women's Club. She and her husband lived at 44 North Second Street, and while no photos exist of Marcella or Charles, the Darling House is pictured at the end of this chapter in the "Images" section, courtesy of John Rojas and the Chula Vista Historical Society. The Darlings are also buried at Greenwood Cemetery.

YEAR/AGE OF DEATH OF WIVES

The year of death of the wives is as follows for the 88% (460) of the wives for whom year of death could be determined:

Chart 6: Year of Death of Civil War Veterans' Wives

Year of Death	Number	% of Total	Cumulative %
1871-1889	13	3%	—
1890-1899	24	5%	8%
1900-1909	50	11%	19%
1910-1919	107	23%	42%
1920-1929	138	31%	73%
1930-1939	75	16%	89%
1940-1949	46	10%	99%
1950-1958	7	1%	100%
Total	460	100%	

Following the cumulative totals on the chart, we see that by 1929, 73% of the wives in this study for whom year of death could be determined had died. By 1939, 89% had died, and by 1949, 99% had died. Seven wives lived into the 1950s. The last two wives still alive then were Laura Elma Thompson, wife of Medal of Honor Winner James Granville Thompson, who died at age 100 on January 15, 1958, and Maude Sullivan, wife (or possible daughter?) of Marcus Sullivan, who died at 77 on December 2, 1958.

The age at death of the wives is as follows for the 82% (430) of wives for whom age of death could be determined:

Amaziah L. Knox Illa Birdseye Knox

Henry Bentzel, Wife Carrie Bentzel
and Son Fred Lithgow Bentzel

Chart 7: Age at Death of Civil War Veterans' Wives

Age at Death	Number	% of Total	Cumulative %
23-49	19	5%	—
50-59	36	8%	13%
60-69	62	14%	27%
70-79	131	31%	58%
80-89	151	35%	93%
90-100	31	7%	100%
Total	430	100%	

In a later part of this chapter, I discuss age of death of the veterans, and it tracked fairly closely with the age of death of the wives. 2% of the veterans died between age 28-49; 6% from 50-59; 19% from 60-69; 35% from 70-79; 32% from 80-89 and 6% died at 90 or older. The difference comes in year of death. No veterans lived after 1943, whereas seven widows lived into the 1950s, as mentioned above.

OCCUPATION OF VETERANS

The veterans who came to San Diego had varied occupations. The only place where occupation was found was on the intake form for Heintzleman Post, and the major occupations in evidence were the following: Farmers and Ranchers (154 veterans), carpenters (92 veterans), merchants (43 veterans), real estate investors (26 veterans), attorneys (25 veterans), ministers (21 veterans), doctors (20 veterans), and engineers (17 veterans).

Attorneys: The following veterans were attorneys who practiced in San Diego; several became judges: David H. Budlong, Patricius H. Casey, Levi Chase, Norman H. Conklin (later a district attorney and judge), Thomas T. Crittenden, J.L. Dryden, William H. Francis, Alfred Haines (later a district attorney and judge), Noah Hodge, David B. Hoffman (later a district attorney), Herman Jackson.

Other attorneys were John D. King, Edwin H. Lamme, Moses A. Luce (later a judge), J. Wade McDonald, John O.W. Paine, Watson Parish, George Puterbaugh (later a judge), Henry J.G. Rogers, Michael Shea (pension attorney or pension agent), Henry W. Talcott, Robert T. Warner, Alexander G. Watson, J.D. Works (later a judge), and Charles H. Wynn.

Doctors: The following veterans were doctors, some of whom practiced during the war but not after: Joseph C. Beam, Thomas J. Burns, J.B. Cooper, Edward C. Folsum, David Gouchenaur, Joseph E. Hall, James W. Hughes, R.G. Hulbert, Miles Hughes, John Ogle, Cassius C. Pillsbury, Robert M. Powers, Francis B. Reed, Peter C. Remondino, Vernon D. Rood, John O. Webster, Homer L. Wells, Augustus J. Wiard, W.A. Winder, and Hiram P. Woodward.

Dentists: Dentistry was represented by: Thomas Coggeswell and James A. Young.

Ministers: Ministers were: Edward H. Bailiff, Henry B. Barnes, James B. Brewington, Benjamin A. Butler, William A. Clark, R.V. Dodge, William H. Dorward, Philip H. Eighmey, F.J. Foot, John A. Frazier, Edwin L. Hill, S.K. Holsinger, Thomas D. Lewes, Henry Lohr, B.F. McDaniel, Samuel J. Neiberger, John L. Pitner, W.H. Stenger, W.S. Trader, William M. Viney, and William A. Waterman.

Architects: Architects were: Milton E. Beebe and Andrew T. Large.

Political Activists: Some veterans held political or elective offices:

    Matthew Sherman (Board of Supervisors 1885-1888; Mayor 1891-1892)

    William W. Bowers (State Assembly 1873; Port Collector 1874-1883, 1898-1906, State Senator 1887-1891; and Congressman 1891-1897)

    David B. Hoffman (Coroner 1855-1857; Board of Supervisors 1857-1858)

    James P.M. Rainbow (Board of Supervisors 1883-1884; 1891-1894)

    Henry U. Emery (Board of Supervisors 1885)

    Martin D. Hamilton (Assessor 1879-1887, County Clerk 1889-1890)

    Sylvester Statler (County Clerk 1878-1882)

    Eli T. Blackmer (Superintendent of Schools 1877-1879; Treasurer 1885-1890)

Additional Occupations:

  Editor--David L. Kretzinger

  Civil Engineer--John G. Fonda, Isaac L. Palmer

  Construction Engineer--Milton L. Slocum

  Publishers--Leroy W. Allum, William Burgess, and Reuben E. Helms

  Hotel Owners/Keepers--Elisha S. Babcock, William W. Bowers, John H. Dodderidge, William A. Dorris, William R. Leonard, Edwin H. Miller, L. Scofield, Peter C. Remondino, and Hampton L. Story.

  Orchardist: Kellogg B. Finley

  Undertaker: James T. Barkley

  Records Searcher: John B. Boyd

  Shorthand Reporter: W.S. Briggs

Many building trades were represented by one or several veterans. There were also bar keepers, blacksmiths, shoemakers, machinists, stone cutters, boat builders, fruit dealers, printers, tinners, painters, cabinet makers and coopers, embalmers, surveyors, lecturers, postal clerks, teachers, and mechanics.

Sometimes veterans appeared in "yellow pages" ads in city directories when they had a business to advertise. Eli T. Blackmer's music store is one example, or Dr. Thomas L. Magee's medical practice. There were those who dealt in real estate and land holdings, and they will be discussed in the "Building the City" section of this chapter, at p. 94.

Finally, Charles E. Anthony became an established expert on mines and mining, and merchant Erastus H. Weegar, emerging from skirmishes with the Navaho Indians in New Mexico during the Civil War, became an expert on Southwestern Indians.

William H. Bailhache, who prior to the Civil War lived in Illinois, was a friend of Abraham Lincoln. He became assistant editor of the San Diego Union in 1892. Hugh G. Gwyn (Confederate Major in the Civil War who was on General Morgan's staff, was postmaster of Coronado for four years, and a principal in the firm of Foster & Gwyn, a company selling fire insurance.

G.A.R. MEMBERSHIP
80% of the Civil War veterans of this study were members of the G.A.R. (Grand Army of the Republic, a national organization of Union veterans.) There were two posts in San Diego, Heintzelman Post #33 (1,076 members), established in 1881, and Datus E. Coon Post #172 (528 members), established in 1894. (The count totals 1,604 "memberships"; only 1,562 were actual members because 42 veterans crossed over and were members of both posts at one time or another. The G.A.R. record for those who joined the two posts accompanies the individual record for each veteran in Chapters Four and Five.

Heintzelman Post #33
As mentioned in an earlier chapter, Captain Matthew Sherman was posted in San Diego for much of the Civil War. "Born in Charlestown, Massachusetts, October 11, 1827, Sherman as a lad of only 13 enlisted in the Navy and served on the USS Columbus and later on the USS Independence."[7] On the latter ship, he sailed around Cape Horn, and served in the Mexican War. After that war, he went back east, but returned to California, was mustered in, and served most of his Civil War time in New San Diego. "In 1862, he was stationed in San Diego, and liked it so well that he came back to settle permanently after his discharge from the Army in 1865."[8]

By 1867, he had met and married Augusta Barrett, and they moved into the old barracks at New Town, where they were "the only inhabitants, [their] nearest neighbor being four miles away at Old Town."[9] Alonzo E. Horton arrived in San Diego on April 15 of the same year, and purchased "Horton's Addition," a large area adjacent to "New San Diego" (see location map, p. 103), for an average of 26 cents an acre.

[By] "...June, 1867, Sherman bought from the City Trustee's Pueblo Lot 1155, a 160 acre tract adjoining Horton's property on the west, for 50 cents an acre. Sherman's Addition (or Sherman Heights as it was called because of its elevation), overlooked the flat lands of what is now downtown San Diego, stretching west to the harbor. Sherman Heights was bounded by 15th and 24th streets, between Market and Commercial Streets, and is one of the oldest subdivisions in New San Diego. Sherman subdivided his land in 1869, and soon recouped his original investment as he sold off lots. The first residence in the southeastern section of New San Diego was the Sherman home, a small cottage near the northwest corner of 19th and J Streets, constructed in 1868."[10]

San Diego went through mini-boom and bust periods, and went "bust" when plans for a railroad connection to the east and north fell through. "Matthew Sherman retired to his farm in El Cajon valley, raising zinfandel grapes. In 1885, the recently-organized California Southern Railroad made connections with the Santa Fe, running a line from San Diego to San Bernardino; at last, San Diego had its transcontinental connection. The population tripled and land sales boomed! Sherman came out of his semi-retirement, sold his El Cajon farm and vineyard, and had plans drawn up for a large new home in Sherman Heights. It was a two-story, 11 room structure, described as "finely furnished", and costing $15,000."[11]

Matthew Sherman donated land for what was later called "Sherman School", and helped develop Mount Hope Cemetery, where many of the Civil War veterans of this study are buried. (Mrs. Sherman gave the cemetery its name). Sherman later served as mayor of San Diego in 1891, a year after Heintzelman Post #33 sponsored a "Civil War Encampment" on Coronado Island. Matthew Sherman lived on until July 5, 1898, and his passing was marked by a large funeral and turnout.[12] Augusta Sherman continued to live in the big house with her son and his family, dying on January 5, 1913.[13] Both are buried at Mount Hope.

"The first G.A.R. post ... in San Diego ... Heintzelman Post #33 ... was organized on October 8, 1881, by Matthew Sherman as mustering officer."[14] The post was named after Samuel P. Heintzelman, discussed in Chapter 1 and below. A partial list of charter members of this group included:

Joseph Farley; Edward Folsom; M.D. Hamilton; W.H. Horrell; Cornelius Huntington; Curtis Johnson, Danville F. Jones; James P. Jones; John A. Kooken; Joseph Leonard; William Leonard; Moses A. Luce; Charles O. Pierce; William Reupsch; Hosea B. Rice, and Matthew Sherman.[15]

Datus E. Coon Post #172
"Datus E. Coon Post #172 was organized November 10, 1894 by George Puterbaugh as mustering officer, with twenty four charter members"[16] as follows:

John Q. Ashton, Joseph Van Castle, W.D. Woodward, Francis C. Higgins, James H. Grovesteen, John Confer, Joseph Martin, Charles Miller, Thomas Crogan, Z.C. Mathes, John Straw, Frank James, C.C. Bailey, W.E. Lewis, John R. Doig, Samuel S. Knoles, Arthur H. Dauchey, Patrick Wellington, Joseph Gray, Peter C. Smith, John O'Brien, Peter Watts, Isaac A. Esleeck, Horace J. Hull.[17]

The death of Datus E. Coon is a sad story. This G.A.R. Post was named after a man who was accidentally shot by a fellow veteran in 1893. As the San Diego Union reported December 17:

> "At 9 o'clock yesterday morning Gen. Datus E. Coon was accidentally shot by his friend, J.H. Grovesteen. The ball of 32 calibre, entered about an inch below and two inches to the right of the navel, inflicting and exceedingly painful and perhaps fatal wound. The manner in which the accident occurred and the circumstances connected with it were described by Mr. Grovesteen to a Union reporter, and his version was corroborated by Gen. Coon in conversations with Gen. Murray and Judge Luce soon after the unfortunate occurrance took place."

> 'I had promised Father Ubach to go out to the old mission this morning to repair an organ at the Indian school', said Mr. Grovesteen, 'and was anxious to have a companion on the trip. In fact, Mrs. Grovesteen insisted that I should not go alone, on account of the large number of tramps said to have been encountered at different times lately by travelers in outlying districts of the city, and in consequence I asked two or three different friends to go along before I thought of Gen. Coon. None of the others could go, but the general was unoccupied and said he would be delighted to take the outing. This was at the Ablemarle hotel, where I met him about 8 o'clock in the morning.'

> 'He went up to his room and got his revolver and then we drove to my house at First and Date streets. The general remained in the buggy while I went in and procured my tools and a lunch to be taken along. When these had been placed in the rear of the vehicle, I stepped into the buggy at the right side. Noticing that the general carried his revolver in his outside upper coat pocket, I thought to put my revolver, an old-fashioned weapon and one which I had not seen for perhaps three years, in the same pocket in my coat. I took the scabbard containing it from my side pocket, and curious to see the condition of the revolver, drew it from the scabbard.'

> 'After a glance I returned it to the scabbard, but in some unaccountable manner, and while the revolver was still in my grasp, the weapon was discharged, blowing out the end of the scabbard. Before I had looked up Gen. Coon, sitting beside me, gasped, 'You have killed me, Grovesteen; I am done for!'

> 'I was horror stricken, but realizing the situation I immediately began to assist the general in getting to the ground, and with but little help from me he walked up the steps to the house and into a room, where he reclined on a bed. I made him as comfortable as possible at a moment's notice, and leaving him in my wife's care, I ran to Dr. Edward's residence.'

HEADQUARTERS
Datus E. Coon Post, No. 172
DEPARTMENT OF
CALIFORNIA AND NEVADA
G. A. R.

GENERAL DATUS E. COON

HEINTZELMAN POST NO. 33
G. A. R.
Department of California and Nevada
Robert Butler, Commander
Meets second and fourth Tuesdays of each month at Woodbine Hall, 346 Fifth Ave.

HEINTZELMAN WOMAN'S RELIEF CORPS NO. 1
Auxiliary to Heintzelman Post No. 33.
Lillian M. Griggs, President
Meets first, second, third and fourth Tuesdays of each month 2 p.m. Woodbine Hall, 346 Fifth Ave.

G. A. R.
Datus E. Coon Post No. 172
and its auxiliary
The Woman's Relief Corps No. 84
Meet at Knights of Pythias Hall, Third and E Streets.
Second and Fourth Saturdays of each month.
Commander of Post, A. S. Stimson.
President of Corps, Elma E. Rhodiner.

Matthew Sherman

Augusta Sherman

'That physician responded at once. He found by a hasty examination that the wound was an exceedingly dangerous one, and called in other physicians. Drs. Magee, Hearne and Burton, the latter the army surgeon at the barracks, were called. From what they told me I fear there is very slight hope for my poor friend. It was a terrible accident.'

"Besides the doctors named, there were numerous friends and acquaintences of the general at the house within a short time after the shooting, but owing to the nature of the unfortunate man's wound, no one was admitted except Capt. [Albert] Dill and one or two other old army friends of the general, who acted in the capacity of nurses during the afternoon."

The article goes on to state the nature of the wound, and that it was inoperable due to the negative effects of ether on General Coon. Meanwhile:

"Many anxious inquiries were made at the house as to his condition throughout the afternoon, and the deplorable accident was but the one subject of conversation among hundreds of persons. No blame is in any way attached to Mr. Grovesteen, but rather keen sympathy, for he has long been an intimate friend of Gen. Coon. The only near relative of Gen. Coon is a daughter, Mrs. Charles Loomis, who is a resident of San Francisco. She was telegraphed to immediately after the accident and is doubtless now far on her way toward this city."

Later--"Gen. Coon died very quietly at 2:44 this morning."[18]

A subsequent article described the funeral planned for General Coon, and details of his war record:

"[General Coon] ... raised a company of calvary and was appointed captain in the Second Iowa Cavalry. In September, 1861, he was promoted to major, commanding the Second battalion. He was in the battles of New Madrid and Island No. 10, Shiloh, and in a desparate charge near Corinth, Miss. Maj. Coon's next engagement was at the battle of Boonville, July 1, 1862, which gained for Sheridan the rank of brigadier general, and promoted Maj. Coon to command of Ed Hatch's regiment."

"Six months later he was placed in command of a brigade of cavalry. In 1864, he was appointed colonel and was ordered to Memphis, where he commanded a brigade of cavalry. He participated in the battle of Franklin, and was driven back to Nashville by Hood's army. At Nashville his command was increased to 5,000 men, and with these in December, 1864, he moved with the whole army to contest with General Hood."

"Col. Coon's command occupied the right of General Thomas' command. In advance of the army Col. Coon's command captured several earth-works, prisoners, artillery, and 200 stand of arms, and at Brentwood Hill, charging as an infantry up a hill, Col Coon's men captured 400 prisoners, two pieces of artillery, and 400 stand of arms. The colonel's horse was killed under him. Immediately after the battle of Nashville Col. Coon was appointed brevet brigadier general by President Lincoln for gallant conduct on that field."[19]

General Coon is buried under a simple tombstone on G.A.R. Hill at Mount Hope Cemetery, his bravery all but forgotten. But he wasn't forgotten by his friends. Almost a year later to the date, James H. Grovesteen and several other veterans called a muster of Datus E. Coon Post #172.

Records of both Datus Coon Post and Heintzelman Post are at the San Diego Historical Society Archives, and are described in Chapter Two, "Research Design." The Heintzelman records are more extensive, containing, in addition to individual war records, address books and records of meetings held by this post.

There are often photos depicting Civil War veterans in newspaper obituaries and also photos like the one of Datus Coon presented on p. 65 which came from a letterhead in the San Diego Historical Society's collection of G.A.R. records. Those records, where available, were transcribed and presented in Chapters Four and Five of this study.

THE ENCAMPMENT

In August, 1890, Heintzelman Post #33 sponsored a Civil War Encampment on Coronado Island, just across the bay from San Diego.

The San Diego Union reported this event in two separate newspaper articles on August 4 and 8, 1890. The first article described the court martial of Camp Commander J.P. Jones for calling the roll of states at the encampment and neglecting to include in the roll call the largest and most populous of all states, the "state of matrimony." The article went on to describe the decoration of the tents, listed names of some of the attendees, and said that thousands of people visited the visitors on the beach. It also described a yacht race held the previous day.[20]

The article indicated that there were delegations arriving from several states, including those from Maine, Vermont, Massachusetts, Connecticut, Rhode Island, New York, Delaware, Pennsylvania, Alabama, Kentucky, Virginia, Ohio, Illinois, Indiana, Michigan, Wisconsin, Missouri, Kansas, Colorado, the District of Columbia, Iowa, California and Minnesota. The states with the largest number of delegates were Illinois (20), Iowa (19), Ohio (17), New York (14), Michigan (13) and Pennsylvania (12).[21]

Also mentioned was the following:

> "The fifer who plays with such animation when the camp drum corps is out is John Comstock and the fife is the same on which he played while marching with the Western army under General Grant. Mr. Comstock was a member of Company K, 45th Regiment Illinois Volunteers, also known as the Lead Mine Regiment, the historic one that undermined and blew up Fort Hill at Vicksburg and then charged into the break and held it for two hours. Because of their heroic conduct during the seige they were given the honor of marching in first, and so it came about that the old fife was the first played in Vicksburg on that memorial Fourth of July morning."[22]

The second article, among other things, stated that:

> "Many things take place in camp life that are not announced in the programmes, and some which do not find their way into print. There is scarcely a night after the ball is over without something going on till nearly daylight that keeps the people more or less astir. One night, which promised to be a quiet one, the camp was thrown into a state of alarm by the firing of cannon at midnight, and it was feared the filibusters had made an attack, but it proved to be only some of the old boys who had stolen a cannon from the Quartermaster and were experimenting with it."[23]

The article went on to describe the attack and storming of "Fort Union":

> "The busy seaport town of Heintzelman, situated on the bay of Glorietta, was thrown into the greatest excitement yesterday when it became known that an invading army under the command of General Coon had gone into quarters in close proximity and an attack was momentarily expected. The State militia was at once called out to protect the city. Commander Jones ordered Commodore Pettingill to report with three gunboats and a ram in Glorietta Bay and also take charge of the land forces. A signal station was established on the bluff near the camp."

"Last evening was the brightest, boomiest, noisiest time which Camp Heintzelman has seen since it was initiated into existence a week ago. The people from the city began to crowd the cars and ferryboats as early as 3:00 o'clock in the afternoon. .... The occasion of all this gathering was the event of the encampment, the storming of Fort Union."

"The attack was begun by the naval force on the bay. The new men of war, Charleston, Boston and San Francisco, steamed in close to the Fort under the command of Commodore Amos Pettingill and began shelling the fort and the iron-clad monitor Montauk, which ...had just [been raised] from her long resting place off Cape Hatteras. A short time at this long distance firing convinced the Commodore that he could not reduce the works, and so drawing off out of range of the fort ceased firing and only sent an occasional shell over the fort, the bursting of which served to remind the commandant of the fort, General D.E. Coon, that he and his fillibusters were being watched."

"While the vessels were at their almost useless by-play...General Coon had dispatched a force under command of Colonel Vestal to engage the land forces under General J.P. Jones. Vestel's force succeeded in partially surprising the land force and Captain Schiller with Co B of the Ninth California had to stand the brunt of the attack three times, driving the enemy almost back to their works, and in turn being driven back almost onto his own quarters."

"At the time that Captain Schiller was driven back, Company A of the same regiment came to his support and Colonel Spileman took command of the forces in the field. .... While the fight was most active, Co A executed a flank movement, going down the ocean side to the rear and south of the fort and began an attack on the weakest side. ... just as they were going in, the flanking party made its attack completely surprising and demoralizing the enemy, and as the Union forces piled over the earth works there was nothing else for the fort to do but surrender. The loss on both sides was heavy and the wounded were numberless."

"Just as the fort surrendered, a parting shot was given to the fleet. The shell entered the forward magazine of the Montauk, exploding the small quantity of power therein contained and setting fire to the monitor. The flames burned slowly but could not be controlled and the crew were forced to abandon her, escaping to the other vessels or to the land. The burning boat formed a pretty sight and the fort having been silenced the army and camp had nothing to do but watch it. The entire fleet drew away from the burning boat expecting every moment that the flames would reach the main magazine and explode it, but for some reason the flames died down and went out before it was reached."

"Prisoners were taken to camp and in accordance with general headquartrers were shot as traitors for taking part in the fillibustering expedition. After the execution, the camp went into a general rejoicing over the victory and the camp fire was continued until early morning, no attention being paid to taps, though they were given."[24]

The article continues:

"Serenades take place nightly. ... Twenty-two tents were visited, which included all the headquarters, all the officers, both outgoing and incoming, and the headquarters of the ... and Union, the Sun and the San Diegan [newspapers]."

"Among the interesting war relics seen in camp are copies of two southern papers, the Daily South Carolinian and the Richmond Sentinal, bearing the dates of 1864 and 1863, respectively. These papers are the property of H.P. Starr of Otay, Lieutenant, Twenty Second Reg. NY Cav, and came into his possession while in prison, being given to the soldiers by the colored men who looked after the prison. This gentleman also has a blank book for which he paid $30 and used it as an autograph book while in prison. The first two pages are handsomely engraved with pen and ink sketches done by an officer--a fellow prisoner--and giving the names of a number of prisons in which Mr. Starr was confined. Then follows the names of the unfortunates who were his companions in misery."

"Quartermaster Kooken has at his headquarters what was once a very handsome silken flag, but now tattered and discolored with age. The blue field contains the Pennsylvania coat of arms and the motto 'Virtue, Liberty, Independence,' surrounded by thirty-three stars and printed in gold letters on the stripes are 'Dranesville, Dec. 20, 1861, 42nd Reg't PV 1st Rifles, Penna Reserve Vol Corps.' This flag is owned by Mrs. General Ord of San Diego, and originally belonged to her husband...Mrs Ord is in feeble health, and would like all comrades and WRCs to visit her."[25]

Needless to say, the August 1890 encampment was a great success, and participants most certainly went home with a favorable impression of San Diego. It was probably an impetus for many of them to find their way back to live here in later years.

PROMINENCE

As the years went by, some of the Civil War veterans included in this study became prominent locally. This section contains a list of city, county, or general histories which name these veterans and/or their wives, and the individuals named in each:

In Clarence Alan McGrew's *City of San Diego and San Diego County: The Birthplace of California*,[26] Vols. 1 and 2, the following veterans are mentioned: Alfred Haines, George W. Hazzard, Myron T. Gilmore, Moses A. Luce, George Puterbaugh, Peter C. Remondino, and Cella B. Slocum.

In Carl H. Heilbron's *History of San Diego County*,[27] the following veteran is mentioned: Alfred Haines.

In *San Diego County, California: A Record of Settlement, Organization, Progress and Achievement*,[28] (author of Vol. 2 is the publisher, S.J. Clarke Publishing Company), the following veterans are mentioned: Charles E. Anthony, Sanford W. Belding, George H. Crippen, Oliver H.P. Forker, Hugh G. Gwyn, George W. Hazzard, William H. Holderness, W.J. Little, Moses A. Luce, Thomas L. Magee, William Ober, George Puterbaugh, Peter C. Remondino, Matthew Sherman, Uzzial Stevens, and J.L. Strawn.

In William E. Smythe's *History of San Diego 1542-1907*,[29] the following veterans are mentioned: Elisha S. Babcock, Eli T. Blackmer, William Wallace Bowers, Levi Chase, Norman H. Conklin, R.V. Dodge, William H. Francis, Myron T. Gilmore, David Gouchenaur, David B. Hoffman, Samuel S. Knoles, Moses A. Luce, George Puterbaugh, and Matthew Sherman.

In Leland Ghent Stanford's *San Diego's Legal Lore & The Bar*[30] the following veterans are mentioned: Norman H. Conklin, Alfred Haines, David B. Hoffman, Moses A. Luce and George Puterbaugh.

In *An Illustrated History of Southern California*,[31] the following veterans are mentioned: William H. Bailhache, Datus E. Coon, Isaac L. Palmer, John D. Palmer, George Puterbaugh, Edward B. Spileman, and John H. Snyder.

In *San Diego County Pioneer Families: A Collection of Family Histories Compiled by Members and Friends of the San Diego Historical Society*,[32] the following veterans are mentioned: William H. Bailhache, Alonzo Bell, Henry M. Bentzel, Nathan H. Downs, Henry W. George, James M. Hartley, Noah Hodge, Moses A. Luce, Edmond L. Matot, Gustavus F. Merriam, John D. Palmer, Matthew Sherman, Hampton P. Sloane, plus their wives and some children, including photos.

In Don Stewart's *Frontier Port: A Chapter in San Diego's History*, [33] the following veterans are mentioned: Albert Dill, Isaac L. Palmer, Robert J. Pennell, and Amos Pettingill.

In Elizabeth MacPhail's *The Story of New San Diego and of its Founder Alonzo E. Horton*,[34] the following veterans are mentioned: William W. Bowers, Myron T. Gilmore, Henry W. Halleck, Moses A. Luce, David B. Hoffman (Huffman in this book), William S. Rosecrans, and Matthew Sherman.

Soldiers who were in San Diego prior to, during, and after the Civil War, including Samuel P. Heintzelman, William S. Rosecrans, and Matthew Sherman, are listed in Ed Scott's *San Diego Soldier Pioneers 1846-1866*.[35]

The following veterans were mentioned in *The City and County of San Diego, Illustrated, and Containing Biographical Sketches of Prominent Men and Pioneers*: Norman H. Conklin, George W. Hazzard, W.H. Holabird, Moses A. Luce, Peter C. Remondino, and John D. Works.[36]

In *Chula Vista Heritage 1911-1986*, published by the City of Chula Vista, the following are mentioned: Charles W. and Marcella Darling, and Alfred Haines.[37]

In Eldonna P. Lays' book, *The History of El Cajon: Valley of Opportunity*, the following are mentioned: Enoch Birdseye, Amaziah and Illa Birdseye Knox, and Levi Chase.[38]

In Thomas Joseph Adema's book, *Our Hills and Valleys: A History of the Helix-Spring Valley Region*, the following veteran is mentioned: David B. Hoffman.[39]

In 1992, a series of eight articles was published in the San Diego Daily Transcript newspaper about Moses A. Luce, Civil War Medal of Honor Winner, which contained excerpts of a life history that he had dictated for his children. The date range of the articles is January 22, 1992 to February 4, 1992, and cover his Civil War experiences (including the activities which led to his winning the Medal of Honor), his marriage, and his work both as an attorney and judge in San Diego. The San Diego Daily Transcript is available on microfilm at the San Diego Public Library Newspaper Room and the San Diego County Law Library. A list of titles to the articles is at Footnote 40 in "Source Notes" at the end of this book, where footnotes to Chapter Three are cited.[40]

Finally, some of the veterans of this study made it into the files of the Coroner's office, as noted in the San Diego Historical Society's *Guide to the Coroner's Inquests, 1853-1905, San Diego County*[41], and they are: Peter Elford, Arthur H.M. Haddock, Miles Hughes, Horace Hull, George Hurd, Henry Lamb, J.W. Langdon, Erasmus Payne, Ludlow Pruden and Simeon Skinner. The Coroner's record for each veteran appears with their individual listing in Chapters Four or Five of this study.

BUILDING THE CITY/SAN DIEGO SOLDIERS' HOME
It was mentioned in Chapter Two that Alonzo E. Horton "...received the juciest slice from the heart of the melon by reaching San Diego ahead of the post Civil War land developers."[42] But he didn't beat them all, however.

First on the scene, (although he went East for the war and died in Washington, D.C.), was Samuel P. Heintzelman, the early commander of troops at San Diego, mentioned in Chapter One. Heintzelman was on the scene at the time when Andrew Gray and Lt. Thomas Denton Johns of the Second U.S. Infantry were siting New Town. "Johns [had] brought with him materials and supplies to construct a supply depot at La Playa. In the interim and acting under instructions from the Colonel of the Boundary Survey Commission ... Gray had sounded and surveyed San Diego Bay. ... Gray and Johns [also] drew up the plan for a town site at [an] old Spanish landfall, Punta de los Muertos."[43]

Alonzo E. Horton

William W. Bowers

Lucy Horton Bowers

The Hotel Florence

"Samuel Peter Heintzelman, commander of the troops in San Diego, wrote in his diary March 21, 1850: 'Mr. Gray has just returned from Sounding the Bay. He has found a point of the Bay where there is eighteen feet of water, even at low tide. He and five others have bought it, and some other land, from the Alcalde for $23,000. They intend to build a wharf and lay out a town. I tried to buy last summer.'"[44]

"By May 29, 1857, there were 14 civilian buildings in San Diego. ... That summer, Heintzelman recorded in his diary that he had ridden out to La Playa, giving up his quarters at the Mission and still too stubborn to take part in the New Town action."[45] While Heintzelman left San Diego to take part in the Civil War and never really returned, he ... was the first garrison commander who purchased land in both town and county."[46]

[After the war,] "Heintzelman yearned to find a permanent home 'for the few remaining years I can expect to live.' More and more he was thinking of settling at San Diego, California, if the Southern Pacific Railroad ever became a reality. He had always liked the sunny and invigorating Southern California climate and had maintained his property in the oceanside town."[47]

"In Washington in December 1872, he thought again of moving to San Diego but instead he finally settled into a house on M Street in the capital. Here old friends from Texas and comrades from the Civil War came to call."[48] ... Samuel Peter Heintzelman, a man of 'intense nature' and 'vehement action,' died in Washington at his residence at 1123 Fourteenth Street in the early morning hours of May 1, 1880. With the Stars and Stripes in the capital at half-mast, and after a small funeral at his residence, his body was accompanied by a military escort to Buffalo, New York, where it lay in state at the City Hall before burial with military honors at Forest Lawn Cemetery next to his infant son. The old general was seventy-four."[49]

Thus an early military leader of the Mexican War, San Diego and Yuma was put to rest. It was just a year later that a local G.A.R. Post was dedicated to his honor by Matthew Sherman and others.

Sherman, having served in the war and having returned shortly thereafter, was the earliest Civil War veteran on the post-war scene, right in time for pending development. "By 1869, it was apparent to even the die hards that South San Diego [New Town] was going to supplant Old Town. Those who a year before were ready to make an affidavit that Horton was insane and should be committed to the state hospital at Stockton were beginning to wonder just who was crazy, Horton or they. Many of the leading residents of Old Town had already moved to New Town, including E.W. Morse and Matthew Sherman. Even before Horton arrived, Sherman was grazing sheep on land he owned just east of Horton's Addition. In 1867, he built a home at Nineteenth and J. In 1869, he subdivided Sherman's Addition, which became known as East San Diego and later as Golden Hill. Like Horton, he donated land for a school ... which became known as the East San Diego School. ... Later the Sherman School was built at Seventeenth and H, and then at Twenty-Second and Island."[50]

Several Civil War leaders took an active interest in the development of San Diego. One was General William Starke Rosecrans[51], who "...had resigned from the army after the Civil War and came to California as one of the incorporators of the Southern Pacific Railroad. He told [Alonzo E.] Horton that he would like to visit San Diego to see if a railroad could be built from San Diego eastward to Yuma. If it could, Horton's property would be worth millions. On Horton's next trip south Rosecrans accompanied him. They hired a team, and with several others went first to Tijuana and then to Jacumba Pass where they could view the desert. General Rosecrans said 'Horton, this is the best route for a railroad through the mountains that I have ever seen in California.' As they returned through Horton's Addition, Rosecrans jokingly remarked that if he ever owned a lot in San Diego, 'I would like it right here.' Horton remembered this casual remark and the approximate location. After the land was surveyed and lots set out Horton made Rosecrans a present of the block bounded by Fifth, Sixth, F and G."[52]

"On September 18, 1869, General ... Rosecrans paid another visit to San Diego. Arriving with a group of railroad officials, he was in town only one day and was royally entertained. While [in San Diego] he sold back to Horton the block that had been given to him a year before. The consideration was said to be $2,000 in cash and two lots. Rosecrans was well satisfied with the deal, and after assuring residents that a railroad was a 'certainty', he extended his best wishes and left on the steamer Senator. ... General Rosecrans served in Congress as a representative from Northern California from 1885 to 1893. He died in 1898, the year Fort Rosecrans was established on Point Loma."[53]

"[Alonzo E.] Horton, although married several times, had no children, but had an abundance of relatives and in-laws. He wrote enthusiastically to his family in Wisconsin, telling them about his new city, and urged them to come West and make their fortunes with him. Many of his relatives did just that. In the summer of 1869 his youngest sister, Lucy, arrived with her husband, W.W. Bowers [Civil War veteran of this study]. ... Soon after Bowers' arrival Horton announced plans for the Horton House, which was to be a lavish hostelry, 'a palatial brick edifice,' one of the finest in Southern California. His brother-in-law [Bowers] would be the architect and builder. ... The site of the Horton House was to be on D between Third and Fourth [present site of the U.S. Grant Hotel.]"[54]

"In 1883, W.W. Bowers announced he had acquired the block bounded by Third, Fourth, Fir and Grape, and would build a luxurious hotel on the site. [The location] was way up on the hill, far from the center of town, with only a rough dirt road leading to it. It had previously been the site of Indian huts, and sheep still grazed in the vicinity. ... The new hotel opened on February 24, 1884 with a gala ball and became the show place of the city during the boom days. It was called The Villa, or The Florence, and the surrounding area became known as Florence Heights. The Florence in later years became the Casa Loma and then was torn down...."[55]

The study of city builders must include Dr. Peter C. Remondino, and it is with gratitude that the following information is quoted from Peter Arnold Ottaviano's Master's Thesis on Dr. Remondino, entitled, *"The Fever of Life: The Story of Peter Charles Remondino,"* available at Copley Library, University of San Diego.

Remondino, an Italian by birth, served in the Civil War "...[b]etween [medical] school terms in 1863 and again in 1864 [and] served in the Union Army in Maryland and Virginia as an Acting Medical Cadet and an Acting Assistant Surgeon. After graduation as an M.D. on March 10, 1865, he served as a Post Surgeon at various Virginia posts. Without doubt, his many months of battlefield medical experiences could supply enough material for a separate study."[56]

"[T]he wartime experience that would most impact Remondino's eventual decision to migrate to the Far West was his acquisition of a malarial type fever in the fall of 1864. The fever that would plague him off and on for the next nine years became a key reason for his move to seek a more healthful climate in Southern California."[57]

"Remondino started his San Diego medical career in Alonzo Horton's New Town, then just seven years old. The City of San Diego Business Directory of 1874 lists an office for Remondino on Fifth Street, near "F" Street. He would have an office within walking distance of that site for the next fifty years."[58]

After marrying Sophia Ann Earle on September 27, 1877, "Examination of several representative transactions discloses that the Remondinos traded nineteen lots, ultimately selling six and holding thirteen for investment purposes. In addition to land deals in the city Remondino bought and sold an 80-acre ranch in Cajon Valley, today's City of El Cajon. This spread was expansive, and included a ten-acre fruit orchard ... [and] a large barn [holding] stalls for 20 horses. ... He was also involved in the buying, building and when necessary, the movement of downtown San Diego buildings, one of which was a book bindery."[59]

Hampton L. Story Elisha S. Babcock

The Hotel del Coronado

With Dr. Thomas Coates Stockton, he opened the growing town's "first private hospital."[59] After selling all his interest in the sanitarium to Dr. Stockton, he entered into the hotel business. "San Diego was in the midst of its greatest boom era in the mid-1880s, the 'Glory Years'. Railroad service between San Diego and the eastern United States commenced on November 19, 1885 after several failed attempts. The railroad was responsible for Southern California's rapid expansion. Remondino was ready to ride the boom with the amenities to travelers and opportunity-seekers afforded by his hotel. ... The mansard roof of the St. James, San Diego's first skyscraper, was covered in decorative round tin plates on the top floors, which reflected the sun and glittered like mirrors."[60]

"The heyday of the hotel ended in 1888 with the collapse of the property boom. A formidable new competitor, the Hotel del Coronado on nearby Coronado Island, opened in February 1888, and the St. James lost its glittering reputation as "the place to be" to the prominent and exclusive island landmark. Remondino leased out the St. James in May 1889, then sold it during the 1890s. ... Remondino experienced the highs and lows of business in the 1880s, as did so many other San Diegans. Unlike Alonzo Horton ... Ephraim Morse [and others], Remondino did not die a poor man. He was able to survive despite serious financial difficulties because he never relinquished his true vocation, his medical practice."[61]

A landmark that was always on the horizon across the bay from New Town was called "the peninsula" or "the island". It was acquired by marriage by Pedro C. Carrillo when he married Josefa Bandini. The property was "...deeded ... as a 'wedding gift'..." by Governor Pio Pico on May 15, 1846."[62]

In *Coronado: The Enchanted Island*, Dr. Ray Brandes and Katherine Eitzen Carlin state, "The boom of the eighties in California was fostered by the coming of the railroads. Cheap and fast transportation attracted the unemployed easterners, health seekers, real estate promoters and a variety of merchants and tradespeople. Their arrival sparked an economic boom, fed by more rapid transportation of goods and supplies, and an era of unbounded construction. By 1885, Hampton L. Story and Elisha S. Babcock, Jr., [along with others] had ownership of the peninsula, and the dream of the Enchanted Island began."[63]

"Hampton L. Story left Cambridge, Massachusetts in 1856 for Chicago. There he opened a music store, served in the Union Army during the Civil War, and after the war farmed in Kansas. ... By 1885, he had spent half a dozen summers and winters in San Diego. ... Here he met Elisha S. Babcock, Jr. a native of Evansville, Indiana. Babcock had joined the Union Army just after graduation from high school ...."[64] They together planned to acquire the peninsula, and selecting "...Major Levi Chase [Civil War veteran of this study], a prominent lawyer who had come to San Diego in 1868 ... the sale was negotiated ... on November 19, 1885."[65]

They went on to develop the peninsula, called by now "Coronado", and constructed the magnificent Hotel del Coronado. They "...hired W.H. Holabird [Civil War veteran of this study] as general agent for the company. Holabird, a native of Vermont had served in the Vermont Volunteer Infantry, and Story had been in the same regiment during the American Civil War. He came to San Diego at Story's urging and was sometimes referred to as the 'Father of the Boom' because of the extraordinary skills he showed in advertising southern California to the rest of the nation."[66]

Wendell Easton, president of the Coronado Beach Company, "...set the date of the formal auction as November 13th" ... and "...put Robert J. Pennell [Civil War veteran of this study] in charge as agent for the Land Bureau. Pennell ... did his job well, inviting investors to take a map and examine the property. ... Bidding began at $500 and moved up to $1,600. Major Levi Chase bought the first lot on the ocean, near the site of the proposed hotel. Before the day had ended the Land Bureau had sold 350 lots for a total of $110,000."[67] The hotel was designed by an Evansville, Indiana firm, to be "...built around a court ..., a garden of tropical trees, shrubs and flowers ... balconies should look down on this court from every story...."[68] The hotel opened its doors in February, 1888.

W.H. Holabird was not only involved with the Hotel del Coronado. He also saw the need for a Soldiers' Home in San Diego for, as the advertising went, "The Government has established homes [in the District of Columbia, Ohio, Virginia, Kansas, Wisconsin and Maine] with accommodations for 12,000 soldiers, with no provisions made for at least 200,000 veterans who will need such a refuge within the next five years."[69]

Holabird presented a proposal to the National Encampment of the GAR in August, 1887, that a Soldiers' Home be built in an area called "Grantville".[70] The proposal, later implemented by Holabird and the Junipero Land and Water Company, was to set apart 200 acres of land near the Mission in Mission Valley, divide it into 25 X 100 foot lots, and,

> "...lay out in the center about 5 acres in the form of an elipse, for the grounds of the Soldiers' Home, and 20 acres of rich bottom land for gardens. ... The lots were to be sold and one third of the net proceeds, together with the two pieces of land mentioned above, put into the hands of three trustees ... to build a home for veteran soldiers belonging to the Grand Army of the Republic. The United States government have established several such Soldiers' Homes, but this one was proposed as a private institution."[71]

In October, 1887, the townsite and grounds were laid out. "...over 400 lots have been sold, a number of houses built and permanently occupied by families, a post office established, a store opened, district school located within a mile, and many improvements made. ... In June the Company commenced erecting one wing of the proposed Soldiers' Home which will be finished during September. This is a neat building, conveniently arranged and costing about $5,000 which will be added too from time to time as sufficient funds are collected."[72]

A map of the location of the Soldier's Home[73] appears on the next page. The location of the campus of the Soldiers' Home was just south of the present location of Kaiser Hospital on Zion Avenue in Grantville, and it is possible that the hospital was partially built on the same property.&n2

In an article for the Allied Gardens Examiner on January 28, 1960, Sophie Jaussaud Jackson stated: "Having been born here in Grantville, I have seen many changes. In 1887, plans for a townsite were laid by the Junipero Land and Water Company. Plans for a Soldiers' Home were in the making. The Grand Army of the Republic could not have chosen a more beautiful site at that time for the erection of its first Soldiers' Home...a place where the old soldiers passed the closing days of their lives amid such historic surroundings as the First Settlement of California and the First Mission of California. The site of the Soldiers' Home was north of the school. This is now called Grant Circle. The home housed 500 veterans. ... I can remember as a small child watching a soldier on guard, with a gun to his shoulder, walking back and forth past the small station building and entrance to the grounds."[74]

The Navajo News continues: "Grantville got its start, but the grand plan of the Junipero Land and Water Company fizzled. The great "bust" of 1888 caused Grantville...to bog down or collapse altogether as money tightened and land values dropped due to the unrealistic speculation. ... Grantville was one of [Holabird's] latest ventures in San Diego County booming and was not successful. Holabird left San Diego in February, 1887. His legacy remains, however. The next time you're on Rainier, Glacier or Vandever Avenues...turn onto the quiet residential road you see there. You'll find yourself on Holabird Street!"[75]

Little additional information was available about San Diego Soldiers' Home; however, there is no indication that burials took place there. This facility is mentioned here because several veterans in Chapter 5 were died or buried at a "Soldiers' Home", but were either not researched or not found by Dave Jackson when he consulted the burial register at Los Angeles National Cemetery. Doing additional research in the "Index to Historical Register of Soldier's Home, Sawtelle" (see p. 32 for a discussion of this Index), several veterans were indeed found to have died at Sawtelle: Augustus H. Moore, John E. Noble, James L.

William H. Holabird

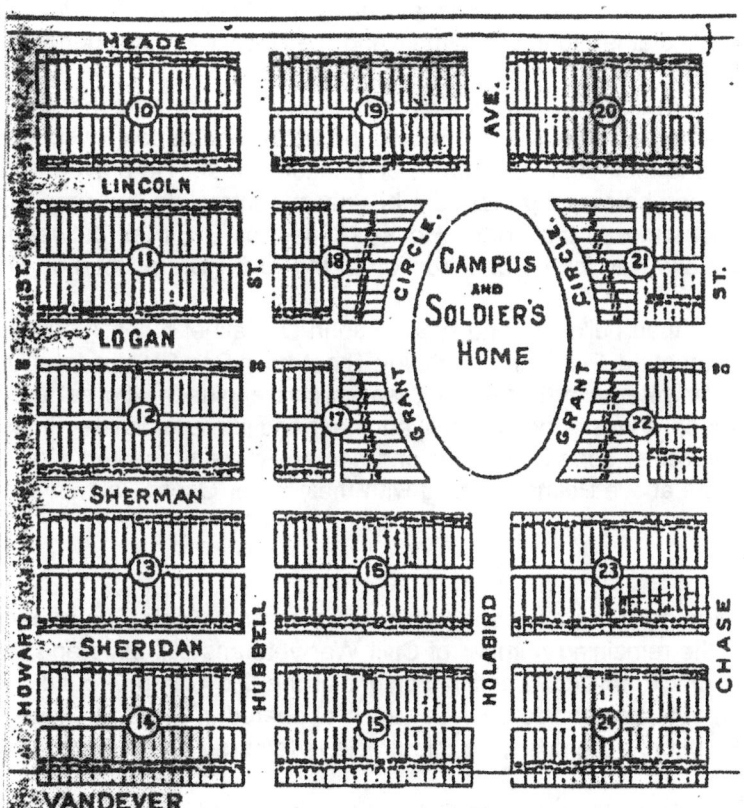

Location of the Campus of the
G.A.R. Soldier's Home in Grantville

A further check in the California Death Index (discussed on p. 34) revealed that others died in Los Angeles (see their death certificates for more information): William H. Bennett, Frederick Brenard, Lyman Brown, William A. Cone, Morris H. Lamb, Charles Lindley, and Charles Morris. One veteran, Stephan Sweetman, died in Alameda County, CA. Two additional "Soldier's Home" veterans died in San Diego, but were buried out of state. A check of their death certificates at the county revealed that William Brandis was buried at Fort Collins, Colorado, and Henry C. Spangler was buried at San Gabriel Cemetery, San Gabriel, California.

Finally, for several "Soldiers' Home" deaths, no record was found for their death or burial, including: Senaca P. Couts, Horace Doesser, A.W. Hogeland, Chief Iodine Josiah Juvenal, Watkins Washington, and William H. Wheaton.

Other Civil War veterans of this study were also developers and builders in San Diego. As the years went by, additional development was done by George W. Hazzard (who erected one of the first brick business blocks at the corner of Sixth and Market Streets, and buildings on other blocks downtown);[76] George H. Crippen (who developed Point Loma);[77] William H. Holderness (Tijuana Valley);[78] William Ober (builder of the first house in Ramona);[79] and Uzzial J. Stevens (El Cajon valley).[80] Attorney Levi Chase settled the title and boundaries of El Cajon Rancho, and as an attorney worked on litigation concerning Warner's ranch.[81]

While the above veterans all had a part in building the city, others helped to move around what had been built. Such was the case with John D. Palmer, (Civil War veteran of this study), who would be a distant cousin if the author had lived in his time. His granddaughter, Bertha Palmer Wohlers, has written a wonderful book entitled *Follow the Light: The Palmer Family and the Savoy Theater*. She described San Diego in the time of her grandfather John D. Palmer, and the lifestyle of later generations.[82]

"After John D. Palmer's saw milling business in Ohio was swept away by a freshet, he packed up his wife Lydia [Swift, whom he married on August 22, 1865 at the home of Charles Swift, Waterford Township, Washington County, OH) and their eight children ... and headed west. He arrived in San Diego in 1884 with $16.00 in his pocket, and before long started a business: contracting, building, and moving houses. In 1906, J.D. Palmer & Sons moved the Horton House [Annex] on D Street, between Third and Fourth, to 1134 Union Street, to make way for the construction of the [U.S.] Grant Hotel on D Street."[83]

City building involved more than buildings and roads. John D. Palmer's son Andrew Scott Palmer was instrumental in the operation of the Pickwick and Savoy Theaters in San Diego. John D. Palmer's brother, Isaac L. Palmer, (Civil War veteran of this study), was a civil engineer who set the first stake for the California Southern Railroad; he was listed as a civil engineer and surveyor in later times. While no photos of Isaac L. Palmer are available, John D. Palmer and his family are presented after this chapter in the "Images" section. All of the above Palmers, along with their father Oscar Palmer, are buried near each other on G.A.R. Hill.

THE DIE-OFF
Charting the die-off of veterans was a poignant moment in the study. Help was at hand from newspaper articles which discussed the remaining number of Civil War veterans still alive and their activities. The first, a San Diego Union article entitled "Tenting Tonight at the Old Camp Ground," was really a group photo showing 53 G.A.R. veterans and four wives which appeared in the San Diego Union on Sunday, January 10, 1932.[84]. The photo accompanying this article is featured on the back cover of this book.

The next article in the San Diego Union was on October 29, 1933, and it stated that two charter members of Datus E. Coon Post were still alive: A.H. Daughy [Dauchey] and W.B. Northern. Others still alive and also mentioned were: A.S. Stimson, Post Commander, A.E. Vest (88), Capt. T.C. Shelly (90); John Gipson (95), Dr. John Ogle (91), and Robert Tillman.[85]

The San Diego Union on June 1, 1937 said "Only Four Members of G.A.R. at Luncheon" given in their honor in the French room of the U.S. Grant Hotel by Mayor Percy Benbough and F. Carl Sherwood.[86] The photo pictured S.R. Shattuck, A.E. Vest, F.W. Northern, C. Kennedy, and R.T. Gilmore, along with several wives.

A much longer article appeared on the front page of the San Diego Union on June 5, 1938 which discussed four San Diego veterans who would march at Gettysburg. The article indicated that "...not so long ago, there were 375 members in Heintzelman Post G.A.R. here, and Datus E. Coon Post boasted more than 560. But now there are 13 in Heintzelman, four in Coon post."[87] Those who were to go on the trip to Gettysburg included Arthur E. Vest, Walter H. Northern, Charles Kennedy and John M. Riddle, a Confederate veteran, who said: "Every year ... I go back to Virginia to raise a crop. Now, I'm going to Gettysburg to raise _____' ... [Mr. Vest] 'hoped to meet O.N. Wilmington of Indianapolis, Ind' [while at Gettysburg, as] 'We bunked together for four years. As far as I know, we are the only survivors of our regiment.'"[88]

The article stated in passing the importance of San Diego as a destination for Civil War veterans, and that it was the destination long popular with G.A.R. veterans in the twilight of life. "Throughout the United States", according to Dr. Overton Mennett, Los Angeles, National Commander, "about 5000 Civil War veterans are living, an average of less than two to a county, and the combined total on the rosters of the local posts is 17!"[89]

The last article of this type appeared on May 30, 1939, and stated: "Grand Army Veterans Honored at Luncheon." "Six members of the Grand Army of the Republic were honored guests when Hammer Club members yesterday devoted its program to a Memorial Day observance."[90] The guests (pictured) were William Hubert, 95 (no further information available); Charles Kennedy, 91; H.A. Cross, 94; A.E. Vest, 94; Thomas Means, 93; and William [Walter] B. Northern, 93. By 1943, all of the veterans were dead.

Year of death could be determined for 66% (1,279) of the veterans of this study, using the records cited in Chapter Two, "Research Design" for those veterans for whom a year of death was available. Chart 8 shows the results of the year of death tabulation.

Chart 8: Year of Death of San Diego Civil War Veterans

Year of Death	Number	% of total	Cumulative %
1863-1889	34	2%	—
1890-1899	104	8%	10%
1900-1909	240	19%	29%
1910-1919	357	28%	57%
1920-1929	383	30%	87%
1930-1939	154	12%	99%
1940-1943	7	1%	100%
TOTAL:	1,279	100%	

Many of the veterans in this study lived a long time into the 20th century...a lot longer than one might expect. In the above chart, the die-off is presented in ten year increments. A small number of veterans is grouped from 1863-1889; the remaining veterans are grouped in 10-year increments. The first death of a veteran of this study was that of James J. Chard of Co G, 4th California Infantry, whose death by drowning in San Diego on January 25, 1863 occurred during the war years.

By 1929, 87% of the veterans of this study had died; by 1939, 99% had died, and by 1943, all were dead. The last to die was Horace Bly Day, who died on June 1, 1943, eighty years after the death of James J. Chard.

AGE AT DEATH

The veterans who came to San Diego generally lived long lives. The youngest veteran death in the study was, again, James J. Chard, who died at 28 during the Civil War. He was subsequently buried at Fort Rosecrans National Cemetery.

For the 1,038 veterans for whom a death age could be determined, the following chart lists the veteran's ages of death in 10 year increments, with the exception of the first group...individuals dying between the ages of 28 (Chard) and 49:

Chart 9: Age at Death of San Diego Civil War Veterans

Age (at death)	Number	% (of total)	Cumulative %
28-49	27	2%	—
50-59	62	6%	8%
60-69	194	19%	27%
70-79	363	35%	62%
80-89	328	32%	94%
90-107	64	6%	100%
TOTAL:	1,038	100%	

Looking at cumulative totals, only 8% of the veterans had died by age 59, only 27% by age 69, and only 62% by age 79. 94% died by age 89, but 64 (6% of the veterans) continued to live into their 90s, with one veteran living until the age of 107! Age of death was determined either by tombstone inscriptions, cemetery office records, or by use of G.A.R. records to generate a rough estimate of age at death.

There are three veterans who should be further mentioned. Arthur E. Vest lived second longest in time, dying in 1943. (Horace Bly Day outlasted him by 22 days in 1943). It was of interest to see what Mr. Vest looked like because at the bottom of his G.A.R. record were the words: "A mighty good soldier".

One day at the San Diego Historical Society, while looking through the "Biographical Files", a photo of Mr. Vest from the San Diego Union appeared (see p. iv). In the photo, Mr. Vest was looking at a picture of himself taken as a young soldier of the Civil War![91] Such is the serendipitous nature of research. Whatever the reason for the serendipity, it was a wonderful experience to find that image.

Horace Bly Day lived the longest in time, dying on June 1, 1943. Two newspaper articles discussed his 90th birthday, and later his obituary. Mr. Day began his career selling horseradish to New York hotels, and the business gradually grew into the H.B. Day Hotel Supply Company. He was also the first New York agent for the Cadillac automobile. Mr. Day was described as an organizer of the Home Telephone Company in San Diego, and also served on the city water commission. "Cherished first among the souveniers of this stalwart builder of empire is memory of his service in the Army of the Confederacy, in the war between the states, where 'I went out in '64 and came back in '65 after smelling plenty of powder.'"[92]

Hiram Reynolds lived to age 107, and an obituary in the San Diego Sun discussed this veteran. He was born in Springwater, NY on March 10, 1829 and came from a long-lived family, one relative dying at age

103 and another relative dying at age 106. When Mr. Reynolds died, he was believed to be the nation's oldest Civil War veteran. He was 35 when he entered the Union ranks, and fought until a broken leg at the battle of Richmond put him out of front line action. He was quoted as saying: "I do not believe in death, and so I do not fear it. What others call death, I think of as 'passing over'--a transition, a further growth. Growth and development is the secret of the universe. Nothing is ever lost."[93]

Nor was Mr. Reynolds. Finding his likeness was another example of serendipity. It was particularly touching to come upon his tombstone at Mount Hope Cemetery one warm September day. Upon looking at the stone, there was an image of Mr. Reynolds as a sweet looking older man, who was looking back! Out of all of the veterans of this study who had tombstones, his was the only tombstone where a likeness appeared on the stone.

BURIAL
Many of the veterans buried in the G.A.R. section at Mount Hope Cemetery were from both Heintzelman and Datus E. Coon G.A.R. Posts. Members of the two Posts were never competitors, but instead cooperated with each other. Heintzelman Post members attended the founding of the Datus E. Coon Post, and supported its activities. It was probably the sad story of the death of General Coon which pulled the men together. Thus, those from Datus E. Coon Post were included in the large numbers of Civil War veterans buried in the Heintzelman-owned plot on G.A.R. hill and Annex.

As such, they were together even in death. Their associations across the barrier of death can be seen in their burial patterns, particularly at Mount Hope Cemetery, where cluster and patterned burials occurred. If the veterans weren't active in the two G.A.R. Posts, they were Masons or Odd Fellows, or they were buried in Catholic cemeteries with other members of their church. The associations stand out at Mount Hope because the older parts of this cemetery were historically divided along association lines (G.A.R., Masonic, Odd Fellows).

Chart 10 presents a breakdown of veterans buried in "associational" locations versus the number of veterans buried at Greenwood, Ft. Rosecrans, Cypress View, those who were cremated, and "All other"-- those buried in the various non-associational "Divisions" of Mount Hope. Not included on this list are those who were buried in cemeteries listed in Chapter Five.

Chart 10: Burial Locations of San Diego Civil War Veterans

Location of Burial	# Buried There	% of Total
G.A.R. Hill/Annex	455	49%
MH/Masonic Cemetery	115	12%
Greenwood Cemetery	84	9%
MH/IOOF Cemetery	49	5%
Catholic	36	4%
MH/Confederate	25	3%
Cremated	22	2%
Fort Rosecrans	4	—
Cypress View	2	—
All other	146	16%
Total	938	100%

An article in the San Diego Union on September 17, 1893 discussed how many of the veterans sealed their pact to be with each other in death. The article stated:

"Ordinance No. 229" An ordinance granting to Heintzelman Post No. 33, Grand Army of the Republic, a certain tract of land for cemetery purposes:" Be it ordained by the common council of the city of San Diego, as follows:

"Section 1: That there is hereby set apart, dedicated to and for the use of Heintzelman Post No. 33, of the Grand Army of the Republic, in trust for cemetery purposes only, all that lot, tract, piece and parcel of land, situate, lying and being in Mount Hope Cemetery, in the city of San Diego, in the county of San Diego, state of California, designated by the letters G.A.R. on the map of said Mount Hope Cemetery, made by O.N. Sanford, CE, in January, 1893."

"Section 2: That the said Heintzelman Post No. 33, of the Grand Army of the Republic, shall have the free and exclusive use and control of said tract of land forever for cemetery purposes only, subject however, to such supervision as may be vested in the corporate authorities of the city of San Diego by the laws of the State of California."

"Section 3: That this ordinance shall take effect and be in force from and after its passage and approval and three publications in the San Diego Union and Daily Bee."[94]

The ordinance was approved and adopted between August 20th and September 5th, 1893 by the Board of Aldermen and president C.C. Brandt; the Board of Delegates and president Sewell F. Barker; and William H. Carlson, Mayor of the City of San Diego. (   ) Seal of George D. Goldman, City Clerk.

THE MORTAR
In 1897, the small mortar that now appears at the top of G.A.R. Hill arrived in San Diego, as the San Diego Union reported on December 14:

"Heintzelman Post G.A.R. has received from the ordnance department at Mare Island a ten-inch mortar and forty-two ten-inch shells, the weapon having been brought down on the steamer Santa Rosa Sunday night. It will be exhibited on the plaza for a few days, after which it will be taken to Mount Hope and occupy a conspicuous place in the G.A.R. section of the cemetery, the shells being sufficient in number to form a pyramid near the mortar. The mortar was procured for Heintzelman post through the efforts of Maj. Smith of Company H, U.S.A., lately stationed here, and other gentlemen."[95]

The mortar still stands at Mount Hope Cemetery G.A.R. section today, protecting the Civil War veterans who are buried there.

In the Civil War, the goal often was to reach the high ground. This goal was of prime importance in the battle of Gettysburg, for example, where many lives were lost in the attempt to reach or secure the high ground of Little Round Top.

It is probably no mistake that a great number of San Diego's Civil War veterans are buried on the the high ground of G.A.R. Hill. The high ground signified safety. The grouping of the veterans signified companionship. The name of the cemetery, Mount Hope, signified a desire for a better experience in the life to come. May God bless them and keep them all.

CHAPTER FOUR: LIST I--CIVIL WAR VETERANS BURIED IN SAN DIEGO

The following codes will be used for the Civil War veterans of this study who were buried in San Diego, and all available information will be entered for each veteran. However, if a veteran, for example, had no "A" or "official government tombstone, no "A" line will be presented for that veteran; if the veteran had no "B" or family stone, no "B" line will be presented below, etc. Veterans with the most complete information would have both official and unofficial tombstones, a wife listing, and will be a member of both G.A.R. Posts. Only a few veterans have this much information available about them, however.

A "JS" record is a Johnson-Saum Knobel Funeral Home record, where available. The reader is urged to consult other information sources available for individual veterans which are mentioned in Chapter 3. Also, any census information included in this list comes from San Diego Genealogical Society's *Leaves & Saplings* newsletter, reporting on the "1880 Census, San Diego County," and selected city and county histories cited below.

Information from the San Diego Herald newspaper appears in the San Diego Genealogical Society's publication "Newspaper Records from the San Diego Herald", published from May 29, 1851 to April 7, 1860. The obituaries in this newspaper report the earliest deaths that occurred in the veteran group, or in the wives group.

Codes used in this chapter are:

A. **Veteran's Official Tombstone:** Information from a veteran's official government tombstone, if available.

B. **Veteran's Unofficial Tombstone:** Information from a veteran's unofficial/family tombstone, if available.

C. **Cemetery Information:** This section identifies the cemetery where each individual in this chapter is buried; gives their grave location within the cemetery, and provides information from the cemetery office for the veteran's date of death, etc. Codes used to identify individual cemeteries are: **CAL**--Calvary Cemetery (also known as Mission Hills Cemetery and Pioneer Cemetery); **CV**--Cypress View Mausoleum; **FR**--Fort Rosecrans National Cemetery; **GW**--Greenwood Cemetery; **HC**--Holy Cross Cemetery; and **MH**--Mount Hope Cemetery.

Cemetery office information is coded as follows: **DOD/B**--Date of death and burial; **A**: Age at death; **N**: Nativity, if available; **M**: Marital status at death, if available. Names in "_____" are additional names found in the cemetery office record rather than on a veteran's tombstone.

D. **Heintzelman Post #33 G.A.R.:** The following are codes used to identify specific information that was collected for members of Heintzelman Post #33 G.A.R. This is the only post that compiled information about age at entry into the post, occupation, residence and length of service; this information was not collected by those who compiled the Datus Coon Post information. The codes used for Heintzelman Post records thus are:

N--Nativity; **A**: Age at time of entry into the post; **O**--Occupation **R**--Residence (reported below only if other than San Diego); **CW**--Civil War unit of service and rank; **E/D**--Dates of enlistment into and discharge from the Civil War; **LOS**: Length of service (also includes unusual reasons for discharge such as wounds, disability); **GAR**: Date veteran entered Heintzleman Post G.A.R.; **SP**: Date suspended from the post; **DR**: Date dropped from the Post; **RE**: Date reinstated into the Post; **D**: Date honorably discharged from the post. At times, there is also a notation of date of death and other additional information.

E. **Datus E. Coon Post #172 G.A.R.:** The following are codes used to identify specific information that was collected for members of Datus Coon Post #172 G.A.R. The information was collected in a large ledger book for members of the post, and is reported below for those who were members. This post collected nativity plus year of birth information (birth year is entered below by last two digits only, i.e. 1/4/46 for a birth on January 4, 1846. Age, occupation, residence or length of service information was not collected by this post. The best way to estimate an individual veteran's length of service for a Datus Coon Post member is to use the E/D notation (dates of enlistment and discharge). The Datus Coon Post codes are as follows:

N--Nativity, with year of birth if available; **CW**: Civil War unit of service and rank; **E/D**: Dates of enlistment into and discharge from the Civil War; **GAR**--Date entered Datus Coon Post G.A.R. There also might be some **SP** (suspended), **DR** (dropped), **RE** (reinstated) and **D** (honorable discharge) codes used for a Datus Coon Post member, as was done for the Heintzelman Post veterans.

NOL/NFI--If no ledger sheet was filled out for an individual veteran, the entry will simply read NOL/NFI, meaning there is "no other listing and no further information" about the veteran. This code involved Datus Coon Post members only.

F. **Information on Veteran's Wife (if located):** If a veteran's wife can be located, information will be included about her. Standards of proof for wives: "Wife" designation on a tombstone; wife buried next to veteran on a cemetery map; wife listed in cemetery office records (internment book, lot card), or, in a few cases, wife listed in a county history, obit, or some source outside of a cemetery record. The usual wife entry will include the information from their tombstone (which is always shown before the "DOD/B" listing); then the **DOD/B** from the cemetery office, followed by **A:** Age at death **N:** Nativity (if available) and **M:** Marital (if available). Again, names in "_____" are names found in the cemetery record rather than on the tombstones.

NOTE: Some citations in this Chapter are long and run to the following page in the text. In order to obtain the entire citation for an individual, please go to the page following their citation to see if the citation runs to that page.

MASTER LIST OF VETERANS BURIED IN THE CITY OF SAN DIEGO

Ackles, Willis
A/B: No stone
C: MH/GAR Hill DOD/B: 7/6-10/1923 A: 75
D: Willis Ackles N: Missouri A: 44 O: Janitor CW: Co E 83 US C T (Pvt/Corp) E/D: 7/63-10/65 LOS: 27 mos GAR: 2/24/1892 SP: 12/27/1898 RE: 12/24/1899 SP: 6/28/1904 DR: 1/22/1907 SP: 12/24/1912 DR: 7/28/1914 RE: 7/9/1918 Died: 7/6/1923 S: H

Ackley, Henry J.
A/B: No stone
C: MH/GAR Hill DOD/B: 12/14-19/1925 A: 78/3/20
D: H.J. Ackley N: Steuben, NY A: 37 O: Soldier CW: Co D 194 NY ___ (Pvt) E/D: 2/65-5/65 LOS: 3 mos GAR: 5/25/1882 D: 7/1/1883 S: H
F: Adelia Ackley DOD/B: No further information Note: Her name on 1880 Census--Born NY; parents from NY; she is 36 in 1880, and wife to Henry Ackley.

Adams, Frederick F.
B. F.F. Adams Co B 43rd Ohio Vol Inf 1861-1864
B: F.F. Adams, October 5, 1842-October 28, 1928
C. MH/Div.4 DOD/B: 10/28/1929-2/23/1930 A: 86/__/23 O: Died Seattle, WA [grave stone says date of death is 1928]
D. Frederick F. Adams N: Ohio A: 39 O: Merchant CW: Co B 43 Ohio Inf (Sgt) E/D: 10/61-9/64 LOS: 34 mos GAR: 3/31/81 SP: 4/30/1890 RE: 12/10/1890 TR: 12/13/1910 S: H
F. Mary Virginia, his wife March 2,1854-October 30,1887 "He giveth His beloved sleep" DOD/B: 10/30-11/1/1887 A: 34 N: California M: Married J/S: "Adams, Mary d. 30 Oct (1887), 35 yrs, mar, bur Mt Hope Cem"

Adams, George
A. Geo. Adams Post QM Sg't USA
C. MH/Masonic O DOD/B: 5/10-12/1896 A: 59/8/20 N: Canada M: Single E. NOL/NFI--DC

Allen, Andrew J.
B. A.J. Allen Oct 1,1840-Oct 18,1927 US Army 1861-1865
C. MH/Div.6 DOD/B: 10/18-20/1927 A: 87/__/17 Died in San Diego
F: Martha J. Ford Allen (probable wife) DOD/B: 12/1-3/1904 A: 60 (from information on lot card)

Allen, Charles Warren
B. Charles Warren Allen 1848-1907
C. MH/Masonic P DOD/B: 9/12-16/1907 A: 58/8/16 N: England M: Married
E. Chas W. Allen N: Greenville, OH 1843 CW: Co C 30th Ind Inf (Pvt) Term: 3 yrs E/D: 9/61-2/63 Indianapolis, Ind due to wounds GAR: 5/9/1923 or 5/9/1925 on transfer from US Grant Post Omaha, Nebraska S: DC

Allen, Seth S.
A. S.S. Allen Co G 25 CT Inf
C. MH/Masonic P DOD/B: 6/27-28/1908 A: 68/11/6 N: CT M: Married Name Seth
D. Seth S. Allen N: Conn A: 65 O: Retired CW: Co G 25 CT Inf (Pvt E/D: 8/62-8/63 LOS: 12 mos GAR: 7/12/1904 Died: 1908--is [grave] stone S: H

Allen, William Tankerville
B. In memory of Major William Tankerville Allen R.M. Second son of Captain Robert Calder Allen C.B.R.N. Born Nov 23,1845 Died Dec 10,1906
C. MH/IOOF DOD/B: 12/10-13/1906 A: 63 N: England M: Single

Allum, Thomas
B. Capt Thomas Allum Father 1818-1897
C. MH/Masonic J DOD/B: 3/7-9/1897; A: 78/9/___; N: American M: Married
D. Thomas Allum N: Penn A: 63 O: Carpenter CW: Co C 22 Iowa Inf (Pvt) Promoted?: Co B 48 Iowa Inf (Lieut) E/D: 8/62-10/64 LOS: 26 mos GAR: 3/22/1888 SP: 6/28/1892 RE: 4/1896 Died: 3/15/1897--is [grave] stone S:H
F. Rebecca Allum Mother 1837-1918 DOD/B: 10/2-5/1918 A: 81/4/27

Anderson, Mark B.
A: M B Anderson Co G 4 Wis Cav
C. MH/GAR Div.2 DOD/B: 3/14-16/1908 A: 86 N: PA M: Married Name Mark "JS record indicates Mark Anderson died of senility at Coronado, CA on 8/14/1908 at age 86; nativity PA; marital--married
E: Mark B. Anderson N: Reading, PA CW: Co G 4 Wis Cav (Pvt) Term: 3 yrs E/D: 12/63-5/65 Brownsville, TX GAR: 4/7/1896 on transfer from Garfield Post Dept. of Minn S: DC

Anderson, William
A/B. No stone
C. MH/GAR Hill DOD/B: 2/27-3/1/1933 A: 89/__/5 O: Died in Chula Vista
D: Wm Anderson R: Chula Vista CW: Co G 16 NY Cav (Pvt) E/D: Not stated LOS: Not stated GAR: 1/1930 RE: 3/22/1932 Died: 2/27/1933 S: H

Angier, Albert Warriner
A. Albert W. Angier Co I 3 Minn Inf
C: MH/Div.6 DOB: 9/14/1909 A: 77 "Removed from a private cemetery north of Del Mar"
D. Albert W. Angier N: New York A: 65 O: Rancher R: Del Mar CW: Co I 1 Minn Inf (Pvt) E/D: 10/61-11/64 LOS: 36 mos GAR: 2/25/1896 SP: 12/27/1898 RE: 5/12/1900 TR: 5/22/1906 Died: 6/__/1908 Los Angeles (Note: The GAR death date is probably in error as the 9/14/1909 death date above reflects a reburial from Del Mar, north of San Diego, where he apparently lived.)
F: Josephine Sumner Angier 1842-1919 DOB: 9/14/1929 A: 77 Died in Los Angeles, CA

Anthony, Charles E.
A/B. "Anthony" stone
C: MH/Masonic N DOD/B: 12/24-26/1918 A: 75/6/14 Note: Charles Anthony was born on June 10, 1843 to Elam and Nancy (Hunt) Anthony. After the Civil War, he married Lucy M. Elmer on November 7, 1863, and moved to San Diego, where he was a chemist and assayer, well informed on mining lands and the value of ore, according to *San Diego County, California: A Record of Settlement*, etc.
D: Charles E. Anthony N: New York A: 48 O: Miner CW: Co A 19 NY Inf (Pvt) Re-Enl?: Co __ 3 NY Art (Musician) E/D: 5/61-6/63 LOS: 24 mos GAR: 6/24/1891 SP: 3/__/1893 DR: 3/28/1899 S: H

Anthony, Charles E. (Con't)
E: Chas E. Anthony B: Union Spgs, NY CW: Co A 19 NY Inf (Pvt) afterword 3rd Art (Musician) Term: 3 yrs E/D:
    5/61-6/63 Auburn, NY GAR: Date not given Died: 12/23/1918 Buried: Masonic Cemetery (Mount Hope)
    S: DC
F: Lucy M. Anthony "Anthony stone" DOB: 5/19-21/1902 A: 55 N: American M: Married "Leny"

Antrobus, John C.
B: John C. Antrobus 1844-1936 Pvt Co I Reg 6 Iowa Inf
C: MH/GAR Div.2 DOD/B: 5/10-13/1936 A: 92/10/12 Died in Los Angeles
E: John C. Antrobus N: Decatar Co, IL CW: Co I 6 IA Inf (Pvt) Term: 3 yrs E/D: 7/61-8/64, Burlington, IA (No
    further information given) S: DC
F: Margaret J. Antrobus 1927 Aged 87 yrs. Margaret Jane DOD/B: 6/17-30/1927 A: 87/3/25 Died in San Diego

Arnold, Don J.
A: Don J. Arnold Co D 5 MO S M Cav
C: MH/GAR Div.3 DOD/B: 4/26-29/1918 A: 76
D: Don J. Arnold N: Ohio A: 70 O: Not stated CW: Co C MO State Militia Mt. Inf (Pvt) Re-enl?: Co C 5th MO Cav
    (Pvt) E/D: __/61-2/62 LOS: Not stated GAR: 3/10/1914 Died: 4/26/1918 S: H

Asher, Bartlett
B: Stone overturned at this location
C: MH/Div.6 DOD/B: 6/14-16/1907 A: 75/3/27 N: Indiana M: Married
D: Bartlett Asher N: Indiana A: 68 O: Railroading CW: Co E 1 Texas Inf (Pvt) E/D: 3/64-3/65 LOS: 12
    mos. GAR: 1/9/1900 Died: 6/14/1907--is [grave] stone S: H
F: Cynthia Ann Asher Stone overturned at this location DOD/B: 1/2-5/1921 A: 81

Ashton, John Quincy
B: John Q. Ashton Sept 22,1830-Jan 2,1919
C: MH/GAR Hill Middle Name: Quincy DOD: 1/2-7/1919 A: 87
D: John Q. Ashton N: Penn A: 52 O: Merchant CW: Co B 12 Kans Inf (Pvt) Re/Enl?: Co ___ 2 Kans Col'd (?)
    (QM Sgt) E/D: 8/62-7/65 LOS: 35 mos GAR: ? date SP: 9/26/1889 DR: 6/30/1891 RE: 11/12/1894 D:
    11/12/1894 S: H
F: Priscilla D. Ashton Jan 13,1839-Feb 20,1916 DOD/B: 2/20-22/1916 A: 77 Full name--Priscilla D. Hamlin Ashton

Atwood, Joseph R.
A/B: No stone
C: MH/Masonic F DOD/B: 2/23-26/1926 A: 81/8/1
D: Joseph R. Atwood N: Illinois A: 77 O: Retired CW: Co C 27 Ill Inf (Corpl) E/D: 8/61-9/65 LOS: 4 yrs
    GAR: 9/13/21 Died: 2/23/1926 S: H

Austin, Henry C.
B: Corpl Henry Austin Co 1 14 NY H A
C: MH/GAR Hill DOD/B: 12/13-16/1929 A: 84/2/22
E: Henry C. Austin N: DePyster, NY CW: Co 1 14 NY H A (Pvt/Corpl) Term: Unstated E/D: 11/63-8/65 GAR: No
    further information Obit: Children lived at Harvey, IL; no wife listed Died: 12/13/1929 A: 84 Bur: Mount
    Hope S: DC
F: Julia A. Austin No stone DOD/B: 1/22-24/1903 A: 58/11/22 N: England M: Married

Avery, Henry J.
A: Henry J. Avery Co A 67 Ill Inf
C: MH/GAR Hill DOD/B: 10/13-15/1929 A: 86/9/5 Died in San Diego

Babcock, Edward A.
B: Edward A. Babcock Co C 89 NY Inf Vol (1st Serg't) 1839-1910
C: MH/GAR Div.2 DOD/B: 4/8-10/1910 A: 68/9/1 N: NY M: Married
F: Fannie Irene 1839-1923 DOD/B: 7/4-6/1923 A: 84

Babcock, Elisha Spurr
B: Elisha S. Babcock Beloved Husband of Isabella Graham Father of E.S. 3rd Arnold and Graham May 1849-Sept 1922
C: MH/Div.3 DOD/B: 9/8-11/1922 A: 73/4/7
   NOTE: Elisha Babcock's father and mother are buried near him. Their stones read: Father Elisha S. Babcock 1814-1890; Mother Agnes S. Babcock 1828-1911 "Agnes Sutherland Babcock" His DOD/B: 4/3-4/1890 A: 75/7/19 Her DOD/B: 10/4/1911-4/21/1912 A: 84/9/20
F: Isabella Graham Babcock Sept 1850-July 1932 DOB: 8/1/1932 A: No further record

Bacon, David G.
A: D.G. Bacon Co E 18 Ill Inf
C: MH/Div. 6 DOD/B: 5/13-14/1901 A: 61 N: American M: Married

Bahl, Perry William
A: Perry W. Bahl Co C 16 Ohio Inf
C: MH/GAR Div.2 DOD/B: 5/15-17/1929 A: 85/7/17 O: Died in San Diego
E: Perry Wm. Bahl N: Wooster, Ohio 1843 CW: Co C 16 OVI (Pvt) Term: 3 yrs E/D: 9/61-10/64 Columbus, OH GAR: 11/27/1920 on transfer from Matthews Post #69 Dept. of MO Died: 5/15/1929 A: 85/7/17 Buried: Mount Hope S: DC
F: Clara E. Bahl July 1, 1846-June 1, 1932 (buried in Masonic A) DOD/B: 6/1-3/1932 A: 85/11/__ Died in San Diego "Clara Edith" (Her name on stone with "Wright, Jetson G. 1880-1955; Madge A. 1875-1962"

Bailey, Clark Charles
A/B: No stone C: GW/Hawthorne DOD/B: 4/15-18/1927 A: 93/8/4
E: Clark C. Bailey N: NY CW: Co I 13th Mich Inf (Pvt) Term: Unstated E/D: 12/61-7/_ GAR: No date Died: 4/15/1927 A: 93/8/4 Buried: Greenwood S: DC
F: Lillie A. Bailey, Wife of Clark C. Bailey, Born Ontario Canada, died Jan. 14, 1907, aged 62 yrs. 7 ms. 10 ds. A Loving Mother, A True Wife, and a Christian DOD/B: 1/14/1907-7/11/1911 A: 61

Bailhache, William Henry
B: William Henry Bailhache 1826-1905 Capt AQM US Vols
C: MH/GAR Hill Name spelled "Barlhache" DOD/B: 3/12-16/1905 A: 78/6/28 N: Ireland M: Single? Note: William H. Bailhache was born in Chillicothe, Ohio, was manager of the Illinois State Journal in Springfield, IL, was a friend and backer of Abraham Lincoln, lived after the war with his wife in Ripon, WI, and moved to Santa Fe, NM (1874) and California (1886). He was assistant editor of the San Diego Union Newspaper until 1892 (Information from *San Diego County Pioneer Families*).
D: W.H. Bailhache N: Ohio A: 49 O: Clerk CW: Co __ 1 US Vol (AQM) E/D: 9/61-6/65 LOS: Not stated GAR: 1887 SP: 3/29/1889 DR: 3/28/1899 RE: 4/10/1900 Died: 3/12/1905 "Died East" S: H
F: Ada Brayman, his wife 1839-1923 DOD/B: 4/2-4/1923 A: 83/10/27 Died: Los Angeles, CA Her ashes buried in grave of William Bailhache Name: Adaline A. Brayman Bailhache

Baird, Charles A.
A: Corpl Chas. A. Baird Co B 19 US Inf
C: MH/Masonic/O DOB: 2/23-28/1909 A: 47/3/19 N: Not stated M: Single

Baker, Eldred
B: Eldred Baker May 12, 1842-December 13, 1916
C: MH/Masonic S DOD/B: 12/13-15/1916 A: 74
E: Eldred Baker N: NY CW: Co F 142 NY Inf (Pvt) Term: 3 yrs E/D: 8/62-6/65 GAR: 7/10/1909 on transfer from John A. Rawlins Post #126 Dept of Minn D: 12/13/1916 A: 74 Buried: Masonic Cemetery (Mount Hope) S: DC

Baker, Oscar Holmes
B: Oscar H. Baker Co L 1st Regt W VA Cav 1848-1919
C: MH/GAR Hill DOD/B: 9/8-11/1919 A: 71/5/1 Title #9 to Abbie J. Baker
D: Oscar H. Baker N: W VA A: 66 O: Farmer CW: Co L 1st WVA Cav (Pvt) E/D: 3/65-8/65 LOS: Not stated GAR: 11/24/14 on transfer from Canby Post #16 Dept. of Oregon Died: 9/8/1919 S: H
F: Abbie J. Baker July 8, 1854-Sept 9,1943 DOD/B: 9/9-15/43 A: 89/2/1 Died: Santa Monica, CA

Banks, Horatio
A: Horatio Banks Co E 74 Ill Inf
C: MH/Div.6 DOD/B: 12/2-6/1916 A: 74
D: Horatio Banks N: Canada A: 61 O: Merchant CW: Co E 74 Ill Inf (Pvt) E/D: 8/62-6/65 LOS: 36 mos GAR: 1/12/1904 (probably from Ellsworth Post #30 Dept of Iowa Died: 12/2/1916 S: H
F: Alice F. Banks Craik (remarried to Robert Craik) DOD/B: 5/1-3/1944 A: 86/2/15

Barlow, Alfred
A: Alf'd Barlow Co G 14th Mich Inf
C: MH/Masonic C DOB: 9/18-20/1897 A: 53 M: Married N: American

Barnes, Barton N.
A: Barton Barnes Co G 22 Ill Inf
C: MH/GAR Div.2 DOD/B: 7/23-26/1910 A: 72/11/13

Barrett, Isaac Stephens
A: Isaac S. Barrett Co E 1 Minn H A
B: Isaac S. 1847-1921
C: MH/GAR Hill DOD/B: 9/11-12/1921 A: 74 O: Title #392 issued to Mrs. Louisa E. Barrett
E: I.S. Barrett N: Southport, PA 10/20/1846 CW: Co E I Minn Hv Art (Pvt) Term: 1 yr E/D: 1/64-10/65 Nashville, TN GAR: 12/9/1911 on transfer from Jamyers Post #60 Dept. of Minn Died: 9/11/1921 A: 74/11/21 S: DC
F: Louisa E. 1853-1927 DOD/B: 12/20-23/1927 A: 74/9/13 Died in San Diego

Barrett, John C.
A: J.C. Barrett Co G 1 VT Cav
C: MH/GAR Div.2 DOD/B: 10/7-10/1906 A: 65 N: Not stated M: Widower "John"

Barrett, William H.
B: "Barrett"
C: MH/Div.6 DOD/B: 12/26-29/1906 A: 62 N: Mass M: Married
D: Wm. H. Barrett N: Nantucket, Mass A: 37 O: Aparian R: Jamul, CA CW: Co I 20 Mass ___ (Pvt) E/D: 7/61-7/64 LOS: 3 yrs GAR: 10/21/1881 SP: 12/31/1883 DR: "Dropped" S: H

Barrick, William N.
A: W.N. Barrick Co B 38th IA Inf
C: MH/GAR Hill DOD/B: 10/28-30/1905 A: 67 N: Ohio M: Single
D: William N. Barrick N: Ohio A: 66 O: Carpenter CW: Co B 38 Iowa Inf (Pvt) Re-Enl?: Co I 34 Iowa Inf (Pvt) E/D: 11/62-4/65 LOS: 29 mos GAR: Date not stated--died after being elected but not mustered Died: 11/27/1905--is [grave] stone S: H

Barrow, Absolom E.
B: A.E. Barrow Born Mar 19,1843 Died Jan 14, 1908 "Confederate Vet"
C: MH/Masonic J DOD/B: 1/14-16/1908 A: 66/10/__ N: Virginia M: Married
F: Emma Barrow Born June 18, 1849 Died Aug 9, 1912 Native of VA DOD/B: 8/14-15/1912 A: 63/1/28 M: Widow

Baxter, Albert Beverly
A: Albert B. Baxter Co H 38 Wis Inf
C: MH/GAR Hill DOD: 11/14/1920-2/24/1921 A: 72 O: Title #213 to Francis M. Elmer
F: Dana E. wife of Albert Baxter 1848-1922 DOD/B: 3/22-24/1922 "Mandana E. Baxter"

Beam, Joseph C. (Dr.)
A/B: No stone
C: MH/Div.1 DOD/B: 3/5-9/1914 A: 87/1/7 "Joseph"
D: J.C. Beam N: Penn A: 57 O: Doctor CW: Co A 43 Ohio Vols (Pvt) E/D: 10/61-2/63 due to Surgeon's Certif. of disability LOS: 16 mos GAR: 6/30/1886 SP: 1/10/1889 DR: 6/30/1891 S: H
F: Margaret J. Beam No stone DOB: 7/8-10/1889 A: 61/6/2 N: Ohio M: Married

Beamer, John
A: Jno. Beamer Co C 10 Ill Inf
C: MH/GAR Hill DOD/B: 5/6-8/1908 A: 67/2/26 N: Ohio M: Married "JS" record indicates John Beamer died of pneumonia on 5/6/1908 at 436 or 8 National Avenue Nativity Ohio Marital--married.
D: John Beamer N: Ohio A: 66 O: Engineer CW: Co C 10 Ill Inf (Pvt) E/D: 8/61-7/65 LOS: 42 mos GAR: 11/27/1906 Died: 5/6/1908--is [grave] stone S: H
F: Mary E. Beamer 1848-1924 DOD/B: 11/20-22/1924 A: 76/8/11

Beamer, Peter Walter
A: Sgt Peter W. Beamer Co K 16 Ill Inf
B: Peter W. Beamer Father
C: MH/GAR Hill DOD/B: 11/25-28/1924 A: About 88 Middle name Walter
D: Peter W. Beamer N: Ohio A: 62 O: Blacksmith R: Lakeside, CA/San Diego CW: Co K 16 Ill Inf (Pvt/Sgt) E/D: 5/61-7/65 LOS: 48 1/2 or 54 mos GAR: 3/12/1900 or 3/13/1900 Died: 11/25/1924 S: H
F: Julia A. Beamer Mother DOD/B: 7/10-13/1927 A: 74/5/21 Name Julia Ann Beamer

Beck, Andrew
A: Corpl And'w Beck Co B 4 Minn Inf
C: MH/GAR Div. 2 DOD/B: 6/12-18/1907 A: 75 N: Germany M: Married

Beck, James Madison
B: James M. Beck Father 1836-1931
C: MH/Masonic P DOD/B: 11/16/31-5/17/1932 A: 95 (ashes in grave with Emma J. Beck)
D: James M. Beck N: New York A: 58 O: Carpenter CW: Co C 1 Mich Eng (Pvt/Sgt) E/D: 12/63-9/65 LOS: 21 mos GAR: 1/22/1895 Died: 11/16/1931 S: H
F: Emma J. Beck Mother 1847-1940 DOD/B: 5/21-24/1941 A: 93/11/10

Belding, Sanford Whitfield
B: "Belding"
B: Sanford W. Sept 1845-May 1930
C: MH/Masonic J DOD/B: 5/24-27/1930 A: 84/8/1 Died in San Diego Note: Sanford Belding was born at Greenwich, OH on September 23, 1845, and after the war was an agent for Pacific Coast Steamship Company. He married (second) Myrtle Hartzell on May 15, 1901. He was elected to the city Board of Public Works, and was also secretary to the city Board of Education, according to *San Diego County, California: A Record of It's Settlement*, etc.
D: S.W. Belding N: Ohio A: 45 O: Clerk CW: Co ? 12 Ohio Independent Bat L A (Pvt) E/D: 9/64-9/65 LOS: 12 mos GAR: 2/11/1891 SP: 6/23/1925 RE: 10/13/1925 Died: 5/24/1930 S:H
F: Lydia M. Belding No stone DOB: 4/13-15/1897 A: 46 N: American M: Married

Bell, Alexander
A: Alex Bell 1840-1901 CSA
C: MH/Confederate DOD/B: 5/18-21/1901 A: 61 N: Canadian
F: Mary Bell 1842-1914 DOD/B: 4/7-10/1914 A: about 77 N: LA M: Widow "Confederate Plot"
Note: Alexander Bell was born in 1840 in Canada and died 5/18/1901 in San Diego. He came to California from Texas. S: UDC document, California Room (see Chapter II, "San Diego Public Library" sources)

Bell, G.U/G.V.
A: Corp'l G.U. or G.V. Bell Co M 2nd US Vol Engr's
C: MH/Div.1 DOD/B: No record in boxes

Bell, Samuel V.
A/B: No stone
C: MH/Div.2 DOD/B: 11/19-20/1887 A: 60 N: American M: Single
D: Samuel V. Bell N: Penn A: 62 O: Retired CW: Co B 10 PA RC (Pvt) E/D: 7/61-1/63 Re-Enl?: Co B 159 PA Inf (Pvt) E/D: 1/63-6/65 LOS: 48 mos GAR: 5/24/1904 S: H

Bennett, DeForest P.
B: DeForest P. Bennett 1836-1929
C: MH/Div.6 DOD/B: 1/22-24/1929 A: 92/4/9 Died in San Diego
E: DeForest P. Bennett N: Batavia, NY CW: Co G 105 NY Inf (Corpl) Term: 3 yrs E/D: 8/62-8/63 Nashville, TN
    due to Surgeon's Certificate of Disability GAR: No further information Obit--Died: 1/22/1929 A: 92/4/9
    Note: To Illinois 1849 to homestead; to Iowa 1872; then to San Diego 1903; wife died 1912--name not listed;
    children listed Buried: Mount Hope S: DC
F: Annie B. Mulville 1869-1948 DOD/B: 2/21-25/1948 A: 78/7/8 Died in San Diego

Bennett, Gilbert P.
A: Sergt G.P. Bennett Co K 27 IA Inf
C: MH/GAR Hill DOD/B: 10/18-19/1910 A: 75/10/19 N: NY M: Married Obit--1911 City Directory, San Diego Public
    Library: "Dr. Gilbert P. Bennett died 10/18/1910 aged 75."
D: G.P. Bennett N: New York A: 72 O: Physician CW: Co K 27 IA Inf (Sgt) E/D: 8/62-8/65 LOS: 33 1/2 mos
    GAR: 11/12/1907 (probably on transfer from Gen. George R. Smith Post #53 Dept of Missouri Died:
    10/18/1910 S: H
F: Alma Bennett No stone DOD/B: No record in boxes

Bennett, Jesse
A: Jesse Bennett Co E 3 IA Inf
C: MH/GAR Div.3 DOD/B: 4/16-18/1919 A: 76/5/4
E: Jesse Bennett N: Harlen Co, Ohio 1841 CW: Co E 3 IA Inf (Pvt) Term: 3 yrs E/D: 4/61-1/63 St. Louis, MO
    due to disability GAR: 1/27/1917 on transfer from E.O. Hord Post #82 Dept. of Cal/Nev Died: 4/16/1919
    A: 77 Buried: GAR Plot (Mount Hope) S: DC
F: Eliza Ann Bennett 1838-1918 DOD/B: 8/1-3/1918 A: 80/2/3

Bentzel, Henry M.
A: H.M. Bentzel Co A 6th Iowa Cav
B: Henry M. Bentzel July 13, 1844-July 17, 1879 Note: Henry M. Bentzel was born in Dover, York County, PA, came
    to San Diego, and was employed at Lankershim's Flower Mill as miller. He married Carrie Victoria Lithgow
    on December 31, 1873. He served one term as City Assessor, and was elected to a second term in May,
    1879, but his health failed and he passed away in July, 1879 at 35 years of age, according to *San Diego
    County Pioneer Families.*
C: MH/Div.3 DOD/B: 7/17-18/1879 A: 35 N: PA M: Married J/S: "Bentzel, H. d. 17 Jul (1879), 35 yrs, b. PA,
    male, mar, bur City Cem" Obit/San Diego Herald, circa 7/15/1879: "In this city July 17, Henry M. Bentzel,
    a native of Pennsylvania, aged 35 years. The funeral will take place from the Baptist Church at 2:00 p.m.
    this Friday afternoon. Friends and acquaintences are invited to attend. Dover, York, PA papers please
    copy."
F: Carrie V. Hackett--MH/Masonic H Tombstone reads: Carrie V. Hackett July 25, 1847-May 21, 1923; family stone
    reads: Samuel Warren Hackett 1836-1920 Carrie V. Hackett 1847-1923. Her DOD/B: 5/21-24/1923 A: 75
    Note: Parents were Adam Lithgow, born of Scottish parents in 1808 in Lancaster, PA; died 1890 in San
    Diego; and Carrie Woodward (1810?-1895). Both buried in MH/Div. 3. Family came across plains by ox train
    in 1853, settling in Chollas Valley, San Diego (farming and bee keeping). Carrie was one of the first school
    teachers in San Diego at the "little pink schoolhouse" at 7th and B Streets. Samuel Hackett ran a stage line
    and mail service between San Diego and Temecula, according to *San Diego County Pioneer Families.*

Berg, Anton
A: Anton Berg Co H 3 or 8 US Inf
C: MH/IOOF DOD/B: 3/27-29/1910 A: 70 N: Austria M: Single

Berry, Riley
A: Riley Berry Co B 133 Ill Inf
C: MH/GAR Div. 3 DOD/B: 8/12-14/1913 A: 67/7/__ M: Married
D: Riley Berry N: Illinois O: Gardener CW: Co B 133 Ill Inf (Pvt) Re-Enl: Co G 149 Ill Inf (Pvt) LOS: Not stated
    GAR: 5/14/1912 TR: To Colorado Springs Post #22 Died: 8/12/1913 S: H
F: Elizabeth Berry No stone DOD/B: 8/22-28/1937 A: 86/__/14

Birdseye, Enoch L.
A: E.L. Birdseye   Co B   123rd Ohio Inf
C: MH/IOOF   DOD: 11/27/1875   A: 40   J/S: "Birdseye, Mr. d. 27 Nov (1875), 40 yrs, b. OH, male, bur IOOF Cem"
    Obit/San Diego Herald 11/27/1875: "Died, Birdseye, at his residence near Cahon Valley, Nov. 27, E.L.
    Birdseye, native of Norwalk Co, OH, aged 34 years. Funeral from Episcopal Church."
F: Illa Birdseye Knox   Buried: GW/Magnolia Place (no tombstone)   DOD/B: 2/2-4/1930   A: 84   Note: Illa Birdseye
    remarried to Amaziah Knox of El Cajon, CA, just east of San Diego. His DOD/B: 7/22-25/1918   A: 84   His
    tombstone reads: "Father Born 12/6/1833 Died 7/22/1918" He is buried next to Illa at GW/Magnolia. Note:
    See Chapter 3, "Marital Status" for more on Illa Birdseye Knox.

Birmingham, Thomas
B: Th's Birmingham   Co D   9 Conn Inf
C: MH/Div.?   DOD/B: No record in boxes

Black, Edwin J.
A/B: No stone
C: MH/GAR Hill   DOD/B: 1/8-11/1924   A: 82/5/4
D: Edwin J. Black   N: New Jersey   A: 80   O: Retired   CW: Co D   20 Conn Inf (Pvt)   E/D: 8/62-6/65   LOS: 3 yrs
    GAR: 4/11/1922   Died: 1/8/1924   S: H

Black, Isaac
B: Isaac Black   Corpl Co B   84th Ind Vol Inf   1843-1922
C: MH/GAR Hill   DOD/B: 10/24-26/1922   A: 79/3/28
D: Isaac Black   N: Indiana   A: 75   O: Grocer   CW: Co B   84 Ind Inf (Pvt/Corpl)   E/D: 9/62-7/65   LOS: 34 mos   GAR:
    11/26/1918 (former post disbanded)   Died: 10/24/1922   S: H
F: Eudora E. Black   1872-1930   DOD/B: 2/20-24/1930   A: 58/4/13   Died in San Diego

Blackmer, Eli T.
A: E.T. Blackmer   Co A   37 Mass Inf
C: MH/GAR Hill   DOD/B: "No records--government stone only"   Died in San Diego   Name: Blackmar
D: Eli T. Blackmer   N: New Braintree, Mass   A: 50   O: Piano Tuner/Dealer   R: National City, CA   CW: Co A   37
    Mass Inf (1st Lieut)   E/D: 7/62-11/62 due to sickness/disability   LOS: 4 mos   GAR: 12/22/1881   SP:
    6/26/1900   RE: 3/26/1901   Post Commander 1895   Died: 7/18/1907--is [grave] stone
F: Louisa H. Blackmer   DOD/B: No further information   Note: 1880 census lists Louisa H. Blackmer, age 48, as wife
    of Eli Blackmer; nativity New Hampshire, as were parents; listed as wife to Eli Blackmer.

Blake, Robert Walter
B: Robert W. Blake   Co G   39 Ill Inft   1841-1931
C: MH/GAR Div. 2   DOD/B: 8/28-31/1931   A: 89/8/3   O: Died in San Diego
D: Robert W. Blake   N: England   A: 80   O: Retired   CW: Co G   39 Ill Inf (Pvt)   E/D: 9/61-12/64   Re-enl? Co H
    2 U.S.V.V. (Pvt)   E/D: 2/65-2/66   LOS: 3 yrs   GAR: 7/25/22   Died: 8/28/1931   S: H
E: R.W. Blake   N: England   CW: Co G   39 Ill Inf (Pvt)   Term: 3 yrs   E/D: 9/61-9/64 Petersburg, VA   Re-enl: Co E
    U.S.V.V. Hancock's Corp (Pvt) 2/65-2/66 Elmira, NY   GAR: ? date on transfer from Jas Mead Post #60
    or #67 Dept. of Nebraska   S: DC
F: Persis A. Blake   1836-1909   DOD/B: 6/21-23/1909   A: 73/5/2   N: VT   M: Married   "Amanda Perris Blake"

Blanchard, George A.
A: Art'fr G.A.Blanchard   Co B   1 MO Eng'r's
B: George A. Blanchard, Member of Co B, 1st Regt MO Engineers   Born Oct 27, 1833   Died Dec 21, 1902
C: MH/GAR Hill   DOD/B: 12/21-24/1902   A: Not stated   N: American   M: Married   Died in San Diego
F: Margaret J. Blanchard Feb 4, 1855-Oct 24, 1914   DOD/B: 10/25-27/1914   A: 59/8/19   N: Ohio   M: Married   Died
    in San Diego   "Margaret Jane"

Bogardus, Byron Frank
A/B: No stone
C: MH/GAR Hill   DOD/B: 11/14-17/1921   A: 85
D: Byron F. Bogardus   N: New York   A: 63   O: Mason   CW: Co __ 19 Ill Inf (Musician)   E/D: 9/61-3/62   LOS: 6 mos
  GAR: 8/28/1883 (probably on transfer from Winthrop Post #28 Dept of NY   S: H
F: Kittie Bogardus   No stone   DOD/B: 9/15-17/1917   A: 69

Bogart, Elias Fetheringale
B: Elias F. Bogart   Co I   88 Ohio   1838-1914
C: MH/GAR Div.3   DOD/B: 4/8-10/1914   A: 75/4/28   N: Ohio   M: Married
F: His wife Elizabeth J. 1814-1918   DOD/B: 4/21-23/1918   A: 78/3/19   "Elizabeth Jane"

Bohanan, Sylvester Lee
A: S.L. Bohanon   Co E   Hatch's Minn Cav
C: MH/GAR Div. 2   DOD/B: 6/11-13/1912   A: 70/4/16   N: Maine   M: Widowed

Bolster, Robert
A: Rob't Bolster   Co 1   3 US Art
C: MH/GAR Div.2   DOD/B: 12/12-16/1912   A: 84

Boodry, George O.
A: Geo. O. Boodry   Co A   39 Mass Inf
C: MH/GAR Div.2   DOD/B: 3/23-27/1906   A: 80/2/297   N: Mass   M: Married
D: George Boodry   N: Mass   A: 74   O: Shoemaker   CW: Co A   39 Mass Inf (Pvt)   D: __/62-6/65   LOS: 36 mos   GAR:
  8/28/1890   Died: Soldier's Home 3/23/1906   S: H
  SAWTELLE: Records for this veteran were not searched at Sawtelle Soldier's Home or Los Angeles National
  Cemetery as he was buried in San Diego.
F: Elizabeth, wife of Geo. Boodry   DOD/B: 2/13-15/1910   A: 73   N: England   M: Widow

Booth, Oliver T.
A/B: No stone found
C: MH/Div.5   DOD/B: 12/24-27/1916   A: 84   Oliver F.
D: Oliver T. Booth   N: Ohio   A: 83   O: Retired   CW: Co E   2 Kans Cav (Capt)   E/D: 7/61-1/64 due to disability
  LOS: Not stated   GAR: 9/26/1916   Died: 12/23/1916   S: H

Boscher, Emil H.
B: Emil Boscher   Born Feb 26, 1844   Died Dec 16, 1913   "Auf Widersehen In Himmellshoehen"
C: MH/Div.5   DOD/B: 12/16-19/1913   A: 69/9/20
D: E.H. Boscher   N: Germany   A: 45   O: Druggist   CW: Co A __ MO L A (Pvt)   E/D: __/61-__/66   LOS: 60 mos
  GAR: 5/7/1884   Died: 12/17/1913   S: H
F: Ida Boscher   Born Oct 16, 1844   Died May 17, 1898   DOB: 5/17-20/1898   A: 54   N: German   M: Married

Bowers, William Wallace
B: "Bowers" stone
B: W.W. Bowers   Born 1834   Died 1917
C: MH/Masonic K   DOD/B: 5/2-4/1917   A: 82
D: W.W. Bowers   N: New York   A: 50   O: Hotel Keeper   CW: Co I   1 Wis Cav (Pvt/Sgt)   E/D: 2/62-3/65   LOS: 27 mos
  GAR: 10/22/1885   SP: 9/28/1897   RE: 10/12/1897   Died 5/2/1917   S: H
F. Lucy Horton Bowers   Born 1835   Died 1917   DOD/B: 11/10/1917-2/2/1918   A: 82/7/3

Boyd, John B.
B: John B. Boyd   Mother Mary Charlie (four persons mentioned on one tombstone)
C: MH/Masonic A   DOD/B: 12/24-26/1902   A: 51   N: American   M: Single
D: J.B. Boyd   N: Northumberland, PA   A: 35   O: Searcher of records   CW: Co F   139 Ill Inf (Pvt)   E/D: 5/64-10/64
  LOS: 5 mos   GAR: 2/8/1883   SP: 9/26/1889   DR: 6/30/1891   S: H

Boyette, William James H.
A: W.J.H. Boyette Co D 14 Ky Cav CSA
C: MH/Confederate DOD/B: 3/9-15/1923 A: 78/11/8 "Confederate"
   Note: William James H. Boyette was born in 1845 and died on 3/9/1923 in San Diego, CA. He was a Private, Co D, 14 Kentucky Cavalry S: UDC document, California Room (see Chapter II, "San Diego Public Library" sources)
F: Lucinda A. Boyette 1850-1923 DOD/B: 2/16-23/1923 A: 73/11/25 "Confederate"

Brabazon, George P.A.
B: Geo. P.A. Brabazon Jan 4, 1845-Oct 10, 1912 Natives of Ireland
C: MH/Masonic T DOB: 10/10/1912 A: 67/9/6
F: Rhoda Jane Dec 14, 1861-Apr 30, 1946 Beloved wife of Capt. Geo. P.A. Brabazon Natives of Ireland
   DOD/B: 4/30-5/3/1946 A: 85/5/16 Died in San Diego

Bradley, Frances William
B: "Bradley" stone
B: Francis William 1848-1912
C: MH/Masonic N DOD/B: 5/3-6/1912 A: 63/11/10 or 18
D: Frances W. Bradley N: Missouri A: 42 O: Bar Keeper/Liq.Dealer CW: Co A 44 MO Inf (Pvt) E/D: 8/64-5/65
   LOS: 9 mos GAR: 7/26/1888 SP: 9/26/1889 RE: 9/__/1891 GAR: 12/13/1892 Died 5/10/1912 S: H

Bradley, Garrett R.
A/B: No stone
C: MH/GAR Hill DOD/B: 3/31-4/2/1931 A: 92/4/30 Died in San Diego
D: Garrett R. Bradley N: Ohio A: 80 O: Retired R: Encanto CW: Co K 2 Iowa Cav (Pvt/Sgt) E/D: 8/61-9/65 LOS: 4 yrs 1 mo GAR: 4/22/1919 SP: 12/31/1928 RE: 10/8/1929 Died 3/31/1931 S: H

Bradwell, Alexander N.
B: Alex N. Bradwell Confederate Veteran Died Nov 13, 1903 age 50 (60?) years
C: MH/Div.6 DOD/B: 11/13-17/1903 A: 60 N: American M: Single

Brayton, George
A: George Brayton Co B 9 Minn Inf
C: MH/GAR Div.3 DOD/B: 1/31-2/3/1915 A: 94/10/7 N: NY M: Widowed
D: George Brayton N: New York A: 94 O: Tailor CW: Co B 9 Minn Inf (Pvt) E/D: 8/62-8/65 LOS: Not stated
   GAR: 3/24/1914 on transfer from L.P. Plummer Post #50 Dept. of Minn Died: 2/2/1915 S: H

Brenner, George A.
A. Geo. A. Brenner 10th Reg't US Cav (Chief Mus'n)
B: George A. Brenner, Chief Musician 10th Regt U.S. Calvary Born in Wertenberg, GER Feb 2, 1840 Died in San Diego Cal May 6, 1896
C: MH/GAR Hill DOD/B: 5/6-7/1896 A: 56 N: French
F: Mary E. Brenner (No grave stone) DOD/B: 7/24-8/6/1928 80/4/0

Brewer, Joseph C./G.
A: Cap't Joseph C./G. Brewer RGS 11 Ill Cav
C: MH/GAR Div.3 DOD/B: 8/9-12/1916 A: 80

Brewington, James B.
A: James Brewington Co A 7 Ind Inf
C: MH/IOOF DOB: 5/23/1917 A: 78
D: Jas B. Brewington N: Indiana 74 O: Minister CW: Co A 7 Ind Inf (Pvt) E/D: 9/61-9/64 LOS: Not stated
   GAR: 8/12/1913 Died: 5/20/1917 S: H

Brimm, Boyd P.
B: Boyd Brimm   1st Lieut   Co F   4 IA Cav   Born June 30, 1833   Died Oct 8, 1906
C: MH/GAR Hill   DOD/B: 10/8-10/1906   A: 73/3/8   N: England   M: Married
D: Boyd P. Brimme   N: Indiana   A: 68   O: Retired   CW: Co F   4 IA Cav (Pvt/1st Lieut)   E/D: 10/61-9/64 due to resignation   LOS: 36 mos   GAR: 12/10/1901   D: 2/27/1906   Died: 10/8/1906   S: H
F: Mary H.   Born Sept 23, 1842   Died Sept 4, 1917   DOD/B: 9/4-6/1917   A: 74   Name Mary Hammond Brimm

Brink, Thomas Edward
B: Thomas E. Brink   Civil War Veteran   May 28, 1843-Jan 1, 1923
C: MH/Masonic F   DOD/B: 1/1-3/1923   A: 79/7/4

Brinkman, Henry F.
A: Henry Brinkman   Co H   4 NY Inf
C: MH/GAR Div.2   DOD/B: 10/27-29/1908   A: 76/2/19   N: Germany   M: Single   "JS" record indicates Henry F. Brinkman died of heart disease 10/27/1908   Nativity Germany   Marital--married.   Place of death 4046 L St.
D: Henry Brinkman   N: Germany   A: 75   O: Cigar maker   CW: Co H   4 NY Inf (Pvt)   E/D: 4/61-8/62 due to disability   LOS: Not stated   GAR: 7/28/1908   Died: 10/27/1908   S: H

Britton, Capt. Thomas
B: In Memory Of Captain Thomas Britton   U S Army Retired   Born April 5, 1828   Died Sept 18, 1896
C: MH/GAR Hill   DOD/B: 9/18-20/1896   A: 68   N: English   M: Widower
F: Katherine Britton (possible wife)   DOD/B: No record in boxes/name on lot card only

Brody, Paul E.
B: Paul E. Brody   Pvt   Nevada Medical Corps
C: MH/Masonic   DOD/B: No record found

Brooks, John L.
A: John Brooks   Co M   2 Minn Cav
C: GW/Magnolia Place   DOD/B: 5/15-19/1922   A: 74/2/23
F: Lydia Brooks   DOD/B: 5/15-19/1922   A: 88

Brooks, John B./P.
B: John Brooks   1845-1928   Native of Indiana
C: MH/GAR Hill   DOD/B: 12/3-5/1928   A: 83/2/15   O: Died in San Diego   Middle Initial B.
E: John Brooks   N: Franklin Co, Ind   1846   CW: Co L   6th Ind Cav (Corpl)   Term: 3 yrs   E/D: 9/63-9/65   Indianapolis, Ind   GAR: 6/14/1924   SP: 9/24/1927   S: DC

Broughton, George W.
A: Geo W. Broughton   U S Navy
C: MH/GAR Div.3   DOD/B: 6/12-15/1915   A: 74   N: "On shipboard"   M: Married

Brouhard, George B.
B: George Brouhard   Feb 23, 1838-Feb 10, 1932   2nd Iowa Cavalry
C: MH/GAR Div.2   DOD/B: 2/10-15/1932   A: 92/11/18   O: Died in San Diego
E: George B. Brouhard   N: Boone Co, Ind   2/23/38   CW: Co B   2nd IA Cav (Pvt)   Term: 3 yrs   E/D: 8/61-11/64   Davenport, IA   GAR: 5/10/1913 on transfer from Stanton Post #55 Dept of Cal/Nev   Died: 2/10/1932 at Naval Hospital, San Diego   A: 94/11/16   S: DC

Brown, George
B: Husband George Brown   Born June 23, 1828   Died July 4, 1903   16th Wis Vol
C: MH/Div. 6   DOD/B: 7/4-5/1903   A: 75   N: English   M: Married
F: Atlanta Brown   His Wife   1834-1915   DOD/B: 1/9-11/1915   A: 80/7/21   N: Not stated   M: Widow

Brown, James Devoe
B: James Devoe Brown Corp Co F 140 Ind Inf Jun 18, 1842-Aug 31, 1916
C: GW/Hawthorne DOD/B: 8/31-9/2/1916 A: 74

Brown, James Edwin
A/B: No stone
C: MH/GAR Hill DOD/B: 12/22-27/1922 A: 76/11/29
D: James Brown N: Ireland A: 75 O: Not stated CW: Co B 196 PA Inf (Pvt) E/D: 7/64-11/64 LOS: Not stated GAR: 2/22/1916 on transfer from Bidwell Williams Post #9 Dept of New York Died: 3/30/1921 A: 80 S: H
    Note: San Diego County records show a James Brown who died on 3/30/1921. The Mount Hope cemetery office record reflects a James Brown with dates of death and burial of 12/22/1922 and 12/27/1922--burial in Lot 278 on GAR Hill. This may or may not be the "James Brown" reflected in the GAR record.

Brown, John B.
B: John Calloway Brown 1839-1923
C: MH/GAR Hill DOD/B: 5/10-12/1923 A: 83/6/23
E: John B. Brown N: Crawford Co, OH 5/16/48 CW: Co G 49 Ohio Inf (Musician) Term: 3 yrs E/D: 3/64-12/65 Columbus, Ohio GAR: 11/12/1927 on transfer from Plains, Montana Died: 9/13/1930 S: DC
    Note: San Diego County records show a John Brown who died on 5/10/1923.

Browning, Thomas Newton
A/B: One stone shown on map--no longer visible
C: MH/GAR Div.2 DOD/B: 1/13-15/1917 A: 72
E: Thos N. Browning N: Harrison Co, Ohio CW: Co F 62 Ill Inf (Mus'n) Term: 3 yrs E/D: 12/61-3/66 Little Rock GAR: 6/8/1912 on transfer from Geo H. Thomas Post #17 Dept of Indiana Died: 1/13/1917 S: DC
F: Sarah Ann Browning No stone DOD/B: 4/12-15/1912 A: 65/8/2 N: Ohio M: Married

Bryan, Solon
A/B: No stone
C: MH/Masonic J DOD/B: 1/9-13/1926 A: 84
D: Solon Bryan N: Ohio A: 49 O: Farmer CW: Co E 4 Ill Cav (Sergt) E/D: 9/61-1/64 LOS: 28 mos GAR: 9/27/1888 SP: 6/28/1892 RE: 3/12/1895 Died: 1/10/1926 S: H
F: Mary Ellen Bryan No stone DOD/B: 11/30-12/5/1921 A: 70/__/21

Bryant, Elden S.
B: Elden S. Bryant Co H 1st Mich Reg Light Art Vol 1814-1900
C: MH/Div.1 DOD/B: 4/18-19/1900 A: 85/8/0
D: E.S. Bryant N: New York A: 74 O: Lumberman CW: Co H 1 Mich L.A. (Pvt) E/D: 3/64-8/65 LOS: 17 mos GAR: 10/25/1888 S: H

Bryant, Richard
A: Rich'd Bryant Co A 4th Cal Inf (tombstone visible at Calvary Cemetery)
C: CAL/Sec.2, South 1/3, Row 33-2D DOD/B: 8/3-5/1894 A: 69 Native of Ireland. Parents: Thomas Bryant/Catherine O'Connell O: Mechanic Cause of Death: Heart Disease
F: Nora Daley (no record of burial at Calvary Cemetery) Source: Death record of daughter Mary Agnes Bryant, buried at Calvary Cemetery 10/28/1886 A: 14 Parents: Richard Bryant and Nora Daley

Buck, Nathan
A: Nathan Buck Co K 56 Ill Inf
B: Nathan 1837-1905
C: MH/GAR Hill DOD/B: 8/31-9/4/1904 A: 67 N: American M: Widowed [grave stone says 1905; rest of sources say 1904]
D: Nathan Buck N: New York A: 60 O: Drayman CW: Co B 4 US Art (Pvt) Re-Enl?: Co A 41 Ill Inf (Pvt) E/D: 7/61-12/63 Re-Enl?: Co K 56 Ill Inf (Pvt) E/D: 12/63-7/65 LOS: 48 mos GAR: 6/13/1899 SP: 6/28/1904 Died: 9/4/1904 (later corrected to 9/1/1904--is [grave] stone S: H
F: Anna 1837-1900 DOD/B 3/14-16/1900 A: 67 N: American M: Married "Eliza Anna"

Buckley, Joseph
B: In memory of Joseph Buckley Member Co H 89 Ill Vol Inf Born Feb 3, 1831 Died Mar 25, 1902
C: MH/Div.6 DOD/B: 3/25-26/1902 A: Not stated N: English M: Married
F: Mary Buckley Born Dec 29, 1830 Died Jan 4, 1909 DOD/B: 1/4-6/1909 A: 78 N: England M: Widow

Buckley, Michael
A. Mich'l Buckley 3 GL Boy USN (tombstone visible at Calvary Cemetery)
C: CAL/Sec.1, South, Row 8 DOD/B: No record found in Catholic cemetery index

Budlong, David H.
B: Lieut Col David H. Budlong 135th U.S.C. Inf 1829-1912
C: GW/Palm Terrace DOD/B: 11/30-12/2/1912 A: 81/7/__
D: David H. Budlong N: New York A: 79 O: Attorney CW: Co C 33 Wis Inf (Pvt) Promoted?: Co __ 135 U.S.C.T
    (Lt Col) E/D: 8/62-10/65 LOS: See prior notes GAR: 7/12/1910 (probably on transfer from Dept of Idaho
    Died: 11/28/1912 S: H
F: Martha D. Budlong Gruell Dec 1, 1844-May 30, 1916 "At Rest" DOD/B: No further record

Bumpus, William Bates
A: Wm.B. Bumpus U.S. Navy
C: MH/GAR Div.3 DOD/B: 4/12-14/1913 A: 72/9/16 N: Mass M: Married
D: William B. Bumpus N: Mass O: Seaman CW: Seaman U.S.S. Kerrington and Ship North Carolina E/D: 2/62-
    2/64 LOS: 24 mos GAR: 2/13/1900 Died: 4/12/1913 S: H
F: Ella M. No stone DOD/B: 2/15-22/1940 A: 71/2/13 (ashes) Died in San Diego

Burbeck, Lucius D.
A. Corpl L.D. Burbeck Co E 4 Mass Vol
B: Lucius D. Burbeck, Co E 4th Mass Vol Born June 30, 1824 Died Oct 20, 1900 Lucus
C: MH/GAR Hill DOD/B: 10/21-23/1900 A: 76 N: Canadian M: Widowed
D: Lucius D. Burbeck N: East Canada A: 58 O: Carpenter CW: Co E 4th Mass Inf (Corpl) E/D: 9/62-8/63 LOS:
    11 mos GAR: 1/8/1882 or 1/8/1883 Post Commander 1894 Died: 10/29/1900--is [grave] stone S: H

Burch, Grenville L.
A: G.L. Burch Co I 98 Ill Inf
C: MH/GAR Div.3 DOD/B: 7/16-19/1917 A: 72 Greenville

Burgoyne, Charles
A: Chas Burgoyne 1845-1916 CSA
C: MH/Confederate DOD/B: No record in boxes
    Note: Charles Burgoyne was born on 6/2/1845 in Virginia; died on 4/13/1916 in San Diego S: UDC
    document, California Room (see Chapter II, "San Diego Public Library" sources)

Burk, Benjamin H.
A. Benj. H. Burk Co A 89 NY Inf
C: MH/Div.2 DOD/B: Called "Benj. H. Buck" 6/2-4/1905 A: 55/3/7 N: American M: Single
D: Benj H. Burk N: New York A: 45 O: Carpenter CW: Co A 89 N Y Inf (Pvt) E/D: 8/61-8/62 due to disability
    LOS: 12 mos GAR: 2/23/1888 SP: 12/27/1898 RE: 5/8/1900 Died: 6/2/1905 S: H
F: Phebe Burk DOD/B: 3/29-31/1919 A: 85 "Phoebe"

Burkhard, Fred
B: Frederick Dec 5, 1844-Feb 4, 1922 Co F 140th Ill's Vol Inf
C: MH/Blk 1 Lot 135 Gr 1 DOD/B: 2/4-8/1922 A: 77/1/30
D: Fred Burkhard N: Switzerland A: 69 O: Manufacturer CW: Co F 140 Ill Inf (Pvt) E/D: 5/64-9/64 LOS: Not stated
    GAR: 4/14/1914 Died: 2/4/1922 S: H
F: Effie E. Dec 15, 1863-Apr 10, 1931 DOD/B: 4/10-13/1931 A: 67/3/25

Burnham, Charles W.
B: Judge Chas W. Burnham of Routt Co, Col Veteran of the Civil War 1847-1906
C: MH/Div.6 DOD/B: 3/26-29/1906 A: 58

Burton, Henry J.
B: Henry J. Burton 1st Mich Lgt Artl'y Mar 26, 1846-Aug 11, 1925
C: MH/GAR Hill DOD/B: 8/11-14/1925 A: 79/4/16 [GAR post date of death probably in error]
E: Henry Burton N: Charleston, NH CW: Co D 1st Mich L A (Pvt) Term: 3 yrs E/D: 1/64-8/65 Jackson, Mich GAR: 8/26/1911 on transfer from Elsmer Post Dept. of Indiana Died: 12/28/1918 S: DC Note: San Diego County death record indicates Henry J. Burton died on 8/11/1925.

Butler, Benjamin A.
B: Benjamin A. Butler 1849-1918
C: MH/IOOF DOB: 4/15/1918 No other information in boxes
D: Benjamin Butler N: Indiana A: 51 O: Minister CW: Co I 55 Mass Inf (Pvt) E/D: 6/63-8/65 LS: 26 mos GAR: 2/25/1895 TR: 4/28/1896 S: H
F: Orpha Butler 1849-1914 DOD/B: 1/20-22/1914 A: 66

Butler, Robert Harris
B: Robert H. Butler Apr 30, 1846-Dec 10, 1934 Co G 40th Wis Inf Vol Co H 49th Wis Inf Vol
C: MH/GAR Hill DOD/B: 12/10-13/1934 A: 88/7/10 O: Died in San Diego "Robert Horris Butler"
D: Robert H. Butler N: Wis A: 75 O: Retired CW: Co G 40 Wis Inf (Pvt) E/D: 5/64-9/64 LOS: 110 days Re-Enl?: Co H 49 Wis Inf (Pvt) E/D: 2/65-11/65 LOS: 9 mos GAR: 9/27/1921 Died: 12/10/1934 S: H
E: Robert H. Butler N: Oakland, Jefferson Co., Wis 4/30/46 Enl: Co G 40th Wis Inf (Pvt) Term: 100 days E/D: 5/64-9/64 Madison, Wis Re-enl: Co H 49 Wis Inf (Pvt/Corpl) D: __/64-11/65 Madison, Wis GAR: 3/14/1895 TR: 9/10/1921 (see D above) S: DC
F: Jennie Adele Dec 31, 1841-Jan 4, 1924 DOD/B: 1/4-7/1924 A: 82/__/4 Name Jennie Adele Ervin Butler

Butschli, Jacob
B: Jacob Butschli Co A 1st Nebraska
C: GW/Masonic Place DOD: 2/21-22/1930 A: 91/3/9
E: Jacob Butschli N: Obeupp, Canton of Berne, Switzerland 11/8/38 CW: Co K 27 Ill Inf (Pvt) Term: 3 yrs E/D: 8/61-9/64 Springfield, IL GAR: Date not stated Died: 2/17/1930 A: 91/3/9 Obit: 6 children who lived at Sacramento, San Diego, and Long Beach, CA, and Braymer, MO; no wife listed S: DC

Cahoon, Charles
A: Chas. Cahoon Co I 1 Mich L A
C: MH/GAR Hill DOD/B: 4/21-23/1921 A: 76
E: Charles Cahon N: Portland, Maine 12/5/45 CW: Co I 1st Mich L A (Pvt) Term: 3 yrs E/D: 1/64-7/65 Detroit, Mich GAR: 6/22/1918 Died: 4/21/1921 A: 75/4/17 S: DC

Caldwell, John G.
A: Jno G. Caldwell 23 US Inf
C: MH/GAR Div.2 DOD/B: 9/25-28/1909 A: 70 N: Illinois M: Widower

Calkins, Joel P.
B: Joel P. Calkins Oct 27, 1840-May 28, 1922
C: MH/GAR Hill DOD/B: 5/28-30/1922 A: 81/7/1
E: J.P. Calkins N: Hancock Co, Ill 10/27/40 CW: Co G 2 Ill Cav (Pvt) Term: 3 yrs E/D: 7/61-8/64 Baton Rouge, LA GAR: 3/23/1907 on transfer from Boston Corbett Post #273 Dept of Nebraska Died: 5/28/1922 A: 81/7/1 S: DC
F: Anna M. Calkins May 27, 1843-Jan 6, 1923 DOD/B: 1/4-6/1923 A: 79/7/8 Name Anna Mary Calkins

Callaghan, Patrick
B: Patrick Callahan Born in Ireland March 19, 1841 Died Nov 28, 1928 Mustered in United States Service Aug 18, 1862 Co H 20th Reg Wisc Vol Inf Discharged Springfield, Missouri Feb 15, 1863 Civil War Veteran
C: HC/St.Bernard, Plot 176, Grave 11 DOB: 12/1/1928 "Pat" No further information available
D: Patrick Callaghan N: Ireland A: 81 O: Retired CW: Co H 20 Wis Inf (Pvt) E/D: 8/62-2/63 due to disability LOS: 8 mos GAR: 7/25/1922 Died: 11/28/1928 S: H

Camacho (Comacho), Lorenzo
A: Sgt Lorenzo Comacho Co D 1st Cal Native Cav (tombstone visible at Calvary Cemetery)
C: CAL/Sec.1, North, Row 9-3 DOD/B: No record found in Catholic cemetery index
F: Elena Valenzuela (no record of burial at Calvary Cemetery) Source: Death record of child Lorenzo Camacho, buried at Calvary Cemetery on 7/18/1896 A: 5 Parents: Lorenzo Camacho and Elena Valencia. Death record of child Juan Camacho, buried at Calvary Cemetery on 11/8/1904 A: 24 Parents: Lorenzo Camacho and Elena Valenzuela

Campbell, George A.
B: Father Geo A. Campbell 1839-1923 Co I PR V C 1st Penn Bucktails
C: MH/GAR Div.2 DOD/B: 6/1-4/1923 A: 84 George H.
D: George A. Campbell N: New York A: 73 O: Carpenter R: La Mesa, CA CW: Co I 1 PA Inf Rifles (Pvt) E/D: 8/61-12/64 LOS: Not stated GAR: 8/13/1912 Died: 6/1/1923 S: H

Campbell, John T.
A/B: No stone
C: MH/GAR Hill DOD/B: 4/22-25/1922 A: 78/6/__ (for John Thomas Campbell)
E: John T. Campbell N: Mt Carmel, Ill 1844 CW: Co B 1st Ore Inf (Pvt) Term: 3 yrs E/D: 12/64-7/65 Ft. Vencomer GAR: 6/25/192__ on transfer from Lawton Post #99 Dept of Washington/Alaska Died: 4/20 or 23/1922 A: 79 S: DC

Capps, Thomas J.
A: Lt Col T.J. Capps 3 Tenn Cav
C: MH/Div. 1 DOD/B: 10/21-23/1902 A: 74 N: American M: Married
D: Thomas J. Capps N: Tenn A: 60 O: Mechanic CW: Co F 1 East Tenn Cav (Capt/Lieut Col) E/D: 3/62-__/63 due to disability LOS: 1 yr or 34 mos GAR: 6/30/1886 SP: 6/20 or 28/1892 RE: 5/11/1897 Died: 10/23/1902 S: H
F: Augusta Skelley Gapps 1836-1922 DOD/B: 4/13-17/1922 A: 85 Augustine Kilbome Capps

Capsel, Louis/Capsul, Lewis
A/B: No stone search undertaken
C: MH/Masonic F DOD/B: 5/24-28/1924 A: 78 "Louis Capsel"
E: Lewis Capsul N: France 5/15/46 CW: Henshaw's Ill Batt (Pvt) Term: 3 yrs E/D: 12/62-7/65 GAR: No further information Died: 5/24/1924 A: 78/__/9 Buried: Masonic Cemetery (Mount Hope) S: DC

Carey, George W. (Dr.)
B: Dr. George W. Carey 1st Ore Inf Co B 102nd Reg 1844-1924
C: MH/GAR Div. 2 DOD/B: 11/17-12/12/1924 A: 80/2/10 (ashes)

Carlin, Patrick
A: Pat'k Carlin Co I 10 NH Inf
C: MH/GAR Div. 3 DOD/B: 9/11-15/1913 A: 75/5/28 N: New York M: Single

Carmichael, Jacob Elson
B: Jacob E. Carmichael Father July 2, 1838-Mar 28, 1922 1st Nebraska Co A
C: GW/Cypress Place DOD/B: 3/28/1922-9/26/1924 A: 83/8/26 NOTE: Prior burial at Mount Hope/GAR Hill DOD/B: 3/29-30/1922 A: 83 Removed to Greenwood on 9/6/1924 GAR HIll lot sold--Veteran Fred Jilson now buried there

Carmichael, Jacob Elson (Con't)
D: Jacob E. Carmichael N: Illinois A: 70 O: Farmer CW: Co A 1 Neb Inf (Pvt) E/D: 5/61-__/63 due to disability
   LOS: Not stated GAR: 3/24/1908 Died: 3/28/1922 S: H
F: Mother Sarah T. Apr 21, 1850-Feb 13, 1931 DOD/B: 2/13-16/1931 A: 80

Carpenter, Charles D.
B: Chas D. Carpenter 1839-1925 Sgt Co D 20 Ohio Vol Inf
C: MH/GAR Div.2 DOD/B: 3/28-4/1/1925 A: 86
F: Maria H. 1845-1933 DOD/B: 10/12-14/1933 A: 88/1/9 Died in San Diego Hannah Maria

Casey, Patricius H.
B: Patricius H. Casey Mason 1844-1913
C: MH/Masonic O DOB: 9/29/1913 A: 69/6/5
D: Patricius H. Casey N: Ireland A: 66 O: Lawyer CW: Co I 31 Mass Inf (Pvt) E/D: 1/64-3/64 LOS: Not stated
   GAR: 5/10/1910 (probably on transfer from Scott Bradley Post #177 Died: 9/29/1913 S: H
F: Louise E.H. Casey 1852-1924 DOD/B: 8/14-19/1924 A: 72

Casteel, Reubin S.
A: Reubin S. Casteel Co G 8 MO SM Cav
C: MH/GAR Div. 2 DOD/B: 5/3-6/1912 75/3/15 N: Tenn M: Married

Castle, William D.
A: W.D. Castle U.S Navy
C: MH/GAR Hill DOD/B: 5/20-22/1906 A: 62 N: Michigan M: Single

Catlin, John
A. Bglr John Catlin Co A 5 NY Cav
C: MH/GAR Hill DOD/B: 10/4-8/1925 A: 76/6/26
D: John Catlin N: Not stated A: 72 O: Retired R: National City, CA CW: Co A 5 NY Cav (Bugler) E/D: 3/61-7/65
   LOS: 4 yrs Re-Enl?: Co K 1 US Cav (Bugler) E/D: 7/65-9/68 LOS: 3 yrs GAR: 3/27/1923 Died: 10/4/1925
   S: H

Cavileer, John Charles
A: John Cavileer Co G 4 NJ Inf
C: MH/GAR Div. 2 DOD/B: 6/9-11/1918 A: Not stated
D: John G. Cavileer N: New Jersey A: 61 O: Mariner R: Coronado, CA CW: Co G 4 NJ Inf (Pvt) E/D: 8/61-4/64
   due to disability LOS: 40 mos GAR: 1/9/1906 S: H
F: Sarah No stone DOD/B: 11/15-16/1910 A: 47/3/8 N: Scotland M: Married

Center, Lewis W.
A: Sergt Lewis W. Center Co F 193 NY Inf
C: MH/GAR Div. 2 DOD/B: 6/24-29/1912 A: 67/2/28 N: New York M: Widower

Chalfant, Alfred
A: Alfred Chalfant Co K 213 PA Inf
C: MH/GAR Div.3 DOD/B: 4/2-5/1916 A: 67
E: Alfred Chalfant N: Chester Co, PA 7/11/49 CW: Co K 213 PA Inf (Pvt) Term: 1 yr E/D: 2/65-11/65 Washington,
   D.C. GAR: 2/14/1914 Died: 4/2/1916 Buried: GAR Plot (Mount Hope) S: DC
F: Josephine S. Chalfant 1858-1946 DOD/B: 10/8-10/1945 A: 85/4/20 Died in San Diego Middle name Stewart

Chapman, George B.
A: Lieut Geo B. Chapman Co F 11 Ind Cav
C: MH/Div.6 DOD/B: 4/23-25/1912 A: 77/2/14
D: George B. Chapman N: Indiana A: 55 O: Carpenter CW: Co __ 9 Ind Batt (Pvt) Re-Enl?: Co F 11 Ind Cav (1st
   Lieut) E/D: __/62-11/65 due to disability LOS: 36 mos GAR: 10/28/1891 DR: 3/28/1899 RE: 4/10/1900
   Died: 4/23/1912 S: H

Chapman, George B. (Con't)
F: Ella Ewing Wife of Geo. B. Chapman Born Aug 8, 1848-Died Nov 16, 1904 DOD/B: 11/16-17/1904 A: 56 N: American M: Married (filed under "Mary Chapman")

Chapman, Joseph
A: Jos Chapman Co C (or G) 48 (or 49) Wis Inf
C: MH/GAR Hill DOD/B: 11/2-6/1919 A: 72
F: Fannie Chapman No stone DOB: 1/21-2/28/1921 A: 76 (ashes) Fannie L.

Chapman, Joseph M.
B: Joseph Chapman Oct 28, 1839-July 7, 1916 45 Iowa Vol
C: GW/Laurel Place DOD/B: 7/7-10/1916
F: Jennie Chapman Barkley 1837-1924 DOD: 1924

Chard, James J.
B: To the memory of 1st Sarg't James J. Chard of Co G 4th Inf Cal Vols Died Jan 25, 1863 Aet. 28 y'rs Native of Cleveland, Ohio [Note: According to Richard H. Orton's *Records of California Men in the War of the Rebellion, 1861-1867*, James J. Chard died in San Diego of drowning on 1/25/1863. No further information]
C: FR/Post Section 4, Grave 1 DOB: 1/25/1863 "1st Sgt"

Chase, Charles M.
A: Charles M. Chase Co I 2 Mich Inf
C: MH/GAR Div. 2 DOD/B: 7/25-27/1912 A: 72 N: Canada M: Married
E: Charles M. Chase N: New York CW: Co I 2 Mich Inf (Pvt) Term: 3 yrs E/D: 5/61-12/61 Alexandria, VA due to disability Re-Enl: Co ___ 7 Wis Indep Batt (Pvt) E/D: 11/62-7/65 Milwaukee, Wis GAR: 6/10/1905 on transfer from Wood Co Post #22 Dept of Wisconsin Died: 7/12/1912 A: 72 Buried: GAR Plot (Mount Hope)--DC
F: Sarah Ann Chase No stone DOD/B: 3/20-23/1921 A: 76

Chase, Thurston Purdy
A/B: No stone
C: Cremated
E: T.P. Chase N: Manchester, VT 1/12/42 CW: Co G 35 Iowa Inf (Pvt) Term: 3 yrs E/D: 8/62-7/65 Vicksburg, Miss LOS: 2 yrs 11 mos 11 days GAR: 6/10/1911 Obit: Died: 6/27/1926 A: 84/5/15 Cremated Married: Emily S. Anderson on 3/30/1884 Socorro Co, New Mexico; children--2 in San Diego, 1 Grass Valley, 1 Pasadena, CA, 1 Los Angeles, CA; 1 Chicago, IL; 1 Cleveland, OH S: DC

Chenault, Leo O.
A: Capt L.O. Chenault 1841-1919 CSA
C: MH/Confederate DOD/B: 1/6-16/1919 A: About 78
   Note: Leo O. Chenault was born in Virginia in 1841; died 1/6/1919 in San Diego, CA; Captain; enlisted 1861, Corinth, Miss S: UDC document, California Room (see Chapter II, "San Diego Public Library" sources)

Christopher, William Henry
A: Sgt Wm. H. Christopher Co C 7 Ill Cav
C: MH/GAR Hill DOD/B: 4/30-5/2/1921 A: 79 Middle name Henry
E: W.H. Christopher N: Northfield, NY CW: Co C 7 Ill Cav (Pvt) Term: 3 yrs E/D: 8/61-2/64 Germantown, TN Re-Enl: Same Company (Pvt/Sgt) E/D: 2/64-11/65 Camp Butler, IL GAR: 10/28/1911 on transfer from Amboy Post #572 Dept of Illinois Died: 4/30/1921 A: 79/5/25 S: DC

Clark, Edwin A.
B: Father Edwin A. 1842-1924
C: MH/Masonic A DOD/B: 3/19-24/1924 A: 82/__/25
D: Edwin A. Clark N: Penn A: 78 O: Retired CW: Co K 1 NJ Inf (Pvt) E/D: 4/61-10/62 LOS: Not stated GAR: 4/27/1920 S: H
F: Mother Martha A. 1840-1918 DOB: 9/17/1918 A: 77/5/5

Clark, George (Robert C.)
A: George Clark Co E 1 Ore Cav
C: MH/GAR Div.2 DOD/B: 1/6-7/1910 A: 78 N: NY M: Single (AKA Robert C. Clark)

Clark, Newton Ambrose
A: QM Sergt Newton A. Clark Co H 15 Kan Cav
C: MH/GAR Div. 3 DOD/B: 8/2-5/1914 A: 79/5/10 N: PA M: Married
D: Newton A. Clark N: Penn A: 70 O: Farmer CW: Co H 15 Kas Cav (Pvt/QM Sergt) E/D: 9/63-6/65 LOS: Not stated GAR: 7/25/1905 Died: 8/2/1914 S: H

Clark, William L.
A: Capt Wm L Clark 13 Mass Inf
C: MH/GAR Hill DOD: 4/18/1886 "Removed 1/1895" (no explanation) A: 58 N: American M: Married J/S: "Clark, W.L., d. 18 Apr (1886), 58 years, b. Boston, MA, mar, bur GAR Cem"

Cleveland, James S.
B: James S. Cleveland 1846-1935
C: MH/Div.6 DOD/B: 6/24-26/1935 A: 89/__/21 Died in San Diego
E: J.S. Cleveland N: Hornellsville, NY CW: Co E 146 Ill Inf (Pvt) Term: 1 yr E/D: 9/64-7/65 Springfield, Ill LOS: 9 mos 26 days GAR: 2/27/1909 on transfer from C.O. Loomis Post #2 Dept of Illinois SP: 1926 RE: 1928 Died: 6/24/1935 A: 89/__/21 Buried: Masonic (Mount Hope) S: DC
F: Charlotte Ann His Wife 1839-1908 DOD/B: 6/28-28/1908 A: 68/5/2 N: Ohio M: Married

Cleveland, Lewis C.
A: L.C. Cleveland Co G 2 Cal Cav
C: MH/GAR Hill DOD/B: 10/23-25/1905 A: 67 N: Illinois M: Widower
E: Louis C. Cleveland N: Barron Co, IL CW: Co G 2 Cal Cav (Pvt) Term: 3 yrs E/D: 10/64-2/66 Camp Union, CA GAR: 3/24/1900 Died: 10/23/1905 A: 66 Buried: GAR (Mount Hope) S: DC

Clevenger, Benjamin C.
A: Corpl B.C. Clevenger Co E 122 Ill Inf
B: Benjamin C. Clevenger 122nd Illinois Inf'try War of the Rebellion Died Nov 15, 1900 aged 67 years
C: MH/GAR Hill DOD/B: 11/15-19/1900 A: 67 N: American M: Widower
E: B.C. Clevenger N: Macoupin, IL CW: Co E 122 Ill Inf (Corpl) Term: 3 yrs E/D: 8/62-8/63 Benton Barracks, MO due to disability GAR: 3/10/1900 on transfer from Scott Post #398 Dept of Kansas Died: 11/15/1900 A: 65 Buried: GAR (Mount Hope) S: DC

Cline, Joseph Henry
A: Jos. H. Cline Co A 26 Ill Inf
C: MH/GAR Div. 2 DOD/B: 2/17-20/1912 A: 69/5/21 N: Illinois M: Married
D: Joseph H. Cline N: Illinois A: 69 O: Plasterer CW: Co A 26 Ill Inf (Pvt) E/D: 8/61-5/64 LOS: Not stated GAR: 12/12/1911 on transfer from Escondido Post #143 Dept of Cal/Nev Died: 2/17/1912 S: H
F: Mother Luvica J. Cline 1856-1930 DOD/B: 4/13-16/1930 A: 74/__/18 Died in San Diego Middle name Jane

Coan, Henry Clay
B: Henry C. Coan Pvt 1 Ohio Hv Arty Dec 15, 1939
C: MH/GAR Hill DOD/B: 12/15-19/1939 A: 93/1/22 Died in San Diego
D: Henry C. Coan N: Ohio A: 54 O: Carpenter CW: Co D 1 Ohio H A (Pvt) E/D: 6/63-7/65 LOS: 24 mos GAR: 2/12/1901 S: H

Coffeen, Lewis/Louis
B: Lewis Coffeen July 8, 1837-Oct 5, 1919
C: MH/GAR Div.2 DOD/B: 10/5-7/1919 A: 87/3/__
E: Lewis Coffeen--NOL/NFI S: DC
F: Elizabeth E. Coffeen His Wife Sept 12, 1834-Dec 9, 1911 DOD/B: 12/9-12/1911 A: 77/2/27 N: NY M: Married

Cole, John C.
A: Sergt John C. Cole   Co K   169 PA Inf
C: GW/Palm Terrace   DOD/B: 6/13-15/1914   A: 73/7/26

Colebaker, Samuel
B: Samuel Colebaker   1849-1932
C: MH/GAR Div.2   DOD/B: 8/4-15/1932   A: About 83   Died in San Diego
E: Samuel Colebaker   N: Hagerstown, MD   1844   CW: Co __ 7 Ind Batt (Pvt)   Term: 3 yrs   E/D: 1/62-7/65   GAR: 4/10/1926   Died: 8/12/1932   S: DC

Coleman, Ezekial A.
B: Lieut. Ezek'l Coleman   Co A   78th US C T
C: MH/GAR HILL   DOD/B: 11/11-12/1898   A: 84   N: American   M: Married   Middle Initial A.
F: "Mrs E.A. Coleman" (wife?)   No stone   DOB: No record in boxes

Coleman, John
A: Jno Coleman   Co A   3 (or 8) NY Prov Cav
C: MH/Div.6   DOD/B: 10/30-11/2/1904   A: 65   N: Ireland   M: Single
F: Delphine Coleman (wife?)   DOD/B: No record in boxes

Coleman, Levi B.
A: L.B. Coleman   Co G   4 Mich Inf
C: MH/GAR Div.2   DOD/B: 5/15-16/1908   A: 85   N: New York   M: Single
   "JS" record indicates that Levi Coleman died of stomach cancer 5/15/1908 Nativity New York Marital--single Died at County Hospital.

College, James
B: James College   1830-1912
C: GW/Magnolia Place   DOD/B: 2/13-15/1912   A: 81   "Colledge"
E. James College, Jr.   N: Northampton, England   CW: Co C   146 NY Inf (Pvt)   Term: 3 yrs   E/D: 8/62-5/65 General Hospital, Philadelphia, PA due to wounds   GAR: 3/14/1904 on transfer from George H. Thomas Post #5 Dept. of Dakota   Died: 2/12/1912   A: 81   Buried: Mount Hope (record in error--buried at GW)   S: DC
F: Mary B. College   1834-1922   DOD/B: 6/13-15/1922   A: 88

Collins, Lewis Rapalee
A: Lewis R. Collins   Co F   50 Ill Inf
B: Lewis R. Collins   1842-1920
C: MH/Div.1   DOD/B: 12/22-24/1920   A: 70/10/8   "Lewis Rapalee Collins"
F: Margaret Bolles Collins   1847-1935   DOD/B: 11/4-7/1935   A: 88/1/22   Died in San Diego   "Margaret Vesta Collins"

Combe, Francis M.
B: Francis M. Combe   1841-1924   6th MO Vol Inf
C: MH/GAR Hill   DOD/B: 9/5-8/1924   A: 83/3/15

Comings/Cummings, L.B. (Dr.)
A: Medical Cadet L.B. Comings   US Army
C: MH/GAR Hill   DOD/B: 7/18-19/1898   A: 54   N: American   M: Widower   "Dr" Cummings (Commings)
F: Mary T. Comings   No stone   DOD/B: 6/22-23/1894   A: 40   N: American   M: Married

Commo, Rubin
B: In memory of Captain R. Commo Departed This Life Mar 29, 1906 aged 65 years
C: MH/Div.6   DOD/B: 3/29-4/1/1906   A: 65/__/17   N: New Brunswick   M: Married

Comstock, John
A: John Comstock   Co K   45 Ill Inf
C: GW/Laurel Place   DOD/B: 10/20-21/1910   A: 72/7/27

Comstock, John (Con't)
D: John Comstock N: New York A: 47 O: Brickmaker CW: Co K 45 Ill Inf (Pvt) E/D: 10/61-12/64 LOS: 38 mos GAR: 12/27/1883 SP: 1/10/1889 DR: 6/30/1891 S: H

Confer, John W.
A: Sgt. Jno. W. Confer Co E 93 Ohio Inf
C: MH/GAR Hill DOD/B: 5/4-6/1902 A: 57/8/4 N: American M: Married
E: John W. Confer N: Miamisburg, OH 8/5/18__ CW: Co E 93 OVI (Pvt) Term: Unstated E/D: 6/61-8/61 Franklin, Ohio due to disability Re-Enl: Same company (Pvt/Sergt) Term: 3 yrs E/D: 6/62-6/65 Nashville, TN GAR: 11/10/1894 Charter Member of Datus Coon Post Died: 5/4/1902 A: 58 S: DC
F: Mother Della L. Confer Sept 22, 1851-May 15, 1927 DOD/B: 5/15-6/22/1927 A: 75/7/23 (ashes) Died in San Diego "Confar"

Conklin, Norman Henry
A: N.H. Conklin Act Ensign US Navy
B: Norman Henry Conklin 1839-1908
C: MH/Masonic A DOB: 6/12/1908 A: 69 "JS" record indicates Norman Conklin died of apoplexy on 6/10/1908 Nativity PA Marital--married Died at 2167 5th Street (Avenue) Note: 1880 census for San Diego indicates Norman Conklin, 41, was born in Pennsylvania; his father was from Connecticut; his mother from Vermont.
D: Norman H. Conklin N: Wyoming Co, Penn A: 43 O: Lawyer CW: Co D 2 KY Inf (Pvt) E/D: __/61-8/61 Re-Enl?: US Navy (Acting Ensign) E/D: Not stated LOS: Not stated GAR: 5/24/1883 SP: 6/26/1900 RE: 8/14/1900 Post Commander 1885 Died: 6/10/1908--is [grave] stone S: H
F: Myra Reese Conklin 1847-1916 DOD/B: 8/6-8/1916 A: 68 Middle name Isabelle Note: 1880 census reveals she is 32, from Indiana; parents from Kentucky, and she is wife to N.J. Conklin.

Connell, Cornelius
A: Corn'l's/Cornelius Connell Co G 7th Kans Cav (2 tombstones/same information, both visible Calvary Cemetery)
C: CAL/Sec.1, North, Row 7-3 (Sec.1-North, Row 2) DOD/B: No record found in Catholic cemetery index

Cook, George H.
B: George H. Cook May 24, 1840-Dec 8, 1926
C: MH/GAR Hill DOD/B: 12/8-11/1926 A: 86/6/14
D: Geo. H. Cook N: Mass A: 79 O: Retired CW: Co C 3 Wis Inf (Corpl/Sgt) E/D: 4/61-7/65 LOS: 4 yrs 3 mos GAR: 1/13/1920 Died: 12/9/1926 S: H Note: San Diego County death record indicates he died 12/8/1926.

Cook, Henry
A: Henry Cook Co G 1 Ohio Inf
C: MH/GAR Div.3 DOD/B: 7/15-17/1913 A: 83/9/11 N: Ohio M: Married
D: Henry Cook N: Ohio A: 68 O: Rancher R: Lakeside CW: Co G 1 Ohio Inf (Pvt) E/D: 8/61-8/64 LOS: 36 mos GAR: 3/27/1900 Died: 7/15/1913 S: H
F: Mary D. Cook No stone DOD/B: 12/25-29/1916 A: 70

Coon, Datus E.
B: Gen'l Datus E. Coon Died Dec 17, 1893 aged 62 y
C: MH/GAR Hill DOD/B: 12/17-19/1893 A: 62 N: American M: Widower Note: Datus Coon was born in DeRuyter, Madison Co, NY on February 20, 1831, son of Luke and Lois (Burdick) Coon. Luke Coon born Petersburg, NY in 1804. Lois Coon born 1808 in Rhode Island of German descent, according to *An Illustrated History of Southern California*.
D: Datus E. Coon N: New York A: 57 O: Real Estate CW: Co I 2 Iowa Cav (Capt) Promoted: Col/Br Brig Gen E/D: 7/61-8/65 LOS: 51 mos GAR: 2/23/1888 Post Cmdr 1891 Died: 12/26/1893--is [grave] stone S: H

Cooper, Daniel C.
B: Daniel C. Cooper Co F 125th OVI 1842-1907
C: MH/Masonic P DOB: 12/26/1907 A: 65/11/16 N: Ohio M: Married
F: His Wife Anna B. 1845-1919 DOD/B: 4/5-8/1919 A: 74/1/23 (AKA Anna Cooper Noyes)

Cooper, J.B.
A: Ass't Surgeon J.B. Cooper 27th Wis Inf
C: MH/GAR Hill DOD/B: No record in boxes
D: J.B. Cooper N: Penn A: 66 O: Physician CW: Co ___ 27 Wis Inf (Asst Surgeon/Surgeon) E/D: 8/62-9/65 LOS: 36 mos GAR: 5/14/1884 Died: 7/26/1888--is [grave] stone S: H
F: Catherine E. Cooper 1838-1924 wife of J.B. Cooper DOD/B: 3/4/1924-11/21/1925 A: 85/1/15 (ashes)

Costello, Thomas
A: Thomas Costello Co K (or R) 15 Conn Inf
B: Costello unofficial stone broken off and gone
C: MH/GAR Hill DOD/B: 6/22-25/1897 A: 58 N: American M: Married
F: Mary Costello No stone DOD/B: 1/15-19/1925 A: 74/8/5

Cotton, John L.
B: John L. Jan 14, 1848-Feb 26, 1923
C: MH/GAR Div.2 DOD/B: 2/26-3/1/1923 A: 74/1/12
D: John L. Cotton N: Indiana A: 72 O: Retired CW: Co D 31 and 47 Iowa Inf (Pvt) E/D: 6/64-9/64 LOS: 100 days GAR: 5/14/1918 Died: 2/26/1923 S: H
F: Della L. May 21, 1855-Jan 5, 1923 DOD/B: 1/5-8/1923 A: 68/7/15 "Della Loretta"

Courtney, James
A: Jas Courtney Co D 16 Mass Inf (tombstone visible at Calvary Cemetery)
C: CAL/Sec.1, Central, Row 3 DOB: 8/16/1897 Native of County Kerry, Ireland Spouse: Julia Courtney (Catholic record)
F: Julia Courtney DOD/B: No record found in Catholic cemetery index (Catholic record)

Coutant, Jacob Benson
A: Jacob B. Coutant Co A 7 Ind Inf
C: MH/GAR Div.3 DOD/B: 9/30-10/3/1916 A: 78
E: J.B. Coutant N: New York CW: Co E 7 Ind Inf (Pvt) Term: 3 mos E/D: 4/61-7/61 Re-Enl: Co A 7 Ind Inf (Pvt) E/D: 8/61-9/62 due to disability GAR: 6/10/1905 on transfer from S. Cowell Post #60 Dept of Iowa Died: 9/30/1916 A: 78 S: DC
F: Sarah E. Coutant No stone DOD/B: 2/27-3/3/1941 A: 98/0/24 Died in Chula Vista, CA

Craigo, Joseph M.
B: Joseph M. Craigo 1842-1925 Co F 2nd Reg Wis Cav
C: MH/GAR Div. 2 DOD/B: 12/31/1925-1/4/1926 A: 83/4/12 Died in San Diego
F: Annie E. 1848-1924 DOD/B: 1/20-23/1924 A: 75/1/25

Crane, Luther Kent
A: Sergt Luther K. Crane Co F 2 Colo Cav
C: MH/GAR Hill DOD/B: 2/27-28/1917 A: 81 "Luther Kent"
D: Luther Crane N: Mass A: 67 O: Rancher CW: Co H 2 Colo Cav (Pvt/Com Sgt) E/D: 9/62-2/65 due to wound LOS: 36 mos GAR: 3/24/1903 Died: 2/27/1917 S: H
F: Mary A. Crane 1835-1897 DOD/B: 2/5-6/1897 A: 62 N: American M: Married Name Mary A. Crain

Crippen, George Henry
B: "Crippen" stone
C: MH/IOOF DOD/B: 12/8-12/1938 A: 92/4/22 Died in Ramona, CA Note: George Crippen was born in Oswego, NY in 1846. After the war, he went to Dowagiac, MI and Burlington, KS, then to San Diego in 1886. He married Melissa C. Daniel (of a prominent Southern family) in 1875. He was member of the city council, and a primary developer of land in the Point Loma area of San Diego.
D: George H. Crippen N: New York A: 62 O: Retired CW: Co ___ Independent NY Batt (Pvt) E/D: 12/63-8/65 LOS: Not stated GAR: 7/28/1908 S: H
F. Melissa Charlotte "Crippen" stone DOB: 1/25-27/1931 A: 78/7/17

Crockett, John
B: John Crockett Co D 68 Ohio April 28, 1844-Mar 17, 1924
C: MH/Masonic F DOD/B: 3/17-21/1924 A: 79/10/8
D: John Crockett N: Ohio A: 72 O: Mason CW: Co D 68 Ohio Inf (Pvt) E/D: 9/61-7/65 LOS: 34 mos GAR: 2/26/1918 on transfer from Farragut Thomas Post #8 Kansas City, MO and J.A. Martin Post #153 Cal/Nev Died: 3/17/1924 S: H
F: Ellen Crockett Sept 28, 1851-Apr 18, 1933 DOD/B: 4/18-21/1933 A: 81/7/17 (AKA Ellen Shook)

Cromwell, Robert
A: Lieut Rob't Cromwell Co G 10 Ill Inf
C: GW/Acacia Place DOD/B: 10/9-10/1918 A: 81/8/17
D: Robert Cromwell N: New York A: 53 O: Rancher R: Fallbrook, CA CW: Co G 10 Ill Inf (Pvt) E/D: 4/61-7/61 Re-Enl?: Co A 10 Ill Inf (Pvt/1st Lieut) E/D: 8/61-7/65 LOS: 46 1/2 mos GAR: 9/20/1890 SP: 6/28/1892 DR: 3/28/1899 RE: 5/22/1900 Died: 10/9/1918 S: H

Cummings, Wallace E.
A: W.E. Cummings Co H 10 ME Inf
C: MH/GAR Div. 2 DOD/B: 6/19-21/1911 A: 79/6/19 N: Maine M: Married Died in San Diego
D: Wallace E. Cummings N: Maine A: 68 O: Carpenter CW: Co C 10 ME Inf (Pvt) E/D: 8/61-3/62 due to disability LOS: Not stated GAR: 4/22/1891 SP: 9/28/1892 or 9/28/1897 DR: 3/28/1899 RE: 11/25/1902 Died: 6/20/1911 S: H
F: Georgiana Louisa Cummings No stone DOB: 1/15-17/1912 A: 78/5/8

Cunningham, Windsor T.
B: Windsor T. 1843-1931
C: MH/IOOF DOD/B: 10/25-28/1931 A: 88/__/13 Died in San Diego
D: W.T. Cunningham N: Albany, NY A: 73 O: Real Estate CW: Co F 70 NY Inf (Pvt) Re-Enl?: Co A 86 NY Inf (Pvt) E/D: 4/61-7/65 LOS: 50 mos GAR: 2/27/1917 SP: 12/31/1928 S: H
F: Ida V. 1858-1911 DOD/B: 11/13-18/1911 A: 53/9/18 N: New York M: Married Died in San Diego

Curby, Augustus W.
B: A.W. Curby 1843-1910 Co K 14 Reg Wis Inf
C: MH/Div. 1 DOD/B: 3/22-24/1910 A: 67 N: PA M: Single

Curby, William Franklin
A: William F. Curby Co E 52 Wis Inf
C: MH/GAR Hill DOD/B: 5/28-6/1/1926 A: 84/3/14 Died in San Diego Middle name Franklin
E: Wm. F. Curby N: Chester Co, PA 3/1840 or 3/1841 CW: Co K 33 Wis Inf (Musician) Term: 3 yrs E/D: 8/62-6/63 due to disability Re-Enl: Co E 52 Wis Inf (Musician) E/D: 3/65-6/65 GAR: 10/10/1917 Died: 5/28/1926 A: 84/3/14 Buried: Mount Hope Obit: Lists wife Nora Curby S: DC
F: Norma Curby (owner of cemetery plot) DOD/B: No record in boxes

Cureton, David
B: David Cureton Serg Maj Co A 32 MO Inf Civil War Sep 17, 1843-Dec 26, 1923
C: MH/Div. 1 DOD/B: 12/27-28/1923 A: 80/3/10

Currier, Charles F.
A: Drummer C.F. Currier Co O 29 IA Inf (Co D?)
C: MH/GAR Hill DOD/B: 10/2-4/1901 A: 56 N: American M: Married

Curtis, David G.
A/B: No stone C: Cremated DOD/C: 8/14-17/1926
E: David G. Curtis N: Oneida, NY CW: Co I 26 Iowa Inf (Pvt) Term: 3 yrs E/D: 8/62-5/63 Davenport, Iowa due to disability LOS: 9 mos 22 days GAR: 2/27/1909 on transfer from Gen. Strong Post #82 Dept of Kansas Died: 8/14/1926 at San Diego Naval Hospital A: 10 days less than 81 years. Cremated 8/17/1926 at Benbough Crematory. Married: Miss Annie C. Southworth at Sarved(?), Kansas in February, 1891; one child S: DC

Curtis, Nathaniel A.
B: Bare stone except for: "Sept 15, 1927"
C: MH/GAR Div.2 DOD/B: 9/15-19/1927 A: 80/5/10 Died in San Diego
E: Nathaniel A. Curtis N: Allen Co, Ohio 1847 CW: Co E 12 Ohio Vol Cav (Pvt) Term: 3 yrs E/D: 8/62-6/65
    GAR: 6/26/1920 Died: 9/15/1927 Buried: GAR Plot (Mount Hope) Obit: Wife Mary E, 4 children: 1 in San
    Diego; 1 in Sanger, CA; 1 in Minnesota, 1 in Indiana S: DC
F: Mary Ellen Curtis Nov 9, 1852-Feb 27,1936 DOD/B: 2/27-29/1936 A: 83/3/18 Died in San Diego

Dailey, Orin V.
A: Orin V. Dailey Co E 1 Neb Inf
C: MH/GAR Div.3 DOD/B: 1/5-7/1916 A: 79 Name spelled Orrin
D: Orin V. Dailey N: New Brunswick A: 71 O: Machinist Co E 1 Neb Inf (Pvt) E/D: 6/61-11/66 LOS: 65 mos
    GAR: 7/9/1907 Died: 1/5/1916 S: H

Daily, Edwin V.
A/B: No stone
C: MH/GAR Div.3 DOD/B: 2/21-3/1/1924 A: About 78
E: Edwin V. Daily N: Camden, ME 1846 CW: Co I 19 ME Inf (Pvt) Term: 1 yr E/D: 2/65-6/65 Washington, DC
    GAR: 12/11/1920 Died: 2/21/1924 A: 78 S: DC
F: Mary Dailey No stone DOB: 3/11-13/1915 A: 53/1/15 N: RI M: Married

Daly, Francis H.
A: Sgt Francis Daly Co E 118 PA Inf
C: MH/GAR Hill DOD/B: 1/30-2/1/1902 A: 75 N: American M: Married
E: Francis Daly N: Philadelphia, PA CW: Co H 17 PA Inf (Pvt) Term: 3 mos E/D: 4/61-8/61 Philadelphia Re-Enl:
    Co E 118 PA Inf (Corpl/Sgt) E/D: 8/62-5/65 Philadelphia GAR: ? date on transfer from John A. Martin Post
    #153 Dept of Cal/Nev Died: 1/30/1902 A: 75 Buried: GAR Plot (Mount Hope) S: DC

Dannals, George M.
A/B: No stone
C: MH/Masonic G DOD/B: 4/21-23/1926 A: 81/5/19
D: George M. Dannals N: Rochester, New York A: 36 O: Bookkeeper CW: Co E 54 NY National Guard (Corpl)
    E/D: __/__-4/66 LOS: Not stated GAR: 12/22/1881 SP: 4/30/1890 RE: 9/28/1897 Post Commander 1884
    Died: 4/21/1926 S: H
F: Lucy L. Dannals No stone DOD/B: 8/6-8/1947 A: 91/3/13 Died: Coronado,CA

Darling, Charles W.
B: Charles W. Darling Co E 32nd Reg New York Vol Inf
B: Charles W. Darling 1844-1922
C: GW/Cypress Place DOD/B: 5/29-6/1/1922 A: 77 "Major Charles Darling"
F: Marcella Rolph Darling 1855-1950 DOD/B: 3/26-29/1950 A: No record found "Marcella Elizabeth Darling"

Darling, Horace
A: Horace Darling Co G 21 MO Inf
C: MH/GAR Div. 2 DOD/B: 8/9-14/1907 A: 80 N: New York M: Widower
D: Horace Darling N: New York A: 55 O: Farmer CW: Co C 24 MO Inf (Pvt) E/D: 7/61-__/64 LOS: 24 or 36 mos
    GAR: 10/19/1885 Died: 8/9/1907--is [grave] stone S: H
F: Mother Darling DOD/B: 5/15-17/1900 A: 73 N: American M: Married Name Mary E. Darling

Darr, Milton B.
A: Corpl Milton Darr Co I 18 Ill Inf
C: MH/GAR Div. 3 DOD/B: 5/2-4/1915 A: 78/3/1 N: PA M: Married
D: Milton B. Darr N: Penn A: 76 O: Glazier CW: Co I 18 Ill Inf (Pvt/Corpl) E/D: 3/65-12/65 LOS: Not stated GAR:
    3/25/1913 on transfer from J.B. Wyman Post Dept of Illinois Died: 5/2/1915 S: H
F: Susan Elixa Darr No stone DOD/B: 10/1-3/1923 A: 81/5/19

Davidson/Davison, Henry O.
B: Henry O. Davison Jan. 25, 1920
C: GW/Acacia Place DOD/B: 1/25-28/1920 A: No record found
E: Henry O. Davidson N: South Hadley, Mass 9/13/43 CW: Co A 46 Mass Inf (Pvt) Term: 9 mos E/D: 8/62-7/63
   Springfield, Mass Re-Enl: Co B 61 Mass Inf (Pvt/Corpl) E/D: 11/64-6/65 Arlington Heights GAR: 2/27/1909
   on transfer from Reno Post #29 Dept of Colorado Died: 1/25/1920 A: 76/4/12 Buried: Greenwood Cemetery
   S: DC
F: Hannah S. Davison Dec. 5, 1915 DOD/B: 12/5-7/1915 A: 62

Davidson, John M.
A/B: No stone
C: Cremated "JS" record indicates he died 12/10/1908 of apoplexy at 1604 Grand Ave. Age: 72/8/14 Nativity KY
   Marital--married Buried La Vista Cemetery, National City, CA (although record below indicates Mount Hope)
E: John M. Davison N: Kentucky 3/25/36 CW: Co B 47 KY Inf (Pvt) Term: 1 yr E/D: 6/63-12/64 Lexington, KY
   GAR: 6/__/1908 Died: 12/__/1908 A: 76 Buried: GAR plot (Mount Hope) S: DC

Davis, George Perkins
B: Father George P. Davis 1844-1920
C: MH/IOOF DOB: 11/24/1920 A: 76
D: George P. Davis N: Ohio A: 74 O: Retired CW: Co B 125 Ohio Inf (Pvt/Sgt) E/D: 10/62-10/65 LOS: 36 mos
   GAR: 1/22/1918 D: 9/10/1918 TR: 9/10/1918 "Transfer expired" S: H
E: Geo. P. Davis N: Kinsman, Ohio 1/19/44 CW: Co B 125 OVI (Pvt/Sgt) Term: 3 yrs E/D: 10/62-10/65 GAR:
   6/14/1919 Died: 11/21/1920 A: 76/11/2 S: DC
F: Mother Ruth C. Davis 1846-1917 DOB: 2/14-16/1917 A: 71

Davis, John Henry
A/B: No stone
C: MH/GAR Hill DOD/B: 8/12-15/1923 A: 76/2/24
D: John H. Davis N: South Carolina A: 66 O: Railroading CW: Co B 3 Del Inf (Pvt) E/D: 12/64-6/65 LOS: Not
   stated GAR: 9/13/1910 (on transfer from Montrose Post #38 Dept of Colo/Wyo?) Died: 8/12/1923 S: H

Davis, Josiah
A: Josiah Davis Co G 8 Ill Inf
C: MH/IOOF DOB: 10/10/1922 A: 85

Davis, L. Murry
B: L. Murry Davis 2nd Lieut Co G 43rd Indiana Born Sept 4, 1846 Died Dec 16, 1898
C: MH/Masonic N DOD/B: 12/16-18/1898 A: 52 N: American M: Single Name Murry F.
D: Murray Davis N: Indiana A: 41 O: Teamster CW: Co G 43 Ind Inf (Pvt) E/D: 11/61-6/64 LOS: 32 mos GAR:
   6/30/1886 D: 2/23/1888 S: H

Davis, Stephen Melvin
A: Lt Col Stephen Melvin Davis Co F 5th VA Inf CSA
C: MH/Confederate DOD/B: 2/23-26/1931 A: 87/10/__
F: Alice E. Davis 1858-1942 DOD/B: 4/24-29/1942 A: 83/10/6
NOTE: Stephen Melvin Davis was born 3/30/1843 in New York State; Died 2/23/1931 in San Diego, CA. Lt Colonel,
5th Virginia Infantry. Surrendered at Appomattox. S: UDC document, California Room (see Chapter II, "San Diego
Public Library" sources)

Davis, Walker
A: Walker Davis Co K 65 US C T
C: MH/GAR Hill DOD/B: 5/8-10/1904 A: 76 N: American M: Widower Race: Black
E: Walker Davis N: Garrett Co, KY CW: Co K 65 US Colored Inf (Pvt) Term: 3 yrs E/D: 12/63-1/67 Baton Rouge
   GAR: 1/24/1895 S: DC

Davis, William H.
B: William H. Davis 1838-1911 Co A 11 Mich Inf
C: GW/Laurel Place DOD/B: 1/8-14/1911 A: No record found
F: Frances E. Davis 1848-1923 DOD/B: 10/14-17/1923 A: No record found

Day, Horace Bly
A/B: No stone
C: GW/CMTD Buried in Sunshine, Tier D, Crypt 2 DOD/B: No record found
D: Horace B. Day N: Newton, NH A: 68 O: Retired Merchant CW: Co ___ 12 Mass L A (Pvt) E/D: 11/64-1/65
    LOS: 2 mos GAR: 6/25/1918 Died: 6/1/1943 (alias Robert Smith) S: H
    Newspaper article states he was in Confederate service (? unit), saying "I went out in '64 and came back in
    '65 after smelling plenty of powder." Obit nativity: Haverhill, MA. Above record nativity: Newton, NH.
F: Mary R. Day DOD/B: No further information Note: She is listed as his widow in 1942 City Directory.

Day, Joshua Davis
B: Joshua D. Day Sept 25, 1839-Mar 24, 1933
C: MH/Masonic B DOD/B: 3/24-27/1933 A: 93/5/27 "Civil War Vet"
D: Joshua D. Day N: Mass A: 61 O: Weigher CW: Co H 12 Mass Inf (Pvt) E/D: 5/61-3/64 Re-Enl?: Co C
    39 Mass Inf (Pvt/Corpl) E/D: 3/64-7/65 LOS: 36 mos GAR: 11/27/1900 Died: 3/24/1933 S: H
F: Mother Mary L. Day 1841-1923 DOB: 1/13-17/1923 A: 81/8/2 "Mary Louise"

Day, William G.
B: William G. Day Co B 74th Illinois Inf Born July 20, 1829 Died April 16, 1900
C: MH/GAR Div. 2 DOD/B: 4/16-17/1900 A: 71 N: American M: Married
F: Mary E. Day Jan 10, 1837-Apr 17, 1923 DOD/B: 4/17-21/1923 A: 86/3/7 Name Mary Elizabeth Day

Dayton, Richard Thomas
A: Richard Dayton US Navy
C: MH/GAR Hill DOD/B: 4/17-20/1928 A: 82/3/0 "Richard Thomas"
E: Richard Dayton N: East Cambridge, Mass 1845 CW: US Navy (Pvt) Term: 3 yrs E/D: 5/62-6/63 due to disability
    GAR: 6/11/1921 on transfer from Lyon Post #8 Dept of Cal/Nev Died: 4/17/1928 A: 83/3/1 Obit: Wife
    Harriet; native of Mississippi (?) No children listed S: DC
F: Harriet Dayton (no stone) DOD/B: 11/22-26/1928 A: 58/1/8

DeBurn, Eugene
B: Eugene DeBurn 1843-1927 Co E 80th Regt Ohio Vols
C: MH/Masonic R DOD/B: 5/9-11/1927 A: 84/1/23
E: Eugene DeBurn N: Harrison Co, Ohio CW: Co E 80 Ohio Inf (Pvt) Term: 3 yrs E/D: 1/62-9/65 Beaufort, SC
    GAR: 7/11/1895 Died: 5/9/1927 A: 84/1/23 Obit: Native of Ohio; born 1843; to San Diego in late '80s;
    Superintendent of Schools in '90s. Wife Mamie Albee De Burn; 3 children (2 San Diego, 1 Alhambra, CA)
    Buried: Masonic (Mount Hope) S: DC
F: Mamie Albee DeBurn 1865-1946 DOD/B: 9/3-5/1946 A: 80/11/19

DeFord, Thomas J.
A: Sergt Thos J. DeFord Co D 46 Ind Inf
C: MH/GAR Div. 3 DOD/B: 10/13-15/1913 A: 71/3/26 N: Indiana M: Married
F. Emma DeFord No stone DOD/B: 7/30-8/1/1914 A: 58/2/24

Dennison, A.R.
B: Maj. A.R. Dennison 27th Mass 1835-1930
C: MH/GAR Hill DOD/B: 11/28-12/1/1930 A: 95/6/__ Died in San Diego "Major"
D: A.R. Dennison N: Maine A: 90 O: Retired CW: Co D 27 Mass Inf (Capt); Promoted: Co ___ 2 US C T (Major)
    E/D: 9/61-11/64 LOS: Not stated GAR: 3/23/1926 Died: 11/27/1930 S:H

DeShanaway, John
B: John DeShanaway 1846-1924
C: MH/GAR Hill DOD/B: 11/15-17/1924 A: 78/7/1919
E: John DeShanaway N: Ohio 1846 CW: Co A 14 OVI (Pvt) Term: 3 yrs E/D: 1/64-7/65 Cleveland, Ohio GAR: 8/14/1920 on transfer from Forsythe Post #15 Dept of Ohio Died: 11/14/1924 A: 78/6/18 S: DC

Devoe, Joseph George
A: Jos G. Devoe Co B 50 Mass Mil Inf
C: MH/IOOF DOB: 12/19/1918 A: 75

Dibble, Edwin D.
B: Edward D. Dibble 1846-1915
C: MH/Masonic T DOD/B: 8/23-26/1915 A: 69/1/8 "Edward D"
D: Edwin D. Dibble N: Missouri A: 64 O: Merchant CW: Co K 45 Iowa Inf (Sgt) E/D: Not stated GAR: 8/9/1910 SP: 12/24/1912 DR: 12/27/1918 S: H
F: Belle M. Dibble 1852-1920 DOD/B: 4/22-26/1920 A: 67/10/18

Dickson/Dixon, George W.
A: Sgt G.W. Dickson Co B 131st PA Inf
C: MH/GAR Hill DOD/B: 3/31-4/2/1892 A: 71 N: American M: Married "Dixon"
D: George W. Dixon N: PA A: 66 O: Farmer CW: Co D 131 PA Inf (Pvt) E/D: 8/62-5/65 LOS: 32 2/3 mos GAR: 2/9/1888 SP: 1/10/1889 DR: 6/30/1891 Died: 3/31/1892--is [grave] stone S: H

Dickson, J.F.
A: J.F. Dickson Co K 2nd Cal Inf
C: MH/GAR Hill DOD/B: "Not on records"
D: J.F. Dickson N: Mass A: 38 O: Tinner CW: Co K 2 Cal Inf (Pvt) E/D: 7/64-6/66 LOS: 23 mos GAR: 7/24/1885 SP: 1/10/1889 DR: 6/30/1891 Died: "Dead"--is [grave] stone S: H
F: Mary Stearns Dickson No stone DOD/B: 6/13-14/1899 A: 77 N: American W: Widowed

Dill, Albert F.
B: Albert F. Dill 1840-1905 Co E 43 Mass Inf 1862-1863 Acting Ensign US Navy 1863-1865
C: MH/GAR Hill DOD/B: 2/2-8/1905 A: 64 N: American M: Married
D: Albert F. Dill N: Mass A: 43 O: Mariner CW: Co E 43 Mass Inf (Pvt) Re-Enl?: US Navy (Act. Ensign) E/D: 9/62-5/65 due to resignation LOS: 27 mos GAR: 11/13/1883 Post Commander 1893; Dept Commander 1899 Dept of Cal/Nev Died: 2/3/1905--is [grave] stone S: H
F: Isabelle Gay Dill 1848-1924 DOD/B: 11/22-24/1924 A: 76/6/20 (ashes)

Dillingham, John
A: John Dillingham US Navy
C: MH/GAR Hill DOD/B: 1/25-27/1895 A: 70 N: American M: Married "Captain"
D: John Dillingham N: Mass A: 62 O: Mariner CW: "Acting Master" E/D: 5/61-12/64 due to resignation; prisoner of war 18 mos in Texas LOS: 43 mos GAR: 12/23/1886 Died: 2/25/1895--is [grave] stone S: H
F: Clara C. Dillingham (no stone) DOD/B: 4/25-27/1912 A: 75/11/13 (buried in Div. 5)

Dixon, Henry G.
A: Henry Dixon Co K 140th PA Inf
C: MH/GAR Hill DOD/B: 7/18-20/1898 A: 74 N: American M: Married "Dixon"

Dodge, Richard Varick
B: Father Rev R.V. Dodge 1821-1885 Springfield, Ill "Servant of God, Well Done"
C: MH/Div. 3 DOD: No record in boxes J/S record: "Dodge, Rev R.V. d. 26 Feb (1885), 68 years, b. IL, mar, "shipped to Springfield, IL" Episcopal Church records also indicate he was "shipped east". [Is he truly buried at Mount Hope? Note: 1880 census indicates he was born in Illinois; his parents born in New York.
D: Richard V. Dodge N: Koskia, Illinois A: 62 O: Clergyman CW: US Vols (Chaplin) E/D: 8/62-2/63 LOS: 6 mos GAR: 4/24/1884 Died: 2/26/1885--no [grave] stone S: H

Dodge, Richard Varick (Con't)
F: Mother Sarah E. Wife of Rev R.V. Dodge 1823-1901 "I Have Kept The Faith" DOD/B: 12/6-8/1901 A: 78/2/__
　　N: American M: Widow "Mrs. Sarah E. Dodge"   Note: In 1880 census, Sarah E. Dodge is 57, wife to Richard V. Dodge, and is from Maryland, as are her parents.

Dodson, Alonzo E.
B: Alonzo E. 1849-1919
C: MH/Masonic Q DOD/B: 4/15-5/19/1919 A: 69/8/2
E: Alonzo E. Dodson NOL/NFI--DC
F: Nannie J. 1849-1931 DOB: 4/4-6/1931 A: 81/4/25

Doig, J. R.
B: John Rankin Doig 1844-1912
C: GW/Laurel DOD/B: 12/22-26/1911 A: 67 Note: John Doig born Wayne Co, OH on March 8, 1846, son of Prof. James R. and Hannah Rankin Doig. At 16, enl. Co C 19 IA Regt; Re-enl 2 IA Cav. Was in battles of Vicksburg and Nashville. Studied medicine at College of Physicians/Surgeons in Chicago. To Ellsworth, KS in 1879. Married Nellie Seaver of Muskegon, MI in 1881. To San Diego in 1886. Practiced medicine in San Diego; then Kansas in 1898. In 1905, back to Ramona, CA (north of San Diego). (See file of San Diego Historical Site Register No. 104, Sherman-Doig House, 136 Fir St, San Diego, at S.D.Historical Society)
E: J.R. Doig (John Rankin Doig?) NOL/NFI S: DC
F: Nell E. Doig 1858-1939 DOD/B: 11/24-27/1939 A: 81

Dolph, Franklin
B: Franklin Dolph Died Oct 7, 1894 Aged 56 Years Lieut 1st Wis Cav
C: MH/Div. 5 DOD/B: 10/8-10/1894 A: 58 N: American M: Widower

Donaldson, Cyrus
A: Corpl Cyrus Donaldson Co H 63 Ind Inf
C: GW/Magnolia Place DOD/B: 3/20-21/1912 A: 80

Dooley, Nate Edward
A: Nate Edward Dooley US Navy
C: MH/GAR Div.2 DOD/B: No record in boxes

Dooley, Patrick
B: Patrick Dooley Civil War Veteran 1861-1865 Retired Soldier 4th U.S. Inf Born in Ireland Died Jan 23, 1910 "A Patriotic and Faithful Soldier"
C: FR/Post Section 5, Grave 76 DOD/B: 1/23-24/1910 "Pvt"

Dort, Levi Morrison
B: Corpl Levi M. Dort Dec 27, 1843-Aug 6, 1918 Co E 84 Ill Vol Inf
C: MH/GAR Hill DOD/B: 8/6-8/1918 A: 74/7/10 Title #27 to Mrs. M.L. Dort
E: Levi M. Dort N: Beechtown, Ohion Co (?), Ohio 12/27/43 CW: Co E 84 Ill Vol Inf (Pvt/Corpl) Term: 3 yrs E/D: 7/62-6/65 Camp Harker, TN GAR: 8/14/1909 on transfer from John Wood Post #96 Dept of Illinois
　　Died: 8/__/1918 Buried: GAR (Mount Hope) S: DC
F: Emma J. his wife Oct 26, 1848-Aug 16, 1931 DOD/B: 8/16-17/1931 A: 82/9/21 Died: SD "Emma Jane Gabriel"

Douay, Francis
B: Father Francis Douay Died April 20, 1911 aged 65 years Co C 31st Mass Vol Reg.
C: MH/GAR Div.?? DOD/B: 4/19-22/1911 A: 65 N: Vermont M: Widower

Dryden, James L.
A/B: No stone
C: CMTD/Benbough Crematory DOD: 11/9/1925 A: 85/3/10
D: J.L. Dryden N: Ohio A: 48 O: Lawyer CW: Co C 36 Ill Inf (Pvt) E/D: 8/61-10/64 LOS: 38 mos GAR: 12/5/1884
　　TR: 1895 S: H

Dryden, James L. (Con't)
E: James L. Dryden (Colonel) N: Pigria, Miami Co, Ohio CW: Co C 36 Ill Inf (Pvt) Term: 3 yrs E/D: 8/61-10/64 Springfield, Ill due to disability GAR: 7/8/1898 on transfer from Heintzelman Post San Diego Died: 11/9/1925 A: 85/3/10 Obit: Married Frances Emily Hill in 1871. S: DC
F: Frances Emily Dryden No stone in MH/Div.1 DOD/B: 6/27-29/1910 A: 59/11/3 "Francis E." Buried in Div.1
OBIT: Col. Dryden served in the 36 Ill Vol Inf and was wounded several times. In 1871, he married Frances Emily Hill, and they had four sons and two daughters. In 1880, Pres. Rutherford B. Hayes appointed Dryden attorney for the United States in the territory of Montana. Came to San Diego in 1887. Was public adminstrator several years, and also served as Coronado postmaster. In 1896, Col. Dryden was elected to the state legislature, and introduced the first California bill for women's suffrage; also active in securing the location of the normal school. He wrote manuscripts for five books on economic and spiritual ideals--one of which was at the printer; the proofs arrived only two days before his death; one son S: DC

Duffy, George M.
A: Corpl Geo M. Duffy Co K 11 W VA Inf
C: GW/Olive DOD/B: 9/27-28/1915 A: 76
E: Geo M. Duffy N: Belmont, Ohio 7/7/39 CW: Co K 11 W VA Inf (Pvt/Corpl) Term: 3 yrs E/D: 8/62-5/65 GAR: 4/10/1915 Died: 9/27/1915 Buried: Greenwood S: DC

Duffy, W.E.
A: W.E. Duffy Co F 48 PA Inf (tombstone visible at Calvary Cemetery)
C: CAL/Sec.1-South, Row 6 DOD/B: No record found in Catholic cemetery index

Dumford, I.S.
A: I.S. Dumford Co K 99th Ill Inf
C: MH/GAR Hill DOD/B: 1/12-13/1893 A: 56 N: American M: Married

Eagan, Michael I.
A: Mich'l I. Egan Co B 2 NE Mo H G Inf
C: MH/GAR Div. 2 DOD/B: 12/10-12/1911 A: 93 Died in San Diego "Michael J. Eagen"
E: Michael I. Eagan N: Newfoundland CW: Co B 2 MO Inf (Pvt/Sgt) Term: 1 yr E/D: 3/61-3/62 Canton, MO Re-Enl: Co M 69 MO Cav ((Pvt) E/D: 3/62-3/64 Canton, MO GAR: 6/8/1901 Died: 12/10/1911 A: 92 Buried: GAR (Mount Hope) S: DC

Earle, Francis S.
B: Maj Francis Sobieski Earle Born in New York City Aug 18, 1836 Died in San Diego Mar 1, 1901 Adjt 4th Mich Inf USV; Asst Adj't General Army Corps Army of the Potomic "Father, in Thy gracious keeping, leave we now thy servant sleeping"
C: MH/IOOF DOD/B: 3/1-3/1901 A: 76 N: American M: Married
D: Francis S. Earle N: New York A: 64 O: Rancher CW: Co __ 4 Mich Inf (Adj/Major) E/D: 6/61-5/64 LOS: 34 mos GAR: 1888 Died: 3/2/1901--is [grave] stone S: H
F: Harriet Frances Earle, Wife of Maj. Francis S. Earle, Dau of Rev. Frederick Miller Born Branford, Conn July 21, 1844 Died San Diego Jan 6, 1924 DOB: 1/8/1924 A: 80

Eastman, Joseph
A: Joseph Eastman Co B 11 Ill Cav
C: GW/Acacia Place DOD/B: No record found

Easton, Orlando W.
A: Capt Orlando W. Easton Co H 47 U S C T
C: GW/Laurel Place DOD/B: 4/24-26/1913 A: 75
F: Martha Lee 1877-1934 At Rest DOD/B: No record found

Eaton, Avery W.
B: Avery W. Eaton Co H 26 ME Inf
C: MH/GAR Div.2 DOD/B: 7/20-23/1909 A: 64/5/16 "JS" record indicates he died on 7/20/1909 of cirrhosis of the liver at County Hospital Nativity Maine Marital--married
D: Avery W. Eaton N: Maine A: 58 O: Merchant CW: Co H 26 ME Inf (Pvt) E/D: 9/62-8/63 LOS: 10 mos GAR: 8/11/1903 Died: 7/20/1909 S: H
F: Vianna Eaton No stone DOD/B: 6/8-11/1919

Edginton, Thomas Jefferson
B: Thomas Jefferson Edginton Co B 47 Iowa Vol Inf 1846-1930
C: MH/GAR Div. 3 DOD/B: 11/30-12/4/1930 A: 84/7/13 Died in Loma Linda, CA "Edgington"
D: Thos. J. Edginton N: Ohio A: 79 O: Retired CW: Co B 47 Iowa Inf (Pvt) E/D: 5/64-9/64 LOS: 100 days GAR: 5/26/1925 Died: 1/4/1929? (date too faint to read) S: H
F: Mary Wykoff 1859-1927 DOD/B: 5/12-14/1927 A: 67/7/29

Edwards, Augustus
A: Aug. Edwards Co K 6 VA Inf
C: MH/IOOF DOB: 9/8-10/11/1909 A: 65/7/11 N: W VA M: Single

Eighmy, Philip H.
B: Rev Philip H. Eighmy Apr 9, 1839-Feb 10, 1916 56th NY Vol Inf
C: MH/Masonic S DOD/B: 2/10-12/1916 A: 76
E: Phillip H. Eighmey N: Middletown, Delaware Co, NY 4/9/39 CW: Co H 56 NY Vol Inf (Pvt) Term: 3 yrs E/D: 8/62-12/62 due to asthma GAR: 12/24/1910 Died: 2/10/1916 A: 76/10/__ Buried: Masonic (Mount Hope) S: DC
F: Durinda C. Eighmy Aug 17, 1840-Mar 25, 1919 DOD/B: 3/25-27/1919 A: 78/7/8 Middle name Christina

Elford, Peter
A. Peter Alford Co E 11 Kas Mil Inf
C: MH/GAR Hill DOD/B: 9/30-10/3/1894 A: 69/9/__ N: English M: Married Note: Coroner's Inquest Report 71-02 402 indicates DOD is 9/30/1894 from heart degeneration. San Diego Historical Society Archives

Ellis, Horace F.
B: My father Horace F. Ellis Killed on the Battlefield May 10, 1864 aged 44 years
C: MH/Div.3? DOD/B: No record; probably grave stone only

Ellis, Thomas G.
A: Corpl Thos G. Ellis Co A 11 Wis Inf
C: MH/Div.5 DOD/B: 4/13-16/1920 A: 83/4/1
E: Thomas G. Ells N: England 12/7/36 CW: Co A 11 Wis Inf (Pvt/Corpl) Term: 3 yrs E/D: 12/61-12/64 Milwaukee, Wis GAR: 10/23/1915 Died: 4/13/1920 S: DC
F: Clara D. Ellis 1845-1924 DOB: 11/11-17/1924 A: 79/3/4

Ellsworth, Chandler W.
A: C.W. Elsworth Co E 1 IA Cav
B: Chandler W. Ellsworth born July 15, 1831 Died July 25, 1900 Asleep in Jesus
C: MH/GAR Hill DOD/B: 7/25-26/1900 A: 69 N: American M: Married
D: Chandler W. Ellsworth N: New York A: 45 O: Real Estate CW: Co E I Iowa Cav (Pvt) E/D: 9/62-12/64 LOS: 27 mos GAR: 5/13/1886 Died: 7/25/1900--is [grave] stone S: H
F: "Helen" D0D/B: 8/1-2/1918 A: 83/2/7

Elmer, Parmenus
A: Parmenus Elmer Co I 37 Ill Inf
C: MH/GAR Hill DOD/B: 2/4-7/1921 A: 79/3/30 Name spelled "Parmenas"
E: Parmenus Elmer N: Allegheny Co, NY CW: Co I 37 Ill Inf (Pvt) Term: 3 yrs E/D: 8/61-2/64 New Orleans, LA Re-enl: Same company (Pvt) E/D: 2/64-5/66 Springfield, Ill GAR: 4/9/1904 on transfer from Lincoln Post

Elmer, Parmenus (Con't)
  #8 Dept of Col/Wyo Died: 2/4/1921 A: 79 S: DC
F: Francis M. Elmer (no stone) DOD/B: 12/21-24/1927 A: 69/7/7 Died in San Diego

Emerson, George D.
B: Geo. D. Emerson Capt Co L 1st Mich Eng 1818-1900
C: MH/Div. 5 DOD/B: 9/28-29/1900 A: Not stated N: American M: Single

Emery, H.U.
A: Corpl H.U. Emery Co F 1 Nev Cav
C: MH/GAR Hill DOD/B: 8/7-11/1888 A: 45/1/7 N: Maine M: Single (?--see below)
D: H.U. Emery N: Rockland, Maine A: 42 O: Farmer R: Pine Valley, CA CW: Co F 1st Batt Nevada Cav (Corpl)
    E/D: 5/64-6/65 LOS: 13 mos GAR: 10/11/1883 Died: 8/7/1888--is [grave] stone S: H
F: Lucy S. Emery (no stone) DOD/B: 9/8-10/1899 A: 79/5/16 N: American M: Married

Emery, Herbert L.
A: Herbert L. Emery Co C 4 Cal Inf
C: MH/GAR Hill DOD/B: 4/29-5/1/1913 A: 69/9/29 N: Maine M: Single "Capt"
D: Herbert L. Emery N: Rockland, Maine A: 40 O: Farmer R: Pine Valley, CA CW: Co C 4 Cal Inf (Pvt) E/D:
    10/64-2/66 LOS: 16-20 mos GAR: 1/10/1884 Died: 4/29/1913 S: H

Emery, J.S.
A: J.S. Emery Co G 4 Cal Inf
C: MH/GAR Hill DOD/B: 11/11-13/1893 A: 76/1/__ N: American M: Married (Record in book is for W.S. Emery)

Enoch, Charles
A: Chas Enoch Co G 41 Wis Inf
C: GW/Palm Terrace DOD/B: No record found A: 69?

Erion, Jacob B.
A/B: No stone
C: Cremated--Bonham Bros 4th & Elm, San Diego, CA
E: Jacob B. Erion N: Ohio 1842 CW: Co A 4 OVI (Pvt) Term: 3 yrs E/D: 6/61-11/62 Harper's Ferry due to disability
    GAR: 7/26/1924 on transfer from Phil Kearney Post Dept of Nebraska Died: 1/14/1929 A: 86/4/15 Cremated
    Obit: Five children, no wife mentioned S: DC

Evans, John H.
A: John H. Evans Co C 135 Ind Inf
C: MH/GAR Div. 2 DOD/B: 5/17-20/1938 A: 93/__/16 Died in San Diego
F: Mary B. Evans 1847-1936 DOD/B: 6/6-10/1936 A: 89/6/20 Died in San Diego "Mary Barton Evans"

Evans, Philip H.
B: Philip H. Evans 1847-1919
C: MH/Masonic S DOD/B: 11/22-25/1919 A: 72/6/17
D: Philip H. Evans N: New York A: 62 O: Carpenter R: National City, CA CW: Co C 14 US Inf (Pvt) Re-Enl?: Co
    L 24 NY Cav (Pvt) E/D: 11/61-6/65 LOS: Unstated GAR: 9/28/1909 SP: 12/24/1912 DR: 12/24/1918 S:H
F: Marietta Evans 1849-1932 DOB: 8/31-9/2/1932 A: 82/8/7

Fabian, Otto E.
B: Otto E. Fabian 1836-1904
C: MH/Confederate DOD/B: 9/20-22/1904 A: 68/3/12 N: Germany M: Married NOTE: Removed to Daughters of
    Confederacy Plot on 9/2/1913
            Note: Otto E. Fabian was born in 1836; Died 9/20/1904 in San Diego, CA. He was a Pvt, Co B, Wirt
            Adams' Mississippi State Troops Cavalry. S: UDC document, California Room (see Chapter II, "San
            Diego Public Library" sources)
F: Caroline E. Fabian 1844-1917 DOD/B: 2/22-28/1917 A: 73 "Caroline Elizabeth" Confederate Plot

Fairbanks, Albert F.
B: Albert Fairbanks 1844-____
C: MH/Div.6 DOD/B: 1/9-12/1933 A: 87/7/1
E: A.F. Fairbanks N: Mass 6/8/44 CW: Co D 43 Mass Inf (Pvt) Term: Unstated E/D: 9/62-7/63 LOS: 10 mos 18 days GAR: 4/21/1896 on transfer from Junction City Post #133 Dept of Kansas Died: 1/9/1933 A: 88/7/1 Buried: Mount Hope S: DC
F: Martha Fairbanks 1854-1914 DOD/B: 10/31-11/2/1914 A: 60 N: Sweden M: Married

Farley, Joseph
A: Jos Farley Co I 20th Ia Inf
C: MH/GAR Hill DOD: 1/4/1887 DOB: 1887 A: 74/3/18
D: Joseph Farley N: Gallatin Co, Ill A: 60 O: Carpenter CW: Co I 30 Iowa Inf (Pvt) E/D: 8/62-8/63 due to wound in left thigh and side, also in neck LOS: 1 yr GAR: 10/8/1881 Charter Member/1st Officer of the Day Heintzelman Post GAR Died: 1/4/1887 S: H

Farnsworth, Robert N.
A: Rob't N. Farnsworth Co G 4 IA Inf
C: MH/Div.7 DOD/B: 4/28-30/1912 A: 73 N: Indiana M: Married
F: Rachel Farnsworth No stone DOD/B: 12/16-20/1920 A: 82/6/13

Farris, J.M.
A: J.M. Farris Co G 10 Minn Inf (stone hard to read)
C: MH/Div. 2 DOD/B: No record found

Farrow, Stephen French
B: Stephen F. 1843-1924
C: MH/Masonic T DOD/B: 2/2-4/1924 A: 81/__/1
D: Stephen F. Farrow N: Illinois A: 65 O: Farmer CW: Co D 3 Ill Cav (Pvt) E/D: 11/64-10/65 due to disability LOS: Not stated GAR: 6/22/1909 SP: 6/27/1916 DR: 12/24/1918 S: H
F: Elizabeth F. 1844-1911 DOB: 1/24/1911 A: 67/15/__

Faulk, Marcus D.
B: Marcus D. Faulk 1833-1909
C: MH/Confederate DOD/B: 6/18-20/1909 A: 76/2/8 N: Georgia M: Married
   Note: Marcus D. Faulk was born 4/10/1833 in Georgia; Died 6/18/1909. S: UDC document, California Room (see Chapter II, "San Diego Public Library" sources)
F: Margaret E. Faulk 1832-1919 DOD/B: 2/17-19/1919 A: 86/9/18 "Confederate Plot"

Fell, Aurelius
A/B: No stone
C: Cremated Died at age 90
E: Aurelius Fell N:Orangeville, Ohio 9/8/39 CW: Co G 10 PA Res Vol Corps E/D: 6/61-3/63 Davids Island due to wounds LOS: See prior notes
   NOTE: DC file from various newspapers: The Penn R C (Mercer's Rifles) encamped at Wilkins, suburb of Pittsburg, from June to July 20, 1861. Entrained for Washington, D.C. Arrived at Harrisburg and mustered into the US Service by General W.T. Sherman; then boarded train for Washington, D.C. First engagement at Drainsville, VA on 12/30/1861, the first victory for the Union forces on the Potomac. Wounded at Gaines Mills, VA on 6/26/1862. Taken prisoner on __/17/1862 at Savage Station, VA. Taken to Libby Prison in 1862. Paroled 9/62. Sent to Parole Camp in MD on 9/62. Exchanged 11/8/62. Wounded at Fredericksburg, VA 12/13/1862 sent to ___ Island Hospital, NY. Discharged for disability due to wounds. Voted for Abraham Lincoln in 1860.
F: Minnie L. Fell DOD/B: No record at Mount Hope Cemetery

Ferdon, Charles M.
A: Chas M. Ferdon Co A 23 Mich Inf
C: MH/GAR Div.3 DOD/B: 11/18-20/1914 A: 78/4/2 or 78/9/2 N: Michigan M: Married

Ferris, Edmond
B: Edmond Ferris 1842-1919 A Native of Ohio, A Soldier of the Civil War 8th, 47th Ind Vol
C: MH/GAR Div. 3 DOD/B: 3/23-28/1919 A: 76/11/10
F: Arlene Marling Ferris A Native of _____ 1854-1916 DOD/B: 3/30-4/1/1916 A: 63 "Adeline (Addie) Clare"

Ferris, John Charles
B: In loving memory John C. Ferris Jan 2, 1834-Nov 30, 1933 Sgt Co F 1 Regt Colo Cav Your Great Grandson
C: MH/GAR Div.2 DOD/B: 11/30-12/8/1933 A: 98/10/28 Died in San Diego
D: John C. Ferris N: New York A: 90 O: Retired CW: Co F 1 Col Cav (Pvt/Sgt) E/D: 9/61-11/64 LOS: 3 yrs GAR: 7/28/1925 Died: 11/__/1933 S: H
E: John C. Ferres N: Cohengo Forks, NY 1/2/35 CW: Co F 1 Col Cav (Pvt/Sgt) Term: 3 yrs E/D: 9/61-10/64 Denver, Colo GAR: 6/22/1923 on transfer from Sundan Post #81 Dept of Montana TR: To Heintzelman Post San Diego S: DC

Ferry, Charles H.
A: Chas H. Ferry Co I 17 Wis Inf
B: Charles H. Ferry 1841-1910
C: MH/Div.6 DOD/B: 1/7-10/1910 A: 68/11/21 N: Wisconsin M: Married
F: Susan A. Ferry 1840-1920 DOD/B: 12/3-6/1920 A: 80

Field, Putnam
A: Captn Putnam Field Co C 10 NY Inf
B: Capt Putnam Field born Leverett, Mass November 10, 1836 Died March 3, 1915 "Capt"
C: MH/GAR Hill DOD/B: 3/3-5/1915 A: 78/3/29 N: Mass M: Widower
D: Putnam Field N: Mass A: 63 O: Printer CW: Co I 10 NY Inf (Pvt) Promoted?: Co C 10 NY Inf (Capt) E/D: 4/61-7/65 LOS: 51 mos GAR: 5/8/1900 (probably on transfer from Winthrop Post #28 Dept of NY Died: 3/3/1915 S: H
F: Anna M. McGaffey, wife of Putnam Field Born Stansted, Quebec February 19, 1847 Died April 4, 1906 DOD/B: 4/4-5/1906 A: 59/1/24 N: Canada M: Married "McGaffery"

Finch, William W.
B: William W. Finch Lieut 128th Ind Vol Inf Born Dec 26, 1839 Died Sept 1, 1916
C: MH/IOOF DOD/B: 9/1-5/1916 A: 76 NO WIFE
D: William W. Finch N: New York A: 68 O: Retired CW: Co D 128 Ind Inf (Pvt/2 Lieut) E/D: 11/63-6/64 due to disability LOS: Not stated GAR: 10/27/1908 TR: 12/13/1910 S: H

Finley, Kellogg B.
B: Kellogg B. Finley QM Sergt Co M 4th NY Hvy Art 1840-1932
C: GW/Laurel Place DOD/B: 2/29-3/3/1932 A: 91
D: Kellogg B. Finley N: New York A: 70 O: Orchardist CW: Co G 8 NY H A (Pvt) Re-Enl?: Co M 4 NY H A (QM Sgt) E/D: 12/63-9/65 LOS: Not stated GAR: 6/13/1911 Died: 2/2/1932 S: H
F: Louise Upton Finley 1843-1917 DOD/B: 1/28-31/1917 A: 73

Fitch, Edwin Peabody
B: Edwin P. Fitch Co I 10th Maine 1861-63 1840 South Bridgton, ME 1931 San Diego, Calif
C: MH/GAR Div.3 DOD/B: 7/1-3/1931 A: 91/3/9 Died in San Diego
E: Edwin P. Fitch N: Bridgeton, ME CW: Co I 1 Maine Inf (Pvt) Term: 3 mos E/D: 4/61-7/61 Portland, ME Re-Enl: Co I 10 Maine Inf (Pvt/Sgt) E/D: 9/61-5/63 Portland, ME GAR: 9/23/1911 Died: 7/1/1931 A: 91 Buried: Greenwood Cemetery, San Diego, CA [although Mount Hope cemetery records read as above]
  Obit: Wife died in 1916; 4 children located in New York City, Vermillion, So Dak, Corona, CA and San Diego, CA. Moved in 1883 from Maine to So.Dakota; member of the state legislature there two years; to San Diego in 1909; charter member of East San Diego Presbyterian Church, 43rd St at Polk Ave, San Diego S: DC
F: Elizabeth Powers Fitch Their children will rise up and call them blessed. DOD/B: 8/25-31/1916 A: 75

Fitzgerald, Edmond
A/B: No stone
C: Cremated
D: Edmond Fitzgerald N: Ireland A: 56 O: Engineer CW: Co K 53 Ill Inf (Pvt/1st Lieut) E/D: 11/61-12/64 LOS: 36 mos GAR: 2/28/1890 SP: 6/27/1903 DR: 1/5/1907 Died: 1/18/1907 Cremated S: H

Fitzgerald, Robert V.
A: 1st Sgt Robt. V. Fitzgerald Co D 155 NY Inf
C: MH/GAR Div. 2 DOD/B: 2/28-3/1/1912 A: 71 N: New York
E: Robt. V. Fitzgerald N: New York CW: Co D 155 NY Inf (Pvt) Term: 3 yrs E/D: 9/62-1/65 Washington, D.C. due to gun shot wound at Cold Harbor GAR: 2/27/1904 on transfer from Askine Post #24 Dept of Maine Died: 2/28/1912 A: 71 Buried: GAR (Mount Hope) S: DC

Fitzgerald, Thomas
A/B: No stone
C: MH/GAR Hill DOD/B: 5/21-24/1921 A: 78 Title #243 to A.A. Mantius
E: Thomas Fitzgerald N: Brewer, Maine CW: Co F 19 Maine Inf (Pvt/Corpl) E/D: 3/64-7/65 GAR: 7/10/1926 S: DC

Flamming, John (Flammang/Flammage)
B: John Flamming Pvt Co B 9 Wis Inf Civil War Jun 24, 1830-Jan 3,1912
C: MH/GAR Div. 3 DOD/B: 1/3-5/1917 A: 84 Name John Flammang
D: John Flammage N: Belgium A: 80 O: Farmer CW: Co K 9 Wis Inf (Pvt) Re-Enl?: Co B 9 Wis Inf (Pvt) E/D: 10/61-1/66 LOS: Not stated GAR: 12/9/1913 on transfer from Gettysburg Post #59 Dept of Tulare, CA Died: 1/3/1917 S: H

Flinn, Daniel L.
A: 1st Sgt Dan'l Flinn Co B 17 Ind Inf (tombstone visible at Calvary Cemetery)
C: CAL/Sec.1, South, Row 7 DOB: 12/13/1900 A: 73 "Flynn"

Fogarty, Patrick
A: Pat'k Fogarty Co A 7 PA Cav
C: HC/St Bernard, Plot 185, Grave 7 DOB: 3/11/1919 No further information available
F: Ellen Fogarty 1842-1929 St. Bernard/Plot 185, Grave 6 DOB: 6/20/1929 No further information available

Foote, John Ward
A: Sergt John W. Foote Co G 16 NY H A
C: MH/Masonic A DOB: 10/18/1913 A: 69/11/12
E: John W. Foot N: Rushville, Yates Co, NY CW: Co G 16 NY H A (Pvt/Sgt) Term: 3 yrs E/D: 12/63-12/65 David's Island, NY GAR: 3/11/1898 Died: 10/13/1913 A: 69 Buried: Masonic (Mount Hope) S: DC
F: Lenora Foote 1849-1926 DOD/B: No record found

Forbes, David
A: Sgt David Forbes Co C 1 Conn Cav
C: MH/Block 1 DOD/B: 2/6-9/1931 A: About 87 Died in San Diego

Ford, Daniel Boon
A: D.B. Ford Co B 1 Prov En MO Mil
B: Daniel B. Ford 1831-1907
C: MH/Masonic P DOD/B: 4/25-28/1907 A: 76/1/29 N: MO M: Married "Boon"
F: Sarah M. Ford 1841-1922 DOD/B: 10/23-27/1922 A: 81/3/12 Middle name Maria

Forker, Oliver H.P.
A/B: No stone
C: MH/Masonic A DOD/B: 2/27/-3/3/1920 A: 83 Note: O.H.P. Forker was born in Clinton, Beaver County, PA on December 29, 1836, and was four when his family moved to Ohio. In 1869, he married Anna Blackburne,

Forker, Oliver H.P. (Con't)
    daughter of Col. W. D. Blackburne, and she died in 1906. After the war, he came to San Diego (in 1880), and became a prosperous fruit grower. "One sleeve of his coat hangs empty, a constant reminder of his valiant services and sacrifices for his country in the dark days of the Civil War." (from *San Diego County, CA: A Record of Settlement*, etc., where details of his war record are given.)
D: Oliver H.P. Forker N: Penn A: 81 O: Retired CW: Co H 59 Ill Inf (Pvt/Sgt) E/D: 8/61-7/64 due to disability
    LOS: 35 mos GAR: 8/27/1918 DR: "Dropped" Died: 2/27/1920 S: H

Forsythe, Thomas Hall
B: Thos H. Forsythe Co A 147 PA Inf
C: MH/Masonic P DOD/B: 3/22-25/1908 A: 65/3/5 N: Connecticut M: Married

Fortescue, William M.
B: Capt Wm. Fortescue April 1, 1835-July 3, 1915
C: GW/Laurel Place DOD/B: 7/3-5/1915 A: No record found
F: Margaret Hook, Wife of Capt W.M. Fortescue March 16, 1856-July 1, 1908 DOD/B: 7/1-8/12/1908 A: 51

Fralich, Zachariah
A: Zack Fralich Co L 9 NY H A
C: MH/GAR Hill DOD/B: 11/9-10/1901 A: 64/11/__ N: American M: Married
D: Zachariah Fralich N: Canada A: 58 O: Carpenter CW: Co L 9 NY H A (Pvt) E/D: 12/63-10/65 LOS: 22 mos
    GAR: 4/13/1897 Died: 11/9/1901--is [grave] stone S: H

Frank, Alonzo
A/B: No stone
C: MH/GAR Div.2 DOD/B: 6/8-11/1932 A: 86/3/2 Died in San Diego "Alonza"
D: Alonzo Frank N: New York A: 84 O: Not stated CW: Co E 89 Ill Inf (Pvt/Corpl) E/D: 8/62-6/65 LOS: Not stated
    GAR: 8/14/1928 Died: 6/7/1932 S: H
E: Alonzo Frank N: Troy, NY 3/6/44 CW: Co E 89 Ill ___ (Pvt/Corpl) Term: 3 yrs E/D: 8/62-6/65 Nashville, TN
    GAR: 8/25/1923 on transfer from Junction City #132 Dept of Kansas TR: 1928 S: DC
F: Almira Frank No stone DOD/B: 2/14-17/1934 A: 77/9/15 Died in San Diego

Franklin, Robert Calvin
A: Robert C. Franklin Co A 29 Ala Inf CSA
C: MH/Confederate DOD/B: 10/29-11/1/1937 A: 92/3/__ Died in San Diego
    Note: Robert Franklin was born 7/29/1845 in South Carolina; Died 10/29/1937 in San Diego, CA. At one time received a Confederate Pension from State of Oklahoma S: UDC document, California Room (see Chapter II, "San Diego Public Library" sources)

Frasier, Peter
B: Peter E. Frasier 1844-1923 GAR
C: MH/IOOF DOB: 1/29/1929 A: Not stated

Frazier, John A.
A: Chaplain J.A. Frazier 73rd Ind Vol
B: J.A. Frazier Chaplain 73rd Ind Vol Died Sep 9, 1898 aged 84 yrs
C: MH/GAR Hill DOD/B: 9/9-11/1898 A: 83/4/__ N: American A: Married

Freeborn, Fremont
A/B: No stone
C: Cremated Bonham Brothers Mortuary
E: Fremont Freeborn N: Rhode Island 12/18/48 CW: Co A 15 US Inf 2 Batt (Pvt) Term: 3 yrs E/D: 6/65-7/66
GAR: 8/28/1920 Died: 3/2/1930 A: 81/9/8 S: DC

Freede, Charles William
B: Father Charles W. Freede 1845-1924
C: MH/GAR Div.2 DOD/B: 11/15-19/1924 A: 79/9/2
D: Charles W. Freede N: Ohio A: 58 O: Clerk Co C 68 Ohio Inf (Pvt) E/D: 1/64-7/65 LOS: 18 mos GAR:
    1/26/1904 S: H

Freeman, Charles H.
A: Yeoman C.H. Freeman US Navy
C: MH/Masonic B DOD/B: 4/14-16/1903 A: 78 Died in San Diego
D: C.H. Freeman N: Charlestown, Mass A: 56 O: Printer R: National City, CA CW: US Navy--Ship Rhode Island
    (Landsman/Master's Mate) E/D: __/61-9/65 LOS: Not stated GAR: 4/1/1883 SP: 1/23/1890 S: H
F: Rebecca C. Freeman No stone DOB: 3/3-6/1910 A: 82/1/27 N: Mass? M: Widow Died in San Diego

French, James Milton
A: Col James M. French 63 VA Inf CSA
C: MH/Confederate DOD/B: 1/3-5/1916 A: 81
    Note: James M. French was born on 9/14/1834 in Giles County, VA; Died 1/3/1916 in Encanto (San Diego),
    CA. Began service as a Major. Promoted to Colonel, 63rd Virginia Infantry after distinguished service at
    Chickamauga. POW at Camp Chase, KY and later Johnson's Island, OH S: UDC document, California Room
    (see Chapter II, "San Diego Public Library" sources)

French, Stephen
B: Stephen French May 23, 1844-Jan 2, 1929 Veteran of US Civil War Co D Regt 11 Ill Vol Inf
C: MH/Div.3, Block 1 DOD/B: 1/2-4/1929 A: 84/7/10
D: Stephen French N: Illinois A: 56 O: Fruit Dealer CW: Co D 111 Ill Inf (Pvt) E/D: 8/62-6/65 LOS: 34 mos GAR:
    6/26/1900 SP: 6/23/1908 DR: 12/24/1918 S: H Note: Tombstone says 11 Ill Inf; GAR rec. says 111 Ill Inf.
F: Alice French, Wife of Stephen French June 17, 1846-Oct 16, 1929 DOD/B: 10/16-19/1929 A: 83/3/29 (record
    is under Margaret Alice French)

Frew, David Webster
B: David W. Frew Dec 25, 1838-Dec 8, 1917
C: MH/GAR Div.3 DOD/B: 12/8-11/1917 A: 79 Died in San Diego Name also David Freer
D: David F. Frew N: Penn A: 66 O: Retired CW: Co B 1 PA L A (Pvt) E/D: 7/61-5/62 Re-Enl: Co B 134 PA Inf
    (Sgt/2nd Lieut) E/D: 8/62-5/63 LOS: 19 mos GAR: 10/10/1905 S: H
F: Mary J. Frew May 22, 1855-June 14, 1933 DOD/B: 6/14-16/1933 A: 78/__/23 Died in San Diego "Mary Jane"

Friend, James Edward
B: Capt James Edward Friend 1841-1898 The Newsboy's Friend
C: MH/Masonic L DOD/B: 3/30-4/1/1898 A: 57 N: American M: Widower "Capt"

Froelich, Godfrey F.W.
B: Sgt Godfrey Froelich Co H 10 MO Inf
C: MH/GAR Div. 3 DOD/B: 10/25-27/1914 A: 79/11/5 N: Germany M: Widower Name Godfrey Frederick William
D: G.F. Wm. Froelich N: Germany A: 76 O: Notary Public R: Miramar (now part of San Diego) CW: Co D 10 Ill
    Inf (Pvt) Re-Enl: Co H 10 MO Inf (Sgt) E/D: 4/61-9/64 LOS: Not stated GAR: 12/12/1911 on transfer from
    Ellsworth Post #172 Dept of Illinois Died: 10/25/1914 Buried: Mount Hope S: H

Fry, George
A: George Fry 1827-1901 CSA
C: MH/Confederate DOD/B: 5/16-19/1901 A: 74 N: English M: Married
    Note: George Fry was born 1827 in England; Died 5/16/1901 in San Diego, CA. Came to Calif. from Texas.
    S: UDC document, California Room (see Chapter II, "San Diego Public Library" sources)

Fuller, Boyd
A: Boyd Fuller Co K 32nd Mass Inf
C: MH/GAR Hill DOD/B: No further information available

Fullerton, James S.
A: Lieut Jas S. Fullerton Co B 1 PA L A
B: James S. Feb 16, 1830-Nov 1, 1907
C: MH/IOOF DOD/B: 11/1-4/1907 A: 77/8/16 N: PA M: Single
F: Amanda J. May 30, 1834-July 13, 1911 DOB: 7/13-18/1911 A: 77/1/13 N: PA M: Widow

Gaches, William Henry
A: Wm H. Gaches Co G 1 MD Cav
C: MH/GAR Hill DOD/B: 2/14-16/1920 A: 74

Gallagher, John
A: Jno Gallagher Co E 5 NH Inf (tombstone visible at Calvary Cemetery)
C: CAL/Sec.1, South, Row 8 (Sec. N2/3-2, Blk D, Lot 25) DOD/B: No record found in Catholic cemetery index
F: Several Gallagher women/girls buried here; one is Katherine Gallagher--tombstone reads: In Loving memory of
      Katherine Gallager Born County Monaghan, Ireland 1870 Died San Diego June 21, 1906 Rest in Peace

Gangwer, Jesse
A: Corpl Jesse Gangwer Co E 28 PA Inf
C: MH/GAR Div. 3 DOD/B: 1/28-31/1913 A: 76 Name Gangmere
D: Jesse Gangwer N: Penn A: 77 O: Carpenter CW: Co E 28 PA Inf (Pvt/Corpl) E/D: 8/62-5/65 LOS: Not stated
      GAR: 12/12/1911 on transfer from Ezra S. Griffin Post #139 Dept of PA Died: 1/29/1913 S: H

Gardner, Warren M.
A: Warren M. Gardner Co B 151 Ill Inf
C: MH/GAR Hill DOD/B: 9/10-22/1934 A: 87 (ashes) Died in San Diego Cremated: Bonham Brothers Crematory
E: Warren Gardner N: Illinois? 4/20/47 CW: Co B 151 Ill Vol Inf (Pvt) Term: Unstated E/D: 2/65-1/66 LOS: 11
      mos 2 days GAR: 4/22/1905 SP: 1/26/1907 RE: 2/14/1925 Died: 9/10/1934 A: 87/4/20 Cremated:
      9/13/1934 S: DC

Gardner, William H.
A: W.H. Gardner Co B 5 Cal Inf
C: MH/GAR Hill DOD/B: 11/15-17/1890 A: 74 N: American M: Single Middle initial "X."?
D: Wm. H. Gardner N: New York A: 71 O: Carpenter CW: Co B 5 Cal Vols (Pvt) E/D: 10/61-12/64 LOS: 38 mos
      GAR: 7/22/1886 SP: 1/10/1889 DR: 8/24/1904 S: H

Garside, Joseph
B: Joseph Garside Private Co B 83rd Illinois Vol Inft 1841-1930
C: MH/GAR Hill DOD/B: 6/4-6/1930 A: 89/3/10 Died in San Diego
E: Joseph Garside N: Yorkshire, England 2/25/41 CW: Co B 83 Ill Inf (Pvt) Term: 3 yrs E/D: 8/62-4/64 due to
      disability Fort Donaldson, TN GAR: 7/26/1913 on transfer from J.W. Owens Post #5 Dept of Arizona Died:
      6/4/1930 S: DC
F: Mary I. Garside Born in Ohio 1848-1933 DOD/B: 12/9-13/1933 A: 85/27/__ Died in San Diego

Gaylord, Levi B.
A: L.B. Gaylord Co C 44 IA Inf
C: MH/GAR Div. 2 DOD/B: 3/4-6/1909 A: 62/11/__ N: Ohio M: Married Name Levi

Geen, William M.
A: Wm. Geen Co B 6 MO S M Cav
C: MH/Masonic K DOD/B: 6/11-15/1920 A: 79/5/17
D: William Geen N: Missouri A: 69 O: Farmer CW: Co M 6 MO State Militia (Pvt) E/D: 2/62-3/65 LOS: Not stated
      GAR: 6/25/1912 SP: 12/10/1918 RE: 9/9/1919 Died: 6/11/1920 age 79/9/17 S: H
F: Anna Ida Geen 1870-1946 DOD/B: 4/13-18/1946 A: 75/4/20

George, _____
B: _____ George 1841-1906 Civil War 80th Regiment Ohio Volunteer Infantry
C: MH/Masonic P DOD/B: No further record Note: This tombstone not located on subsequent walk-through of cemetery.

George, Henry Wesley
A: Henry W. George Co D 44 NY Inf
B: Father Henry Wesley Feb 20, 1839-Apr 22, 1916
C: MH/GAR Hill DOD/B: 4/23-25/1916 A: 77 "Henry Wesley"
E: Henry W. George N: Jay, Essex Co, NY 2/23/39 CW: Co D 44 NY Inf (Pvt) Term: Unstated E/D: 9/61-10/64
    Albany, NY GAR: 4/23/1897 Died: 4/22/1916 A: 77/2/2 S: DC
F: Mother Caroline Bigler Nov 24, 1848-Dec 8, 1911 DOD/B: 12/8-11/1911 A: 63/__/14 N: Ohio M: Married
    Note: Henry, of Puritan stock, moved to Iowa after being wounded at Chancellorsville in the Civil War. In 1872, he married Caroline Bigler, born in New Philadelphia, Ohio in 1848 to John and Mary Hagy Bigler, natives of Switzerland. Family moved to San Diego in 1892. Farmed in Nestor and Tijuana Valley; home in Golden Hill; seven children, according to *San Diego County Pioneer Families.*

Gibbons, Homer W.
B: Father Ho_____ Gibbons 18_6-1924 Co I 80 Inf Ohio
C: MH/GAR Hill DOD/B: 2/21-26/1924 A: 86/7/17 "Homer W."

Gibbs, Artemus
B: Artemus Gibbs Co K 1st Reg New York Dragoons 1841-1920
C: MH/GAR Hill DOD/B: 12/18-20/1920 A: 79/11/8 Title #176 to Rosetta N. Gibbs
F: Rosetta N. Gibbs DOD/B: No record found Note: Called "Rose" in 1919 City Directory.

Giddings, J.R.B.
A: Corp'l J.R.B. Giddings Co D 22 V R C (tombstone visible at Calvary Cemetery)
C: CAL/Sec.1, South, Row 9 DOD/B: No record found in Catholic cemetery index

Gillett, George A.
A: Corpl George A. Gillett Co E 1 Ohio L A
C: MH/GAR Div.3 DOD/B: 3/25-27/1918 A: 76
E: Geo. A. Gillett N: Champlain, Ohio CW: Bat E 1 Ohio L A (Pvt/Corpl) Term: 3 yrs E/D: 8/61-4/63 due to disability
    GAR: 1/26/1918 Died: 3/25/1918 A: 76 S: DC

Gilmore, Myron Tyrrel
B: Myron Tyrrel Gilmore 15th Regt Maine Vol Inf January 11, 1847-June 9, 1939
C: GW/Hawthorne DOD: 6/9/1939 A: No record found
D: Myron T. Gilmore N: Dedham, Maine A: 40 O: Blacksmith CW: Co B 15 ME Inf (Pvt) E/D: 2/65-11/65 LOS: 9 mos GAR: 2/28/1884 Post Commander 1898 S: H
F: Mary Parker Gilmore January 10, 1918 DOD: 1/10/1918 A: 81
    Note: A book by Theodore Davie entitled *San Diego Trust & Savings Bank 1889-1989* states (pp. 132-133) that Myron Gilmore was born on 1/11/1847 in Dedham, ME. After the Civil War, he migrated to San Diego in 1883, and became assistant cashier at First National Bank. In April, 1889, he assisted Joseph Sefton, Sr. in organizing San Diego Savings Bank and became its first cashier there. Elected bank president in 1909 after Mr. Sefton died; became the bank's President Emeritus until his death on 6/9/1939 at 92. "From his desk near the front door of the Watts Building and then at Sixth and Broadway, Gilmore assisted in guiding the Bank through its years of transition from small town bank to metropolitan institution." Considered the "Dean of Pacific Coast Bankers." Memberships: First Congregational Church; Chamber of Commerce, San Diego Club, Heintzelman Post G.A.R., Tuesday Club, honorary chairman of YMCA.

Gilpatrick, Jeremiah H.
A: J.H. Gilpatrick Co F 1 ME L A
C: MH/GAR Hill DOD/B: 1/1-3/1907 A: 61/9/20 N: Maine M: Married "JS" record indicates he died of ___nation of the heart at 903 F Street on 1/3/1907 Nativity Maine Marital--married Age 61/9/25
D: Jeremiah H. Gilpatrick N: Maine A: 59 O: Laborer CW: Co __ 6 ME L A (Pvt) E/D: 12/64-6/65 LOS: 6 mos
    GAR: 6/14/1904 Died: 1/1/1907--is [grave] stone S: H
F: Leelah R. Gilpatrick No stone DOB: 4/28/1908 Note: Called "Leelah R. in 1907 City Directory; also listed as widow of Jeremiah H. Gilpatrick.

Gipson, John C.
B: Sgt. John C. Gipson Btry C 1 NY L Art 1842-1933
C: MH/GAR Div.2 DOD/B: 10/26-28/1933 A: 91/5/1 Died in San Diego "Civil War Vet"
E: John C. Gipson N: Jefferson Co, NY 5/25/42 CW: Bat C 1 NY LA (Pvt/Sgt) Term: 3 yrs E/D: 7/61-9/64 City

Gipson, John C. (Con't)
Point, VA GAR: 12/9/1915 on transfer from H.H. Webber Post #300 Dept of New York Died: 10/26/1933
A: 91/5/1 S: DC
OBIT: Wife Mary E. Gipson; son in San Diego; son in Jamul, CA. OBIT: Returning to Dakota Territory after the Civil War, Mr. Gipson became a leading figure in forming North and South Dakota to statehood. Elected to the North Dakota state normal school board; first state oil inspector; state commander of North Dakota GAR in 1882. To Oklahoma in 1903--organized bank at Temple, Oklahoma; was US land commissioner. To San Diego in 1914; member First Methodist church; married nearly 67 years. S: DC
F: Mary E. Gipson No stone DOD/B: 1/14-18/1938 A: 87/7/9 Died in San Diego

Gleason, Henry J.
A: Capt H.J. Gleason Co G 72 Ill Inf
C: MH/Div.6 DOD/B: 7/12-14/1902 A: 58 N: American M: Married Name Henry Gleson or Glesow
F: Mother Fannie L. Gleason 1844-1933 DOD/B: 10/24-26/1933 A: 89/3/19 Died in La Mesa, CA "Fannie E."

Goodspeed, John Willard
A: John W. Goodspeed Co D 136 NY Inf 1831-1920 GAR
C: MH/GAR Hill DOD/B: 11/1-3/1920 A: 89/6/__
E: J.W. Goodspeed, J.W. N: Perry, Wyoming Co, NY 6/1/31 CW: Co D 136 NY Inf (Pvt/Sgt) Term: 3 yrs E/D: 8/62-6/65 Rochester, NY GAR: 11/13/1915 on transfer from Colorado Springs Post #22 Dept of Colorado Died: East San Diego A: 89/5/__ S: DC

Gordon, Richard
A: Richard Gordon Co A 55 VA Inf CSA
C: MH/Confederate DOD/B: 9/18-21/1923 A: 70 "Confederate Plot" Note: Pvt, Co A, 55th Virginia Infantry S: UDC document, California Room (see Chapter II, "San Diego Public Library" sources)
F: Sallie L. Gordon, 1842-1919 DOD/B: 4/1-3/1919 A: 77

Gould, William P.
A: Wm. P. Gould Co H 17 Wis Inf
C: GW/Laurel Place DOD/B: 11/16-19/1924 A: 80

Grant, George W.
B: George W. Grant 1840-1926
C: MH/IOOF DOB: 6/7/1926 A: 86 "George W."
D: George W. Grant N: Boston/Roxbury, Mass A: 42 O: Clerk R: National City, CA CW: US Navy Steamer Chocure (Pay Steward/Pay Clerk) E/D: 8/62-10/64 LOS: 26 mos GAR: 5/25/1882 SP: 9/26/1889 RE: 5/2/1891 SP: 12/10/1918 S: H
F: Marie D. Wife of Geo. W. Grant Born March 30, 1841 Died March 19, 1901 "Come Unto Me And I Will Give You Rest" DOD/B: 3/19-21/1901 A: 59 N: American M: Married "Marie D."

Granville, John H.
B: J.H. Granville 1812-1909 Co K 15 NY Cav
C: MH/GAR Div.2 DOD/B: 3/6-8/1909 A: 97/8/29 N: England M: Married Died in San Diego
  NOTE: Another DOD/B: 2/7-9/1938 A: 76/3/22 GAR Div.2 "JS" record indicates John "Granrelle" died on 3/6/1909 of heart disease at "Archer near Palm" Nativity England Marital--married
D: John H. Granville N: England A: 75 O: Gardener CW: Co E 124 NY Inf (Pvt) E/D: 8/62-1/63 Re-Enl?: Co K 15 NY Cav (Pvt) E/D: 12/63-7/65 LOS: 24 mos GAR: 9/27/1892 Died: 3/6/1909--is [grave] stone S: H
F: Catherine Granville (stone written as "B.C. Granville") DOB: 5/26-28/1921 A: 86

Gray, Capt. J.S.
B: Capt J.S. Gray 1835-1889 (Civil War?--"Capt" designation only) (tombstone visible/Calvary Cemetery)
C: CAL/Sec.2, Block A, Lot 26 DOB: No record found in Catholic cemetery index
F: Mary J. Smith 1830-1891 DOD/B: (On same stone with J.S. Gray/same burial location) DOD/B: No record found in Catholic cemetery index

Gray, William
A: William Gray Co I 22 Ill Inf
B: William Gray Born in Scotland Feb 10, 1830 Died in National City Aug 6, 1891 How sleep the brave who sink to rest with all their countrys honour blest
C: MH/GAR Hill DOD/B: 8/6/1891-6/13/1899 A: 58 N: Scotland M: Married
F: "Mother" (probable wife Elizabeth M. Gray) DOD/B: 9/21-23/1913 A: 73/5/2 N: VA M: Widow

Green, Elias S.
B: Elias S. Green Feb 17, 1846-May 28, 1917 Co A 140 Ind Vol
C: MH/IOOF DOB: 5/28-31/17 A: 72
D: Elias S. Green N: Indiana A: 62 O: Retired CW: Co H 117 Ind Inf (Pvt) Re-Enl?: Co A 140 Ind Inf (Sgt) E/D: 7/63-7/65 LOS: Not stated GAR: 7/28/1908 Died: 5/28/1917 S: H
F: Lucy M. Green Mar 6, 1851-July 29, 1928 DOB: 8/1/1928 A: 77

Green, Henry Clay
A. Henry C. Green Co D 127 Ill Inf
C: MH/BLK 6 DOD/B: 1/15-18/1932 A: 87/10/4
D: Henry C. Green N: Michigan A: 71 O: Not stated CW: Co D 127 Ill Inf (Pvt) Re/Enl?: Co D 125 Ill Inf (Pvt) E/D: 8/62-5/65 LOS: Not stated GAR: 11/25/1915 S: H
F: Angeline A. Green 1862-1943 DOD/B: 3/23-25/1943 A: 80/9/26 "Angelina A."

Green, William
B: William Green Co D 140 NY Inf Oct 31, 1844-July 26, 1922
B: William Green 1844-1922
C: MH/Masonic F DOB: 7/28/1922 A: 77/8/27
F: Alice K. Green 1851-1924 DOD/B: 6/8-13/1924 A: 72/__/6

Green, William M.
B: William M. Green 1835-1906 At Rest (GAR)
C: MH/Masonic O DOD/B: 12/24-26/1906 A: 71/__/8 N: New York M: Married "Greene"
F: Antoinette M. Green 1845-1925 DOD/B: 11/6-9/1925 A: 80/1/8

Greenleaf, William Charles
B: William Chas. Greenleaf June 22, 1834-May 18, 1917 R.I.P. (tombstone no longer at Calvary Cemetery)
C: CAL/Sec.3, South 1/3, Row H-3 (Sec.3, Block H, Lot 3) DOB: 5/18/1917 A: 83 Born: 6/22/1834
D: William Greenleaf N: Ohio A: 65 O: Farmer CW: Co E 11 Ind Inf (Pvt/Corpl) E/D: 7/61-9/65 LOS: Not stated GAR: 1/25/1910 Died: 5/17/1917 S: H

Gregory, A.E.
A: Lieut A.E. Gregory 12th? Ohio Batty
C: MH/GAR Hill DOD/B: 6/27-28/1897 A: 54 N: American M: Married
D: A.E. Gregory N: Ohio A: 45 O: Abstractor CW: Co D 25 Ohio Inf Bat (Pvt) Re-Enl?: Co __ 12 Ohio Inf Batt (1st Lieut) E/D: 6/61-6/64 LOS: 36 mos GAR: 4/25/1889 Died: 7/13/1897--is [grave] stone S: H

Gregory, Starr Cozier
A: Starr C. Gregory Co A 105th Ill Vol
B: Starr Cozier Gregory 1842-1924
C: MH/Div.5 DOD/B: 6/26-28/1924 A: 81/10/5
D: Star C. Gregory N: Illinois A: 77 O: Retired CW: Co A 105 Ill Inf (Pvt) E/D: 10/62-5/63 due to sickness LOS: 7 mos GAR: 4/13/1920 Died: 6/26/1924 S: H
F: Maria Marcia, Wife of Starr C. Gregory
F: Maria Marcia 1846-1928 DOD/B: 1/27-31/1928 A: 81/11/24 Died in San Diego

Griggs, John R.
A: John R. Griggs Co G 91 NY Inf
C: MH/Div.6 DOD/B: 5/15-28/1936 A: 80/9/19 (If he was born 1856, is he too young for the Civil War? Yet his service

Griggs, John R. (Con't)
    record on tombstone matches the GAR record below)
D: John R. Griggs N: New York A: 74 O: Retired CW: Co H 76 NY Inf (Pvt) Re-Enl?: Co G 91 NY Inf (Pvt) E/D:
    10/61-7/65 LOS: 44 mos GAR: 4/23/1918 by transfer Died: 4/29/1924 S: H
F: Mary A. Griggs Aug 24, 1843 DOD/B: Division 6 burial

Grinnell, Oliver C.
A: O.C. Grinnell Co D 5th Mich Inf
C: MH/GAR Hill DOD/B: 2/24-27/1899 A: 53/11/26 N: American M: Married Died in San Diego

Grinnell, William W.
A: Wm W. Grinnell Co E 97 NY Inf
C: MH/Div.5 DOD/B: 5/31-6/2/1913 A: 76 "Frederika Home Plot"

Grisswell, Robert H.
A: Hosp Stewd Robt H. Grisswell USA
C: MH/Div. 6, near Pirnie in Lot 34 DOD/B: No record in boxes

Griswold, Jesse
A: Jesse Griswold Co F 5 PA Cav
B: Jessie Griswold Died Nov 11, 1911 aged 68 years At Rest
C: GW/Laurel Place DOD/B: 11/11/1911-2/14/1914 A: 68 NOTE: Prior burial in MH/GAR Div.2 DOD/B: 11/11-
    13/1911 A: 68/5/27 N: PA M: Married Approved to transfer to Greenwood on 2/14/1914
F: Alice Griswold 1838-1923 DOD/B: 12/2-4/1923 A: 85

Grosvenor, Royal W.
B: Royal W. Grosvenor 1845-1922 94 Regt Ohio Vol Inf
B: Royal W. Grosvenor 1845-1922 (smaller stone)
C: GW/Palm Terrace DOD/B: 3/24-28/1922 A: 76
E: R.W. Grosvenor N: Shelby Co, Ohio 12/22/45 CW: Co C 94 OVI (Pvt) Term: 3 yrs E/D: 8/62-7/65 Springfield,
    Ill Captured 9/1/1862 near Lexington, KY. Exchanged 12/10/1862. Wounded 5/14/1864 Battle of Resaca
    Transferred to Co B 15 VRC (? rank) In six engagements GAR: 4/24/1895 on transfer from Alexander Post
    #158 Dept of Ohio Died: 3/24/1922 A: 76/3/2 S: DC
F: Mother Mary C. Stannard 1853-1915 (wife?) DOD: 1915 A: 71

Gwyn, Hugh Garvin
B: Major Hugh G. Gwyn 1835-1925
C: MH/BLK 3 DOD/B: 3/16-20/1925 A: 85/8/24 "Garvin" Note: Major Hugh G. Gwyn was born in the north of Ireland
    on June 20, 1840, and as a small boy accompanied his parents to America, to settle in Louisville, KY. After
    the war, he became secretary of the Home Fire Insurance Company in Nashville, TN, and moved to San
    Diego in 1878. He was postmaster at Coronado, and started a fire insurance company Foster & Gwyn; later
    Gwyn & Lancaster. "When the GAR groups from California and Nevada met at San Diego in 1895, Major
    Gwyn organized and headed the parade, an honor never before or since conferred upon a Confederate
    officer." (from *San Diego County, California: A Record of Settlement*, etc.
F: Mary V. Gwyn 1864-1923 DOD/B: 10/10-11/2/1923 A: 59/2/8 (ashes) "Gwynne"

Haddock, Arthur H.M.
A: A.H.M. Haddock Co E 3 Iowa Inf
C: MH/GAR Hill DOD/B: 4/25-28/1892 A: 49 N: American M: Married (Coroner Inquest Report 57-02 336 indicates
    "Arthur" Haddock died an accidental death--morphine poisoning--4/25/1892--SD Historical Society Archives)

Haden, John Franklin
A: J.F. Haden Co G 4th Miss Cav CSA
C: MH/Confederate DOD/B: 2/14-16/1934 A: 87/8/14 Died in San Diego
    Note: John Franklin Haden was born 5/31/1846 in Hernando, DeSoto County, Miss; died 2/14/1934 in San
    Diego, CA He was Pvt, Co G, 4th Miss Cav S: UDC document, California Room (see Chapter II, "San Diego

Haden, John Franklin (Con't)
   Public Library" sources)
F: Sarah Ophelia Haden 1857-1937 DOD/B: 1/22-23/1937 A: 80/__/7 Died in San Diego

Hahn, Joseph
A: Jos. Hahn Co I 7 NY Inf
C: MH/GAR Div. 3 DOD/B: 2/10-16/1914 A: 83 N: France M: Widower
E: Joseph Hahn N: Alsace, France 8/27/31 CW: Co I 7 NY Inf (Pvt) Term: 3 yrs E/D: 7/62-2/63 Frederick, MD
   for disability GAR: 9/13/1903 on transfer from Lyon Post Dept of Illinois Died: 2/10/1914 A: 82/5/13 S: DC

Haines, Alfred
B: Alfred Haines 1845-1934
C: GW/Hawthorne DOD/B: 10/15-18/1934 A: 88/10/29
D: Alfred Haines N: Penn A: 57 O: Lawyer R: San Diego/Chula Vista, CA CW: Co C 47 Iowa Inf (Pvt) E/D: 5/64-
   9/64 LOS: 4 mos GAR: 1/27/1903 Died: 10/15/1934 S: H
F: Flora Conklin Haines 1858-1905 DOB: 6/11/1910 A: 46 "Removed from Mount Hope Cemetery." Mount Hope
   information: DOD/B: 1/8-10/1905 A: 46 Buried in Div. 4 "Flora C. Haines" Note: Lot reclaimed by cemetery
   on 8/1991.

Hale, John A.
B: John A. Hale May 23, 1825-June 11, 1911
C: MH/Masonic Q DOD/B: 6/11-15/1911 A: 84/__/17 N: Indiana (probably state of enlistment) M: Married (First
   buried GAR Div.2 Lot 62; removed to Div.6 Lot 2 on 11/10/1911; removed to Masonic Q Lot 2 on 6/25/1917)
E: J.A. Hale N: Kennebeck, Maine CW: Co A 99 Ind Inf (Pvt) Term: 3 yrs E/D: 6/62-10/65 Washington, D.C. GAR:
   2/27/1904 Died: 6/13/1911 A: 84 Buried: GAR plot (Mount Hope) S: DC
F: Susan His Wife July 16, 1834-July 26, 1920 DOD/B: 7/25-28/1920 A: 86

Hall, Francis
A: Francis Hall Co A 1 NJ Inf
C: MH/IOOF DOB: 1/23-26/1910 A: 70

Hall, George P.
A: George P. Hall Co B 2 Neb Cav
B: George P. Hall Apr 22, 1841-May 12, 1915
C: MH/GAR Div. 2 DOD/B: 5/12-17/1915 A: 74/__/20 or 79/__/20 N: England M: Married
D: George P. Hall N: England A: 54 O: Rancher R: Lemon Grove, CA CW: Co B 2 Neb Inf (Pvt) E/D: 8/61-9/62
   Re-Enl?: Co D 2 Neb Inf (Pvt) E/D: 2/63-1/65 LOS: 36 mos GAR: 5/24/1898 TR: 12/22/1903
   TR cancelled: 3/8/1904 Died: 5/12/1915 S: H
F: Mary Elizabeth Hall, his wife Dec 28, 1847-Feb 26, 1932 DOD/B: 2/26-29/1932 A: 84/1/29 Died in San Diego

Hall, William Henry
B: William H. Hall Co E 58 Ill Inf 1848-1925
C: MH/GAR Hill DOD/B: 7/12-14/1925 A: 77/__/11

Halversen, Soren
B: Father Soren Halversen Feb 25, 1845-June 11, 1921 Co K 3rd Reg Wisc Inf'try
C: MH/BLK 1 DOD/B: 6/11-14/1921 A: 76
F: Mother Mary Anna Halversen Apr 29, 1851-Jan 30, 1920 DOD/B: 1/30-2/2/1920 A: 67/9/1 "Anna Marie"

Hamilton, Beverly
A: Beverly Hamilton US Navy
C: MH/IOOF DOB: 3/16/1917 A: 71
D: Beverly Hamilton N: Washington A: 63 O: Barber CW: USS Verlena (Landsman) E/D: __/64-5/65 LOS: Not
   stated GAR: 2/13/1912 Died: 3/14/1917 S: H

Hamilton, Martin Douglas
B: Martin D. Hamilton Apr 28, 1843-Aug 4, 1926 Co G 17 Ind Vol
C: MH/GAR Hill DOD/B: 8/4-6/1926 A: 83/3/7 Died in San Diego
D: M.D. Hamilton N: Jackson, Ind A: 37 O: Farmer R: San Diego, Los Angeles CW: Co G 17 Ind Vol (Pvt/1st Sgt)
    E/D: 6/61-8/65 due to loss of right arm, wound in left thigh LOS: 4 yrs GAR: 10/8/1881 Charter Member
    Heintzelman Post GAR 1st SV Commander Post Commander 1882 SP: 1/30/1893 SP: 1/30/1894 DR:
    3/28/1899 RE: 8/27/1912 Died: 8/4/1926 S: H
F: Fayette Lemon, wife of M.D. Hamilton Born Jan 23, 1840 Died July 27, 1887 DOB: 7/27/1887 A: 47/6/4 "Fayette
    Lemar Hamilton" J/S: "Hamilton, Mrs Fayette, d. 27 Jul (1887), 40 years, b. IN, mar, bur Mt Hope Cem"

Hampson, Robert/Rufus A.
A: 1st Sgt R.A. Hampson Co D 1 Ohio Inf
C: MH/GAR Hill DOD/B: 2/18-19/1899 A: 69 N: American M: Widower "Robert A. or Rufus A.)

Handy, John H.
A: Mus'n John H. Handy Band 9 ME Inf
C: MH/GAR Hill DOD/B: 7/10-12/1922 A: 82/3/__
D: John H. Handy N: Maine A: 55 O: Blacksmith CW: Co __ 9 ME Inf (Musician) E/D: 9/61-11/62 LOS: 14 mos
    GAR: 11/28/1893 SP: 3/28/1899 DR: 10/25/1904 RE: 1/10/1922 Died July 10, 1922 S: H
F: Emma J. Handy (no stone) DOD/B: 3/20-22/1907 A: 68/5/29 N: Maine M: Divorced

Hanson, Martin
A. Martin Hanson Co H 4 NY Cav
C: MH/GAR Div.2 DOD/B: 9/4-5/1907 A: 60/8/2 N: Denmark M: Single "Hansen"
E: Martin Hanson N: Denmark CW: Co H 4 NY Cav (Pvt) Term: 3 yrs E/D: 10/61-11/64 Pulaski, TN GAR:
    2/28/1903 on transfer from J.B. Steadman Post #24 Dept of Wash/Alaska Died: 9/7/1907 A: 65 Buried:
    GAR (Mount Hope) S: DC

Hardy, Albert
A: Albert Hardy Co K 100 Ill Inf
C: MH/Div.6 DOD/B: 4/4-6/1928 A: 81/9/2 Died in San Diego
E: Albert Hardy N: Meggs Co, Ohio CW: Co K 100 Ill Inf (Pvt) Term: Unstated E/D: 7/62-6/65 LOS: See prior
    notes GAR: 8/14/1926 Died: 4/4/1928 Buried: Mount Hope S: DC
F: Elizabeth H. Hardy Aug 4, 1871 DOD/B: No record found

Hardy, Daniel Elson
A: Dan'l E. Hardy Co H 5 Mass Inf (or 6 Mass Inf?) (hard to read)
C: MH/Masonic Q DOB: 10/14-16/1909 A: 72/7/5 N: MA M: Married

Harlan, John
A: Jno Harlan Co H 116 PA Inf
C: MH/Div.4 DOD/B: 10/28-29/1890 A: 60 N: American M: Married
F: Mary Francis Harlan No stone DOD/B: 5/21-28/1934 A: 80/5/14 (ashes) Died in San Diego

Harmon, Ole Oleson
A: Ole O. Harmon Co B 153 Ill Inf
C: MH/BLK 5 DOD/B: 3/7-11/1932 A: 86/11/8
D: Ole O. Harmon N: Norway A: 73 O: Retired CW: Co B 153 Ill Inf (Pvt) E/D: 2/65-9/65 LOS: 7 mos GAR:
    6/11/1918 Died: 3/7/1932 S: H
F: Mother Laura Harmon May 9, 1851-July 7, 1940 DOD/B: 7/7-12/1940 A: 89/1/28 Died in San Diego

Harper, Joseph H.
B: Joseph H. Harper May 22, 1844-May 27, 1927
C: MH/Masonic C DOD/B: 5/27-31/1927 A: 83/__/5
D: Joseph H. Harper N: Ohio A: 71 O: Farmer CW: Co I 89 Ohio Inf (Pvt) E/D: 8/62-9/64 Re-Enl?: Co I 117 Ill
    Inf (Pvt/Sgt) E/D: 8/62-8/65 LOS: Not stated GAR: 3/14/1916 Died: 5/27/1927 S:H

Harper, Joseph H. (Con't)
F: Tamar Alice Harper Feb 28, 1850-May 29, 1892 DOD/B: 5/29-31/1892 A: 40 N: American M: Married

Harrigan, James
A: Jas Harrigan Co E 5 IA Inf
C: MH/GAR Div.2 DOD/B: 9/16-17/1908 A: 65/2/6 N: New York M: Married "JS" record indicates he died on
    9/16/1908 of acute alcoholism at 1737 Atlantic (Avenue?) Nativity New York Marital--married
E: James Harrigan N: East Bloomfield, Ontario Co, NY CW: Co E 5 IA Inf (Pvt) Term: 3 yrs E/D: 7/61-3/64
    Evansville, Ind GAR: 6/25/1904 Died: 9/18/1908 A: 64 Buried: GAR (Mount Hope) S: DC

Harris, Avril
A: Corpl Avril Harris Co A 89 NY Inf
C: MH/Masonic R DOD/B: 11/22-25/1922 A: 85/2/2
F: Marietta Harris No stone DOD/B: 1/24-28/1937 A: 96/4/4 Died in San Diego

Harris, L.W.
A: L.W. Harris Co B (or Co G) 3 Ind Cav
C: MH/GAR Hill DOD/B: 5/2-4/1901 A: 76/8/18 N: American M: Married "Leander"

Harris, Moses Cox
B: Moses C. Harris 1842-1923 Prvt Co C 77 Ohio Inf
C: MH/GAR Hill DOD/B: 12/15-18/1923 A: 81/6/25

Hartley, James Monroe
B: James M. Hartley 44 Iowa Inf 1904; also James Monroe 1846-1904
C: MH/Div.3 DOD/B: 7/23-24/1904 A: 59/11/__ N: American M: Married
D: James M. Hartley N: Lee Co, Iowa A: 36 O: Speculator CW: Co D 44 Iowa Inf (Pvt) E/D: 5/64-1/65 LOS: 3
    1/3 mos (100 days) GAR: 7/12/1883 SP: 6/30/1888 DR: 11/30/1891 RE: 5/10/1898 Died: 7/23/1904--is
    [grave] stone S: H
F: Mary Jane Tibbetts 1852-1940 DOD/B: 12/9-11/1940 A: 88/7/9 Died in San Diego
    Note: James/Mary Jane to San Diego w/4 children in 1882; he sold insurance throughout Pacific States;
    offspring developed North Park area of San Diego, according to *San Diego County Pioneer Families*

Hartzell, Thomas B.
A: Sgt T.B. Hartzell Co G 3 IA Cav
B: T.B. Hartzell 1842-1902 Co G 3 Iowa Cav
C: MH/GAR Hill DOD/B: 5/6-8/1902 A: 60 N: American M: Married
D: Thomas B. Hartzell N: Iowa A: 40 O: Carpenter R: Poway, CA CW: Co G 3 Iowa Cav (Corpl/Sgt) E/D: 8/61-
    8/65 LOS: Not stated GAR: 10/26/1882 SP: 9/24/1895 RE: 5/26/1896 Post Commander 1888 Died:
    5/6/1902--is [grave] stone S: H
F: Letta E. Hartzell 1848-1933 DOD: 1/24/1933 DOB: 1933 A: 85 No records of burial; could have been interred
    by family; above [this information] from family 10/5/1957

Harvey, Rufus D./W.
A: Rufus D. Harvey Co D 13 Wis Inf
C: MH/GAR Hill DOD/B: 6/27-30/1934 A: 90/6/19 Died in National City, CA
E: Rufus W. Harvey N: ? location 2/28/47 CW: Co B 1 Ill L A (Pvt) E/D: 5/63-7/65 Term: Unstated GAR:
    7/24/1926 on transfer from Phil Sheridan Post, Marshalltown, IA and Crocker Post, Des Moines IA. D:
    10/12/1929 (Discharged at own request; totally blind 14 years from 1912) S: DC

Haskell, John Lincoln
A/B: No stone
C: MH/GAR Div.3 DOD/B: 8/5-7/1914 A: 76 "John Lincoln Haskell"
E: John L. Haskell N: Norway, Maine 3/25/38 CW: Co A 5 ME Inf (Pvt/2nd Sgt) Term: 3 yrs E/D: 4/61-5/64
    Portland, ME Re-Enl: Co B 8 Vet Inf (Pvt) E/D: 7/64-7/65 GAR: 6/13/1914 Died: 8/5/1914 A: 76
    Buried: GAR (Mount Hope) S: DC

Haskins, William A.
A: Mus'n W.A. Haskins Co H 1 Wash Terr Inf
C: MH/GAR Hill DOD/B: 7/15-17/1906 A: 61 N: Illinois M: Single
D: William A. Haskins N: Illinois A: 41 O: Rancher Clerk/Musician CW: Co H 1 Wash Terr Inf (Pvt/Musician) E/D: 9/62-7/65 LOS: 34 mos GAR: 8/25/1887 SP: 1/10/1889 or 6/10/1889 DR: 6/30/1891 GAR: 2/8/1898 Died: 7/16/1906--is [grave] stone S: H

Hathaway, Franklin
B: Frank June 2, 1836-July 4, 1917 115th O.Vol.Inf
C: MH/GAR Div.2 DOB: 7/4-7/1917 A: 81
D: Frank Hathaway N: Ohio A: 58 O: Printer CW: Co E 13 Ohio Inf; Co B 115 Ohio Inf; and Co A 188 Ohio Inf (Mus'n) E/D: 4/61-9/62 LOS: 16 mos GAR: 11/26/1895 Died: 7/4/1917 S: H
F: Emma Nov 29, 1844-Oct 13, 1934 DOD/B: 10/13-16/1934 A: 89/10/14

Hayes, Thomas
A: Thomas Hayes Band 18 NY Inf (tombstone visible at Calvary Cemetery)
C: CAL/Sec 1, North, Row 2 DOD/B: No record found in Catholic cemetery index

Haynes, George E.
A: Mus'n Geo. E. Haynes Co D 5 RI H A
B: George E. Haynes 1844-1917
C: MH/BLK 7 DOD/B: 6/14-18/1917 A: 74
E: Geo. E. Haynes N: Wilmington, VT 2/9/44 CW: Co D 5 RI Inf (Pvt) Term: 3 yrs E/D: 11/61-6/65 New Burn, NC GAR: 10/27/1906 on transfer from C.B. Lawton Post #44 Dept of VT Died: 6/15/1917 A: 73/4/__ Buried: GAR Annex (Mount Hope) S: DC
F: Estella A. Smith, Wife of George E. Haynes 1851-1911 DOD/B: 11/20-22/1911 A: 60/10/13 N: VT M: Married

Hays, John
B: John Hays 1842-1924 46 Ohio Inf
C: MH/GAR Div.2 DOD/B: 8/14-16/1924 A: 82/4/3

Hayward, William H.
A: Wm. H. Hayward Co A 1 Ohio L A
C: MH/GAR Div.3 DOD/B: 5/18-20/1915 A: 80/7/22 N: New York M: Married
E: W.H. Hayward N: New York CW: Co A 1 Ohio L A (Pvt) Term: 3 yrs E/D: 9/61-9/64 Chattanooga, TN Re-Enl: Co D 4 US Vet Vols (Pvt) E/D: 3/65-3/66 GAR: 6/10/1905 on transfer from Col. Eli Post #158 Dept of Michigan Died: 5/18/1904 A: 81 S: DC Note: This death date is probably the author's transcription error, as San Diego County records indicate he died on 5/18/1915.
F: Marie A. Hayward Feb 4, 1836 -June 18, 1927 DOD/B: 6/18-21/1927 A: 91/4/14 Died in Los Angeles

Hazzard, G.R.
A: G.R. Hazzard Co 8 5th US Art
C: MH/Div.2 DOD/B: No further record

Hazzard, George W.
B: George W. 1845-1942
C: MH/IOOF DOD/B: 4/3-6/1942 A: 97/2/__ Died in San Diego "George W." Note: George W. Hazzard was born in Cambridge City, Wayne Co, Indiana in February, 1845. Arriving on December 8, 1868 in San Diego, he took up a claim in the Otay Valley. He married Alice Curtis, South Carolina native, in 1870. He later established a general merchandise store, and sold it in 1882. He was an incorporator of the San Diego Water Company and the City Gas Company, member of the Chamber of Commerce, and socially prominent. (from *San Diego County, California: A Record of Settlement*, etc.)
D: George W. Hazzard N: Indiana A: 52 O: Real Estate CW: Co B 134 Ind Inf (Pvt) E/D: 4/64-9/64 LOS: 5 mos GAR: 11/23/1897 Died: 4/3/1942 S: H
F: Alice 1844-1940 DOD/B: 9/13-28/1940 A: 96/6/27 Note: 1880 census says "Allie Hazzard," 34, is wife of George Hazzard. She is native of Missouri, with Massachusetts mother and South Carolina father.

Healey, Bernard
A: Sgt Bernard Healey Co A 8th US Inf (tomestone visible at Calvary Cemetery)
C: CAL/Sec.1, North, Row 9-3 DOD/B: No record found in Catholic cemetery index
D: Bernard Healey N: Dublin, Ireland A: 50 O: Soldier CW: Co G 8 US Inf (Pvt) Re-enl?: Co A 8 US Inf (Sgt)
    E/D: 3/61-12/82 due to disability LOS: 21 9/12 years GAR: 10/28/1881 Died: 3/28/1893--is [grave] stone
F: Margaret Healy (no record of burial at Calvary Cemetery) Source: Death record of child Simon Healy DOD/B: 1/5-
    7/1894 A: 48 N: Ireland Parents: Bernard and Margaret Healy

Heath, James A.
B: James A. 1840-1920
C: MH/Div.3 DOD/B: 4/29-5/1/1920 A: 79/11/25
D: James A. Heath N: Maine A: 40 O: Ship Chandler CW: Co K 35 Mass Inf (Pvt) E/D: 9/62-7/65 LOS: 34 mos
    GAR: 9/19/1881 Died: 4/29/1920 S: H
F: Anna T. 1850-1927 DOB: 1/20-3/4/1927 A: 76/6/23 (ashes) Died in Berkeley, CA "Anna True Heath"

Hefflin, Frederick
A: Fred'k W. Hefflin Co E 8 CT Inf
C: MH/GAR Div.3 DOD/B: 5/24-26/1913 A: "around 76"
D: Fred W. Heflon N: Conn A: 39 O: Painter CW: Co E 8 Conn Inf (Pvt) E/D: 2/64-6/65 LOS: 14 mos GAR:
    3/25/1886 SP: 6/30/1888 DR: 11/30/1891 S: H

Heller, Moses
B: Moses Heller Born Feb. 10, 1839 Died April 20, 1927
C: GW/Palm Terrace DOD/B: 4/20-25/1927 A: 88
D: Moses Heller N: Ohio A: 68 O: Machinist CW: Co I 123 Ohio Inf (Pvt/Corp) E/D: 8/62-6/65 LOS: 34 mos GAR:
    6/14/1906 on transfer from Morton Post #12 Dept of North Dakota Died: 4/20/1927 S: H
F: Martha J. Heller Born June 1, 1844 Died Sept. 30, 1914 DOD/B: 9/30-10/2/1914 A: 71

Hendershot, Lorenzo
A: L. Hendershot Co K 174 Ohio Inf
C: MH/Div.3 DOD/B: 2/19-29/1916 A: 69 "Lorenza"
E: Lorenzo Hendershot N: Layfayette, Monroe Co, NJ 7/2/46 CW: Co K 174 OVI (Pvt) Term: 1 yr E/D: 9/64-6/65
    Charlotte, NC GAR: 5/12/1906 Died: 2/19/1916 A: 69/8/__ S: DC

Henderson, William P.
A: Wm.P. Henderson Co E 8 Ill Inf
C: MH/GAR Hill DOD/B: Record only contains name and GAR Hill Lot 13
D: Wm P. Henderson N: Illinois A: 43 O: Printer CW: Co I 17 Ill Inf (Pvt) Re-Enl?: Co E 8 Ill Inf (Pvt) E/D: 5/61-
    6/65 LOS: 4 yrs GAR: 9/22/1884 Died: 7/3/1888--is [grave] stone S: H
F: Mother Anna E. Henderson 1852-1943 DOD/B: 8/18-23/1943 A: 91/3/30 Died in San Diego "Anna Eliza"

Henneberry, Garret Joseph
A: Heneby/Henery Garrett Co H 69 Ill Inf (name misspelled) (both tombstones visible at Calvary Cemetery)
B: Garrett Joseph Henneberry Sept 14, 1846-Dec 3, 1914 Co H 69 Ill Inf
C: CAL/Row 7 Grave 5 (unsurveyed area) DOD/B: 12/4-6/1914 A: 68 Spouse: Nora Henneberry
F: Nora Henneberry (no record of burial at Calvary Cemetery) Source: DOD/B information on husband

Hennion, Martin
A: Lieut Martin Hennion Co G 2 Colo Cav
B: Martin 1836-1908
C: MH/Div.6 DOD/B: 6/11-13/1908 A: 72/6/10 N: New York M: Married "Hinnion"
D: Martin Hennion N: New Jersey A: 69 O: Retired CA: Co S 3 Colo Inf (Orderly) Re-Enl?: Co __ 2 Colo Cav
    (2nd Lieut) E/D: 9/62-9/65 LOS: 36 mos GAR: 9/12/1905 Died: 6/11/1908--is [grave] stone S: H
F: Nannie J. 1834-1918 DOD/B: 4/18-20/1918 A: 83/10/18

Herrick, Amos P.
A: Sgt Amos P. Herrick Co C 1 US Cav
C: MH/Div.7 DOD/B: 5/6-9/1914 A: 82/7/21
D: Amos P. Herrick N: Concord, New York A: 52 O: Farmer R: Campo, CA CW: Co C 1 US Cav (Duty Sgt) E/D: 7/58-7/63 LOS: 60 mos GAR: 11/8/1883 SP: 6/30/1892 SP: 3/28/1896 DR: 3/28/1899 RE: 5/8/1900 Died: 5/6/1914 S: H
F: Arcella Stowe Herrick No stone DOB: 9/9-11/1912 A: 85/6/20 N: NY M: Married

Hesser, Wilber F.
A: W.F. Hesser Co C 124 Ill Inf
C: MH/GAR Div.2 DOD/B: 8/26-28/1907 A: 65/11/16 N: Virginia M: Married "Wilbur"
E: Wilber F. Hesser N: Louisa Court House, VA CW: Co C 124 Ill Inf (Pvt) Term: 3 yrs E/D: 8/62-8/65 Chicago, Ill GAR: 5/25/1907 on transfer from McPherson Post #6 Dept of Col/Wyo Died: 8/26/1907 A: 65 Buried: GAR (Mount Hope) S: DC

Hewson, James
B: Capt James Hewson Newark, NJ Feb 14, 1834 Redlands, CA Dec 31, 1907
C: MH/Masonic L DOB: 12/31/1907 A: 73/10/6 N: NJ M: Widower
F: Tetuanuie A. Fanaue Hewson Tahiti Mar 24, 1844-July 5, 1902 Wife? DOD/B: 7/5-7/1902 A: 57 N: Tahiti M: Married (record under "T.F. Hewson")

Hiatt, Marvin
A: Marvin Hiatt Co C 181 OH Inf
C: MH/Div.6 DOD/B: 3/23-25/1912 A: 75/__/6
E: M.B. Hiatt N: Rainsborough, Ohio CW: Co C 181 Ohio Inf (Pvt) Term: 3 yrs E/D: 9/64-7/65 Salisbury, NC GAR: 8/8/1908 Died: 3/23/1912 A: 75 Buried: GAR (Mount Hope) S: DC

Hicks, James V.
A: Jas V. Hicks Co H 7 Mich Cav
B: James V. 1848-1917
C: GW/Knights of Pythias DOD/B: 2/15-17/1917 A: 68
D: J.V. Hicks N: New York A: 36 O: Mail Contr/Carrier R: Fallbrook, CA CW: Co H 7 Mich Cav (Pvt) E/D: 2/65-12/65 LOS: 11 mos GAR: 9/5/1884 SP: 9/26/1889 RE: 3/26/1895 RE: 5/30/1896 Post Commander 1899 Died 2/16/1917 S:H
F: Emma L. 1850-1885 (wife?) DOD/B: 12/19/1885-8/28/1917 A: 35 Died at Fallbrook, CA

Hicks, John J.
A: Lieut J.J. Hicks Co H 7th Mich Cav
B: John J. 1826-1891
C: GW/Knights of Pythias DOD/B: 12/31/1891-8/28/1917 A: 65
D: John J. Hicks N: New York A: 62 O: Farmer CW: Co H 7 Mich Cav (Lieut) E/D: 10/62-9/63 due to disability LOS: 11 mos GAR: 8/23/1888 DR: 6/30/1891 Died: 12/31/1891--is [grave] stone S: H

Higbee, Elbert R.
A/B: (stone buried/no longer visible)
C: MH/GAR Div.2 DOB: 12/29-31/1914 A: 72
E: E.R. Higbee N: Ohio 10/10/43 CW: Co C 125 OVI (Pvt) Term: 3 yrs E/D: 8/62-8/63 due to Surgeon's Certificate of Disability GAR: 5/13/1905 on transfer from N.L. Morris Post #40 Dept of Ohio Died: 12/29/1914 A: 71 S: DC
F: Hattie Goodman Higbee (stone buried/no longer visible) DOD/B: 1/6-9/1922 A: 75

Higgins, Robert Walter
A: Corpl Rob't W. Higgins Co B 17 Kans Inf
C: MH/GAR Div. 3 DOD/B: 6/8-13/1916 A: 73 "Robert Walter Higgins"

Hill, William F.
B: William F. Hill Jan 18, 1837-May 24, 1918 Co G 23rd Iowa Inf At Rest in Jesus
C: GW/Cypress Place DOD/B: 5/24-27/1918 A: 81
D: William F. Hill N: Not stated A: 65 O: Retired CW: Co C 23 Iowa Inf (Pvt) LOS: Not stated GAR: 7/27/1909
 TR: 1/23/1912 S: H
F: His Wife Mary M. Hill Oct 28, 1854-Mar 13, 1923 DOD/B: 3/13-15/1923 A: 68

Hilliard, Lanson
A: Lanson Hilliard Co K 193 NY Inf
C: MH/GAR Div. 3 DOD/B: 2/15-17/1914 A: 79 N: New York M: Married

Himebaugh, Henry H.
A: Lieut Henry H. Himebaugh Co D 49 Wis Inf
C: MH/IOOF DOB: 3/23/1925 A: 85
E: H.H. Himebaugh N: Green Township, Erie Co, PA CW: Co E 40 Wis Inf (Corpl) Term: 100 days E/D: 5/64-9/64
 Madison Re-Enl: Co D 49 Wis Inf (Recruiting 2nd Lieut/Asst.Lieut/1st Lieut) E/D: 1/65-11/65 Benton
 Barracks GAR: 7/14/1900 Died: 3/18/1925 Buried: Mount Hope S: DC
F: Ada J. Himbaugh No stone DOB: 1/15/1936 A: 87 "Himbaugh"

Himmell, Charles S.
A: Chas S. Himmell Co F 25 NY Cav
C: MH/GAR Div. 2 DOD/B: 1/25-27/1911 A: 66 N: Bavaria M: Married Name Himel
E: Charles Himmell N: Zweybreiken, Bavaria CW: US Navy (Landsman) Term: 1 yr E/D: __/63-__/__ Charleston,
 SC Re-Enl: Co F 25 NY Cav (Pvt) E: 11/64-6/65 GAR: 11/23/1898 Died: 1/25/1911 A: 66 Buried: GAR
 (Mount Hope) S: DC
F: Susan H. Himmell (no stone) DOD/B: 3/5-8/1928 A: 83 Died in San Diego

Hinckle, William S.
A: Capt W.S. Hinckle Co D 1 Ind H A
C: MH/GAR Hill DOD/B: 11/29-12/1/1904 A: 74 N: American M: Married "Capt"
D: Wm. S. Hinkle N: Indiana A: 53 O: Farmer CW: Co D 21 Ind Inf (Lieut/Capt) E/D: 7/61-12/64 LOS: 41 mos
 GAR: 2/23/1888 SP: 9/26/1889 DR: 6/30/1891 Died: 11/30/1904--is [grave] stone S: H
F: Mary Hinckle (no stone) DOD/B: 10/29-31/1917 A: 81

Hodge, Noah Note: To San Diego in 1887; lived in Golden Hill, according to *San Diego County Pioneer Families*
B: Noah Hodge Born in Springfield, Ill Feb 6, 1842 Died in San Diego, Cal May 17, 1891
C: MH/IOOF DOD/B: 5/17-22/1891 A: 49 N: American M: Married
D: Noah Hodge N: Illinois A: 47 O: Lawyer CW: Co C 124 Ill Inf (Pvt) Promoted?: Co __ 52 US C T (1st Lieut)
 E/D: 7/62-7/65 due to resignation LOS: 36 mos GAR: 9/12/1889 Died: 5/17/1891--is [grave] stone S: H
F: Sarah W. Ashmun Wife of Noah Hodge Born in Hudson, O Aug 29, 1843 Died in San Diego, Cal Sept 12, 1907
 DOD/B: 9/12-14/1907 A: 64 N: Ohio M: Widow

Hodges, John
A/B: No stone search undertaken
C: GW/Crematory Niche 194, Room #2 DOD: 2/9/1927 A: 87
D: John Hodges N: New York A: 75 O: Farmer CW: Co I 28 Wis Inf (Pvt) E/D: 8/62-8/65 LOS: Not stated GAR:
 7/14/1914 (probably on transfer from John Ingham Post #96 Dept of Nebraska TR: 9/10/1916 S: H
E: John Hodges N: Scriba or Scuba, NY 1838 CW: Co I 28 Wis Vol Inf (Pvt) Term: 3 yrs E/D: 8/62-8/65
 Brownsville, TX GAR: 1/13/1917 on transfer from Heintzelman Post San Diego Died: 2/9/1927 Cremated:
 Greenwood Cemetery S: DC

Hoeffle, Jacob
A/B: No stone
C: MH/GAR Hill DOD/B: 7/3-4/1887 A: 53 N: German M: Married "removed 7/27/1897 from GAR Lot 37 to Lot 148
D: Jacob Hoeffle N: Germany A: 46 O: Saloon CW: __ Batt Artl'y (Capt.Pennington) (Pvt) E/D: 9/61-9/62 LOS:
 1 yr GAR: 5/27/1886 Died: 7/4/1887--no [grave] stone S: H

Hoffman, David Bancroft
A: Lieut David B. Hoffman Asst Surg'n 4 Cal Inf (both his/her tombstones visible at Calvary Cemetery)
C: CAL/Sec. 1, North, Row 3 DOD/B: No record found in Catholic cemetery index
   Note: First American physician/surgeon to San Diego; born in New York (parents Chauncey B. and Mary (Beal) Hoffman; to San Diego as ship's surgeon in 1851; returned 1854 to establish office/drug store at Old Town plaza; built house/office in "New Town" in 1869; president of San Diego County Medical Society; represented San Diego County (1861) in the state legislature; 12 years post surgeon at U.S. Army hospital, located near old army barracks; nine children, five survived; died 1891 at Helix (probably Mt. Helix, La Mesa--near San Diego), age 64 S: San Diego Historical Society Biographical File)
F: Maria Dolores Beloved Wife of Dr. David B. Hoffman Died Aug 12 A.D. 1887 aged 48 years (she buried same location as he) DOD/B: 8/12-14/1887 A: 48 Spouse: Dr. David B. Hoffman Parents: Peter and Guadalupe Wilder. Also death record for child Chamer David Hoffman DOB: 12/19/1900 A: 27 Parents: Dr. David Hoffman and Maria Dolores Wilder Note: 1880 census says Mary D. Hoffman, 41, was wife of D.B. Hoffman. She was a California native, with Massachusetts father and California mother.

Hoine, Samuel P.
A: Samuel P. Hoine Co M 2 Wis Cav
C: MH/Div.1 DOD/B: 5/21-23/1931 A: 84/9/28 Died in San Diego
F: Orrinda Estella No stone DOD/B: 11/30-12/10/1940 A: 81/8/19 Died in San Diego

Holcomb, Herman
A: Herman Holcomb Co C 2 Neb Cav
B: Herman Mar 15, 1830-Sept 20, 1913
C: MH/GAR Div.2 DOD/B: 9/20-22/1913 A: 83/6/5 N: PA M: Married
F: Louisa March 27, 1833-Dec 26, 1914 DOD/B: 12/26-28/1914 A: 81 N: NY M: Widow "Nancy Louisa Holcomb"

Holman, Franklin
A/B: No stone
C: Cremated
E: Franklin Holman N: Princeton, KY CW: Co F 114 Ill Inf (Pvt) Term: 3 yrs E/D: 8/62-8/65 Vicksburg, Miss GAR: 4/25/1903 on transfer from Eutill Post #71 Dept of Illinois Died: 12/27/1907 A: 84 Cremated S: DC

Holmes, Philander
A: Philander Holmes Co A 12 Ind Cav
C: GW/Acacia Place DOD/B: 11/9-19/1918 A: 68

Holt, William J.
A: Wm. J. Holt Co B 186 OH Inf
C: MH/IOOF DOD/B: No further record

Honeycutt, Daniel
B: Daniel Honeycutt 1842-1928 Co H 50 Ind Vol Inf
C: MH/GAR Hill DOD/B: 2/25-27/1928 A: 85/5/30 Died in San Diego
F: Sarah E. Honeycutt 1848-1922 DOD/B: 2/10-16/1922 A: 73 Middle name Elizabeth

Hood, Alan/Allen R.
A: Corpl Allen R. Hood Co B 1 NH Vol Cav
B: Allen R. April 8, 1842-Dec 28, 1923 GAR
C: MH/Div.1 DOD/B: 12/28/1923-1/2/1924 A: 81/8/20 "Allen"
E: Alan R. Hood N: Dearing, NH 4/8/42 CW: Co C 16 NH Inf (Pvt) Term: 9 mos E/D: 9/62-8/63 Concord, NH Re-Enl: Co B 1 NH Cav (Pvt) E/D: 3/64-7/65 Cloud's Mills, VA GAR: 11/27/1920 on transfer from O.W. Lull Post #11 Dept of New Hampshire Died: 12/28/1923 A: 81/8/20 S: DC
F: Ellen R. Feb 18, 1848-Oct 31, 1928 WRC DOB: 10/31-11/3/1928 A: 80/8/13 Died in San Diego

Hopkins, Archibald
A: Corpl Archibald Hopkins Co E 8 Tenn Cav

Hopkins, Archibald (Con't)
C: MH/Masonic Q DOD/B: 2/28-3/3/1916 A: 74
F: Martha A, Wife of A. Hopkins May 10, 1843-May 18, 1912 DOB: 5/18-23/1912 A: 68/__/10 N: NC M: Not stated

Hopkins, Eugene
A: Eugene Hopkins Co H 14 NY H A
B: Eugene Hopkins Mar 14, 1848-Dec 27, 1911
C: GW/Laurel Place DOD: 12/27/1911 A: 62 Note: Wife's stone below reads "Good Night, Good Morning"
F: Emma F. Hopkins April 6, 1860-Sept 23, 1932 DOD/B: 9/23/1932 A: 75 Died San Francisco

Horton, George R.
A: G.R. Horton Co I 3rd Mich Cav
B: Geo R. Horton Mbr of Mich Cav 3rd Regt Co 1 1841-1898
C: MH/GAR Hill DOD/B: 10/16-18/1898 A: 57 yrs N: American M: Married
D: George R. Horton N: Michigan A: 51 O: Jeweler CW: Co I 3 Mich Cav (Pvt) E/D: 9/63-2/66 LOS: 53 mos
    GAR: 5/23/1893 SP: 6/25/1895 Died: 10/17/1898--is [grave] stone S: H

Hoskin, O.F.
B: O.F. Hoskin Oct 8, 1827-Sept 3, 1903
C: MH/Masonic M DOD/B: 9/3-6/1903 A: 76 N: American M: Married
E: O.F. Hoskins NOL/NFI S: DC

Hough, Charles Warren
A: C.W. Hough Co G 18 US Inf
C: MH/GAR Hill DOD/B: 2/18-19/1905 A: 74/10/4 "Charles Warren"
D: Hough, Charles W. N: New York A: 69 O: Retired CW: Co G 18 US Inf (Pvt) E/D: 5/62-5/65 LOS: 36 mos
    GAR: 5/14/1891 SP: 12/23/1902 RE: 2/28/1905 Died: 4/17/1905--is [grave] stone (error in date?) S: H

Houston, John
A/B: No stone (cremated)
E: John Houston N: Buffalo, NY CW: Co B 3 US Inf (Pvt) Term: Unstated E/D: 4/61-4/64 GAR: 10/23/1926 on
    transfer Died: 6/30/1934 Cremated Bonham Brothers S: DC

Hover, Aaron S.
A: Aaron S. Hover Co A 20 NY Mil
C: GW/Palm Terrace DOD: 5/11/1914 A: 77
D: Aron S. Hover N: New York A: 66 O: Sewing M. Agent CW: Co A 20 NY Mil (Pvt) E/D: __/61-7/61 LOS: 3 mos
    GAR: 12/25/1900 Died: 5/11/1914 S: H

Howard, Henry A.
A: Henry A. Howard Co K 7 Cal Inf
C: MH/GAR Div.2 DOD/B: 3/9-11/1911 A: 78

Howell, William
B: William Howell GAR 1847-1932
C: MH/GAR Div.2 DOD/B: 2/19-24/1932 A: 82/10/6 Died in San Diego
D: William Howell N: New York A: 70 O: Retired CW: Co F 52 Ill Inf (Pvt) E/D: 12/64-3/65 LOS: 3 1/2 mos due
    to disability GAR: 7/9/1918 DR: "Dropped mem" Died: 2/18/1932 S: H
F: Lida Howell WRC 1864-1927 DOD/B: 3/13-17/1927 A: 62/6/13 Died in San Diego

Huddleston, John
B: John Feb 23, 1845-Apr 25, 1928 Co G 5th Reg of Minn Vol Wagoner
C: MH/GAR Div.2 DOD/B: 4/25-5/2/1928 A: 83/2/2 Died in San Diego
D: John Huddleston N: New York A: 78 O: Retired CW: Co G 5 Minn Inf (Pvt/Wagoner) E/D: __/62-9/65 LOS:
    3 yrs GAR: 8/23/1921 Died: 4/25/1928 S: H
F: Salina Y. Dec 25, 1832-June 27, 1926 DOD/B: 6/27-30/1926 A: 93/6/2 Died in San Diego "Huddlestown"

Hudgins, Amos Edward
A: Amos Hudgins Co K 2 Kans Inf
C: MH/GAR Div. 2 DOD/B: 2/9-12/1926 A: 81/4/1 Race: Black Died in Coronado, CA
D: Amos E. Hudgins N: Missouri A: 69 O: Barber CW: Co K 2 Kans Inf (Pvt) Re-enl?: Co K 2 Kans Cav (Pvt)
  E/D: 9/63-10/65 LOS: Not stated GAR: 5/27/1913 Died: 2/9/1926 S: H
F: Cynthia Ann Hudgins No stone DOD/B: 6/27-30/1934 A: 80/1/24 Race: Black Died in Coronado, CA

Huey, G.L.
A: Lieut G.L. Huey RQM 55th KY Inf
C: MH/GAR Hill DOD/B: 9/21-25/1898 A: 75 N: American M: Married

Hughes, James Douglas
A: Jas Douglass Hughes Co 1 1 Ala Inf
C: MH/Confederate DOD/B: 6/24-25/1929 A: 82/5/9 Died in San Diego
  Note: James D. Hughes was born 1/14/1847 in Jackson, Miss; Died on 6/24/1929 in San Diego, CA. In 1861, he ran away from home to join John H. Morgan's command in Tennessee. Transferred to Co A 5th Tennessee Cavalry. After Shiloh battle, transferred to Co I 1st Alabama Infantry (Private). Wounded at Altoona in left hip and right eye by a shell explosion. Served balance of war in enrolling department in Alabama and later medical examining board. Was last surviving member of the John H. Morgan Camp 1198 of the United Confederate Veterans, San Diego. His wife, Louisa (or "Nona") Roldam was born 1837 in Long Beach, CA. She was of Mexican heritage. Her father had been killed in the early 1850's at San Pasqual in San Diego County while serving under Cave J. Couts against the Indian insurrection. S: UDC document, California Room (see Chapter II, "San Diego Public Library" sources)
F: Louisa Hughes 1838-1928 DOD/B: 2/26-29/1928 A: about 90 Died in San Diego

Hughes, James W.
B: Maj J.W. Hughes Surgeon 152 NY Inf
C: MH/GAR Hill DOD/B: 3/1-2/1899 A: 64 N: American M: Married
D: James W. Hughes N: New York A: 62 O: Physician CW: Co __ 59 NY Inf (Asst.Surg.) Promoted?: Co __ 152 NY Inf (Surgeon) E/D: 5/63-7/65 LOS: 26 mos GAR: 8/11/1896 SP: 12/27/1898 Died: 3/1/1899--is [grave] stone S: H

Hughes, John Henry
B: John H. Hughes Co H 95th Ill Reg
C: MH/GAR Hill DOD/B: 10/8-10/1921 A: 76
D: John Hughes N: Illinois A: 67 O: Farmer CW: Co H 95 Ill Inf (Pvt) E/D: 7/62-5/65 LOS: Not stated GAR: 3/10/1914 (probably on transfer from Plummer Post #50 Dept of Minnesota Died: 10/8/1921 S: H

Hughes, Miles
A: Miles Hughes Co I 10th Ill Inf
B: Miles Hughes Co I 10th Ill Inf Born Mar 16, 1847 Died Mar 26, 1892
C: MH/GAR Hill DOD/B: 3/26-28/1892 A: 46 N: American M: Married (Coroner Inquest File 56-05 337--accidental death at South Coronado--gunshot--3/26/1892--San Diego Historical Society Archives)
D. Miles Hughes N: Illinois A: 40 O: Physician & Surgeon CW: Co I 10 Ill Inf (Pvt) E/D: 2/65-7/65 LOS: 4 1/2 mos GAR: 2/9/188 SP: 1/10/1889 DR: 6/30/1891 Died: 3/26/1892--is [grave] stone S: H

Hull, Horace J.
A: H.J. Hull Co M 50th NY Inf
C: MH/GAR Hill DOD/B: 11/7-10/1897 A: 50 N: American M: Married (Coroner Inquest File 113-1 523--accidental death--drowning--11/7/1897--San Diego Historical Society Archives)
E: Horace J. Hull N: Athens, PA CW: Co M 50 NY Engineers (Artificer) Term: 3 yrs E/D: 12/63-6/65 GAR: 11/10/1894 Charter Member Datus Coon Post Died: 11/7/1897 A: 68 S: DC

Humphrey, E.O.
A: E.O. Humphrey Co I 102 Ill Inf
C: GW/Olive DOD/B: 12/4/1913 A: 66
F: Clara DOD/B: 10/19-22/1926 A: 81

Hunt, George W.
A: 1 Lt George W. Hunt Co K 1 Kans Mtd Inf
C: GW/Palm Terrace DOD/B: No record found

Hunt, Ishabel/Ashbel
A: Ishabel Hunt Co A 21 Conn Inf
C: MH/GAR Div.2 DOD/B: 10/27-11/2/1923 A: 76/6/25 "Ashbel"
F: Mrs. Annie Hunt (on stone) DOD/B: 2/17-3/6/1926 A: 70 Died in Denver, Colorado (ashes) "Anna W."

Hunt, Nathan
B: Nathan Hunt 1847-1935 GAR Co H 2 Iowa Cav
C: MH/GAR Div.2 DOD/B: 8/23-27/1935 A: 88/6/14 Died at Los Angeles Military Home (Sawtelle?)
D: Nathan Hunt N: Ohio A: 49 O: Physician CW: Co H 2 Iowa Cav (Pvt) E/D: 2/64-9/65 LOS: 15 mos GAR: 10/22/1895 SP: 9/28/1897 RE: 3/26/1901 Died: 8/23/1935 S: H
F: Ida 1851-1936 DOD/B: 8/1-5/1936 A: 85/5/__ Died in National City, CA "Ada Ellen"

Hunt, William Foster
A: William F. Hunt Co E 22 NY Inf
B: William F. Hunt 1844-1927
C: HC/St. Paul's, Plot 582, Grave 5 DOB: 5/11/1927 No further information available
E: William Hunt N: White Hall, NY 1845 CW: Co E 22 NY Inf (Pvt) Term: 2 yrs E/D: 11/61-6/63 LOS: See prior notes GAR: 4/9/1921 on transfer from Dept of Oklahoma Died: 5/8/1927 Obit: Lists wife Elizabeth R. Hunt, although she is not buried with him at Holy Cross Cemetery S: DC

Hurd, George S.
A: Geo. S. Hurd Co E 1 Wis H A
C: MH/GAR Hill DOD/B: 5/4-6/1899 A: 62 N: American M: Married (Coroner Inquest File 119-3 587 indicates suicide--Laudanum poisoning--5/4/1899--San Diego Historical Society Archives)
E: Geo. S. Hurd N: Wishauka, Indiana CW: Co E 1 Wis H A (Pvt) Term: Unstated E/D: 8/64-6/65 Madison GAR: 3/10/1899 Died: 5/3/1899 A: 61 Buried: GAR (Mount Hope) S: DC
F: Mary, wife of G.S. Hurd died 1916 DOD/B: 9/29-10/3/1916 A: 77 Name Mary Whitney Hurd

Hurley, Cornelius G.
A: Corpl Cornelius G. Hurly Co M 1 Cal Cav
C: MH/GAR Div.2 DOD/B: 7/15-17/1911 A: 74/3/__ N: Iowa M: Not stated "Hearley"

Hutchinson, G.O.
A: G.O. Hutchinson Co B (or Co D) 1 ME H A
C: MH/? DOD/B: No record found

Hutchison, Ezra P.
B: Ezra P. 1847-1935 Note: Same tombstone lists Ezra and Catherine plus George S. and Viola (next record)
C: MH/Div.5 DOD/B: 10/20-11/1/1935 A: 87/11/30 Died in National City, CA
D: Ezra P. Hutchison N: Ohio A: 72 O: Retired CW: Co A 169 Ohio National Guard (Pvt) E/D: 5/64-9/64 LOS: 100 days GAR: 7/13/1920 Died: 10/30/1935 S: H
F: Catherine B. 1825-1902 DOD/B: 3/29-31/1902 A: 77 N: American M: Married

Hutchison, George S.
B: George S. 1846-1926 Note: Same tombstone lists George S. and Viola plus Ezra and Catherine (record above)
C: MH/Div.5 DOD/B: 9/25-29/1926 A: 80/1/18 Died in National City, CA
D: George S. Hutchison N: Ohio A: 73 O: Retired CW: Co H 102 Ohio Inf (Pvt/Corpl) E/D: 2/64-7/65 LOS: 1 1/2

Hutchison, George S. (Con't)
  yrs GAR: 7/13/1920 Died: 9/26/1926 S: H
F: Viola 1853-1926 DOB: 12/25-28/1926 A: 73/4/6 Died in National City, CA

Imberie, James M.
B: Rev James M. Imberie 1841-1926 23 Ohio Inf
C: GW/Cypress Place DOD/B: 9/14-17/1926 A: 85
F: Katherine R. 1845-1932 DOD/B: 12/7-9/1932 A: 88

Ingraham, Andrew
A: Andrew Ingraham Co B 1 NY NG L A
C: MH/GAR Div.2 DOD/B: 9/10-11/1910 A: 76/5/18
E: Andrew Ingraham N: Monroe Co, NY CW: Bat B 1st Batt NY L A (Pvt) Term: 100 days E/D: 8/64-11/64
  Rochester, NY GAR: 5/12/1906 Died: 5/10/1910 A: 76 Buried: GAR (Mount Hope) S: DC Note: San Diego
  County death record indicates he died on 9/10/1910.

Irgens, John S.
A: J.S. Irgens Co K 15 Wis Inf
C: MH/GAR Hill DOD/B: 12/31/1901-1/2/1902 A: 69/10/20 N: Norway M: Married
F: Louisa Irgens 1827-1916 DOD/B: 6/22-24/1916 A: 88 "Louise P."

Jackson, Johiel
A: Johiel Jackson Co E 4 Wis Cav 1836-1914
C: MH/GAR Hill DOD/B: 7/19-21/1914 A: 78 Removed 6/2/1920 from GAR Div.3 to GAR Hill
F: Rebecca Ann Jackson No stone DOD/B: 5/19-21/1920 A: 81/2/7

Jackson, Thomas Miller
B: Civil War Veteran Thomas Miller Jackson Born Hanisonville, KY Mar 1, 1845 Died Dec 21, 1931
C: MH/GAR Div.2 DOD/B: 12/21-23/1931 A: 87/9/20 Race: Black Died in San Diego
E: Thomas M. Jackson N: Kentucky CW: Batt A 2 Regt US Col L A (Pvt) Term: 3 yrs E/D: 11/63-10/65 Nashville,
  TN Re-Enl: Co M 9 US Cav (Pvt) E/D: 2/67-2/72 McKavet, TX GAR: 11/26/1904 S: DC

James, Charles P.
A: Sgt C.P. James Co G 58 PA Inf
C: MH/GAR Hill DOD/B: 2/24-25/1891 A: 51 N: American M: Single "Charles P."

Jamison, Alexander
A: Alex Jamison Co D 122 Ill Inf
C: MH/GAR Div.3 DOD/B: 2/15-17/1913 A: 78/4/6 N: Scotland M: Married
D: A.A. Jameson N: Ohio A: 65 O: Merchant Co F 8 MO Inf (Pvt/Capt) E/D: 6/61-7/64 LOS: 37 mos
  GAR: 8/13/1890 TR: 12/15/1892 S: H

Jenkins, Andrew J.
A: A.J. Jenkins Co K 2 NY Cav
C: MH/GAR Hill DOD/B: 7/4-7/1889 A: 52 N: American M: Widower

Jenks, Park M.
A: Park M. Jenks Co B 109 NY Inf
C: GW/Cypress Place DOD/B: 1/30-2/1/1919 A: 73
D: Park M. Jenks N: Penn A: 73 O: retired CW: Co B 109 NY Inf (Pvt) E/D: 8/62-5/65 LOS: Not stated GAR:
  1/3/1918 Died: 1/30/1919 S: H
F: Augusta Jenks Aug 31, 1847-June 11, 1916 DOD/B: 6/11-13/1916 A: 69

Jenness, Walter B.
A: Capt W.B. Jenness Co H 1 ME Inf
C: MH/GAR Div. 2 DOD/B: 2/20-24/1908 A: 67/9/___ N: Maine M: Married

Jewell, William S.
B: William S. Jewell Born April 28, 1834 Died March 12, 1894
C: MH/Masonic K DOD/B: 3/12-14/1894 A: 59 N: American M: Married (GAR date of death below is probably in error; grave stone/office record say 1894)
D: William S. Jewell N: Philadelphia, PA A: 48 O: Merchant CW: Co G 6 MO ___ (Pvt/1st Lieut) E/D: 4/62-2/63 due to resignation LOS: 10 mos GAR: 6/22/1882 SP: 12/31/1883 Died: 1893--is [grave] stone S: H
F: Emilia F. Jewell Born March 5, 1839 Died Oct 25, 1911 DOB: 10/25-30/1911 A: 72/7/21 N: Germany M: Widow

Jilson, Fred E.
B: Frederic E. Jillson 1843-1926 Co F 2nd Kansas Vol Cav
C: MH/GAR Hill DOD/B: 3/9-17/1926 A: 83/1/15 Died in San Diego This lot formerly Jacob Carmichaels--he buried Greenwood Cemetery on 9/16/1924 by Permit #686 "Jillson"
E: F.E. Jilson N: Pautucket, Mass 1843 CW: Co F 2 Kans Cav (Pvt) Term: 3 yrs E/D: 12/61-1/65 Levenworth, Kans GAR: 10/24/1925 on transfer from Hartrauft Post #3 Dept of Oklahoma Married Mary Ella Sawyer at Topeka on 9/1/1867 Married 58/6/9 yrs Died: 3/9/1926 A: 83/1/15 S: DC
F: Mary E. Jillson Wife 1846-1936 DOD/B: 1/22-24/1936 A: 87/6/25 Died in San Diego

Johns, Adam
A: Adam Johns Co F 13 Ohio Cav
C: MH/GAR Div. 2 DOD/B: 2/14-16/1910 A: 64/4/6 N: Ohio M: Married
F: Elizabeth Johns May 3, 1848-Mar 19, 1938 DOD/B: 3/19-21/1938 A: 89/10/16 Died in San Diego

Johnson, Nathaniel S.
A: Lieut N. S. Johnson Co F 134 Ohio Inf
C: MH/GAR Div. 2 DOD/B: 6/6-8/1910 A: 81/3/22 N: VA M: Widower

Johnson, Peder
A: Peder Johnsen Chf Bos'n Mate US Navy (tombstone visible at Calvary Cemetery)
C: CAL/Sec.3, North 2/3, Row 9-26-C (Block C, Lot 26) DOD/B: No record found in Catholic cemetery index

Johnson, Thomas G.
A: Thomas G. Johnson Co D 8 (or 9) Ind Inf
C: MH/GAR Hill DOD/B: 3/13-16/1933 A: 87/7/___ Civil War Vet Died: Spring Valley, CA

Johnson, William M. A.
A: Wm. Johnson Co C (or Co G) 10 Ohio Inf
C: MH/GAR Div. 3 DOD/B: 6/7-10/1913 A: 73/9/15 N: Ohio M: Married "Wm M.A."

Jones, Danville P.
B: Father Danville P. Jones Co D 20 ME Inf
C: MH/GAR Hill DOD/B: 11/10-14/1917 A: 71 "Danville F."
D: Danville F. Jones N: Solon, Maine A: 37 O: Painter CW: Co D 20 Maine Inf (Pvt) Re-Enl?: Co A 6 VRC (Pvt) E/D: 7/62-7/65 LOS: 36 mos GAR: 10/8/1881 Charter member of Heintzelman Post GAR; first Officer of the Guard Post Commander 1886 Died: 11/11/1917 S: H
F: Mother Sadie M. Jones Dec 20, 1850-Feb 22, 1933 DOD/B: 2/22-24/1933 A: 82/2/2 Died in San Diego

Jones, David R.
B: David R. Jones 1836-1914 Co G 39 IA Inf
C: MH/GAR Div.3 DOD/B: 10/29-30/1914 A: 77/2/29
E: David R. Jones N: North Wales, Great Britain CW: Co G 39 IA Inf (Pvt) Term: 3 yrs E/D: 8/62-6/65 Washington, D.C. GAR: 3/27/1909 on transfer from Lookout Mountain Post #88 Dept of Cal/Nev Died: 10/29/1914 A: 78/2/29 S: DC
F: Sarah E. 1844-1922 DOD/B: 2/6-8/1922 A: 77 "Mrs. Sarah Effie"

Jones, Henry Houston
B: Henry Houston Jones 1st Lt Co B 65 Regt Ill Inf Civil War 1828-1910
C: MH/IOOF DOD/B: 10/26-27/1910 A: 82 N: Illinois M: Single "Henry H."

Jones, James P.
A: Jas. P. Jones US Navy
C: MH/GAR Hill DOB: 11/29/1913 (his ashes buried in wife's grave the same day she was buried) (record under J.P. Jones)
D: James P. Jones N: Madison, ME A: 47 O: Painter/Cabinet Maker CW: US Navy/Gun Boat Sagamore (Fireman) E/D: 11/61-__/__ LOS: 2 yrs GAR: 10/8/1881 Charter Member Heintzelman Post GAR; first J.V. Commander Post Commander 1883 Died: 11/13/1913 S: H
F: Mary I. Jones No stone DOD/B: 11/27-29/1913 A: 73/6/16 N: Maine M: Widow

Jones, Richard A.
A: R.A. Jones Co F 11 Kan Cav
C: MH/Div.1 DOD/B: 8/4-6/1905 A: 64 N: Indiana M: Single
D: Richard A. Jones N: Not stated A: 48 O: Real Estate CW: Co F 11 Kans Inf (Pvt) E/D: 8/62-8/65 LOS: 36 mos GAR: 2/27/1894 SP: 12/27/1898 RE: 6/14/1904 Died: 8/4/1905--is [grave] stone S: H

Jones, Samuel
A: Sam'l Jones Co I 8th US Inf
C: MH/GAR Hill DOD/B: 9/13-15/1891 A: 50 N: England M: Single

Judd, Charles L.
A: Sergt C.L. Judd Co E 1 Ohio L A
B: Charles L. Judd 1832-1907
C: MH/Masonic P DOD/B: 9/2-5/1907 A: 74/9/12 N: Ohio M: Married
F: Kate E. Judd 1838-1914 God in His wisdom has recalled, the boon his love had given, and though their bodies slumber here, their souls are safe in heaven DOB: 4/7/1914 A: 74

Kastner, Joseph
A: Joseph Kastner Co B 11 Ill Cav
C: GW/Acacia Place DOD/B: 1/4-6/1934 A: 88

Kearney, Eli S.
B: Eli P. Kearney Mar. 24, 1845 - Jan. 3, 1927
C: GW/Laurel Place DOD/B: 1/3-5/1927 A: 81
D: Eli S. Kearney N: New Brunswick A: 76 O: Retired R: National City, CA CW: Co G 21 Mich Inf (Pvt) E/D: 2/64-6/65 LOS: 1 yr 4 mos GAR: 11/22/1921 TR: 12/22/1925 S: H
E: Eli S. Kearney N: New Brunswick British Province 3/24/45 CW: Co G 21 Mich Inf (Pvt) Term: 3 yrs E/D: 2/64-6/65 Detroit GAR: 9/9/1916 on transfer from McCrosky Post #110 Dept of Missouri TR: 11/12/1926 RE: On transfer from Heintzelman Post San Diego Died: 1/3/1927 Funeral 1/5/1927 "Post did not officiate on account of Miss Alice Groghan" Buried: Greenwood Obit: Residence was National City, CA Wife Francis L. Kearney S: DC
F: Francis L. Kearney Sept. 14, 1841 - Sept. 5, 1927 DOD/B: 9/5-8/1927 A: 85

Keeney, Thomas Benton
B: Thomas B. Aug 25, 1835-Feb 24, 1915
C: MH/GAR Div.3 DOD/B: 2/24-26/1915 A: 79/5/30
E: T.B. Keeney N: PA 1836 CW: Co G 3 Minn Vol Inf (Pvt) Term: 3 yrs E/D: 8/64-7/65 Jacksonport, Arkansas GAR: 5/13/1905 Died: 2/24/1915 A: 79/6/__ S: DC
F: Esther A. June 23, 1843-April 5, 1926 DOD/B: 4/5-7/1926 A: 82/9/13 Died in San Diego "Esther Awilda"

Keith, Alymer D.
A: QM Sgt Alymer Keith Co G 2 Colo Cav
C: MH/GAR Hill DOD/B: 6/26-30/1905 A: 67 N: New York M: Married "Alyma"

Keith, Alymer D. (Con't)
D: Alymer D. Keith N: New York A: 49 O: Merchant C/W: Co G 2 Col Cav (Pvt/QM Sgt) E/D: 7/62-6/66 LOS: 36 mos GAR: 2/10/1881 SP: 9/26/1889 DR: 6/30/1891 RE: "Reinstated" Died: 6/24/1905 Buried: GAR--is [grave] stone S: H
F: Lizzie E. Keith 1842-1927 DOD/B: 2/20-22/1927 A: 84/8/10 Died in San Diego

Kelder, Abram
A: Sergt Abram Keldar Co G 88 Ill Inf
C: MH/GAR Div.3 DOD/B: 11/25-27/1918 A: 79
E: Abram Keldar N: Belisle, NY 6/12/39 CW: Co G 88 Ill Inf (Pvt/Sgt) Term: 3 yrs E/D: 8/62-6/65 Nashville, TN GAR: 11/12/1910 from Hot Springs, So. Dakota Died: 11/25/1918 A: 79/5/__ S: DC

Kelly, Abraham
A: Abraham Kelly Co K 23 Ind Inf
B: Father Abraham Sept 16, 1844-Dec 21, 1921
C: MH/GAR Hill DOD/B: 12/21-24/1921 A: 77 Died in San Diego
E: Abraham Kelly N: Henry Co, Ohio CW: Co C 118 Ind Inf (Pvt) Term: 6 mos E/D 8/63-3/64 Indianapolis Re-CW: Co K 23 Ind Inf (Pvt) E/D: 10/64-7/65 Louisville, KY GAR: 8/27/1910 Died: 12/21/1921 S: DC
F: Mother Anna M. Jan 29, 1846-Feb 10, 1922 DOD/B: 2/10-13/1922 A: Not stated Died in San Diego "Annie Marie"

Kelly, Eli C.
A: E.C. Kelly Co A 125 Ohio Inf
C: MH/GAR Hill DOD/B: 7/6-7/1900 A: 67 N: American M: Married Died in San Diego
D: Eli C. Kelley N: Penn A: 70 O: Wheelwright CW: Co A 125 Ohio Inf (Pvt) Re-Enl?: Co B 15 VRC (Pvt) E/D: 8/62-7/65 LOS: 36 mos GAR: 5/24/1898 Died: 7/6/1900--is [grave] stone S: H

Kelly, John L.
A: J.L. Kelly Co G 7 Cal Inf
C: MH/GAR Hill DOD/B: 7/3-5/1901 A: 77 N: American M: Widower "John Kelley"

Keltner, George Frances
A/B: No stone
C: MH/Masonic S DOD/B: 2/27-3/2/1918 A: 76
D: George F. Keltner N: Maryland A: 61 O: Musician CW: Co E 2 Iowa Inf (Pvt) E/D: 9/62-5/65 LOS: 30 mos GAR: 3/24/1903 TR: 1/26/1904 S: H
E: Geo F. Keltner N: Baltimore, MD CW: Co E 2 Iowa Inf (Pvt) Term: 3 yrs E/D: 9/62-5/65 Washington, D.C. GAR: 2/22/1908 on transfer from Patrick Collins Post #4 Dept of Idaho Died: 12/29/1917 Buried: Masonic (Mount Hope) S: DC

Kennedy, Nathaniel
A/B: Stone broken off and gone
C: MH/GAR Hill DOD/B: 12/7-14/1920 A: 78/8/5
D: Nathaniel Kennedy N: Penn A: 42 O: Merchant CW: Co H 149 PA Vols (Pvt) E/D: 8/62-6/65 LOS: 34 or 39 mos GAR: 6/30/1886 SP: 6/__/1894 RE: 1/1/1897 SP: 9/28/1897 DR: 10/12/1897 Post Commander 1889 Died: 12/7/1920 S: H
F: Sarah Kennedy Stone broken off and gone DOD/B: 11/9-11/1903 A: 56 N: American M: Married

Kenney, Robert D.
A: R.D. Kenney Co E 5 Cal Inf
C: MH/GAR Hill DOD/B: 11/17-19/1903 A: 68 N: American M: Married Died in San Diego "Robt. D."
F: Anna M. Kenney No stone DOD/B: 5/18-26/1932 A: 89 In grave of R.D. Kenney Died in San Diego

Kerr, John M.
A: John M. Kerr Co F 25 Ohio Inf
B: John M. Kerr Nov 2, 1841-May 10, 1909
C: MH/Div.6 DOD/B: 5/10-12/1909 A: 67/6/8

Kerr, John M. (Con't)
E: John M. Kerr N: Jefferson Co, Ohio CW: Co D 1 VA Inf (Pvt) Term: 3 mos E/D: 5/61-8/61 Re-Enl: Co F 25
   Ohio Inf (Pvt) E/D: 9/61-8/65 GAR: 5/10/1906 on transfer from Eggleston Post Dept of Kansas Died:
   5/10/1909 A: 67 Buried: GAR (Mount Hope) S: DC
F: Emma Kerr April 26, 1855-Feb 23, 1908 DOD/B: 2/23-25/1908 A: 52/9/28 N: Indiana M: Married

Kidder, John W.
A: John W. Kidder Co D 3 Wis Inf
C: MH/GAR Hill DOD/B: 6/21-23/1927 A: 83/4/25 Died in San Diego
E: John W. Kidder N: Manitowoc Co, Wis 1/27/44 CW: Co D 3 Wis Inf (Pvt) Term: 3 yrs E/D: 5/61-12/65 Madison
   LOS: 4 yrs 6 mos 15 days GAR: 5/26/1923 Died: 6/21/1927 A: 83/4/25 Died at Pacific Beach, San Diego,
   CA Obit: Lists 11 (?) children, no wife mentioned S: DC

King, Albert J.
A: Alb't J. King Co G 15 Ohio Inf
C: MH/GAR Div.2 DOD/B: 6/24-27/1910 A: 73/3/10 N: Poland M: Single
F: Mother Martha E. King 1835-1923 DOD/B: 5/12-16/1923 A: 88/7/15 "Martha Elizabeth"

King, William C.
B: William C. King 1845-1925 Corp Co B 125th Ill Inf
C: GW/Cypress Place DOD/B: 11/17/1925 A: 75
E: W.C. King N: Ohio 1846 CW: Co B 125 Ill Inf (Pvt/Corpl) Term: 3 yrs E/D: 8/62-7/65 Chicago, IL GAR:
   5/14/1921 on transfer from Dept of Illinois S: DC
F: Alice C. King 1869-1951 DOD/B: Record not found

Kingsland, Henry Edmund
A: H.E. Kingsland Co F 35 IA Inf
C: MH/IOOF DOB: 10/1-3/1916 A: 79

Knapp, John
A: Lieut Jno Knapp Co I 97 PA Inf
C: MH/GAR Div.2 DOD/B: 1/29-2/3/1908 A: 71/5/11 N: PA M: Married
F: Christina Knapp No stone DOD/B: 12/19-21/1916 A: 83 "Christiana"

Knoles, Samuel S.
A: Sergt S.S. Knoles Co K 114 Ill Inf
C: MH/Masonic P DOB: 7/31-8/2/1908 A: 68/4/11 N: Indiana M: Married
E: Samuel S. Knoles N: Indiana CW: Co K 114 Ill Vol Inf (Pvt/Sgt) Term: 3 yrs E/D: 8/62-7/65 GAR: 11/10/1894
   Charter Member Datus Coon Post Died: 7/31/1908 A: 68 S: DC
F: Lois B. Knoles No stone DOB: 1/19/1915 A: 76

Knowles, Amos Pendleton
B: "Knowles" stone
C: MH/Masonic A DOD/B: 1/24-26/1892 A: 63 N: American M: Married
D: A.P. Knowles N: Northport, ME A: 51 O: Aparian CW: Co A 8 Cal ___ (Lieut) E/D: 8/64-11/65 LOS: 13 mos
   GAR: 12/22/1881 Died: 1/24/1892--is [grave] stone S: H
F: Anna Knowles "Knowles" stone Note: 1880 census lists Anna, 40, as wife of A. P. Knowles. She is 40, is from
   Germany, as are her parents.

Kooken, John A.
A: J.A. Kooken Co G 3rd PA H A
C: MH/GAR Hill DOD/B: 12/13-16/1894 A: 62 N: American M: Married "John"
D: J.A. Kooken N: Johnstown, PA A: 48 O: Carpenter CW: Co C 152 PA ___ (Pvt) Re-Enl?: Co E 1st MO ___
   (Pvt) E/D: 9/62-2/65 LOS: 29 mos GAR: 10/8/1881 Charter member of Heintzelman Post GAR; first Adjutant
   Died: 12/13/1894--is [grave] stone S: H
F: Anna E. Kooken 1834-1924 WRC DOD/B: 4/14-16/1924 A: 89/10/15 Middle Name Ewalt

Krebs, Augustus
A: August Krebs Co K 3 US Inf
C: MH/GAR Div.2 DOD/B: 9/3-7/1909 A: 80/4/2 N: Poland M: Single "Augustus"

Kretsinger, David L.
A: Lieut D.L. Kretsinger Co G 56 U S C I May 1844-Dec 1910
C: GW/Hawthorne DOD/B: 12/4/1910 A: 66
D: David L. Kretsinger N: Indiana A: 42 O: Editor CW: Co A 10 Kansas Inf (Pvt) Promoted?: Co G 56 US C T
    E/D: 7/61-11/65 due to resignation LOS: 48-55 mos GAR: 8/23/1888 SP: 9/26/1889 DR: 6/30/1891 RE:
    2/11/1896 Post Commander 1900 Died: 12/4/1910 S: H
F: Susan E. Kretsinger Feb 7, 1846-Nov 5, 1940 DOD/B: 11/5/1940 A: No record found

Kroff, Samuel W.
A: S.W. Kroff Co C 12 Ohio Inf
B: Samuel W. Kroff 1841-1906
C: MH/Masonic O DOD/B: 4/7-10/1906 A: 65 N: Ohio M: Married Name Kropp
D: Samuel W. Kroff N: Ohio A: 45 N: Printer CW: Co C 12 Ohio Inf (Pvt) E/D: 6/61-6/62 LOS: 16 mos GAR:
    5/20/1886 SP: 1/30/1888 RE: 8/9/1888 SP: 1/10/1889 RE: 4/10/1900 Died: 4/7/1906--is [grave] stone
    S: H
F: Carla E. Kroff 1849-1943 DOD/B: 12/29-31/1943 A: 94/6/27 Died in San Diego Middle name Exuma or Exuna

Kurth, Andrew H.
B: And'w Kurth Co I 1 Kans Inf
B: Andrew H. Aug 23, 1836-Aug 13, 1912
C: MH/GAR Div.2 DOD/B: 8/13-19/1912 A: 76/2/21 N: Germany M: Married
D: Andrew Kurth N: Germany A: 63 O: Carpenter CW: Co I 1 Kans Inf (Pvt) E/D: 4/61 or 5/61-1/63 due to
    disability LOS: 20 mos GAR: 7/25 or 8/25/1899 Died: 8/13/1912 S: H
F: Susan Wife of A.H. Kurth Born Oct 7, 1844 Died Feb 2, 1904 DOD/B: 2/2-7/1904 A: 57/3/26 N: Amer. M: Marr.

Lamb, Harvey Willard
B: Harvey W. Lamb Nov 9, 1845-Feb 6, 1916 Co C 125 O V I
C: MH/GAR Div.3 DOD/B: 2/6-9/1916 A: 75 "Harvey Willard Lamb"

Lamb, Henry
A: Henry Lamb Co I 2nd Iowa Cav
C: MH/GAR Hill DOD/B: 7/9-??/1897 A: 69 N: American M: Married Coroner's Inquest Report 111-5 513 indicates
    DOD was 7/9/1897 and cause morphine poisoning/suicide San Diego Historical Society Archives record
F: Bertha A. Lamb Aug 29, 1850-June 21, 1936 DOD/B: 6/21-26/1936 A: 86/9/23

Lampman, Granville L.
A: G.L. Lampman Co G 184 NY Inf
C: MH/GAR Div. 2 DOD/B: 5/6-8/1909 A: 75 N: Not stated M: Widower "Granville" "JS" record indicates he died
    of heart disease at 453 5th (Avenue?) on 5/6/1909 Nativity unknown Marital--widower

Langdon, John W.
A: J.W. Langdon Co A 95 Ill Inf
B: John W. Langdon of Co A 95th Ill Reg't Born in Friendship, NY Died May 31, 1896 aged 65 years
C: MH/Div.1 DOD/B: 5/31-6/2/1896 A: 65 N: American M: Widower Coroner's Inquest Report 100-7 476 indicates
    DOD is 5/31/1896 and cause is heart disease San Diego Historical Society Archives record
D: John W. Langdon N: Racine, Wis A: 48 O: Blacksmith CW: Co A 95 Ill Inf (Pvt) E/D: 7/62-8/65 LOS: 36 mos
    GAR: 3/28/1884 SP: 1/10/1889 DR: 6/30/1891 Died: 5/31/1896--is [grave] stone S: H
F: Emily Langdon Born in London, England Died Dec 13, 1895 aged 62 years DOD/B: 12/13-14/1895 A: 59
    "Emily B."

Langdon, Samuel J.
A: Sergt Sam'l Landgon Co G 94 Ill Inf
C: MH/GAR Div.2 DOD/B: 6/4-6/1909 A: 80/__/28 N: Ohio M: Widower
D: Samuel J. Langdon N: Ohio A: 78 O: Retired CW: Co G 94 Ill Inf (Pvt/Sgt) E/D: 8/62-8/65 LOS: Not stated
    GAR: 6/11/1907 (probably on transfer from Major Anderson Post #5 Dept of Idaho Died: 6/1/1909 S: H

Large, Andrew T.
A/B: No stone
C: MH/GAR Hill DOD/B: 5/21-22/1889 A: 71 N: New Jersey M: Widower
D: A. T. Large N: New York A: 40 O: Architect CW: Co D 36 Wis Inf (Pvt/Corpl) E/D: 3/64-7/65 LOS: 16 mos
    GAR: 3/3/1884 D: 11/10/1898 S: H
F: Sarah A. Large No stone DOD/B: 2/14-15/1888 A: 64/10/14 N: Missouri M: Married "Sarah Ann"

Laws, William Henry
A: Wm. Laws Co F 20 US C T
C: MH/GAR Div.3 DOD/B: 7/8-10/1914 A: 64/4/__ R: Black N: PA M: Married "William Henry Laws"
D: William Laws N: Penn A: 46 O: Cook CW: Co F 20 US C T (Pvt) E/D: 12/63-7/65 LOS: 22 mos GAR: 5/8/1894
    SP: 12/27/1898 RE: 5/12/1900 SP: 6/25/1907 S: H
F: Rosetta Laws No stone DOD/B: 10/31-11/4/1943 A: 82/5/14 Race: Black Died in San Diego

Leaming, Edwin R.
B: Edwin R. Leaming 1827-1914 Co F 16th Reg Kansas Cav
C: MH/GAR Hill DOD/B: 1/21-24/1914 A: 87/11/1917 N: New Jersey M: Married "Edward"
F: Minerva L. Leaming 1841-1923 DOD/B: 9/22-25/1923 A: 81/13/__

Lee, Charles P.
A: Chas P. Lee Co K 10 NY H A
C: MH/GAR Hill DOD/B: 10/20-24/1921 A: 78 Title #314 to Mrs. Chas P. Lee
E: Chas P. Lee N: Essex Co, NY 5/8/43 CW: Co K 10 NY H A (Pvt) Term: 3 yrs E/D: 3/64-8/65 Staten Island
    GAR: 8/23/1921 on transfer from Post #78 Dept of Kansas Died: 10/20/1921 A: 78/5/12 S: DC

Lehman, Peter
A/B: No stone
C: MH/GAR Div.3 DOB: 8/6-9/1918 A: 80
D: Peter Lehman N: Germany A: 70 O: Retired CW: Co I 9 Mich Inf (Pvt) E/D: 12/63-9/65 LOS: Not stated GAR:
    1/14/1908 Died: 8/6/1918 S: H

Leibey, Edward Hamilton
A: Edgar H. Leibey Cpl 2 Col Cav
C: MH/GAR Div. 3 DOD/B: 1/1-4/1928 A: 85/4/7 Died in San Diego "Edgar Hamilton"
E: Edward H. Leibey N: Miamisburg, Ohio 8/25/__ CW: Co E 2 Colo Cav (Pvt/Corpl) Term: 3 yrs E/D: 2/63-9/65
    Fort Leavenworth; wounded in Battle of Little Blue, MO during Price Raid GAR: 5/23/1908 on transfer from
    Reynolds Post #33 Dept of Wyoming Died: 1/2/1928 at San Diego Naval Hospital Buried: 1/4/1928 at Mount
    Hope S: DC
F: Virgilla E. Leibey May 22, 1840-Nov 19, 1914 DOD/B: 11/19-21/1914 A: 74/5/27 N: NY M: Married

Leonard, Joseph
A: Major Jos Leonard 96th Ohio Inf
C: MH/Div.4 DOD/B: 8/27/1885-9/2/1887 A: 63 N: Holland M: Married J/S: "Leonard, Joseph, d. 27 Aug (1885),
    63 years, mar, no burial data"
D: Joseph Leonard N: Amsterdam, Holland A: 59 O: Cabinet Maker CW: Co B 96 Ohio ___ (Capt/Major) E/D:
    7/62-11/64 LOS: 2 yrs GAR: 10/8/1881 Charter Member of Heintzelman Post GAR; first Quartermaster
    Died: "Died"--is [grave] stone S: H
F: Maria C. Leonard No stone DOD/B: 2/21-22/1877 A: 55/4/__ N: Vermont M: Married Obit/San Diego Herald,
    2/21/1877: "In this city on Wednesday 2/21, Mrs. Maria C. Leonard, aged 53 yrs 6 mos, a native of
    Montpelier, VT, wife of Joseph Leonard. Funeral at the Episcopal Church."

Leonard, William
A: Wm. Leonard Co K 2nd NJ Inf
C: MH/GAR Hill DOD/B: 1/2-4/1893 or 6/2-4/1893 A: 57 "John William Lenard"
D: Wm Leonard N: Baltimore, MD A: 45 O: Tailor CW: CO K 2 NJ __ (Pvt) E/D: 5/61-6/64 LOS: 3 yrs GAR: 10/8/1881 Charter Member of Heintzelman Post GAR; first QM Sergeant Died: 1893 S: H

Leslie, G. H.
B: Serg't G.H. Leslie Co D 4th NY H A
C: MH/Div.6 DOD/B: 2/24-26/1905 A: 64 N: American M: Married

Levings, John K.
A/B: No stone
C: Cremated
E: John K. Levings N: Canada 1844 CW: Co D 1 Nev Cav (Pvt) Term: 3 yrs E/D: 8/63-11/65 GAR: Date not stated "Commander of Post Cal/Nev" Died: 3/18/1929 Cremated S: DC

Lewis, Charles W.
A: Charles W. Lewis Colonel 7 Calif Inf
C: MH/IOOF DOB: 1891 A: Not stated Died in San Diego "Capt"

Light, Jacob J.
A: J.J. Light Co C 31 Ind Inf (or Co G)
C: MH/Div.6 DOD/B: 10/30-11/1/1905 A: 70 N: Indiana M: Widower

Lilley, James
A: James Lilley Co K 114 US C Inf
C: MH/GAR Div.2 DOD/B: 7/15-19/1934 A: 88/11/14 Race: Black Died in San Diego

Limebeck, George H.
A: Geo. H. Limebeck Co E 30 Mich Inf
B: GW/Laurel Place DOD/B: 1/16-20/1911 A: 69
D: George H. Limebeck N: New York A: 45 O: Mechanic CW: Co E 30 Mich Inf (Pvt) E/D: 11/64-6/65 LOS: 7 mos GAR: 2/2/1882 SP: 6/30/1888 SP: 1/10/1889 DR: 6/30/1891 RE: 3/11/1899 Post Commander 1910 (date hard to read) Died: 1/16/1911 S: H
F: Emma Limebeck DOD/B: 3/9/1905-9/11/1909 A: 65

Lince, Cornelius
A: Cornelius Lince Co C 44 Wis Inf
C: MH/GAR Div.2 DOD/B: 6/1-3/1911 A: 87/5/7 N: New York M: Married
D: Cornelius Lince N: New York A: 86 O: Retired CW: Co C 44 Wis Inf (Pvt) E/D: __/64-9/65 LOS: Not stated GAR: 2/8/1910 Died: 6/1/1911 S: H
F: Esther E. Lince No stone DOD/B: 5/3-6/1912 A: 78/__/28 N: NY M: Widow

Lindsey, Dennis
A: Dennis Lindsey Co A 48 Wis Inf
C: MH/Masonic U DOD/B: 9/17-19/1928 A: 81/10/__ (record filed under "Lindsay")

Lingenfelter, Deliscus
A: Lieut D. Lingenfelter Co D 68 Ind Inf
C: MH/Div.4 DOD/B: 1/26-29/1912 A: 82/4/9 N: KY M: Widower
F: Elizabeth Lingenfelter Died Nov 3, 1894 aged 65 years "Oh Loving Wife and Mother Gone from Us But Safe With Jesus" DOD/B: 11/3-5/1894 A: 65 N: American M: Married

Livingston, Frederick W.
A: F.W. Livingston Asst Hosp Stwd 14 Ill Cav
C: MH/GAR Hill DOB: 5/28-31/1908 A: 74/8/16

Livingston, Frederick W. (Con't)
E: F.W. Livingston N: Jerico, Chittenden Co, VT CW: Co A 14 Ill Cav (Pvt/QM Sgt) Term: 3 yrs E/D: 9/62-7/65
    Pulaski, TN GAR: 7/25/1895 on transfer from San Jacinto Post #121 Dept of Cal/Nev Died: 5/28/1908
    A: 75 Bur: GAR (Mount Hope) S: DC
F: Mary E. Livingston 1849-1934 DOD/B: 3/25-27/1934 A: 84/8__ Died in San Diego

Lockwood, Nathan S.
A: N.S. Lockwood Co A 2nd Ind Cav
C: MN/GAR Hill DOD/B: 9/14-16/1896 A: 59/9/6 N: American M: Married
D: Nathan Lockwood N: Springfield, Ohio A: 46 O: Builder CW: Co A 2 Ind Inf (Pvt) E/D: 9/61-10/64 LOS: 36 mos
    GAR: 3/22/1883 Died: 9/22/1896--is [grave] stone S: H
F: Ella D. Lockwood No stone DOD/B: 12/29-31/1918 A: 73/1/14

Logan, William King
B: William King Logan 1847-1928 Confederate Soldier
C: MH/Confederate DOD/B: 11/10-12/1928 A: 81/8/6 Died in San Diego
        Note: William K. Logan was born in 1847; Died in 1928 in San Diego, CA S: UDC document,
        California Room (see Chapter II, "San Diego Public Library" sources)

Lohr, Henry
B: Henry Lohr Co K 18 Penn Cav
B: Rev. Henry July 2, 1846-Sept 17, 1922
C: MH/Div.6 DOD/B: 9/17-20/1922 A: 76/2/15
D: Henry Lohr N: Penn A: 50 O: Minister R: Otay (near San Diego) CW: Co K 18 PA Cav (Corpl) E/D: 9/62-7/65
    LOS: 36 mos GAR: 11/9/1897 SP: 12/27/1898 RE: 10/23/1900 TR: 10/23/1900 GAR: 9/23/1919 Died:
    9/17/1922 S: H
F: Hattie Mar 2, 1866 DOD/B: 10/21-25/1951 A: 85 Died in San Diego

Lombardy, Frank K.
A: Sergt Frank K. Lombardy Co C (or Co G) 29 US Inf
B: Frank K. Lombardy
C: MH/Masonic P DOD/B: 6/21-23/1917 A: 68
F: His Wife Elizabeth Lombardy DOD/B: 7/1-5/1924 A: 84/8/19

Loomis, M.S.
A: M.S. Loomis Co B 5th Cal Inf (tombstone visible at Calvary Cemetery)
C: CAL/Sec.1, North, Row 14-4 DOD/B: No record found in Catholic cemetery index
D: M.S. Loomis N: Missouri A: 54 O: Miner CW: Co B 5 Cal Inf (Pvt) E/D: 10/61-9/66 LOS: 58 mos GAR:
    9/22/1887 Died: 10/20/1888--is [grave] stone S: H
F: "Mrs. Loomis" on group pioneer commemorative marker at Calvary Cemetery DOD/B: No record found

Loper, Newton
B: Newton Loper Co A 69 NY Inf Civil War Mar 29, 1850-Oct 26, 1921
C: MH/GAR Hill DOD/B: 10/26-31/1921 A: 71

Loring, William Edward
B: Wm E. Loring 1842-1924 Co E 141st Regt Penn Vols
C: MH/GAR Hill DOD/B: 5/3-7/1924 A: 82/1/25
E: W.E. Loring N: Newark Co, NY CW: Co E 141 PA Inf (Pvt/Sgt) Term: 3 yrs E/D: 8/62-5/64 Philadelphia, PA due
    to disability GAR: 8/28/1898 Died: 5/3/1924 A: 82/6/25 S: DC
F: Anne Cameron Loring No stone DOD/B: 2/2-7/1947 A: 87/11/21 Died in San Diego

Louck, James H.
A/B: No stone
C: MH/GAR Hill DOD/B: 11/25-27/1891 A: 54 N: American M: Married "Louks"

Louck, James H. (Con't)
D: J.H. Loucks N: New York A: 48 O: Bath House Keeper CW: Co D 2 NY L A (Pvt) E/D: 9/62-5/65 LOS: 32 mos GAR: 3/10/1887 SP: 9/26/1889 DR: 6/30/1891 Died: 11/25/1891--is [grave] stone S: H

Loud, Charles A.
A: Lieut Chas A. Loud Co G 88 U S C T
C: MH/IOOF DOD/B: 10/2-4/1913 A: 70/5/14
D: Charles A. Loud N: Maine A: 66 O: Retired CW: Co F 41 Mass Inf (Pvt) Promoted?: Co G 88 US C T (2nd Lieut) E/D: 8/62-6/64 due to resignation LOS: Not Stated GAR: 3/23/1910 Died: 10/2/1913 S: H
F: Rhoda W. Tay Loud Born in Medford, Mass March 2, 1854 Died in San Diego Nov 6, 1917 DOB: 11/6-8/1917 A: 62

Low, Francis M.
A: Francis M. Low Co G 137 Ill Inf
C: MH/GAR Div.3 DOD/B: 2/19-23/1915 A: about 70

Luce, Moses A.
B: Moses A. Luce May 1842-April 1933
C: GW/Hawthorne DOD/B: 4/23-25/1933 A: 90
D: Moses A. Luce N: Payson, Ill A: 39 O: Attorney CW: Co E 4 Mich Vols (Pvt/Sgt) E/D: 6/61-6/64 LOS: 3 yrs GAR: 10/8/1881 Charter Member/1st Post Commander of Heintzelman Post GAR SP: 1/30/1893 RE: 3/26/1895 Died: 4/25/1933 S: H (Medal of Honor Winner)
Note: In *Medal of Honor Winners 1863-1963* (Washington: Government Printing Office, 1964), prepared for the Subcommittee of Veterans' Affairs of the Committee on Labor and Public Welfare, U.S. Senate, Government Printing Office, 1964, p. 500, the entry for Moses A. Luce is: Rank and Organization: Sergeant, Company E, 4th Michigan Infantry. Place and date: At Laurel Hill, VA, 10 May 1864 Entered service at: _____ Birth: _____ Date of issue: 7 February 1895. Citation: Voluntarily returned in the face of the advancing enemy to the assistance of a wounded and helpless comrade, and carried him, at imminent peril, to a place of safety." [This reference book is at the Family History Center, San Diego, CA, Call No. 973.0 M2y]

Note: On p. 46 of Samuel F. Black's *San Diego County, California: A Record of Settlement, Organization, Progress and Achievement*, Vol 1 (Chicago: S.J. Clarke Publishing Company, 1913) (copy at the Family History Center, Call No. 979.498 H2b Vol 1) is stated: "He [Moses A. Luce] was awarded the Congressional Medal of Honor for bravery displayed at the Battle of Spottsylvania and, while yet in his teens at the time of enlistment, his valor and loyalty equalled that of many a Veteran twice his years."
F: Adelaide Mantania Luce Sept 1858-May 1928 (Note: Daughter of James Mantania, Civil War Veteran of this study, and Olive B. Mantania) DOD/B: 5/7-10/1928 A: No record found

Luckett, Alexander
A: Alex Luckett Co G 32 US C T
C: MH/GAR Hill DOD/B: 9/16-17/1896 A: 80 N: American Race: Black M: Married
D: Alexander Luckett N: Penn A: 77 O: Laborer CW: Co G 32 US C T (Pvt) E/D: 2/64-8/65 LOS: 18 mos GAR: 6/26/1894 Died: 9/26/1896--is [grave] stone S: H
F: Martha J. Luckett No stone DOD/B: 2/20-22/1909 A: 83/1/29 N: PA M: Widow Race: Black Died in San Diego

Lufbery, George F.
B: Geo F. Lufbery 1839-1911 Veteran of the Civil War
C: GW/Laurel Place DOD/B: 4/19-24/1911 A: 71
F: Martha Adeline Linn 1824-1911 At Rest (wife?) DOD/B: No record found

Lyman, James O.
A: Jas O. Lyman Co A 9 Ind Cav
C: MH/GAR Div.3 DOD/B: 3/23-26/1914 A: 76/8/27 N: Ohio M: Widower Died in San Diego
E: J.O. Lyman N: Andover, Ashtabula Co, Ohio 6/26/37 CW: Co A 9 Ind Cav (Com Sgt) Term: 3 yrs E/D: 10/63-

Lyman, James O. (Con't)
    5/65 Vicksburg, Miss due to sickness (McPherson General Hospital) GAR: 11/26/1904 Died: 3/23/1914
        A: 76/8/__ Buried: GAR (Mount Hope) S: DC

Mackey, Clarke D.
A: Clarke D. Mackey Co E 3 NY Inf
C: MH/Masonic M DOB: 2/1/1915 A: About 75

Magee, Thomas Lee
A/B: No stone
C: MH/Masonic K DOD/B: 1/1-3/1929 A: 92/2/18
D: Thos L. Magee N: Ohio A: 49 O: Physician CW: Co __ 51 Ill Inf (Asst. Surg/Surg) E/D: 11/62-9/65 LOS: 34
    mos GAR: 10/22/1885 SP: 3/28/1899 RE: 12/22/1903 D: 12/22/1903 Post Commander 1890 S: H
E: Thomas L. Magee N: Guernsey Co, Ohio CW: Co __ 51 Ill Vol Inf (Asst Surg/1st Lieut/Major/Surgeon) Term:
    3 yrs E/D: 11/62-9/65 Camp Erwin GAR: 12/26/1903 from Heintzelman Post San Diego S:DC
F: Elizabeth S. (Sarah Elizabeth) No stone DOD/B: 10/9-11/1904 A: 70/2/25 N: American Married
    OBIT: Notable career as a Civil War surgeon, leaving the service with the rank of Major. Gen. Phil Sheridan
    praised him for his excellent war record. Youngest surgeon in command at age 26. With Gen. Sheridan at
    the battle of Stone River and Chicamauga; amputated hundreds of legs and arms in field hosptals; attended
    thousands of soldiers on some of the bloodiest fights of the Sheridan campaign. His great-grandfather
    crossed the Delaware with George Washington. Member Baptist Church 77 years; Master Mason; 4 terms
    as city health officer in San Diego; surgeon with Santa Fe railroad in San Diego; member US Pension Board;
    survived by two sons.

Majors, Archibald C.
A/B: No stone
C: Cremated
E: Archib.C. Majors N: Adams Co, IL 8/31/43 CW: Co B 43 MO Inf (Pvt) Term: 1 yr E/D: 2/65-7/65 Benton
    Barracks due to disability Re-Enl: Co A 50 MO Inf (Pvt) E/D: 7/65-____ GAR: 10/10/1927 Died:
    11/13/1930 A: 87 Cremated S: DC

Malson, Nathan
A: Nathan Malson Co B 2 Wis Inf
C: MH/GAR Hill DOD/B: 6/20-22/1892 A: 49 N: American M: Married
F: Lizzie Malson died Feb 4, 1898 aged 54 years DOD/B: 2/4-5/1898 A: 47 N: American M: Widow "Lizzie V."

Manning, Phillip
B: Phillip Manning Jan 31, 1838-Oct 1, 1909 Co F 2nd PA Heavy Art
C: MH/GAR Div.2 DOD/B: 10/1-3/1909 A: 71/8/__ N: PA
F: Barbara A. Manning Feb 9,1850-Oct 9,1935 DOD/B: 10/9-11/1935 A: 85/8/0 Died in San Diego "Barbara Ann"

Mantania, James D.
A: Corpl J.D. Mantania Co I 72nd Ill Inf
B: James D. Mantania 1808-1880
C: MH/Div.3 DOD/B: 4/24-26/1880 A: 52 N: New York M: Married "Mantania" J/S: Mantania, J.D., bu 24 Apr
    (1880), 52 yrs, b. NY, male, mar, bur City Cem" Obit/San Diego Herald, 4/24/1880: "In this city April 23,
    James D. Mantania, a native of Orange Co, VT(?) and late of Avon, IL, aged 52 yrs. Notice of funeral
    hereafter."
F: Olive B. Mantania 1831-1909 DOD/B: 12/23-24/1909 A: 78/10/1 N: NY M: Widow "Mantana"

Marrs, David L.
A: David Marrs Co B 48 IA Inf
C: MH/GAR Div.2 DOD/B: 2/26-28/1918 A: 69/11/2
D: David L. Marrs N: Indiana A: 43 O: Rancher CW: Co B 48 IA Inf (Pvt) E/D: 5/64-10/64 LOS: 5 mos GAR:
    12/23/1891 SP: 12/27/1894 RE: 5/11/1897 Died: 2/26/1918 S: H
F: Mary M. Marrs No stone DOD/B: 5/11-14/1917 A: 73

Marshall, Edmund
B: Edmund Marshall 1833-1928 Co D 118 Reg Inf
C: MH/GAR Hill DOD/B: 5/25-28/1928 A: 95/6/28 Race: Black Died in San Diego
D: Edmund Marshall N: Kentucky A: 50 O: Laborer CW: Co D 118 US C T (Pvt) E/D: 8/64-2/66 LOS: 18 mos
    GAR: 11/26/1890 SP: 6/26/1894 RE: 12/30/1894 Died: 5/25/1928 S: H
F: Martha 1838-1896 DOD/B: 4/5-6/1896 A: 58 N: American M: Married Race: White "Mrs. Martha"

Marshall, John H.
B: Capt John H. Marshall Born June 19, 1845 Died September 7, 1905 Our Beloved Husband
C: MH/Div.5 DOD/B: 9/8-11/1905 A: 60/4/10 N: Maine M: Married "vault" burial
F: Ellen M. Marshall, An Adored and Adoring Wife and Mother Died December 8, 1892 aged 46 years DOD/B:
    12/8-11/1892 A: 46 N: American M: Married "Vault--removed Dec. 1893"

Marshall, William P.
B: Wm. P. Marshall Band Master 30 Regt Wis Vol Inf 1840-1923
C: MH/GAR Hill DOD/B: 10/16-20/1923 A: 83/7/3
D: William P. Marshall N: Indiana A: 63 O: Farmer CW: Co K 30 Wis Inf (Pvt/Drum Major) E/D: 8/62-8/65 LOS:
    36 1/2 mos GAR: 11/22/1904 Died: 10/18/1923 S: H
F: Caroline F. 1847-1924 DOD/B: 6/17-19/1924 A: 77/3/13

Marston, George
B: Col Geo. Marston died at Horton House San Diego, Calif Aug 16, 1888 aged 64 years.
C: MH/Div.3 DOD/B: 8/16-28/1888 A: 64 N: New Hampshire M: Widower
F: Miss Etta L. Marston 1845-1924 DOD/B: 2/23-3/1/1924 A: 78 "Etta L. Marston"

Martin, Elihu G.
A: E.G. Martin Co G 29 IA Inf
C: MH/IOOF DOB: 8/22-23/1906 A: 74/5/16 N: Ohio M: Widower "Elihu" (probable veteran)

Martin, Joseph
A: Joseph Martin Co I 6th NY H A
C: MH/GAR Hill DOD/B: 12/25-26/1897 A: 56 N: Hungarian M: Single
D: Joseph Martin N: Hungary A: 53 O: Druggist CW: Co I 5 NY Art (Pvt) E/D: 3/64-8/65 LOS: 16 mos GAR:
    3/27/1894 TR: 10/22/1894 S: H
E: Jos. Martin N: Comowy, Austro/Hungary 1841 CW: Co I 5 NY H A (Pvt) Term: 1 yr E/D: 3/64-9/65 GAR:
    11/10/1894 Charter member of Datus Coon Post Died: 12/5/1897 A: 56 Obit: He enlisted in Co I 6 NY
    Art (Pvt) on 3/23/63; on re-enl, made a U.S. Army Hospital Steward in 1869; se'rved 30 years, retiring on
    10/28/1893 S: DC Note: County death record indicates he died on 12/25/1897.

Mate, W.B.
A: W.B. Mate Assistant Steward US Navy
C: MH/Near GAR Hill DOD/B: No record found

Mathenia, William Samuel
B: Wm. S. Mathenia 1839-1930 Co D 64th Ill Vol Inf
C: MH/GAR Div.2 DOD/B: 3/23-29/1930 A: About 86 Died in San Diego
E: Saml Mathenia N: Tuscarowa, Ohio 1842 CW: Co D 64 Ill Inf (Pvt) Term: 3 yrs E/D: 1/65-6/65 GAR:
    6/28/1924 SP 9/24/1927 Died: 3/23/1930 S: DC

Matot, Edmund L.   Note: Family moved from Vermont to San Diego in 1887, lived in "New Town",
A: Edmond Matot 2 VT L A   according to *San Diego County Pioneer Families*
C: MH/Div.6 DOD/B: 11/1-4/1918 A: 76/9/12
E: Edmund L. Matot N: Sudsbury, VT 1/20/42 CW: Co __ 2 Vt Batt (Pvt) Term: Unstated E/D: 12/61-1/63 New
    Orleans due to disability GAR: 11/27/1896 on transfer from C.J. Ormsbee Post #18 Dept of VT
    T: 1/8/1916 Died: 12/1918 Buried: Mount Hope S: DC
F: Emma B. No stone DOD/B: 12/12-14/1902 A: 53/10/__ N: American M: Married

Matson, Albert E.
A: Albert E. Matson Co I 132 Ill Inf
C: MH/Div.3 DOD/B: 12/4-6/1909 A: 68/5/__ N: Ohio M: Married
F: Belle Matson No stone DOD/B: No record found

Mattern, Henry J.
B: Henry J. Mattern Co E 1st Reg Ill Light Artillery 1845-1924
C: MH/GAR Div.2 DOD/B: 11/24-26/1924 A: 79/9/14
F: Josie W Wife of Henry J. Mattern 1852-1935 DOD/B: 10/6-8/1935 A: 83/1/3 Died in San Diego
    "Josephine W."

Matthews, Thomas
B: In memory of Captain Thomas E. Matthews Born Dec 6,1831 Died Jan 23,1903
C: MH/Div.1 DOD/B: 1/23-25/1903 A: 71/1/18 N: American M: Married

Maxwell, Wilton P.
B: Major W.P. Maxwell June 1, 1832-Mar 30, 1919 A native of Hamilton, Ohio
C: MH/Confederate DOD/B: 3/30-4/1/1919 A: 86/9/29
    Note: Wilton P. Maxwell was born 6/1/1832 in Hamilton, Ohio; Died 3/3/1919 in San Diego, CA. He
    was Pvt, Co C 4th Texas Infantry. Discharged 6/2/1862 because of loss of right hand at Battle of
    Gaines Mill, Virginia. Called "Major". S: UDC document, California Room (see Chapter II, "San
    Diego Public Library" sources)

Maynard, Chauncey J.
A: Capt C.J. Maynard Co C 31 IA Inf
C: MH/Div.6 DOD/B: 12/1-4/1910 A: 75/5/27
D: Chauncey J. Maynard N: New York A: 68 O: Printer CW: Co C 31 Iowa Inf (Capt) E/D: 7/62-2/63 LOS: 8 mos
    GAR: 1/26/1904 (probably on transfer from Reno Post #35 Dept of South Dakota) Died: 12/1/1910 S:H
F: Cordelia B. Maynard No stone DOD/B: 3/16-19/1923 A: 91/1/17

Maynard, Cloice S.
B: Cloice S. Maynard Oct 12, 1846-July 16, 1927 Co D 64 Ohio Inf
C: MH/GAR Hill DOD/B: 7/15-23/1927 A: 80 Died in San Diego
E: Cloice S. Maynard N: Marseilles, Ohio 10/12/46 CW: Co I 135 Ohio N G (Pvt) Term: 100 days E/D: 5/64-9/64
    Columbus, Ohio Re-Enl: Co D 64 Ohio Inf (Pvt) E/D: 5/65-1/66 Columbus, Ohio LOS: 1 yr, 1 mo, 10 days
    GAR: 1/14/1913 Died: 7/18/1927 Phoenix, AZ A: 80/9/6 Buried: 7/20/1927 S: DC
F: Theodara E. May 20, 1853-Apr 20, 1925 DOD/B: 4/20-25/1925 A: 72/11/__ "Theodora Estelle"

McCarty, John
A: Jno McCarty Co F 3rd NY L A (tombstone visible at Calvary Cemetery)
C: CAL/Sec.3, North 2/3, A-14 DOD/B: There is a burial record for John McCarthy DOD/B: 5/15-18/1891 A: 51 N:
    Canada Parents: Bart McCarthy and Margaret Luskin Cause of death: Heart disease

McClelland, William Thomas
A: Wm. T. McClelland Co G 30 Ill Inf
C: MH/GAR Div.3 DOD/B: 4/11-14/1913 A: 79 M: Married
D: William T. McClelland N: Penn A: 52 O: Farmer R: Campo, CA CW: Co G 30 Ill Inf (Pvt/Sgt) E/D: 9/61-11/62
    due to wounds LOS: 14 mos GAR: 8/17/1886 DR: 6/30/1891 RE: 5/14/1901 Died: 4/11/1913 S: H
F: Mattie A. McClelland No stone DOD/B: 2/7-8/1934 A: 77/8/13 Died in Chula Vista, CA

McConnell, James E.
A: James E. McConnell Sgt Co B 11 PA Cav
C: MH/GAR Hill DOD/B: 5/29-6/2/1932 A: 89/__/27 Died in La Mesa, CA
E: Jas E. McConnell N: ? location 5/2/43 CW: Co B 11 PA Cav (Pvt) Term: 3 yrs E/D: 10/61-1/64 Williamsburg,
    VA Re-Enl: Co B 4 PA Cav (Sgt) E/D: 2/64-8/64 Richmond, VA GAR: 4/23/1923 on transfer from John
    A. Logan Post #180 Dept of Cal/Nev SP: 9/24/1927 S: DC

McConnell, James E. (Con't)
F: Lulu M. McConnell No stone DOD/B: 1/8-10/1892 A: 23 N: American M: Married "Lula M. AKA Mary Louisa Ashton McConnell"

McConville, Patrick Henry
A: P.H. McConville Co G 12 US Inf (only this tombstone is visible at Calvary Cemetery)
B: In memory of Patrick Henry McConville Born in New York City Died Jan 17, 1907 aged 63 yrs 10 mos 7 d's May his soul rest in peace
C: CAL/Sec.3, North 2/3, Row B-17 (Block B, Lot 17) DOD/B: 1/17/1907 and 1/17/1908 (two dates listed) A: 63 N: New York City "JS" record indicates a "Patrick Henry Mc(Conyer?) died on 1/17/1907 of paralysis Nativity New York Marital: Married Age: 63/6/7
D: Patrick H. McConville N: New York A: 57 O: Lumberman CW: Co C 12 US Inf (Pvt) E/D: 5/62-5/65 LOS: 36 mos GAR: 12/10/1901 Died: 1/18/1907--is [grave] stone S: H
F: Katherine McConville DOD/B: No record found in Catholic cemetery index Note: Katherine is listed in the 1909 City Directory as being widow to Patrick McConville.

McCoy, William Hill
B: W.H. McCoy 1844-1922
C: MH/Confederate DOD/B: 4/8-10/1922 A: 77
   Note: William H. McCoy was born 4/15/1844 in Virginia; Died 4/3/1922 in San Diego, CA. S: UDC document, California Room (see Chapter II, "San Diego Public Library" sources)

McCrumb, John W.
A: Sergt J.W. McCrumb Co A 14 PA Cav
C: MH/GAR Hill DOD/B: 8/12-16/1903 A: 68 N: American M: Single

McDonald, J. Wade
B: J. Wade McDonald Into Thy Hand, Oh Judge of Judges, I Commit My Cause and Close My Case
C: GW/Laurel Place DOD/B: 7/27-28/1910 A: 66/10/17
D: J. Wade McDonald N: Illinois A: 47 O: Lawyer CW: Co E 20 Ill Inf (Pvt) E/D: 6/61-9/62 due to wounds LOS: 15 mos GAR: 7/22/1891 Died: 7/27/1910 S: H
F: Ann McDonald Steffes DOD/B: 4/4-7/1942 A: 78

McDowell, C.H.
A: Corpl C.H. McDowell Co G 2 DC Inf
C: MH/Div.7 DOD/B: 9/24-26/1912 A: 71/6/11 N: New York M? Married
F: Elizabeth McDowell No stone DOD/B: 2/15-18/1927 A: 75/5/19 Died in National City "Mrs. Elizabeth"

McDuell, James H.
A: Jas H. McDuell Co I 123 Ohio Inf
C: MH/Div.1 DOD/B: 9/8-9/1911 A: 79 N: Washington, D.C. M: Married
F: Norma M. McDuell July 23, 1869-July 19, 1952 DOD/B: 7/19-28/1952 A: 83 (ashes) Died: Glendale, CA Date of Birth: 7/23/1869 "Nora Melvina"

McGirl, Barney
A: Barney McGirl Co ___ 2nd Regt Kansas Inf (tombstone not visible at Calvary Cemetery; FHC information)
B: Barney McGirl Born County Leitrim, Ireland Died Oct 27, 1906 aged 77 years
C: CAL/Sec.3, Block B, Lot 15 DOD/B: No record found in Catholic cemetery index

McIntosh, Daniel
A: Sergt Dan'l McIntosh Co E 5 US Cav B: Daniel McIntosh 1844-1912 Bat D 3rd Art
C: MH/Div.3 DOD/B: 11/18-21/1912 A: 67/11/19 N: Scotland M: Single

McIntosh, F.J.
A: F.J. McIntosh Co B 10 NY H A
C: MH/GAR Hill DOD/B: 4/26-30/1900 A: 72 N: American M: Married

McIntosh, F.J. (Con't)
D: F.J. McIntosh N: New York A: 57 O: Shoe Maker CW: Co B 10 NY Arty (Pvt) E/D: 8/62-6/65 LOS: 2 11/12 yrs GAR: 5/20/1886 SP: 1/10/1889 DR: 6/30/1891 Died: 4/10/1900--is [grave] stone S: H

McIntosh, Henry Curtis
A: Henry G. McIntosh Co G 2 Ill L A
C: MH/IOOF DOB: 1/10/1918 A: 73
D: Henry C. McIntosh N: Elmira, NY A: 72 O: Retired CW: Co F 67 Ill Inf (Pvt) E/D: 5/62-__/__ Re-Enl?: Co G 2 Ill L A (Pvt) E/D: 1/63-9/65 LOS: 40 mos GAR: 8/14/1917 on transfer from Post #31 Dept of Iowa. Died: 1/10/1918 S: H
F: Mary E. Rhodes McIntosh 1844-1945 DOD/B: 2/24-27/1945 A: 100/4/16 Died in San Diego "Mary Elizabeth"

McKenna, Augustine P.
B: Augustine P. McKenna Corporal Co G 61st Ohio Reg Born January 6, 1842 Perry Co, Ohio Died March 1, 1897 San Diego, CA (tombstone visible at Calvary Cemetery)
C: CAL/Sec.2, North 2/3, D-26 (Block D, Lot 26) DOD/B: No record found in Catholic cemetery index

McLaren, Benjamin F.
A/B: No stone
C: MH/GAR Hill DOD/B: 3/16-21/1930 A: 90 Died in Yuma, AZ
D: Benjamin McLaren N: Vermont A: 55 O: Civil Engineer CW: USS Pensacola (Landsman/Yeoman) E/D: 1/63-6/64 LOS: 17 mos? GAR: 8/27/1895 SP: 9/28/1897 RE: 6/__/1898 SP: 3/26/1907 RE: 12/24/1907 Died: 3/16/1930 S:H
F: Martha M. McLeran 1836-1912 DOB: 5/4-7/1912 A: 75/10/15 N: MA M: Married

McPheeters, Alpheus Leroy
A: Corpl A.W. McPheeters Co H 5 Wis Inf
C: MH/Div.6 DOD/B: 7/16-17/1929 A: 68/__/27 Died in San Diego "Alphius Leroy"
F: Mary McPheeters (possible wife) No stone DOD/B: 11/25-28/1927 A: 78 Died in National City, CA Buried in Div.5

McSurely, Anderson
A/B: No stone search undertaken
C: CMTD DOD/B: No record found
E: Anderson McSurely N: Van Buren Co, Iowa 1845 CW: Co G 3 Iowa Inf (Pvt) Term: 3 yrs E/D: 5/63-8/65 GAR: 6/28/1924 Died: 2/25/1926 Cremated S: DC

Means, Thomas Decater
B: Thos D. Means 1846-1939 7th Ill Cav GAR
C: MH/Div.6 DOD/B: 9/20-23/1939 A: 93/7/9 Died in San Diego "Decater"
F: Viola Means 1857-1928 DOD/B: 5/11-15/1928 A: 70/8/13 Died in San Diego

Mellus, Frances G.
A: Frances G. Mellus Co E 2 ME Cav
C: MH/GAR Hill DOD/B: 10/22-25/1909 A: 67/7/9 N: Maine M: Married
D. Frank G. Mellus N: Maine A: 55 O: Mariner CW: Co C 4 ME Inf (Pvt) Re-Enl?: Co __ 2 ME Cav (Pvt) Re-Enl?: U.S.S. Louisville (Seaman) E/D: 6/61-9/62 LOS: 15 mos GAR: 4/12/1898 Died: 10/22/1909 S: H
F: Mary Josephine Mellus No stone DOD/B: 8/3-5/1913 A: 64 N: Not stated M: Widow

Merritt, Thomas W.
A: Thos W. Merritt Co G 11 PA Inf 1837-1913
C: GW/Cypress Place DOD/B: 1/28-2/1/1913 A: 76
F: Alma C. Merritt 1839-1921 DOD/B: 8/7-10/1921 A: 82

Meserve, William N.
A: William M. Meserve Major 4 Mass Hv Art'y
C: MH/GAR Div.6 DOD/B: 10/6-10/1928 A: 84/5/27 Died in San Diego

Meyer, Christian Y.
B: Capt C. Meyer 1835-1920 Civil War Veteran
C: MH/GAR Hill DOD/B: 4/24-28/1920 A: 85/4/28 "Christian Y." "Capt"
F: Addie Meyer No stone DOD/B: 11/6/1929-3/11/1931 A: 40 Died in San Diego "Addie Meyers"

Miles, John F.
A/B: No stone
C: MH/Masonic J DOD/B: 12/4-5/1902 A: 84 N: American M: Single Is this him?
D: J.F. Miles N: Illinois A: 65 O: Druggist CW: Co __ 35 Ill Inf (RQM) E/D: 7/61-9/64 LOS: 38 mos GAR: 6/28/1883 Died: "Dead"--is [grave] stone S: H

Milford, David
A: David Milford Co A 6 PA H A
C: MH/GAR Div. 3 DOD/B: 11/26-27/1916 A: 88 E 1/2 lot reserved for wife
F: Jane Milford No stone DOB: 3/29-29/1920 A: about 90

Miller, Albert Judson
A: A.J. Miller Co B 25 (or 26) Ill Inf
C: MH/Div.6 DOD/B: 6/7-8/1905 A: 69/1/4 N: American M: Married
E: Albert Judson Miller N: Franklin Co, VT CW: Co A 11 Ill Inf (Pvt) Term: 3 mos E/D: 4/61-__/__ S: DC
F: Lucretia Miller No stone found DOD/B: No record in boxes/name on lot card only

Miller, Charles F.
A: Corpl C.F. Miller Co F 6 US Cav
C: MH/GAR Hill DOD/B: 5/5-7/1901 A: 68 N: German M: Widower
D: Charles Miller N: Germany A: 59 O: Soldier CW: Co F 6 US Cav (Pvt) E/D: 4/62-4/65 LOS: 36 mos GAR: 10/11/1892 TR: 8/8/1893 S: H
E: Chas Miller N: Germany CW: Co F 6 US Cav (Pvt) Term: 3 yrs E/D: 4/62-4/65 GAR: 11/10/1894 Charter Member of Datus Coon Post Died: 5/5/1901 A: 66 S: DC

Miller, John G.C.
A: Lieut John G.C. Miller Co E 14 Ind Inf
C: MH/GAR Hill DOD/B: "no records--govt. stone only" Died in San Diego "John C."

Miller, Swan A.
B: Swan A. Miller Mar 11, 1941 GAR
C: GW/Cypress Place DOD/B: No record found
F: Eda M., Wife of S.A. Miller Mar 18, 1921 DOD/B: Call cemetery office for information.

Miller, William Keith
A: Wm. Miller Co E 3 IA Cav
C: MH/GAR Hill DOD/B: 5/8-10/1921 A: 77/1/26 "Wm Keith"
D: William Miller N: Indiana A: 58 O: Farmer CW: Co E 3 Iowa Cav (Pvt) E/D: 8/61-8/65 LOS: 48 mos GAR: 3/24/1903 SP: 12/27/1904 DR: 12/24/1918 S: H

Millichamp, Stephen W.
A: Sergt W. Millichamp Co F 1 Mich Cav
B: Stephen W. Millichamp Born Sept 23, 1844 Died April 28, 1911 2nd Lieut 1st Michigan Cav
C: MH/Masonic O DOD/B: 4/28-5/1/1911 A: 67/7/5 (Moved to Masonic Cemetery 5/26/1919)
E: Stephen Millichamp N: St. Claire, Michigan CW: Co F 1 Mich Cav (Pvt/Sgt) Term: 3 yrs E/D: 3/62-3/65 Winchester, VA GAR: 3/26/1897 on transfer from Emmet Crawford Post #19 Dept of Texas Died: 4/28/1911 A: 67 Buried: Mount Hope S: DC

Millichamp, Stephen W. (Con't)
F: Julia A. Millichamp 1846-1927 DOD/B: 3/29-31/1927 A: 81/2/18

Milliron, Joseph C.
B: Lieut/Sgt Joseph C. Milliron Co I 8 Ind Inf Born Feb 24, 1842 Died Apr 2, 1895
C: MH/GAR Hill DOD/B: 4/2-4/1895 A: 52 N: American M: Married
D: J. C. Milliron N: Penn A: 51 O: Jeweler CW: Co I 8 Ind Inf (Pvt/Lieut) E/D: 8/61-8/65 LOS: 50 mos GAR: 3/27/1894 Died: 4/9/1895--is [grave] stone S: H
F: Fanny M. His Wife DOD/B: 10/19-23/1941 A: 89/__/4 Died in Los Angeles, CA "Fanny M." Milliron

Mills, Charles A.
A/B: No stone
C: MH/IOOF DOD/B: 9/5-11/1941 A: 90 3/16 Died in San Diego (ashes) IS THIS HIM??
D: C.A. Mills N: Rhode Island A: 47 O: Mechanic CW: Co E 11 RI Inf (Pvt) E/D: 9/62-7/63 LOS: 11 mos GAR: 11/23/1891 TR: 2/25/1892 S: H
F: E.M. Mills (on stone) DOB: 4/26-29/1916 A: 55 "Emma"

Mills, Cleveland W.
B: C. W. Mills 1841-1927
C: GW/Ivy Place DOD: 4/16-19/1927 A: 85
E: Cleveland W. Mills N: Morgenstown, Ohio 1842 CW: Co K 10 Ind Cav (Pvt/1st Sgt) Term: Unstated E/D: 8/63-6/65 Indianapolis GAR: 6/21/1921 on transfer from Bucklin Post #466 Dept of Kansas Died: 4/16/1927 at La Mesa, CA Buried: Greenwood Cemetery Wife: Laura B. Mills S: DC
F: Laura B. Mills 1868-1960 DOD/B: 10/17-21/1960 A: 92

Miner, August
A: Aug Miner Co G 17 Wis Inf (tombstone visible at Calvary Cemetery)
C: CAL/Sec.1, C, Row 4 DOD/B: An "August Mincur" was buried 2/13/1904

Miner, Samuel G.
A: Lieut S.G. Miner 9th Ohio Cav
C: MH/Masonic C DOD/B: 1/9-12/1906 A: 68 N: Ohio M: Widower "Samuel D. Miner 9th Ohio Cav"

Mingus, Cyrus L.
A: Cyrus L. Mingus Co G 130 Ind Inf
B: Cyrus Luther Mingus Dec 29, 1846-Sept 30, 1914
C: MH/IOOF DOB: 9/30-10/3/1914 A: 68 N: CA? M: Married Note: Nativity of California probably inaccurate
F: Rebecca Viola Dille His Wife Aug 24, 1860-Sept 9, 1922 DOB: 9/11/1922 A: 62 "Rebecca V."

Minor, Mitchell A.
B: Mitchell A. Minor 1842-1937
C: MH/Masonic Q DOD/B: 12/20-22/1937 A: 95/4/5 Died in Ramona, CA
D: Mitchell A. Minor N: Conn A: 76 O: Farmer R: Ramona, CA CW: Co A 24 Ohio Inf (Pvt) E/D: 4/61-6/64 LOS: 3 yrs GAR: 7/22/1919 S: H
F: Lucy G. Minor 1848-1919 DOD/B: 4/23-24/1919 A: 72/2/4

Mitchell, Charles G./C.K.
A/B: No stone
C: MH/IOOF DOD/B: 7/11-13/1906 A: 52 N: American M: Single "Charles Goetschins Mitchell"
E: C.K. Mitchell N: Hillsboro Co, NH CW: Co D 18 US Inf (Pvt) Term: 3 yrs E/D: 8/62-3/65 due to loss of arm GAR: 2/8/1908 on transfer from J.B. Matthews Post #6 Dept of Oregon S: DC (Possible GAR record for Charles G. Mitchell, buried at this location in Mount Hope Cemetery)

Mitchell, James P.
B: James Mitchell 1851-1913
C: MH/Masonic L DOB: 7/30/1913 A: 62/4/20

Mitchell, James P. (Con't)
D: J.P. Mitchell N: Tenn A: 60 O: Farmer CW: Co E 29 Ill Inf (Sgt/Capt) E/D: 8/61-12/64 LOS: 39 mos
    GAR: 11/6/1888 SP: 4/30/1890 DR: 11/30/1891 S: H
F: Matilda Mitchell No stone DOD/B: She is on lot card, but not buried with him Note: She is listed as widow to him in City Directory after his death.

Moffatt, Henry G.
A: Henry G. Moffatt Co G 32 Wis Inf
C: MH/GAR Hill DOD/B: 12/15-20/1926 A: 87/11/17 Died in San Diego
D: Henry G. Moffett N: Virginia A: 82 O: Retired CW: Co G 32 Wis Inf (Pvt) E/D: 5/62-7/65 LOS: 3 yrs 2 mos
    GAR: 12/13/1921 Died: 12/15/1926 S: H

Montney, Levi
A: Levi Montney Corpl Co L 18 Mich Inf
C: MH/GAR Hill DOD/B: 1/2-5/1938 A: 93/4/17 Died in San Diego
E: Levi Montney N: Jefferson Co Township, Clayton, NY CW: Co F 16 Mich Inf (Corpl) Term: 3 yrs E/D: 3/64-7/65
    Jeffersonville, Ind GAR: No further information S: DC

Moore, Alanson O.
A: Sergt Alanson O. Moore Co E 4 Vet Res Corps
C: MH/Masonic H DOB: 7/5/1911 A: 81
E: A.O. Moore N: Troy, Bradford Co, PA CW: Co F 95 Ill Inf (Pvt/Sgt) Term: 3 yrs E/D: 8/62-7/65 Rock Island, Ill
    GAR: 10/28/1905 on transfer from D.C. Morris Post #90 Dept of Iowa Died: 7/2/1911 A: 81 Buried: Masonic
    (Mount Hope) S: DC

Moore, Alexander
A: Alex Moore Co G 2 Cal Inf
C: MH/Div. 7 DOD/B: 12/23-26/1913 A: 86/__/2 N: Ireland M: Married

Moore, John Gollis
B: Confederate Veteran Colonel John Gollis Moore Died Oct 19, 1902 aged 81 years
C: MH/Masonic M DOD/B: 10/19-21/1902 A: 81 N: English M: Widower "John Collis" or "Collins"

Morey, A.B.
A: A.B. Morey Co E 124th Ill Inf (First stone [corner stone] of Mount Hope Cemetery)
C: MH/Div.1 DOB: 12/10/1869 A: 40 N: Not stated M: Married NOTE: He is the first burial at Mount Hope
    Cemetery. Notes say: Bet[ween] Div.1 and Div.2 Sec: Park--front of old office--see lot owner's old book p.
    5--single grave only--gov. marker J/S: "Mourie, Mr. A., d. 10 Dec (1869), San Diego, 40 years, b: American,
    marr, bu City Cem"
[NOTE: Ann Christine Kelly's, *History and Documentation of Five Major Local Cemeteries in the City of San Diego*, 36, states: "Mount Hope's first burial was A.B. Morey (1829-1869). Morey fought with an Illinois Infantry Regiment during the Civil War. He died after suffering a fatal heart attack at the age of 40," citing an article by Herbert Lockwood, "Mount Hope Filling Up But There's Still Room," *San Diego Union*, undated. Thesis is at Copley Library, University of San Diego.]

Morgan, James M.
A: Jas. M. Morgan Co D 17 Ind Inf
B: MH/GAR Div.3 DOD/B: 2/12-19/1913 A: 70/2/13 N: Indiana M: Not stated

Morris, Samuel G.
A: Sam'l G. Morris Co G 1 Ill Cav
C: MH/GAR Div.2 DOD/B: 11/28-30/1912 A: 78/8/__ N: Ohio M: Widower
E: Sam G. Morris N: Norwalk, Ohio CW: Co G 1 Ill Cav (Pvt) Term: 3 yrs E/D: 4/61-10/61 St Louis, MO POW at
    Lexington, MO 9/20/61 released on parole Re/Enl: Co A 83 Ill Inf (Pvt) E/D: 8/62-6/65 Nashville, TN GAR:
    ? date on transfer from Kirkwood Post #81 Dept of Illinois Died: 11/12/1912 A: 71 Buried: GAR (Mount
    Hope) S: DC

Morrison, David
B: David Morrison Died May 12, 1914 Aged 73 years Co B 129 Ill Inf
C: MH/Masonic T DOB: 5/13/1914 A: 73/4/11

Morse, Edward A.
B: Edward A. Morse Co B 23 OVI Apr 29, 1845-Nov 15, 1920
C: MH/GAR Hill DOD/B: 11/15-17/1920 A: 75/6/16
D: E.A. Morse N: Penn A: 75 O: Retired CW: Co B 23 Ohio Inf (Pvt) E/D: 1/64-7/65 LOS: 1 yr 6 mos GAR: 11/9/1920 Died: 11/15/1920 S: H
F: Rosetta E. July 28, 1853-Aug 16, 1925 DOD/B: 8/16-19/1925 A: 72/__/19

Morton, James Ami
A/B: No stone
C: MH/GAR Div.3 DOD/B: 3/24-27/1919 A: 80/9/2
D: James A. Morton N: New York A: 60 O: Not stated CW: Co H 10 PA Inf (Pvt) E/D: 7/61-__/__ LOS: Not stated GAR: 12/9/1902 Died: 3/24/1919 S: H

Mosher (Moshier), William Henry
A: 1st Sgt Wm. H. Mosher Co B 1 Wis Inf
C: MH/GAR Div.3 DOD/B: 10/6-9/1916 A: 76 "William Henry"
D: Wm. H. Moshier N: New York A: 75 O: Retired CW: Co B 1 Wis Inf (Pvt/1st Sgt) E/D: 8/61-10/64 LOS: Not stated GAR: 5/25/1915 Died: 10/5/1916 S: H
E: Wm. H. Moshier NOL/NFI--DC

Munhall, Thomas T.
B: Thomas T. Munhall Captain Co D 11 Ill Cav 1841-1926
C: MH/GAR Hill DOD/B: 3/15-17/1926 A: 84/9/10 Died in Chula Vista, CA "Capt"
D: Thos T. Munhall N: Ohio A: 83 O: Retired R: Chula Vista, CA CW: Co B 11 Ill Vol Cav (Pvt/Capt) E/D: 9/61-10/65 LOS: 4 yrs GAR: 1/27/1925 Died: 3/15/1926 S: H
F: Ella Grant, wife of Capt T.T. Munhall 1864-1945 DOD/B: 4/29-5/2/1945 A: 80/9/1 Died in Chula Vista, CA

Murdock, George L.
B: George L. Murdock 1836-1911 Capt 34 Reg Mass Vol 1862, 1863-5
C: GW/Laurel Place DOD/B: 12/30/1911-1/2/1912 A: 75
F: His Wife Anna Frances Peck 1830-1918 A Native of Rhode Island DOD/B: 1/5-8/1918 A: 89

Murdock, John Pierpont
B: John P. Murdock Corpl Co C 3rd W VA Inf Oct 4, 1842-Sept 30, 1925
C: MH/Masonic F DOD/B: 9/30-10/6/1925 A: 82
D: John Murdock N: Virginia A: 75 O: Jeweler CW: Co C 3 VA Inf (Corpl) E/D: 6/61-7/64 LOS: 25 mos GAR: 1/8/1918 Died: 9/30/1925 S: H

Murphy, Charles H.
B: Charles H. Murphy April 16, 1845-Nov 18, 1915
C: MH/GAR Hill DOD/B: 11/18-20/1915 A: 70/7/2 N: New York M: Married
D: Charles H. Murphy N: New York A: 64 O: Carpenter CW: Co H 13 Iowa Inf (Pvt) E/D: 10/61-11/64 LOS: Not stated GAR: 1/11/1910 (probably on transfer from Lyon Post #24 Dept of Idaho) Died: 11/18/1915 S: H
F: Nancy M. Murphy March 28, 1848-March 3, 1916 DOD/B: 3/3-4/1916 A: 67 "Mrs. Nancy Murphy"

Murray, George L.
B: George L. Murray May 5, 1848-Sept 20, 1927
C: MH/Div.7 DOD/B: 9/22-27/1927 A: 81/4/1910 Died in San Diego
D: George Murray N: Missouri A: 52 O: Cook CW: Co H 2 MO Art (W C A D) E/D: 12/63-11/65 LOS: 23 mos GAR: 1/8/1901 Died: 9/20/1927 S: H
F: Minnie Murray (wife?) No stone DOD/B: No record found Note: City Directory of 1927 lists George L. Murray as cook. City Directory of 1929 lists Minnie Murray as cook.

Neer, Barton B.
A/B: No stone
B: Cypress View Mausoleum, Garden Court, Corridor B, Tier 6, Crypt 30 DOD/B: None further information, although crypt sold to Mrs. Barton B. Neer on 1/19/1929. Mortician: Benbough Mortuary
E: Barton Neer N: Kendall Co, Ill 3/30/48 CW: Co H 46 Ill Inf (Pvt) Term: 3 yrs E/D: 2/64-1/66 Baton Rouge, LA severely wounded in battle of Jackson, Miss on 7/7/64 GAR: 1/13/1912 on transfer from Edward Bridge Post #24 Dept of IL Died: 10/9/1934 A: 86 Buried: Cypress View S: DC Obit: No wife, children listed.
F: Mrs. Barton B. Neer DOD/B: No further information

Neill, Dyas
B: Dyas Neill Feb 10, 1837-Sept 28, 1923 1st Iowa Cavalry
C: MH/GAR Div.2 DOD/B: 9/28-10/1/1923 A: 86/7/18
D: Dyas Neill N: Ireland A: 84 O: Retired CW: Co H 1 IA Cav (Pvt) E/D: 5/61-3/66 LOS: 4 yrs GAR: 8/23/1921 Died: 9/28/1923 S: H
F: Elizabeth A. Neill Mar 3, 1849-Jan 4, 1935 DOD/B: 1/4-7/1935 A: 85/10/1 Died in San Diego "Elizabeth Augusta"

Nelson, George L.
A: George L. Nelson Co A 2 Colo Cav
C: MH/GAR Div.3 DOB: 6/12-16/1914 A: about 70 N: Not stated M: Single

Nelson, Nelson Edward
B: Nelson Edward Nelson Serg Co A 1 Minn Vols Civil War Dec 25, 1832-Dec 24, 1913
C: GW/Palm Terrace DOD/B: 12/24-29/1913 A: 89

Nesbitt, Jeremiah
B. Jeremiah Nesbitt Co G 162 Ohio Inf Pvt Civil War 1844-1937
C: MH/GAR Hill DOD/B: 8/25-30/1937 A: 92/8/7 Died in San Diego
D: Jeremiah Nesbitt N: Ohio A: 83 O: Not stated CW: Co G 162 Ohio Inf (Pvt) E/D: 5/64-8/64 LOS: Not stated GAR: 2/28/1928 Died: 8/25/1937 S: H

Nettlebeck, Herman
A: Sergt H. Nettlebeck Co B 4 MO SM Cav
C: MH/GAR Div.2 DOD/B: 3/17-18/1911 A: Not stated M: Married

Nevenhuisen, William W
A: Wm. W. Nevenhuisen Co H 111 PA Inf
C: MH/Masonic M DOB: 4/9-13/1912 A: 67/11/26 N: PA M: Married

New, Edward
A/B: Edward New Co A 9 US Inf (tombstone not at Calvary Cemetery Source: FHC record)
C: CAL/Sec.1, South, Row 4 DOB: 2/1/1905 A: 74

Nichols, George Ewing
A: G.E. Nichols US Navy
C: MH/GAR Div.2 DOD/B: 12/21-24/1908 A: 65/9/28 N: Wisconsin M: Married
F: Mrs. Francis Nichols No stone DOD/B: No further information.

Nichols, James G.B.
A: James G. B. Nichols Co F 4th Mich Cav
C: MH/Masonic L DOB: 12/13/1913 A: 71
D: James G.B. Nichols N: New York A: 40 O: Farmer/Harness Maker CW: Co F 4 Mich Cav (Pvt) E/D: 8/62-5/65 LOS: 33 mos GAR: 9/13/1888 SP: 9/24/1895 RE: 6/26/1900 Died: 12/10/1913 S: H
F: Sabra E. Wife of J G B Nichols April 30, 1845-May 20, 1905 DOD/B: 5/20-22/1905 A: 60 N: Amer. M: Married

Nickens, Samuel I.
A: S.I. Nickens US Navy
C: MH/GAR Hill DOD/B: 4/11-13/1905 A: 61 N: American Race: Black N: American M: Married
D: Samuel L. Nickens N: Penn A: 50 O: Waiter CW: US Navy U.S.S. Tuscarowa (Landsman) E/D: 12/61-1/65
 LOS: 36 or 48 mos GAR: 1/26 or 6/26/1894 DR: 3/28/1899 RE: 4/24/1900 Died: 4/12/1905--is [grave]
 stone S: H

Noble, Thomas P.
A: Corpl T.P. Noble Co K 14 ME Inf
C: GW/Laurel Place DOD/B: 11/30-12/2/1908 A: 71
D: Thomas P. Noble N: Maine A: 48 O: Carpenter CW: Co K 14 ME Inf (Corpl) E/D: 3/63-8/65 LOS: 37 mos
 GAR: 11/25/1886 SP: 12/27/1889 or 12/27/1898 RE: 3/11/1899 Died: 11/30/1908--is [grave] stone S:H

Nosler, James Mylan/Mylon
A: J.M. Nosler Co D (or Co O) 2nd Iowa Cav
C: MH/GAR Hill DOD/B: No record in boxes except name/burial location   J/S: "Nosler, James Mylan, d. 22 Jun
 (1886), 42 years, b. IN, mar, bur GAR Cem" Note: Name "Mylon" comes from Episcopal Church records,
 where his baptism is noted on the same day that he later died (May 8, 1886). Record reads: Nosler, James
 Mylon. 8 May 1886. At house, 12th and C. Age 50. H.H. Wilcox and Mrs. Nosler, witnesses. (Died the
 same night). (from: Record of Baptisms of Holy Trinity Church, in *Episcopal Church Records*, p. 11-B).
F. Esther L. Beloved wife of W.H. Nosler Born May 28,1841 Died Nov 14,1887 Dearest Mother, thou has left us
 We thy loss most deeply feel But tis God who hath bereft us He can all our sorrows heal DOB: 11/14/1887
 A: 43 Died in San Diego (possible wife of J.M.Nosler?)

Nute, Charles N.
A: Corpl Chas N. Nute Co G 2 DC Inf
C: MH/GAR Div.3 DOD/B: 9/24-25/1912 A: 77/4/15 N: Maine M: Married
E: Charles Nute N: Maine CW: Co G 2 DC Inf (Pvt/Corpl) Term: 3 yrs E/D: 1/62-5/62 Washington, D.C. due to
 disability GAR: ? date on transfer from Silas A. Slickland Post #13 Dept of Arkansas Died: 9/24/1912
 A: 77 Buried: GAR (Mount Hope) S: DC
F: Elizabeth Nute No stone DOD/B: 5/3-28/1936 A: 92/8/28 (ashes) Died in San Diego

Nutt, Henry Walker
A: H.W. Nutt Co A 2 Cal Inf
C: MH/Div.1 DOD/B: 4/6-8/1903 A: Not stated N: American M: Married

Ober, William
B: William Ober Aug 24, 1847-Aug 16, 1923
C: MH/GAR Div.2 DOD/B: 8/16-20/1923 A: 75/11/1922 Note: William Ober was born in Somerset County, PA on
 August 24, 1847. After the war, he came on the Orizaba to San Diego in the fall of 1870. He married Cora
 Leabo, Kentucky native, in 1882. He built the first house in Ramona (North San Diego County), and later
 farmed in the Tijuana Valley, where he used scientific agricultural standards. (from *San Diego County,
 California: A Record of Settlement*, etc.)
D: William Ober N: Somerset Co, PA A: 34 O: Blacksmith R: Bernardo (probably Rancho Bernardo) CW: Co G
 93 PA Inf (Pvt) E/D: 9/64-6/65 LOS: 8 mos GAR: 3/23/1882 SP: 1/10/1889 DR: 6/30/1891 S: H
E: William Ober N: Somerset Co, PA 9/24/49 CW: Co G 93 PA Inf (Pvt) Term: 3 yrs E/D: 9/64-6/65 GAR:
 6/28/1919 Died: 8/17/1923 A: 76/11/24 S: DC
F: Cora Ober Oct 13, 1859-Sept 2, 1948 DOD/B: 9/2-9/1948 A: 88/10/9 Died in Sacramento, CA

O'Farrell, William Morris
A: Wm Morris O'Farrell Co I 26 NY Inf
C: MH/Div.3 DOD/B: 3/10-14/1934 A: 93/10/__ Died in San Diego
D: Wm M. O'Farrell N: New York A: 62 O: Retired CW: Co I 26 NY Inf (Pvt) E/D: 5/61-5/63 LOS: 24 mos GAR:
 4/9/1901 S: H
F: Ellen G. 1853-1935 DOD/B: 9/8-11/1935 A: 83/3/7 Died in San Diego "Ellen Cecelia"

O'Neill, Patrick
A: Pat'k O'Neil Co D 2 Cal Inf (his/her tombstones visible at Calvary Cemetery)
B: Ptk O'Neill July 29, 1822-March 29, 1900
C: CAL/Sec.2, North 2/3, Row E-8 DOB: 3/23/1900 A: 77 Parents: Constantine O'Neil and Sarah Campbell
F: Lorenza O'Neill Feb 28, 1832-Jan 1, 1904 RIP (she buried next to him) DOB: 1/5/1904 A: 79 Spouse: Patrick
    O'Neil Parents: Nicholas Silvas and Maria Antonia Machado Also: Child John O'Neil DOB: 2/21/1902 A:
    28 Native of Old Town San Diego Parents: Patrick O'Neil and Lorenza Silvas

Ogden, Tully
A: Tully Ogden Co C 2nd Cal Inf
C: MH/Div.2 DOD/B: 5/31-6/2/1895 A: 52 N: Norwegian M: Married
D: Tully Ogden N: Norway A: 42 O: Speculator CW: Co C 2 Cal Inf (Pvt) E/D: 12/64-5/66 LOS: 17 mos GAR:
    10/11/1883 SP: 7/1/1890 RE: 12/10/1890 Died: 1/1/1895--is [grave] stone S: H Note: County death record
    indicates he died on 5/31/1895.
F: Mina 1849-1934 DOD/B: 8/13-15/1934 A: 83/10/3 Died in San Diego "Mina"

Ogle, John Joseph
A: John J. Ogle Co K 3 PA Hv Arty
C: MH/GAR Hill DOD/B: 2/4-5/1934 (or 8/1934?) A: 87/1/2 Died at Patton, CA "Dr."
E: Dr. John Joseph Ogle N: Penn 1847 CW: Co K 3 PA H A (Pvt) Term: 1 yr E/D: 2/64-__/__ GAR: 12/9/1922
    on transfer from Dept of Indiana Died: 2/4/1934 Obit: He is "Dr. Ogle" Buried: Mount Hope S: DC
F: Irene A. Ogle No stone DOD/B: 2/13-15/1939 A: 83/10/1 Died in San Diego

Olin, Dyer W.
A/B: No stone
C: MH/Masonic E DOD/B: 8/24-26/1922 A: 78/6/__
E: Dyer W. Olin N: Maconogo, Wis (sp?) 1/30/45 CW: Co I 50 Wis ___ (Pvt) Term: 1 yr E/D: 2/65-6/65 Madison
    GAR: 1/27/1917 on transfer from Coeur d'Alene Post #19 Dept of Idaho Died: 8/24/1922 A: 76/7/__ S: DC
F: Alma Olin No stone DOD/B: 6/22-24/1929 A: 76/9/__

Oliphant, John A.
B: John A. Oliphant Feb 22, 1847-Nov 13, 1930 Civil War Veteran Co A 124th Indiana Vol
C: MH/Div.6 DOD/B: 11/12-14/1930 A: 83/8/21 Died in San Diego (GAR death date probably a mistake)
D: John A. Oliphant N: Indiana A: 79 O: Retired CW: Co A 124 Ind Inf (Pvt) E/D: 10/63-10/65 LOS: 3 yrs GAR:
    10/13/1925 Died: 11/12/1930 S: H
F: Delphine C. Oliphant Jan 14, 1849-Mar 7, 1938 DOD/B: 3/7-9/1938 A: 89/1/21 Died in San Diego

Orcutt, Herman C.
A: H.C. Orcutt Co G 6th Vt Inf
C: MH/Div.4 DOD/B: 7/23-29/1892 A: 66/10/19 N: American M: Married "H.C." Note: Name "Herman" from the
    1880 census of San Diego, where he was 54, a farm hand, and was born in Massachusetts of Connecticut-
    born parents.
D: H.C. Orcutt N: Mass A: 59 O: Farmer CW: Co C 6 VT Inf (Pvt) E/D: 9/64-5/65 LOS: 8 7/30 mos GAR:
    12/13/1883 SP: 1/10/1889 DR: 6/30/1891 Died: "Dead"--no [grave] stone S: H
F: Eliza E. Orcutt No stone DOD/B: 6/28-30/1909 A: 84/4/8 N: VT M: Widow Note: In the 1880 census for San
    Diego, she is 55, wife to Herman, and was born in Vermont of a Vermont father and New Hampshire mother.

Orrick, Ephraim M.
B: Ephraim M. Orrick April 18, 1831-Oct 7, 1906 At Rest
B: MH/Confederate DOD/B: 10/7-9/1906 A: 75/4/24 N: Arkansas M: Married "Ephream M. Ouick"
F: Emaline Sept 10, 1828-Jan 13, 1910 DOD/B: 1/13-15/1910 A: 81/4/3 N: NC M: Widow "Emmaline"
    "Confederate Plot"
    Note: Ephraim Orrick was born 4/13/1831 in Arkansas; Died 10/7/1906 in San Diego, CA. Private. Served
    in Texas Rangers and later in Texas Scouts S: UDC document, California Room (see Chapter II, "San Diego
    Public Library" sources)

Otis, Elmer
B: Col. Elmer Otis USA Feb 27, 1830-Aug.18, 1897 (tombstone visible at Calvary Cemetery)
C: CAL/Sec.2, Block D, Lot 8 DOB: 8/19/1897 Spouse: Agnes Boone Parents: Homer Otis and Laura Chapman
D: Elmer Otis N: Mass A: 63 O: Retired Officer CW: Cadet for life--retired from active list E/D: __/49-2/91 LOS: 42 years GAR: 6/27/1893 Died: 8/24/1897--is [grave] stone S: H
F: Agnes Otis (name on pioneer monument at Calvary Cemetery) DOD/B: No record found in Catholic cemetery index

Outcalt, Lewis S.
A: Lewis S. Outcault Co F 86 Ill Inf
B: Lewis S. Outcault June 6, 1844-Nov 17, 1917
C: MH/GAR Hill DOD: 11/17-20/1917 A: 73
D: Lewis A. Outcalt N: Ohio A: 52 O: Rancher CW: Co F 26 Ill Inf (Pvt) E/D: 11/61-7/65 LOS: 32 mos GAR: 11/24/1896 (probably on transfer from Wm. T. Sherman Post #21 Dept of Idaho TR: 6/25/1901 TR: 6/13/1905 Died 11/17/1917 (killed by street car) S: H
F: Mary L. Whitmore, wife of Lewis S. Outcault Jan 29, 1848-Sept 30, 1907 DOD/B: 9/30-10/2/1907 A: 59/8/11 N: Ohio M: Married

Oviatt, William H.
A: Lieut Wm. H. Oviatt Co C 6 IA Inf (or Co G?)
B: William 1842-1911
C: MH/IOOF DOB: 9/25-27/1911 A: 69/17/8 N: Ohio M: Married
F: Augusta 1844-1924 DOB: 9/22/1924 A: 80 (ashes)

Owens, William T.
B: William T. Owens 1840-1921 Born in Wales 2nd Wisconsin Cavalry GAR
C: MH/Masonic S DOD/B: 5/19-21/1921 A: 80
D: W.J. Owens N: Wales A: 79 O: Carpenter CW: Co I 2 Wis Cav (Pvt) E/D: 1/64-11/65 LOS: 1 yr 11 mos GAR: 1/29/1921 Died: 5/19/1921 S: H

Paine, John O.W.
A: Capt Jno O.W. Paine Co E 14 ME Inf
C: MH/Masonic A DOB: 6/1-3/1910 A: 72/4/24 "J.O.W."
D: John O.W. Paine N: Chaleston?, Maine A: 43 O: Lawyer CW: Co D 14 ME Inf (2nd Lieut) Promoted?: Co E 14 ME Inf (Capt) E/D: 12/61-8/65 LOS: 44 mos GAR: 2/9/1882 SP: 12/27/1898 RE: 3/14/1899 Died: 6/1/1910 S: H
F: Jane Price Paine 1837-1883 DOB: 3/16/1883 A: 46 "Jennie" J/S: "Payne, Mrs. J.O.W., d. 15 Mar (1883), 46 years, b. MD, mar, bur Masonic Cem" Obit/San Diego Herald, 3/16/1883: "In this city Mar 15, Mrs. Jennie P. Paine, wife of J.O.W. Paine, esq. died yesterday morning of consumption after a lingering illness. Funeral at 2:00 p.m. today from family residence, 5th Street on the hill. The bereived husband and motherless children have the heartfelt sympathy of the community."

Palmateer, Charles Daniel
A: Charles D. Palmateer Co D 62 Ill Inf
C: MH/GAR Hill DOD/B: 8/21-24/1929 A: 83/7/1 Died in San Diego

Palmer, Isaac Lassell
A: I.L. Palmer Co A 36 Ohio Inf
C: MH/GAR Hill DOD/B: 12/20-22/1891 A: 46/5/29 N: American M: Married Died in San Diego Note: Isaac Palmer was born in Marietta, OH, according to *An Illustrated History of Southern California*. He is brother to John Dresser Palmer; both are descendants of Walter Palmer of Stonington, CT, who arrived at Salem and Charlestown, MA in 1629. Note: 1880 census indicates "J.L.Palmer" is 34, a grocer, and born in Ohio, with Ohio-born parents.
D: I.L. Palmer N: Ohio A: 37 O: Clerk CW: Co A 36 Ohio Inf (Pvt) E/D: 7/62-7/65 LOS: 48 mos GAR: 11/9/1882 Died: 12/20/1891--no [grave] stone S: H
F: Maria W. 1842-1932 DOD/B: 12/29-31/1932 A: 90/5/23 Died in San Diego Note: Maria Palmer is 37 in the 1880 census for San Diego; wife to "J.L.Palmer", and from Ohio, with Ohio-born parents.

Palmer, John Dresser
A: 1st Sgt John D. Palmer Co G 182 Ohio Inf
B: John D. Palmer June 5, 1843-Jan 15, 1906 Note: Middle name "Dresser" is from *San Diego County Pioneer Families*. (See also a book by his granddaughter Bertha Palmer Wohlers, entitled: *Follow the Light: The Palmer Family and the Savoy Theater*, San Diego Public Library Call No. 929.20973/Palmer). Both he and his brother Isaac Lassell Palmer are descendants of Walter Palmer of Stonington, CT, who arrived at Salem and Charlestown, MA in 1629.
C: MH/GAR Hill DOD/B: 1/15-17/1906 A: 62/7/10 M: Married
D: John D. Palmer N: Ohio A: 43 O: Carpenter CW: Co C 3 Ohio Inf (Pvt) Re-Enl?: Co C 182 Ohio Inf (Sgt) E/D: 4/61-7/65 LOS: 51 mos GAR: 7/22/1886 SP: 4/30/1890 DR: 6/30/1891 RE: 1898 Post Commander 1902 Died: 1/15/1906--is [grave] stone S: H
F: Lydia S. Palmer May 2, 1844-12/1/1913 DOD/B: 12/1-3/1913 A: 69/6/29 N: Ohio M: Widow

Parker, Edson O.
A: Mus'n Edson O. Parker Co F 10 NY HA
C: MH/Div.1 DOD/B: 10/25-29/1913 A: 60/6/21
D: Edson O. Parker N: New York A: 71 O: Land Agent CW: Co F 10 NY Art (Musician) E/D: 8/62-5/65 LOS: 33 mos GAR: 10/25/1904 S: H
F: Jane A. Parker (Mother?) No stone DOD/B: 6/11-13/1899 A: 77 N: American M: Widow

Parker, George W.
A: Lieut Geo.W.Parker Adjt 126 Ill Inf
B: Geo.W.Parker Dec 4, 1832-Oct 6, 1909
C: MH/GAR Hill DOD/B: 10/7-9/1909 A: 76/10/__ N: PA M: Widower
D: George H. Parker N: Penn A: 59 O: Druggist CW: Co H 126 Ill Inf (Pvt/Adjt) E/D: 8/62-2/64 due to disability LOS: 18 mos GAR: 7/12/1892 SP: 3/26/1895 DR: 3/28/1899 Died: 10/7/1909--no [grave] stone S: H
F: Mary A, wife of _____ July 25, 1837-Feb 3, 1895 DOD/B: 2/3-4/1895 A: 57 N: American M: Married

Parsons, Benjamin F.
A: Benj Parsons Co I 1 US Art (tombstone not visible at Calvary Cemetery
C: CAL/Sec.1 DOB: 9/29/1896 A: 72 N: Virginia Spouse: Frances Tenley
F: Frances Tenley/Talley DOD/B: No record found in Catholic cemetery index Source: DOB information on husband Also: Child Nettie Parsons DOB: 8/13/1871 Parents: Benjamin Parsons and Frances Talley Baptized by (Dona) Felipa Marron

Patterson, James Lloyd
A: 2 Lt James L. Patterson Co D NC Inf CSA
C: MH/Confederate DOD/B: 11/29-12/4/1913 A: 73/7/8
Note: James L. Patterson was born 1837, Henderson Co, NC; Died 11/29/1913 Imperial Valley, CA. Enlisted 8/5/1862 at Asheville, NC as Sgt. Promoted to 1st Sgt. Promoted to 2nd Lt, Co D, 25 NC Inf. Surrendered at Appomattox S: UDC document, California Room (see Chapter II, "San Diego Public Library" sources)

Patton, Morand D.
A: Moran D. Patton Co I 18 IA Inf
C: MH/GAR Div.3 DOD/B: 3/2-4/1915 A: 70/4/12 or 70/9/12 N: Ohio M: Married Name Marand
E: Morand D. Patton N: Findley, Hancock Co, Ohio 10/18/44 CW: Co I 18 Iowa Inf (Pvt) Term: 3 yrs E/D: 8/62-7/65 Little Rock, Ark GAR: 8/22/1914 Died: 3/2/1915 A: 70 S: H

Paull, Charles M.
A: Charles M. Paull Co H 33 IA Inf
C: MH/GAR Hill DOD/B: 7/29-8/1/1924 A: 79/11/2
D: Chas. M. Paul N: Kane Co, Ill A: 74 O: Retired R: National City, CA CW: Co H 33 Iowa Inf (Pvt) E/D: 8/62-7/65 LOS: 35 mos GAR: 8/13/1918 Died: 7/29/1924 S: H

Payne, Erasmus
A: Erasmus Payne Co G 115 Ohio Inf
C: MH/GAR Hill DOD/B: 9/20-22/1900 A: Not stated N: American M: Single (Coroner Inquest Report 129-3 648
    death from head injury due to fall--9/20/1900--San Diego Historical Society Archives)

Pearce, Jacob
B: Jacob Pearce Sgt 151 Regt Ill Infantry Civil War April 26, 1845-Jan 11, 1915
C: MH/GAR Div.3 DOD/B: 1/8-11/1915 A: 68/8/13 N: Penn M: Widower

Peck, Hiram H.
A: H.H. Peck Co L 16 NY H A
C: MH/GAR Div.3 DOD/B: 1/19-22/1917 A: 75 "Hiram"
E: Hiram H. Peck N: Hanega Falls, NY (sp?) 12/26/41 CW: Batt 16 NY H A (Pvt/Corpl) Term: 3 yrs E/D: 1/64-8/65
    New York City; wounded in both legs by gun shot GAR: 8/28/1909 on transfer from John F. Miller Post #31
    Dept of Wash/Alaska Died: 1/20/1917 S: DC
F: Nellie E. Wife of H.H. Peck 1844-1924 DOD/B: 1/27-30/1924 A: 79/8/17 "Mellie"

Pells, James William
B: James William 1838-1923
C: MH/Masonic S DOD/B: 10/17-20/1923 A: 85/8/16
D: James W. Pells N: New York A: 68 O: Merchant CW: Co C 156 NY Inf (Pvt) Re-Enl? Co G 156 NY Inf (Corpl)
    E/D: 9/62-10/65 LOS: 36 mos GAR: 4/25/1905 Died: 10/18/1923 S: H
F: Francis A. Pells July 17, 1845-Dec 1, 1942 "My Precious Mother is Resting in the Arms of Jesus" DOD/B: 12/1-
    3/1942 A: 97/4/15 Died at Coronado City Hospital

Pennell, Robert J.
A: R.J. Pennell US Navy
C: MH/Masonic K DOB: 8/27-29/1889 A: 42/5/__ N: American M: Married
D: Robert J. Pennell N: New York A: 41 O: Salesman CW: US Mayflower (2nd Officer) 6/63-6/65 due to sickness
    LOS: 24 mos GAR: 6/28/1888 SP: 3/28/1889 Died: 8/27/1889--is [grave] stone S: H

Peterson, George
A: Geo Peterson Co B 1 Nev Cav
C: MH/GAR Div.2 DOD/B: 2/16-28/1923 A: 84 "Co B 1st Batt Nevada Cavalry Born in Norway Aug 15, 1839)
F: Bergette Peterson No stone DOD/B: 4/22-25/1931 A: 78/6/25 Died in San Diego

Pettingill, Amos
A/B: No stone
C: MH/GAR Hill DOD/B: 1/20-23/1898 A: 65/10/16 N: American M: Married
D: Amos Pettingill N: Mass A: 53 O: Boat Builder CW: Co B 35 Mass Inf (Corpl) E/D: 8/62-11/62 due to disability
    LOS: 4 mos GAR: 9/27/1870 Died: 1/24/1898--is [grave] stone S: H
F: Frances Pettingill No stone DOD/B: 8/25-29/1901 A: 73 N: American M: Widow

Pettit, John Wycliffe
A: 1 Lt John W. Pettit Co K 14 Wis Inf
C: MH/GAR Hill DOD/B: 3/4-6/1933 A: 91/1/20 "Civil War Vet" Died in San Diego "John Wickiffe"
E: John Wycliffe Pettit N: Illinois 7/12/42 CW: Co K 14 Wis Inf (Pvt/1st Lt) Term: 3 yrs E/D: 11/61-10/65 GAR:
    2/27/1915 on transfer from Garfield Post #57 Dept of Iowa Died: 3/4/1933 A: 91 Obit lists wife Mary J. Pettit
    S: DC
F: Mary Pettit No stone DOD/B: No record found

Petty, John W.
A: J.W. Petty Co B 47 Ill Inf
C: MH/GAR Hill DOD/B: 8/16-22/1906 A: 60 N: Not stated M: Widower

Pfaff, George
A: Geo Pfaff Co H 24 Ohio Inf
C: MH/GAR Div. 2 DOD/B: 3/12-14/1907 A: 64 N: Germany M: Single

Pfister, Adam
A: Adam Pfister Co D 4 KY Cav
C: MH/Div.6 DOD/B: 3/6-7/1906 A: 65 N: Germany M: Widower

Pfister, Ferdinand
B: Ferdinand Pfister Co A 9th Ohio Vol Inf Born Apr 18, 1838 Died Jan 16, 1903
C: MH/GAR Div.2 DOD/B: 1/16-18/1903 A: 64/10/__ N: German M: Married
D: Ferdinand Pfister N: Germany A: 45 O: Machinist CW: Co A 9 Ohio Inf (Pvt) E/D: 4/61-6/64 or 5/61-6/64 LOS: 37 mos GAR: 6/4/1883 SP: 9/26/1889 RE: 6/25/1895 Died: 1/16/1903--is [grave] stone Buried: GAR Plot (Mount Hope) S: H
F: "Mother" DOD/B: 10/28-31/1922 A: 81/7/2 Died in San Diego "Francis"

Piburn, Thomas Benton
B: Thos B. Piburn 1847-1918 Co C 48th Iowa Inf
C: MH/GAR Div.3 DOD/B: 5/17-21/1918 A: 70/11/__ Name Thomas Benton Pilburn
F: Mary E. 1845-1927 DOD/B: 2/3-5/1927 A: 81/10/13 "Buried box to box with Thomas B. Piburn"

Picken, John
A: John Picken US Navy
B: MH/GAR Div.2 DOD/B: 3/9-11/1908 A: 65/9/3 N: Scotland M: Married "JS" record indicates he died on 3/9/1908 of paralysis at County Hospital Nativity Scotland Marital--married

Pickett, William T.
A: W.T. Pickett Co G 5 (or 6) IA Cav
C: MH/GAR Hill DOD/B: 8/21-24/1902 A: 62 N: American M: Single

Pickett, Zedekiah
A: Zedekiah Pickett Co F 7 Ind Inf
C: MH/GAR Hill DOD/B: 8/27-28/1898 A: 77 N: American M: Widower Name Jedekiah
D: Zedekiah Pickett N: Indiana A: 54 O: Contractor R: National City, CA CW: Co F 7 Ind Inf (Pvt) E/D: 4/61-8/61 Re-Enl?: Co E 76 Ind Inf (Pvt) E/D: 7/62-8/64 LOS: Not stated GAR: 7/9/1890 SP: 9/22/1896 Died: 9/13/1898--is [grave] stone S: H
F: Cynthia Pickett No stone DOD/B: 10/25-26/1893 A: 51 N: American M: Married "Mrs. Cynthia"

Pierce, Charles O.
A: C.O. Pierce Co B 7th US Inf
C: MH/IOOF DOD/B: 2/20-24/1889 A: 48 N: American M: Married
D: Chas O. Pierce N: Lowell, Mass A: 39 O: Painter CW: Co B 7 US Inf (Pvt) E/D: 7/60-7/65 LOS: 5 years GAR: 10/8/1881 Charter Member of Heintzelman Post GAR Died: 2/20/1889 S: H
F: Mother Sarah J. Pierce Born Jan 23 (or 25), 1815 (1816?) Died April 29, 1893 DOD/B: 4/29-5/2/1893 A: 78/3/__ N: American M: Widow "Mrs Sarah" Note: This is his mother, not wife listed as a "Mother"

Piher, William
A: Sgt Wm Piher US Army
C: MH/Div.3 DOD/B: 2/2-6/1910 A: 74/11/14 N: Scotland M: Married
E: Wm Piher N: Scotland CW: 2 US Art Luttons Bat (Sgt) Term: 5 yrs E/D: 8/61-8/65 St Louis, MO GAR: 8/11/1900 on transfer from Hartroft Post #151 Dept of Cal/Nev Died: 2/2/1910 A: 78 B: GAR (Mount Hope) S: DC
F: Rachel Adair Piher 1833-1915 DOD/B: 2/10-13/1915 A: 84/6/9 N: MD M: Widow

Pirnie, Alexander
B: Alexander Pirnie June 11, 1846-____ Born at Argill, Scotland 7th NY Battery L A
C: MH/Div.6 DOD/B: 9/14-22/1932 A: 86 (ashes) Died in San Diego
D: Alexander Pirnie N: Scotland A: 57 O: Stone Cutter CW: Co K 3 NY L A (Pvt) E/D: 10/64-6/65 LOS: 8 mos
  GAR: 4/26/1904 Died: 9/13/1932 S: H
F: Ida Lillian Palmer Wife of Alex. Pirnie Mar 14, 1860-Dec 10, 1909 Born at Webster Hill, Oneida Co, NY DOD/B:
  12/10-12/1909 A: 49/8/26 N: NY M: Married
M: Mary Sophia Palmer, Mother of Ida L. Pirnie Oct 24, 1838-Feb 17, 1907

Pivers, David Hart
B: David Hart Pivers Capt
C: MH/Masonic H DOD/B: 1/10-12/1907 A: 56/9/23 N: Maine M: Married Record filed under "Rivers" "JS" record:
  David (C.?) Rivers died 1/10/1907 of heart rupture, San Diego Nativity Maine Marital: Married

Place, Samuel S.
A: Sam'l S. Place Co A 2 Ill Cav
C: MH/GAR Div.2 DOD/B: 12/27-30/1908 A: 68/__/2 N: New York M: Widower

Polhamus, Adelbert C./Albert Howard
A: Adelbt C. Polhamus Sgt Co D 192 NY Inf
C: MH/GAR Div. 2 DOD/B: 7/2-6/1926 A: 85/1/23 Died in San Diego Name Adelbert C.
D: Adelbert C. Polhamus N: New York A: 80 O: retired CW: Co F 9 NY Inf (Pvt) Re/Enl?: Co __ 198 NY Inf
  (Sgt) E/D: 7/61-8/65 LOS: 4 yrs GAR: 9/27/1921 Died: 7/2/1926 S: H
E: A.C. Polhamus N: 29 Cannon St, New York City 5/9/41 CW: Co F 9 NY Inf (Pvt) Term: 2 yrs E/D: 7/61-7/63
  Camp Alford, VA Re-Enl: Co D 192 NY Inf (Pvt/Sgt) E/D: 1/65-8/65 Cumberland, MD "Comrade Polhamus
  was under the name of Albert Howard" GAR: 6/9/1899 on transfer from Moses F. Odell Post #443 Died:
  7/1/1926 at Naval Hospital S: DC

Pollock, Samuel S.
B: Samuel S. Oct 23, 1833-April 3, 1921 Co D 14 PA Cav
C: MH/GAR Hill DOD/B: 4/3-7/1921 A: 87
D: S.S. Pollock N: Penn A: 82 O: Carpenter CW: Co D 14 PA Cav (1st Sgt/2nd Lieut) E/D: 9/62-6/65 LOS: Not
  stated GAR: 10/24/1881 SP: 3/28/1899 DR: "Dropped" RE: 5/27/1913 Died: 4/3/1921 S: H
E: Samuel S. Pollock NOL/NFI S: DC
F: Wife Emma July 30, 1848-June 18, 1911 DOD/B: 6/18-20/1911 A: 63/10/19 N: KY M: Married

Pope, William W.
B: Capt W.W. Pope 92nd Ill Mtd Inf 1844-1929
C: MH/GAR Hill DOD/B: 1/11-14/1929 A: 84 Died in Los Angeles
D: Wm. W. Pope N: New York A: 74 O: Electrician CW: Co F 92 Ill Inf (Pvt) E/D: 8/62-6/65 LOS: 32 mos GAR:
  2/26/1918 Died: 1/11/1929 S: H
F: Evaline Hendrix, wife of Capt W.W. Pope 1855-1927 DOD/B: 6/8-11/1927 A: 71/7/__ Died in San Diego "Eva"

Porter, John P.
A/B: No stone
C: MH/GAR Div.2 DOD/B: 7/8-11/1931 A: 96/1/11 Died in Chula Vista, CA
D: John P. Porter N: Penn A: 69 O: Retired CW: Co B 58 PA Inf (Pvt) E/D: 10/61-10/64 LOS: Not stated GAR:
  4/8/1913 on transfer from George H.Thomas Post #9 Dept of Idaho TR: 4/22/1913 S: H

Potter, Milton M.
A/B: No stone
C: GW/CMTD/Cathedral Mausoleum #E DOD/B: 11/15-18/1932 A: 94 (cremated elsewhere than GW)
E: Milton M. Potter N: Penn 1/29/38 CW: Co D 55 Ill Inf (Pvt/2 M.Sgt) Term: 3 yrs E/D: 8/61-8/65 GAR:
  12/9/1922 Died: 11/15/1932 A: 94/9/17 Buried: Greenwood Mausoleum S: DC

Powell, A.H.
A: Chaplain A.H. Powell 24 MO Inf
C: MH/Div.6 DOD/B: 9/28-30/1905 A: 77/6/__ N: Kentucky M: Widower "Rev. Powell"

Powers, Marion
A: Sergt Marion Powers Co K 137 Ind Inf
C: MH/GAR Div.2 DOD/B: 11/30-12/2/1908 A: 66/7/8 N: Indiana M: Single "JS" record indicates he died on 11/30/1908 of insanity at County Hospital Nativity Indiana Marital--widower
D: Marion Powers N: Indiana A: 60 O: Farmer R: Dehesa, CA CW: Co K 137 Ind Inf (Sgt) E/D: 5/64-10/4 LOS: 5 mos GAR: 10/14/1902 SP: 3/26/1907 S: H

Powers, Robert A.
A: Rob't A. Powers Co B 13 Vt Inf
B: Robert A. Powers 1841-1911
C: MH/GAR Div. 2 DOD/B: 2/10-12/1911 A: 69/9/8 N: VT M: Married
F: Anna E. Powers 1857- _____ DOD/B: No record in boxes/wife?

Pruden, Ludlow
A/B: No stone
C: MH/Div.6 DOD/B: 3/11-21/1904 A: 70 N: American W: Widowed "Civil War Veteran" (Coroner Inquest File 14912 000--death due to heart disease on 3/11/1904--San Diego Historical Society Archives)

Pugh, Theophilus J.
A/B: No stone
C: MH/GAR Div.3 DOD/B: 5/2-10/1915 A: 86 (he probably died in 1925--cemetery record is probably in error)
D: T.J. Pugh N: Indiana A: 80 O: Retired CW: Co I 7 Ind Inf (Pvt) E/D: 9/61-10/62 due to wounds LOS: 12 mos GAR: 12/14/1920 Died: 4/4/1925 S: H Note: Does this GAR record match this burial--the DODs are so far apart; however, because of the unusual name, it could be the same person

Puterbaugh, George
A: Capt Geo Puterbaugh Co E 47 Ill Inf [Born 8/6/1842, Mackinaw, IL, son of Jacob & Hannah (Hittle) Puterbaugh]
B: George Puterbaugh Died Nov 20, 1918
C: GW/Magnolia Place DOD/B: 11/20-22/1918 A: 76 M: 1st wife Carrie Troyer James on 9/13/1866; death 3/1870.
D: George Puterbaugh N: Illinois A: 42 O: Lawyer CW: Co F 8 Ill Inf (Corp) Re-Enl?: Co E 47 Ill Inf (Capt) E/D: 4/61-10/64 LOS: 41 mos GAR: 5/13/1886 SP: 12/27/1898 or 1899 RE: 6/23/1903 Died: 11/20/1918 S:H
F: Catherine H. Puterbaugh died July 22, 1905 DOD: 7/22/1905-9/26/1917 A: 61 (removed from Mount Hope)
  He married 2nd Catherine Hall Wagoner on 10/1/1874; married 3rd Amy C. (Young) Wood [no record at GW] on 8/25/1909, daughter of Capt. J.F. Young, great-grandson of Betsy Ross, maker of 1st American Flag.

Quigley, George Beard
A/B: No stone
C: Cremated
E: George B. Quigley N: Warren Co, PA CW: Co D 13 PA Inf (Pvt) Term: Unstated E/D: 3/61-6/63 due to disability GAR: 9/11/1926 Died: 4/22/1927 A: 86 Cremated Merkley Mortuary S: DC

Rainbow, James P.M.
B: James P.M. Rainbow Born March 20, 1836 Beaver Co, Penn Died Oct 19, 1907
C: MH/IOOF DOD/B: 10/19-21/1907 A: 71/6/29 N: PA M: Married "J.P.M."
D: James P. Rainbow N: Beaver Co, Penn A: 46 O: Farmer/Apiarian R: Rainbow/FallBrook, CA CW: Co E 1 Cal Inf (Pvt/Corpl) E/D: 8/61-8/64 LOS: 36 mos GAR: 3/2/1883 SP: 9/26/1889 DR: 6/30/1891 RE: 2/24/1892 Died: 10/19/1907--is [grave] stone S: H
F: Augusta Rainbow-Lockwood Born September 30, 1846 Died April 24, 1928 DOB: 5/1/1928 A: 82 "In same grave as James P.M. Rainbow" Record under "Augusta Rainbow"

Ramsey, Simmons
A: Sergt Simmons Ramsey Co E 10 Kans Inf
C: MH/GAR Hill DOD/B: 4/17-18/1909 A: 72/9/29 N: Indiana M: Married
D: Simmons Ramsey N: Indiana A: 64 O: Farmer R: Merle CW: Co I 3 Kans Inf (Pvt) Re-Enl?: Co E 10 Kans Inf (Sgt) E/D: 7/61-8/64 LOS: 36 1/2 mos GAR: 8/8/1902 (probably on transfer from Dan Pratt Post #50 Dept of Indiana Died: 4/17/1909--is [grave] stone S: H
F: Ada J. Ramsey Meehan 1849-1934 DOD/B: 12/23-27/1934 A: 85/10/15 Died in San Diego

Reames, Bartlett
B: Bartlett Reames 1835-1913 1st Lieut Co A 7th Inft MO Vol
C: GW/Palm Terrace DOD/B: 8/8-11/1913 A: 78
F: Rebecca B. Reames 1844-1923 DOD/B: 6/28-7/2/1923 A: 78 "Rebecca Boothman Reames"

Redfern, Alfred
A: Alf'd Redfern Co K 91 Ind Inf
C: GW/Magnolia Place DOB: 4/10/1919 A: 67

Reed, James C.
A: Jas C. Reed Co A 13 Ohio Inf
C: MH/GAR Div.3 DOD/B: 2/13-15/1918 A: 70/10/6
E: James C. Reed N: Chili, Ohio (Chillicothe?) 4/7/44 CW: Co A 13 OVI (Pvt) Term: 3 yrs E/D: 4/61-6/64 Columbus, Ohio GAR: 9/25/1909 on transfer from Maywood Post #184 Dept of Cal/Nev Died: 2/13/1918 A: 73/10/6 S: DC

Reed, John P.
B: Capt. John P. Reed Native of Maine 1834-1897
C: MH/Masonic G DOD/B: 4/1-4/1897 A: 63

Remondino, Peter Charles
B: Located Sophia Remondino's crypt and inscription only
C: GW/Cathedral Mausoleum, Corridor A, Tier D, Crypt 4 DOD/B: 12/10-13/1926 A: 80 Note: 1880 census indicates "R.C. Remondino" is 43, a physician, and born in Italy of Italian-born parents. Note: Dr. Remondino was born in Turin, Italy on February 10, 1846, and left Italy with his father in 1854 for New York City, then to Wabasha, MN, according to *San Diego County, California: A Record of Settlement*, etc. (see more about him in Chapter 3 in the "Building the City" section.
D: Peter C. Remondino N: Italy A: 37 O: Physician CW: US Vols (Medical Cadets) E/D: 5/64-10/65 LOS: 17 mos GAR: 2/22/1883 DR: 6/30/1891 RE: 5/14/1901 Died: 12/10/1926 S: H
F: Sophia Ann Remondino 1861-1944, Corridor A, Tier D, Crypt 22 DOD/B: 10/13-16/1944 (born 6/26/1861) A: No record. 1880 census: Sophia is 18, wife of "R.C. Remondino, b. France; father French; mother English

Rench, Lyman T.
A: Lyman T. Rench Co K 77 Ill Inf July 13, 1915
C: GW/Hawthorne DOD/B: 7/13/1915-5/18/1916 A: 76 Prior burial: MH/GAR Div.3 DOD/B: 7/13-15/1915 A: 76/6/6 N: Maryland M: Married Removed to Greenwood 5/18/1916
F: Susan Agnes Wife 1846-1926 DOD/B: 12/19-21/1926 A: 80

Reupsche, William
B: William Reupsch 1836-1913
C: MH/Div.3 DOD/B: 2/12-14/1913 A: 87/__/4 "Reupsch"
D: William Reupsche N: Germany A: 42 O: Shoe Maker CW: Co F 41 NY Inf (Pvt) E/D: 11/62-12/65 LOS: 3 yrs GAR: 10/8/1881 Charter Member Heintzelman Post Died: 2/12/1913 S: H
F: Dorothy Reupsch 1846-1925 DOD/B: 2/10-11/1925 A: 79/1/4

Reynolds, Hiram H.
B: Hiram H. Reynolds Mar 10, 1829-Jan 29, 1937 (tombstone photo p. 64)
C: MH/Div.6 DOD/B: 1/29-2/3/1937 A: 107/10/19 Died in San Diego Oldest lived Civil War veteran

Reynolds, Hiram H. (Con't)
D: Hiram H. Reynolds N: New York A: 90 O: Retired CW: Co K 148 NY Inf (Pvt) E/D: __/62-__/65 LOS: 3 years GAR: 6/24/1924 SP: 12/22/1925 RE: 6/14/1927 TR: 8/6/1935 to Stanton Post Died: "Deceased" S: H
F: Amelia Maria Oct 14, 1838-Mar 13, 1922 DOD/B: 3/3-15/1922 A: 83

Reynolds, Joshua Thomas
B: Joshua T. Reynolds Apr 22, 1915 aged 80 yrs 6 mos Capt Co F 9th Reg Penn Reserves
C: MH/GAR Div.3 DOD/B: 4/22-24/1915 A: 80/6/2 N: PA M: Single
D: Joshua T. Reynolds N: Penn A: 78 O: Engineer CW: Co F 9 PA Reserves (Pvt/Capt) E/D: 4/61-__/64 due to resignation LOS: Not stated GAR: 3/11/1913 on transfer from Farragut Post #8 Dept of Kansas Died: 4/22/1915 S: H

Reynolds, Lewis D.
A/B: No stone C: Cremated
D: Lewis D. Reynolds N: New York A: 64 O: Mechanic CW: Co B 3 NY Cav (Pvt) E/D: 7/61-1/65 LOS: 38 mos GAR: 4/12/1904 Died: 1/13/1918 "Cremated" S: H

Rice, Almeron F.
A: A.F. Rice Co E 9 Mich Inf
B: Almeron F. Rice Newark, Wayne Co, NY Sep 9, 1847 Seattle, Wash Nov 30, 1902
C: MH/Div.2 DOD/B: 11/30-12/7/1902 A: 55 N: American M: Married
E: A.F. Rice N: Wayne Co, NY CW: Co E 9 Mich Inf (Pvt) Term: 1 yr E/D: 3/65-9/65 Nashville, TN GAR: 2/12/1896 Died: 11/30/1902 A: 56 Buried: Mount Hope S: DC

Rice, John H.
A: Act Ensign J.H. Rice US Navy
C: MH/GAR Hill DOD/B: 7/29-31/1903 A: 75/8/24 N: American M: Widower
D: John H. Rice N: Maine A: 69 O: Mariner CW: US Navy (Acting Ensign) E/D: __/62-10/65 LOS: 34 mos GAR: 8/27/1896 TR: 4/3/1897 S: H
E: Rice, John H. N: Norway 11/5/27 CW: US Navy (Act.Ensign/Act.Master) Term: Duration of war E/D: 12/62-10/65 Charlestown Mass GAR: ? date on transfer from Heintzelman Post San Diego Died: 7/29/1903 A: 76 Buried: GAR Plot (Mount Hope) S: DC
NOTE: Enlisted at Charlestown, Mass. Transferred to Brooklyn Navy Yard, NY; then to Cairo, Ill and Cincinatti, Ohio. Executive officer of Flag Ship Moose. Served in district of Upper Mississippi. Promoted to Master and placed in command of Steamship Reindeer for 1 year. Transferred to command of Steamer Brilliant until close of war S: DC

Rice, Laban W.
A: Bglr Laban Rice Co D 1 Tex Cav CSA
C: MH/Confederate DOD/B: 10/18-19/1914 A: 74/__/24 N: Texas M: Widower "Labon"
Note: Laban W. Rice died 10/18/1914 in San Diego, CA. Pvt, Co D 1 Texas Calvary (State organization). Was Bugler. S: UDC document, California Room (see Chapter II, "San Diego Public Library" sources)

Richards, George J.
B: Col. George J. Richards Feb 26, 1848-Feb 15, 1921
C: MH/Masonic R DOD/B: 2/15-18/1921 A: 72/11/11 "Col"
D: George J. Richards N: New York A: 65 O: Not stated CW: Co D 14 NY H A (Sgt) E/D: 12/63-8/65 LOS: Not stated GAR: 6/24/1913 Died: 2/15/1921 S: H
F: Hermina A. Richards Aug 15, 1867-Mar 21, 1937 DOD/B: 3/21-23/1937 A: 69/7/4 Died in San Diego

Richardson, Charles D.
B: Charles Dana Richardson 1841-1919 Co G 30th Mass Vol Inf
C: GW/Laurel Place DOD: 1919 A: No record found
D: Charles D. Richardson N: Mass A: 61 O: Farmer CW: Co C 30 Mass Inf (Pvt/QM Sgt) E/D: 10/61-7/66 LOS: 57 mos GAR: 8/11/1903 Died: 12/7/1919 S: H
F: Sarah Titlon 1841-1926 DOD: 1926 A: 84

Richey, Jay Harvey
A/B: No stone
C: MH/GAR Hill DOD/B: 11/15-20/1929 A: 82/__/24 (ashes) Died in San Diego "Jay"
E: J. Harvey Richey N: Maryville, Ohio CW: Co H 136 Ohio Inf (Pvt) Term: 90 days E/D: 5/64-10/64 Camp Chase, Ohio GAR: 1/26/1900 DR: 12/9/1916 S: DC
F: Flora G. Richey Aug 25, 1857-April 24, 1924 DOD/B: 4/24-26/1924 A: 66/7/3 "Flora Garvin"

Richmond, Jonathan Edward
B: Jonathan Richmond 1845-1924 Co E 44 MO Inf
C: MH/GAR Div.2 DOD/B: 3/14-17/1932 A: 71/5/2 Died in San Diego "John"
F: Margaret A. Richmond No stone DOD/B: 1/4-16/1946 A: 75/3/23 (ashes) Died in Los Banos, CA

Ricksecker, Lucius Edgar
A: Corpl L.E. Ricksecker Co A 153 PA Inf
C: MH/GAR Div.3 DOD/B: 1/30-2/3/1913 A: 72/__/16 N: PA M: Married

Riddle, George Henry
A: Geo H. Riddle Co K 8 IA Cav
B: George H. Riddle 1845-1921
C: MH/GAR Hill DOD/B: 9/19-21/1921 A: 76
E: Geo. H. Riddle N: PA 3/23/45 CW: Co K 8 Iowa Cav (Pvt) Term: 3 yrs E/D: 7/63-6/65 GAR: 10/23/1915 on transfer from J.B. Steadman Post #24 Dept of Wash/Alaska Died: 9/19/1921 A: 76/5/24 S: DC
F: Catherine C. Riddle 1853-1941 DOD/B: 6/21-25/1941 A: 88/2/24 Died in San Diego

Riddle, James D.
A: James D. Riddle Co C 69 Ill Inf Sept 29, 1844-July 11, 1934
C: MH/GAR Div.2 DOD/B: 7/11-14/1934 A: 89/9/11 Died in San Diego

Riley, William T.
B: William T. Riley 1843-1917 Co D 86th NY Inf
C: GW/Acacia Place DOD/B: 8/10-13/1917 A: 74
D: Wm. T.Riley N: Allegheny Co, NY A: 74 O: Retired CW: Co D 86 NY Inf (Pvt) E/D: 10/61-10/64 LOS: 36 mos Re-Enl?: Co K 5 Hancock's Vet Vol (Pvt/Sgt) E/D: 3/65-3/66 LOS: 12 mos GAR: 6/26/1917 on transfer from Post #6 Dept of Idaho Died: 8/10/1917 S: H
F: Frances M. Riley 1845-1916 DOD/B: 10/25-27/1916 A: 71

Roach, Henry
B: (See long grave stone inscription below)
C: MH/GAR Hill DOD/B: 7/24-27/1902 A: 57/4/12 N: English M: Married Name Harry
  Note: Stone reads: Henry Roach Born March 12, 1846 Died July 24, 1902 Civil War Private Co E 11th Mich Vol Inf Sept 15, 1861-Oct 4, 1865 Regular Army 19th Inf 1st Sergt 1866-1872 Spanish American War 1st Lieut and RQM 34th Mich Vol Inf Appointed aid on staff of Gen. Lawton August 13, 1898 To live in the hearts of those we leave behind is not to die.
F: Viola M. Carling Died Jan 15, 1910 DOD/B: No record in boxes (buried near him on map; her name on large tombstone to him) Note: City Directory for 1903 lists Viola as widow to Henry Roach.)

Roach, William Henry
A: W.H. Roach Co F 7 Tenn Cav CSA
C: MH/Confederate DOD/B: 7/13-16/1928 A: 82/7/7 Died in National City, CA
F: Hattie Lee Roach 1862-1937 DOB: 1/23/1937 (no record further record available)
  Note: William H. Roach was born 12/6/1845 in Williams Co, Tenn; Died 2/14/1934 in San Diego, CA. Pvt Co F 7 Tenn Cav. S: UDC document, California Room (see Chapter II, "San Diego Public Library" sources)

Roark, James A.
A: James A. Roark Co F 6 Ill Cav
C: MH/GAR Div. 3 DOD/B: 6/3-4/1913 A: 82/__/26 N: PA M: Married
D: James A. Roark N: Illinois A: 55 O: Stock Raiser CW: Co F 6 Ill Cav (2nd Lieut) E/D: 10/61-10/62 due to resignation LOS: 12 mos GAR: 6/30/1886 SP: 3/28/1889 DR: 3/28/1899 SP: 12/27/1904 DR: 1/22/1907 RE: 10/10/1911 SP: 12/24/1912 DR: 12/24/1918 Died: 6/2/1913 S: H

Roberts, Joseph W.
A: Sergt J.W. Roberts Co L 97 Ohio Inf
C: MH/Div.5 DOD/B: 10/1-4/1904 A: 73/8/__ "J.W."
D: Joseph W. Roberts N: Ohio A: 56 O: Shoemaker CW: Co C 97 Ohio Inf (Pvt) E/D: 8/62-6/65 LOS: 34 mos GAR: 3/22/1888 Died: 10/11/1904--is [grave] stone S: H
F: Matilda Roberts No stone DOB: 1/9-11/1913 A: 84/8/21 N: Ohio M: Widow

Roberts, Luzerne L.
A: L.L. Roberts Co L 6 Ohio Cav
C: MH/GAR Hill DOD/B: 2/25-26/1900 A: 58 N: American M: Married
D: L.L. Roberts N: Ohio A: 39 O: Machinist CW: Co L 6 Ohio __ (Pvt) Re/Enl?: Co G 18 Ohio __ (Pvt) E/D: 10/61-10/64 LOS: 42 mos GAR: 5/25/1882 SP: 9/26/1889 DR: 11/30/1891 Died: 2/25/1900--is [grave] stone S: H

Robinson, Culbert Byron
A: Corp'l C.B. Robinson Co B 52nd PA Inf
C: MH/GAR Hill DOD/B: 8/27-30/1890 A: 52 N: American M: Married "Culbert Byron"
D: C.B. Robinson N: Penn A: 47 O: Railroad Conductor CW: Co B 52 PA Inf (Pvt/Corpl) E/D: 2/62-8/65 LOS: 41 mos GAR: 7/8/1886 SP: 1/10/1889 Died: 8/29/1890--is [grave] stone S: H

Robinson, George Cromwell
B: Corpl Geo. C. Robinson 1838-1925 Co B 7th Ohio Inf
C: MH/GAR Hill DOD/B: 7/11-13/1925 A: 87/5/7 "Cromwell"
E: Geo C. Robinson N: England CW: Co B 7 Ohio Inf (Pvt) Term: 3 yrs E/D: 6/61-6/64 Columbus, Ohio GAR: 10/10/1908 on transfer from Frank P. Blair Post Dept of Missouri DR: 12/9/1916 S: DC

Robinson, Melvin W.
A: M.W. Robinson Co H 3 Ohio Cav
C: MH/GAR Hill DOD/B: 3/12-14/1904 A: 63/7/19 N: American M: Married Died in San Diego "Melvin M."
E: M.W. Robinson N: Washington Co, Ohio CW: Co H 3 Ohio Cav (Pvt) Term: 3 yrs E/D: 10/61-10/62 Cincinnati, Ohio due to Surgeon's Certificate of Disability GAR: 5/26/1901 on transfer from John Anderson Post Dept of Kansas Died: 3/12/1904 A: 66 Buried: GAR (Mount Hope) S: DC

Roby, David B.
B: David B. Roby 1845-1925 Pvt Co B 63 Ohio Vol Inf
C: MH/GAR Div.2 DOD/B: 1/3-7/1925 A: 79/8/27
D: David B. Roby N: Ohio A: 73 O: Retired CW: Co B 63 Ohio Inf (Pvt) E/D: 8/62-7/65 LOS: 35 mos GAR: 5/28/1918 Died: 1/3/1925 S: H

Roby, Rheuben Theodore
A: Rheuben Roby Co H 38 Wis Inf
C: MH/GAR Div.2 DOD/B: 4/11-12/1910 A: 66/6/13 N: Ohio M: Married Name Reuben
D: Reuben T. Roby N: Ohio A: 58 O: Carpenter CW: Co H 38 Wis Inf (Pvt) E/D: 6/64-__/__ LOS: Not stated GAR: 2/9/1904 SP: 3/26/1907 Died: 4/11/1910 S: H

Rodgers, Henry J.G.
A: H.J.G. Rodgers Co D 133 NY Inf
C: MH/GAR Div.2 DOD/B: 12/12-14/1899 A: 79 N: American M: Married "Rogers"
D: Henry J.G. Rogers N: New York A: 68 O: Lawyer CW: Co D 133 NY Inf (Pvt/Corp) E/D: 8/62-6/65 LOS: 35

Rodgers, Henry J.G. (Con't)
    1/2 mos GAR: 2/9/1888 Died: 12/12/1899--is [grave] stone S: H
F: Ellen Rogers aged 71 years DOD/B: 4/25-27/1911 A: 71/10/16 N: England M: Widow Died in San Diego

Rodig, Charles Herman
B: Herman Rodig Co O 6 Ohio Cav
C: MH/GAR Hill DOD/B: 9/24-27/1934 A: 89/__/3 Died in San Diego
F: Mother Mary Rodig Apr 9, 1868-July 6, 1942 DOD/B: 7/6-9/1942 A: 74/1/27

Rood, Vernon Dudley
B: Vernon Dudley Rood, M.D. Born April 20, 1842 Died Oct 26, 1906
C: MH/IOOF DOD/B: 10/26-11/1/1906 A: 64/6/6 N: Vermont M: Married "Dudley"
D: Vernon D. Rood N: Vermont A; 45 O: Physician CW: Co H 2 VT Inf (Pvt) E/D: 4/61-6/64 LOS: 38 mos GAR:
    2/9/1888 SP: 6/25/1901 DR: 12/24/1901 Died: "Dead"--no [grave] stone S: H

Root, Eleaser Talcut
A: Eleaser Root Co I 65 Ill Inf
C: MH/GAR Div.2 DOD/B: 1/20-22/1913 A: Not stated N: Connecticut M: Married Middle name Talcut
E: Eleaser Root N: Coventry, CT CW: Co I 65 Ill Inf (Pvt) Term: 3 yrs E/D: 3/62-7/65 Orensboro (Oakboro?), NC
    GAR: 4/23/1912 on transfer from Rawlins Post #35 Dept of Nebraska. Died: 1/17/1913 A: 67 Buried: GAR
    (Mount Hope) S: DC
F: Francis E. Root No stone DOD/B: No further record Note: City Directory for 1914 lists Francis as widow of E.T.
    Root.

Rose, George W.
A. Lieut Geo W. Rose Co L 33 Mass Inf
C: MH/Masonic C DOD/B: 2/21-24/1904 A: 70/6/19 N: American M: Married

Rose, John
A: John Rose Co G 16 PA Cav
C: MH/GAR Hill DOD: 11/9-12/1903 A: 61/10/4 N: American M: Married
D: John Rose N: Penn A: 47 O: Carpenter CW: Co M 16 PA Cav (Pvt) E/D: 9/62-6/65 LOS: 34 mos GAR:
    4/25/1889 Died: 11/9/1903--is [grave] stone S: H
F: Clara Rose No stone DOD/B: 7/29-8/1/1932 A: 83/2/14 Died in San Diego

Ross, James
A: Jas Ross Co B 1 US Cav
C: GW/Magnolia Place DOD/B: 2/11-14/1912 A: 73

Rosswell, Edwin
A: Edwin Rosswell Co H 2 Mass H A
C: MH/Masonic U DOB: 8/1/1913 A: 70

Rowe, Charles Carroll
B: Charles C. Rowe Co G 12 NH Vols Civil War Nov 6, 1845-June 8, 1925
C: MH/GAR Hill DOD/B: 6/8-10/1925 A: 78/7/2
D: Chas C. Rowe N: New Hampshire A: 79 O: Retired CW: Co G 12 NH Inf (Pvt) E/D: 8/62-10/63 due to wounds
    LOS: 1 yr GAR: 11/27/1923 TR: 11/25/1924 S: H
E: Chas. C. Rowe N: Guilford, NH 1845 CW: Co G 12 NH Inf (Pvt) Term: 3 yrs E/D: 8/62-10/63 at Concord, NH
    due to wounds GAR: 12/13/1924 on transfer from Dept of New Hampshire Died: 6/8/1925 A: 78/7/2 Buried:
    Mount Hope S: DC

Rowe, Josiah Lemeul
A: Josiah L. Rowe Co K 2 Mich Inf
C: MH/Div.3 DOD/B: 7/19-21/1880 A: 39 N: Michigan M: Married J/S: "Rowe, Josiah L., d. 19 Jul (1880), 39 yrs,
    b: MI, mar, bu City Cem" Obit/San Diego Herald, 7/19/1880: "In this city Monday July 19, Josiah Lemuel

Rowe, Josiah Lemuel (Con't)
   Rowe, a native of Highland, Oakland Co, Michigan aged 39 yrs. Notice of funeral will be given in tomorrow's Union. Obit/San Diego Herald, 7/21/1880: "Funeral this p.m. at 2:00 from residence. Friends invited to attend."

Roys, S.W.
B: In memory of Capt S.W. Roys Born in Pultneyville Wagner Jan 1, 1827 Died in San Diego March 21, 1876
C: MH/IOOF DOB: 3/21/1876 A: Not stated "Cap. S.W. Roys"

Ruff, Francis B.
A: F.B. Ruff Co D 21 IA Inf
B: In memory of Francis B. Ruff Died Jan 31, 1907 aged 85 years
C: MH/Masonic L DOD/B: 2/2-4/1907 A: 85 N: NY M: Married
E: Francis B. Ruff N: Dearborn, Mich CW: Co D 21 Iowa Inf (Pvt) Term: 3 yrs E/D: 8/62-8/65 Clinton, Iowa GAR: 7/13/1901 Died: 2/2/1907 A: 86 Buried: GAR (Mount Hope) S: DC
F: Mary Ann Tiffin his wife a native of England Died May 9,1914 aged 79 yrs 6 mos DOB: 5/11/1914 A: 79/6/0

Rule, George
A: Geo A. Rule Co B 30 Wis Inf
B: George A. 1835-1913
C: MH/IOOF DOD/B: 2/21-22/1913 A: 78/4/__
F: Elizabeth A. 1845-1923 DOB: 8/7/1921 A: 78 (stone/office record differ)

Russell, Hiram W.
A: Sergt Hiram W. Russell Co I 1 Ill L A
B: Hiram W. June 17, 1842-Aug 20, 1910
C: GW/Hawthorne DOD/B: 8/20/1910-10/7/1919 A: 68
F: Evaline April 18, 1842-Oct 29, 1919 DOD/B: No record found except "Evaline" name appears on the back of Hiram's cemetary record card

Russell, John I.
A/B: No stone
C: Cremated
D: John I. Russell N: New York A: 78 O: Retired CW: Co A 1 Iowa Cav (Pvt/2nd Lieut) E/D: 6/61-2/65 due to resignation LOS: Not stated GAR: 10/27/1914 Died: 12/13/1917 Cremated: 12/17/1917 S: H

Salazar, Jose Maria
A: Jose M. Salazar Co A 1 Cal Cav (tombstone not at Calvary Cemetery; photo of tombstone in Calvary Cemetery photo collection at San Diego Historical Society)
C: CAL/Sec.1, South, Row 4 DOD/B: No record found in Catholic cemetery index
D: Jose Maria Salazar N: Mexico A: 78 O: Laborer CW: Co A 1 Cal Cav (Pvt) E/D: 2/65-5/66 LOS: Not stated GAR: 9/12/1911 Died: 3/3/1913 S: H

Sammis, Marsden H.
B: Marsden H. Sammis Co B 178th Ohio Inf 1844-1918
C: GW/Hawthorne DOD/B: 5/11-14/1918 A: 74
D: M.H. Sammis N: Westerville, Ohio A: 73 O: Pension Attorney CW: Co A 5th Ind Cav (Pvt) Re-enl?: Co A 5th Ind Inf (Sgt) E/D: 7/63-2/64 Re-enl?: Co B 178 Ohio Vol Inf (Sgt) E/D: 8/64-7/65 LOS: 18 mos GAR: 5/22/1917 on transfer from A. Lincoln Post #4 Dept of Col/Wyo S: H
F: Frances E. Sammis 1846-1933 DOD/B: 12/22-23/1933 A: 87

Saum, Augustus B.
B: Augustus B. Saum G.A.R. 1844-1934
C: GW/Elks Rest DOD/B: 11/20-23/1934 A: 90
D: Augustus B. Saum N: Homer, OH A: 74 O: Contractor CW: Co I 14 Iowa Inf (Pvt) E/D: 8/61-11/64 LOS: 39 mos GAR: 6/25/1918 Died: 11/20/1934 S: H
F: Mary Emily Saum 1848-1937 DOD/B: 6/26-28/1937 A: 89

Saunders, Charles K.
B: Chas. K. Saunders Co G 15 Ohio Inf Vols Died Feb 23, 1895
C: MH/GAR Hill DOD/B: 2/23-26/1895 A: 76 N: England M: Widower

Savage, George B.
A: George B. Savage Co E 19 VA Hv Art'y CSA
B: MH/Confederate DOD/B: 10/20-22/1923 A: 80/2/3 "Confederate Plot"
    Note: George Savage was born in 1843; Died 10/20/1923 in San Diego, CA. Pvt Co I 39 VA Inf. Enlisted in this unit 9/11/1861 at Harper's Ferry. Discharged 2/3/1862. Re-Enlisted 2/21/1862 in 19 VA Heavy Artillery Battalion. S: UDC document, California Room (see Chapter II, "San Diego Public Library" sources)

Scarbrough, B.F.
A: Sgt B.F. Scarbrough Co A 12 KY Cav
C: MH/GAR Hill DOD/B: 5/20-22/1903 A: 62 N: American M: Single

Schaler, Julius G.
B: Julius Schaler 1833-1924 Co E 5 Minn Inf Vol
C: MH/Div.2 DOD/B: 10/21-25/1924 A: 90/10/13
F: Amalia Schaler 1847-1927 DOD/B: 5/10-13/1927 A: 80 Died in Chula Vista, CA

Scherrer, Hieronimus
B: Hieronimus Scherrer Co D 16 Reg Ill 1835-1916
C: MH/GAR Div.3 DOD/B: 8/2-3/1916 A: 85 "Hieronimus"
D: Heronimus Scherrer N: Germany A: 70 O: Retired CW: Co D 16 Ill Cav (Pvt) E/D: 2/63-10/64 LOS: Not stated GAR: 7/27/1909 Died: 8/2/1916 S: H
F: Catherine, His Wife 1831-1919 (tombstone has been pushed over since this record made) DOD/B: 4/18-21/1919 A: 89/__/5 Died in San Diego

Schiller, Henry J.
A: Henry Schiller Co G 1 MO Inf
C: MH/IOOF DOB: 5/12-15/1917 A: 77
D: Henry J. Schiller N: Prussia A: 70 O: Retired CW: Co G 1 MO Inf (Pvt) E/D: 11/61-12/64 LOS: Not stated GAR: 10/25/1910 Died: 5/13/1917 S: H

Schrader, Adolph
B: Adolph 1842-1933
C: MH/Div.6 DOD/B: 11/21-25/1933 A: 91/2/9 Died in San Diego
D: Adloph Schrader N: Germany A: 79 O: Retired CW: Co K 38 Ind Inf (Pvt) E/D: 8/61-8/65 LOS: 4 yrs GAR: 12/13/1921 SP: 12/22/1925 RE: 3/22/1932 S: H
F: Mother 1847-1905 DOD/B: 4/1-3/1905 A: 57/3/27 N: American M: Married "Adalia Layden Schrader"

Schudey (Shudy), John
A: John Schudey 1 NE MO Inf
C: MH/Div.7 DOD/B: 1/13-5/__/1912 A: 71/9/6 N: PA M: Married Record found under "Shudy" for husband/wife
F: Leah Shudy No stone DOD/B: 1/4-8/1931 A: About 95 Died in San Diego

Schultheiss, Frederick L.
B: Frederick Schultheiss 1826-1909
C: GW/Hawthorne DOD/B: 7/11/1909-11/4/1924 A: 83 (prior burial at Mount Hope: DOD/B: 7/11-13/1909 A: 83/11/25 N: Germany M: Widower "F.L. Schultheiss" "Removed to Greenwood Cemetery in 1924")
E: Fred Scheiltheiss N: Germany CW: Co I 1 Kans Inf (Pvt) Term: 3 yrs E/D: 5/61-6/64 Leavenworth, Kansas GAR: 4/23/1897 Died: 7/11/1909 A: 84 Buried: GAR (Mount Hope) S: DC
F: Fredericka Schultheiss 1836-1908 DOD/B: 4/5/1908-11/4/1924 A: 73

Schultz, James T.
A/B: No stone
C: MH/Div.3 DOD/B: 10/20-23/1916 A: 69
D: James T. Schultz N: Illinois A: 45 O: Rancher R: Oneonta, CA CW: Co F 26 Ill Inf (Pvt) E/D: 2/64-7/65 LOS: 17 mos GAR: 9/9/1891 SP: 3/__/1893 DR: 3/28/1899 S: H
F: Florence K. Schultz No stone DOD/B: 10/26-30/1940 A: 89/2/3 Died in Palm City

Scidmore, G.B.
A: G.B. Scidmore Co K (or Co N) 2nd Colo Cav
C: MH/GAR Hill DOD/B: 3/18-21/1898 A: 82 N: Not stated M: Single "Seidmore"

Scoby, Thomas Hertell
A: Thos. H. Scoby Co A 96 Ohio Inf
C: MH/GAR Hill DOD/B: 4/4-6/1914 A: 64/__/4 N: Ohio M: Married "Scobey"
D: Thomas H. Scoby N: Ohio A: 36 O: Plasterer CW: Co A 196 Ohio Inf (Pvt) E/D: 2/65-9/65 LOS: 7 mos GAR: 6/30/1886 Post Commander 1901 Died 4/5/1914 S: H
F: Clara C. Scobey May 8, 1854-Dec 21, 1935 DOD/B: 12/21-24/1935 A: 81/7/13 (ashes) Died in San Diego "Scobey"

Scott, Winfield
B: Winfield Scott Chaplain USA Feb 26, 1837-Oct 19, 1910
C: MH/GAR Hill DOD/B: 10/19/1910-4/4/1911 A: 73 N: Michigan
F: Helen Louise Scott Jan 8, 1838-Nov 17, 1931 DOD/B: 10/17-20/1931 A: 93/10/9 Died in San Diego

Scruby, John
B: John Scruby July 14, 1842-Feb 28, 1920 Co D 25 Wis Vol Inf
C: MH/GAR Hill DOD/B: 2/28-3/1/1920 A: 77

Seabold(t), Gilbert L.
A: G.L. Seabold Co A 33 Ill Inf
C: MH/GAR Hill DOD/B: 9/16-18/1906 A: 70 N: Illinois M: Widower "Seybolt"

Seavy, James
A: James Seavy Co D 19 Wis Inf
C: MH/GAR Div.3 DOD/B: 2/28-3/5/1915 A: 72/4/9 N: PA M: Married
F: Helen Seavy No stone DOD/B: 11/16-22/1920 A: 79/3/2

Sechrist, Jacob
A: Jacob Sechrist Co K 7 PA Cav
C: MH/GAR Hill DOD/B: 6/24-26/1892 A: 48 N: American M: Married
F: Mother Lucy E. Sechrist 1852-1934 DOD/B: 4/12-16/1934 A: 81/11/29 Died in San Diego "Lucy Enfield Sechrist"

Sedgewick, Thomas S.
B: Col Thomas Stewart Sedgwick Zanesville, Ohio Aug 13, 1828 San Diego Cal June 23, 1904 A Soldier of the Civil War
C: MH/IOOF DOD/B: 6/23-25/1904 A: 76 N: American M: Widower "Col T.S. Sedgwick"

Seidell, Charles W.
A/B: No stone
C: MH/Masonic P DOD/B: 12/28/1905-1/4/1906 A: 66 N: Germany M: Married "Sidell"
D: Charles W. Seidell N: Germany A: 61 O: Rancher R: Bostonia, CA CW: Co C 105 Ill Inf (2nd Sgt/1st Sgt) Promoted?: Co G 16 US C T (1st Lieut/Capt) E/D: 8/62-5/66 LOS: 45 mos GAR: 1/9/1900 Died: 12/28/1905--is [grave] stone S: H

Sennock (Sennett), Judson L.
A: J.L. Sennock Co E 3 NY L A
C: MH/GAR Hill DOD/B: 3/12-14/1909 A: 75/1/13 N: New York M: Widower "Judson Sennett" "JS" record indicates a Judson L. Se___ett died 3/12/1909 of Brights Disease at 813 5th (Avenue?) Nativity New York Marital--widower
D: Judson L. Sennett N: New York A: 56 O: Agent CW: Co E 3 NY Art; 3 NY H A (Pvt) E/D: 8/62-5/65 LOS: 45 2/3 mos GAR: 5/28/1890 D: 6/23/1903 Rejoined: By transfer from Stanton Post Died: 3/12/1909--is [grave] stone S: H

Servoss, Freeman
B: Freeman Servoss Nov 18, 1837-Oct 7, 1925
C: MH/GAR Hill DOD/B: 10/7-11/1925 A: 88/10/19
D: Freeman Servoss N: New York A: 76 O: Farmer CW: Co C 52 Ill Inf (Musician) E/D: 10/61-8/62 LOS: Not stated GAR: 6/24/1913 Died: 10/7/1925

Seymour, W.C.
A: W.C. Seymour US Navy
C: MH/Masonic O DOD/B: 10/23-26/1896 A: 60/9/28 N: American M: Married "W.C. or H.C. Seymore"

Sharp, James L.
A: James L. Sharp Co L 1 Ind Hv Art'y
C: MH/GAR Hill DOD/B: 1/22-25/1934 A: 87/5/3 Died in San Diego
E: James L. Sharp N: Richland, Indiana 1847 CW: Co L 1st Ind H A (Pvt) Term: 3 yrs E/D: 4/63-1/66 GAR: 9/13/1924 on transfer from H.W. Lawton Post Dept of Indiana Died: 1/22/1934 A: 87 S: DC

Shattuck, John
A: John E. Shattuck 4 Mass Cav
C: FR/Section A Grave 203 CA DOB: 11/6-8/1937 No other information available
E: John Shattuck N: Petersburg, Ill 1845 CW: Batt A 3 Ill L A (Pvt) Term: 3 yrs E/D: 6/62-6/65 GAR: 5/28/1932 Died: 11/6/1937 A: 89 Buried: Bennington Cemetery, Fort Rosecrans S: DC

Shaughnessey, William M.
B: W.M. Shaughnessey 36th Wis Inf 1839-1922
C: MH/GAR Hill DOD/B: 2/26-3/1/1922 A: 83 "William Shonessy"

Shaw, Frank A.T.
B: Francis A.T. Shaw June 7, 1848-Sept 28, 1921
C: MH/IOOF DOB: 10/1/1921 A: 73 Note: 1880 census indicates he was 31, a teamster, and was born in Pennsylvania, as was his father. (Mother's place of birth not given on this record.)
D: Frank A.T. Shaw N: Philadelphia, Penn A: 34 O: Teamster/Road Overseer CW: Co H 7 Cal Cav (Pvt) E/D: Not stated LOS: Not stated GAR: 2/8/1883 SP: 12/31/1883 GAR: 7/9/1890 SP: 12/28/1892 SP: 12/31/1893 DR: 3/28/1899 RE: 6/8/1909 Died: 9/28/1921 S: H
F: Brigida M. Shaw Oct 28, 1847-Aug 25, 1940 DOB: 8/25-27/1940 A: 92/9/28 Died in San Diego Note: The 1880 census for San Diego County indicates that Brigida Shaw was born in California, was 29 at the time of the census, and was the wife of Francis Shaw. Her father was born in California; her mother in France.

Shaw, Joseph M.
B: Joseph M. Shaw 1841-1919 Co F 1 US Cav
C: GW/Cypress Place DOD/B: 12/9-15/1919 A: 78

Shay, William
A: Wm. Shay Co K 23 Ill Inf (tombstone visible at Calvary Cemetery)
C: CAL/Sec.1, C, Row 1 DOD/B: No record found in Catholic cemetery index

Sheldon, Richard Henry
A/B: No stone
C: MH/GAR Hill   DOD/B: 5/26-29/1916   A: 74
D: Richard H. Sheldon   N: Ohio   A: 45   O: Carpenter   CW: Co F 3 Ohio Cav (Pvt)   Re/Enl?: Co F 12 Ohio Cav (Pvt)
   E/D: 9/61-11/65   LOS: 37 mos   GAR: 12/25/1886   SP: 12/26/1905   RE: 4/10/1906   Died: 5/26/1916   S: H
F: Annie W. Sheldon Born Aug 12, 1842 Died: Jan 18, 1897 WRC 1883   DOD/B: 1/18-21/1897   A: 54/6/__
   N: English   M: Married   "Mrs. Annie W."

Sherman, Edward
A: Edw'd Sherman Co K 153 Ill Inf
C: MH/Masonic M   DOB: 3/31/1913   A: 67/4/26

Sherman, Francis M.
B: Francis M. Sherman Born Aug 6, 1841 Died Dec 15, 1903 Corpl Co I 9 Ind Inf
C: MH/GAR Hill   DOD/B: 12/15-17/1903   A: 62/9/9   N: American   M: Widower
D: Francis Sherman   N: Indiana   A: 50   O: Rancher   CW: Co I 9 Ind Inf (Pvt)   E/D: 4/61-1/63   LOS: Not stated   GAR:
   ? date   Died: 12/15/1903--is [grave] stone   S: H
F: Jennie Dawley, wife of F.M. Sherman Born Oct 9, 1842 Died Feb 14, 1903   DOD/B: 2/14-22/1903   A: 60/4/5   N:
   American   M: Married

Sherman, Matthew
B: Captain Matthew Sherman Charlestown, Mass Oct 11, 1827 San Diego, Cal July 5, 1898 A Veteran of the
   Mexican and Civil Wars
C: MH/Div.3   DOD/B: 7/5-7/1898   A: 70/8/5   N: American   M: Married   "Capt"
D: Matthew Sherman   N: Charlestown, Mass   A: 54   O: Real Estate   CW: Co G 4 Cal Vols (1st Lieut/QM)   E/D: 1/__
   to 11/65   LOS: Not stated   GAR: 9/28/1881 First Mustering Officer of Heintzelman Post GAR   Died: 7/5/1898-
   -is [grave] stone
F: Augusta J. His wife April 17, 1839 to Jan 5, 1913   DOD/B: 1/5-7/1913   A: 73/8/19   N: Maine   M: Widow

Sherwood, James
A: James Sherwood Co F 10 NJ Inf
C: MH/GAR Div.3   DOD/B: 12/9-11/1913   A: About 68   N: Not stated   M: Single

Shryock, Seymour
B: Seymour Shryock Indiana Cpl Co K 5 Regt Iowa Inf Civil War July 6, 1839-Aug 4, 1931
C: GW/Cypress Place   DOD/B: 8/4-8/1931   A: 92
D: Seymour Shryock   N: Indiana   A: 79   O: Gardener   R: Paradise Valley   CW: Co K 5th Iowa Inf (Pvt/Corpl)   E/D:
   7/61-8/64   LOS: 3 yrs 1 mo   GAR: 5/13/1919   DR: 1926   Died 8/4/1931   S: H
F: Mary E. Shryock 1851-1928   DOD/B: 5/6-8/1928   A: 77   "Mary Elizabeth Shryock"

Simon(s), John
A: Jno Simon Co E 94 Ill Inf
C: MH/GAR Hill   DOD/B: 6/18-20/1905   A: 74/2/28   N: Switzerland   M: Married   "Simons"
F: Johanna B. Simon Beloved Wife of John Simon Born Nov 11, 1834 Died Oct 22, 1902   DOD/B: 10/22-24/1902
   A: 67/11/12   N: German   M: Married   "Johanna Simons"

Simpson, John H.
A: Sergt John H. Simpson Co I 5 US Inf
B: John H. Simpson 1830-1912
C: MH/Masonic A   DOD/B: 11/22-25/1912   A: 82/__/19   N: England   M: Married   "Captain"   Note: 1880 census of San
   Diego indicates he was 49, a clerk with "PCCS", and was born in England, as were his parents.
F: Anna Simpson 1842-1924   DOD/B: 4/6-8/1924   A: 82/__/28   "Anna Nancy"   Note: The 1880 census for San Diego
   indicates that Anna Simpson was born in Missouri, was 38 at the time of the census, and was married to G.H.
   Simpson. Her parents were both born in Kentucky.

Singleton, J.A.
A: J.A. Singleton Co D 5th Cal Inf (tombstone visible at Calvary Cemetery)
C: CAL/Sec.1, North, Row 10-3 (burial site for a "J.A. Singleton") DOD/B: No record found in Catholic cemetery index

Sinks, John F.
A: QM Sgt John F. Sinks 61 Ohio Inf
C: MH/Div.5 DOB: 11/25-26/1909 A: 67/5/7 N: Ohio M: Married
F: Anna E. McKinney 1861-1943 DOB: 5/1-4/1943 A: 82/3/24 Died in San Diego "Anna Elizabeth"

Skinner, Simon
A: Simon Skinner Co D 50 NY Eng'rs
C: MH/GAR Hill DOD/B: 2/16-18/1903 A: 80 N: American M: Widower "Simeon" (Coroner Inquest Report
        14417 000 indicates death from heart degeneration on 2/16/1903--San Diego Historical Socity Archives)
F: Mary T. Skinner No stone DOD/B: 8/9-12/1918 A: 72/1/26

Slack, Andrew J.
A: A.J. Slack Co A 7th W VA Cav
C: MH/GAR Hill DOD/B: 6/26-29/1892 A: 51 N: American M: Single "Andrew"

Sloan, James L.
B: Jas L. Sloan Co A 68 Ind Inf
C: MH/GAR Div.3 DOD/B: 2/19-20/1918 A: About 75
E: James L. Sloan N: Fairfield, Ind CW: Co A 68 Ind Inf (Pvt) Term: 3 yrs E/D: 8/62-6/65 Indianapolis GAR:
        11/27/1909 Died: 2/19/1918 A: 84 Buried: GAR (Mount Hope) S: H

Slocum, Milton L.
B: Col M.L. Slocum Oct 23, 1832-July 14, 1919
C: MH/Confederate DOB: 7/14/1919 A: 45 (ashes) "Col M.L."
F: Cella B. (ashes of) DOB: 3/17/1944-5/9/1944 A: 87 Died in San Diego Note: As mentioned in Chapter 3 under
        "Marital Status", Cella B. Slocum was born in Missouri; married in Cowan, TN, and later lived in National City,
        CA (just south of San Diego), finally settling in San Diego.
    Note: Milton L. Slocum was born 10/23/1832 in Charlotte Co, VT; Died 7/1/1919 in San Diego, CA. Pvt Co
        A 8 Alabama Cavalry S: UDC document, California Room (see Chapter II, "San Diego Public Library")

Sly, George Elliott
A: Mus'n Geo E. Sly Co A 4 Minn Inf
C: MH/Masonic M DOD/B: 4/28-5/3/1912 A: 66/1/26

Smith, Charles F.
A: C.F. Smith Co G 94 Ohio Inf
C: MH/GAR Hill DOD/B: 6/5-7/1898 A: 57 N: American M: Married

Smith, Charles F.
A: Chas F. Smith Co H 65 Ill Inf
C: MH/GAR Hill DOD/B: 9/10-11/1895 A: 76 N: American M: Married
F: Harriet H. Smith No stone DOD/B: 12/21-22/1905 A: 75/4/21

Smith, Frederick A.
B: Frederick A. Smith, Civil War Veteran 1861-1865 1st Reg Co B 1844-1925
C: MH/Masonic S DOD/B: 6/29-7/1/1925 A: 80/10/29

Smith, G.C.
A: G.C. Smith Co C 10 Tenn Cav
C: MH/Div.6 DOD/B: 10/7-9/1931 A: 79/3/8 Died in San Diego "George W. Smith" (only "G" Smith buried Div.6)

Smith, George H.
B: Major Geo H. Smith US Military Telegraph Corps 1833-1905
C: MH/GAR Div.2 DOD/B: 4/29-5/3/1905 A: 71/10/7 N: American M: Married
F: Mary F.B. Smith 1835-_____ DOD/B: 11/28-12/1/1931 A: 96/2/3 Died in New Mexico "Mary Francis Brown Smith"

Smith, George H.
A: Geo H. Smith Co M 3 Mich Cav
B: George H. Smith 1843-1917
C: MH/Masonic S DOD/B: 3/21-24/1917 A: 74
D: George H. Smith N: New York A: 71 O: Farmer R: El Cajon, CA CW: Co M 3 Mich Cav (Pvt) E/D: 9/61-1/63 due to disability LOS: Not stated GAR: 9/23/1913 on transfer from C.F. Doors Post #61 Dept of Michigan Died: 3/21/1917 S: H
F: Adelaide A. Smith 1850-1934 DOD/B: 3/24/1934-9/20/1940 (ashes) A: 84/3/30 Died in New York City

Smith, George William
B: Col Geo W. Smith 1840-1926 Confederate Veteran
C: MH/Div.1 DOD/B: 9/10-13/1926 A: 85/11/1 Died in San Diego
F: Sarah C. 1854-1924 DOD/B: 1/6-8/1924 A: 69/6/8

Smith, Henry
A: Henry Smith Co E 10 Ill Inf (tombstone visible at Calvary Cemetery)
C: CAL/Lot A DOD/B: No record found in Catholic cemetery index
F: Ana Smith (possible wife) DOB: 2/18/1889 A: 54 Spouse: H. Smith Parents: V. Garcia and Francisca Bonilia

Smith, Henry
A: Henry Smith Co B 51 Wis Inf
C: MH/GAR Div.2 DOD/B: 10/26-29/1934 A: 86/7/19 Died in San Diego

Smith, James A.
B: James A. Smith May 10, 1846-May 20, 1910 "Oh Happy Condition, Death Vanquished. Eternal Life Supreme. To God Be All The Praise For Our Salvation"
C: MH/Masonic T DOD/B: 5/20-23/1910 A: 64/__/10
D: James A. Smith N: Indiana A: 60 O: Paint Merchant CW: Co F 5 Kans Cav (Pvt) Re-Enl?: Co D 10 Kans Inf (Sgt) E/D: 8/61-8/65 LOS: 49 mos GAR: 5/8/1906 Died: 5/18/1910 S: H
F: Priscilla A. Smith DOD/B: 1/11-15/1944 A: 91/__/22 Died at Alhambra, Los Angeles County, CA

Smith, James K.
B: James K. Smith 1839-1925 Co F 55th Regiment Ill Inf
C: MH/IOOF DOB: 10/17/1925 A: 85
D: James K. Smith N: Ohio A: 78 O: Retired CW: Co F 55 Ill Inf (Pvt) E/D: __/61-10/64 due to wounds LOS: Not stated GAR: 4/22/1919 Died: 10/15/1925 S: H

Smith, Joseph H.
B: Captain Joseph H. Smith 97th NY Vol Inf 1841-1927
C: GW/Hawthorne DOD: 6/25/1927 A: 86
D: Joseph Smith N: Boston, Mass A: 43 O: Land Agent CW: Co E 97 NY Inf (Pvt/Capt) E/D: 10/61-10/64 LOS: 36 mos GAR: 9/11/1884 SP: 6/26/1894 RE: 5/30/1896 Died: 6/25/1927 S: H
F: Jeanette Fiske, Wife of Capt. Joseph H. Smith 1837-1909 DOD/B: 12/30/1909-1/2/___ (no further information on date of burial) A: 71

Smith, Julius S.
A: Julius S. Smith Corpl Co B 141 Ohio Inf 1845-1932
C: MH/GAR Div.2 DOD/B: 10/6-8/1932 A: 87/6/25 Died in San Diego
E: Julius S. Smith N: Athens, Ohio 1845 (March, 1845?) CW: Co B 141 OVI (Corpl) Term: Unstated E/D: 5/64-9/64 LOS: 4 mos 15 days GAR: 4/14/1917 on transfer from Burnside Post #23 Dept of Oregon Died: 10/6/1932 S: DC
F: Mary W. Smith 1846-1931 DOD/B: 12/1-3/1931 A: 85/5/26 Died in National City, CA

Smith, O. Cincinatus
A: O.C. Smith Co C 10 Tenn Cav CSA
C: MH/Confederate DOD/B: 10/27-31/1911 A: 68/7/27 "O.C."
Note: Cincinatus Smith was born 3/1/1843 in Waverly, Tenn; Died 10/27/1911 in San Diego, CA. Pvt Co C 10 Tenn Cav. Re-Enlisted 8/2/1862 at Humphrey County, Tenn. S: UDC document, California Room (see Chapter II, "San Diego Public Library" sources)

Smith, Peter C.
A: Peter C. Smith Co G 7 Ind Inf
C: MH/GAR Hill DOD/B: 12/15-18/1911 A: 82 N: Indiana M: Married "Peter O."
E: Peter C. Smith N: Indiana CW: Co G 7 Ind Inf (Pvt) Term: Unstated E/D: 4/61-9/61 GAR: 11/10/1894 Charter Member of Datus Coon Post Died: 12/15/1911 A: 82 S: DC
F: Eleanor M. Wife of Peter C. Smith Oct 18, 1829-Feb 19, 1913 DOD/B: 2/19-21/1913 A: 83/3/2 N: PA M: Widow

Smith, Richard
A: Chf Bugler Rich'd Smith 1 Wis Cav
C: MH/Div.1 DOD/B: 10/13-15/1910 A: 64/6/5 N: NY M: Married
F: Martha Smith No stone DOB: 12/1-4/1940 A: 91/__/17 Died in Alhambra, CA

Smith, Samuel C.
A/B: No stone
C: MH/GAR Div.3 DOD/B: 6/19-23/1915 A: 74/11/19
D: Samuel C. Smith N: Penn A: 74 O: Mariner CW: Co F 4 Cal Inf (Pvt) E/D: 10/61-11/64 LOS: 37 mos GAR: 4/14/1903 S: H

Smith, Samuel W.
B: Samuel W. Smith Sept 17,1840-Sept 24,1908
C: MH/Masonic P DOD/B: 9/24-26/1908 A: 68/__/7 N: New York M: Married (GAR death date off a little from tombstone and cemetery office record)
D: Samuel W. Smith N: New York A: 59 O: City Marshall R: National City, CA CW: Co B 73 NY Inf (Pvt) E/D: 8/62-5/65 LOS: 32 mos GAR: 11/14/1899 SP: 6/25/1901 RE: 10/11/1904 SP: 3/26/1907 Died: "Dead"--is [grave] stone S: H
F: Kittie L. Smith Oct 18,1855-May 3,1919 DOD/B: 5/3-6/1919 A: 63/6/15 "Kittie Loree Smith"

Smouse, Daniel F.
A: 1st Sgt Dan'l F. Smouse Co F 11 PA Res Inf
C: GW/Acacia Place DOD/B: No record found under "Daniel"--is a "David" Smouse DOD/B: 1/14-15/1920 A: 78
F: In memory of Lizzie M. Smouse Aug 31, 1851-June 4, 1921 DOD/B: 7/4-6/1921 A: 69 "Lizzie Miller Smouse"

Smout, Basil
B: Basil Smout 2nd Lt Co K 23rd Wis Inf 1835-1930
C: GW/Ivy Place DOD/B: 7/15-17/1930 A: 95
D: Basil Smout N: England A: 86 O: Retired CW: Co K 23 Wis Inf (Pvt/2nd Lieut) E/D: 8/62-12/64 due to disability LOS: 2 yrs 4 mos GAR: 5/11/1921 Died: 7/15/1930 S: H
F: Mrs. Emma L. Smout 1839-1927 DOD/B: 4/3-5/1927 A: 88

Snead, William B.
A: William B. Snead Co E 14 KY Inf
C: MH/GAR Div. 2 DOD/B: 11/15-17/1932 A: 87/7/23 Died in San Diego "Smead AKA William B. Snead"
E: Wm.B. Snead N: Charlston?, Washington Co, VA 3/22/48 CW: Co E 14 KY Inf (Pvt) Term: 3 yrs E/D: 8/61-2/64 Cattlesburg, KY Re-Enl: (same company) (Pvt) Discharged from Co A Bat 14 KY ___ (Pvt) E/D: 2/64-10/__ Louisville GAR: 3/22/1924 on transfer from Daniel Tyler Post, Alabama Died: 11/14/1932 A: 84/7/23 Naval Hospital Buried: Mount Hope Obit: Lists wife Della Snead S: DC
F: Della Margaret Smead (no stone search undertaken) (wife?) DOD/B: 8/22-29/1949 A: 96 Died: Patton, CA Buried: Masonic U

Snedecor, Isaac D.
A. Capt I.D. Snedecor Co A 1 MO Prov En Mil
C: MH/GAR Hill DOD/B: 2/14-16/1904 A: 77 N: American M: Married
D: Isaac D. Snedecor N: Missouri A: 61 O: Carpenter CW: Gov Staff--MO (Major) E/D: 12/61-3/65 LOS: 39 mos GAR: 7/26/1888 SP: 6/30/1891 RE: 1/24/1892 Died: 2/14/1904--is [grave] stone S: H

Sneer, Philetus E.
A/B: No stone
C: GW/CMTD DOD: 11/20/1932 A: 85 (record says a cremation marker out in cemetery, but no burial at GW)
E: Philetus E. Sneer N: Richland Co, Ohio 1/23/47 CW: Co G 12 Ind Cav (Pvt) Term: 3 yrs E/D: 11/63-9/65 Columbus, Miss due to disability GAR: 6/21/1925 Died: 11/20/1932 A: 85/9/28 Cremated Buried: Greenwood Cemetery S: DC

Snyder, Edward
B: Sacred to the Memory of Edward Snyder Lieut of Co G 178th NY Inf Born Oct 7, 1835 Died Sept 12, 1903 Member of the Loyal Legion U.S.A Prof. Emeritus of University of Ill.
C: MH/IOOF DOD/B: 9/13-16/1903 A: 68 N: Poland M: Married
F: Mary Stoddard Snyder Born Nov 18, 1838 Died Jan 7, 1926 DOB: 1/13/1926 A: Not stated

Snyder, John H.
B John Harrison Snyder Aug 29, 1843-May 14, 1924 Co F 13th Kan Inf
C: GW/Arbor Vitale/CMTD DOD/B: 5/14/1924 A: 80 (GW record indicates he was cremated)
D: John H. Snyder N: Ohio A: 69 O: Merchant CW: Co F 13 Kans Inf (Pvt) E/D: 9/62-6/65 LOS: 33 mos GAR: 6/30/1886 SP: 9/26/1889 DR: 3/28/1899 RE: 6/22/1909 Died: 5/14/1924 S: H
F: Jennie Whiteley Snyder His Wife May 13, 1849-Jan 9, 1924 San Diego Pioneers DOD/C: 1/9-12/1924 (date of death; latter date is date of cremation) A: 77

Snyder, Lorenzo
B: Lorenzo Snyder Co E 9th Reg Indiana Inf 1836-1927
C: MH/GAR Div.2 DOD/B: 5/11-16/1927 A: 90/10/24 Died in San Diego "Snider"
F: Martha J. Snyder No stone DOB: 8/21/1924 A: 74/2/20

Speers, Gustav
A: Gustav Speers Co G 46 NY Inf
C: MH/GAR Div.2 DOD/B: 9/26-29/1908 A: 76 N: Germany S: Single "August"/"Gustave" "JS" record says an "August" Spear died 9/26/1908 of senile debility at St. Joseph's Sanitarium Nativity Germany M: Married

Spence, Samuel R.
B: Samuel R. Spence 1823-1899 Comp A 62 Regt PA Vol
C: MH/IOOF DOD/B: 5/10-12/1899 A: 76 N: American M: Married
D: Samuel R. Spence N: PA A: 61 O: Merchant CW: Co __ 2nd Batt Vet Reserves (Pvt/1st Sgt) E/D: 7/61-7/64 LOS: 3 yrs GAR: 6/12/1885 SP: 6/10/1893 DR: 3/28/1899 Died: Ju..23d 1899 or 5..23 1899 (GAR record difficult to read)--no [grave] stone S: H Note: County death record indicates he died 5/10/1899.
F: Sarah Spence 1834-1909 DOD/B: 7/3-6/1909 A: 75 N: Ohio M: Widow (possible wife--buried in another IOOF location; tombstone also has name of Wood L. Jackson 1858-1923 on it)

Spencer, Jonathan Richmond
B: Jonathan Richmond Spencer 1845-1924 Co E 44th MO Inf
C: MH/GAR Hill DOD/B: 11/7-10/1924 A: 79/6/26
D: J.R. Spencer N: Missouri A: 40 O: Not stated CW: Co E 44 MO Inf (1st Sgt) E/D: 8/64-8/65 due to disability
    LOS: 1 yr GAR: 1/14/1884 SP: 1/10/1889 DR: 5/23/1889 SP: 6/28/1892 DR: 1/12/1894 S: H
F: Sarah Jane 1850-1889 DOD/B: 4/26-28/1889 A: 39 N: Ohio M: Married

Spileman, Edward Barnett
A: E.B. Spileman Co D 11 NJ Inf
B: Col E.B. Spileman 1841-1915
C: MH/Masonic S DOD/B: 12/3-6/1915 A: 74/4/__
D: Edward B. Spileman N: Mass A: 45 O: Merchant CW: Co D 11 NJ Inf (Pvt) Re-Enl?: Co H 2 VRC (Pvt) E/D:
    8/62-4/65 LOS: 32 mos GAR: 9/27/1888 SP: 9/28/1891 RE: 4/24/1900 Died: 12/3/1915 S: H

Sprague, Joseph Benjamin
B: Sergn't Joseph B. Sprague Co K 15 Ind Inft 1841-1912
C: MH/Masonic T DOD/B: 12/19-21/1912 A: 70/11/28
D: Joseph B. Sprague N: New Jersey A: 63 O: Merchant CW: Co K 15 Ind Inf (Pvt/Sgt) E/D: 5/61-6/64 LOS: Not
    stated GAR: 5/25/1905 (probabaly on transfer from Eaton Post #55 Dept of Ohio Died: 12/19/1912 S: H
F: Jennie Sprague No stone DOD/B: No further information available

Stambaugh, William H.
A: Wm. H. Stambaugh Co A 49 Ind Inf
C: MH/GAR Div.2 DOD/B: 3/26-27/1912 A: 71/1/19 N: Ohio M: Widower "Stambough"
D: Wm. H. Stambaugh N: Ohio A: 49 O: Farmer CW: Co A 149 Ind Inf (Pvt) E/D: 1/65-9/65 LOS: 8 mos GAR:
    12/26/1889 SP: 6/30/1891 DR: 3/28/1899 RE: 9/24/1907 Died: 3/26/1912 S: H
F: Evaline Stambaugh No stone DOD/B: 2/3-4/1907 A: 53/1/2 N: Ohio M: Married "Evalyne Stambough"

Stancliff, William Henry
A/B: No stone
C: MH/GAR Hill DOD/B: 3/25-27/1925 A: 84/10/25 (her ashes buried with him on 3//27/1925)
E: Wm. Henry Stancliff N: McKean, Erie Co, PA 4/1/40 CW: US Navy (Landsman) Term: 3 yrs E/D: 6/61-9/61
    Brooklyn, NY on Doctor's Certificate Re-Enl: US Navy (Ordinary Seaman) E/D: 8/64-7/65 at "Prinston" GAR:
    4/24/1920 Died: 3/25/1925 A: 84/10/25 Buried: GAR (Mount Hope) S: DC
F: Florence Stancliff No stone DOB: 3/27/1925 A: 61/1/19

Stark, Nathaniel Jasper
A: N.J. Stark 1844-1913 Co C 150 Ill Inf
C: MH/GAR Hill DOD/B: 1/23-25/1913 A: 69/7/24
D: Nath'l J. Stark N: Indiana A: 42 O: Carpenter CW: Co C 150 Ill Inf (Pvt) E/D: 2/65-1/66 LOS: 11 mos GAR:
    7/8/1886 SP: 9/28/1897 SP: 9/28/1897 RE: 5/22/1900 Died: 1/23/1913 S: H
F: Elizabeth, his wife 1851-1929 DOD/B: 12/28-30/1929 A: 78/4/18 Died: Santa Ana, CA

Statler, Sylvester
B: Sylvester Statler Born August 21, 1843 Died March 8, 1891
C: MH/Div.3 DOD/B: 3/8-10/1891 A: 47/5/__ N: American M: Married
D: Sylvester Statler N: Miami Co, Ohio A: 39 O: Clerk CW: Co K 1 Ohio Inf (Pvt) E/D: 9/61-9/64 LOS: 36 mos
    GAR: 2/8/1883 Died: 3/8/1891--is [grave] stone S: H
F: M.E. Statler Rogers Born Mar 7, 1850 Died Dec 23, 1917 DOB: 12/26/1917

Stearns, Hiram Allen
A: H.A. Stearns Co I 6 Mass Mil Inf
B: Hiram A. Stearns Died Mar 23, 1908 aged 73 yrs 7 mos 24 ds
C: MH/Masonic Q DOD/B: 3/23-26/1908 A: 73/7/24 N: Mass M: Not stated
F: Melissa A. Stearns 1843-1917 DOD/B: 4/3-6/1917 A: 73 "Melissa Ann Stearns"

Steele, Augustus F.
B: Augustus F. Sept 1, 1841-July 4, 1929 [Husband/Wife both] Natives of New York
C: MH/GAR Hill DOD/B: 7/4-8/1929 A: 87/10/3 Died in San Diego
D: Augustus F. Steele N: New York A: 72 O: Farmer CW: Co D 1 NY Dragoons (Pvt) E/D: 8/62-6/65 LOS: Not stated GAR: 7/28/1914 on transfer from Iman (?) GAR post in Oklahoma Past Post Commander Died: 7/4/1929 S: H
F: Julia C. July 21, 1850-July 27, 1928 DOD/B: 7/27-30/1928 A: 78/__/6 Died in San Diego

Steele, S.G. (Seumere G.?)
B: Capt S.G. Steele died Feb 5, 1887 aged 69 years
C: MH/GAR Hill DOB: 2/5/1887 A: 69 "Capt" Note: Name "Seumere G." from the 1880 census for San Diego. He was 63 at the time of the census, and was born in New York, as were his parents.
F: Mary, Wife of Capt S.G. Steele Died July 14, 1896 aged 62 years DOD/B: 7/14-16/1896 A: 62/6/__ N: American W: Widowed "Mary A." Note: Mary A. Steele was 46 at the time of the 1880 San Diego census; was married to Seumere G. Steel, and was born in Maine, as were her parents.

Stephen, Robert
A: Rob't Stephen Co A 1 Minn Inf
C: MH/GAR Hill DOD/B: 8/1-2/1901 A: 69/7/__ N: Scotland M: Married

Stephens, David
A: David Stephens Co L 1st Wis H A
B: David 1844-1917
C: MH/GAR Div. 3 DOD/B: 4/3-5/1917 A: Not stated
D: David Stephens N: Tenn A: 59 O: Grocer CW: Co L 1 Wis Art (Pvt) E/D: 8/63-6/65 LOS: 22 mos GAR: 11/24/1903 SP: 6/28/1910 RE: 4/25/1911 Died: 4/3/1917 S: H
F: Mary E. 1851-1934 DOD/B: 4/14-18/1934 A: 83/1/18 Died in San Diego "Mary Ellen"

Stephens, Walter
B: Father Walter 1845-1925
C: MH/GAR Div.2 DOD/B: 6/11-15/1925 A: 79/10/22
D: Walter Stephens N: England A: 59 O: Carpenter CW: Co D 169 NY Inf (Pvt) E/D: 3/65-8/65 LOS: 17 mos GAR: 10/25/1904 TR: 4/14/1908 RE: 2/11/1910 Died: 6/10/1925 S: H
F: Mother Catherine 1843-1933 DOD/B: 7/10-12/1933 A: 90/1/19 Died in San Diego "Catherine Elizabeth"

Stevens, Edward R.
A/B: No stone
C: MH/Div.6 DOD/B: 7/21-23/1909 A: Not stated N: New York M: Married "Capt Edwin R."
D: Edward R. Stevens N: New York A: 63 O: Merchant CW: Co C 3 Wis Cav (Capt) E/D: 9/61-2/64 LOS: 28 mos GAR: 6/30/1886 SP: 4/30/1890 DR: 3/28/1899 Died: 7/20/1909--no [grave] stone S: H
F: Esther Stevens No stone DOD/B: 10/6-8/1915 A: 84 N: New York M: Widow Died in San Diego

Stevens, Uzzial J.
A: Capt Uzzial J. Stevens Co N 3 Iowa Cav
C: MH/GAR Div.2 DOD/B: 11/26-30/1912 A: 75 N: Not stated M: Married Note: Uzzial J. Stevens was born in Knox Co, OH, on 3/17/1837, according to *San Diego County, CA: A Record of Settlement, Organization, Progress and Achievement*. He came to California in 1875; was married first to Sylvania Jones; next to Gertrude Good, whom he married in 1911. No record of her burial was found at Mount Hope Cemetery. He died on Thanksgiving Day, 1912.
D: Uzzial Stevens N: Ohio A: 63 O: Rancher R: Bostonia, CA CW: Co M 3 Iowa Cav (Pvt/Corpl) E/D: 9/61-9/64 LOS: 36 mos GAR: 1/9/1900 Died: 11/28/1912 S: H

Stewart. E.B.
A: E.B. Stewart Co E 184th Ohio Inf
C: MH/GAR Hill DOD/B: No other record available
D: E.B. Stewart N: Maryland A: 44 O: Clerk CW: Co E 184 Ohio Inf (Pvt) E/D:11/64-11/65 due to wounds LOS: 12 mos GAR: 9/19/1887 D: 2/2/1888 Died: 2/2/1888--no [grave] stone S: H

Stewart, Samuel W.
B: "Father"
C: MH/GAR Hill DOD/B: 10/24-29/1926 A: 77/__/21 Died in San Diego
D: S.W. Stewart N: Penn A: 70 O: Retired CW: Co C 4 Penn Cav (Pvt) E/D: 2/64-8/65 LOS: 1 1/2 yrs GAR: 8/24/1920 Died: 10/24/1926 S: H
F: "Mother" DOD/B: 6/19-23/1919 A: 67/1/19 Died in San Diego Frances Stewart

Stewart, Thomas J.
A/B: No stone
C: MH/IOOF DOB: 12/31/1917 A: 78 (probable DOD/B record for this veteran)
D: Stewart, Thomas J. N: New York A: 48 O: Painter CW: Co D 28 NY Militia (QM Sgt) E/D: 9/61-11/64 LOS: 36 mos GAR: 10/17 or 11/27/1887 SP: 12/26/1905 DR: 1/22/1907 DR: 12/24/1918 S: H

Stewart, W.B.
A: W.B. Stewart US Navy Mate Asst
C: MH/Div.5 DOD/B: 4/2-7/30/1929 A: About 60 Died in San Diego (probable DOD/B record for this veteran)

Stiles, Alonzo R.
A: Alonzo R. Stiles Co F 21 IA Inf
C: MH/GAR Div. 2 DOD/B: 11/27-29/1909 A: 64/__/18 N: Iowa M: Married
E: Alonzo Stiles N: Dubuque, Iowa CW: Co F 21 Iowa Inf (Pvt) Term: 3 yrs E/D: 10/64-8/65 Galveston, TX GAR: 3/26/1904 Died: 11/27/1909 A: 68 Buried: GAR (Mount Hope) S: DC

Stimson, Albert S.
A: Albert S. Stimson Co A 28 Mich Inf
C: MH/GAR Hill DOD/B: 4/4-6/1934 A: 88/8/29 Died in San Diego
E: Albert S. Stimson N: Lawrence, Michigan 1845 CW: Co A 28 Mich Inf (Pvt) Term: 3 yrs E/D: 8/64-6/66 Raleigh, NC GAR: 7/27/1918 on transfer from Stanton Post #5 Dept of Cal/Nev Died: 4/4/1934 A: 88 Obit: Lists wife Jessie Hall Stimson S: DC
F: Jessie Hall Stimson No stone DOD/B: 6/24-7/10/1939 A: 66 Died in Orlando, Florida

Stone, George M.
A: Artf'r G.M. Stone Co G 1 Mich Eng
C: MH/Div.3 DOD/B: 3/6-8/1900 A: 57 N: American M: Married
D: Geo M. Stone N: Michigan A: 40 O: Farmer R: Ballena, CA CW: Co A 2 Mich Inf (Pvt) Re-Enl: Co G 1 Mich Eng (Artificer) E/D; __/61-9/65 LOS: 4 yrs GAR: 12/10/1885 SP: 1/10/1889 DR: 6/30/1891 Died: 3/8/1900--is [grave] stone S: H
F: Susan Farley Stone 1861-1928 DOD/B: 10/29-11/1/1928 A: 67/1/5 Susan Emma Died in San Diego

Stopher, Edgar A.
B: Edgar A. Stopher Feb 27, 1842-Aug 9, 1918 Co C 14 Regt Iowa Inf
C: MH/GAR Hill DOD/B: 8/9-12/1918 A: 74/5/13
F: Susie L. His Wife Oct 22, 1848-July 15, 1930 DOD/B: 7/15-19/1930 A: 81/8/23 Died in San Diego

Storey, William Henry
A: Sergt W.H. Storey US Sig Corps
C: MH/Div 4 DOD/B: 4/4-6/1908 A: Not stated N: New York M: Married Note: He is 29 in the 1880 census of San Diego; he was born in New York; his parents were born in England. He worked for U.S. Telegraph.
F: Clara Choate Storey No stone DOD/B: 11/4-16/1891 A: 35 N: American M: Married Note: Born in California, in 1880 San Diego census, she was 24 years old, married to Wm. Storey. Father born Ohio; mother Maine

Stover, Joseph W.
B: 1st Lieut J.W. Stover Co E 62nd Ill Inf Father Feb 13, 1842-Feb 27, 1899
C: MH/GAR Hill DOD/B: 2/27-3/1/1899 A: 57/__/14 N: American M: Married
F: Fannie M. Stover No stone DOD/B: 5/31-6/3/1940 A: 86/6/__ Died in San Diego

Stratton, Samuel S.
A: Sergt Sam'l S. Stratton Co A 181 Ohio Inf
C: MH/Masonic M DOD/B: 12/31/1910-1/1/1911 A: 81/7/14 N: Ohio M: Married

Strawn, James C.
A/B: Stone overturned/cannot read inscription
C: MH/Div.6 DOD/B: 4/2-7/1931 A: About 87 Died in San Diego
E: James C. Strawn N: Delaware Co, Ind 8/18/44 CW: Co C 9 Kans Cav (Corpl) Term: 3 yrs E/D: 9/61-11/64 Levenworth, Kans GAR: 10/22/1927 on transfer from Chetopa Post Dept of Kansas. Died: 4/2/1931 at Sawtelle National Home Buried: Mount Hope S: DC SAWTELLE: Records for this veteran were not searched at Los Angeles National Cemetery because his burial record was in San Diego
F: Lida G. Strawn Stone overturned/cannot read inscription DOD/B: 6/13-16/1925 A: 70/9/26

Sullivan, John Cornwall
B: John C. Sullivan 1842-1921
C: MH/Masonic T DOD/B: 8/2-4/1921 A: 79
D: John C. Sullivan N: Illinois A: 70 O: Carpenter CW: Co B 3 Cal Cav (Pvt) E/D: 8/64-12/64 LOS: Not stated GAR: 5/27/1913 Died: 8/2/1921 S: H
F: Margaret Wife of John C. Sullivan 1849-1913 DOB: 10/6/1913 A: 64/2/10 "Margarett"

Sullivan, Marcus M.
B: Marcus M. 1844-1919
C: MH/GAR Div.3 DOB: 4/9-11/1919 A: 75/3/20
E: Marcus M. Sullivan N: Boston, Mass 12/20/40 CW: Co G 1 Mass Inf (Pvt) Term: 3 yrs Discharged from Co E 3 Mass Cav (Com Sgt) E/D: 5/61-9/65 GAR: 3/25/1916 on transfer from Harlen Post #146 Dept of Ohio Died: 4/9/1919 A: 78 S: DC
Service record: Participated in the engagements of Fairfax Court House 3/7/61; Bull Run 7/4/62; Plantation 10/25-27; Mattawan Creek 11/2; Yorktown 4/16-5/4/62; ___burg 5/5; Fair Oaks 5/31- 6/1; Seven days before Richmond to 7/1; Oak Grove 6/25; Savage Station 6/29; White Oak and Malvern Hill 7/1; Harrison's Landing 8/15; Grovesters 8/29-30 Fredericksburg 12/12-15 Rapahanoc Bridge 2/5-7/65 Chancellorsville 5/1-5; Gettysburg 7/1-3; Kelly's Ford 11/7; Payne Farm 11/__ Wilderness 7/5-7/64; Spottsylvania Ct. House 5/12 S: DC
F: Maude B. 1880-1958 DOD/B: 12/2-8/1958 A: 77 Died in San Diego "Maude Belle" (wife or daughter?)

Sunnocks, Melvin D.
A: M.D. Sunnocks Co D 40 Wis Inf
C: MH/GAR Hill DOD/B: 1/17-19/1903 A: 55/11/2 N: American W: Widower
E: M.D. Sunnucks N: St. Lawrence Co, NY CW: Co D 40 Wis Inf (Pvt) Term: 100 days E/D: 5/64-9/64 Madison, Wis GAR: 7/11/1895 Died: 1/17/1903 A: 57 Buried: Mount Hope S: DC
F: Eliza Sunnucks No stone 9/20-22/1899 A: 53/4/5 N: American M: Married

Sutemeier, Henry
A: Corpl Henry Sutemeier Co C 4 US R C MO Inf
C: GW/Hawthorne DOD/B: 7/12-15/1914 A: 80
D: Henry Sutemier N: Germany A: 73 O: Merchant CW: Co C 4 MO Inf (Pvt/Corpl) E/D: 4/61-7/61 LOS: Not stated GAR: 6/9/1908 Died: 7/13/1914 S: H
F: Mary E. Sutemeier Mar 22, 1843-Jan 5, 1922 DOD/B: 1/5-7/1922 A: 78

Sutherland, Thomas J.
A: Thomas J. Sutherland Co L 1 Mich Cav
C: MH/Masonic U DOB: 12/4-8/1928 A: 86/11/9

Sweeney, Henry
B: Capt Henry Sweeney 1831-1900 4th US Cavalry (his/her tombstones visible at Calvary Cemetery)
C: CAL/Sec.2, North 2/3, E-24 DOD/B: No record on Catholic cemetery index
D: Henry Sweeney N: Ireland A: 58 O: Soldier CW: Co H 2 US Dragoons (Pvt) Re-Enl?: Co K 4 US Cav (Capt)
    E/D: 9/54-4/86 due to retirement LOS: Not stated GAR: 7/9/1890 SP: 6/26/1900 RE: 6/10/1900 D:
    7/10/1900 Died: 12/9/1900--is [grave] stone S: H
F: Agnes T. Sweeney 1835-1917 (she buried in same location as he) DOD/B: No record on Catholic cemetery index

Swetnam, James S.
A: Sgt J.S. Swetnam Co A 2 MO Sharpshooters CSA
C: MH/Confederate DOD/B: 12/1-5/1924 A: 82/9/16 "Confederate Plot"
E: J.S. Swetnam NOL/NFI--DC
    Note: James S. Swetnam was born 3/1/1842; Died 12/1/1924 in San Diego, CA. Sgt Co A 2 Missouri
    Sharpshooters Bn. S: UDC document, California Room (see Chapter II, "San Diego Public Library" sources)

Taft, Byron Parker
B: Byron P. Taft Co F 10th Reg Wis Inf 1857-1924
C: MH/GAR Hill DOD/B: 2/9-13/1924 A: 77/6/10
E: Byron P. Taft N: Wetutown (Watertown?), Wis 10/30/43 CW: Co F 10 Wis Inf (Pvt) Term: 3 yrs E/D: 9/61-11/64
    Madison, Wis GAR: 11/13/1920 on transfer from Lake City Post Dept of Colorado Died: 2/9/1924 A: 80/3/9
    Buried: Mount Hope S: DC
F: Sarah Taft July 5, 1850-May 21, 1944 DOD/B: 5/21-24/1944 A: 93/10/16 Died in San Diego

Talcott, Henry W.
A: H.W. Talcott Mus'n 13 Ind Inf
B: Henry W. Talcott 1838-1907
C: MH/GAR Div.2 DOD/B: 10/6-8/1907 A: 68/7/27 N: Indiana M: Married
D: Henry W. Talcott N: Indiana A: 55 O: Lawyer CW: Co __ 13 Ind Inf (Mus'n) E/D: 6/61-8/62 LOS: 14 mos GAR:
    8/28/1894 SP: 9/28/1897 RE: 3/27/1900 SP: 6/26/1900 RE: 9/24/1901 Died: 10/6/1907--is [grave] stone
    S: H
F: Emma Jane, His Wife 1858-1909 DOD/B: 3/8-10/1909 A: 51 N: Iowa M: Widow

Taylor, George O.
A: Geo.O. Taylor US Navy
C: MH/GAR Div.2 DOD/B: 2/26-27/1912 A: 68 N: CT M: Not stated

Teeters, Loftus
A: Loftus Teeters Co I 33 Ohio Inf
C: MH/Masonic Q DOD/B: 1/2-4/1912 A: 63/2/8 N: Ohio M: Married
F: Rebecca Teeters No stone DOD/B: 3/16-23/1943 A: 80/9/14 Died at Patton, CA

Tenny, Silas B.
B: Silas B. Tenny 1836-1926 Private Co C 3rd Wis Cav
C: GW/Acacia Place DOD/B: 2/21-22/1926 A: 89
D: Silas B. Tenny N: New York A: 86 O: Retired CW: Co C 3 Wis Cav (Pvt) E/D: 12/61-2/65 LOS: 3 yrs GAR:
    8/8/1922 Died: 2/21/1926 S: H

Thieme, Charles B.
A: Chas B. Thieme Co A 26 Wis Inf
C: MH/Div.1 DOD/B: 4/7-11/1909 A: 67/8/4
E: C.B. Thieme N: Germany 10/30/42 CW: Co A 26 Wis Inf (Pvt) Term: 3 yrs E/D: 8/62-6/65 David's Island M.
    City due to disability GAR: ? date on transfer from Robert Chevis Post #2 Dept of Wisconsin Died:
    4/7/1909 A: 67 Buried: GAR (Mount Hope) S: DC
F: Theresa Thieme No stone DOD/B: 11/21-27/1916 A: 71

Thompson, James Granville
B: James G. Thompson Medal of Honor Pvt Co K 4 NY H A Civil War 1849-1921 Note: Official Medal of Honor tombstone
C: MH/GAR Hill DOD/B: 5/23-27/1921 A: 71
E: James Thompson N: Sandy Creek, NY 1849 CW: Co K 4 NY H A (Pvt) Term: 3 yrs E/D: 2/64-10/65 GAR: 4/10/1920 Died: 5/23/1921 A: 71 S: DC
F: Laura Elma Thompson No stone DOD/B: 1/15-17/1958 A: 100 Died a widow in San Diego Death Certificate says she died 1/15/1958 at 100. She was born in Indiana on 10/4/1857. Father: William DePoy; mother Caroline King, both of Ohio. William D. Thompson, informant. Buried 1/17/1958 at Mount Hope. Funeral home: Lewis Colonial Benbough, 3051 El Cajon Blvd, San Diego.

Note: In *Medal of Honor Recipients 1863-1963* (Washington, D.C., Government Printing Office, 1964), prepared for the Subcommittee on Veterans' Affairs of the Committee on Labor and Public Welfare, U.S. Senate, Government Printing Office, 1964, p. 591, the entry for James Thompson is: Rank and organization: Private, Company K, 4th New York Heavy Artillery. Place and date: At White Oak Road, VA 1 April 1865. Entered service at: Sandy Creek, NY. Birth: Sandy Creek, NY. Date of issue: 22 April 1896. Citation: Made a hazardous reconnaisance through timber and slashings, preceding the Union line of battle, signaling the troops and leading them through the obstructions." [This book is available at the Family History Center, San Diego, Call No. 973.0 M2y]

Please also note that on p. 590, Allen Thompson, the brother of James Granville Thompson had virtually the same citation. The only difference in the citation was his company: Private, Co I, 4th NY Heavy Artillary. His Medal of Honor was issued the same day and for the same reason cited as the one issued to James Granville Thompson. Allen Thompson does not appear to have migrated to San Diego, however, and is not a veteran included in this study.

Thompson, Samuel
A: Corpl Sam'l Thompson Co I 132nd Ill Inf
C: MH/GAR Hill DOD/B: 12/31/1893-1/2/1894 A: 67 N: Norway M: Single "Saul Thompson"

Tibballs, Joseph B.
A: J.B. Tibballs Co B 146th Ohio Inf
C: MH/GAR Hill DOD/B: 4/25-27/1898 A: Not stated N: American M: Married Name Joseph H.
F: Rena Tibballs No stone DOD/B: 6/14-15/1916 A: 77

Tillman, Robert
A: Robert Tillman Co A 127 US Cld Inf
C: MH/GAR Div.3 DOD/B: 12/11-15/1936 A: About 89 Race: Black Died in San Diego
E: Robert Tillman N: Fairfax, VA CW: Co A 127 US Colored Inf (Pvt) Term: 3 yrs E/D: 8/64-10/65 Brazos, Santiago, TX GAR: 5/28/1897 Died: 12/11/1936 A: 89 S: DC

Tinker, Edgar C.
B: Edgar C. Tinker 1844-1932
C: MH/GAR Div.2 DOD/B: 3/22-25/1932 A: 88/6/3 Died in San Diego
E: Edgar C. Tinker N: Bedford, Ohio 1844 CW: Co D 84 OVI (Pvt) E/D: 5/62-9/62 Term: 100 days Re-Enl: Co H 150 OVI (Pvt) E/D: 5/64-8/64 GAR: 6/28/1919 Died: 3/24/1932 S: DC
F: Adelia J. Sholes 1838-1927 DOD/B: 12/31/1927-1/2/1928 A: 89/6/6

Tinker, William H.
A/B: No stone
C: MH/Masonic K DOD/B: 2/8-14/1923 A: 84/7/__
D: William H. Tinker N: Maine A: 50 O: Civil Engineer R: Coronado, CA; San Diego, CA CW: Co H 6 ME Inf (Pvt) Re-Enl?: US Signal Corps (Sgt) E/D: 4/61-7/64 LOS: 38 mos GAR: 7/26/1888 Died: 2/9/1923 S: H

Todd, Eugene
B: Eugene Todd 1834-1927
C: GW/Ivy Place DOD/B: 12/22-24/1927 A: 93
E: Eugene Todd N: New Jersey 11/3/34 CW: Co B 138 Ill Inf (Pvt) Term: 3 yrs E/D: 6/64-10/64 Springfield, Ill due
    to disability LOS: 3 mos 23 days GAR:12/13/1924 on transfer from Mason City Post Dept of Illinois Died:
    12/22/1927 A: 93/1/19 Buried: 12/24/1927 Greenwood Cemetery S: DC
F: Grace E. Todd 10-11-87 - 1-20-55 (daughter?) DOD/B: 1/20-25/1955 A: 67

Todd, James
A: James Todd Co B 139th Ill Inf
C: MH/GAR Hill DOD/B: 8/6-9/1888 (no other information except "Died at San Diego or National City")

Tout, Henry Clay
A: Henry C. Tout Co B 117 Ind Inf
C: MH/GAR Hill DOD/B: 12/2-7/1933 A: 89/__/27 "Civil War Vet" Died in San Diego Middle name Clay
E: Henry C. Tout N: Danville, Ind 1844 CW: Co B 117 Ind Inf (Pvt) Term: 18 mos E/D: 6/62-2/64 GAR:
    10/23/1920 on transfer from E.D. Baker Post #6 Dept of Idaho Died: 12/2/1933 A: 89 S: DC
F: Neville S. Clay No stone DOD/B: 12/26-29/1938 A: 79/__/21 Died in San Diego

Towers, Justus A.
A: Justus A. Towers Co F 7 IA Cav
C: MH/GAR Div.2 DOD/B: 7/31-8/2/1934 A: 87/1/12 Died in San Diego

Townsend, Daniel W.
A: Saddler D.W. Townsend Co I 15 Ill Cav
C: MH/GAR Hill DOD/B: 9/3-5/1901 A: 57/10/20 N: American M: Married Name Daniel

Tracy, J.E.
A: J.E. Tracy Co D 189 NY Inf
C: MH/? DOD/B: No further information available
D: J.E. Tracy N: New York A: 56 O: Merchant R: Fallbrook, CA CW: Co D 189 NY Inf (Sgt) E/D: 8/64-5/65 LOS:
    9 14/30 mos GAR: 9/22/1884 SP: 7/30/1889 DR: 7/30/1891 Died: 12/27/1905--is [grave] stone S: H

Tracy, James H.
A: J.H. Tracy Co B 2 IA Inf
C: MH/GAR Div.2 DOD/B: 7/29-31/1902 A: 65/9/20 N: American M: Married
D: James H. Tracy N: Michigan A: Not stated O: Carpenter CW: Co B 2 Iowa Inf (Pvt) E/D: 5/61-6/62 Re/Enl?:
    Co C 14 Iowa Inf (Pvt) E/D: 9/64-5/65 LOS: 21 mos GAR: 3/27/1900 Died: 7/29/1902--is [grave] stone S: H

Tracy, John
A: Jno. Tracy Co K 5th NY H A
C: MH/GAR Hill DOD/B: 5/31-6/2/1895 A: 55 N: Ireland M: Single

Travers, Jones
B: Jones Travers Quarter Gunner US Navy
C: MH/GAR Div.3 DOD/B: 11/6-8/1913 A: 71/5/__ N: MA M: Widower "Jonas"

Tucker, Samuel F.
B: Samuel F. Tucker 2nd Regt Calif Cav 1861-1863 2nd Regt Mass Cav 1863-1865 Veteran of the Civil War
    1834-1915
C: GW/Palm Terrace DOD/B: 6/21-7/17/1915 A: 81
F: Emma R. Tucker His Wife 1846-1924 DOD/B: 6/5-8/26/1924 A: 78

Turner, Asbury
B: Asbury 1848-1928 [Both he and she are natives of Greensburg, Indiana]
C: MH/Div.6 DOD/B: 1/22-24/1928 A: 79/6/3 Died in San Diego
D: Asbury Turner N: Indiana A: 79 O: Retired CW: Co A 146 Ind Inf (Pvt) E/D: __/64(?)-__/65 LOS: Not stated GAR: 4/26/1927 Died: 1/20/1928 S: H
F: Virginia A.   July 23, 1855-May 23, 1947 DOB: 5/23-29/1947 A: 91/10/__ Died in Albequerque, NM

Turner, John Castle
B: Father John C. Nov 6, 1838-Jan 20, 1928
C: MH/IOOF DOB: 6/22/1928 A: 90
D: John Turner N: Ireland A: 48 O: Carpenter CW: Co G 1 US Engineers (Artificer) E/D: 10/64-9/65 LOS: 11 1/2 mos GAR: 9/22/1887 SP: 1/10/1889 DR: 6/30/1891 S: H
F: Mother Hester S. Nov 24, 1843-Mar 31, 1926 DOB: No further record available

Tyler, Joseph H.
A: J.H. Tyler Co K 6 Minn Inf
C: MH/Div.6 DOD/B: 8/18-22/1905 A: 87/4/18 N: New York M? Widower Name Joseph
D: J.H. Tyler N: New York A: 65 O: Expressman CW: Co K 6 Minn Inf (Pvt) E/D: 1/64-8/65 LOS: 19 mos GAR: 12/27/1883 SP: 1/28/1892 DR: 10/25/1904 S: H
F: Martha Tyler No stone DOD/B: 2/20-21/1904 A: 73/9/24 N: American M: Married "Mrs Martha"

Tyrell, John D.
B: "He Giveth His Beloved Sleep" John D. Tyrell Born Dec 20, 1847 Died Jan 21, 1929
C: MH/Div.4 DOD/B: 1/21-23/1929 A: 82/1/1 Died in San Diego
D: John Tyrell N: England A: 48 O: Seaman CW: Co __ 4 NY L A (Pvt) Re-Enl?: USS Kenawae (Seaman) E/D: __/63-__/64 LOS: 12 mos GAR: 10/28/1891 SP: 6/26/1894 DR: 3/28/1899 SP: 5/28 or 6/28/1904 RE: 9/11/1906 Died: 1/21/1929 S: H
F: His Wife Julia D. Walker Born Aug 23, 1846 Died Dec 27, 1906 DOD/B: 12/28-31/1906 A: 60/4/5 N: Maine M: Married "Mrs Julia"

Underwood, Hugh
A: Hugh Underwood Co K 42 Ohio Inf
C: MH/GAR Div.3 DOD/B: 8/19-20/1913 A: 80/5/16 N: PA M: Widower

Unger, August
A: August Unger Co D 69 NY Inf
C: MH/GAR Hill DOD/B: 1/22-25/1932 A: 86/4/22 Died in San Diego
D: August Unger N: Germany A: 75 O: Retired CW: Co B 69 NY Inf (Pvt) E/D: 6/64-10/65 LOS: 1 yr GAR: 10/26/1920 TR: 10/25/1921 Rejoined: 3/28/1922 Died: 1/22/1932 S: H

Van Arman, John
B: Col. John Van Arman Born in Plattsburg, NY Died April 6, 1890 aged 70 yrs 3 dys
C: MH/Div. 3 DOD/B: 4/6-7/1890 A: 70/__/1 N: American M: Married
F: Amanda Convis, Wife of John Van Arman 1824-1903 DOD/B: 3/17-20/1903 A: 79 N: American M: Widowed

Van Buskirk, Marshall
B: Marshall Van Buskirk Co I 1st Regt Wis Cavalry Died Jan 9, 1904 aged 66 years Rest in Peace
C: MH/Masonic N DOD/B: 1/9-11/1904 A: 66 N: American M: Married
F: Emily Van Buskirk No stone DOD/B: 6/16-21/1927 A: 77/10/24

Van Castle, Joseph
A/B: No stone search undertaken
C: GW/CMTD DOD/C: 5/5-7/1926 A: 86 (5/7 date is cremation date; ashes scattered at GW)
D: Joseph Von Castle N: Germany A: 50 O: Soldier CW: Co G 17 PA Cav (Pvt/Corpl) E/D: 8/64-8/65 LOS: 12 mos GAR: 3/25/1891 TR: 9/11/1894 S: H

Van Castle, Joseph (Con't)
E: Joseph Van Castle N: Germany or Belgium CW: Co G 17 PA Cav (Pvt/Corpl) Term: 3 yrs E/D: 8/64-8/65 GAR: 11/10/1894 Charter Member of Datus Coon Post Died: 5/5/1926 A: 86/8/11 Buried: Greenwood (Cremated) S: DC
F: Jennie Van Castle No stone DOD/B: 5/27-31/1911 A: 67/2/17 N: NY M: Married Buried in MH/Div.1 (no record of her being buried at GW)

Van Ostrand, J.E.
A: J.E. Van Ostrand Co B 56 NY N G
C: MH/GAR Div.2 DOD/B: 1/31-2/5/1935 A: 84 Died in San Diego

VanDine, George B.
A: Geo. B. VanDine Co F 36 Ohio Inf
C: GW/Palm Terrace DOD/B: 4/28-30/1915 A: 82/5/13

Veile, George C.
A/B: No stone
C: Cremated
E: George C. Veile N: Denmark 4/27/41 CW: Co B 15 Wis Inf (Pvt) Term: 3 yrs E/D: 12/61-1/62 Nashville, TN Re-Enl: Co __ 8 Batt Wis L A (Corpl) E/D: 1/62-8/65 Milwaukee, Wis LOS: See prior notes GAR: Date Not stated Died: 7/16/1934 A: 94 Cremated: Bonham Brothers Crematory Obits: War veteran, retired Federal judge, no wife mentioned, 2 sons S: DC

Velbert, John (Velvet)
A: John Velbert Co I 42 NY Inf
C: MH/GAR Div.3 DOD/B: 8/13-15/1919 A: 81
E: John Velbert N: Germany 2/15/38 CW: Co I 42 NY Tammany & 50 (Pvt) Term: 3 yrs E/D: 6/61-1/65 Long Island GAR: 2/9/1918 Died: 8/19/1919 A: 81/5/__ Buried: GAR (Mount Hope) S: DC

Vest, Arthur E.
A/B: No stone
C: Cypress View Mausoleum/Shepard Lane, Main Corridor, Tier 2, Crypt 41 "Major Arthur E. Vest" DOD: 1943 No further information
E: Arthur E. Vest N: Ohio 11/25/45 CW: Co F 57 Ind Inf (Pvt/Sgt) Term: 3 yrs E/D: 12/61-12/65 Victoria, TX GAR: ? date "A mighty good soldier!" S: DC
F: Ann Vest Cypress View Mausoleum/Shepard Lane, Main Corridor, Tier 2, Crypt 40 DOD: 1946 No further information
NOTE: Death certificate for Arthur E. Vest, San Diego "Civil War Veteran" who lived for the longest time into the 20th century indicates: Place of death--San Diego, U.S. Naval Hospital. Resided in San Diego and California: 36 years DOD: 5/10/1943 A: 97/5/15 Date of Birth: 11/25/1945 Place: Cincinnati, Ohio Occupation: Carpenter (retired) Father: Roland Vest, born Franklin Co, VA Mother: Edith Edwards, born Cincinatti, Ohio. Wife: Anna E. Vest, age 86.

Wade, Nelson Walker
B: "Wade/Russell" stone
C: MH/Masonic Q DOD/B: 12/11-17/1921 A: 79/8/4 (ashes)
D: Nelson W. Wade N: New York A: 79 O: Retired R: National City, CA CW: Co G 21 NY Inf (Pvt) E/D: 5/61-7/61 LOS: 3 mos GAR: 5/24/1921 Died: 12/12/1921 Buried: "Greenwood" (but see above) S: H
F: Martha V. Wade No stone DOB: 2/1-7/1933 A: 87 (ashes) Died in National City, CA

Walker, Fletcher Jackson
A/B: No stone
C: MH/Div.6 DOD/B: 5/1-4/1932 A: 88/5/__ Died in San Diego
D: Fletcher J. Walker N: Ohio A: 64 O: Retired CW: Co A 1 Iowa Cav (Pvt) E/D: 6/61-3/66 LOS: 55 mos GAR: 11/12/1907 (probably on transfer from Tipbest (sp?) Post #32 Dept of Iowa S: H

Warburton, Percival D.
A: P.D. Warburton Co B 11 RI Inf
C: MH/GAR Div.2   DOD/B: 1/17-23/1929   A: 81/7/13   Died in San Diego
D: P.D. Warburton N: Rhode Island A: 50 O: Engraver CW: Co H 9 RI Inf (Pvt) E/D: 5/62-9/62 Re-Enl?: Co B
  11 RI Inf (Pvt) E/D: 9/62-7/63 LOS: 13 mos GAR: 4/12/1898 Died: 1/17/1929 S: H
F: Eliza R. Warburton No stone DOD/B: 3/11-16/1932 A: 80/10/13 Died in San Diego

Ward, Adolphus
B: Adophus Ward A member of 244 A O U W, Topeka, Kansas Born June 2, 1846 Died Feb 15, 1902
C: MH/Masonic F DOD/B: 2/15-21/1902 A: 55/8/13 N: American M: Married
F: Elizabeth Ward Conklin Died July 20, 1915 aged 57 years DOB: 7/23/1915 A: Not stated

Ward, G.G./George H.
B: G.G. Ward Co 11 5 VT Inf
C: MH/GAR Div.3 DOD/B: 8/25-9/1/1917 A: 75 (probable record for veteran...only "G. Ward" in records)

Ward, Jerome L.
A: Jerome L. Ward Co I 1 Wis Cav
B: J.L. Ward 1833-1913
C: MH/IOOF DOB: 9/26-29/1913 A: 80/4/21 N: NY M: Widower

Ward, Peter
A/B: No stone
C: MH/GAR Hill DOD/B: 9/13-20/1923 A: 83/2/20
E: Peter Ward N: Bellvue, Ill 6/24/40 CW: Co I 1st Colo Cav (Pvt) Term: 3 yrs E/D: 11/61-11/65 Denver, CO
  GAR: 10/13/1917 on transfer from Redondo Post #203 Dept of Cal/Nev Died: 9/13/1923 S: DC

Warner, Francis H.
B: Francis H. Warner 11 Mass Battery April 12, 1848-Dec 6, 1906
C: MH/GAR Div.2 DOD/B: 12/6-9/1906 A: 63/7/1929 N: Mass M: Married
D: Francis H. Warner N: Mass A: 62 O: Printer CW: Co __ 11 Mass Batt (Pvt) E/D: 12/63-6/65 LOS: 41 mos
  GAR: 7/25/1905 Died: 12/5/1906--no [grave] stone S: H
F: His wife Elizabeth A. Warner DOD/B: No further record available

Warren, Jones K.
B: Jones K. Warren Jan 19, 1824-April 26, 1922
C: MH/GAR Hill DOD/B: 4/26-28/1922 A: 98
E: Jones K. Warren N: Canada 1/19/24 CW: Co B 125 Ohio Inf (Pvt/Sgt) Term: 3 yrs E/D: 8/62-6/65 Nashville,
  TN GAR: ? date on transfer from John W. Geary Post #15 Dept of Kansas Died: 4/26/1922 A: 98/3/17
  S:DC
F: Antoinette A. Peck His wife Sept 26, 1829-May 14, 1905 DOD/B: 5/15-16/1905 A: 68 N: American M: Married
  "Mrs A.A. Warren"

Washington, S.W.
A: Corpl S.W. Washington 1 HGO Ohio S.S.
C: MH/IOOF DOD/B: No record found

Wasson, John
B: Jno. Wasson Co D 45 MO Inf
C: MH/GAR Div.2 DOD/B: 10/25-30/1910 A: 75 N: Indiana M: Married
D: John Wasson N: Missouri A: 52 O: Laborer CW: Co F 50 MO Inf (Pvt) E/D: 8/64-7/65 LOS: 10 mos GAR:
  4/26/1888 SP: 3/28/1889 DR: 6/30/1891 RE: 11/13/1906 Died: 10/28/1910 S: H
F: Cynthia Wasson No stone DOD/B: 10/21-23/1918 A: 80

Watson, Alexander G.
B: Alexander G. Watson Born in Burlington, Vermont Died in San Diego, Calif Jan 7, 1893 Aged 54 Years Capt 1st Vermont Cavalry
C: MH/Masonic K DOD/B: 1/7-9/1893 A: 54 N: American M: Married
D: Alexander G. Watson N: Vermont A: 48 O: Lawyer CW: Co L 1 VT Cav (Pvt/Capt) E/D: 8/62-6/65 LOS: 34 mos GAR: 1/27/1887 Died: 1/7/1893--no [grave] stone S: H
F: Delia Haskell Watson Wife of A.G.W. Burlington May 31, 1844 San Diego Oct 23, 1902 DOB: 10/23-25/1902 A: 58/4/23 N: American M: Widowed "Mrs Delia"

Watson, Joseph M.
B: Jos M. Watson 1828-1919 Capt Co H 2 Iowa Inf
C: GW/Laurel Place DOD/B: 7/7-8/1919 A: 90
F: Jennie B. Watson His Wife 1844-1911 DOD/B: No record found

Watts, Peter
A: Sergt Peter Watts Co F 2 IA Inf
C: MH/GAR Hill DOD/B: 3/17-20/1911 A: 74/3/__ N: Scotland M: Married
E: Peter Watts N: Dundee, Scotland CW: Co F 2 Iowa Inf (Pvt/Sgt) Term: 3 yrs E/D: 5/61-5/64 GAR: 11/10/1894 Charter Member of Datus Coon Post Died: 3/11/1911 A: 69 S: DC

Waugh, Samuel
A: Sam'l Waugh Co B 14 Ill Inf
C: MH/Div.1 DOD/B: 1/1-3/1903 A: 67 N: American M: Married
D: Samuel Waugh N: Penn A: 54 O: Carpenter CW: Co B 14 Ill Inf (Pvt) E/D: 7/61-7/65 LOS: 48 mos GAR: 2/14/1889 SP: 9/26/1889 RE: 3/12/1895 SP: 12/27/1898 RE: 4/10/1900 Died: 1/1/1903--is [grave] stone S: H
F: Susan Devoted Mother and Grandmother, Faithful Christian In Loving Memory 1842-1934 Additional stone: Mother Susan Waugh Sept 1, 1842-July 8, 1934 DOD/B: 7/8-11/1934 A: 91/10/7 Died in San Diego

Wearing, John
A: Jno Wearing Co L 2 PA H A
C: MH/GAR Hill DOD/B: 12/8-10/1902 A: 56/7/4 N: American M: Married Name spelled Warenig and Wareing in this record
E: John Wareing N: Wayne Co, PA CW: Co L 2 PA H A (Pvt/Color Bearer) Term: 3 yrs E/D: 2/64-7/65 Chester, PA due to gun shot wound at Cold Harbor resulting in amputation of left leg GAR: ? date on transfer from Dept of PA Died: 12/8/1902 A: 56 Buried: GAR (Mount Hope) S: DC
F: Mother Darling Eleanor Wearing Bray 1873-1947 DOD/B: 4/27-29/1947 A: 73/5/28 Died in Los Angeles, CA Buried as "Eleanor Jane Bray"

Weaver, Charles S./W.
A: Chas S. Weaver Co B Bracket's Minn Cav
C: MH/GAR Div.2 DOD/B: 3/31-4/1/1911 A: 69/7/__ N: Illinois M: Married
D: Charles W. Weaver N: Illinois A: 57 O: Mechanic CW: Co B Brackett's Batt Minn Cav (Pvt) E/D: 3/64-6/66 LOS: 27 mos GAR: 6/30/1882 Died: 3/31/1911 S: H
F: Nettie Weaver No stone DOD/B: 2/9-12/1924 A: 77/8/22

Weaver, Thomas F.
B: Thomas F. Weaver Co D 2 Colo Vol Cav 1831-1924
C: MH/GAR Div.2 DOD/B: 4/9-12/1924 A: 91/5/18
D: Thomas F. Weaver N: Ohio A: 74 O: Farmer CW: Co F 2 Colo Cav (Pvt) E/D: 6/62-6/65 LOS: 36 mos GAR: 8/22/1905 Died: 4/10/1924 S: H
F: Emily J. 1848-1925 DOD/B: 10/19-22/1925 A: 77/6/29 "Emma J."; also "Emily"

Webb, Charles Aden
A: Charles A. Webb Co G 8 VT Inf Nov 20, 1845-Mar 10, 1935
C: MH/GAR Hill DOD/B: 3/10-13/1935 A: 89/3/18 Died in San Diego "Charles Aden Webb"
E: Chas. A. Webb N: Middlefield, Mass 11/20/45 CW: Co G 8 VT Vol Inf (Pvt) Term: 1 yr E/D: 8/64-6/65
   Washington, D.C. GAR: 2/12/1909 on transfer from Johnson Post #23 Dept of VT Died: 3/10/1935 Buried:
   3/13/1935 (Mount Hope) S:DC
F: Flora Webb June 13, 1853-July 11, 1948 DOD/B: 7/11-16/1948 A: 96/__/28 Died in Santee, CA "Flora L."

Weber, Frances J.
A: F.J. Weber US Navy
C: MH/GAR Div.2 DOD/B: 6/7-9/1908 A: 61/__/29 N: New York M: Married "Webber"
F: Mary Weber 1845-1924 DOD/B: 8/26-28/1924 A: 78/5/6 "Webber"

Webster, Albert I.
A/B: No stone
C: MH/Div.2 DOD/B: 10/24-26/1927 A: 83/6/19 Died in San Diego
D: Albert I. Webster N: Illinois A: 70 O: Farmer CW: Co E 113 Ill Inf (Pvt) E/D: 8/62-6/65 LOS: Not stated GAR:
   9/9/1915 SP: 4/22/1925 RE: 1/12/1926 Died: 10/24/1927 S: H
F: Sylvia A Webster No stone DOB: 5/6/1924 No other information available

Webster, Calvin R.
B: Calvin R. Webster Artificer Battery B 1st NJ Lt Artillery Born Newark, NJ Jan 26, 1840 Died May 27, 1928
C: MH/Masonic F DOD/B: 5/27-29/1928 A: 88/4/1 NO WIFE
D: Calvin R. Webster N: New Jersey A: 73 O: Merchant CW: Co __ 1 NJ Lt Art (Artificer) E/D: __/61-9/64 LOS:
   Not stated GAR: 6/24/1913 Died: 5/27/1928 S: H

Webster, Francis E.
A: Sergt Francis E. Webster 10 US Inf
C: MH/GAR Hill DOD/B: 5/14-21/1923 A: 62

Webster, John O.
A/B: No stone
C: MH/Div.5 DOD/B: 9/5-7/1896 A: 52 N: American M: Married
D: John Webster N: Maine A: 51 O: Physician CW: Co A 8 ME Inf (Pvt/Sgt) E/D: 9/61-8/65 LOS: 48 mos GAR:
   1/23/1894 Died: 9/5/1896--is [grave] stone S: H
F: Anna Bartlett Webster No stone DOB: 8/31-10/22/1942 A: 97 Died in La Mesa, CA

Weegar, Erastus Henry
B: Erastus H. Weegar Died June 21, 1931 Aged 86 Years
B: E.H. Weegar
C: MH/Div.6 DOD/B: 6/21-23/1931 A: 86/4/4 Died in San Diego
D: E.H. Weegar N: Canada A: 41 O: Merchant CW: Co C 1 Cal Vols Inf (Pvt) E/D: 4/65-5/66 LOS: 1 year
   GAR: 5/20/1886 SP: 1/10/1889 DR: 6/30/1891 S: H
E: Erastus H. Weegar N: Williamsburg, Canada 1846 CW: Co C 1 Cal Inf (Pvt) Term: 1 yr E/D: 4/65-8/66 Santa
   Fe, NM LOS: "In service 1 yr 4 mos 3 days" GAR: 6/14/1924 on transfer from Heintzelman Post San Diego
   Died: 6/21/1931 A: 86 Buried: Mount Hope
   OBIT: "A noted friend of the South West Indians" No wife listed; 2 children
   OBIT: 56 years in San Diego County. Enlisting Co C, 1st regulars of Calif.Volunteers in 1865, Mr. Weeger
   helped quell Indian disturbances in New Mexiso, where Navajos threatened troubles at the close of the Civil
   War. His regiment rounded up 10,000 Indians and held them on the reservation at Las Cruces until danger
   of outbreaks had passed. His kindly manner made him greatly beloved by the Indians. He would often give
   from his own pocketbook when they were threatened with starvation. He was made Indian agent at Campo
   in 1899. S: DC
F: Mother Mary Ann Weegar Born Oct 26, 1846 Died Jan 25, 1918 (second stone says "Mother Mary Ann Weeger")
   DOB: 1/25-31/1918 A: 72/3/2 Obit for wife Mary Ann indicates native of Troy, NY; died at 72; church St.
   Pauls; three girls: 1 San Diego, 1 Chicago, 1 Clexico, MX S: DC

Welch, James
A: Jas Welch   Co G   34 US V. Inf   (tombstone visible at Calvary Cemetery)
C: CAL/Sec.3, North 2/3, Row 17A (Block A, Lot 17)   DOD/B: No record in Catholic cemetery index

Wellington, Edwin W.
A: E.W. Wellington   Co F   111th PA V Inf
B: Edwin W. Wellington   Mar 5, 1838-Jan 12, 1914   Co K   102 (or 162) PA V Inf
C: MH/GAR Hill   DOD/B: 1/12-14/1914   A: 81/10/7   N: New York   M: Married
F: Mary E, Wife of Edwin W. Wellington   July 15, 1833-Feb 21, 1899   DOD/B: 2/21-22/1899   A: 65   N: American

Wells, Alpheno W.
A: A.W. Wells   Co H   9 VT Inf
C: MH/GAR Hill   DOD/B: 9/23-25/1902   A: 54/7/9   N: American   M: Married

Wells, Homer L.
A/B: No stone
C: MH/GAR Hill   DOD/B: 2/6-11/1924   A: 84/3/7
D: H.L. Wells   N: Iowa   A: 42   O: Physician   CW: Co A   57 Ohio Inf (Pvt/1st Lieut)   E/D: 9/61-3/65   LOS: 42 mos
   GAR: 7/13/1882   TR: 12/9/1891   S: H

Wells, Leonard Bates
A: 1st Sgt. Leonard B. Wells   Co A   8 Ill Inf
C: MH/GAR Div.3   DOD/B: 5/22-24/1912   A: 85/3/23   Died in San Diego   "Bates"
F: Susan Wells   Sept 25, 1842-Sept 12, 1928   DOD/B: 9/12-14/1928   A: 85/11/18   Died in San Diego

West, Joseph G.
A: Jos G. West   Co K   9th Ill Cav
C: MH/GAR Hill   DOD/B: 9/27-29/1899   A: 56   N: American   M: Widower   "John A." in record

Weston, Charles D.
A: C.D. Weston   Co F   28th ME Inf
B: Charles D. Weston   1844-1896   Member of Co F   28 Reg Maine Vol
C: MH/Div.2   DOD/B: 6/6-9/1896   A: 52   N: American   M: Married
F: Mary Weston is lot owner, but is not buried at Mount Hope; no further information available on her

Wheeler, Lyman
B: Lyman S.   Srgt   Co 1   25th Mass Vet Vol Inf   Apr 11, 1837-Feb 18, 1929
B: Lyman S. Wheeler   Apr 11, 1837-Feb 18, 1929
C: MH/BLK 2   DOD/B: 2/18-23/1929   A: 92   Died: Tuscon, AZ
D: Lyman Wheeler   N: Mass   A: 77   O: Farmer   CW: Co I   25 Mass Inf (Corpl/Sgt)   E/D: 9/61-4/65 due to wounds
   LOS: Not stated   GAR: 1/26/1915 on transfer from Robert Anderson Post #32 Dept of Nebraska   DR:
   12/31/1928   S: H
F: Mary E. Wife of L.S. Wheeler   Nov 26, 1834-Sept 7, 1920   DOD/B: 9/7-10/1920   A: 86
F: Mary E. Wheeler   Nov 26, 1834-Sept 7, 1920

Whims, Joshua K.
A/B: No stone
C: MH/GAR Div.2   DOD/B: 10/28-30/1912   A: 76   N: PA   M: Widower   "Joshua W."
E: J.K. Whims   NOL/NFI--DC

Whipple, Charles
A: Lt Col Chas Whipple   19 Wis Inf
C: MH/Div.4   DOD/B: 1/12-14/1882   A: Not stated   N: New York   M: Married   J/S: "Whipple, Charles, d. 12 Jan
   (1882), 56 years, b: NY, mar, bur City Cem"   Obit/San Diego Herald, 1/12/1882: "In this city January 12, Col
   Charles Whipple, a native of Wayne Co, NY, aged 67. Friends and acquaintences are invited to attend the
   funeral on Saturday January 14 at 10:00 at his late residence, corner of 10th and G Streets. San Francisco

Whipple, Charles (Con't)
papers please copy."
F: Dotba Whipple No stone DOD/B: 7/13/1919-10/9/1920 A: 89 (ashes) (wife?) Also tombstone next to his reads: "Caroline Lee 1845-1930" (wife/sister?) DOD/B:

Whipple, S.G.
B: Lt Col S.G. Whipple 1st Batt'y Cal Mount'rs
C: MH/Div.2 DOD/B: 8/30-31/1887 A: 40 N: Rhode Island M: Single Record under "G. Whipple"
Note: Above tombstone information is correct, but not cemetery office information. His actual burial may be at Myrtle Grove Cemetery in Eureka, Humboldt Co, CA. DOD: 10/21/1895, according to cemetery office record. Tombstone there reads: S.G. Whipple Lieu't. Col. 1 Mount'rs. Cal. Inf., according to *Humboldt County Cemeteries* by Gene Duvall (copy in California Room, San Diego Public Library, Call No. RCC 929.5/Humboldt, Vol. 1.) Another veteran in same cemetery belonged to "Col. Whipple Post #49 GAR" (in Eureka?.) Contact City of Eureka employee Barbara (707) 441-4191 for more information. A citation to Whipple is also in book *Canary Yellow and Infantry Blue: Army Officers in Arizona between 1851-1886*, by Constance Altshuler (published by Arizona Historical Society), cited as "Stephen Girard Whipple", born Burlington, VT (Nov. 5, 1825); edited paper in Humboldt Bay, CA in 1886; died Eureka. 1 daughter, 2 sons.
F: Georgia E. (Lord) Whipple (Lord is married name by prior marriage; he met her at "Camp Apache", probably in Arizona DOD: 5/13/1925 (probably Myrtle Grove Cemetery, although he is buried in GAR section.)

White, Asa G.
A: A.G. White Co K 6 IA Cav
B: Asa G. White 1817-1891
C: MH/Div.1 DOD/B: 9/15-17/1891 A: 71 N: American M: Married
F: Martha B. Keyes, Wife of Asa G. White 1826-1902 DOD/B: 7/17-19/1902 A: 76 N: American M: Widow

White, Nicander
A: Nicander White Co D 8 Ohio Cav
C: MH/Div.6 DOD/B: 3/1909-3/22/1909 A: 68/10/__
E: Nicander White N: Highland Co, Ohio CW: Co D 8 Ohio Inf (Pvt) Term: 3 yrs E/D: 2/64-6/64 Camp Dennison, Ohio due to disability GAR: 7/11/1908 on transfer from Mitchell Post #45 Dept of Ohio Died: 3/__/1909 A: 68 Buried: GAR (Mount Hope) S: DC

Whitlock, Sidney Winder
A: Sidney W. Whitlock Co K 2 MO S.M. Cav
C: MH/Div.6 DOD/B: 11/24-28/1922 A: 89/9/18 Middle name "Winder"
F: Mina Elizabeth L. Whitlock No stone DOD/B: 6/23-27/1905 A: 72/1/9 N: American M: Married

Wiard, Augustus J.
A: Augustus J. Wiard Co E 17 Wisc Inf
C: MH/GAR Div.2 DOD/B: 2/8-10/1912 A: 87/6/3 N: PA M: Married
D: Augustus J. Wiard N: Penn A: 77 O: Physician R: Otay (near San Diego) CW: Co E 17 Wis Inf (Pvt) E/D: 9/64-6/65 LOS: 9 mos GAR: 8/27/1901 Died: 2/8/1912 S: H
F: Mary J. Wiard Aug 26, 1833-Mar 9, 1923 DOD/B: 3/9-12/1923 A: 89/6/11

Wiggens, Francis C.
B: Francis C. Wiggens Oct 6, 1840-May 23, 1936 Co F 2nd Ohio Cav
C: MH/Div.6 DOD/B: 5/23-26/1936 A: 93/7/17 Died in San Diego
E: Francis Wiggins NOL/NFI
F: Lucy J. Wiggins Sept 29, 1841-June 23, 1907 DOD/B: 6/23-25/1907 A: 65 N: New York M: Married

Wilcox, David Elias
B: David E. Wilcox Pvt Co F 76 Regt PA Inf Civil War Jun 4, 1844-Oct 26, 1925
C: MH/GAR Hill DOD/B: 10/26-28/1925 A: 81/4/22
E: David Wilcox N: Mt Pleasant, Wayne Co, PA 6/4/44 CW: Co F 76 PA Inf (Pvt) Term: 3 yrs E/D: 9/64-6/65 Raleigh, NC GAR: 11/22/1913 from Warren Ricks Post Dept of PA Died: 10/26/1925 A: 81/4/22 S: DC

Wiley, George O.
A: George O. Wiley Co B 34 Mass Inf
C: MH/GAR Div.2 DOD/B: 8/18-22/1911 A: 67/1/24 N: Mass M: Married
F: Genevieve Wiley No stone DOD/B: 11/24-30/1932 A: 71/1/15 Died in New York State "Wiley"

Wilkins, George A.
B: Capt Geo A Wilkins Co H 47 Reg Ill Vol
C: MH/GAR Hill DOD/B: 9/2-4/1895 A: 74 N: Ireland M: Single "Capt"

Willey, John Alexander
A/B: No stone
C: MH/Masonic U DOD/B: 2/17-20/1928 A: 84/5/23
E: John A. Willey N: Knox Co, Ill 8/25/43 CW: Co G 67 Ill Inf (Pvt) Term: 3 mos E/D: 5/62-10/62 Camp Douglas, Chicago, IL GAR: 11/26/1927 on transfer from E.O.C.Ord Post, San Antonio, TX Died: 2/19/1928 S: H

Willey, Norris M.
A: N.M. Willey Co A 8 Mass Inf
B: Norris M. Willey Died Jan 10, 1905 aged 64 years
C: MH/Div.6 DOD/B: 1/10-14/1905 A: 60 N: American M: Married "Wiley"

Williams, Charles H.
A: Mus'n Chas H. Williams Band 20 Brig Corps D'Afrique
C: MH/GAR Div.2 DOB: 10/15-17/1910 A: 80/6/10
D: Charles H. Williams N: New York A: 79 O: Carpenter CW: Co K 13 Mass Inf (Pvt) Re-enl: Co __ 81 U S C T (Musician) E/D: 4/61-8/65 LOS: Not stated GAR: 8/24/1909 Died: 10/15/1910 S: H
F: Sarah L. Williams 1841-1913 DOB: 3/16-18/1913 A: 72/7/10 N: MA M: Widow

Williams, Clarence J.
A: Lieut C.J. Williams QM 2 Kans Cav
C: MH/GAR Div. 2 DOD/B: 1/21-23/1912 A: 73 N: NY M: Married "Clarance"

Williams, Henry H.
A: Major H.H. Williams 10 Kansas Inf
C: MH/Masonic G DOD/B: 3/28-30/1906 A: 77/5/29 N: New York M: Married
D: Henry H. Williams N: New York A: 59 O: Merchant CW: Co __ 3 Kans Inf (Major) also: Co __ 10 Kans Inf (Major) E/D: 6/61-2/65 LOS: 41 mos or 43 mos GAR: 3/22/1888 SP 3/29/1889 DR: 3/28/1899 RE: 4/24/1900 Died: 3/28/1906--is [grave] stone S: H
F: Mary A. Williams No stone DOB: 2/17-20/1922 A: 80

Williams, James
A: Serg't Jas Williams Co B 162 NY Inf (tombstone visible at Calvary Cemetery)
C: CAL/Sec.1, C, Row 3 (Sec.1--Central) DOD/B: Two records in Catholic cemetery information as follows: James Williams DOB: 11/24/1893 A: 47 Native of Kentucky Spouse: Nora Maloney Cause of death: Accidental drowning; County record: James Williams DOD: 11/13/1893 A: 57 Cause of death: Gunshot wound
F: Nora Maloney DOD/B: No record in Catholic cemetery index Source: DOD/B information on husband

Williams, L.A.
A: Corpl L.A. Williams Co A 2 VRC
C: GW/Hawthorne DOD/B: 2/19/1906-5/16/1913 A: 76 Prior burial in MH/GAR Hill DOD/B: 2/19-20/1906 A: 76/5/2 N: Maryland M: Married Removed to Greenwood Cemetery 5/16/1913

Williams, Morgan Thomas
B: Morgan T. Williams Sergt 1st NY Cav 1841-1926
C: MH/GAR Div.2 DOD/B: 9/29-10/1/1926 A: 84/11/_ Died in San Diego
D: Morgan T. Williams N: New York A: 83 O: Retired CW: Co K 1 NY Cav (Pvt) E/D: 8/61-7/65 LOS: 4 yrs GAR: 4/14/1925 Died: 9/29/1926 S:H

Wilson, Alexander
A: Alex Wilson Co H 78 PA Inf
C: MH/GAR Hill DOD/B: 9/10-10/4/1928 A: 82/2/26 Died in San Diego
D: Alexander Wilson N: Penn A: 55 O: Sheet Metal Worker CW: Co H 78 PA Inf (Pvt) E/D: 2/65-9/65 LOS: 8 mos
  GAR: 4/24/1906 Died: 9/30/1928 ("8" of 1928 is hard to read) S: H

Wilson, Hiram J.
A: H.J. Wilson Co D 18 Mich Inf (or Co B?)
C: MH/IOOF DOD/B: 2/14-16/1905 A: 68 N: American M: Married "Hiram J."

Wilson, Silas
B: Silas Wilson 1846-1925
C: MH/Div.6 DOD/B: 12/29/1925-1/2/1926 A: 79/7/13 Died in San Diego To Div.6 on 8/20/1927 from GAR Div.2 Lot 200
E: Silas Wilson N: Moundville, West VA 5/6/46 CW: Co A 7 W VA Inf (Pvt) Term: 3 yrs E/D: 8/62-7/65 LOS: 2 yrs 11 mos 22 days GAR: 9/13/1924 on transfer from G.A. Hobart Post #27 Dept of Idaho. Died: 12/29/1925 at San Diego A: 70 S: DC
  Note: In 1871, he removed from West VA to Atlanta, Iowa where he established an extensive nursery business. He married Miss Edna Aylesworth of Atlanta, IA on 9/29/1875. They have two children, both sons--Fred W. Wilson of San Diego; W.H. Wilson of Nampa, Idaho. He was Commissioner of Iowa at the Exposition at St. Louis, MO in 1904. In 1886 he was elected a member of the Iowa Legislature, and was re-elected for second and third terms. During his third term, he was Speaker of the House. He sold his nursery at Atlanta in 1904, and spent two years on the West Coast looking for a new location. In 1906, he bought 640 acres of land near Nampa, Idaho and planted it to apples. He spent several winters in San Diego prior to 1923, and in that year removed here and started a home. He was during his whole manhood a member and Deacon of the United Presbyterian Church. He was married in 1875 by a cousin of the writer of this obituary, T.C. Shelly, Adjt, Datus E. Coon Post No 172. S: DC
F: Edna Wilson 1853-1933 DOD/B: 8/26-29/1933 A: 80/7/27 Died in San Diego Born: Atlanta, IA (see above).

Winchester, Lewis K.
B: Lewis K. Winchester Sgt 1 Ark Cav May 12, 1837-May 9, 1922
C: MH/GAR Hill DOD/B: 5/9-11/1922 A: 84 "Louis K."
D: Lewis K. Winchester N: Hardin Co, KY A: 81 O: Retired CW: Co H 1 Ark Cav (Pvt/Sgt) E/D: __/61-5/64 LOS: See prior notes GAR: 6/25/1918 Died: 5/9/1922 S: H

Winscott, James Clayton
B: James Clayton Winscott Pvt Co B 33 Mo Inf Civil War Feb 22, 1846-Feb 23, 1928
C: MH/Masonic U DOD/B: 2/23-27/1928 A: 82/__/1
E: James Clayton Winscott N: Hannibal, MO CW: Co A 50 Ill Inf (Pvt) Term: 3 yrs E/D: 4/61-12/62 Re-Enl: Co B 33 MO Vol Inf (Pvt) E/D: 12/62-2/66 GAR: 6/9/1906 on transfer from Custer Post #21 Dept of Indian Territory Died: 2/24/1928 Buried: Masonic (Mount Hope) S: DC

Winslow, Charles Caffin
B: Charles C. Winslow 1834-1918
C: MH/Masonic Q DOD/B: 3/20-22/1918 A: 84
E: Chas C. Winslow N: Maine CW: Co H 21 Maine Inf (Pvt) Term: Unstated E/D: 5/65-11/65 Augusta, Maine GAR: 12/26/1908 DR: 12/9/1916 S: DC
F: Lusanna G. His Wife 1834-1913 DOB: 7/17/1913 A: 78/5/27

Wishmeyer, Frederick C.
B: C.F. Wishmeyer Corpl Co H 1 Reg Ind Vol Inf died at San Diego, Cal on Dec 2, 1897 aged 76 yrs
C: MH/GAR Hill DOD/B: 12/2-3/1897 A: 73 yrs "Frederick C. Wisheneyer"

Wood, Aaron
B: Aaron Wood 1845-1924
C: MH/Confederate DOD/B: 2/4-9/1924 A: 78/7/30 N: "Confederate" "Aron"
F: Annie J. 1849-1924 DOD/B: 10/18-23/1924 A: Not stated N: "Confederate" "Mrs. Aaron Wood"
        Note: Aaron Wood was born 6/5/1845 in Mississippi; Died 2/4/1924 in San Diego. S: UDC document, California Room (see Chapter II, "San Diego Public Library" sources)

Wood, Augustus M.
A: Mus'n Aug's M. Wood Co A 44 Iowa Inf
B: Augustus M. Wood Husband of Amy C. Born 1851 Died 1905
C: GW/Magnolia Place DOD/B: No record found
F: Amy C. Wood DOD/B: 11/7-9/1928 A: No record found Buried: GW/Masonic "Annie C."

Wood, Calvin Maples
B: 1st Lieut Calvin M. Wood Forge, NY 1837-San Diego 1923 Co I 19 Wis Vol 1862-1865
C: MH/Div.6 DOD/B: 1/14-18/1923 A: 85/11/16 "Maples"
E: Calvin M. Wood N: Cairo, Green Co, NY 1837 CW: Co I 19 Wis Inf (Ord Sgt/1st Lieut) Term: 3 yrs E/D; 1/62-7/65 due to disability GAR: 6/11/1921 Died: "Died" S: DC
F: Esther M. Wood Catskill, NY 1837-San Diego 1904 Ladies of the GAR DOD/B: 10/24-25/1904 A: 66/11/9 N: American M: Married "Ester"

Wood, H.F.
B: Sacred to the memory of Capt. H.F. Wood US Navy Born at Swanzi, Mass Nov 27, 1837 Died in San Diego March 20, 1888
C: MH/GAR Hill DOD: 3/29/1888 "No record of burial--[date of death] taken from [grave] stone"

Wood, Thomas E.
A: Capt T.E. Wood Co H 123 Ill Inf
C: MH/GAR Hill DOD/B: 3/30-4/1/1894 A: 54 N: American M: Married

Woodman, Ezra E.
A: Ezra E. Woodman Co G 11 ME Inf
C: MH/GAR Div.3 DOD/B: 11/13-15/1913 A: 78/7/13 N: Maine

Woodruff, George A.
A: 1st Sgt Geo A. Woodruff Co H 113 Ill Inf
C: MH/GAR Div.2 DOD/B: 3/4-6/1912 A: 79/4/6 N: CT M: Married
D: Geo. H. Woodruff N: Conn A: 64 O: Foundryman R: San Diego/National City CW: Co H 113 Ill Inf (Pvt/Sgt) E/D: 8/62-6/65 LOS: 34 mos GAR: 4/12/1898 TR: 6/27 or 8/27/1901 GAR: 5/13/1908 TR: 5/14/1908 Died: 3/4/1912 S: H
F: Elizabeth Woodruff 1840-1915 DOB: 10/22-23/1915 A: 74/11/21 N: IN M: Widow

Woodruff, Joseph D.
A/B: Stone no longer visible
C: MH/Div.5 DOD/B: 3/9/1923-9/30/1926 A: 79/8/__ (ashes) Died in San Diego
D: Joseph D. Woodruff N: New York A: 60 O: Cheese Maker CW: Co I 61 NY Inf (Pvt) E/D: 10/61-4/63 due to disability LOS: 18 mos GAR: 10/14/1902 Died: 3/7/1923 (GAR death date is slightly in error) S: H
E: Joseph D. Woodruff NOL/NFI--DC
F: Emily Jane Woodruff No stone DOD/B: 9/21-22/1926 A: 87/4/17 Died in San Diego

Woodward, Hiram P. (Horace P.)
A: H.P. Woodward MD Asst Surgeon 15 & 18 Mich Vol Inf 1824-1901
C: MH/GAR Hill DOD/B: 10/24-26/1901 A: 77/6/7 N: American M: Married
D: Hiram P. Woodward N: New York A: 57 O: Physician CW: Co __ 15 Mich Vols (2nd Lieut/Capt) E/D: 2/62-5/63 due to disability LOS: 15 mos GAR: 7/8/1886 SP: 9/26/1889 RE: 1/14/1890 or 12/10/1890 Died:

Woodward, Hiram P. (Horace P.) (Con't)
    10/24/1901--is [grave] stone S: H
F: Emma A. Wife of H.P. Woodward 1841-____ DOD/B: 2/6-8/1921 A: 79 "Emma Arvilla"

Woolsey, George Sylvester
A/B: No stone
C: MH/Div.6 DOD/B: 8/8-11/1921 A: 89 (ashes)
E: Geo. S. Woolsey NOL/NFI--DC
F: Mother Alvira R. Woolsey Died Mar 13, 1915 "Love Shall Bring My Own To Me" DOB: 3/11-13/1914 A: 82 N: Ohio M: Married "Alvira Rebecka"

Worth, Jehoiada
B: Jehoiada Worth 1836-1920
C: MH/Masonic S DOD/B: 6/13-16/1920 A: 84/1/16
D: Jehoiada Worth N: Penn A: 65 O: Merchant R: Coronado, CA CW: Co D 4 Iowa Cav (Pvt) E/D: 9/61-8/65 LOS: 47 mos GAR: 8/11/1893 Died: 6/13/1920 S: H
F: Mary E. Worth 1860-1918 DOB: 2/4-9/1918 A: 59 "Mary Emma"

Worth, John C.
A: John C. Worth Co D 41 IA Cav
C: GW/Hawthorne DOD/B: 8/25/1910-2/23/1911 A: 72 (removed from MH)
E: John C. Worth N: Lucerne Co, PA CW: Co D 4th Iowa Cav (Pvt) Term: 3 yrs E/D: 9/61-8/65 Davenport, Iowa GAR: 11/27/1896 on transfer from Escondido Post #143 Dept of Cal/Nev Died: 8/25/1910 A: 71 Buried: Greenwood S: DC
F: Mother Margaret E. Worth 1848-1920 DOD/B: 5/11-15/1920 A: 72

Worthing, Ranford
A: Lieut Ranford Worthing Co L 12 S C H A
B: Ranford Worthing 1839-1910
C: MH/Div.4 DOD/B: 6/2-4/1910 A: 70/8/5
D: Ranford Worthing N: Maine A: 62 O: Mining Engineer CW: Co M 1 ME H A (Pvt) Re-Enl?: Co L 12 ____ H A (2 Lieut) E/D: 1/64-4/66 LOS: 26 mos GAR: 8/12/1902 SP: 12/27/1904 RE: 3/28/1905 TR: 3/28/1905 S: H
F: Celia A. Worthing 1843-1898 DOD/B: 2/10-12/1898 A: 54 N: American M: Married

Wright, George P.
A: Hosp Stwd Geo. P. Wright 7 VT Inf
C: MH/GAR Div.2 DOD/B: 8/2-4/1910 A: 66 N: VT M: Single
D: George P. Wright N: Vermont A: 50 O: Contractor CW: Co K 7 VT Inf (Pvt) E/D: 2/62-2/64 Re-Enl?: Co __ 7 VT Inf (Hosp Stwd) E/D: 2/64-5/66 LOS: 39 mos GAR: 9/10/1895 Died: 8/5/1910 S: H

Wright, Henry Q.
A: H.Q. Wright Co I 11 Ill Inf
C: MH/GAR Hill DOD/B: 7/21-23/1902 A: Not stated N: American M: Widower
D: Henry Q. Wright N: New York A: 54 O: Carpenter CW: Co I 11 Ill Inf (Pvt) Re-enl?: Co A 64 Ill Inf (Pvt) E/D: 4/61-5/65 LOS: 48 or 49 mos GAR: 7/18/1893 Died: 7/21/1902--is [grave] stone S: H

Wright, Philander D.
B: Philander D. Wright April 14,1844-April 2,1929
C: MH/GAR Div.2 DOD/B: 4/2-4/1929 A: 84/11/19 Died in Lemon Grove, CA
E: Philander Wright N: Wilmington, IL CW: Co C 14 Iowa Inf (Pvt) Term: 3 yrs E/D: 11/62-9/65 Davenport, Iowa GAR: 11/28/1908 on transfer from Sedan Post #74 Dept of Kansas Died: 4/2/1929 "Interred" S: DC
F: Emma Wright Sept 2,1842-May 18,1923 DOD/B: 5/18-22/1923 A: 81/8/16

Wright, Walter W.
B: Walter W. Wright 1844-1925 Co C 1st Batt 12 US Inf
C: MH/GAR Hill DOD/B: 8/9-12/1925 A: 81/4/11
D: Walter W. Wright N: Ohio A: 76 O: Retired CW: Co C 12 US Inf (Pvt) E/D: 5/62-5/65 LOS: 3 years GAR: 10/12/1920 Died: 8/9/1925 S: H

Wroughton, William H.
A: Wm. H. Wroughton Co D 49 Ind Inf
C: MH/GAR Div.3 DOD/B: 5/27-31/1917 A: 87 Title #1378 to Wm. Wroughton
D: Wm H.Wroughton N: Indiana A: 79 O: Not stated CW: Co D 49 Ind Inf (Corpl) E/D: 11/61-12/62 LOS: Not stated GAR: 12/26/1915 on transfer from Datus Coon Post San Diego Dismissed: 1/2/1917 TR: 1/9/1917 S: H
E: Wm. H. Wroughton N: Clark Co, Indiana 4/16/37 CW: Co D 49 Ind Inf (Pvt/Corp) Term: 3 yrs E/D: 10/61-12/62 due to disability Louisville, KY GAR: 10/13/1906 TR: 12/25/1915 to Heintzelman Post GAR San Diego RE: 1/13/1917 from Heintzelman Post GAR San Diego D: 5/27/1917 S: DC

Wyatt, Charles C.
A: Corpl C.C. Wyatt Co H 22nd Iowa Inf
C: MH/Masonic J DOD/B: 4/6-7/1896 A: 60 N: American M: Married
D: Charles C. Wyatt N: Kentucky A: 55 O: Capitalist CW: Co H 22 Iowa Inf (Pvt) Re-Enl?: Co G __ VRC (Pvt) E/D: 8/62-6/65 LOS: 34 mos GAR: 12/10/1890 TR: 12/28/1892 Died: 4/29/1896--is [grave] stone S: H
F: Kate Wyatt No stone DOB: 12/13/1941-1/6/1942 A: 81 (ashes) Died in Los Angeles

Wyllis, Sidney A.
A/B: No stone
C: MH/GAR Div.3 DOD/B: "Died in San Diego" No other information available
D: Sidney A. Willis N: Michigan A: 56 O: Farmer R: Chollas Valley (near San Diego) CW: Co H 4 Mich Inf (Corpl/Sgt) E/D: 6/61-6/64 LOS: 36 mos GAR: 12/8/1896 Post Commander 1904 Died: 1/__/1928 S: H
F: Ida B. A good wife DOD/B: 7/19-21/1916 A: 61 "Ida D."

Wynn, Charles Harmon
A/B: No stone
C: MH/Div.3 DOD/B: 5/12-15/1926 A: 78/__/19 Died in Orland, CA
D: Charles H. Wynn N: New York A: 58 O: Lawyer CW: Co I 35 Ill Inf (Pvt) E/D: 4/62-4/65 LOS: 36 mos GAR: 9/11/1906 Died: 5/12/1926 S: H
F: Myra Euphemia Wynn (or Myra Euphrenia) No stone DOB: 12/1-3/1909 A: 63/10/__ N: PA M: Married Record under name "Euphemia Wynn"

Young, Edgar S.
A: E.S. Young Co G 14th Mich Inf
C: MH/Masonic C DOD/B: 8/17-20/1893 A: 48/1/21 N: American M: Married

Young, J.F.
A: Capt J.F. Young Co K 10 MO Cav
C: GW/Magnolia Place DOD/B: 9/1/1913-4/17/1917 A: 78 "J.T. Young"
F: Amy E. Young Nov. 22, 1925 DOD/B: 11/22-25/1925 A: 81 "Amy S. Young"
  Note: Is J.F. Young the possible father of Amy C. Young, third wife of veteran George Puterbaugh (see p. 196 above). If so, he is the great-grandson of Betsy Ross, maker of the 1st American flag.

Young, John A.
A: Sergt of Ord. John Young U.S.A.
C: FR/Post Sec.5 Grave 67 DOD: 5/26-29/1915 "Sgt"
E: John Young N: Philadelphia, PA CW: Co F 6 PA Cav (Pvt) Term: 3 yrs E/D: 11/61-10/64 Harper's Ferry, VA Re-Enl?: Co E 88 PA Inf (Corpl) E/D: 1/65-6/65 GAR: 2/27/1909 Died: 5/26/1915 Buried: Ft. Rosecrans S:DC

Young, Robert C.
B: Robert C. Young 84 Ill Inf 1844-1922
C: MH/GAR Hill DOD/B: 10/20-23/1922 A: 78
D. Robert C. Young N: Kentucky A: 75 O: Retired CW: Co E 84 Ill Inf (Pvt) E/D: 8/62-6/65 LOS: 3 yrs GAR: 12/14/1915 GAR: 3/8/1920 Died: 10/20/1922 S: H

Young, William A.
B: William A. Young Co F 28 Ill Inf Dec 31, 1838-Feb 4, 1924
C: MH/Masonic F DOD/B: 2/4-8/1924 A: 85
E: William A. Young N: Petersburg, Ill 12/30/38 CW: Co F 28 Ill Inf (Pvt) E/D: 8/61-1/64 St. Louis, MO due to wounds GAR: 12/9/1916 Died: Soldier's Home 2/4/1924 age 85 S: DC

SAWTELLE: No records were found for this veteran at Los Angeles National Cemetery.
S: Los Angeles National Cemetery

CHAPTER FIVE: LIST 2--CIVIL WAR VETERANS WITH BURIAL LOCATIONS UNKNOWN

This list contains veterans for whom no local burial information could be determined (except for a few internments in areas near San Diego: La Vista Cemetery in National City, Glen Abbey Cemetery in Bonita, and El Cajon Cemetery in El Cajon.) Additionally, some veterans died and were buried at Sawtelle Soldier's Home in Los Angeles.

A good number of veterans on this list, however, may be buried locally at Greenwood Cemetery, Holy Cross Cemetery, Cypress View Mausoleum, Fort Rosecrans Cemetery or in cemeteries on the outskirts of the San Diego city limits. If the researcher feels that a veteran on this list might have died in the city of San Diego, a call to local cemeteries would help to clarify that. Cemetery records for Greenwood and Holy Cross Cemeteries (where many of the veterans may be buried) could not be accessed personally, but staff members are there to assist you. Be aware of the dates of opening of these cemeteries: Greenwood opened in 1907; Holy Cross opened in 1919, Cypress View opened in 1927, and Fort Rosecrans opened after 1883). They may have a burial record for your veteran.

In this list, the following codes are used:

N: Nativity **A**: Age **O**: Occupation **CW**: Civil War unit of service and rank **Term:** Term of enlistment (for Datus Coon Post members only) **E/D**: Dates of entry/discharge from Civil War **LOS**: Length of Service **GAR**: Date of entry into Heintzelman Post or Datus Coon Post G.A.R. (indicative of approximate time of arrival in San Diego) **D**: Honorably discharged from G.A.R. **SP**: Suspended from G.A.R. **DR**: Dropped from G.A.R. **RE**: Reinstated in G.A.R. **S**: Source of record, whether from H: Heintzleman Post records or from DC: Datus Coon Post records **NOL/NFI**: There is no other listing, no further information about this veteran, other than that he joined the Datus Coon Post G.A.R. at one time or another. Only his name was listed on a roster for that organization, and no other information.

Reason for discharge is only noted if other than for expiration of term of service, close of war, or general orders. Reasons thus noted include "disability," "wounds," etc.--anything out of the ordinary.

Some veterans of this study were buried at Sawtelle Soldier's Home (Los Angeles National Cemetery), and they are included below. The Sawtelle information will be noted just under the G.A.R. information for these veterans, and flagged with the word "SAWTELLE." Again, several burials are also included below from La Vista Cemetery in National City, two from Glen Abbey in Bonita, and one from El Cajon Cemetery in El Cajon. Only tombstone inscriptions are reported for the veterans buried at these facilities. Researchers should call the cemetery offices at Sawtelle, La Vista, Glen Abbey or El Cajon Cemeteries for the cemetery office record for these individuals. However, the San Diego Genealogical Society's publication *San Diego Cemetery & Burial Records* does contain an indexed listing of burial information for those buried in La Vista Cemetery. For further information about this publication, see pages 18 and 19 of this study.

NAME OF VETERAN	**VETERAN HISTORY**
Abrahams, W.F.	N: Steubensville, Ohio CW: Co F 84 Ohio Vol Inf (Pvt) Term: 90 days E/D: 5/62-9/62 Camp Delaware, Ohio GAR: 5/28/1904 Died: 3/31/1915 age 63 Buried: Los Angeles S: DC
Ackerman, Frank	N: France A: 81 O: Retired CW: Co M 17 Ind Cav (Pvt) E/D: 7/63-5/65 LOS: 1 yrs 8 mos GAR: 10/27/1925 Died: 3/6/1929 S: H
Adair, Marion	N: Columbus, OH, 7/7/48 CW: Co ___ 33 IA Inf (Pvt) Term: Unstated E/D: 2/64-8/65 GAR: 7/11/1934 DR: For nonpayment of dues S: DC
Adams, Calvin J.	N: Michigan A: 78 R: La Mesa O: Gardener CW: Co E 50 Ill Inf (Pvt) E/D: 1/64-7/65 LOS: 18 mos GAR: 9/11/1923 Died: 3/8/1924 S: H
Adams, Stephen J.	N: England A: 79 O: Retired CW: Co D Marine Brigade (Pvt) E/D: 2/64-4/65 LOS: 1 yr GAR: 7/8/1924 TR: 9/19/1927 S: H
Ainsley, G.W.	Corpl G.W. Ainsley 25 N Y L A (official tombstone). Buried in La Vista Cemetery, National City, CA.

Albee, Timothy M.	N: Conn A: 75 O: Painter CW: Co A 44 Ind Inf (Pvt); Re-enl?: Co C 152 Ind Inf (Sgt) E/D: 8/61-6/65 LOS: 46 mos GAR: 10/10/1893 SP: 12/22/1896 DR: 3/28/1899 RE: 3/10/1914 Died: 5/11/1919 S: H
Alcorn, Robert A.	N: Beaver, PA 9/9/44 CW: Co H 19th Regt IA Inf (Corpl) Term: 3 yrs E/D: 8/62-7/65, Mobile, AL GAR: ? date on transfer from Miles Keller Post S: DC
Alexander, W.F.	N: Maine A: 40 O: Carpenter CW: Co E 1 MO Cav (Pvt) E/D: 12/63-8/65 LOS: 1 yr, 8/12 mos GAR: 5/13/1886 SP: 1/10/1889 DR: 6/30/1891 S: H
Alford, Robert	N: Indiana A: 66 R: Lakeside O: Rancher CW: Co K 136 Ind Inf (Pvt) Re-enl?: Co I 152 Ind Inf (Pvt) E/D: 5/64-8/65 LOS: Not stated GAR: 10/22/1912 S: H
Alhoun, William H.	N: PA A: 68 O: Farmer CW: Co C 52 Ind Inf (Pvt) E/D: 9/64-10/65 LOS: Not stated GAR: 3/9/1915 SP: 12/28/1920 S: H
Allen, Henry E.	N: Buffalo, NY CW: Co K 2nd Wis Inf (Pvt) Term: 3 yrs E/D: 5/61-10/63 Washington, DC Re-enl: Co A 1st Wis Art. (Corp) 10/__-8/64 Milwaukee, WI GAR: 9/25/1920 on transfer from F.A. Warden Post, Wisconsin S: DC
Allen, Horatio D.	N: Salem, Mass CW: Co A 23 Mass Inf (Pvt/Corpl) Term: 3 yrs E/D: 9/61-1/64 Newport News, VA Re-Enl: Co A 23 Mass Inf (Corpl) E/D: 1/64-7/65 Boston, Mass GAR: 12/14/1914 on transfer from Stanton Post #2 Dept of Florida S: DC
Allen, John W.	NOL/NFI S: DC
Allen, William	N: Ohio 1841 CW: Co I 16th Rgt Maine Vols (Pvt) Term: 3 yrs E/D: 6/62-7/__ (possibly 7/65) Washington, D.C. GAR: ? date on transfer from A.E. Bennett Post Calif. S: DC
Allen, William W.	N: Iowa A: 63 O: Surveyor CW: Co A 11 Ill Inf (Pvt) Re-Enl?: Co H 26 Ill Inf (1st Lieut) E/D: 4/61-4/65 due to resignation LOS: 48 mos GAR: 9/9/1891 SP: 3/25/1902 RE: 2/28/1905 SP: 6/23/1908 RE: 8/13/1912 Died: 10/1/1913 S: H
Allum, Leroy W.	N: Penn A: 44 O: Publisher CW: Co C 22 Iowa Inf (Pvt/Color Sgt) E/D: 8/62-10/65 LOS: 38 mos GAR: 2/14/1889 SP: 3/26/1895 TR: 4/25/1895 S: H
Amick, Daniel B.	N: Miflin, PA A: 47 R: Oceanside/San Diego O: Teacher/Rancher CW: Co E 3 PA HA (Pvt) E/D: 1/64-11/65 LOS: 21 or 36 mos GAR: 5/4/1883 SP: 1/10/1889 DR: 3/28/1899 SP: 6/24/1902 DR: 1/22/1907 RE: 8/13/1912 Died: 10/2/1920 S: H
Andre, Zacheriah T.	N: PA CW: Co B 2 MO L A (Pvt) Term: 3 yrs E/D: __/63-__/65 St Louis GAR: 8/22/1925 on transfer Died: 8/26/1928 at Naval Hospital A: 80/9/20 Buried: The Presidio, San Francisco Obit: Brother Charles Andre in Rockford, IL S: DC "Zacheriah Taylor Andre"
Angstedt, Albert	N: Reading, PA 4/27/46 CW: Co B 205 PA Inf (Pvt) Term: 1 yr E/D: 8/64-6/65 Alexandria, VA GAR: 9/8/1923 on transfer from George Wright Post #1 Dept of Oregon Died: 3/21/1928 A: 81/10/23 Buried: Cleveland, OH Obit: Wife Louise Angstedt; two children, one in Cleveland, OH, and in Finley, OH S: DC
Anthony, David R.	N: Penn A: 80 O: Blacksmith CW: Co B 143 PA Inf (Pvt) E/D: 8/62-6/65 LOS: 3 yrs GAR: 2/8/1921 TR: 7/13/1921 S: H
Archer, John R.	N: Indiana A: 61 O: Merchant CW: Co G 70 Ill Inf (Sgt) E/D: 6/62-10/62 LOS: 5 1/3 mos GAR: 8/22/1902 TR: 12/22/1908 S: H

Arey, A.R.	N: Maine A: 39 O: Seaman CW: SS Niphon (Ordinary Seaman/Masters Mate) E/D: 11/62-11/64 LOS: 24 mos GAR: 8/13/1885 SP: 1/10/1889 DR: 6/30/1891 S: H
Arment, J.A.	N: Hagentown, Ind CW: Co H 140 Ind Inf (Pvt) E/D: 10/64-7/65 GAR: 2/6/1927 on transfer from Lewis Post #294, Kansas S: DC
Armstrong, Nelson	N: Canada A: 73 O: Retired CW: Co L 8 NY HA (Pvt/Corpl) Term: 3 yrs E/D: 12/63-6/65 GAR: 1/14/1918 on transfer from Post #57 Cal/Nev SP: 12/23/1924 DR: 6/23/1925 TR: 11/25/1930 S: H
Arnold, E.M.	N: Ohio A: 49 O: Carpenter CW: Co C 2 Minn Inf (Pvt) E/D: 9/61-9/65 LOS: 48 mos GAR: 6/28/1888 TR: 9/27/1888 S: H
Arnold, James M.	N: Hardy Co, VA CW: Co E 3 MO Cav (Pvt) Term: Unstated Re-Enl: Co I 12 Kans Inf (Sgt) E/D: 9/61-6/65 Little Rock GAR: No information given Buried: Oklahoma S: DC
Arnold, James M.	N: Virginia A: 63 O: Farmer CW: Co E 3 MO Cav (Sergt) Re-Enl?: Co I 12 Kans Inf (Sgt) E/D: 9/61-6/65 LOS: 41 mos GAR: 1/24/1889 TR: 5/15/1891 Died: "Dead, no date" [Record then states]--"Died Apr 14, 1898--is [grave] stone" S: H
Ashton, J.M.	NOL/NFI S: DC
Atwood, John R.	N: Maine A: 77 O: Retired CW: Co H VRC (Pvt) E/D: 8/62-7/65 LOS: 3 yrs GAR: 3/8/1920 Died: 4/2/1924 S: H
Augenbaugh, W.L.	NOL/NFI S: DC
Auld, George	N: Canada A: 68 O: Agent CW: Co B 70 NY Inf (Pvt) E/D: 4/61-7/64 LOS: Not stated GAR: 12/14/1913 from post in North Dakota? SP: 6/27/1916 Died: 8/10/1916 at Soldier's Home S: H
	SAWTELLE: DOD/B: 8/9-12/1916 Soldier's Home, Sawtelle, CA Bur: "Branch USA", Sec.30, Row B, Grave 15 with tombstone inscription "Capt Geo Auld Co K 1 N.O. Inf Sp. Am. War" S: Los Angeles National Cemetery
Averill, Charles W.	N: Maine A: 55 O: Miner CW: Co B 28 Maine Inf (Pvt) E/D: 9/62-5/63 due to disability LOS: 8 mos GAR: 12/12/1899 SP: 12/11/1900 DR: 10/25/1904 S: H
Babcock, Charles H.	N: Maine A: 64 O: Farmer CW: Co F 43 Ohio Inf (Pvt) E/D: 10/61-11/64 LOS: 37 mos GAR: 2/26/1907 Died: 5/14/1931 S: H
Baer, Charles J.	N: Germany A: 82 O: Not stated CW: Co A Bat #1 NJ (Pvt) E/D: 9/64-6/65 LOS: Not stated GAR: 3/13/1928 SP: 12/31/1928 Re: 1/14/1930 Died 9/4/1932 S: H
Baer, N.	N: Germany A: 40 O: Merchant CW: Co G 3 Md Inf (Pvt) Re-enl?: Co A 3 Md Inf (Pvt) E/D: 12/61-7/65 LOS: 43 mos GAR: 7/8/1886 SP: 12/28/1892 DR: 3/28/1899 S: H
Bailey, Benjamin E.	N: Wisconsin A: 64 O: Blacksmith CW: Co A 36 Wis Inf (Pvt) E/D: 2/63-7/65 LOS: 29 mos GAR: 7/28/1903 Died: 10/31/1912 S: H
Bailey, G.W.	N: Ohio A: 53 R: Bear Valley O: Laborer CW: Co E 2 Ohio Cav (Pvt) Re-enl?: Co E 10 Ohio Cav (Sgt) E/D: 9/61-7/65 LOS: 46 mos GAR: 11/7/1885 SP: 3/26/1895 RE/D: 9/8/1896 S: H
Bailiff, E.H.	NOL/NFI S: DC

Bailiff, Edward H.	N: Ohio A: 70 O: Preacher CW: Co F 148 Ind Inf (Sgt) E/D: 1/65-9/65 LOS: 8 mos GAR: 2/10/1903 Died: 9/2/1904 Riverside, CA S: H
Baird, John R.	N: Ohio A: 76 O: Not stated CW: Co H 81 Ohio Inf (Pvt/Sgt) E/D: 8/62-7/65 LOS: Not stated GAR: 9/28/1915 Died: Colorado in 1916 or early 1917 S: H
Baker, August Cesar	N: Belgium 2/12/42 CW: US Navy Ship Morse & Mystic (Carpenter's Mate) Term: 1 yr E/D: 8/63-8/64 Re-Enl: Co I 3rd Penn Cav (Pvt) 10/64-7/65 GAR: 2/14/1920 on transfer S: DC
Baker, Edward	N: England A: 63 O: Farmer CW: Co F 12 NY Inf (Pvt) E/D: 4/61-7/61 LOS: 3 mos GAR: 4/10/1906 D: 12/11/1906 S: H
Baker, James	N: Bloomington, Ill 1846 CW: Co F 113 Ill Inf (Pvt) Term: 3 yrs E/D: 10/63-6/65 Chicago, IL GAR: 5/25/1921 on transfer from Hayward Post #349 Dept of Nebraska SP: 9/24/1927 S: DC
Baldwin, C.W.	NOL/NFI S: DC
Bales, Dillon	N: Missouri A: 70 O: Retired CW: Co B 51 MO Inf (Pvt) E/D: 3/65-6/65 LOS: 4 mos GAR: 8/24/1920 Died: 3/9/1926 S: H
Ball, Thomas P.	N: Ohio A: 80 O: Retired CW: Co D 152 Ind Inf (Pvt) E/D: 8/65-12/65 LOS: Not stated GAR: 3/13/1928 S: H
Barber, George	N: New York A: 83 O: Retired CW: Co H 120 NY Inf (Mus'n) E/D: 8/62-4/63 due to disability LOS: Not stated GAR: 4/13/1926 Died: 5/2/1932 S: H
Barkley, James T.	N: New York A: 69 O: Undertaker CW: Co F 70 NY Inf (Pvt) Promoted?: Co E 70 NY Inf (2nd Lieut) E/D: 4/61-3/64 due to resignation LOS: Not stated GAR: 7/12/1910 (probably on transfer from Lincoln Post #1 Dept of Kansas) S: H
Barnes, Rev. Henry B.	N: White Oak, Estill Co, KY 10/14/39 O: Minister CW: Co F 30 Iowa Inf (1st Sgt) Term: Unstated E/D: 8/62-6/65 Davenport, Iowa GAR: 10/9/1926 on transfer from Torrence Post #2 Dept of Iowa; also a member of GAR Post #154, Portland, Ind. Notes: Classical graduate Wesleyan University with degree of A.M. Died: 4/26/1935 age 96, Sawtelle, CA Obit: Boyhood in Bloomfield, Iowa; Methodist Minister 70 yrs; patient at Naval Hospital San Diego before move to Sawtelle Soldier's Home Age at death: 96 Wife: Ida L Barnes; 2 children San Diego, one in Kahoka, MO S: DC SAWTELLE: DOD: 4/6/1935 at Soldier's Home, Sawtelle, CA Bur: "Branch ____", Sec.76, Row C, Grave 3 with tombstone inscription: "Henry B. Barnes 1st Sgt Co F 30 Iowa Inf" S: Los Angeles National Cemetery.
Barnes, William H.	N: NY 1845 CW: Co I 2 NY HA (Pvt) Term: 3 yrs E/D: 8/61-9/65 GAR: 12/18/1919 on transfer TR: 7/10/1920 S: DC
Barnum, Henry P.	N: Canada A: 65 O: Retired CW: Co C 96 Ill Inf (Pvt/Corpl) E/D: 8/62-1/65 due to disability LOS: Not stated GAR: 2/27/1910 (probably from Waukegan Post #374 Dept of Ill) Died: 12/26/1927 S: H
Barrett, J.J.	NOL/NFI S: DC
Barrett, Michael	N: New Jersey A: 76 O: Not stated CW: US Navy (Landsman) E/D: 8/64-5/65 LOS: Not stated GAR: 12/28/1915 on transfer from Phil Sheridan Post #74(?) Dept of Idaho TR: 11/28/1916 S: H

Barton, R.H.	N: Ohio A: 77 O: Retired CW: Co D 17 Ohio Inf (Pvt) Re-enl?: Co B 1 Ohio Cav (2 M Sgt) E/D: 4/61-9/65 LOS: 4 yrs 5 mo GAR: 12/9/1919 S:H
Bartwistle, James	NOL/NFI S: DC
Bassett, Edwin F.	N: Mass A: 45 O: Perfumer CW: Co H 29 Mass Inf (Pvt) E/D: 11/61-6/65 LOS: 43 mos GAR: 5/11/1890 SP: 12/31/1890 DR: 3/28/1899 S: H
Bates, Daniel O.	N: New York CW: Co K 16th(?) Mich Inf (Pvt) Term: 3 yrs E/D: 2/62-11/62 due to disability Quincy, Ill GAR: 5/14/1904 Died: 10/9/1909 A: 72 Bur: NY S: DC
Bates, R.O.	N: Ohio A: 39 O: Mechanic CW: Co H 9 __ Ind? Cav (Pvt) Re-enl?: Co A 29 Ind ___ (rank?) E/D: 6/62-8/65 LOS: 38 mos GAR: 6/30/1886 SP: 9/30/1893 DR: 6/12/1894 S:H
Battles, Edgar C.	N: Lowell, Mass 8/7/1846 CW: Co __ 11 Mass Infty (Pvt) Term: Unstated E/D: 6/64-9/64 GAR: 8/13/1927 on transfer S: DC
Battroff, Martin P.	N: Salem, MA? 1841 CW: Co I 81 Ind Inf (Pvt) Term: 3 yrs E/D: 8/62-6/13/__, Indianapolis GAR: No further information S: DC Note: Martin B. Battroff and his wife are buried at El Cajon Cemetery, 2080 Dehesa Road, El Cajon, CA (a community east of San Diego--phone (619) 442-0052). His official government tombstone reads: Martin B. Battroff Co I 81 Ind Inf 1841-1936. His wife's tombstone reads: Margaret E. Battroff, 1855-1930.
Battrum, Alexander	N: England A: 82 O: Retired CW: Co I 16 Ill Inf (Pvt) E/D: 4/61-Fall/62 due to disability GAR: 8/9/1921 Died: 12/10/1923 S: H
Baughman, Henry J.	N: Illinois A: 61 O: Miner CW: Co C 10 Ill Inf (Pvt) E/D: 2/64-7/65 LOS: 17 mos GAR: 4/24/1906 (probably on transfer from Greenwood Post #10 Dept of Col/Wyo Died: 5/29/1917 Buried: Cannon City, Col S: H
Baughman, Samuel K.	N: Illinois A: 67 O: Postal Clerk CW: Co C 10 Ill Inf (Pvt/1st Lieut) E/D: 8/61-7/65 LOS: Not stated GAR: 11/22/1910 Died: 6/3/1915, Chicago, IL S: H
Beach, Wade	N: Fairfield, Wayne Co, Ill CW: Co G 18 Ill Inf (Pvt) Term: 3 yrs E/D: 5/61-6/64 Springfield, Ill Re-Enl: Co D 1st Colo Cav (Pvt) 12/64-10/65 Denver, CO GAR: No further information S: DC
Beach, Wade	N: Illinois A: 84 O: Retired CW: Co G 18 Ill Inf (Pvt) E/D: 5/61-6/64 ReEnl?: Co D 1 Vet Bat Colo Cav (Pvt) E/D: 10/64-3?/65 LOS: Not stated GAR: 2/14/1928 SP: 12/30/1928 S: H
Beardsley, John	N: Newfield, Thompson Co, NY CW:Co I 179 NY Inf (Corp) Term: 1 yr E/D: 8/64-6/65 Elmira, NY GAR: No further information S: DC
Beck, Albert A.	N: New York A: 44 O: Clerk CW: Co B 157 NY Inf (Pvt) E/D: 8/62-4/65 LOS: 33 mos GAR: 8/23/1888 SP: 6/30/1891 RE: 12/9/1891 TR: 12/9/1891 S: H
Beck, Sanford	NOL/NFI S: DC
Beebe, Daniel L.	N: New York A: 68 O: Carpenter CW: Co D 4th Ill Cav (Pvt/Sgt) E/D: 9/61-11/64 LOS: Not stated GAR: 8/10/1909 (probably from Duke Calvin Post #143 Dept. of S.Dakota TR: 7/12/1910 S: H
Beebe, Milton E.	N: New York A: Not stated O: Architect CW: Co K 9 NY Cav (Pvt) E/D: Not stated; discharged due to disability GAR: 5/14/1912 Died: 2/4/1923 S: H

Bell, Alonzo	N: Not stated O: Rancher R: Fallbrook, CA CW: Co F Hatch's Minnesota Cavalry Notes: Belonged to GAR, post unknown. Died: Sawtelle Soldier's Home after an operation Wife: Margaret Phelan, daughter of James & Catherine Phelan S: *San Diego County Pioneer Families* (San Diego: San Diego Historical Society, 1977). See citation to this book in "Source Notes," Chapter III, Source Note #32.

SAWTELLE: Records for this veteran were not researched at Los Angeles National Cemetery. |
Bell, Harrison W.	N: Wayne Co, Mich CW: Co M 1 Mich Eng'rs (Pvt) Term: 3 yrs E/D: 10/63-9/65 Nashville, TN GAR: 5/28/1896 Died: 1/1922 at Pacific Grove, CA A: 80 S: DC
Bell, John B.	N: Stanford, KY 1833 CW: Co C 144 Ill Inf (Pvt) Term: 3 yrs E/D: 9/64-7/65 GAR: 7/29/1919 on transfer S: DC
Bell, John R.	N: Indiana A: 56 O: Carpenter CW: Co I 25 Ind Inf (1st Lieut/Captain) E/D: 8/61-1/62 LOS: 6 mos due to resignation GAR: 3/30/1882 SP: 1/10/1889 DR: 3/28/1899 Died: 5/23/1900--no [grave] stone S: H
Bennett, William H.	N: Kokomo, Ind 1842 CW: Co __ 21 Batt Ind Art (Pvt) Term: 3 yrs E/D: 12/63-__/65 Indianapolis, Ind GAR: 9/10/1921 on transfer from Gordon Post Dept of Indiana Died: 2/1924 at Soldier's Home S: DC

SAWTELLE: Records for this veteran were not searched at Los Angeles National Cemetery, although California Death Index indicates he died in Los Angeles County |
Bent, Judson	N: Mass A: 69 O: Retired CW: Co K 5 Mass Inf (Pvt) E/D: 8/62-7/63 LOS: 11 mos GAR: 3/28/1905 Died 1/5/1932 S: H
Bergman, Jacob	N: Germany A: 52 O: Farmer R: Oak Grove CW: Co B 1 US Dragoons (Pvt) E/D: 8/58-7/62 LOS: 5 yrs GAR: 7/24/1884 Dead--no [grave] stone S: H
Bigelow, Lyman G.	N: Michigan A: 74 O: Retired CW: Co D 10 Mich Cav (Pvt) Promoted?: Co H 1 US C T (1st Lieut) E/D: 9/63-3/66 LOS: Not stated GAR: 2/22/1916 S: H
Bill, Douglas G.	N: Ohio A: 65 O: Farmer CW: Co C 49 Wis Inf (Pvt) E/D: 2/65-11/65 LOS: Not stated GAR: 5/28/1912 on transfer from Star King Post #52 C & N (Col/Nev?) Died 7/18/1921 S: H
Billingsley, L.W.	N: Putnam Co, Ind CW: Co I 7 Ind Inf (Pvt) Term: 3 mos E/D: 4/61-8/61 Indianapolis, Ind Re-enl?: Co K 4th Ind Cav (Corp) 8/62-7/___ Promoted? Co K 14 US Colored (2nd Lt) Promoted? Co A 44 US Colored Troops (Capt) E/D: 3/64-2/65 Chattanooga, TN GAR: 9/23/1911 on transfer from Farragut Post #25 Dept of Nebraska. S: DC
Bird, Frank	N: Maine A: 80 O: Retired CW: Co __ 4 Mass Bat (Pvt) E/D: 1/64-10/65 LOS: 1 yr 10 mos GAR: 2/12/1924 SP: 12/31/1928 Died 7/10/1930 S: H
Birdsall, S.H.	N: Penn A: 84 O: Teacher R: Encanto CW: Co K 150 PA Bucktails (Pvt) E/D: 8/62-8/63 Promoted?: Co C 1 U S C T (1st Lieut/QM) E/D: 8/63-10/65 LOS: 3 yrs GAR: 1/14/1921 TR: 4/12/1921 S: H
Blair, Samuel M.	N: Harden Co, OH CW: Co I 7th Iowa Inf (Pvt) Term: 3 yrs E/D: 2/64-7/65 Louisville, KY GAR: 10/13/1928 Died: 12/1931 S: DC

Blaisdell, S.(?) G.	N: Vermont A: 48 O: Farmer R: Poway CW: Co F? 12 NH Inf (Pvt/Sgt) E/D: 6/62-6/65 LOS: 36 mos GAR: 10/26/1882 SP: 1/10/1889 DR: 6/30/1891 Died 1897--no [grave] stone S: H
Blakely, Joseph H.	N: Ohio 6/12/41 CW: Co D 11 Iowa Inf (Pvt) E/D: 9/61-10/64 Galesville, Ill GAR: 2/14/1914 on transfer from Henry Kading Post Dept of Iowa Died: 1/10/1929 A: 87 Buried: Afton, Iowa Obit: four children, 3 in San Diego, one in Clovis, _____. S: DC
Blanchard, Oliver C.	N: Ohio CW: US Navy (Landsman) Discharged from Co A 179 Ohio __ (Corpl) Term: Unstated for both enlistments E/D: 8/63-6/65 GAR: 3/28/1903 on transfer from Julius Bassett Post #173 Dept of Michigan Buried: Ohio S: DC
Blankinhom, William F.	N: Germany A: 70 O: Not stated CW: Co D? 27 Penn Inf (Pvt) E/D: 5/61-6/64 LOS: Not stated GAR: 8/24/1915 S: H
Bleak, Oscar	NOL/NFI S: DC
Bleeck, Oscar W.	N: Germany A: 74 O: Civil Engineer CW: Co A 104 NY Inf (Pvt) E/D: 7/63-7/65 LOS: 24 mos GAR: 12/22/1903 TR: 2/9/1904 S: H
Blodgett, Clark A.	N: New York A: 66 O: Retired CW: Co C 185 NY Inf (Pvt) E/D: 9/64-5/65 LOS: Not stated GAR: 2/10/1914 SP: 12/26/1923 Died: 9/17/1932 S: H
Bogart, C.F.	N: New York A: 42 O: Farmer CW: Co I 109 NY Inf (Pvt/Corpl) E/D: 8/62-6/65 LOS: 34 mos GAR: 4/24/1887 TR: 4/9/1890 S: H
Bolting, Charles J.	N: Portland, Maine C/W: US Navy (Ordinary Seaman/Petty Officer) Term: 3 yrs E/D: 9/64-9/67 (Petty Officer) Brooklyn Navy Yard, NY GAR: 1/11/1908 on transfer from Buklin Post Dept of Rhode Island S: DC
Booth, George H.	N: New York A: 87 O: Retired CW: Co K 98 NY Inf (Pvt/1st Lieut) E/D: 11/61-12/64 LOS: 3 yrs 1 mo GAR: 4/25/1911 TR: 3/27/1917 GAR: 1/13/1920 SP: 12/26/1923 DR: 12/23/1924 S: H
Bortel, Peter	NOL/NFI S: DC
Botruff, M.F.	NOL/NFI S: DC
Boutwell, William T.	N: NH A: 61 O: Farmer CW: Co B 13 NH Inf (Pvt) Re-enl?: Co F 13 Vet R C (Pvt) E/D: 8/62-6/65 LOS: 34 mos GAR: 1/12/1904 Died: 8/3/1904 "North" S: H
Bowen, John W.	N: Wales A: 76 O: Retired CW: Co E 15 Iowa Inf (Pvt) E/D: 8/62-7/65 LOS: 3 yrs GAR: 11/9/1920 Died: 6/16/1925 S: H
Bowen, W.T.	N: Indiana A: Not stated R: Moosa O: Merchant CW: Co B 4 VA Cav (Pvt) E/D: 12/63-8/65 LOS: 20 mos GAR: 5/28/1889 SP: 9/26/1889 DR: 3/28/1899 Died Escondido, CA S: H
Bowman, John H.	N: New York A: 45 O: Rancher CW: Co I 20 NY Cav (Pvt) E/D: 9/63-7/65 LOS: 22 mos GAR: 4/11/1889 SP: 4/30/1890 D: 6/30/1891 S: H
Boyd, David O.	N: Penn A: 75 O: Retired CW: Co K 1 Del Inf (Pvt/Sgt) E/D: 9/61-8/65 due to wounds LOS: 4 yrs GAR: 1/27/1920 Died: 1/19/1921 at Buckeye, AZ S: H
Bradt, Jacob A.	N: New York A: 66 O: Farmer CW: Co G 2 NY Cav (Pvt) E/D: 9/64-6/65 LOS: 9 mos GAR: 2/23/1888 TR: 2/28/1889 S: H

Bragg, A.L.	N: Maine A: 44 O: Contractor CW: Co A 6 ME Inf (Pvt) E/D: 5/61-9/64 LOS: 40 mos GAR: 5/24/1888 DR: 11/30/1891 S: H
Brandis, William	N: Germany CW: Co E 1st Col Cav (Pvt/Bugler) Term: 3 yrs E/D: 11/61-12/64 Denver, CO GAR: 4/27/1907 on transfer from Gen.Thomas Post #7 Dept of Col/Wy Died 12/19/1912 A: 71 Buried: GAR plot (Mount Hope) S: DC Note: Death certificate indicates this veteran died in San Diego, but is buried at Ft.Collins, Colorado.
Brandley, Arnold	N: Switzerland 1843 CW: Co F 18 OVI (Pvt) Term: 3 mos E/D: 4/61-8/61 Athens, OH Re-Enl: Co H 23 KY Inf (Pvt/1st Lieut) E/D: 11/61-12/65 GAR: 6/28/1919 from Dept of Kansas S: DC
Brandt, Otto	N: Germany 5/22/43 CW: Co A 72 Ill Inf (Pvt) Term: 3 yrs E/D: 8/62-7/65 Memphis, TN Participated in seige of Vicksburg, Franklin, Nashville & Atlanta to the Sea. GAR: 11/28/1908 on transfer from Thomas Post Dept of Illinois S: DC
Branson, James	N: Muncie, Ind 1850 CW: Co C 42 MO Inf (Pvt) Term: 1 yr E/D: 4/64-4/65 St.Louis, MO GAR: 12/28/1925 Died 11/16/1936 S: DC
Bray, John	N: Morgan Co, Ind CW: Co H 1st MO Cav (Pvt) Term: 3 yrs E/D: 3/62-3/65 Warrensburg, MO GAR: 8/9/1902 on transfer from W.S. Robertson Post #428 Dept of Kansas Died 4/6/1936 A: 91 S: DC
Breedlove, R.D.	N: Missouri A: 41 O: Farmer R: Bear Valley CW: Co D 8 MO Cav (Corpl) E/D: 8/62-8/65 LOS: 3 yrs GAR: 2/11/1886 D: 3/12/1888 S: H
Brenard, Frederick	N: Auburn, Crawford Co, Ohio CW: Co I 3rd Ohio Cav (Pvt/Capt) Term: 3 yrs E/D: 8/61-11/64 Louisville, KY GAR: 5/26/1906 Died: 6/20/1910 A: 73 Buried: Soldier's Home S: DC

SAWTELLE: Records for this veteran were not found at Los Angeles National Cemetery, although California Death Index reveals he died in Los Angeles County. |
Bridges, Otis S.	N: Maine A: 63 O: Carpenter CW: Co __ 5 Wis Bat LA (Corpl) E/D: 9/61-6/65 LOS: 42 mos GAR: 12/24/1901 S: H
Briggs, W.S.	N: Penn A: 41 O: Shorthand Reporter CW: Co K 14 Penn Cav (Pvt) E/D: 9/62-6/65 LOS: 33 mos GAR: 5/8/1886 TR: 11/10/1887 S: H
Bristinstine, Matthias	N: Mercer Co, Ohio CW: Co C 13 Ill Cav (Pvt) Term: 3 yrs E/D: 9/61-1/64 Re-Enl: Co E 13 Ill Cav (Pvt) 1/64-8/65 GAR: 1/22/1916 on transfer from Riverside Post #118 S: DC
Brobst, Albert M.	N: Catarwissa, PA A: 75 O: retired CW: Co G 15 Iowa Inf (Pvt) E/D: 10/61-12/64 Promoted to Co I 63 US C T (1st Lieut) E/D: 5/64-1/66 LOS: 50 1/2 mos GAR: 5/28/1918 TR: 8/10/1920 (name also "Allert") S: H
Brook, James F.	N: Not stated A: Not stated O: Real Estate CW: Co F 39 Iowa Inf (Pvt) E/D: 8/62-6/65 LOS: 34 mos GAR: 8/23/1888 GAR: 7/12/1892 SP: 3/26/1895 RE: 3/14/1898 or 3/14/1899 SP: 12/24/1901 DR: 12/13/1904 SP: 3/26/1907 DR: 12/24/1918 S: H
Brooks, John H.	N: York Co, PA 1834 CW: Co B 38 IA Inf (1st Sgt) Term: 3 yrs E/D: 7/62-1/65 Morgan, LA GAR: 6/5/1910 on transf. from Phil Kearney Post Buried: LA, Calif. S: DC

SAWTELLE: A "John Brooks" is buried at Soldier's Home, Sawtelle DOD: 4/30/1917 Bur: "Branch USA", Sec.31, Row D, Grave 9 with tombstone inscription: "John Brooks Co H 10 US Cav" S: Los Angeles National Cemetery |

Broughton, John B.	N: New York A: 54 O: Contractor CW: Co __ 2 Penn LA (Pvt) E/D: 6/62-6/65 due to disability LOS: 23 mos GAR: 10/14/1891 SP: 3/31/1893 DR: 3/28/1899 TR: 8/8/1904 S: H
Brown, Benjamin W.	N: New York A: 76 O: Retired CW: Co H 29 Wis Inf (Pvt/Corp) E/D: 8/62-6/65 LOS: 34 mos GAR: 11/13/1917 on expired transfer from Eagle Post #57, Eau Claire, Wis Died: 1/30/1921 S: H
Brown, Carleton L.	N: Edwardsburg, Mich 1848 CW: Co K 11 Mich Cav (Pvt/Corpl) Term: 3 yrs E/D: 9/63-7/65 Detroit, MI GAR: 2/12/1921 on transfer from Elwood Post Dept of Nebraska Buried: Bangor, MI S: DC
Brown, Charles A	N: Maine A: 55 O: Farmer CW: Co A 8 Minn Inf (Pvt/Corpl) E/D: __/62-__/65 LOS: 36 mos GAR: 9/26/1884 SP: 1/10/1889 DR: 6/30/1891 S: H
Brown, J.H.	N: Wyandot, Ohio A: 43 O: Druggist CW: Co A 49 Ohio Inf (Pvt) E/D: 8/61-7/64 due to wounds in action LOS: 1 yr 21/30? (LOS too short) GAR: 11/8/1883 SP: 1/10/1889 DR: 10/25/1904 S: H
Brown, Lyman	N: Wyoming Co, NY CW: Co H 1st Mich Eng'rs (Pvt) Term: 3 yrs E/D: 12/63-9/65 Nashville, TN GAR: 9/11/1909 on transfer from E.H. Ewing Post #203 Dept of Mich Died: 12/22/1919 Buried: Soldier's Home S: DC SAWTELLE: Records for this veteran were not found at Los Angeles National Cemetery, although the California Death Index indicates he died in Los Angeles County.
Brown, Max	N: Illinois A: 73 O: Retired CW: Co H 1st MO Eng (Pvt) E/D: 9/61-__/64 LOS: Not stated GAR: 8/13/1912 TR: 4/13/1915 S: H
Brown, Rodney D.	N: Mass A: 53 O: Custom Inspector CW: Str U.S. Rhode Island (Master's Mate) E/D: 9/62-9/66 due to resignation LOS: 48 mos GAR: 5/13/1891 SP: 6/30/1894 DR: 10/25/1904 S: H
Browne, William S.	N: New York A: 63 O: Laborer CW: Chicago Mtd Bat (Pvt) E/D: 9/64-7/65 LOS: 8 mos GAR: 10/11/1883 SP: 9/26/1888 RE: 6/15/1889 Died: 6/22/1900--is [grave] stone S: H
Brownlee, Alex	N: Iowa A: 72 O: Contractor CW: Co B 3 Iowa Cav (Pvt) E/D: 8/63-8/65 LOS: 24 mos GAR: 3/27/1917 on transfer from Post #6 Dept of Texas Died: 10/3/1922 S: H
Brunemer, James H.	N: Ohio CW: Co H 7 Wis Inf (Pvt/Corpl) Term: 3 yrs E/D: 8/61-4/63 due to loss of leg GAR: 4/11/1914 on transfer from Lincoln Post #3 Dept of Potomic Died: 1/1926 S: DC
Bruner, Adam B.	N: Woodville, Ind CW: Co A 22 Kans State Militia (Pvt) Term: Unstated E/D: 10/64-11/64 due to close of Price campaign in MO GAR: 7/10/1926 Story/Photo in file--born Ill; to San Diego in 1869; 4 children in Los Angeles S: DC
Brunner, Leo F.	N: France, 1847 CW: Co __ __ Ohio Lt Art (Pvt) Term: 3 yrs E/D: 5/63-7/65 Camp Chase GAR: 5/27/1921 from Ontario Post #124 Cal/Nev S: DC
Bryan, William	N: Brantford, Canada CW: U.S.S. North Carolina/U.S.S. Shomoken (Landsman/Seaman) Term: 3 yrs E/D: 3/65-12/68 Washington, DC GAR: ? date on transfer from Ventura Post #42 Col/Wyo Died: 11/24/1910 A: 66 S: DC
Buck, Elijah	N: New York A: 57 O: Farmer R: Spring Valley/San Diego CW: Co A 7 Ill Inf (Pvt/Corpl) E/D: 4/61-8/62 due to disability LOS: 16 mos GAR: 5/9/1889 SP: 4/30/1890 RE: 3/28/1899 TR: 5/23/1905 Died: Sacramento (very faint writing) S: H

Burgess, William	N: Bucks Co, PA A: 60 O: Publisher R: National City CW: Co E 203 PA Inf (Pvt) E/D: ___/64-6/65 LOS: 9 16/30 mos GAR: 7/12/1883 SP: 6/30/1888 RE: 7/12/1888 D: 7/12/1888 S: H
Burk, William	N: Charlton, Saratoga Co, NY 7/11/42 CW: Co D 13 Wis Vol Inf (Pvt) Term: 3 yrs? E/D: 8/61-12/__ San Antonio, TX GAR: 4/8/1916 on transfer from Heintzelman Post GAR San Diego S: DC
Burk, William	N: New York A: 71 O: Painter CW: Co D 13 Wis Inf (Pvt) E/D: 8/61-6/64? LOS: Not stated GAR: 9/9/1913 on transfer from T.S. Scatpin (sp?) Post #41 Dept of Wisconsin TR: 3/14/1916 (see citation above) S: H
Burke, C.M.	N: Penn A: 41 O: Plasterer CW: Co F 7 Penn Cav (Pvt) E/D: 2/64-8/65 LOS: 1 yr 6/12 mos GAR: 2/11/1886 SP: __/26/1889 RE: 12/10/1890 D: 12/10/1890 S: H
Burnap, Silas A.	N: Ohio A: 79 O: Retired R: Coronado CW: Co F 18 Ohio Inf (Pvt) Re-enl?: Co H 18 Ohio Inf (Pvt) E/D: 4/61-8/61 Promoted?: Co __ 7 Ohio L A (Capt) E/D: 4/61-1/65 LOS: 27 mos GAR: 7/25/1905 Died: 1/6/1910 S: H
Burnham, E.H.	N: New York A: 42 O: Painter CW: Co B 3 US Arty (Pvt) Re-enl?: Co D 2 US Arty (Pvt) E/D: 3/65-3/68 LOS: 36 mos GAR: 3/24/1884 D: 7/7/1890 Died: 9?/25/1894--is [grave] stone S: H
Burns, A.J.	N: Ohio A: 41 O: Tinner CW: Co H 42 Ohio Inf (Pvt); Promoted?: Co B 53 US C T (1st Lieut) E/D: 11/61-3/66 LOS: 52 mos GAR: 12/21/1881 TR: "Transferred" S: H
Burns, Thomas J.	N: NH A: 62 O: Medical Elec(?) CW: Co F 4 NH Inf (Pvt/Sgt) E/D: 7/61-9/64 LOS: 36 mos GAR: 2/5/1902 TR: 3/28/1903 S: H
Burr, Charles M.	N: Norfolk, CT 2/6/1843 CW: Co E 19th Conn Vol Inf (Pvt) Term: 3 yrs E/D: 8/62-6/65 Transferred to Co __ 2nd Conn HA (? rank) E/D: 8/62-6/65 GAR: 5/10/1913 TR: 7/10/1915 RE: 2/24/1917 Died: "Died" S: DC
	Service/Marital record: Joined 6th Corp; fought in the campaign of '64 from the Wilderness and Spottsylvania to Cold Harbor and Petersburg. Transferred to Army of West Virginia under Gen. Sheridan. Fought in battles of Winchester, Fisher's Hill, Cedar Creek where wounded, lost a leg. Taken prisoner and recaptured when Sheridan arrived on the field from "20 miles away." Transferred to Central Park Hospital, NY City Married 6/5/1870 Lydia Barton in Milford, Delaware S: DC
Burt, John P.	N: Franklinville, NY CW: Co C 12 US Inf (2nd Batt) (Pvt) Term: Unstated E/D: 12/61-12/62 Providence, RI with Surgeon's Certificate of Disability GAR: 1/22/1896 Died: 2/22/1915 Buried: Los Angeles S: DC
Byers, John T.	N: Ohio A: 85 O: Retired CW: Co L 8 Iowa Cav (Pvt) E/D: 10/61-8/65 LOS: Not stated GAR: 4/14/1927 Died: 7/16/1934 S: H
Cadman, James P.	N: Michigan A: 65? O: Secretary CW: Co I 11 Mich Cav (2nd Lieut) Re-enl?: Co I 8 Mich Cav (Capt) E/D: 10/63-10/65 LOS: Not stated GAR: 3/26/1912 on transfer from Geo H. Thomas Post #5 Dept of Illinois Died: 2/2/1933? (year hard to read) S: H
Camp, Guy R.	N: Penn A: 70 O: Farmer CW: Co E 2 Iowa Inf (Pvt) E/D: 10/64-5/65 LOS: 8 mos GAR: 1/26/1904 TR: 12/27/1904 S: H

Camp, James H.	N: Bradford Co, PA 1839 CW: Co A 141 PA ___ (Pvt) Term: 3 yrs E/D: 8/62-5/__ Bailey Crossroads, VA GAR: 7/23/1921 on transfer from Wilson Post #2 Dept of Nebraska Died: 4/1/1934 A: 96 S: DC
Campbell, B.P.	N: Maryland A: 56 O: Farmer CW: Co G 8 Cal Inf (Pvt) E/D: __/61-10/65 LOS: 48 mos GAR: 9/22/1887 SP: 9/26/1889 DR: 6/30/1891 S: H
Campbell, David	N: Ohio A: 66 O: Gardener CW: Co I 90 Ohio Inf (Pvt) E/D: 1/64-1/65 LOS: Not stated GAR: 5/27/1913 SP: 12/10/1919? S: H
Campbell, Milton K	N: Ohio A: 68 O: Farmer R: National City CW: Co B 5 Iowa Inf (Pvt) E/D: 7/61-7/64 LOS: 36 mos GAR: 8/14/1906 TR: 4/9/1912 S: H
Canfield, William J.	N: New York A: 71 O: Clerk CW: Co K 1 NY LA (Pvt/Lieut/Adjt) E/D: 9/61-10/64 LOS: Not stated GAR: 6/22/1915 Died: 6/15/1923 S: H
Carls, Frank	N: Providence, RI A: 75 O: Laborer CW: Co D 115 NY Inf (Pvt) E/D: 9/63-6/65 as a prisoner LOS: 21 mos GAR: 11/19/1918 Died: 5/12/1919 S: H
Carpenter, Albert	N: Ohio A: 65 O: Farmer CW: Co F 4 Mich Inf (Pvt) E/D: 9/61-9/64 LOS: 36 1/2 mos GAR: 11/14/1905 TR: 6/26/1906 S: H
Carpenter, Stephen H.	N: Genessee, NY A: 49 O: Miner CW: Co E 7th Cal ___ (Corpl) E/D: 11/64-6/66 LOS: 19 mos GAR: 4/13/1882 TR: 6/30/1891 S: H
Carpinter, H.L.	N: New York A: 54 O: Carpenter CW: Co F 4 NY H A (Pvt) Promoted?: Co H 4 NY H A (Capt) E/D: 12/61-9/65 LOS: 45 mos GAR: 3/22/1888 SP: 1/10/1889 DR: 10/25/1904 S: H
Carter, John H.	N: Illinois A: 78 O: Retired CW: Co C 117 Ill Inf (Pvt) E/D: 8/62-11/64 due to wounds LOS: 2 yrs GAR: 9/13/1921 Died: 8/14/1924 S: H
Cary, Charles A.	N: New York A: 62 O: Merchant CW: Co F 3 NJ Cav (Pvt/Sgt) E/D: 12/63-8/65 LOS: Not stated GAR: 4/12/1910 TR: 11/11/1919 S: H
Casebeer, W.J.	N: Ohio A: 45 O: Carpenter CW: Co I 1 Ohio Inf (Pvt) E/D: 4/61-9/65 LOS: 49 mos GAR: 1/26/1888 SP: 6/30/1891 DR: 10/25/1904 S: H
Casey, Wilson	N: West Canada A: 80 O: Retired CW: Co A 5 Mich Cav (Pvt) E/D: 2/65-3/66 LOS: 1 yr 1 mo GAR: 5/13/1924 Died: 12/22/1928 S: H
Chamberlin, Jacob	N: Addison, Michigan CW: Co B 8 NY Cav (Corp/1st Lieut) Term: 3 yrs E/D: 9/61-5/65 GAR: 7/11/1903 on transfer from Milo Warner Post #232 Dept of Michigan Died: 3/12/1912 A: 70 Buried: Los Angeles S: DC
Chaney, O.F.	N: New York A: 46 O: Carpenter CW: Co K 1 Vt Cav (Corpl/Sgt) E/D: 10/61-6/65 LOS: 1 yr 5/12 mos GAR: 2/11/1886 SP: 3/28/1899 DR: 10/25/1904 S:H
Charland, Maxim	N: New York A: 84 O: Retired CW: U.S.S. Sabine (Landsman/Qtr Gunner) E/D: __/58-7/61 LOS: 3 yrs GAR: 8/24/1920 Died 1/24/1925 S: H
Chase, Charles E.	N: Maine A: 69 O: Engineer CW: Co L 31 Maine Inf (Pvt) E/D: 8/64-7/65 LOS: Not stated GAR: 10/14/1913 SP: 12/26/1916 DR: 12/24/1918 S: H

Chase, Levi	N: Maine 10/26/23 DOD: 5/31/1906 at San Diego A: 82/7/5 O: Retired Attorney Buried: Morristown, NJ 6/4/1906; lived 36 years at residence in San Diego at date of death; was a widower (no wife named); cause of death was cancer. Undertakers: Johnson & Connell, San Diego. Parents Moses Chase, born Massachusetts; Sarah Greenlaw, born Canada. Informant Charles Chase S: San Diego County death certificate Note: See additional information about Levi Chase in Chapter III, "Building the City" section.

Note: San Diego Obituary on 6/1/1906: Levi Chase, San Diego resident since 1868, was a native of Calias, ME and born on October 26, 1823. He married 1st Elizabeth Wheeler, who died in 1848. He married 2nd Cornelia King of Morristown, NJ in 1853. She died about 10 years before his death. |
Chase, Samuel D.	N: Michigan A: 80 O: Retired R: Encanto CW: Co H 1 Mich Inf (Pvt) E/D: 3/62-6/65 LOS: 3 yrs GAR: 12/__/1925 Died 10/22/1928 S: H
Chatfield, James L.	N: Barton, Ohio CW: Co D 10th OVI (Pvt/Sgt) Term: 3 yrs E/D: 10/62-4/64 Washington, D.C. due to disability GAR: 11/27/1909 S: DC
Chester, D.R.	N: Ohio A: 45 O: Surveyor CW: Co G 88 Ill Inf (2nd Lieut/Capt) E/D: 9/62-6/65 LOS: 33 mos GAR: 2/28/1889 TR: 9/3/1889 S: H
Chilcott, E.	N: Penn A: 52 O: Blacksmith CW: Co B 129 Ill Vol (2nd Lieut) E/D: 8/62-6/65 LOS: 34 mos GAR: 6/30/1886 SP: 9/26/1889 RE: 7/11/1890 D: 7/14/1890 S:H
Childs, Benjamin F.	N: Ohio 9/17/39 CW: Co E 11 Ill Cav (Pvt) Term: 3 yrs E/D: 1/62-1/65 GAR: 1/10/1920 TR: 8/13/1927 S: DC
Chrisman, Leonard	N: Indiana A: 70 O: Retired CW: Co A 47 Iowa Inf (Pvt) E/D: 5/64-9/65 LOS: 16 mos GAR: 2/26/1918 Died 11/14/1936 S: H
Clapp, E.S.	N: Lawrence Co, NY 1842 CW: Co K 1st Ill Art (Pvt) Term: 3 yrs E/D: 2/64-8/65 Chicago, Il GAR: 4/22/1921 on transfer from Illinois Died: 10/21/1924 A: 81/10/13 S: DC
Clark, Charles E.	N: Indiana A: 68 O: Lawyer CW: Co L 1 Ind Art (Pvt) E/D: 6/63-11/65 due to disability LOS: Not stated GAR: 10/27/1908 TR: 1/23/1912 TR cancelled 10/8/1912 SP: 6/27/1916 DR: 12/24/1918 S: H
Clark, Dillard H.	N: KY A: 78 O: Retired CW: Co D 14 KY Cav (Pvt) E/D: 8/62-9/63 LOS: 1 yr GAR: 8/26/1924 Died: 2/20/1926 S: H
Clark, J.C.	N: Indiana CW: Co A 80 Ill Vol Inf (Pvt) Term: 3 yrs E/D: 7/62-6/65 LOS: 2 yrs, 11 mos, 18 days GAR: 10/9/1920 on transfer from Lou Gore Post #100 Dept of Kansas DR: 9/24/1927 S: DC
Clark, James S.	N: Johnson Co, Indiana A: 75 O: Retired R: La Jolla, CA CW: Co F 1 Iowa Inf (Pvt) E/D: 4/61-8/61 LOS: 4 mos Promoted?: Co C 34 Iowa Inf (Pvt/Capt) E/D: 8/62-8/65 LOS: 36 mos GAR: 6/26/1917 on expired transfer from Post #12 Des Moines, IA Died 8/1/1920 S: H
Clark, James S.	N: Penn A: 50 O: Real Estate CW: Co L 102 PA Inf (Sgt) E/D: 8/61-9/64 LOS: 37 mos GAR: 10/1/1881 RE: 3/28/1899 SP: 3/22/1904 SP: 10/25/1904 DR: 1/22/1907 RE: 2/11/1908 TR: 2/11/1908 S: H
Clark, John J.	N: New York A: 54 O: Miner CW: USS Minnesota (Seaman) E/D: 10/61-11/64 LOS: 11 mos GAR: 6/14/1898 SP: 9/25/1899 DR: 12/24/1918 S: H

Clark, Sheldon C.	N: Penn A: 59 O: Mining Engineer CW: Co I 2 Minn Inf (Pvt) E/D: 10/64-6/65 LOS: 8 mos GAR: 3/14/1905 TR: 11/27/1906 S: H
Clark, William A.	N: Indiana A: 68 O: Minister CW: Co K 72 Ind Inf (Pvt) E/D: 8/62-7/65 LOS: Not stated GAR: 10/22/1912 on transfer from McPherson Post #1 Dept of Arkansas SP: 6/27/1916 DR: 12/24/1918 S: H
Clarke, Frank	N: Illinois A: 40 O: Stevedore CW: Co I 7 Iowa Inf (Pvt) E/D: 4/64-6/65 LOS: 14 1/3 mos GAR: 10/13/1887 SP: 1/10/1889 DR: 6/30/1891 S: H
Clemens, Carl	NOL/NFI S: DC
Clothier, W.B.	NOL/NFI S: DC
Coats, Henry	N: England 2/21/41 CW: Co B 3 Reg Cal Inf (Pvt) Term: 3 yrs E/D: 4/64-10/65 GAR: Reinstated 1/23/1915 on transfer from McLain Post #1 Dept of Utah S: DC
Coffey, John	NOL/NFI S: DC
Coggswell, Thomas	N: New Hampshire A: 55 O: Dentist CW: Co B 50 Mass Inf (Pvt) E/D: 9/62-8/63 LOS: 11 mos GAR: 3/25/1891 SP: 6/28/1892 SP: 3/27/1894 RE: 5/9/1899 "Dead" S: H
Colbert, Robert	N: New York A: 79 O: Retired R: East San Diego CW: Co H 14 Wis Inf (Pvt) E/D: 12/61-7/62 due to disability LOS: 7 mos GAR: 6/14/1921 Died: 12/14/1926 (1926 hard to read) S: H
Colby, Lloyd H.	N: New Hampshire A: 59 O: Farmer CW: Co B 6 Wis Inf (Pvt/Sgt) E/D: 2/64-5/65 LOS: 13 mos GAR: 7/25/1905 Died: 5/11/1922 S: H
Cole, W.I.	N: Canada 4/23/48 CW: Co D 3 Mich Inf (Pvt) Term: 1 yr E/D: 10/64-8/65 Detroit, Mich GAR: 6/24/1916 S: DC
Coleman, Patrick	N: Ireland A: 47 O: Mechanic CW: Co F 2 Wis Inf (Pvt) E/D: 6/61-7/65 due to "wounded in spine" (this injury may belong to name listed just above Patrick Coleman in the GAR roster--Hiram Fosnot. Perhaps Fosnot was the one so wounded) LOS: 4 1/2 yrs GAR: 4/8/1886 SP: 1/30/1889 DR: 6/30/1891 S: H
Collier, J.H.	N: Ohio 1846 CW: Co L 4 Mich Cav (Pvt) Term: 3 yrs E/D: 12/63-8/65 GAR: ? date on transfer from John A. Martin Post Dept of Cal/Nev TR: 1927 S: DC
Collins, John T.	N: Virginia A: 51 O: Merchant CW: Co D 1 Del Inf (Pvt) E/D: 4/61-7/65 LOS: 51 mos GAR: 8/23/1888 TR: 5/27/1892 S: H
Comer, Allen	N: Hutton Co, Ohio 9/18/43 CW: Co D 17 Ohio Inf (Pvt) Term: 3 yrs E/D: 9/61-11/63 Louisville KY due to disability Re-Enl: Co A 58 Ohio Inf (Pvt) E/D: 8/64-10/65 Columbus, Ohio GAR: 11/12/1927 S: DC
Comings, J.H.	N: New Jersey A: 57 O: Soldier CW: Co I 15 NJ Inf (Pvt) Promoted?: Co C 15 NY Inf (Brvt Maj) E/D: 8/62-6/65 LOS: 50 mos GAR: 7/12/1892 TR: 9/11/1894 S: H
Cone, William A.	N: Athens Co, Ohio 1847 CW: Co B 53 OVI (Pvt) Term: 3 yrs E/D: 2/64-8/65 GAR: 4/24/1920 on transfer from Custer Post #6 Dept of Wash/Alaska Died: 2/11/1922 A: 74/5/___ Soldier's Home S: DC
	SAWTELLE: Records for this veteran were not searched at Los Angeles National Cemetery, although the California Death Index reveals he died in Los Angeles County.

Conner, Samuel P. N: Vernon Co, Indiana CW: Co F 18 Ill Inf (Pvt/2nd Lieut) Term: 3 yrs E/D: 4/61-7/63 Helena, Arkansas due to resignation Re-Enl: Co C 124 Ind Inf (Pvt/Capt) E/D: 10/63-3/65 due to resignation GAR: 1/25/1908 on transfer from Mitchell Post Dept of Indiana Died: 3/29/1915 A: 77 Soldier's Home S: DC

SAWTELLE: Died 3/28/1915 Soldier's Home, Sawtelle, CA Bur: "Branch USA", Sec. 26, Row D, Grave 4 under name "Sam'l P. Connor", Co C 124 Ind Inf S: LA Nat'l Cemetery

Connor, James N: Ireland A: 65 O: Farmer CW: Co M 2 US Art (Pvt) E/D: 7/61-2/66 LOS: 56 mos GAR: 9/12/1905 SP: 12/24/1912 DR: 12/24/1918 RE: 11/23/1920 Died: 1/30/1922 S:H

Connors, John N: Ireland A: 62 O: Laborer CW: Co B 4 US Art (Pvt) E/D: 8/57-7/62 LOS: 60 mos GAR: 3/28/1899 SP: 6/26/1900 DR: 1/22/1907 S: H

Cook, Augustus N: New York A: 56 O: Printer CW: Co D 3 NY Inf (Pvt/Sgt) E/D: 5/61-5/65 LOS: 48 mos GAR: 11/12/1895 Died: Soldier's Home S: H

SAWTELLE: Died: 8/22/1909 Buried: "Service USA" Sec 16 Row D Grave 13 under "Se__ Aug Cook Co D 3 NY Inf". S: Los Angeles National Cemetery.

Cook, Jacob L. N: Wallingford, VT 1840 CW: Co B 5 Vt Inf (Pvt) Term: 3 yrs E/D: 8/61-6/65 Washington, D.C. GAR: 1/27/1917 S: DC

Cook, Joseph N: Austria A: 52 O: Farmer CW: Co B 8 Ill Inf (Pvt) LOS: 9/64-9/65 LOS: 1 yr GAR: 12/10/1885 SP: 1/10/1889 DR: 6/30/1891 S: H

Coonwell, Robert N: New York A: 53 O: Rancher CW: Co G 10 Ill Inf (Pvt) E/D: 4/61-7/61 Re-Enl?: Co A 10 Ill Inf (Pvt/1st Lieut) E/D: 8/61-7/65 LOS: 46 1/2 mos GAR: 9/24/1890 SP: 6/28/1892 DR: 3/28/1899 S: H

Cooper, Jesse N: Leesburg, OH CW: Co K 3 IA Inf (Pvt/Sgt) Term: 3 yrs E/D: 4/61-4/64 Boonsboro, NC Re-Enl: Same unit (Sgt/1st Lieut) E/D: 4/64-3/65 Boonsboro, NC GAR: 7/11/1908 on transfer from Brownell Post #222 Dept of Iowa Died: 2/15/1915 A: 79 Buried: Soldier's Home S: DC

SAWTELLE: Died 2/1/1915 at Soldier's Home and buried in "Branch USA" Sec. 26, Row A, Grave 3 with tombstone inscription "Lieut Jesse Cooper Co A 3 IA Inf" S: Los Angeles National Cemetery

Copeland, W.A. NOL/NFI S: DC

Corben, James G. N: Ohio A: 51 O: Gardener CW: Co D 11 Ind Inf (Pvt) E/D: 8/61-6/62 due to disability LOS: 10 mos GAR: 4/26/1888 SP: 6/28/1888 DR: 6/30/1891 Died: ? date--no [grave] stone S: H

Cordes, Charles S. N: St Joseph, MO CW: Co A 5 MO Cav (Pvt) Term: 3 yrs E/D: 7/62-6/65 GAR: 8/13/1907? S: DC

Corey, Albert W. N: Wisconsin A: 45 O: Farmer CW: Co H 30 Wis Inf (Pvt) E/D: 11/63-9/65 LOS: 22 mos GAR: 2/11/1889 SP: 9/28/1897 DR: 10/25/1904 S: H

Couchman, E.H. N: Indiana A: 72 O: Retired CW: Co C 18 Iowa Inf (Pvt) E/D: 7/62-8/65 LOS: 3 yrs 1 mo GAR: 12/23/1919 Died: 10/26/1924 S: H

Couts, Seneca P.	N: Boston, Mass CW: Co E 13th Wis Inf (Pvt) Term: Unstated E/D: 7/61-1/63 Leavenworth, Kansas due to Surgeon's Certificate of Disability GAR: 10/25/1902 Died: 12/31/1903 A: 83 Buried: Soldier's Home S: DC

SAWTELLE: No records for this veteran were found at Los Angeles National Cemetery, the Sawtelle Index, the California Death Index, or at the County of San Diego. |
Cowan, Allen	NOL/NFI S: DC
Cowels, Frederick H.	N: Illinois A: 69 O: Miner CW: Co H 3 Cal Inf (Pvt) Re-Enl?: Co H 6 Cal Inf (Pvt) E/D: 12/61-10/65 LOS: 44 Mos GAR: 3/13/1906 TR: 5/22/1906 S: H
Cox, Isaac S.	N: Ohio A: 60 O: Carpenter CW: Co F 63 Ind Inf (Corpl/Sgt) E/D: 8/62-6/65 LOS: 34 mos GAR: 12/24/1901 SP: 3/26/1907 RE: 7/9/1907 SP: 6/23/1914 Died: 11/23/1917 S: H
Craig, George W.	N: Illinois A: 82 O: Retired CW: Co E 132 Ill Inf (Pvt/Sgt) E/D: Not stated LOS: Not stated GAR: 11/9/1926 S: H
Crater, Cornelius	N: New York A: 59 O: Cook CW: Co C 72 NY Inf (Pvt) Re-Enl?: Co E 14 US ___ (Sgt) E/D: 4/61-9/68 LOS: 74 mos GAR: 1/8/1901 TR: 1/26/1904 S:H
Cravath, J.B.	N: Penn A: 39 O: Farmer R: Poway, CA CW: Co B 32 Iowa Inf (Pvt) E/D: 8/62-8/65 LOS: 36 mos GAR: 9/5/1884 DR: 3/28/1899 S: H
Craw, Frank W.	N: New York A: 82 O: Carpenter CW: Co K 35 Wis Inf (Pvt) E/D: 2/64-6/65 LOS: 1 yr GAR: 10/10/1922 Died: 6/11/1932 S: H
Crittenden, Thomas T.	N: Alabama A: 76 O: Lawyer CW: Co A 6 Ind Inf (Capt) Promoted: US Vols (Brig Gen) E/D: 4/61-5/63 due to disability LOS: 24 mos GAR: 10/22/1885 D: 7/22/1897 GAR: 9/24/1901 Died: 9/6/1905 (Died "East") S: H
Croghan, Thomas	NOL/NFI S: DC
Crombie, L.J.	N: Scotland A: 46 O: Tanner R: Fallbrook, CA CW: Co C 1 Nev Vol (Pvt) E/D: 2/64-12/65 LOS: 22 mos GAR: 6/30/1886 SP: 1/10/1889 DR: 6/30/1891 Died: "Dead"--no [grave] stone S: H
Crook, George H.	N: Conn A: 78 O: Retired CW: Co H 23 Conn Inf (Pvt) E/D: 8/62-8/63 LOS: 1 yr GAR: 10/24/1922 Died: 4/20/1923 S: H
Crosby, T.W.	NOL/NFI S: DC
Cross, Harlow A.	N: Champlain, NY 1845 CW: Co G 26 NY Cav (Pvt) Term: 1 yr E/D: 6/65-7/__ Plattsburg, NY GAR: 4/12/1924 D: 11/12/1927 per p.64 of Adjt report S: DC
Cross, Harlow A.	N: New York A: 83 O: Not stated CW: Co G 26 NY Cav (Pvt) E/D: 1/65-7/65 LOS: 6 mos GAR: 9/10/1929 TR: 4/12/1932 RE: 3/12/1935 S: H
Crouch, George	NOL/NFI S: DC
Culp, John W.	N: Illinois A: 77 O: Retired CW: Co M 2 Neb Cav (Pvt) E/D: 2/63-12/63 LOS: 9 mos Re-Enl?: Co G 1 Neb Cav (Pvt) E/D: 2/64-12/64 LOS: ? mos GAR: 10/10/1922 Died: 5/4/1925 S: H

Cundall, Benjamin M.	N: Illinois A: 62 O: Miner CW: Co D 53 Ill Inf (Pvt) E/D: 2/62-7/65 LOS: 41 mos GAR: 7/11/1905 SP: 3/26/1907 DR: 12/24/1918 S: H
Cushing, Allen D.	N: Aurora, Ill 6/28/45 CW: Co F 146 Ill Inf (Pvt) Term: 1 yr E/D: 9/64-7/65 GAR: 10/22/1927 on transfer from D.D. Porter Post #169 Dept of Cal/Nev Died: 6/29/1930 Article: Served as guard when Abraham Lincoln lay in state at the State Capital Rotunda in Springfield, IL; all of his brothers were in the Civil War; he was the only one left S: DC
Cushman, Edmond S.	N: Ogle Co, Ill 1846 CW: Co E 92 Ill Inf (Corpl) Term: 3 yrs E/D: 8/62-6/65 GAR: 8/22/1925 on transfer from Geo H. Thomas Post Died: 8/27/1926 A: 85/10/27 Buried: Nampa, Idaho (Obit: Children in San Diego; Los Angeles; Alene, Oklahoma; Nampa, Idaho; no wife listed; veteran's middle name "Solomon") S: DC
Dakin, Horace E.	N: New York A: 69 O: Farmer R: Jamul, CA CW: Co E 1 Ohio Inf (Pvt) Re/Enl?: Co F 124 Ohio Inf (Capt) E/D: __/61-8/61 due to disability LOS: 5 mos GAR: 12/11/1900 Died 12/26/1904 Soldier's Home S: H
	SAWTELLE: Died 12/23/1904 and buried at Soldier's Home, Sawtelle, CA in "Branch USA", Sec.11, Row C, Grave 3 with tombstone inscription "Capt H.E. Dakin Co F 124 ___ Inf" S: Los Angeles National Cemetery
Dale, John H.	N: New York A: 47 O: Iron Moulder CW: Co F 10 V R Corps (Pvt) E/D: __/64-9/65 LOS: 12 mos GAR: 5/13/1891 SP: 3/31/1893 RE: 9/28/1897 SP: 6/25/1900 DR: 10/25/1904 S: H
Daley, Francis H.	N: Penn A: 55 O: Mechanic R: National City, CA CW: Co B 9 MO Cav (Pvt) E/D: 6/62-2/65 LOS: 36 mos GAR: 7/26/1886 SP: 4/30/1889 RE: 6/30/1890 SP: 3/22 or 24/1904 DR: 1/22/1907 RE: 1/14/1908 S: H
Dame, Luther	N: Maine A: 70 O: Teacher CW: Co C 11 Mass Inf (Capt) E/D: 10/61-8/64 LOS: 34 mos GAR: 2/2/1868 TR: 4/13/1897 S: H
Dampf, Louis	N: Germany A: 39 O: Manufacturer R: Fruitland, CA CW: Co D 7 NY Inf (Pvt) E/D: 8/61-3/63 LOS: 19 mos GAR: 6/13/1878 SP: 4/30/1889 RE: 6/30/1890 D: 2/12/1895 Died: "Dead"--no [grave] stone S: H
Dana, William	N: Ohio A: 44 O: Butcher CW: Co G 27 MO Inf (Pvt) E/D: 9/62-10/63 LOS: 13 1/3 mos GAR: 10/13/1887 SP: 1/10/1889 DR: 6/30/1891 Dead: "Dead"--no date given--Soldier's Home S: H
	SAWTELLE: Died 11/26/1903 at Soldier's Home, Sawtelle, CA Bur: "Branch USA" Sec.4, Row D, Grave 41 with tombstone inscription "Wm Dana Co G 27 MO Inf" S: Los Angeles National Cemetery
Dann, Edward F.	N: Stanford, CT CW: Co D 28 Wis Inf (Pvt) Term: 3 yrs E/D: 6/62-8/65 Brownsville, TX GAR: 2/13/1926 on transfer from Seigle Post #60 Dept of South Dakota Died: 8/14/1936 A: 90 Article: He was a doctor who practiced in Minesota for many years; was 81 at time of article S: DC
Darkes, William W.	N: Indiana A: 60 O: Farmer CW: Co D 43 Ind Inf (Pvt) E/D: 7/64-6/65 LOS: Not stated GAR: 12/28/1909 SP: 12/24/1912 DR: 12/24/1918 S: H
Darrough, James W.	N: Kentucky A: 72 O: Farmer CW: Co F 113 Ill Inf (Pvt) E/D: 8/62-5/65 due to disability LOS: Not stated GAR: 4/26/1910 SP: 12/26/1916 Died: 12/28/1918 S: H

Dauchey, Arthur H.	N: CT O: Jeweler CW: Co B 5 Minn Inf (Pvt) Term: Not stated E/D: 11/64-6/65 GAR: 11/10/1894 Charter Member of Datus Coon Post Died: 4/17/1935 A: 87 Buried: Forest Lawn Mausoleum, Los Angeles, CA Obit: Enlisted when 18 years old; severely wounded in the battle of Mobile. One daughter in Los Angeles; no wife mentioned Middle name "Homer" S: DC
Davidson, J.M.	J.M. Davidson, Co B 47 KY Inf (official tombstone). Buried at La Vista Cemetery, National City, CA.
Davis, Charles S.	N: Ohio A: 37 O: Carpenter CW: Co G 11 Tenn Cav (Bugler) E/D: 9/63-9/65 LOS: 24 mo GAR: 10/28/1886 SP: 1/10/1889 DR: 6/30/1891 SP: 6/26/1900 RE: 5/24 or 9/27/1904 SP: 6/23/1914 RE: 7/9/1918 SP: 12/27/1921 Died: 4/21/1930 S: H
Davis, Edwin P.	N: Virginia 1845 CW: Co B 2nd MD Potomic Home Brigade (Pvt) Term: 3 yrs E/D: 8/61-9/64 Cumberland, MD GAR: 6/24/1916 Died: 8/7/1924 A: 79 S: DC
Davis, I.R./J.R.	N: Wales A: 94 O: Retired CW: Co G 14 PA Cav (Pvt/Corpl) E/D: 5/61-__/65 LOS: Not stated GAR: 11/8/1927 SP: 12/31/1928 S: H
Davis, Leonard F.	N: Vermont A: 70 O: Retired CW: Co A 21 Wis Inf (Pvt/Sgt) E/D: 8/62-5/65 LOS: 33 mos GAR: 2/26/1895 Died: 11/24/1906 Vista, CA--is [grave] stone S: H Burial: La Vista Cemetery, National City, CA. Sergt. L.F. Davis, Co A 21 Wis Inf (official tombstone). Unofficial tombstone: Leonard F. Davis, 1825-1906. Wife: Sarah E. Trimble, Wife of Leonard F. Davis Born Aug 6, 1831, Died Oct 13, 1890.
Davis, Wilber F.	N: Watertown, NY CW: Co B 45 Ill Inf (Pvt) Term: 3 yrs E/D: 3/64-7/65 GAR: 8/10/1929 S:DC
Deakins, Henry C.	N: Illinois A: 86 O: Not listed CW: Co A 14 Ill Inf (Pvt?) E/D: 1/64-9/65 LOS: 1 yr 8 mos GAR: 8/9/1932 S: H
Deasdorff, Wm. P.	N: Des Moines, IA 5/29/50 CW: Co C 7th Cal Inf (Pvt) Term: 3 yrs E/D: 10/64-4/66 San Francisco, CA GAR: 5/13/1916 on transfer from Appomattox Post #50 Dept of Cal/Nev S: DC
Deash, Jacob N.	N: Penn A: 74 O: Retired CW: Co I 56 PA Inf (Pvt) E/D: 2/62-6/62 due to disability LOS: 5 mos GAR: 2/8/1921 S: H
Denny, Eliza M.	N: Indiana A: 58 O: Clerk CW: Co F 81 Ind Inf (Pvt) E/D: 8/62-8/65 LOS: 36 mos GAR: 3/27/1900 SP: 3/26/1907 RE: 5/26/1908 Died: 3/19/1909--no [grave] stone S: H
Derbyshere, Wm. H.	N: Putnam Co, NY 6/30/39 CW: Co E 1 NY Eng (Pvt/Artificer) Term: 3 yrs E/D: 9/61-10/64 Burmuda Hundred, VA due to being wounded with sabre over eye GAR: 3/26/1910 on transfer from Stanton Post #5 Dept of Cal/Nev TR: 3/15/1915 S: DC
Desmont, Chas.E.	N: Detroit, Mich 1847 CW: Co A 23rd OVI (Pvt) Term: 3 yrs E/D: 7/63-7/65 Cleveland, Ohio GAR: 8/22/1925; trans. from Dept of Michigan S: DC (Name also spelled Dermont?)
Detrick, Frank	N: Prussia A: 65 O: Brick Layer CW: Co K 3 Colo Cav (Pvt) E/D: 9/64-12/64 LOS: 100 days GAR: 4/23/1907 Died: 10/18/1924 or 1927? (date hard to read) S: H
Diamond, C.W.	C.W. Diamond, Co E, 2nd NH Inf (official tombstone); "Lieut" in cem. transcr. Buried 8/19/1876 age 34 La Vista Cemetery, National City, CA (Charles Warren Diamond, son Ira & Lucy Kimball Diamond).
Diamond, I.K.	I.K. Diamond, Co O 16th NH Inf (official tombstone). Buried 4/6/1871, age 26-29, La Vista Cemetery, National City, CA (Ira Kimball Diamond, son of Ira & Lucy Kimball Diamond).

Diamond, L.W.	L.W. Diamond, Co H 2nd NH Inf (official tombsone). Buried 12/29/1878, age 32, La Vista Cemetery, National City, CA. Levi Woodbury Diamond, son of Ira & Lucy Kimball Diamond (two other brothers are on p. 213). These three Diamond brothers were all born in Concord, NH and were nephews of Frank A. Kimball, the founder of National City, CA.
Dickens, Charles	NOL/NFI S: DC
Dissinger, David	N: Napuville, Ill 1846 CW: Co H 16 Ill Cav (Pvt) Term: 3 yrs E/D: 12/63-12/65 Springfield, IL GAR: 1/8/1921 on transfer from Dept. of Illinois Died: 2/17/1921 S: DC
Dixon, R.L.	N: Tenn A: 80 O: Retired CW: Co K 56 Ill Inf (Pvt) E/D: __/64-8/65 LOS: Not stated GAR: 1/10/1928 SP: 12/31/1928 S: H
Dodderidge, John H.	N: England A: 41 O: Hotel Keeper CW: USS Great Western (Landsman) E/D: 7/63-9/64 LOS: 14 mos GAR: 5/24/1888 SP: 9/__/1900 RE: 3/8/1904 SP: 12/27/1921 S: H "John "John Henry Dodderidge"
Dodge, John G.	N: NH A: 50 O: Plasterer CW: Co G 17 Ill Inf (Pvt) E/D: 5/61-6/64 LOS: 36 mos GAR: 2/14/1893 S: 3/28/1899 DR: 10/24/1904 S: H
Doesser, Horace	N: New York A: 82 O: Farmer/Laborer CW: Co F 4 Minn Cav (Pvt) E/D: 8/64-5/65 LOS: 9 mos GAR: 5/5/1896 Died: 8/25/1904 Soldier's Home S: H
	SAWTELLE: No records for this veteran were found at Los Angeles National Cemetery, the Sawtelle Index, the California Death Index, or at the County of San Diego.
Donovan, J.W.	N: Oswego Co, NY A: 38 O: Farmer R: Tijuana, MX CW: Co H 43 PA Inf (Pvt) E/D: 11/63-7/65 LOS: 24 mos GAR: 11/8/1883 RE: 2/28/1899 D: 2/28/1899 S: H
Donovan, M.	NOL/NFI S: DC
Dorris, William A.	N: Tenn A: 49 O: Hotel Keeper CW: Co E 2 Cal Vol (Pvt) E/D: 12/64-6/66 LOS: 18 mos GAR: 6/30/1886 SP: 1/10/1889 DR: 6/30/1891 RE: 5/9/1899 Died: 10/14/1899--is [grave] stone S: H
Dorey, Westly B.	N: Missouri A: 76 O: Retired CW: Co __ 30 Ill Inf (Musician) E/D: 3/61-4/62 LOS: Not stated GAR: 3/14/1916 on transfer from Hicker Post #443 Dept of Illinois Died: 9/__/1921 S: H
Dorward, William H.	N: England A: 60 O: Minister CW: Co E 29 Wis Inf (Pvt) E/D: 8/62-6/65 LOS: 34 mos GAR: 3/26/1901 TR: 3/25/1902 S: H
Dostal, James C.	N: Bohemia A: 82 O: Retired CW: Co K 22 Iowa Inf (Pvt) E/D: 6/62-8/65 LOS: 3 yrs 2 mos GAR: 12/23/1924 Died: 11/9/1925 S: H
Dougherty, Louis C.	N: Westmoreland, PA CW: Co B 59 Ill Inf (Pvt) Term: Unstated E/D: 6/61-11/63 Re-Enl: Same unit (Corpl) E/D: 11/63-9/65 GAR: 2/26/1927 S: DC
Douis, Walker	NOL/NFI S: DC
Dow, Francis I.	N: Wayne Co, PA CW: Co A 23 Wis Inf (Pvt) Term: 3 yrs E/D: 8/63-7/65 Mobile, AL GAR: 2/13/1926 S: DC
Downs, Nathan H.	N: Vermont CW: Co G 11 Wis Inf (Pvt/1st Lieut) Term: 3 yrs E/D: 10/61-1/63 St Louis, MO, disabled Re-Enl: Co K 40 Wis Inf (1st Lieut) E/D: 5/64-11/64 Madison, Wis GAR: 6/22/1907 on trans. from Gen. Shields Post #1 Dept of Dakota Died: 10/25/1903 A: 94/7/__ Buried: Nestor, CA S: DC Actual burial La Vista Cem, National City?: Liet Nathan H. Downs, Co G 11 Wis Inf (official tombstone).

Duling, John	N: Coshocton Co, Ohio 2/15/46 CW: Co G 1 Neb Bat Cav (Pvt) Term: Unstated E/D: 3/64-7/66 Omaha, Nebraska GAR: 8/9/1913 on transfer from E.B. Stevens Post #103 Dept of Cal/Nev. TR: 6/10/1916 S: DC
Dunham, George B.	N: Indiana A: 70 O: Farmer CW: Co H 87 Ind Inf (Pvt) E/D: 8/62-6/65 LOS: 35 mos GAR: 7/25/1905 Died: 4/6/1909 S: H
Dunn, W.T.	N: Indiana A: 47 O: Carriage Painter CW: Co B 14 Ind Inf (Pvt); Re-Enl?/D: Co G 80 Ind Inf (1st Lieut) E/D: 6/61-2/64 due to disability LOS: 20 mos GAR: 1/4/1885 D: 10/28/1886 S:H
Duvall, William H.	N: Arkansas A: 54 O: Soldier CW: Co H 6 Ohio Inf (Pvt) E/D: 6/61-6/64 Re-Enl?: Co E 5 US Art (Pvt) E/D: 1/66-6/__ LOS: 36 mos GAR: 7/24/1900 Died: 9/28/1902 Los Angeles S: H
	SAWTELLE: Date of death/burial are 9/28-30/1902, Soldier's Home, Sawtelle, CA Buried "Branch USA", Sec.7, Row C-10, Grave 10 with tombstone inscription "W.H. Duvall Co H 6 Ohio Inf Wife on back of tombstone: "Hansine O G Died 23 Nov 1932" S: Los Angeles National Cemetery
Dye, Bloomfield U.	N: Michigan A: 71 O: Rancher CW: Co E 1 Mich Eng (Pvt) E/D: __/63-__/65 LOS: 2 yrs GAR: 5/27/1886 SP: 1/10/1889 DR: 6/30/1891 GAR: 4/22/1913 RE: 4/22/1913 Died: 6/6/1916 S: H
Dye, J.W.	NOL/NFI S: DC
Dye, John W.	N: Michigan A: 63 O: Engineer CW: Co F 9 Ill Inf (Pvt) Re-Enl? Co __ 2 Batt V R C (Pvt) E/D: 4/61-5/65 LOS: 39 mos GAR: 7/25/1899 or 9/26/1899 TR: 9/25/1900 Re-Joined by transfer S: H
Eagle, J.O.	N: Maryland A: 50 O: Farmer CW: Co I 2 MD Inf (Pvt) E/D: 8/61-?/?? LOS: Not stated GAR: 9/23/1886 SP: 1/10/1889 DR: 6/30/1891 S: H
Eardley, Josiah	N: Derbyshire, England 1842 CW: Co B 1st Utah ___ (Mus'n/Pvt) Term: 4 mos E/D: 4/62-8/62 Salt Lake GAR: 9/12/1925 Died: 12/30/1931 at San Diego S: DC
Easling, Henry L.	N: Iowa A: Not stated O: Farmer CW: Co I 19 Iowa Inf (Corpl) E/D: 8/62-7/65 LOS: Not stated GAR: 10/8/1912 Died: 4/10/1918 at Bonafast, IA S: H
Eastman, Gilman E.	N: York Co, Maine CW: Co E 30 Maine Inf (Pvt) Term: 3 yrs E/D: 12/63-8/65 GAR: 11/24/1917 S: DC
Eastman, H.D.	N: Manlius, NY 1845 CW: Co I 11 NY Cav (Pvt) Term: 3 yrs E/D: 1/64-5/65 Memphis, TN due to sickness GAR: 2/24/1923 on transfer from L.H. Drimley Post #107 Dept of Illinois S: DC
Eaton, Benjamin	N: Mass A: 46 O: Rancher CW: Co K 47 Mass Inf (Pvt) E/D: 11/62-9/63 Re-Enl: Co L 56 Mass Inf (Pvt) E/D: 12/63-7/65 LOS: 28 mos GAR: 6/27/1893 SP: 7/24/1895 DR: 10/23/1904 S: H
Edgar, James A.	N: Mumfordsville, Hunt Co, KY CW: Co A 89 Ill Inf (Pvt) Term: 3 yrs Re-Enl?: Co B 59 Ill Inf (Pvt) E/D: 9/63-12/65 New Braunfields, TX GAR: 9/11/1909 on transfer from G.K. Warren Post #5 Dept of New Mexico TR: 7/8/1916 S: DC
Edwards, John W.	N: Kentucky A: 61 N: Embalmer CW: Co F 14 Ind Inf (Pvt) E/D: 5/61-6/64 Re-Enl?: Co A 4 US Inf (Pvt) E/D: 3/65-3/66 LOS: 48 mos GAR: 4/25/1905 TR: 8/28/08 S: H

Edwards, Nathan — N: Conn A: 67 O: Farmer CW: Co D 1 Conn H A (Pvt) E/D: 5/61-5/64 LOS: 36 mos GAR: 8/22/1905 SP: 6/23/1908 DR: 12/24/1918 S: H

Eggleston, H.J. — N: England A: 74 O: Farmer CW: Co K 3 Wis Inf (Pvt) E/D: 1/64-7/65 LOS: 18 1/2 mos GAR: 2/25/1908 SP: 12/24/1912 DR: 12/24/1918 S: H

Ellibee, Erastus T. — N: Dayton or Phillipsburg, OH 9/1/41 CW: Co D 99 Ind Inf (Pvt) Term: 3 yrs E/D: 8/62-6/65 Washington, D.C. LOS: 2 yrs, 9 mos, 26 days GAR: 1/10/1914 on transfer from Ransom Post #4 Dept of Arizona TR: 9/10/1921 RE: 4/24/1926 on transfer from A.G. Burnet Post #196 Dept of Cal/Nev San Jose Died: 10/26/1935 at San Diego A: 94/1/26 S: DC

Elliot, Robert J. — NOL/NFI S: DC

Ellis, Alvin R. — N: Maine A: 76 O: Retired CW: Co B 19 Maine Inf (Pvt/Corpl) E/D: 7/62-8/65 LOS: 3 yrs GAR: 2/8/1921 Died: 5/6/1921 S: H

Embler, James W. — N: Rome, NY 3/8/41 CW: Co G 1 NY LA (Pvt) Term: 3 yrs E/D: 8/61-2/62 due to disability Re-Enl: Co C 147 NY Inf (1st Sgt) E/D: 8/62-2/65 New Petersburg, VA GAR: 10/22/1927 on transfer from Walter C. Hull Post Dept of NY S: DC

Emiron, George W. — N: Penn A: 74 O: Retired R: Lemon Grove, CA CW: Co B 186 PA Inf (Pvt) E/D: 2/64-8/65 LOS: 18 mos GAR: 2/25/1919 Died: 12/4/1923 S: H

Emmons, Ira J. — N: New York A: 84 O: Retired CW: Co D 3 NY Cav (Pvt) E/D: 8/61-8/65 LOS: 4 yrs GAR: 5/26/1925 TR: 4/6/1926 S: H

Endly, C.F. — N: Ohio A: 76 O: Retired CW: Co E 3 Ohio Cav (Pvt) E/D: 9/61-10/64 LOS: 3 yrs GAR: 8/26/1919 SP: 12/26/1923 DR: 12/28/1924 S: H

Engle, C.B. — NOL/NFI S: DC

Englehorn, John K. — N: Germany A: 84 O: Retired CW: Co E 9 Iowa Cav (Pvt) E/D: 9/63-2/66 LOS: Not stated GAR: 12/14/1926 Died: 10/7/1930 S: H

Erickson, Mathias — N: Sweden 3/23/39 CW: Co D 7 Ill Cav (Pvt/Chief Bugler) Term: 3 yrs E/D: 8/61-11/65 Nashville, TN GAR: 10/14/1911 on transfer from James Randolph Post #116 Dept of Iowa Died: 9/27/1915 Buried: Iowa S: DC

Erwin, James — NOL/NFI S: DC

Esleek/Esleck, Issac A. — N: Washington, D.C. CW: Co L 3 RI HA (Pvt) Term: 3 yrs E/D: 1/62-3/65 Hilton Head, SC GAR: 11/10/1894 Charter Member of Datus Coon Post Died: 1/31/1918 S: DC

Estay, Amos — N: Canada 1845 CW: Co B 21 Wis Inf (Pvt) Term: 3 yrs E/D: 8/62-6/65 Milwaukee, Wis GAR: 10/12/1925 Died: 9/12/1925 (death date is in error if he entered the GAR on 10/12/1925--perhaps he entered the GAR on 9/12/1925 and died on 10/12/1925) S: DC

Eubanks, J.J. — N: Tenn A: 58 O: Carpenter CW: Co C 124 Ill Inf (Pvt/Sgt) 7/61-7/64 LOS: 3 yrs GAR: 7/16/1883 SP: 1/10/1889 DR: 6/30/1891 RE: 12/24/1896 D: 12/26/1896 S: H

Evans, William V. — N: Missouri A: 63 O: Carpenter R: La Mesa, CA CW: Co B 42 MO Inf (Pvt) E/D: 7/64-5/65 LOS: Not stated GAR: 5/25/1909 SP: 6/23/1914 TR: 7/9/1918 S: H

Ewing, Edward	N: New York A: 64 O: Blacksmith R: Otay (near San Diego) CW: Co D 10 Mich Cav (Pvt) E/D: 12/64-12/65 due to disability LOS: 12 mos GAR: 9/28/1897 SP: 12/27/1898 RE: 6/27/1899 Died: 5/1/1900 Soldier's Home S: H
	SAWTELLE: Died 5/27/1900 at Soldier's Home, Sawtelle, CA Bur: "Branch USA", Sec.5, Row F, Grave 13 with tombstone inscription "Edward Ewing Co D 10th Mich Cav" S: Los Angeles National Cemetery
Ewing, William E.	N: Goforth, KY 1847 CW: Co G 28 Ind State Guard Inf (Pvt) Term: 1 yr E/D: 8/63-7/64 Re-Enl: Co G 28 PA Inf (Pvt) E/D: 1/65-7/65 GAR: 12/11/1920 on transfer from Lyon Post #10 Dept of New Jersey S: DC
Falkenstein, John	N: West Virginia A: 52 O: Farmer CW: Co C 3 W VA Cav (Sgt/QM Sgt) E/D: 10/61-1/65 LOS: 39 mos GAR: 6/30/1886 SP: 9/26/1889 RE: 6/30/1898 SP: 9/25/1900 DR: 10/25/1904 Died: 11/4/1914 S: H
Farrow, D.S.	N: Ohio 1843 CW: Co G 2 W VA Cav (Pvt) Term: 3 yrs E/D: 10/61-11/64 Wheeling, VA GAR: ? date by transfer DR: 9/24/1927 S: DC
Fassett, Charles B.	N: Sanderson, Mich CW: Co D 6 Mich Inf (2nd Lieut/Capt) Term: Unstated E/D: 8/61-8/65 GAR: 8/13/1910 on transfer from T.O. Howe Post #33 Dept of South Dakota Buried: South Dakota S: DC
Fay, William A.	N: Grafton, Mass CW: Co G 32 Wis Inf (Pvt) Term: 3 yrs E/D: 12/63-5/65 Prairie du Chein, Wis GAR: 5/27/1898 on transfer from Simon Mix Post #95 Dept of Minnesota Died: 2/1/1913 A: 67 Buried: Mount Hope S: DC Note: No record of burial for William A. Fay at Mount Hope Cemetery.
Feathers, D.H.	N: Canada A: 57 O: Farmer CW: Co C 31 Wis Inf (Pvt) E/D: 8/62-6/65 LOS: 34 mos GAR: 3/28/1893 SP: 9/22/1896 DR: 3/28/1899 S: H
Fesler, William H.	N: Iowa A: 88 O: Not stated CW: Co K 8 Ind Inf (Pvt) E/D: __/62-__/65 LOS: Not stated GAR: 9/10/1929 DR: 12/__/1935 S: H
Field, William B.	N: Chicago, Ill CW: Co C 89 Ill Inf (Pvt) Term: 3 yrs E/D: 11/61-6/65 Nashville, TN Re-Enl: Co F 59 Ill ___ (? rank) E/D: ___/__-12/65 Springfield, IL GAR: 7/23/1909 Died: 1913 Buried: Soldier's Home S: DC
	SAWTELLE: Died 6/3/1913 Soldier's Home, Sawtelle, CA and buried in "Branch USA", Sec. 23, Row D, Grave 15 with tombstone inscription "Wm B Field, Co C 89 Ill Inf" S: Los Angeles National Cemetery
Fitzgerald, Charles R.	N: New Jersey A: Not stated O: Accountant R: La Mesa, CA CW: Co A 26 NJ Inf (Pvt) E/D: 9/62-6/63 LOS: 9 mos GAR: 4/9/1918 on transfer Died: 1/28/1919 S: H
Fitzgerald, Nathan W.	N: Ripley Co, Ind A: 73 O: Lecturer CW: Co A 132 Ind Inf (Pvt) E/D: 5/64-9/64 LOS: 4 mos GAR: 3/13/1917 SP: 12/10/1918 S: H
Fitzpatrick, W.	N: Canada A: 45 O: Engineer CW: Co F 1 Cal ___ (Pvt) E/D: 8/61-8/64 LOS: 36 mos GAR: 7/13/1882 D: 12/28/1883 S: H
Fletcher, B.F.	N: Troy, Maine A: 44 O: Carpenter CW: Co A 16 Maine ___ (PVt) Re-Enl? US Navy (Seaman) E/D: 9/63-8/65 LOS: 23 mos GAR: 8/10/1882 SP: 9/24/1895 RE: 5/26/1896 Died: 5/14/1889 (true date 1899?)--is [grave] stone S:H Burial: B.E. Fletcher Co A 16 ME Inf (official tombstone) La Vista Cemetery, National City, CA

Fletcher, Henry H.	N: New York A: 51 O: Farmer CW: Co G 3 Iowa Cav (Corpl) E/D: 8/61-8/65 LOS: 47 2/3 mos GAR: 12/25/1887 RE: 12/13/1892 Died: 9/2/1928 S: H
Folkin, Samuel J.	N: Montreal, Canada A: 75 O: Retired CW: US Navy (Master Mate) E/D: 4/64-6/65 LOS: 1 yr GAR: 10/28/1919 Died: 12/29/1925 S: H
Folks, John H.	N: Ohio A: 65 O: Rancher CW: Co F 26 Ill Inf (Pvt/Capt) E/D: 8/61-9/64 LOS: 37 mos GAR: 4/22/1891 SP: 3/28/1899 RE/D: 2/24/1903 S: H
Folsum, Edward C.	N: Gray, Maine A: 36 O: Physician CW: Signal Corps (Pvt) E/D: 3/64-1/65 due to disability LOS: 9 mos GAR: 10/8/1881 Charter Member Heintzelman Post DR: 12/28/1882 S: H
Fonda, John G.	N: New York A: 77 O: Civil Engineer R: National City CW: Co G 2 Ill Inf (1st Lieut/1st Post Surgeon) E/D: 7/61-12/61 Promoted: Co __ 12 Ill Inf (Major) E/D: 12/61-11/62 Promoted: Co __ 118 Ill Inf (Lt Col/Col/Brvt Brig Gen) E/D: 11/62-6/65 LOS: 47 mos? GAR: Date not stated--possibly in mid-1899 S: H
Foot, F.J.	N: Conn A: 52 O: Clergyman CW: Co __ 13 Wis Inf (Chaplain) 8/63-12/65 LOS: 28 mos GAR: 4/12/1888 SP: 3/28/1889 DR: 6/30/1891 Died: 7/19/1899--is [grave] stone S: H
Foote, Andrew J.B.	N: Ohio A: 75 O: Bricklayer CW: Co H 2 Ohio Inf (Pvt) E/D: 4/61-8/61 Re-Enl: Co D 1 W VA L A (Pvt) E/D: 8/62-6/65 LOS: Not stated GAR: 6/24/1913 SP: 12/26/1916 DR: 12/24/1918 S: H
Foote, Thomas J.	N: England A: 78 O: Cottage Maker? CW: Co G 20 Iowa Inf (Pvt) E/D: 8/62-7/65 LOS: Not stated GAR: 11/13/1916 (probably on transfer from Lincoln Post Dept Colo/Wyo) Died: 12/13/1917 S: H
Forest, Harry Clay	N: Philadelphia, PA 1843 CW: Co C 196 PA Inf (Pvt) Term: Unstated E/D: 6/64-11/64 GAR: 5/9/1925 D: 11/11/1926 Naval Hospital S: DC
Fortier, Zephraim	N: Not stated 10/20/42 CW: Co K 3 NH ___ (Pvt) Term: 1 yr E/D: 2/65-8/65 Concord, NH GAR: 3/9/1918 TR: 9/13/1919 S: DC
Fosnot, Hiram H.	N: Penn A: 46 O: Carpenter R: Fallbrook, CA CW: Co C 24 Ohio Inf (Pvt) E/D: 5/61-8/61 due to disability [possibly due to being wounded in spine--this entry in the GAR record blends with that of Patrick Coleman, the name just below Fosnots, so it is difficult to say who was injured] LOS: 3 mos GAR: 3/25/1886 SP: 9/26/1889 DR: 6/30/1891 S: H
Foster, Nehemiah D.	N: Maine A: 71 O: Retired CW: Co D 48 Ill Inf (Corp) E/D: 8/61-__/__ due to disability LOS: Not stated GAR: 2/11/1913 on transfer from U.S. Grant Post #28 Ilinois SP: 6/27/1916 DR: 12/24/1918 S: H
Fowler, Elijah P.	N: Rochester, NY 9/25/44 CW: Co K 4 NY HA (Pvt/Corpl) E/D: 12/63-9/65 Fort Richardson GAR: 5/26/1923 on transfer from John A. Martin Post Dept of Cal/Nev TR: 1/15/1929 to Rochester, NY S: DC
Fox, Joseph	N: Penn A: 80 O: Retired CW: Co G 87 PA Inf (Pvt/Corpl) E/D: 9/61-6/65 LOS: 4 yrs GAR: 1/22/1924 Died: 2/18/1927 or 2/19/1927 S: H
Francis, William H.	N: Michigan A: 50 O: Lawyer CW: Co B 2 Mich Cav (Pvt) E/D: 9/61-10/64 LOS: 37 mos GAR: 7/11/1893 SP: 9/24/1895 DR: 10/25/1904 RE: 1/22/1907 S: H

Frantz, Henry	N: Penn A: 72 O: Retired CW: Co H 15 Iowa Inf (Pvt/Corpl) E/D: 11/61-7/65 LOS: 44 mos GAR: 3/27/1917 Died: 4/17/1926 S: H
Frazell, Warren	N: Franklin Co, Ohio 1/8/43 CW: Co E 10 Ill Inf (Pvt) Term: 3 yrs E/D: 2/64-7/65 Chicago, IL GAR: 9/13/1913 S: DC
Fredericks, William M.	N: Denmark A: 45 O: Bricklayer CW: Co A 80 NY Inf (Pvt) E/D: 11/63-1/66 LOS: 26 mos GAR: 4/24/1888 TR: 8/22/1889 S: H
Freeman, William	NOL/NFI S: DC
Frees, Benjamin M.	N: Maine A: 67 O: Lumber Dealer CW: Co H 38 Wis Inf (Pvt/Capt) E/D: 8/64-6/65 LOS: Not stated GAR: 12/10/1912 on transfer from U.S. Grant Post #28 Dept of Illinois Died: 5/28/1920 S: H
Fry, Edward J.	N: Illinois A: 77 O: Retired CW: Co F 22 Ind Inf (Pvt) 7/61-7/62 due to wounds LOS: 12 mos GAR: ? date (probably 2/26/1918) on transfer from Bartlett Logan Post #6 Cal/Nev S:H
Fuller, Andrew J.	N: Michigan A: Not stated O: Retired CW: Co I 5 Mich Inf (Pvt) E/D: __/61-__/62 LOS: LOS: 1 yr Promoted?: Co F 9 Mich Cav (2nd Lieut/1st Lieut) E/D: __/62-__/65 LOS: 3 yrs GAR: 6/26/1923 Died: 1/3/1928 or 1929 S: H
Gaffney, P.H.	N: Ireland CW: Co K 20 Iowa Inf (Pvt/Sgt) Term: 3 yrs E/D: 8/62-7/65 Mobile, AL GAR: 5/26/1906 on transfer from S.H. Seward Post #8 Dept of North Dakota Died: 12/7/1908 A: 72 Buried: Dakota S: DC
Gallager, Patrick	N: Ireland A: 42 O: Miner R: "National" (probably National City, CA) CW: Co C 4 NH Inf (Pvt) E/D: 10/64-8/65 LOS: 10 mos GAR: 12/25/1887 SP: 9/28/1897 DR: 3/28/1899 S: H
Ganoung, William H.	N: New York A: 71 O: Not stated CW: Co E 64 NY Inf (Pvt) E/D: 9/61-9/64 LOS: Not stated GAR: 3/11/1913 on transfer from Farragut T. #8 Dept of Kansas Died: At Sawtelle S: H
	SAWTELLE: Died 11/3/1915, Soldier's Home, Sawtelle, CA Bur: "Branch USA", Sec.27, Row D, Grave 15 with tombstone inscription "Wm Ganoung Co E 64 NY Inf S: Los Angeles National Cemetery
Gardner, Charles	N: Maine A: 76 O: Farmer CW: Co I 37 Iowa Inf (Pvt) E/D: 8/62-5/65 LOS: Not stated GAR: 6/22/1915 on transfer from Gordon Granger Post #64 Dept of Iowa S: H
Gardner, Horace	N: Penn A: 61 O: Not stated CW: Co K 105 Ill Inf (Pvt) E/D: 8/62-1/65 LOS: 34 or 36 mos GAR: 1/23/1894 SP: 9/24/1895 DR: 3/28/1899 SP 12/24/1901 DR: 1/22/1907 Died: 1/__/1907 (Name also spelled "Gartner" in record) S: H
Garrett, James W.	N: Ohio A: 72 O: Not stated CW: Co __ 13 Batt Ind L A (Pvt) E/D: 1/62-7/65 LOS: Not stated GAR: 8/24/1915 Died: 12/10/1925 S: H
Garwood, John F.	N: Ohio A: 80 O: Not stated CW: Co E 82 Ohio Inf (Corpl) E/D: 11/61-12/63 Re-Enl: Co E 83 Ohio Inf (Corpl) E/D: 1/64-7/65 LOS: 4 yrs GAR: 2/23/1923 Died: 1/7/1930 S: H
Gates, William Klugh	N: Penn A: 42 O: Carpenter CW: Co I 55 PA Inf (Pvt) E/D: 2/64-9/65 LOS: 19 mos GAR: 2/28/1889 DR: 6/30/1891 S: H

Gay, John	NOL/NFI S: DC
Gaylord, Orvin N.	N: West Hartland, Hartford Co, Ct 10/2/42 CW: Co G 16 Ct Vol Inf (Pvt) Term: 3 yrs E/D: 7/62-3/63 New Haven, CT due to disability GAR: 2/13/1926 on transfer from Memorial Post Dept of Cleveland, Ohio Died: 1/1931 Obit: 5 children listed; wife not named "Orvin Nathaniel Gaylord" S: DC
George, Charles W.	N: Germany A: 54 O: Merchant CW: Co H 11 Wis Inf (Pvt) E/D: 10/61-12/62 due to disability LOS: 15 mos GAR: 8/__/1882 SP: 8/28/1900 RE: 6/12/1906 SP: 12/26/1916 DR: 12/24/1918 S: H
Germain, O.	NOL/NFI S: DC
Gibson, Emory M.	N: New York A: 65 O: Apiarian R: Jamul, CA CW: Co G 105 Ill Inf (Pvt) E/D: Not stated LOS: Not stated GAR: 7/28/1903 SP: 12/27/1904 DR: 12/24/1918 RE: 4/23/1912 SP: 6/23/1914 S: H
Giffod, F.	NOL/NFI S: DC
Gilbert, Henry H.	N: Moudy Township, Genessee Co, Mich 8/12/40 CW: Co C 66 Ill Inf Western Sharpshooters (Pvt) Term: 3 yrs E/D: 9/61-1/64 due to disability GAR: ? date on transfer from Shields Post #68 Dept of Michigan S: DC
Gilbert, John A.	N: Mass A: 66 O: Railroad Conductor CW: Co C 25 Mass Inf (Pvt) E/D: 11/64-3/65 LOS: Not stated GAR: 2/13/1912 on transfer from Hartrauft Post #3 Dept of Oklahoma SP: 6/23/1914 DR: 12/24/1918 S: H
Giles, Albert L.	N: New Hampshire A: 46 O: Yard Master CW: Co G 32 Mass Inf (Pvt/Sgt) E/D: 5/62-6/65 LOS: 36 mos GAR: 7/26/1888 SP: 9/26/1889 Died: 6/25/1891--no [grave] stone S: H
Gilman, Benjamin W.	N: New York A: 55 O: Railroader CW: Co B 1 Wis Inf (Pvt) Re-Enl: Co B McCl Drag (Pvt) E/D: 4/61-6/63 for disability LOS: 27 mos GAR: 5/13/1891 TR: 11/11/1891 S: H
Gilson, Sylvester	N: New York A: 72 O: Merchant R: Julian, CA CW: Co B 2 Colo Cav (Pvt) E/D: 12/61-1/64 LOS: 36 mos GAR: 8/15/1907 S: H
Gimelich, Christ	N: Germany A: 79 O: Retired CW: Co G 36 Ill Inf (Pvt) E/D: 9/64-6/65 LOS: Not stated GAR: 11/26/1912 on transfer from Streator Post #68 Dept of Illinois S: H
Gleason, Nathan B.	N: New York A: 76 O: Merchant CW: Co E 7 Iowa Cav (Pvt) E/D: 4/63-1/66 due to disability LOS: 33 mos GAR: 11/28/1893 Died: "Dead"--no date, no [grave] stone S: H
Glenn, James H.	N: Tennessee A: 73 O: Retired R: Lemon Grove, CA CW: Co F 3 US Vol Inf (Corpl) E/D: __/64-__/65 LOS: 1 yr GAR: 9/13/1921 Died: 1937 S: H
Glidden, A.P.	N: New Hampshire A: 41 O: Carpenter CW: Co G 1 NH Cav (Pvt) E/D: 3/62-7/65 LOS: 3 4/12 yrs GAR: 5/27/1886 SP: 1/10/1889 DR: 6/30/1891 RE: 12/9/1902 D: 12/9/1902 GAR: 5/13/1913 SP: 6/27/1916 DR: 12/24/1918 S: H
Goetsch, Ferdinand	N: Prussia A: 53 O: Carpenter CW: Co E 69 NY Inf (Pvt) E/D: 8/64-6/65 LOS: 10 mos GAR: 12/8/1896 SP: 9/25/1899 DR: 10/25/1904 S: H
Goetze, William	N: Germany A: 57 O: Musician CW: Co M 2 Cal Cav (Pvt) E/D: 2/62-2/65 LOS: 36 mos GAR: 12/22/1896 TR: 12/12/1905 S: H

Gomer, John H.	N: New York A: 56 O: Carpenter CW: Co E 11 NY Inf (Pvt) E/D: 4/61-6/61 Re-Enl: Co H 1 NY Eng (Corpl) E/D: 10/61-8/62 due to disability LOS: 13 or 16 mos GAR: 5/8/1894 SP: 12/27/1904 DR: 1/22/1907 S: H
Goodell, Maximilian	N: Conn A: 78 O: Retired CW: Co E 1 NY Cav (Pvt) E/D: 10/64-6/65 Re-Enl: Co M 3 US Cav (Pvt) E/D: 1/65-10/68 LOS: 3 yrs GAR: 9/__/1925 Died: 3/11/1930 S: H
Goodrich, James M.	N: Vermont A: 68 O: Farmer CW: Co D 14 VT Inf (Pvt/Corpl) E/D: 9/62-7/63 LOS: 10 mos GAR: 7/6/1888 SP: 12/24/1912 DR: 12/24/1918 S: H
Goodrich, V.R.	NOL/NFI S: DC
Goodspeed, Chas.E.	N: New York A: 84 O: Retired CW: Co D 74 Ill Inf (Corpl) E/D: 7/62-6/65 LOS: 3 yrs GAR: 3/9/1926 Died: 4/2/1932 S: H "Charles E. Goodspeed"
Goodwin, Oliver R.	N: New York CW: Co I 14 Ohio Inf (Pvt) Term: Unstated E/D: 9/61-12/63 GAR: 12/26/1903 on transfer from Lyon Post #8 DR: 9/24/1927 S: DC
Gouchenaur, David	N: Penn A: 50 O: Physician CW: Commisary Dept (Pvt) Re-enl?: Co G 202 PA Inf (Capt) E/D: __/63-8/65 LOS: 24 mos GAR: 5/11/1897 Died: 2/27/1917 or 2/29/1917 S:H
Gould, Francis C.	N: Windham, Maine CW: U.S.S. Housatania (Landsman) Term: 1 yr E/D: 8/62-9/63 GAR: 5/25/1912 TR: 6/24/1916 S: DC
Gould, William H.	N: Penn A: 83 O: Retired CW: Co D 3 Colo Cav (Pvt) E/D: 8/64-12/65 LOS: Not stated GAR: 9/13/1927 Died: 3/__/1932 S: H
Gracy, Robert A.	N: Auburn, Lincoln Co, MO 1841 CW: Co A 1 Oregon Cav (Pvt/Sgt) Term: 3 yrs E/D: 11/61-11/64 Fort Vancouer, Washington Sgt GAR: 7/23/1921 on transfer from Chester A. Arthur Post #47 Dept of Oregon. Died 5/4/1926 at Soldier's Home, Sawtelle, CA. Buried there because he was blind before he died. S: DC SAWTELLE: Records were not searched for this veteran at Los Angeles National Cemetery
Graeter, Henry A.	N: Ohio A: 63 O: Carpenter CW: Co C 16 Ohio Inf (Pvt) E/D: 4/61-__/__ LOS: Not stated GAR: 10/13/1887 D: 9/26/1889 SP: 6/30/1891 RE: 12/__/1893 SP: 9/25/1899 RE: 6/23/1903 SP: 6/25/1907 DR: 12/24/1918 S: H
Gragg, William H.	N: Mass A: 86 O: Farmer CW: Co B 1 Cal Cav Mountaineers (Pvt) E/D: 4/63-5/65 LOS: Not stated GAR: 8/13/1912 SP: 12/22/1914 DR: 12/24/1918 S: H
Graham, Burton F.	N: Illinois A: 76 O: Retired CW: Co I 1 Ill Cav (Sgt) E/D: 5/61-7/62 LOS: 14 mos GAR: 11/27/1917 SP: 12/28/1920 S: H
Graham, Isaac A.	N: Ohio A: 49 O: Carpenter CW: Co E 9 Ill Cav (Sgt) E/D: 9/61-11/62 due to disability LOS: 14 mos GAR: 7/26/1888 SP: 9/26/1889 DR: 6/30/1891 RE: 9/__/1892 DR: 12/24/1918 S: H
Graham, Robert A.	N: Ireland A: 38 O: Merchant R: Bernardo (probably Rancho Bernardo, CA) CW: Co A 90 Penn Inf (Drummer) E/D: 11/61-11/64 LOS: 3 yrs GAR: 1/22/1885 D: 3/22/1888 S:H
Grant Henry S.	NOL/NFI S: DC
Gray, Joseph	N: Illinois CW: Co I 96 Ill Inf (Pvt) Term: 3 yrs E/D: 8/62-6/65 GAR: 11/10/1894 Charter member of Datus Coon Post GAR DR: 12/9/1910 or 12/9/1916 S: DC

Gray, Robert A.	NOL/NFI S: DC
Green, J.N.	N: Canada A: 53 O: Real Estate CW: Co __ 19 Ind Inf (Asst Surgeon) E/D: 9/61-12/61 due to resignation LOS: 15 mos? GAR: 1/19/1886 SP: 9/26/1889 RE: ? Date DR: 12/24/1918 S: H
Green, James	N: Ireland A: 60 O: Farmer CW: Co K 141 NY Inf (Pvt) E/D: 8/62-6/65 LOS: 33 mos GAR: 11/22/1892 Died: 12/12/1911 at Soldier's Home S: H
	SAWTELLE: Died 2/7/1911 at Soldier's Home, Sawtelle, CA Buried: "Branch USA" Sec.19, Row F, Grave 9 with tombstone inscription "Jas. Green Co K 141 NY Inf" S: H, Los Angeles National Cemetery
Green, John A.	N: Central Falls, RI A: 49 O: Machinist CW: Co A 8 Cal Inf (Pvt) E/D: 11/64-10/65 LOS: 13 mos GAR: 2/22/1883 SP: 1/10/1889 DR: 6/30/1891 RE: 4/9/1901 SP: 2/10/1918 S: H
Greenfield, John	N: Muskingham Co, Ohio 9/8/41 CW: Co K 48 Ind Inf (Pvt) Term: 3 yrs E/D: 11/61-6/64 Indianapolis, Ind due to a disability GAR: 11/8/1913 on transfer from W.J. Palmer Post Dept of Col/Wyo TR: 11/12/1921 S: DC
Greenlee, James L.	N: Penn A: 78 O: Retired CW: Co G 37 Ind Inf (Pvt) E/D: __/61-7/64 LOS: 3 yrs GAR: 1/27/1920 SP: 12/31/1925 or 1928 S: H
Gregory, Hugh M.	N: New York A: 54 O: Sea Captain CW: US Navy (Acting Mate/Lieut) E/D: 5/61-2/64 due to resignation LOS: 33 mos GAR: 12/27/1888 TR: 4/25/1889 S:H
Grinell, Calvin	N: Indiana A: 82 O: Retired CW: Co D 33 Ind Inf (Sgt) E/D: 7/62-7/65 GAR: 3/14/1916 Died: 5/28/1920 S: H
Griswold, Benson	N: Troy, Ohio CW: Co F 2 Minn Cav (Pvt) Term: 3 yrs E/D: 11/63-12/65 Ft Snelling, MN GAR: 8/24/1912 on transfer from John A. Dix Post #43 Dept of Cal/Nev Died: 2/28/1926 at Chula Vista, CA (near San Diego) S: DC
Grovesteen, J.H.	N: New York A: 41 O: Piano Tuner CW: Co H 8 NY SM (Pvt) Re-Enl: Co G 174 NY Inf (Sgt) E/D: 5/62-8/66 LOS: 39 mos GAR: 8/21/1886 TR: 9/25/1894 S: H
Grovesteen, James H.	N: New York 1844 CW: Co B 2 Ohio Inf (Pvt) Term: Unstated E/D: 6/61-12/61 due to disability (pneumonia) Re-Enl: Co H 8 NY SM (Pvt); then Co G 174 NY Inf (Sgt) E/D: 5/62-11/65 GAR: 11/10/1894 Charter Member of Datus Coon Post Died 7/23/1921 A: 77 at Los Angeles, CA S: DC
Guilford, Andrew J.	N: Ohio A: 48 O: Miller CW: Co F 11 Mich Cav (Pvt/2nd Lieut) E/D: 8/63-10/65 LOS: 36 mos GAR: 8/21/1886 SP: 6/30/1888 DR: 6/30/1891 RE: 4/28/1903 TR: 4/28/1903 S: H
Gunn, John W.	N: Morgan Co, Ill 7/24/42 CW: Co I 14 Ill ___ (Pvt) Term: 3 yrs E/D: 6/61-6/64 Springfield, IL Re-Enl: Co E 58 Ill Inf (2nd Lieut) 4/65-3/66 Montgomery, AL GAR: 9/8/1923 on transfer from Havensville Post #144 Dept of Kansas DR: "Dropped" S: DC
Guthrie, Roger C.	N: Maine A: 50 O: Machinist CW: Co C 7 Mass Inf (Wagoner) E/D: 6/61-6/64 LOS: 36 mos GAR: 6/27/1889 TR: 7/11/1892 S: H

Guy, Isaac J.C.	N: Wayne Co, Ind CW: Co K 134 Ind Inf (2nd Lieut) Term: 100 days E/D: 2/64-9/64 Indianapolis, Ind Re-Enl: Co C 151 Ind Inf (1st Lieut/Acting Adj) E/D: 2/65-__/__ Nashville TN GAR: 10/22/1927 at age 89 on transfer from Syracuse Post Dept of Kansas Died: 1/1928 S: DC
Hall, H.I.	N: Penn A: 51 O: Not stated CW: Co D 2 Cal Cav (Sgt/Lieut) E/D: 9/61-3/64 LOS: Not stated GAR: 6/30/1886 SP: 1/10/1889 DR: 6/30/1891 S: H
Hall, Harvy R.	NOL/NFI S: DC
Hall, Joseph E.	N: Penn A: 46 O: Physician CW: Co I 148 PA Inf (Pvt); Re-Enl? Co __ 183 PA Inf (Adjutant) E/D: 8/62-7/65 LOS: 35 mos GAR: 8/23/1888 TR: 2/13/1890 S:H
Hallowell, H.B.	N: New York A: 87 O: Retired CW: U S M C (Pvt) E/D: 5/60-__/__ LOS: Not stated GAR: 10/25/1927 Died: 12/19/1927 S: H
Hallowell, Henry B.	N: New York City 1839 CW: US Marine Corps (Pvt) Term: 4 yrs E/D: 5/60-5/65 Philadelphia, PA LOS: 5 yrs GAR: 4/9/1927 on transfer from McPhereson Post Dept of Kansas TR: 10/25/1927 to Heintzelman Post GAR San Diego (see above) Died: 12/14/1927 at San Diego S: DC
Ham, Charles	N: Saratoga Co, NY 11/1/39 CW: Co D 1 NY LA (Pvt) Term: 3 yrs E/D: 12/63-6/65 Elmira, NY GAR: 3/9/1907 on transfer from Pickway Post Dept of Ohio Died: 5/1920 S: DC
Hamilton, James T.	N: Mass A: 49 O: Mechanic CW: Co E 43 Mass Inf (Pvt) E/D: 10/62-7/63 LOS: 9 mos GAR: 2/9/1888 SP: 1/10/1889 RE: 6/10/1890 DR: 6/30/1891 S: H
Haney, Henry F.	N: Vermont A: 78 O: Carpenter CW: Co K 6 Mich Cav (Pvt) E/D: 9/62-10/65 LOS: 37 1/2 mos GAR: 2/9/1904 Died: 2/22/1910 S: H
Hanna, John J.	N: New York A: 82 O: Retired CW: Co K 148 NY Inf (Pvt) E/D: __/62-__/65 LOS: Not stated GAR: 11/8/1927 SP: 12/31/1928 RE: 1/22/1929 S: H
Hanretty, John	N: Ireland A: 39 O: Laborer CW: Co F 3 US Arty (Pvt); Re-Enl? Co P 3 US Arty (Pvt) E/D: 5/61-5/64 LOS: 3 yrs GAR: 10/21/1881 TR: 1/14/1883 S: H
Hanson, Parker W.	N: Maine A: 59 O: Carpenter R: National City, CA CW: Co G 4 ME Inf (Pvt) E/D: 5/61-5/64 Re-enl?: Co __ 7 Mass Inf or H A (Pvt) E/D: 12/61-__/__ LOS: 32 mos GAR: 7/25/1905 Died: 12/25/1926 S: H
Hargrave, William	N: Canada A: 52 O: Retired CW: Co F 141 Ill Inf (Pvt) E/D: 5/64-10/64 LOS: 5 mos GAR: 4/13/1897 SP: 12/24/1912 DR: 12/24/1918 S: H
Harkins, Henry A.	N: New York A: 84 O: Retired CW: Co B 35 NY Inf (Pvt) Re-Enl?: Co L 20? NY Cav (Sgt) E/D: 10/61-__/64 LOS: Not stated GAR: 6/12/1923 Died 7/22/1928 S: H
Harrington, David G.	N: Vermont A: 74 O: Farmer R: Oceanside, CA CW: Co C 1 Minn Inf (Sgt) E/D: 2/65-7/65 or 2/65-8/65 LOS: Not stated GAR: 4/28/1908 Died: 9/7/1914 S: H
Hart, James	N: Virginia A: 47 O: Laborer CW: Co K 2 D C Vol Inf (Pvt) E/D: 1/65-9/65 3 mos? GAR: 4/26/1888 DR: 3/23/1892 Died: "Died", no date--no [grave] stone S: H
Haskins, Alonzo	N: New York A: Not stated O: Stone Manufacturer CW: Co A 23 NY Cav (Pvt) E/D: 1/63-7/65 LOS: 30 mos GAR: 1/24/1889 TR: "Transfer" S: H

Haughn, Francis J.	N: Fayette Co, Ind 1847 CW: Co A 124 Ind Inf (Pvt) Term: 3 yrs E/D: 11/62-8/65 Greensboro, NC LOS: 2 yrs, 9 mos, 22 days GAR: 4/23/1927 on transfer from George H. Thomas Post #17 Dept of Indiana Died: 2/25/1929 A: 82 Obit: Lists wife Anna Haughn S: DC
Hayward, R.E.	N: Clarksville, MO A: 40 O: Engineer R: National City, CA CW: Co D 4 Iowa ___ (Pvt) E/D: 5/61-6/62 gunshot wound, left shoulder, Pea Ridge LOS: 13 mos GAR: 8/10/1882 SP: 3/22/1883 DR: 12/24/1918 S: H
Healey, Michael	N: Ireland A: Not stated O: Merchant CW: Co D 10 NY Art (Pvt) E/D: 9/62-6/65 LOS: 33 mos GAR: 4/14/1887 D: 10/27/1887 Died: "Dead", no date--no [grave] stone S: H
Heath, James/John W.	N: New York A: 76 O: Retired R: National City, CA CW: Co E 10 Minn Inf (Pvt/Capt) E/D: 8/62-3/64 due to disability LOS: 19 mos GAR: 1884 Died: 4/13/1902--is [grave] stone S: H
Hebbard, A.W.	N: Maine A: 56 O: Station Agent R: Fallbrook, CA CW: Co E 28 Wis Inf (1st Sgt/2nd Lieut) E/D: 8/62-8/65 LOS: 3 yrs GAR: 1/28/1886 SP: 1/28/1892 RE: 6/26/1894 D: 12/22/1896 S: H
Hefflin, William H.	N: Canada A: 71 O: Farmer CW: Co D 95 Ill Inf (Pvt/Sgt) E/D: 8/62-8/65 LOS: Not stated GAR: 1/27/1914 SP: 12/27/1921 S: H
Hege, Jacob	NOL/NFI S: DC
Helms, Ruben E.	N: Monmouth, Illinois CW: Co E 40 Wis Vol Inf (Pvt) Term: 100 days E/D: 6/64-9/64 Madison, Wis GAR: 11/28/1914 on transfer from Riverside Post #118 Died: 5/13/1916 at 68/8/__ S: DC
Helms, Reuben	N: Illinois A: 60 O: Publisher CW: Co D 40 Wis Inf (Pvt) E/D: __/64-9/64 LOS: Not stated GAR: 3/24/1908 SP: 6/28/1910 Died: 5/13/1916 S: H
Helpinstine, J.A.	NOL/NFI S: DC
Henderson, Eliel F.	N: Fayette Co, PA CW: Co ___ 101 Ill Inf (Asst.Surgeon) Term: 3 yrs E/D: 2/62-7/65 GAR: 5/8/1909 S: DC
Herffendirfer, Jacob	N: Penn A: 68 O: Shoe Maker CW: Co B 203 PA Inf (Pvt) E/D: 6/64-9/64 LOS: Not stated GAR: 1/12/1915 SP: 12/28/1920 S: H
Herriman, Albert	N: Illinois A: 81 O: Retired CW: Co D 41 Ohio Inf (Pvt) E/D: 9/61-11/65 LOS: 4 yrs GAR: 11/27/1923 SP: 6/23/1925 S: H
Herrington, Beverly A.	N: New York A: 63 O: Farmer CW: Co H 10 Iowa Inf (Pvt) E/D: 8/61-4/62 due to disability LOS: 8 mos Re-Enl?: Co D 24 Iowa Inf (Pvt) E/D: 12/63-7/65 LOS: Not stated GAR: 3/14/1899 Died: 9/27/1903 Soldier's Home S: H
	SAWTELLE: Died 9/26/1903 at Soldier's Home, Sawtelle, CA Bur: "Branch USA", Sec.4, Row D, Grave 7 with tombstone inscription "B.A. Herrington Co H 10 IA Inf" S: Los Angeles National Cemetery
Heustis, Thomas B.	N: Indiana A: 61 O: Drummer CW: Co K 12 Kas Inf (Pvt/Drummer) E/D: 11/62-6/65 LOS: 32 mos GAR: 7/11/1905 RE?: 8/11/1914 Died: 6/28/1926 S: H
Hickox, L.M.	N: Michigan A: 40 O: Carpenter CW: Co H 50 Ohio Inf (Pvt) E/D: 8/62-6/65 LOS: 34 mos GAR: 12/25/1887 SP: 9/26/1889 DR: 6/30/1891 S: H

Higbee, George	N: Ohio CW: Co B 7 OVI (Pvt) Term: 1 yr E/D: 2/65-7/65 GAR: 12/14/1907 Died: "Dropped dead" S: DC
Higgens, M.L.	N: Ohio A: 63 O: Agent CW: Co H 118 Ohio Inf (1st Lieut) E/D: 9/62-3/63 due to sickness LOS: 7 mos GAR: 10/22/1890 DR: 3/23/1892 S: H
Higgins, William	N: Ireland A: 50 O: Mechanic CW: Co B 5 US Inf (Pvt/Corpl Ordinance) E/D: 12/62-4/66 LOS: 40 mos GAR: 1/6/1885 SP: 3/28/1889 DR: 6/30/1891 S: H
Hill, Ambrose	NOL/NFI S: DC
Hill, Charles H.	N: Penn A: 42 O: Merchant CW: Co H 23 Ill Inf (Pvt) E/D: 2/65-7/65 LOS: 4 1/2 mos GAR: 7/26/1888 DR: 3/28/1899 S: H
Hill, Edwin L.	N: Ohio A: 83 O: Minister R: National City, CA CW: Co A 4 Iowa Inf (Pvt/1st Lieut) E/D: 7/61-8/65 LOS: 4 yrs GAR: 8/23/1921 D: 12/9/1922 S: H
Hill, John	N: Canada A: 65 O: Cooper CW: Co H 2 Ill Cav (Sgt) E/D: 8/61-8/64 LOS: 36 mos GAR: 3/14/1893 TR: 8/14/1894 S: H
Hills, Ralph H.	N: Buller Co, Ohio 1845 CW: Co E 145 Ohio Inf (Pvt) Term: 100 days E/D: 5/64-9/64 GAR: 9/9/1922 on transfer from El Paso, TX Died: 2/4/1924 S: DC
Hilsher, Harmon	N: New York A: 87 O: Retired CW: Co A 13 Ind Cav (Pvt) E/D: 7/64-11/65 LOS: 1 yr 10 mos GAR: 2/14/1933 Died: 1/3/1937 (Second to last veteran to join Heintzelman Post GAR Last veteran to join was Andrew L. Reid) S: H
Hilscher, Herman	N: New York City CW: Co H 26 PA Reserves (Pvt) Term: 3 mos E/D: 6/63-7/63 when Lee retreated from the State of Pennsylvania Re-Enl: Co E 16 Ind Mtd Inf (Pvt) E/D: 11/64-11/65 Indianapolis, Ind GAR: ? date on transfer from Hulbert Post #177 Dept of Cal/Nev S: DC
Hinchcliff, E.D.	NOL/NFI S: DC
Hinckley, Oscar S.	N: Mass A: 68 O: Engineer CW: Co D 127 Ill Inf (Pvt) E/D: 6/62-5/65 or 8/62-5/65 LOS: 33 mos GAR: 9/22 or 10/22/1907 TR: 12/26/1911 TR Returned: 9/10/1916 SP: 12/28/1920 S:H
Hipwell, Richard J.	N: Illinois A: 48 O: Salesman CW: Co I 17 Ill Cav (Pvt); Promoted?: Co I 29 U S C T (Lieut) E/D: 1/64-11/65 LOS: 21 mos GAR: 5/13/1891 SP: 12/27/1898 RE: 4/10/1900 SP: 6/28/1910 SP: 12/26/1916 DR: 12/24/1918 S: H
Hixon, D.W.	N: Lowell, IA 1845 CW: Co C 30th Iowa Inf (Pvt) Term: 3 yrs E/D: 8/62-12/63 or 12/62-12/63 Keokuck, IA due to gun shot wounds GAR: 6/26/1920 on transfer from Stanton Post #33 Dept of Iowa TR: 10/12/1929 S: DC
Hixon, George W.	N: Ohio CW: Co I 8 IA Cav (Pvt/Corpl) Term: 3 yrs E/D: 8/62-8/65 GAR: 6/23/1917 on transfer from Frank Thomas Post #94 Dept of Iowa S: DC
Hobingnist, C.A.	N: Sweden A: 79 O: Milkman CW: Co I 16 Mich Inf (Pvt) E/D: 3/65-7/65 LOS: Not stated GAR: 8/25/1914 (probably on transfer from Oliver O. Howard Post #7 Dept of Utah) SP: 6/23/1925 S: H
Hodge, William C.	N: New York A: 71 O: Lecturer CW: Co I 22 Wis Inf (Pvt/Corpl) E/D: 8/62-5/65 LOS: 34 mos GAR: 1/11/1907 D: 9/28/1915 S: H

Hodges, George W.	N: Logan's Port, Indiana CW: Co C 155 Ind Inf (Pvt) Term: Unstated E/D: 3/65-7/65 due to disability GAR: 9/11/1926 S: DC
Hodgkins, Emery	N: Gloucester, Mass 1834 CW: Co B 29 Mass Inf (Pvt/Sgt) Term: 3 yrs E/D: 6/61-6/65 GAR: 5/12/1917 on transfer from Col. Allen Post #45 Dept of Mass Died: 5/24/1925 A: 89/2/__ Seattle, Washington S: DC
Hoffman, John S.	N: Virginia A: 68 O: Engineer CW: Co I 5 Ind Cav (Pvt/Corpl) E/D: 8/62-6/65 LOS: Not stated GAR: 1/8/1901 SP: 6/28/1910 RE: 6/27/1911 TR: 6/27/1911 S: H
Hoffman, W.E.	N: Ohio A: 58 O: Retired Off. CW: Co B 98 Ill Inf (Pvt/Capt) E/D: 7/62-7/65 LOS: 36 mos GAR: 11/26/1895 TR: 7/27/1897 S: H
Hogarty, M.J.	N: Ireland 4/19/35 CW: Co I 141 NY Inf (Pvt) Term: 3 yrs E/D: 8/63-9/64 Re-Enl: Same company (Pvt/1st Lieut) E/D: 9/__-6/65 GAR: 4/24/1920 on transfer from Greeley U.S. Grant Post #13 Dept of Colorado Died: 11/21/1925 S: DC
Hogeland, A.W.	N: New York CW: Co I 47 Ill Inf (Pvt/Corpl) Term: 1 yr E/D: 3/65-2/66 Springfield, Ill GAR: 3/23/1901 on transfer from Lookout Mountain Post #94 Dept of Illinois Buried: Mount Hope S: DC Note: No record of burial for A.W. Hogeland at Mount Hope Cemetery.
Holabird, W.H.	N: Vermont A: 43 O: Real Estate Agt CW: Co C 12 VT Inf (Pvt) E/D: 8/62-3/63 LOS: 10 3/4 mos GAR: 2/9/1888 TR: "Transfer" S: H
Holcomb, B.	N: Granby, Conn A: 37 O: Farmer R: Valley Center, CA CW: Co L 1 Conn Arty (Pvt) E/D: 7/63-9/65 LOS: 25 mos GAR: 5/22/1884 D: 11/24/1887 S: H
Holderness, William H.	N: Adams Co, Ohio R: Chula Vista, CA CW: Co K 8 Ill Inf (Pvt) Term: 3 yrs E/D: 8/61-8/64 GAR: 8/24/1901 on transfer from Republic Post Dept of Kansas Died: 6/12/1926 "The Post did not officiate at the funeral" Obit: Died 6/12/1926 A: 82/3/2. Wife Leona B. Holderness; 5 children, who lived in Mexico, La Grange, Ill, Oneota and Hanford, CA and Portland, Oregon Buried: Glen Abbey Memorial Park, Chula Vista, CA (near San Diego) S: DC
	Note: Glen Abbey tombstone listing reads: "Father William H. Holderness 1884-1926" (From Glen Abbey tombstone inscription book at Family History Center--see Chapter 2 for citation. His is the only Holderness name listed in the index for this cemetery.)
	Note: William H. Holderness was born in Adams County, OH on February 10, 1844, and moved to McLean County, IL at age 11. After the war, he worked in publishing in New York City; taught and farmed in McLean County, and came to California in 1886. He married Leona B. Vance, native of Illinois, in 1873. He was a pioneer in the Tijuana Valley, eventually placing 4,000 acres of alfalfa and vegetables under cultivation. (from *San Diego County, California: A Record of Settlement*, etc.)
Holmes, Augustus	N: Georgia A: 77 O: Retired CW: Co D 10 Tenn Cav (Pvt) E/D: 12/63-8/65 LOS: 2 yrs GAR: 9/12/1922 SP: 12/23/1924 DR: 6/23/1925 S: H
Holsinger, S.K.	N: Tennessee A: 57 O: Minister CW: Co D 13 East Tenn Cav (Pvt) Re-Enl?: Co D 1 East Tenn Cav (Pvt) E/D: 8/62-6/63 due to disability LOS: 10 mos GAR: 5/26/1896 TR: 5/__/1897 S: H
Holt, D.H.	N: Maine A: 48 O: Carpenter CW: Co H 6 Cal Inf (Sgt) E/D: 3/63-2/65 LOS: 35 mos GAR: 4/26/1888 SP: 9/26/1889 DR: 6/30/1891 S: H
Holtz, Fred	NOL/NFI S: DC

Holverson, Thomas	N: Wisconsin A: 59 O: Merchant CW: Co D 43 Wis Inf (Pvt) E/D: 6/64-6/65 LOS: 12 mos GAR: 7/25/1905 TR: 9/14/1909 GAR: 2/13/1918 TR: "Transferred" ("Tostine Holverson") S: H
Hooker, J.B.	N: Brooklyn, NY A: 42 O: Printer CW: Co K 2 Minn ___ (Pvt) E/D: 9/61-3/62 due to hernia LOS: 6 mos GAR: 7/27/1882 SP: 1/10/1889 DR: 6/30/1891 S:H
Hopkins/Hoskins, Ira K.	N: Vicksburg, Miss CW: Co D 11 Ill Cav (Pvt) Term: 3 yrs E/D: 11/61-11/65 Memphis, TN due to disability GAR: 3/24/1900 GAR: 10/25/1902 on transfer from Stanton Post #55 Dept of Cal/Nev DR: 12/9/1916 for nonpayment of dues S: DC
Hopkins, Jerome	N: Iowa CW: Co C 57 Ill Inf (Drummer) Term: 3 yrs E/D: 10/61-7/62 Corinth, Miss due to disability Re-Enl: Co I 113 Ill Inf (Drummer/Principal Mus'n) E/D: 10/62-6/65 GAR: 3/10/1900 on transfer from Geo. H. Mead Post #144 Dept of Illinois S: DC
Hopkins, L.C.	N: Indiana A: 77 O: Retired CW: Co I 12 MO Cav (Pvt) E/D: 3/64-4/66 LOS: 2 yrs GAR: 12/11/1923 Died: 8/25/1924 S: H
Horder, George W.	N: England A: 52 O: Tinsmith CW: Co H 31 Wis Inf (Musician) E/D: 1/62-6/65 LOS: 41 mos GAR: 12/27 or 12/28/1888 SP: 9/26/1889 DR: 6/30/1891 RE: 5/11/1897 SP: 12/24/1901 DR: 1/22/1907 S: H
Horrele, W.H.	N: Davis Co, Indiana A: 36 O: Farmer CW: Co B 27 Ind Inf (Pvt) E/D: 8/61-9/64 LOS: 3 yrs GAR: 10/8/1881 Charter Member of Heintzelman Post DR: "Dropped" S: H
Horst, Henry F.	N: Ohio A: 51 O: Shoemaker CW: Co A 16 Ind Inf (Pvt) E/D: __/61-5/62 LOS: 12 mos GAR: 12/23/1891 SP: 9/22/1896 DR: 10/25/1904 S: H
Howell, Frank	N: Ohio A: 74 O: Retired CW: Co K 1 Ohio V H A (Pvt) E/D: __/63-__/__ LOS: Not stated GAR: 8/26/1919 SP: 6/23/1925 S: H
Hubbard, Martin	N: Indiana A: 74 O: Retired CW: Co L 7 Ind Cav (Pvt) E/D: 9/63-2/66 LOS: 2 yrs GAR: 6/12/1923 Died: 8/16/1925 S: H
Hubbs, Charles L.	N: New York A: 56 O: Custom Inspector CW: Co F 1 Minn Inf (Pvt) E/D: 5/61-5/64 Re-Enl?: Co A 9 US V Vol (Pvt) E/D: 3/65-3/66 LOS: 36 mos? GAR: 11/28/1899 Died: 4/13/1931 Post Commander 1903 S: H
Hudson, John	N: Maryland A: 45 O: Painter CW: Co A 54 Ark Inf (Pvt) E/D: 5/63-2/65 due to disability LOS: 21mos GAR: 2/24/1892 SP: 6/26/1894 RE: 12/24/1894 SP: 12/24/1912 Died: 1/18/1918 (accidentally killed) S: H
Hughes, James	N: England CW: U.S.S. Florida/Colorado/Lafayette (Ord.Seaman/Seaman) Term: 3 yrs E/D: 9/61-10/64 Cairo, Ill GAR: 1912 on transfer from Fred Winthrop Post Dept of Montana SP: "Suspended" S: DC
Hulburd(t), Eben.W.	N: Vermont A: 68 O: Rancher R: San Diego/Descanso, CA CW: Co I 60 Ill Inf (Pvt/2 Lieut) E/D: 9/61-7/62 due to disability LOS: 9 mos GAR: 3/10/1896 Died: 4/23/1916 S:H First name "Ebenezer"
Hulburt, R.G.	N: Missouri A: 39 O: Physician CW: Co C 12 MO Cav (Pvt) E/D: 3/64-6/65 due to disability LOS: 15 mos GAR: 4/24/1888 SP: 3/28/1889 DR: 6/30/1891 S: H
Hunt, Cephas B.	N: Mass A: 69 O: Farmer CW: Co I 112 Ill Inf (Pvt/Sgt) E/D: 8/62-6/65 LOS: Not stated GAR: 11/12/1912 on transfer from Homer C. Jones Post #43 Dept of Oklahoma D: 1/22/1917 TR: 1/23/1917 Past Post Commander S: H

Huntington, C.	N: Chatauqua, NY A: 36 O: Clerk CW: Co H 16 NY ___ (Pvt/Sgt) E/D: 9/61-10/65 wound in left thigh and side; also in neck LOS: 3 yrs GAR: 10/8/1881 Charter Member/1st Officer of the Day for Heintzelman Post SP: 1/10/1889 DR: 6/30/1891 S: H
Huntley, Matthew	N: Trawbridge, England CW: Co A 2 Mass Inf (Pvt/Corpl) E/D: 5/61-3/64 due to Certificate of Disability LOS: See prior record GAR: 5/26/1900 on transfer from Garfield Post #85 Dept of Massachusetts Died: 8/16/1906 Buried: Massachusetts S: H
Huntley, Matthew	N: Trawbridge, England CA: Co A 2 Mass Inf (Pvt/Corpl) Term: 3 yrs E/D: 5/61-3/64 York, PA due to Surgeon's Certificate of Disability GAR: 5/26/1900 on transfer from Garfield Post #85 Dept of Mass Died: 8/16/1906 A: 68 Buried: Massachusetts S: DC
Hurd, Lavinus S.	N: Michigan A: 65 O: Farmer CW: Co C 11 Wis Inf (Pvt/Sgt) E/D: 10/61-9/65 LOS: 38 mos GAR: 2/12/1907 Died: 9/8/1925 S: H
Hurd, Warren H.	N: New Hampshire A: 70 O: Retired R: Coronado, CA CW: Co A 2 NH Inf (Pvt); Promoted? Co B 23 or 28 U S C T (Capt) E/D: 4/61-12/65 LOS: Not stated GAR: 5/27/1913 Died: 12/4/1913 at Witchita, Kansas S: H
Hutchison, William N.	N: Virginia A: 66 O: Book Keeper CW: Co E 1 RI L A (Pvt/Sgt Major) E/D: 8/63-6/65 LOS: Not stated GAR: 5/13/1908 Died: 1/18/1913 S: H
Hutt, George W.	N: New York City 8/6/37 CW: Co K 1st Kans Inf (Pvt/1st Lieut) Term: 3 yrs E/D: 6/61-7/64 Re-Enl: Co E 17 Kans Inf (1st Sergt) E/D: 9/64-11/65 GAR: 11/25/1911 on transfer from Haughey Post #491 Dept of Kansas Died: 9/13/1923 S: DC
Iodine, Chief	N: Oswego, NY 1828/9 (Iroquois Tribe) CW: US Navy S.S. Galena (Seaman) Term: 3 yrs E/D: 1/62-2/65 Philadelphia, PA Re-Enl: 2/65-5/68 Boston, Mass GAR: 10/22/1904 on transfer from Memorial Post #141 Dept of Ohio Died: 1/1/1918 at Soldier's Home OBIT: Went to reservation school until age 15; ran away and joined Clark and Fremont on their trip to the Coast; also with Kit Carson in Arizona. Served as government scout; acquainted with Sitting Bull; Chief Rain-in-the-Face and many other famous Chiefs; at Battle of Wounded Knee; acquainted with Custer. S: DC
	SAWTELLE: Records for this veteran were not found at Los Angeles National Cemetery, the Sawtelle Index, the California Death Index, or the County of San Diego.
Jackson, Herman	N: Illinois A: 77 O: Lawyer CW: Co E 2nd Wis Inf (2nd Lieut); Re-Enl?: Co G 2nd Wis Inf (2nd Lieut) E/D: 4/61-9/61 due to disability LOS: Not stated GAR: 1/12/1915 on transfer from Oshkosh Post #10 Dept of Wisconsin Died: 4/26/1924 S: H
Jackson, J.M.	N: Penn A: 63 O: Miner R: Julian, CA CW: US Navy--Monitor (Ensign) E/D: 1/65-4/67 LOS: 26 mos GAR: 10/28/1886 SP: 1/10/1889 D: 9/8/1896 RE: 2/10/1898 S: H
Jackson, Mason	N: Johnsonville, Ohio A: 72 O: Engineer CW: Co C 26 Iowa Inf (Pvt/Corpl) E/D: 8/62-6/65 LOS: 34 mos GAR: 4/24/1917 on transfer from Santa Monica Post #191 Dept of Cal/Nev SP: 12/28/1920 S: H
Jacobs, John W.	N: West Virginia A: 63 O: Contractor CW: Co C or Co G 1 W VA Inf (Pvt) E/D: 5/61-9/61 Re-enl: Co C 1 W VA Art (Pvt/1st Lieut) E/D: 3/62-6/65 LOS: 43 mos GAR: 6/27/1905 SP: 3/26/1907 DR: 12/24/1918 S: H
Jacobs, L.C.	N: New York A: 42 O: Farmer R: Valley Center, CA CW: Co B 36 Wis Inf (Pvt/2nd Lieut) E/D: 2/64-7/65 LOS: 17 mos GAR: 9/22/1884 SP: 1/10/1889 DR: 6/30/1891 RE: 6/26/1894 D: 7/26/1894 S: H

Jacoby, Henry M.	N: Illinois A: 73 O: Retired CW: Co G 42 MO Inf (Pvt/Sgt/Major) E/D: 8/64-6/65 LOS: 10 mos GAR: 1/13/1920 Died: 3/16/1924 S: H
Jaggers, Thomas	N: Illinois 1842 CW: Co D 8 Ill Inf (Pvt) Term: 3 yrs E/D: 4/61-4/64? Vicksburg, Miss Re-Enl: Co A 59 Ill Inf (Pvt) E/D: __/64-10/65 New Brunswick GAR: 8/9/1924 Died: 9/24/1927 S: DC
James, Frank	NOL/NFI S: DC
James, Francis	N: Canada A: 43 O: Carpenter CW: Co A 135 Ind Inf (Pvt) E/D: 5/64-9/64 LOS: 4 mos GAR: ? date RE: 11/12/1894 TR: 11/12/1894 S: H
James, William F.C.	N: Ohio A: 35 O: Farmer R: Bear Valley, CA CW: Co E 63 Ohio ___ (Sgt) E/D: 7/61-7/65 LOS: 4 yrs GAR: 5/28/1885 D: __/12/1888 S: H
Jenkins, Robert J.	N: Ireland A: 83 O: Retired CW: Co E 64 NY Inf (Pvt) E/D: 1/65-5/65 due to wounds LOS: Not stated GAR: 11/8/1927 SP: "Sus" S: H
Jenney, Royal A.	N: Michigan A: 77 O: Retired CW: Co D 22 Mich Inf (Pvt) E/D: 3/65-9/65 LOS: 6 mos GAR: 3/14/1922 Died: 1935 S: H
Jerman, Thomas	N: Norway A: 54 O: Druggist R: Ramona, CA CW: Co B 17 Wis Inf (Pvt) E/D: 10/64-7/65 LOS: 36 mos? GAR: 8/28/1900 S: H
Jobes, Charles Colic	N: Ohio A: 51 O: Nurseryman CW: Co E 1 Iowa Cav (Pvt) E/D: 8/62-8/65 LOS: 36 mos GAR: 4/26 or 4/28/1888 SP: 9/26/1889 RE: 3/12 or 12/12/1895 Died: 11/9/1906 Buried: Escondido, CA--is [grave] stone S: H
Johns, James B.	N: Ohio A: 73 O: Farmer CW: Co G 43 Ind Inf (Pvt/Sgt) E/D: 10/64-6/65 LOS: 9 mos GAR: 2/13/1918 TR: 10/28/1924 S: H
Johnson, Curtis	N: St Albans, Vermont A: 47 O: Farmer CW: Co E 6 Kans ___ (Pvt); Promoted? Co E 15 Kans ___ (Capt) E/D: __/61-11/65 LOS: 4 yrs GAR: 10/8/1881 Charter Member Heintzelman Post SP: 12/28/1882 DR: 12/24/1918 S: H
Johnson, Edward	N: Mass A: 86 O: Retired CW: Co F 17 Ill Inf (Pvt) E/D: 5/61-6/64 LOS: 3 yrs GAR: 10/23/1923 TR: 4/22/1925 S: H
Johnson, Edward	N: Ohio A: 62 O: Retired CW: Co C 4 Ohio Cav (Pvt/Sgt) E/D: 8/62-10/64 LOS: 24 mos GAR: 3/5/1898 SP: 12/27/1898 SP: 6/26/1900 DR: 1/22/1907 S: H
Johnson, J.J.	N: New Hampshire A: 57 O: Farmer R: Otay (near San Diego) CW: Co I 13 NH Inf (Pvt) E/D: 1/63-6/65 LOS: 29 mos GAR: 10/14/1891 Died: 5/22/1894--is -[grave] stone S: H
Johnson, James A.	N: Indiana A: 77 O: Retired CW: Co H 4 Minn Inf (Pvt) E/D: 12/64-7/65 LOS: 8 mos GAR: 11/14/1922 Died: 8/12/1926 S: H
Johnson, John W.	N: Penn A: 73 O: Photographer CW: Co D 2 Ohio Cav (Pvt) E/D: 4/61-5/62 Promoted? Co E 12 Ohio Cav (Lieut/Capt) E/D: 8/63-11/63 LOS: 27 mos GAR: 12/13/1898 TR: 12/26/1899 S: H
Johnson, William H.	N: New York A: 65 O: Painter CW: Ship "Colorado"? (1st Class Apprentice/Ordinary Seaman) E/D: 8/64-10/67 LOS: Not stated GAR: 11/14/1911 Died: 11/19/1920 S: H
Johnston, John	N: Sweden A: 71 O: Janitor CW: Co D 9 Ill Cav (Pvt/Sgt) E/D: 12/61-10/65 LOS: Not stated GAR: 5/28/1912 Died: 12/30/1927 S: H

Jones, Albert	N: Penn A: 65 O: Miner CW: Co C 8 PA Cav (Pvt) E/D: 2/65-11/65 LOS: Not stated GAR: 1/23/1912 TR: 11/28/1922 S: H
Jones, Alfred	N: Penn A: 40 O: Not stated CW: Co E 16 PA Cav (Pvt) E/D: 2/65-8/65 LOS: 5 2/3 mos GAR: 11/24/1887 SP: 6/10/1889 DR: 6/30/1891 S: H
Jones, Charles P.	N: Bangor, Maine 10/__/28 CW: Co D 5 Wis Inf (Pvt) Term: 3 yrs E/D: 5/61-11/63 due to Surgeon's Certificate of Disability GAR: 7/13/1912 Died: 7/14/1914 A: 84 Buried: Ashland, Oregon beside his wife "Comrade Jones was stole by the Indians when he was 5 months old and remained with them until he was 15 years old" S: DC
Jones, J.O.	N: Maine A: 43 O: Miner CW: Co K 2 ME Cav (Pvt) E/D: 3/64-12/65 LOS: 21 mos GAR: 10/13/1887 SP: 3/28/1889 DR: 6/30/1891 S: H
Jones, Levi J.	N: New York A: 79 O: Retired CW: Co A 179 NY Inf (Pvt) E/D: 2/64-6/65 LOS: 1 yr GAR: 1/22/1924 TR: 10/28/1924 S: H
Judd, Alex	N: ? location 1843 CW: Co G 2 MO Cav (Pvt) Term: 3 yrs E/D: 10/61-9/65 GAR: No further information S: DC
Juvenal, Josiah	N: Illinois A: 57 O: Farmer CW: Co K 150 Ill Inf (Pvt) E/D: 2/65-1/66 LOS: 11 or 13 mos due to disability GAR: 4/7/1891 or 12/13/1898 TR: 9/27/1904 Died: 4/2/1905 Soldier's Home S: H
	SAWTELLE: Records for this veteran were not found at Los Angeles National Cemetery, the Sawtelle Index, the California Death Index, or the County of San Diego.
Kautz, George	N: Ohio A: 63 O: Farmer CA: Co B 140 Ohio Inf (Pvt) E/D: 5/63-9/63 LOS: 4 mos GAR: 4/9/1907 (probably on transfer from Reno Post #49 Dept of Colo/Wyo Died: 10/7/1923 S: H
Kay, Thomas	N: England 7/20/183__ CW: Co F 29 PA Inf (Pvt) Term: 3 yrs E/D: 7/61-7/64 Philadelphia, PA GAR: 9/11/1915 on transfer from Dan Bidwell Post #140 Dept of Cal/Nev Died: 5/4/1923, Stockton (CA?) S: DC
Keacht, Frederick	N: Germany 8/18/45 CW: Co F 5th MO Cav (Pvt) Term: 3 yrs (Co F was consolidated with Co H, then Co D) E/D: 8/62-6/65 Rexburg, Miss GAR: 9/8/1923 on transfer from Turlock Post #197 Dept of Cal/Nev DR: 9/24/1927 RE: 4/14/1928 TR: 4/28/1928 S: DC
Keeler, Ezra	N: Michigan A: 82 O: Retired CW: Co B 22 Mich Inf (Pvt/Sgt) E/D: 8/62-6/65 LOS: 3 yrs GAR: 8/8/1922 Died: 8/12/1924 S: H
Keeney, C.W.	N: Conn A: 50 O: Farmer CW: Co H 16 Conn Inf (Pvt) E/D: 8/62-6/65 LOS: 34 1/2 mos GAR: 8/25/1887 SP: 6/30/1888 DR: 6/30/1891 S: H
Kehoe, William	N: Nova Scotia A: 51 O: Miner CW: Co H 1 Mass Cav (Pvt) E/D: 9/61-10/64 LOS: 3 yrs GAR: 2/25/1886 SP: 9/26/1893 DR: 3/28/1899 S: H
Kellend, Robert	N: England A: 78 O: Retired CW: Co K 34 Mass Inf (Pvt) E/D: 7/62-7/65 LOS: 3 yrs GAR: 10/8/1921 Died: 12/2/1934 S: H
Kellend, Robert	N: England 11/13/43 CW: Co K 34 Mass Inf (Pvt) Term: 3 yrs E/D: 8/62-7/65 Trenton, NJ GAR: 5/18/1918 on transfer from A.J. Smith Post #26 Dept of Oregon TR: 5/22/1920 S: DC

Kennedy, Charles	N: Penn A: 79 O: Retired CW: Co C 14 Kans Cav (Pvt) E/D: 7/64-9/65 LOS: Not stated GAR: 7/26/1927 Died: 2/15/1942 S: H
Kepler, Peter L.	N: Penn A: 77 O: Retired CW: Co I 150 PA Inf (Pvt) E/D: 8/62-6/65 LOS: 2 yrs 8 mos GAR: 11/22/1921 Died: 11/23/1922 S: H
Key, Joseph F.	N: Virginia Grove, IA CW: Co K 2 Iowa Cav (Mus'n) Term: 3 yrs E/D: 8/61-11/64 GAR: 6/26/1920 on transfer from McDonough Post Dept of Illinois Died: 6/26/1923 A: 79 S: DC
Keyes, Hiram	N: Not stated A: Not stated O: Farmer CW: Co K 11 Kans Inf (Pvt) E/D: 9/62-__/65 LOS: 36 mos GAR: 12/9/1886 SP: 1/10/1889 DR: 6/30/1891 S: H
Kilrain, John G.	N: Canada 6/13/43 CW: Co B 26 Iowa Inf (Pvt) Term: 3 yrs E/D: 8/62-6/65 GAR: 1/23/1915 on transfer from Farragut Thomas Post #84 Dept of MO Died: 3/1/1925 S: DC
Kincaid, Orlando D.	N: Elk Co, PA A: 42 O: Miner CW: Co E 1 Iowa Cav (Pvt/Sgt) E/D: 7/61-2/66 LOS: 4 yrs GAR: 11/10/1881 D: 12/28/1882 S: H
King, Burley W.	N: New York A: 71 O: Store Keeper CW: Co B 2 Cal Cav (Pvt) E/D: 9/61-10/64 LOS: Not stated GAR: 2/22/1916 on transfer from Warren Post #54 or #59 Dept of Cal/Nev Died: 9/28/1924 S: H
King, George V.	N: New York A: 37 O: Miner CW: Co G 13 NY ___ (Pvt) E/D: 11/63-6/65 LOS: 18 mos GAR: 6/22/1882 DR: 10/25/1904 Died: "Dead"--no [grave] stone S: H
King, John D.	N: Ohio A: 69 O: Lawyer CW: Co A 33 Ill Inf (Pvt) E/D: 8/61-10/64 LOS: Not stated GAR: 3/24/1908 (probably on transfer from Casey Post #5 Dept of Nebraska) Died: 1/25/1911 S: H
Kinne, Orlando W.	N: New York A: 74 O: Woodworker CW: Co G 14 NY Inf (Pvt) E/D: 5/61-5/63 LOS: Not stated GAR: 7/22/1913 (probably on transfer from Washington Post #85 Dept of Wash/Wyo SP: 12/31/1928 Past Post Commander S: H
Kinsly, Samuel	N: Ohio A: 73 O: Retired R: Encanto (near San Diego) CW: Co F 10 MO? Inf (Pvt) E/D: 8/61-2/63 due to disability LOS: Not stated GAR: 3/23/1915 Died: 1/27/1925 S: H
Klaus, Carl	N: Switzerland 1841 CW: Co B __ Wis ___ (Pvt) Term: 3 yrs E/D: 8/62-8/65 Brownsville, TX GAR: 8/12/1920 on transfer from Miller Post #3 or #31 Dept of Wash/Alaska Died: 10/12/1925 in Washington State A: 84 S: DC
Knott, Peter	NOL/NFI S: DC
Knowles, John	N: Michigan A: 39 O: Insurance CW: Co K 1 Mich Cav (Trumpeter/QM Sgt) E/D: 11/63-7/65 LOS: 20 mos GAR: 11/21/1885 D: 12/23/1886 S: H
Koehler, Edward	N: Franklin Co, Ohio 6/29/36 CW: Co K 79 OVI (Pvt) Term: 3 yrs E/D: 8/62-5/65 due to disability GAR: 6/28/1919 Died: 1/9/1923 A: 86/7/10 S: DC
Kohuly, John	N: Germany 1847 CW: Co K 9 Ohio Cav (Pvt) Term: 3 yrs E/D: 10/63-7/65 Camp Chase, Ohio GAR: 8/14/1920 on transfer from J. B. McClelland Post Dept of Colorado S: DC
Kronskop, George W.	N: Belfontaine, Ohio 1841 CW: Co L 2 Ohio HA (Pvt) Term: 3 yrs E/D: 8/63-8/65 Nashville, TN GAR: 10/23/1920 on transfer from W. R. Cronman Post #57 Dept of Cal/Nev Died 8/15/1925 S: DC

Kruger, Julius G.	N: Germany 7/25/42 CW: Co I 24 Ill Inf (Pvt) Term: 3 yrs E/D: 7/61-8/64 Chicago, Ill LOS: 3 yrs GAR: 10/10/1914 on transfer from Nathaniel Lyon Post #6 Dept of Colo Died: 3/19/1916 A: 73/7/__ Buried: Boulder, CO S: DC
Kuhns, W.P.	NOL/NFI S: DC
Kurtz, Albert A.	NOL/NFI S: DC
Kurtz, Albert A.	N: Ohio A: 70 O: Retired CW: Co K 143 Ill Inf (Pvt) E/D: 5/64-9/64 Re-Enl?: Co F 149 Ill Inf (Drummer) E/D: 1/65-1/66 LOS: 16 mos GAR: 6/12/1917 (probably dropped from Post #172 Dept of Cal/Nev) Died: 10/7/1923 S:H
Kuttnauer, Isador	N: France 1842 CW: Co B 2 MO LA (Pvt) Term: 3 yrs E/D: 8/63-12/66 St Louis, MO GAR: 11/14/1925 S: DC
Lakin, Cyrus B.	N: Columbus, Ohio 2/6/49 CW: Co C 90 Ohio Inf (Musician) Term: 3 yrs E/D: 1/64-10/65 Victoria, TX GAR: 8/25/1923 on transfer from John A. Martin Post Dept of Cal/Nev Died 4/14/1927; buried at Inglewood Cemetery, Los Angeles area Obit: Age at death 78/1/27. Lists 2 children in Los Angeles, one in Vacaville, CA and one in La Mesa, CA (near San Diego); no wife mentioned in obit S: DC
Lamb, Morris H.	N: Madison Co, Ohio CW: Co F 11 Minn Inf (Pvt/Corpl) Term: 1 yr E/D: 8/64-6/65 Gallatin, TN GAR: 11/27/1896 on transfer from M.L. Deveraugh Post #43 Dept of Minnesota Died 11/18/1911 A: 74 Buried GAR Cemetery (Mount Hope) S: DC Death certificate indicates this veteran was buried in Los Angeles, CA (no cemetery noted)
Lamme, Edwin H.	N: Ohio A: 65 O: Lawyer CW: Co I 110 Ohio Inf (Pvt) E/D: 6/62-5/65 LOS: Not stated GAR: 5/23/1911 SP: 12/26/1916 Died: 4/1/1920 S: H
Lane, Ansel S.	N: Old Town, Maine A: 76 O: Real Estate R: Pacific Beach area of San Diego CW: Co B 6 Minn Inf (Pvt) E/D: 8/62-8/65 LOS: 36 mos GAR: 11/27/1917 Died: 10/18/1927 at Sawtelle S: H SAWTELLE: Died 10/18/1927 at Soldier's Home and buried in "Branch USA", Sec.52, Row E, Grave 16 with tombstone inscription "Ansel S. Lane, Co B 6 Minn Inf" S: Los Angeles National Cemetery
Lane, M.W.	N: Indiana A: 77 O: Retired CW: Co E 1 Ind H A (Pvt) E/D: 3/64-1/66 LOS: 1 yr 9 mos GAR: 8/10/1920 TR: 3/16/1925 S: H
Lashmit, W.E.	N: North Carolina A: 52 O: Brickmaker CW: Co I 14 Ill Inf (Pvt) E/D: 6/61-6/64 LOS: 36 mos GAR: 5/24/1888 SP: 9/26/1889 DR: 6/30/1891 S: H
Laufer, Loammi	N: Penn A: 85 O: Retired CW: Co H 35 Iowa Inf (Corpl) E/D: 8/62-8/65 LOS: 3 yrs GAR: 4/28/1925 S: H
Laverty, Leander	N: Indiana A: 72 O: Retired CW: Co A 48 Iowa Inf (Pvt) E/D: 5/64-10/64 LOS: 100 days GAR: 1/28/1919 on transfer from Garfield Post #25 Dept of Kansas S:H
Lawless, Stephen	N: Ireland A: 39 O: Laborer CW: Co C 11 Mass Inf (Corpl) E/D: 8/63-7/65 LOS: 23 mos GAR: 3/13/1884 D: 12/5/1885 S: H
Lawrance, John C.	N: Tioga Co, NY CW: Co E 86 NY SVI (Pvt) Term: 3 yrs E/D: 8/61-4/63 Falmouth, VA for wounds at the Battle of Fredericksburg, VA GAR: 9/25/1909 on transfer from June Sanders Post #3 Dept of Montana TR: 12/10/1913 S: DC

Layton, Robert	N: Lafayette, Indiana 1846 CW: Co D 40 Ind Inf (Pvt) Term: 3 yrs E/D: 11/__-5/63 Nashville, TN due to sickness Re-Enl: Co A 3 Ind Cav (Pvt) E/D: 3/63-5/65 Madison, Indiana GAR: 8/27/1921 DR: "Dropped" S: DC
Leader, J.M.	N: Penn A: 53 O: Laborer CW: Seaman E/D: 12/61-12/64 LOS: 36 mos GAR: 10/27/1887 SP: 9/26/1889 DR: 6/30/1891 S: H
Leatherman, George	N: Elgin, Indiana 1850 CW: Co I 47 Wis Inf (Pvt) Term: 3 yrs E/D: __/65-9/65 Madison, Wis GAR: ? date on transfer from Glendale Post Dept of Cal/Nev Died: 12/23/1935 A: 87 S: DC
Leheu, R.M.	N: Ohio A: 76 O: Retired CW: Co G 11 Iowa Inf (Pvt) E/D: 1/64-7/65 LOS: 1 yr 7 mos GAR: 9/13/1921 SP: 12/22/1925 RE: 1/12/1926 Died: 12/29/1928 S:H
Leoinge, James	NOL/NFI S: DC
Leonard, George D.	N: Vermont A: 37 O: Carpenter CW: Co A 1 Mass H A (Pvt) E/D: 11/63-11/65 LOS: 24 mos GAR: 7/25/1883 TR: 12/15/1892 S: H
Leonard, William R.	N: Ohio A: Not stated O: Hotel Keeper CW: Co B 1 Ohio L A (Pvt) E/D: 8/62-6/65 LOS: Not stated GAR: 2/11/1913 Died: 6/7/1922 S: H
Lewes, Thomas D.	N: Jefferson Co, PA A: 40 O: Clergyman R: National City, CA (near San Diego) CW: Co B 100 PA Inf (Pvt) E/D: 7/64-9/64 LOS: 3 mos GAR: 11/8/1883 DR: "Dropped" S: H
Lewis, Charles	N: Wisconsin A: 76 O: Retired CW: Co B 49 MO Inf (Pvt) E/D: 8/62-8/65 LOS: 3 yrs GAR: 12/13/1921 TR: 8/14/1923 RE: 6/24/1925 SP: 12/31/1928 S:H
Lewis, Charles H.	N: East Hartford, CT A: 84 O: Retired CW: Co D 42 Mass Inf (Pvt) E/D: 7/64-11/64 LOS: 4 mos GAR: 9/10/1918 on transfer from Palo Alto Post #187 Dept of Cal/Nev TR: 6/24/1919 S: H
Lewis, J.C.	N: PA A: 75 O: Retired CW: Co H 146 Ill Inf (Pvt) E/D: 9/64-9/65 LOS: 1 yr GAR: 4/22/1924 S: H
Lewis, John	N: Indiana CW: Co B 50 Ind Inf (Pvt) Term: 3 yrs E/D: 3/62-3/65 Re-Enl: Co B 52 Ind Inf (Pvt) E/D: 3/64-9/65 GAR: 3/10/1917 on transfer from Morgan Post Dept of Indiana DR: "Dropped" S: DC (No explanation of overlap in above terms of service)
Lewis, William W.	N: Kentucky A: 56 O: Real Estate CW: Co B 24 KY Inf (Pvt) E/D: 11/61-6/62 due to disability LOS: 7 mos GAR: 8/22/1899 TR: 7/13/1915 Died: 2/__/1916 S: H
Lindley, Charles	N: Harrisburg, PA CW: Co G 40 Ind Inf (Pvt) Term: 3 yrs E/D: 12/63-6/65 GAR: 6/9/1906 Died 12/19/1907 A: 75 Buried GAR (Mount Hope) S: DC Note: The California Death Index indicates this veteran died in Los Angeles County.
Lingenfelter, Alford	N: Carrelton, KY 1848 CW: Co H 148 Ind Inf (Pvt/Drummer) Term: 1 yr E/D: 2/65-9/65 Nashville, TN GAR: 8/22/1925 on transfer from George H. Thomas Post Dept of Indiana TR: 2/27/1926 S: DC
Lisher, O.B.	N: Ohio A: 67 O: Canvasser CW: Co __ 12 Ind Inf (Band Leader) E/D: 10/61-5/62 LOS: 7 mos GAR: 1/26/1888 SP: 3/28/1889 RE: 11/14/1889 D: 11/14/1889 S: H
Little, William J.	N: Rhode Island A: 71 O: Farmer CW: Co C 12 Iowa Inf (Pvt) E/D: 9/61-2/64 Re-Enl?: Co B 2 Ill Cav (Pvt) E/D: 9/64-6/65 LOS: Not stated GAR: 10/13/1914 Died: 12/28/1928 S: H

Lockwood, Munson M.	N: St Lawrence Co, NY A: 76 O: Retired CW: Co F 5 VT Inf (Pvt/Sgt) E/D: 9/61-6/65 LOS: 45 1/2 mos GAR: 7/24/1917 on transfer from Sumner Post #12 Dept of Oregon Died: 12/13/1918 S: H
Logan, John H.	N: Kentucky 1844 CW: Co B 2 Neb Cav (Pvt) Term: 1 yr E/D: 9/62-9/63 GAR: ? date on transfer from John A. Martin Post #153 Dept of Cal/Nev TR: 10/28/1916 S: DC
Lohr, John	N: Penn A: 61 O: Liveryman CW: Co D 133 PA Inf (Pvt) E/D: 8/62-10/63 Re-Enl?: Co G 93 PA Inf (1st Lieut) E/D: 10/63-6/65 LOS: 33 mos GAR: 8/8/1905 Died: 7/22/1909 S: H
Lohr, N.	N: New York A: 71 O: Retired CW: Co A 69 NY Inf (Pvt) E/D: 10/64-8/65 LOS: 10 mos GAR: 7/12/1921 Died: 10/26/1921 S: H
Long, Porter	N: Michigan A: 40 O: Carpenter CW: Co A 8 Ill Cav (Pvt) E/D: __/63-7/65 LOS: 2 yrs GAR: 5/13/1886 SP: 1/10/1889 DR: 6/30/1891 Died: "Dead"--no [grave] stone S: H
Lopshire, Adam Jos.	N: Allen Co, Indiana 1847 CW: Co B 118 Ind Inf (Pvt) Term: 6 mos E/D: 8/63-2/__ Roanoke, Indiana GAR: 12/26/1925 Obit: Lists two children; no wife named S: DC
Loudon, J.H.	N: Indiana A: 49 O: Trader CW: Co M 11 Ill Cav (Pvt) E/D: 11/61-3/62 due to disability LOS: 4 mos GAR: 6/9/1887 SP: 3/28/1889 DR: 6/30/1891 S: H
Loughrey, William	N: Penn A: 58 O: Farmer CW: Co C 11 MO Cav (Pvt) E/D: __/62-__/65 LOS: 36 mos GAR: 6/9/1887 TR: 3/22/1888 S: H
Lowell, Marcus L.	N: New York A: 63 O: Cooper CW: Co F 101 Ohio Inf (Pvt) E/D: 8/62-6/65 LOS: 46 mos GAR: 5/25/1897 Died: 3/20/1900 Soldier's Home S: H
	SAWTELLE: Died 3/16/1900 at Soldier's Home and buried in Sec 5, Row E, Grave 8 with tombstone inscription "M.L. Lowell Co F 101st Ohio Inf" S: Los Angeles National Cemetery.
Lucas, Joseph H.	N: Indiana Co, PA 11/14/47 CW: Co G 2 PA Vol (Pvt) Term: 6 mos E/D: 6/63-1/64 Pittsburgh, PA Re-Enl: US Signal Corps (Pvt) E/D: 2/64-8/65 New Orleans GAR: 5/26/1906 Died 8/24/1937 A: 90 S: DC
Luckadoe, Joseph	N: Maryland A: 48 O: Soldier CW: Co H 4 U S Inf (Drummer/Pvt) E/D: 5/61-5/66 LOS: 60 mos GAR: 4/14/1896 TR: 5/26/1896 S: H
Lucy, Timothy J.	N: Allegheny Co, PA 1846 CW: Co C 2 MD ___ (Pvt) Term: 3 yrs E/D: 6/64-5/___ Camp Bradford, MD GAR: 4/24/1920 on transfer from Uncle Sam Post #177 Dept of Cal/Nev DR: "Dropped" S: DC
Lundaker, Peter	NOL/NFI S: DC
Lynch, Thomas	N: Coshocton, Ohio CW: Co K 1 Wis Cav (Pvt/Com Sgt) Term: 3 yrs E/D: 8/62-7/65 Edgefield, TN GAR: 9/28/1912 on transfer from Mead Post Dept of Wash/Alaska S: DC
Lyon, E.C.	N: Illinois A: 40 O: Janitor CW: Co E 2 Ill Cav (Pvt) E/D: 11/63-11/65 LOS: 25 mos GAR: 8/13/1885 DR: 3/28/1899 S: H
Lyon, Edward	N: Eastford, CT 9/2/43 CW: Co K 7 CT Cav (Pvt) Term: 3 yrs E/D: 9/61-12/63 Hilton Head, SC Re-Enl: Same company (Corpl) E/D: 12/63-7/65 Goldsboro, NC GAR: 1/26/1900 on transfer from Warner Post #25 Dept. of the East Died: 1/3/1931 S: DC

Lyon, Theodore	N: Penn A: 74 O: Farmer CW: Co G 1 Ohio Cav (Pvt) E/D: 5/62-5/65 LOS: Not stated GAR: 7/25/1911 Died: 8/3/1914 S: H
MacDonald, Duncan H.	N: New York A: 78 O: Capitalist CW: Co B 1 Ohio Cav (Pvt) E/D: 10/61-10/64 LOS: Not stated GAR: 10/14/1913 on transfer from Bartlett Logan Post #6 Los Angeles SP: 12/26/1916 DR: 12/24/1918 S: H
MacKinnon, Hector	N: Scotland A: 72 O: Farmer CW: Co A 12 Ohio Inf (Pvt) E/D: 5/61-6/64 LOS: Not stated GAR: 12/26/1911 Died: 9/24/1912 S: H
Madden, Joseph	N: Quincy, Mass 12/25/46 CW: US Navy SS Nephron & Ohio (1st Class Boy) Term: 1 yr E/D: 4/63-4/64 Charlestown, Mass GAR: 12/14/1914 on transfer from Amasa B. Watson Post Dept of Michigan Died: 11/11/1936 S: DC
Magee, Paris A.	N: Ohio A: 56 O: Grocer CW: "Clara D" (Messenger Boy) E/D: 10/62-4/63 due to disability LOS: Not stated GAR: 12/22/1903 TR: 10/27/1908 S: H
Magoon, George A.	N: Harmony, Maine 6/28/44 CW: Co I 4th Maine Bat LA (Pvt) Term: 3 yrs E/D: 12/61-2/64 Brandy Station, VA Re-Enl: Co _ 4th Maine Bat LA (Pvt/Corpl) E/D: 2/64-6/65 Augusta, Maine LOS: 3 yrs, 5 mos, 27 days GAR: 12/13/1913 on transfer from H.R. Loomis Dept of Wash/Alaska Died: 12/11/1926 San Diego A: 82/5/13 S: DC
Mahan, Dr.	NOL/NFI--DC
Mahoney, Henry	N: Ireland 1842 CW: Ship Sybil (Seaman) Term: Unstated E/D: 10/64-8/65 GAR: 6/22/1918 S:DC
Mallett, John	N: Cayahotz, Ohio CW: Co H 72 Ohio Inf (Pvt) Term: 3 yrs E/D: 11/61-1/64 Germantown, TN Re-Enl: Same company (Pvt) E/D: 11/63-9/65 Vicksburg, Miss GAR: 11/10/1906 on transfer from Custer Post #6 Dept of Wash/Alaska S: DC
Malloy, William	N: Ireland A: 80 O: Retired CW: Co F 18 NY Inf (Pvt) E/D: 5/61-5/63 LOS: 24 mos GAR: 11/19/1918 S: H
Mandeville, F.H.	N: Maryland A: 43 O: Book Keeper CW: Co K 23 NY Inf (Pvt) E/D: 5/61-5/63 LOS: 24 mos GAR: 10/22/1885 SP: 4/30/1890 Died: Comitted suicide at Los Angeles--no [grave] stone S: H
Manners, William A.	N: Penn A: 55 O: Dyer CW: Co C 11 Iowa Inf (Pvt) E/D: 3/64-7/65 LOS: 16 mos GAR: 4/9/1901 TR: 1/14/1902 S: H
Marsh, George W.	N: New York A: 41 O: Farmer R: Encinitas, CA CW: Co __ 8 Batt Wis Arty (Pvt/Sgt) E/D: 12/61-8/65 LOS: 41 1/2 mos GAR: 7/28/1881 Died: 8/12/1913 S: H
Martin, George M.	N: Ohio A: 55 O: Painter CW: Co A 11 Ohio Inf (Pvt) E/D: 4/61-8/64 LOS: 40 mos GAR: 1/26/1887 SP: 9/26/1889 DR: 6/30/1891 S: H
Martin, John	N: Illinois A: 84 O: Retired CW: Co A 8 Iowa Cav (Pvt/Sgt) E/D: 8/63-__/65 LOS: Not stated GAR: 6/26/1923 "Never signed roll" S: H
Martin, Nelson	N: Illinois A: 78 O: Retired CW: Co E 12 Ill Cav (Pvt) E/D: 2/62-3/65 LOS: 3 yrs GAR: 8/28/1923 Died: 2/3/1930 S: H
Mathes, Z.C.	N: Indiana CW: Co B 18 Ind Inf (Pvt) Term: 3 yrs E/D: 9/61-9/64 GAR: 11/10/1894 Charter member of Datus Coon Post S: DC

Mathis, Frederick B.	N: Taylorsville, KY 1841 CW: Co A 15 IA Inf (Pvt) Term: 3 yrs E/D: 1/62-1/63 Keokuk, IA due to disability GAR: ? date on transfer from McPherson Post Dept of Missouri TR: "Transferred" S: DC
Maxwell, James F.	N: Knox Co, Illinois 1848 CW: Co F 102 Ill Vol Inf (Pvt) Term: 1 yr E/D: 3/65-6/65 Blackland, IL GAR: 5/24/1924 DR: "Dropped" S: DC
Maxwell, James H.	N: Missouri A: 67 O: Farmer CW: Co A 32 Ind Inf (Pvt) E/D: 9/63-12/65 LOS: Not stated GAR: 4/8/1913 TR: 12/9/1913 S: H
Maxwell, James T.	N: Canton, Fulton Co, Ill 10/27/38 CW: Co H 17 Ill Inf (Pvt/Sgt) Term: 3 yrs E/D: 5/61-9/62 Boliver, TN due to disability GAR: 7/26/1913 TR: "Transferred" S: DC
McCartin, Francis	N: New York A: 81 O: Retired CW: USS Augusta (Landsman) Re-Enl?: USS Metacomet (Ordinary Seaman) E/D: 9/61-10/64 LOS: 3 yrs GAR: 4/11/1922 SP: 12/31/1928 RE: 1/22/1929 Died: 3/9/1938 S: H
McCauliff, Thomas M.	N: Boston, Mass A: 42 O: Printer CW: Co L 2 Cal Cav (Pvt) E/D: 9/61-10/64 LOS: 36 mo GAR: 1/25/1883 SP: 1/10/1889 DR: 6/30/1891 Died: "Died"--no [grave] stone S: H
McClerken, David W.	N: Illinois A: 74 O: Watchman CW: Co A 10 MO Inf (Pvt) Re-Enl?: Co C 10 MO Inf (Capt) E/D: 8/61-8/64 LOS: Not stated GAR: 3/10/1914 on transfer from Lincoln Post #1 Dept of Cal/Nev TR: 4/11/1916 or 1918 (hard to read) S: H
McClure, Joseph A.	N: Ohio A: 82 O: Not stated CW: Co B 8 Iowa Inf (Pvt) E/D: 9/64-7/65 LOS: Not stated GAR: 4/22/1930 TR: 5/15/1935 S: H
McClure, William P.	N: Indiana A: Not stated O: Druggist CW: Co H 51 Ind Inf (Pvt/Capt) E/D: 10/61-12/65 LOS: Not stated GAR: 6/24/1913 on transfer from Lincoln Post #1 Dept of Kansas Past Post Commander Died: 2/10/1921 S: H
McCoy, Thomas	N: Penn A: 68 O: Foundry Man CW: Co D 114 PA Inf (Corpl) E/D: 8/62-5/65 LOS: Not stated GAR: 6/11/1913 Died: 3/14/1914 S: H
McDaniel, B.F.	N: Penn A: 37 O: Clergyman CW: Co D 81 Penn Inf (Pvt) Re-Enl?: Co __ 1 Batt Penn LA (Pvt) E/D: 4/61-7/65 LOS: 51 mos GAR: No further information D: 1/10/1894 S: H
McDonald, Edward	N: New York A: 67 O: Farmer CW: Co H 1 Wis Inf (Pvt) E/D: 10/61-10/64 LOS: Not stated GAR: 9/24/1912 SP: 12/22/1914 DR: 12/24/1918 S: H
McFarland, Jesse	N: Colesville, Schenectady Co, NY 1846 CW: Co E 90 NY Inf (Pvt) Term: 3 yrs E/D: 10/61-3/62 Key West, FL due to disability Re-Enl: Co F 1st NY Veteran Corps (Pvt) E/D: 8/63-7/65 Camp Pratt, WVA GAR: 6/11/1921 on transfer from Dept of Colorado TR: 8/13/1923 to St. Louis, MO S: DC
McFarland, Schuler	N: Missouri 8/15/39 CW: Co A Hickory Co MO Home Guard (Pvt) Term: 6 mos E/D: 6/61-12/61 Jefferson City, MO due to a disability "This home guard organized by General Fremont" GAR: 4/11/1914 Died: 2/28/__ A: 80 Obit: Lists wife Sarah McFarland S: DC
McGee, William J.	N: Pittsburg, PA A: 78 O: Retired CW: Co E 15 PA Inf (Pvt) E/D: 9/64-6/65 LOS: 9 mos GAR: 8/9/1921 Died: 2/25/1924 S: H
McKnight, Eugene V.	N: Mount Vernon, Ill 12/19/40 CW: Co A 1st Minn HA (Pvt/Sgt) Term: 1 yr E/D: 9/64-6/65 Chattanooga, TN GAR: 7/13/1918 Died: 11/8/1934 at Jamul, CA A: 93/10/13 S: DC

McNally, W.G.	N: Ireland A: 44 O: Grocer CW: Co C 21 NY Inf (Pvt) Re-Enl?: Co H 150 O.N.G. (Sgt) E/D: 5/61-5/66 LOS: 60 mos GAR: 8/23/1888 SP: 9/26/1889 Died: 1899--no [grave] stone S: H
McPheeters, James H.	N: Illinois A: 50 O: Carpenter CW: Co E 16 Wis Inf (Pvt) Re-Enl?: Co __ 1 Minn Batt (Pvt) E/D: 10/61-7/65 LOS: 45 mos GAR: 10/25/1888 DR: 6/30/1891 SP: 12/27/1904 DR: 12/26/1905 S: H
McQuinston, Thomas	N: Ohio A: 59 O: Merchant CW: Co C 1 Miss Marine Brig (Pvt) E/D: 2/64-1/65 LOS: 10 mos GAR: 5/25/1907 S: H
Meagher, John O.	N: St John, New Brunswick 1847 CW: Co I 129 Ind Inf (Pvt) Term: 3 yrs E/D: 3/64-__/__ Indianapolis GAR: ? date on transfer from Thomas Post Dept of MO S: DC
Mendelson, Louis	N: Russia A: 65 O: Custom Broker CW: Co M 4 US R C (Pvt) E/D: 5/61-8/61 LOS: Not stated GAR: 6/9/1903 Died: 9/12/1908 S: H
Menhennet, Wm. H.	N: England A: 65 O: Retired CW: Co D 1 W VA Cav (Pvt/Corpl) E/D: 2/64-7/65 LOS: Not stated GAR: 7/27/1909 (probably on transfer from Shiloh Post #60 Dept of Cal/Nev TR: 1/11/1910 "William H. Menhennet" S: H
Merriam, G.F.	N: Leyden, NY A: 46 O: Farmer R: Apex (near San Diego?) CW: Co F 3 NY Art (1st Lieut) Promoted?: 3rd Batt 5 NY Art (Major) E/D: 11/61-3/65 LOS: 3 4/12 years GAR: 12/22/1881 TR: 12/31/1888 S: H
Merrill, Augustus	N: Maine A: 48 O: Publisher CW: Co A 7 Maine Inf (Pvt/Major) E/D: 5/61-7/65 LOS: 51 mos GAR: 11/22/1888 SP: 10/__/1893 DR: 12/__/1893 S: H
Meth, J. H.	N: Penn A: 80 O: Retired R: National City, CA CW: Co D 97 Ill Inf (Pvt) E/D: 8/62-__/65 LOS: 3 yrs GAR: 6/27/1922 Died: 6/16/1928 S: H
Michener, A.D.	N: Senaca Co, Ohio 1843 CW: Co C 49 OVI (Pvt) Term: 3 yrs E/D: 7/63-6/66 Columbus, Ohio GAR: 9/10/1921 on transfer from Syracuse Post Dept of Kansas Died: 3/12/1925 A: 82. S: DC
Middleton, John	N: New York A: 78 O: Retired CW: Co G 110 NY Inf (Pvt) E/D: 7/62-11/64 due to disability LOS: 2 yrs Re-Enl?: Co B 184 NY Inf (Pvt) E/D: 8/64-11/65 LOS: 1 yr GAR: 3/14/1922 Died: 4/1/1932 S: H
Miller, Admiral N.	N: Rhode Island A: 68 O: News Dealer CW: Co D 21 Conn Inf (Pvt) E/D: 8/62-6/65 LOS: Not stated GAR: 6/25/1912 TR: 1/9/1917 Dismissed: 1/9/1917 S: H
Miller, Edwin H.	N: Ohio A: Not stated O: Hotel Keeper CW: Co I 10 Iowa Inf (Pvt) E/D: 8/64-9/65 LOS: 11 mos GAR: 1/24/1889 SP: 12/23/1893 DR: 3/28/1899 Post Commander 1892 S: H
Miller, Jacob L.	N: Indiana A: 75 O: Retired CW: Co H 20 Ind Inf (Pvt) E/D: 9/63-7/65 LOS: 2 yrs 11 mos GAR: 8/23/1921 Died: 1/27/1922 S: H
Miller, Joseph H.	N: Penn A: 70 O: Farmer CW: Co H 2 PA Inf (Pvt) Re-Enl?: Co E 57 PA Vet Vol (Pvt) E/D: __/__ to 6/65 LOS: Not stated GAR: 3/9/1915 Died: 2/26/1922 S: H
Miller, William F.	N: Germany A: 68 O: Retired CW: Co F 17 Ind Inf (Pvt/Corpl) E/D: 5/61-12/62 Re-Enl?: Co M 4 US Art (Pvt) E/D: 12/62-12/65 LOS: 36 mos GAR: 5/12/1903 Died: 7/3/1904 S: H

Miner, H.W. N: Western Ohio A: 77 O: Retired CW: Co C 1 Mich Engineers (Artificer) E/D: 12/63-3/65 LOS: Not stated GAR: 3/26/1912 (probably on transfer from Dept of South Dakota) SP: 12/28/1920 S: H

Mitchell, Ira N: Indiana A: 74 O: Nurseryman CW: Co I 14 Iowa Inf (Corpl/Sgt) E/D: 9/61-2/63 due to disability LOS: Not stated GAR: 8/24/1909 TR: 10/12/1915 S: H

Mitchell, J.H. N: Illinois A: 42 O: Sign Painter CW: Co G 13 Ill Cav (Pvt) Re-Enl?: Co _ 13 Ill Inf (Regt QM Sgt) E/D: 12/63-8/65 LOS: 20 mos GAR: 5/26/1887 SP: 1/10/1889 DR: 6/30/1891 RE: 2/12/1895 TR: 2/12/1895 S: H

Mitchell, Reuben H. N: Nova Scotia A: 71 O: Carpenter CW: Co E 1 Batt Mass HA (Pvt) E/D: 7/64-6/65 LOS: Not stated GAR: 5/23/1911 SP: 12/24/1912 RE: 1/14/1913 SP: 12/26/1916 DR: 12/24/1918 S: H

Mitchell Winfield L. N: Indiana A: 76 O: Retired CW: Co F 25 MO Inf (Pvt) E/D: 8/61-9/64 LOS: 3 yrs GAR: 4/13/1920 S: H

Mixter, Horace D. N: Warren, Mass CW: Co A 2 US Sharpshooters (Pvt) Term: Unstated E/D: 10/61-10/64 GAR: 10/9/1926 Died: 1/1928 S: DC

Mogle, William N: Ohio A: 50 O: Carpenter CW: Co B 9 Minn Inf (Pvt) E/D: 8/62-6/65 due to sickness LOS: 34 mos GAR: __/__/1884 SP: 1/10/1889 DR: 6/30/1891 S: H

Mohr, Daniel N: Ireland A: 77 O: Farmer CW: Co A 2 Colo Cav (Pvt) E/D: 11/61-12/64 LOS: Not stated GAR: 3/9/1915 SP: 12/26/1916 DR: 12/24/1918 S: H

Montius, Augustus N: Mass A: 81 O: Retired CW: US Navy (Engineer) E/D: 5/62-5/66 due to resignation LOS: 4 yrs GAR: 2/28/1922 Died: 1/3/1924 S: H

Moore, Augustus H. N: Mass A: 61 O: Barber CW: Co L and Co H 3 Mass Inf (Pvt) E/D: 4/61-7/61 LOS: 3 mos Re-Enl?: Co F 47 Mass Inf (Pvt) E/D: 9/62-6/63 LOS: 13 mos GAR: 11/23/1897 TR: 12/26/1899 Died: 11/14/1902 Soldier's Home S: H

SAWTELLE: No records for this veteran found at Los Angeles National Cemetery, although the Sawtelle Index indicates he died at Sawtelle Soldier's Home.

Moore, Francis T. N: Illinois A: 65 O: Cabinet Job. R: National City, CA CW: Co L 2 Ill Cav (Pvt/Capt) E/D: 7/61-6/65 LOS: 48 mos GAR: 6/9/1903 (probably on transfer from Kilpatrick Post #42 Dept of Colorado Died: 12/22/1912 S: H

Moore, George M. N: Louisburg, Ohio A: 72 O: Retired CW: Co G 87 Ohio Inf (Pvt) E/D: __/62-__/62 LOS: 3 mos Re-Enl?: Co L 1 Ohio H A (Pvt) E/D: 8/62-7/65 LOS: 35 mos GAR: 10/23/1917 Died: 9/__/1921 S: H

Moore, John C. N: Michigan A: 41 O: Carpenter CW: Co G 30 Mich Inf (Pvt) E/D: 12/64-6/65 LOS: 6 mos GAR: 1/27/1887 SP: 1/10/1889 DR: 6/30/1891 S: H

Moore, Patrick H. N: Mass A: 40 O: Not stated CW: Co E 15 Mass Inf (Pvt) E/D: 7/61-7/64 LOS: 3 yrs GAR: 5/20/1886 D: 4/24/1891 S: H

Moore, William H. N: Indiana A: 77 O: Farmer CW: Co D 84 Ind Inf (Pvt) E/D: 8/62-6/65 LOS: 2 yrs 10 mos GAR: 9/13/1921 SP: 12/26/1923 DR: 12/23/1924 S: H

Moore, William Roby N: Indiana A: 76 O: Retired CW: Co K 19 MD Inf (Pvt) E/D: 7/61-8/64 LOS: 3 yrs 1 mo GAR: 7/12/1921 TR: 5/23/1922 S: H

Moran, Edward H.	N: Vermont A: Not stated O: Miner CW: Co B 6 Wis Inf (Pvt/Sgt) E/D: __/61-7/65 LOS: 48 mos GAR: 12/11/1900 Died: 11/4/1921 S: H
Moran, George E.	N: Mass A: 69 O: Paper Maker CW: Co I 1 Conn Art (Pvt) E/D: 5/61-5/64 LOS: Not stated GAR: 5/9/1911 TR: 9/14/1916 S: H
Morey, F.A.	NOL/NFI S: DC
Morgan, Adam	N: Muskingham Co, Ohio CW: Co A 9 Ohio Cav (Pvt) Term: Unstated E/D: 1/64-8/65 GAR: 6/10/1911 on transfer from Stanton Post #5 Dept of Cal/Nev TR: "Transferred" S: DC
Morris, Charles	N: Canada A: 60 O: Teamster R: Del Mar, CA CW: Co D 2 US Troops (Pvt) E/D: Not stated LOS: 60 mos GAR: 5/25/1892 SP: 3/31/1893 DR: 3/28/1899 RE: 7/10/1900 Died: 1/17/1907 at Soldier's Home S: H

SAWTELLE: Records for this veteran were not found at Los Angeles National Cemetery, although the California Death Index indicates he died in Los Angeles County. |
Morrison, J.A.	NOL/NFI S: DC
Morrisy, Jessy M.	N: Indiana A: 81 O: Retired CW: Co I 3 Iowa Cav (Pvt/Corpl) E/D: 8/61-8/65 LOS: 4 yrs GAR: 4/28/1925 SP: 12/31/1928 S: H
Morrow, Hugh P.	N: Canada A: 69 O: Real Estate CW: Co M 3 Colo Cav (Pvt) E/D: 9/64-12/64 LOS: Not stated GAR: 5/26/1914 on transfer from Belden Post #59 Dept of Iowa Died: 3/16/1926 S: H
Morse, Nixon	N: Vermont A: 80 O: Retired CW: Co D 3 VT Inf (Pvt) E/D: 4/61-11/61 LOS: 7 mos Re-Enl?: Co F 1 VT Cav (Pvt) E/D: 6/62-8/63 LOS: 1 yr 2 mos GAR: 5/24/1921 Died: 1/11/1926 S: H
Moseley, William C.	N: England A: 77 O: Retired CW: Co A 75 Ill Inf (Pvt/Corpl) E/D: 8/62-4/65 LOS: 2 1/2 yrs GAR: 8/24/1920 Died: 1/21/1929 S: H
Mouter, John P.	N: Sweden A: 90 O: Manufacturer CW: Co G 13 NY Art (Pvt) E/D: 10/64-8/65 LOS: Not stated GAR: 9/22/1914 on transfer from Washington Post #573 Dept of Illinois Died: 10/7/1921 Chicago, Ill S: H
Moylan, Miles	N: Mass A: 55 O: Retired Off. CW: Co C 2 US Drag (Pvt/1st Sgt) E/D: 6/54-4/62 Re-Enl?: Co C 2 US Cav (1st Sgt/2 Lieut) 4/62-3/63 LOS: 48 mos GAR: 1/23/1894 TR: 1/9/1900 S: H
Muclish, Otto	NOL/NFI--DC
Mullaney, James	N: Ireland A: 74 O: Clerk CW: Co K 11 Minn Inf (Pvt) E/D: 7/64-6/65 LOS: 11 mos GAR: 11/14/1922 Died: 1/11/1938 or 1939 S: H
Mulville, Martin	N: Ireland CW: Co A 10 Wis Inf (Pvt) Term: 3 yrs E/D: 8/61-6/64 Madison, Wis due to loss of arm GAR: 1/27/1903 on transfer from Simon Mix Post #95 Dept of Minnesota Died 3/6/1922 at Ocean Beach area of San Diego A: 78 S: DC
Murdock, David H.	N: Ohio CW: Co H 77 Ill Inf (Corpl/Sgt) Term: 3 yrs E/D: 8/62-7/65 GAR: 7/10/1896 Died: [Record said he died on 8/27/1892 but entered the GAR in 1896] S: DC

Mussey, Albert W.	N: Vermont A: 44 O: Farmer R: [El] Cajon, CA CW: Co E 2 Cal Cav (Pvt) 8/64-6/66 LOS: 22 mos GAR: 8/10/1882 SP: 12/31/1883 RE: 9/22/1884 SP: 1/10/1889 DR: 6/30/1891 RE: 5/12/1900 Died: 12/27/1922 S: H
Nace, Uriah P.	N: Penn A: 76 O: Rancher R: Encanto, CA CW: Co B 81 Ohio Inf (Pvt) E/D: 2/65-7/65 LOS: 5 mos GAR: 10/12/1920 TR: 6/8/1926 S: H
Nagle, W.C.	N: Ireland A: 53 O: Mason CW: Co I 193 Ohio Inf (Pvt/Sgt) E/D: 3/65-8/65 LOS: 5 mos GAR: 6/27/1889 SP: 9/24/1895 RE: 11/14/1899 TR: 11/14/1899 S: H
Neiberger, Samuel J.	N: Ohio A: 70 O: Physician CW: Co I 44 Ohio Inf (Pvt) E/D: 9/61-11/62 due to disability LOS: Not stated GAR: 9/22/1908 TR: 6/22/1909 S: H
Neisus, F.G.	N: Prussia A: 40 O: Watch Maker CW: Co G 7 Conn Inf (Bugler) E/D: 9/61-8/65 LOS: 48 mos GAR: 7/4/1886 SP: 1/10/1889 DR: 6/30/1891 S: H
Nelson, J. Martin	N: Illinois A: 65 O: Mf.d Agent CW: Co E 12 Ill Inf (Pvt) E/D: 1/62-2/65 LOS: Not stated GAR: 3/25/1913 TR: 4/27/1920 S: H
Nesbitt, Everett G.	N: Penn A: 72 O: Druggist CW: Co A 14 Iowa Inf (Pvt/Sgt) E/D: 8/62-11/64 LOS: 38 mos GAR: 2/27/1906 SP: 12/10/1918 S: H
Newsom, Eli	N: Bartholomew Co, Indiana 9/28/47 CW: Co A 120 Ind Inf (Pvt/Corpl) Term: 3 yrs E/D: 11/63-1/66 Raleigh, NC GAR: 12/28/1918 on transfer from Jasper Packard Post #589 Dept of Indiana TR: 1922 to Heintzelman Post San Diego S: DC
Newsome, Eli	N: Indiana A: 76 O: Retired CW: Co A 120 Ind Inf (Pvt/Corpl) E/D: 11/63-1/66 LOS: 3 yrs 2 mos GAR: 1/8/1924 Died: 10/4/1924 S: H
Newton, George A.	N: Ohio A: 69 O: Clerk R: Coronado, CA CW: Co E 129 Ill Inf (Pvt) E/D: 8/62-6/65 LOS: Not stated GAR: 3/25/1913 on transfer from Fred C. Jones Post Dept of Ohio? Died: 2/3/1930 (another death date on same line of 11/6/1920) S: H
Nichols, Absalom W.	N: Virginia A: 82 O: Farmer CW: Co F 3 Iowa Inf (Pvt); Re-Enl?: Co F 3 Iowa Cav (Pvt) E/D: 5/61-5/64 LOS: Not stated GAR: 11/24/1914 Died: 12/14/1915 S: H
Nichols, Edmund	N: New York A: 45 O: Carpenter CW: Co I 109 NY Inf (Pvt) E/D: 7/62-__/__ due to gun shot wound LOS: Not stated GAR: 12/2/1885 SP: 1/10/1889 DR: 6/30/1891 S: H
Nichols, F.A.	NOL/NFI S: DC
Nichols, Franklin P.	N: New Hampshire A: 55 O: Hotel Keeper CW: Co B 25 Mich Inf (Pvt); Re-Enl?: Co A 7 Mich Cav (Lieut) E/D: 7/62-7/64 due to disability LOS: 24 mos GAR: 4/26/1888 TR: 9/24/1890 S: H
Nichols, H.H.	N: New York A: 44 O: Carpenter CW: Co G 46 Penn Vols (Pvt) E/D: 9/61-5/65 LOS: 33 mos GAR: 12/2/1885 SP: 1/10/1889 DR: 3/28/1899 S: H
Nichols, Wilmont D.	N: Penn A: 54 O: Teamster CW: Co D 17 Kans Inf (Pvt) E/D: 8/64-12/64 LOS: 3 1/3 mos GAR: 9/24/1901 TR: 12/28/1915 S: H
Nickels, Edgar A.	N: Maine A: 70 O: Pensioner CW: Co C 11 Maine Inf (Pvt/Capt) E/D: Not stated GAR: 5/28/1912 on transfer from Canby Post #5 Dept of Arkansas SP: 12/26/1916 DR: 12/24/1918 Past Commander S: H

Noble, John	N: Chesterfield Co, VA A: 69 O: Farmer R: San Diego/Bernardo (probably the present Rancho Bernardo) CW: Co D 5 Cal Inf (Pvt/Sgt) E/D: 1/62-12/66 LOS: Not stated GAR: 2/23/1882 Died: 11/14/1902 Soldier's Home S: H

SAWTELLE: Sawtelle Index indicates veteran died at Sawtelle Soldier's Home |
Noble, Patrick	N: Ireland A: 50 O: Laborer CW: Co E 11 PA Cav (Pvt) E/D: 9/62-6/65 LOS: 34 mos GAR: 4/25/1889 SP: 9/28/1897 RE: 11/22/1898 SP: 5/28/1904 DR: 1/22/1907 S: H
Northern, Walter B.	N; Lawrenceburg, Ind 7/15/47 CW: Co I 139 Ind Vol Inf (Pvt) Term: 100 days E/D: 5/64-9/64 Indianapolis, Ind GAR: 5/26/1900 Died: 1/17/1941 S: DC
Norton, Daniel A.	N: Maine A: 40 O: Carpenter CW: Co G 125 NY Inf (Pvt) E/D: 8/62-9/63 due to disability LOS: 11 mos GAR: 9/27/1888 SP: 9/26/1889 DR: 6/30/1891 S: H
Norton, Harry	N: New York A: 42 O: Police Officer CW: Co B 23 NY Inf (Pvt); Re-Enl?: Co G 1 NY Cav (Pvt) E/D: 5/61-7/65 LOS: 48 mos GAR: 1/15/1884 SP: 9/26/1889 DR: 6/30/1891 S: H
Noyce, Wm.D.	N: Hudson, NY CW: Co A 39 Wis Inf (Pvt) Term: 100 days E/D: 5/64-9/64 Milwaukee, Wis Re-Enl: Co E 50 Wis Inf (Pvt) E/D: 2/65-4/66 Madison, Wis GAR: 7/24/1915 on transfer from Chester Harding Post Dept of Missouri DR: 7/14/1917 S: DC
Noyes, Ira	N: New Hampshire A: 51 O: Farmer R: San Diego/Otay, CA CW: Co G 12 NH Inf (Pvt); Re-Enl?: Co K 2 NH Inf (Pvt) E/D: 2/65-12/65 LOS: 10 1/2 mos GAR: 5/2/1882 Died: 11/28/1910 S: H
Nulton, O.D.	N: Morgan Co, Ohio A: 35 O: Farmer CW: Co G 21 MO ___ (Musician) E/D: 10/61-1/64 LOS: 38 mos GAR: 2/9/1882 TR: 11/24/1887 S: H
Nulton, Sylvanus D.	N: Morgan Co, Ohio CW: Co G 21 MO Inf (Mus'n/Principal Mus'n) Term: 3 yrs E/D: 10/61-4/66 Ft Morgan, AL GAR: 5/26/1900 on transfer from Escondido Post #143 Dept of Cal/Nev Died: 9/19/1912 A: 77 Buried: Escondido, CA S: DC
O'Brien, James	N: Michigan A: 60 O: Retired CW: Co H 10 Minn Inf (Pvt/Sgt) E/D: 8/62-7/65 LOS: 24 mos GAR: 8/8/1905 SP: 3/26/1907 DR: 12/24/1918 S: H
O'Brien, James	N: Kalamazoo, Mich 1846 CW: Co H 10 Minn Inf (Sgt) Term: 3 yrs E/D: 8/62-7/65 St Paul, MN GAR: 10/4/1922 on transfer from Post #21 Dept of Minnesota D: Died at Soldier's Home 1/8/1924 S: DC Sawtelle Soldier's Home Index confirms he died there.
O'Donnell, John F.	N: Ireland 1839 CW: US Navy (Seaman) Term: 3 yrs E/D: 5/61-7/62 due to wounds GAR: 6/26/1920 on transfer from Veteran Post #436 Dept of New York DR: "Dropped" S: DC
O'Leary, Stephen	N: Ireland A: 46 O: Laborer CW: US Navy U.S.S. Glautus & Galatea (Landsman) E/D: 4/64-1/65 LOS: 6 mos GAR: 6/27/1889 SP: 7/1/1890 DR: 3/28/1899 SP: 3/25/1902 DR: 1/22/1907 S: H
Olney, Eugene C.	N: New York A: 76 O: Retired CW: Co G 30 Mich Inf (Corpl) E/D: 11/64-6/65 LOS: 6 mos GAR: 1/27/1920 Died: 10/24/1920 S: H
Oltman, Richard H.	N: Bremen (Germany?) A: 48 O: Saloon CW: Co F 6 Kans ___ (Pvt) E/D: 10/61-11/64 LOS: 37 mos GAR: 7/13/1882 SP: 12/28/1882 DR: 10/25/1904 S: H
Oman, George B.	NOL/NFI S: DC

Osgood, Isaac P.	N: Lowell, Mass 4/5/42 CW: Co B 32 Mass Inf (Pvt) Term: 3 yrs E/D: 11/61-12/62 due to disability GAR: 5/25/1918 Died: 7/20/1919 A: 77/3/__ Buried: Body shipped to Massachusetts S: DC
Ott, George K.	N: Philadelphia, PA 1846 CW: Co G 138 Ill Inf (Sgt) Term: 90 days E/D: 4/__(64?)-10/64 Re-Enl: Co A 156 Ill Inf (Sgt) E/D: 2/65-9/65 Springfield, Il GAR: 8/28/1920 on transfer from Salt Lake Post #1 Dept of Utah Died: 10/30/1923 A: 66/10/27 S: DC
Owen, George B.	N: Tomkins Co, NY 1846 CW: Co E 3rd Wis Inf (rank?) With Sherman's March to the Sea No further information Buried: Waubun, Wis 2 obits; children listed, no wife GAR: No further information S: DC
Owens, John	N: England A: 64 O: Mechanic CW: Co L 2 Conn H A (Pvt) E/D: 2/64-6/65 LOS: 16 mos GAR: 1/28/1902 TR: 3/24/1903 S: H
Owings, Luthur	N: Indiana A: 52 O: Miner CW: Co D 33 Ind Inf (Pvt) E/D: 3/65-7/65 LOS: 3 mos GAR: 12/22/1896 SP: 3/24/1908 DR: 12/24/1918 S: H
Packard, P.L.	N: Winnebago Co, IL 1847 CW: Co D 154th Ill Inf (Pvt/Corpl) Term: 1 yr E/D: 2/65-9/65 Nashville, TN GAR: 8/12/1922 Died: 1/8/1924 S: DC
Painter, Samuel	N: Penn A: 79 O: Retired CW: Co F 7 Penn Inf (Pvt/Corpl) E/D: 9/61-9/65 LOS: 4 yrs GAR: 7/14/1925 Died: 9/15/1929 S: H
Palmanteer, David	David Palmanteer, Co K 69 PA Inf (official tombstone). Buried in La Vista Cemetery, National City, CA
Palmer, Ernest	N: Ohio A: 59 O: Miner CW: Co A 5 Kans Cav (Pvt) E/D: 7/61-8/64; Re-Enl?: Co H 9 R 1st Army E/D: 3/65-3/66 LOS: 48 mos GAR: 1/26/1904 SP: 6/28/1910 DR: 12/24/1918 S: H
Palmer, J.H.	N: New York A: 63 O: Merchant R: Chula Vista, CA CW: Co I 26 NY Inf (Capt) E/D: 3/61-8/61 LOS: 5 mos GAR: 4/26/1888 SP: 9/26/1889 DR: 6/30/1891 RE: 9/9/1891 TR: 9/9/1891 S: H
Palmer, M.J.	NOL/NFI S: DC
Palmer, T.R.	N: Herkimer Co, NY CW: Co C 13 Mich Inf (Captain/Lt. Col) Term: 3 yrs E/D: 10/61-6/65 Savannah, GA GAR: 12/8/1900 on transfer from Bolder, Col D: 7/2/1920 A: 90 S: DC Burial: Rev. T.R. Palmer Lt Col 13th Mich Vol Inf 12/6/1829-7/2/1920 (unofficial tombstone). Buried in La Vista Cemetery, National City, CA
Pardo, Horace	N: Whitehall, NY 1/22/43 CW: Co C 123 NY Inf (Pvt) Term: 3 yrs E/D: 8/62-4/63 due to disability GAR: 1/26/1918 S: DC
Parish, Watson	N: Tenn A: 46 O: Lawyer CW: Co G 39 Ill Inf (Pvt/Corpl) E/D: 8/61-9/64 LOS: 37 mos GAR: 8/10/1883 SP: 12/27/1898 RE: 4/11/1899 SP: 12/24/1912 DR: 12/24/1918 S: H
Parker, Charles H.	N: New York A: 79 O: Retired CW: Co G 1 NY Eng (Pvt) E/D: 10/61-11/64 LOS: 3 yrs 1 mo GAR: 12/9/1924 TR: 4/28/1925 S: H
Parker, Dexter	N: Mass A: 55 O: Carpenter CW: Co F 105 Ill Inf (Pvt) E/D: 8/62-5/65 LOS: 33 mos GAR: 7/28/1881 SP: 6/30/1888 RE: 12/14/1890 D: 12/24/1890 S: H
Parker, Edwin A.	N: Vermont A: 65 (or 69) O: Retired CW: Co K 4 Minn Inf (Pvt/Corpl) E/D: 12/64-7/65 LOS: Not stated GAR: 10/8/1912 TR: 12/9/1919 S: H

Parker, Stephen H.	N: Ohio A: 72 O: Retired CW: Co B 2 Wis Cav (Sgt) E/D: 8/61-11/65 LOS: Not stated GAR: 8/23/1910 Died 6/12/1911 S: H
Parker, William T.	N: Mass A: 65 O: Mag. Healer CW: Co I 52 Mass Inf (Pvt/Sgt) E/D: 9/62-8/63 LOS: 11 mos GAR: 2/26/1907 SP: 6/23/1908 DR: 12/24/1918 S: H
Parks, Milton B.	N: New York A: 49 O: Brick Layer CW: Co I 28 Wis Inf (Pvt) E/D: 8/62-8/65 LOS: 36 mos GAR: 10/11/1892 TR: 8/8/1893 S: H
Parmenter, William P.	N: Illinois A: 61 O: Farmer CW: Co K 58 Ill Inf (Pvt) E/D: 3/65-3/66 LOS: 12 mos GAR: 4/10/1906 Died: 3/1/1918 or 3/2/1918 S: H
Partsch, Emil C.	N: Texas A: 51 O: Agent CW: Co G 82 Ill Inf (Musician) E/D: 8/62-7/65 LOS: 36 mos GAR: 1/20/1890 TR: 8/25/1908 S: H
Patrick, Wellington	N: Illinois CW: Co E 13 Ill Cav (Pvt) Term: 3 yrs E/D: 12/63-8/65 GAR: 11/10/1894 Charter Member of Datus Coon Post TR: 4/2/1910 S: DC
Paull, Benjamin B.	N: Illinois A: Not stated O: Retired R: National City, CA CW: Co K 9 Iowa Cav (Pvt) E/D: 9/63-2/66 LOS: 100 days GAR: 6/22/1920 TR: 8/__/1923 S:H
Paull, Benjamin B.	N: Illinois 1846 CW: Co K 9 Iowa Cav (Pvt) Term: 3 yrs E/D: 9/63-2/66 Little Rock, AK LOS: 3 yrs GAR: 8/25/1923 on transfer from Heintzelman Post San Diego Died: 5/3/1927 A: 79/11/17 Obit: Children in Orago and Brandon, Oregon and Oroville, CA; wife not mentioned Buried: Sawtelle, CA S: DC
	SAWTELLE: Died 5/3/1927 at Soldier's Home, Sawtelle, CA and buried in "Branch USA" Sec 51, Row H, Grave 2 with tombstone inscription "Benj B Paull Co K 9 IA Cav"--records at Sawtelle also name him "B.B. Pull" S: Los Angeles National Cemetery
Payton, William N.	N: "Ken" (Kentucky?) A: 70 O: Retired CW: Co I 26 MO Inf (Pvt) E/D: 12/62-7/65 LOS: Not stated GAR: 10/14/1916 SP: 12/28/1920 S: H
Payton, William N.	N: Anderson Co, KY 1846 CW: Co I 26 MO Inf (Pvt) Term: 3 yrs E/D: 12/62-8/65 Little Rock, AK GAR: 6/28/1924 SP: 9/24/1927 S: DC
Peak, Jacob	N: Lorraine, France 7/18/43 CW: Co G 34 Ohio Inf (Pvt/Mus'n) Term: 3 yrs E/D: 7/61-9/64 Columbus, Ohio GAR: 2/25/1911 on transfer from Geo H. Thomas Post #13 Dept of Ohio S: DC
Pearson, M.R.	N: Scott Co, KY A: 38 O: Painter CW: Co A 4 Iowa Inf (Pvt) E/D: 7/61-10/64 LOS: 39 mos GAR: 9/8/1883 SP: 1/10/1889 DR: 6/30/1891 RE: 9/28/1897 SP: 12/24/1912 DR: 12/24/1918 S: H
Pearson, Thomas J.	N: Indiana A: 55 O: Farmer CW: Co H 4 Iowa Inf (Pvt) E/D: 7/61-4/65 LOS: 45 mos GAR: No further information SP: 6/26/1900 DR: 10/25/1904 S: H
Pease, John Melvin	N: Wilton, ME 1842 CW: Co H 25 ME Vol Inf (Pvt) Term: 3 yrs E/D: 9/62-7/65 GAR: 5/12/1917 on transfer from Riverside Post #118 Dept of Cal/Nev Died: 5/29/1929 A: 80/8/29 Obit: Lists children, no wife named S: DC
Peebles, L.R.	NOL/NFI S: DC
Peer, James A.	N: Putnam Co, Ohio 1/20/43 CW: Co E Benton Company MO Cadets (Pvt) Term: 3 yrs E/D: 9/61-1/62 Benton Barracks, MO Re-Enl: Co K 20 Ohio Inf (? rank) E/D: 1/62-1/65 GAR: 12/14/1914 on transfer from Farragut Post #95 Dept of Iowa Died: 6/1932 S: DC

Peirson, J. Lacy	N: New York A: 41 O: Not stated CW: Co D 5 NJ Inf (Pvt/2 Lieut) E/D: 8/61-8/62 Re-Enl?: Co I 26 NJ Inf (Pvt/Capt) E/D: 9/62-6/65 LOS: Not stated GAR: 10/8/1895 Died: 10/29/1896 Buried: "Shipped East" S: H
Pendland, Alonzo	N: Elkhart Co, Ind CW: Co B 33 Ind Inf (Pvt) Term: 1 yr E/D: 2/65-5/65 Indianapolis, Ind GAR: 9/8/1928 S: DC
Perigo, William	N: Susquehanna Co, PA A: 52 O: Cabinet Maker CW: Co A 151 Penn ___ (Sgt) E/D: 9/62-7/63 LOS: 10 mos GAR: 10/28/1881 SP: 3/__/1893 DR: 3/28/1899 S: H
Perkins, Harrison	N: Greenbriar Co, West Virginia 1839 CW: Co H 57 Ind Inf (Corpl) Term: 3 yrs E/D: 9/61-4/65 GAR: 12/9/1922 DR: "Dropped" S: DC
Perrin, William H.	N: England CW: Co H 25 Mich Inf (Pvt) Term: 3 yrs E/D: 8/62-5/65 Knoxville, TN GAR: 5/28/1904 on transfer from Phil Karney Post Dept of Minnesota DR: "Dropped" Died 6/1935 S: DC
Phelps, F.A.	N: Wisconsin A: 40 O: Teamster CW: Co E 3 Wis Cav (Pvt) E/D: 8/61-6/65 LOS: 46 mos GAR: 12/23/1886 SP: 1/10/1889 DR: 6/30/1891 S: H
Phillips, Lionel D.	N: Maine A: 65 O: Mining Engineer CW: Co H 1 Mass Inf (Pvt/Sgt) E/D: 4/61-5/64 Re-Enl?: Co E 61 Mass Inf (Pvt/Sgt) E/D: 9/64-12/64 Promoted?: Co A 6 U S C T (2nd Lieut/1st Lieut) E/D: 12/64-10/65 LOS: 50 2/3 mos GAR: 6/28/1904 Post Commander 1905 Died: 6/17/1908 Los Angeles S: H
Pickens, Frank	N: Illinois A: 75 O: Retired CW: Co A 104 Ill Inf (Corpl/1st Sgt) E/D: 8/62-6/65 LOS: 3 yrs GAR: 8/26/1919 S: H
Pierce, Maris	N: Penn A: 65 O: Real Estate CW: Co C 97 Penn Inf (Pvt/Corpl) E/D: 9/61-9/64 LOS: 36 mos GAR: 8/18/1885 TR: 1/27/1903 S: H
Pierce, Sylvester L.	N: Olney, Rockland Co, IL 7/25/46 CW: Co B 98 Ind Inf (Pvt) Term: 3 yrs Re-Enl: Co B 61 Ill Inf (Pvt) E/D: 10/63-6/65 GAR: 9/18/1917 Died: 6/11/1923 A: 76/10/16 S: DC
Pierson, Ed. Aug.	N: New York A: 83 O: Retired CW: Co C 1 Mich L A (Pvt) E/D: 8/61-1/64 LOS: 3 yrs GAR: 5/25/1926 Died: 3/8/1929 S: H
Pillsbury, Cassius C.	N: Maine A: 56 O: Physician CW: Co F 39 Wis Inf (1st Sgt) E/D: 5/64-9/64 LOS: 3 1/2 mos GAR: 12/23/1902 Post Commander 1906 Died: 9/1/1930 S: H
Pine, Albert B.	N: New York A: 73 O: Retired CW: Co C 74 NY Inf (Pvt) E/D: 4/61-8/64 LOS: Not stated GAR: 7/11/1916 Died: 3/12/1922 S: H
Pitner, John L.	N: Illinois A: 53 O: Minister CW: Co D 5 Ill Cav (Pvt/Corpl) E/D: 12/63-5/65 LOS: 24 mos GAR: 5/5/1894 TR: 3/26/1901 S: H
Place, Daniel C.	N: Ohio A: 43 O: Miller CW: Co D 2 Ohio H A (Pvt) E/D: 6/63-8/65 LOS: 26 mos GAR: 10/22 or 11/22/1888 SP: 9/26/1889 DR: 6/30/1891 or 12/93 RE: 8/14/1906 Died: 2/27/1908 S: H
Poland, Martin	N: Mass A: 87 O: Retired CW: Co __ 7 RI Cav (Pvt) E/D: 6/62-9/62 Re-Enl?: Co A 10 Mass Cav (Pvt) E/D: __/64-9/64 LOS: Not stated GAR: 1/25/1927 Died: 9/9/1929 S: H
Pontious, Wilson	N: Ohio A: 72 O: Farmer CW: Co G 85 Ohio Inf (Pvt) E/D: 5/62-9/62 LOS: Not stated GAR: 1/12/1915 on trans. from Col. Baker Post #84 Dept of Michigan SP: 12/14/1929 S:H

Pool, Chester W.	N: Indiana A: 79 O: Retired CW: Co D 40 Wis Inf (Pvt) E/D: 6/64-9/64 LOS: 3 mos GAR: 6/14/1927 TR: 3/18/1928 RE: 3/12/1929 Died: 12/__/1934 S: H
Porter, John	N: Brown Co, Ohio 1835 CW: Co E 23 Iowa Inf (Pvt) Term: 3 yrs E/D: 8/62-10/64 Jefferson Barracks due to wounds GAR: 6/11/1921 on transfer from Dept of Iowa S: DC
Porter, Stephen	N: Indiana A: 66 O: Carpenter CW: Co A 9 Indep Ind Inf (Sgt) E/D: 7/62-8/62 LOS: 30 days GAR: 6/26/1906 Died: 4/15/1914 S: H
Porter, Watson B.	N: Illinois A: 90 O: Retired R: La Jolla, CA CW: Co F 4 Iowa Cav (Capt) E/D: __/61-__/65 LOS: 4 yrs GAR: 6/22/1926 Died: 1/5/1929 S: H
Potter, Daniel	N: Ohio A: 59 O: Accountant CW: Co G 179 Ohio Inf (1st Sgt) E/D: 9/64-6/65 LOS: 9 mos GAR: 1/14/1902 Died: 11/20/1910 S: H
Powell, John C.	N: Penn CW: Co E 8 Penn Inf (Pvt/Sgt) Term: 3 yrs E/D: 4/61-5/64 GAR: 7/28/1917 on transfer from Gordon Granger Post #64 Dept of Iowa Died: 8/7/1930 S: DC
Powers, Robert M.	N: Alden, NY A: 38 O: Physician CW: Co M 2 Ohio H A (Pvt) E/D: 9/62-9/64 LOS: 24 or 36 mos GAR: 6/28/1883 Post Commander 1887 Died: 1/14/1927 S: H
Pratt, C.W.	N: Mass A: 54 O: Carpenter CW: Co C 2 Mass Cav (Pvt) E/D: 9/64-6/65 LOS: 9 mos GAR: 5/13/1886 SP: 9/26/1889 DR: 6/30/1891 S: H
Pratt, Charles E.	N: Wisconsin A: 79 O: Shoe Maker CW: Co F 48 Wis Inf (Sgt) E/D: 3/65-2/66 LOS: 11 mos GAR: 6/12/1923 Died: 8/1/1924 S: H
Prescott, C.W.	N: Penn A: 75 O: Retired R: National City, CA CW: Co L 16 Kans Cav (Corpl) E/D: 2/64-11/65 LOS: 1 yr 9 mos GAR: 9/14/1920 S: H
Preston, Charles	NOL/NFI S: DC
Price, Levi	N: Penn A: 51 O: Merchant R: Lakeside, CA CW: Co G 11 U S Inf (Pvt/Ord Sgt) E/D: 8/61-8/64 LOS: 36 mos GAR: 6/27/1889 TR: 3/13/1891 GAR: 6/11/1895 or 6/11/1896 TR: 9/22/1903 S: H
Probert, John	N: Patterson, NJ 1839 CW: Co B 15 NJ Inf (Pvt) Term: 3 yrs E/D: __/62-7/65 GAR: 3/27/1926 DR: "Dropped" S: DC
Purvis, George	N: Scotland A: 82 O: Retired CW: Co B 51 Ohio Inf (Pvt) E/D: 2/64-10/65 LOS: Not stated GAR: 10/25/1927 Died: 9/16/1935 S: H
Putnam, C.S.	N: New York A: 39 O: Painter CW: Co E 106 NY Inf (Pvt) E/D: 8/62-5/65 LOS: 35 mos GAR: 2/18/1887 SP: 6/30/1888 DR: 6/30/1891 S: H
Putnam, George	N: Mass A: 70 O: Clerk CW: Co E 2 Colo Cav (Pvt) E/D: 9/62-2/64 due to disability LOS: Not stated GAR: 12/22/1908 SP: 6/23/1914 S: H
Quackenbush, C.	N: New York A: 66 O: Realty Agent CW: Co __ 11 NY Indep. Batt (Pvt) E/D: 8/64-6/65 LOS: 10 mos GAR: 11/12/1907 "Chauncey Quackenbush" S: H
Radford, Thomas	N: New York A: 63 O: Merchant CW: US Navy--U.S.S.Vesuvius (Seaman) E/D: 6/61-10/62 LOS: Not stated GAR: 4/24/1900 S: H
Rafferty, E.G.	N: Dearborn Co, Ind 1846 CW: Co G 43 Ind Inf (Pvt) Term: 3 yrs E/D: 10/64-10/65 GAR: 3/27/1926 on transfer from Long Beach Poast #181 Dept of Cal/Nev S: DC

Randall, Thomas J.   N: Michigan A: 80 O: Retired CW: Co A 4 Iowa Inf (Pvt) E/D: 7/61-8/64 LOS: 3 yrs GAR: 2/10/1920 Died: 8/6/1923 S: H

Rapeleye, A.W.   N: Fishkill, NY CW: Co H 1st Cal Cav (Farrier) E/D: 3/64-4/65 Fort Macy, New Mexico Re-Enl: Same company (Veterinary Surgeon) E/D: 4/65-12/66 Presidio, CA GAR: 1/24/1895 Died: 3/19/1908 A: 82 Buried: Soldier's Home. S: DC

SAWTELLE: No records for this veteran were found at Los Angeles National Cemetery, although the Sawtelle Soldier's Home Index indicates this veteran died at Sawtelle Soldier's Home.

Read, John W.   N: Ohio A: 59 O: Farmer CW: Co A 87 Ind Inf (Pvt); Re-Enl?: Co B 42 Ind Inf (Pvt) E/D: 12/63-7/65 LOS: 17 mos GAR: 5/9/1905 (probably on transfer from G.K. Warren Post #5 Dept of New Mexico) Died: 9/9/1929 (same date of death in GAR record as John Reed, below. One of these men died on this date. The best way to discover which one did is to check their death certificates) S:H

Reece, O.M.   N: Iowa A: 43 O: Merchant R: Oceanside, CA CW: Co E 5 Iowa Cav (Pvt) E/D: 8/61-8/65 LOS: 48 mos GAR: 7/8/1886 Died: 1890--is [grave] stone S: H

Reed, A.   N: Maine A: 45 O: Carpenter CW: Co C 23 Maine Inf (Corpl) E/D: 9/62-7/63 LOS: 10 mos GAR: 7/21/1886 SP: 9/26/1889 DR: 6/30/1891 S: H

Reed, Francis B.   N: Ohio A: 64 O: Physician CW: Co I 1 Neb Inf (Pvt) E/D: 10/62-2/63 due to disability LOS: 4 mos GAR: 3/28/1893 SP: 12/31/1893 DR: 10/25/1904 S: H

Reed, John   N: Penn A: 79 O: Retired CW: Co B 1 PA L A (Pvt) E/D: 6/61-6/64 LOS: 3 yrs GAR: 8/24/1920 Died: 9/9/1929 (same date of death in GAR record as John W. Read above. One of these men died on this date. The best way to discover which one did is to check their death certificates) S: H

Reeder, T.W.   NOL/NFI S: DC

Reid, Andrew D.   N: Johnstown, NY A: 70 O: Laborer R: Carlsbad, CA CW: Co D 153 NY ___ (Pvt) E/D: 1/65-10/65 LOS: 10 mos GAR: 7/9/1918 RE: 11/12/1935 (Last member named on roster of Heintzelman Post GAR--he first joined the Post on 7/9/1918, as noted above) S: H

Reintanz, O.J.   N: Germany A: 40 O: Barber CW: Co L 3 NJ Cav (Pvt/Sgt) E/D: 11/63-5/65 LOS: 18 mos GAR: 12/6/1877 SP: 6/28/1892 RE: 6/26/1894 TR: 6/26/1894 S:H

Rhoads, Abraham   N: Ohio A: 65 O: Butcher CW: Co F 63 Ohio Inf (Pvt/Sgt) E/D: 8/62-7/65 LOS: 37 mos GAR: 9/24/1907 Died: 10/8/1922 S: H

Rhodes, Ransom E.   N: New York A: 75 O: Farmer CW: Co E 9 Mich Inf (Pvt) E/D: 8/64-6/65 LOS: 10 mos GAR: 2/9/1904 TR: 10/25/1904 S: H

Rice, Hosea B.   N: Howard, NY A: 36 O: Laborer CW: Co E 14 US Inf (Pvt) E/D: 12/62-12/65 LOS: 3 yrs GAR: 10/8/1881 Charter Member of Heintzelman Post GAR DR: "Dropped" S: H

Richards, George W.   N: Hamilton Co, Ohio 1846 CW: Co C 144 Ind Inf (Pvt) Term: 1 yr E/D: 1/65-8/65 Stevenson Station GAR: 8/10/1918 on transfer from Elmwood Post #61 Dept of Indiana DR: 9/24/1927 S: DC

Richardson, A. Tappen   N: Mass A: 60 O: Retired CW: USS Ohio (1st Class Fireman) E/D: 6/64-9/67 LOS: Not stated GAR: 1/22/1901 Died: 4/1/1917 Cremated--Ashes sent to Lowell, Mass S: H

Richmond, John	N: Indiana CW: Co A 39 Iowa Inf (Pvt) Term: 3 yrs E/D: 8/62-6/65 Washington, D.C. GAR: 2/25/1911 on transfer from J.D. Craven Post #192 Dept of Iowa. TR: 10/23/1915 S: DC
Rickard, Charles W.	N: Ohio A: 77 O: Retired CW: Co G 24 Iowa Inf (Pvt) E/D: 8/62-7/65 LOS: 3 yrs GAR: 8/14/1923 Died: 2/16/1931 S: H
Rickit, H.V.	N: France A: 41 O: Laborer CW: Co B 1 Wash Ter'y (Pvt) Re-Enl?: US Navy (Acting Ensign) (This re-enlistment entry may not be true--it looks as if this was added to the GAR record later. It is written above his true service information) E/D: 2/62-3/65 LOS: 36 mos GAR: 5/24/1883 D: 12/1/1883 S: H
Riedelbauch, John	N: Belvaria (Bavaria?) A: 69 O: Farmer CW: Co A 44 Ill Inf (Pvt) E/D: 9/64-6/65 LOS: 8 2/3 mos GAR: 10/25/1904 TR: 4/14/1908 S: H
Riggs, Joseph	N: England A: Not stated O: Blacksmith CW: Co C 39 Wis Inf (Pvt) Re-Enl?: Co E 9 Ill Cav (Pvt) E/D: 5/64-10/65 LOS: 17 mos GAR: 11/22/1888 SP: 4/30/1890 RE: 12/20/1890 TR: 5/25/1892 S: H
Rimbach, Charles/Carl	N: Germany A: 53 O: Carpenter R: Del Mar/San Diego CW: Co A 3 US Arty (Artificer) E/D: 8/61-2/67 LOS: 66 mos GAR: 10/12/1882 or 10/28/1882 SP: 9/26/1889 DR: 6/30/1891 DR: 3/28/1899 RE: 4/24/1900 S: H
Roberts, Samuel L.	N: Lee Co, Ohio CW: Co C 75 Ill Inf (Pvt) Term: 3 yrs E/D: 8/62-5/63 Evansville, Ind due to physical disability GAR: 3/26/1904 DR: 12/9/1916 S: DC
Robertson, Simon	N: Monmouth, Ill A: 74 O: Retired CW: Co A 14 Ill Cav (Pvt) E/D: 3/63-8/65 LOS: 30 mos GAR: 1/14/1918 TR: 9/26/1922 RE: 5/8/1923 Died: 4/29/1927 S:H
Robinson, A.S.	N: Jefferson, PA 1843 CW: Co A 7 Minn Inf (Pvt/Corpl) Term: 3 yrs E/D: 8/62-8/65 Ft Snelling, MN GAR: 6/11/1921 DR: 9/24/1927 S: DC
Robinson, George	N: Lancaster Co, PA 2/14/43 CW: Co B 3 US Colored Inf (Pvt) Term: 3 yrs E/D: 6/63-11/65 Enlisted Philadelphia, PA; discharged Jacksonville, Florida Re-Enl: Co H 9 US Cav (Pvt) E/D: 11/66-11/71 Ft Quitman, TX GAR: ? date on transfer from Uncle Sam Post #177 Dept of Cal/Nev S: DC
Rockwood, George	N: Kane Co, Ill CW: Co G 15 Kans Cav (Pvt) Term: 3 yrs E/D: 9/63-10/65 Leavenworth, Kans GAR: 2/13/1926 on transfer from D.A. Russell Post #35 Dept of Wash/Alaska Died: 3/12/1934 Buried: Oklahoma City Obit lists wife Mary Rockwood S: DC
Roderick, Edward	N: New York A: 66 O: Farmer CW: Co E 5 Iowa Inf (Pvt); Re-Enl?: Co G 5 Iowa Cav (Corpl) E/D: 5/61-8/65 LOS: Not stated GAR: 9/22/1908 SP: 12/10/1918 S: H
Rogers, Eli	N: Seneca Co, Ohio 1846 CW: Co K 139 Ohio NGVI (Pvt) Term: 100 days E/D: 5/64-8/64 Camp Dennison GAR: 9/10/1921 Died: 1/16/1929 A: 81/9/20 Obit: Lists wife Mary W. Rogers S: DC
Roneau, Charles F.W.	N: Hamburg, Germany 9/18/40 CW: S.S. Fredonia (Pvt/Seaman) Term: 3 yrs E/D: 7/61-7/65 Calloa, Peru GAR: 4/11/1914 SP: 7/14/1917 S: DC
Root, M.S.	N: Medina, Ohio A: 45 O: Jeweler CW: Co K 103 Ohio Inf (Pvt/2nd Lieut) due to resignation E/D: 8/62-2/64 LOS: Not stated GAR: 2/22/1883 Died: "Dead"--no [grave] stone S: H

Rose, Bowers L.	N: New York A: 59 O: Plasterer, San Diego; Rancher, Smithdale and Dehesa, CA CW: Co K 2 PA Inf (Pvt) E/D: 2/65-7/65 LOS: 5 mos GAR: 6/23/1887 SP 1/10/1889 DR: 6/30/1890 GAR: 3/14/1899 SP: 6/25/1901 DR: 1/22/1907 RE: 8/24/1909 SP: 6/28/1914 RE: 9/10/1918 Died: 9/13/1929 S: H
Rose, John L.	N: New York A: 65 O: Retired CW: Co L 14 NY Art (Pvt) E/D: 12/63-8/65 LOS: Not stated GAR: 8/27/1912 Died: 9/26/1929 S: H
Rosengarden, Moses	NOL/NFI S: DC
Ross, Daniel	N: Holland CW: Co A 1 Cal Cav (Pvt) Term: 3 yrs E/D: 8/61-8/64 Las Cruces, NM GAR: 3/13/1909 on transfer from E.E. Cross Post #90 TR: 9/13/1913 S: DC
Ross, R.H.	N: New York A: 44 O: Carpenter CW: Co F 12 Iowa ___ (Pvt) E/D: 9/61-4/62 due to disability LOS: 7 mos GAR: 12/9/1886 SP: 3/28/1889 RE: 9/12/1889 D: 9/12/1889 S:H
Rouark, Nathan L.	N: Maryland A: 70 O: Clerk CW: Co D 1 MD Inf (Pvt) E/D: 10/61-7/65 LOS: Not stated GAR: 4/25/1912 on transfer from Colorado Springs Post #22 Dept of Col/Wyo SP: 12/26/1916 DR: 12/24/1918 S: H
Routson, John G.	N: Columbiana Co, OH CW: Co C 104 OVI (Pvt) Term: 3 yrs E/D: 8/62-7/65 Indianapolis, Ind GAR: 1/27/1906 on transfer from Post #9 Dept of Nebraska Died: 2/21/1909 A: 65 Buried: National City, CA (near San Diego) S: DC
Rowley, Samuel B.	N: New York 4/5/35 CW: Co I 1 Mich Inf (Pvt) Term: 3 yrs E/D: 11/61-3/62 GAR: 4/14/1928 Died: 12/16/1929 A: 93 Obit states one son in Sunnyside, CA; no wife mentioned Buried: Glenn Abbey Cemetery, Chula Vista, CA (near San Diego) S: DC Note: Glenn Abbey tombstone record says: "Samuel B. Rowley Father Mar 2, 1836-Dec 16, 1928" Wife's tombstone reads: "Clara M. Rowley Mother May 7, 1845-Feb 4, 1927" S: Glenn Abbey tombstone records, Family History Center, San Diego.
Rudrauff, William H.	N: Penn A: 62 O: Real Estate CW: Co K 19 PA Inf (Pvt) E/D: 4/61-7/61 Re-Enl?: Co F 82 PA Inf (Pvt/2nd Lieut) E/D: 8/61-12/64 due to wounds LOS: 44 mos GAR: 5/25/1905 Died: 7/23/1916 S: H
Rumpf, August	N: Germany CW: Co A 39 NY Inf (Pvt/2nd Lieut) Term: 3 yrs E/D: 6/61-5/63 Washington, D.C. Re-Enl: Co D 1st US Vet Vol (1st Sgt) E/D: 1/65-1/66 Wilmington GAR: 1/23/1904 on transfer from Folks Post #32 Dept of NY Died: 10/5/1903 A: 75 Soldier's Home S: DC SAWTELLE: Died on ? date (not in records) and buried in "Branch USA" Sec 24, Row A, Grave 6 with tombstone inscription "1st Sgt Augustus Rumpf Co D 1 U.S.V.V. Inf" S: Los Angeles National Cemetery
Runk, Joseph B.	N: Penn A: 59 O: Miner CW: Co H 22 PA Cav (Pvt) E/D: Not stated LOS: Not stated GAR: 1/9/1906 SP: 6/23/1908 DR: 12/24/1918 S: H
Russell, Enoch	N: Indiana A: 62 O: Carpenter CW: Co C 12 US Inf (Pvt) E/D: 10/61-10/64 LOS: 36 mos GAR: 1/22/1907 SP: 12/22/1914 DR: 12/24/1918 S: H
Ryan, John T.	N: Ireland A: 45 O: Cooper CW: Co ___ 2 Ind Batt (Pvt) E/D: 11/64-7/65 LOS: 9 mos GAR: 5/23/1889 TR: 1/9/1890 S: H
Sackett, Charles H.	N: Ohio A: 57 O: Farmer CW: Co A 2 Ohio Inf (Pvt/Corpl) E/D: 8/61-4/63 due to disability LOS: 20 mos GAR: 6/8/1897 SP: 12/27/1898 DR: 12/24/1918 S:H

Sanborn, E.B.	N: Maine A: 43 O: Farmer CW: Co C 8 Maine Inf (Pvt) E/D: 9/61-6/65 LOS: 52 mos GAR: __/__/1886 TR: 2/28/1889 S: H
Santee, Milton	N: Penn A: 55 O: Surveyor CW: Co A 13 Ill Inf (Pvt); Re-Enl?: Co __ 11 MO Cav (1st Lieut) E/D: 4/61-7/65 LOS: 51 mos GAR: 3/25/1891 SP: 9/28/1897 Died: "Died"--no date S: H
Sawtelle, Arthur M.	N: Ohio A: 70 O: Real Estate CW: Charleston Navy Yard (Marine Engineer) E/D: 2/64-10/65 LOS: Not stated GAR: 4/13/1909 TR: 4/9/1912 S:H
Schaeffer, Jason	N: Tuscarora Co, Ohio 6/4/33 CW: Co H 152 Ind Inf (Pvt) Term: 1 yr E/D: 2/65-8/65 Charleston, VA GAR: 11/13/1915 SP: "Suspended" S: DC
Schill, Charles	N: Germany A: 41 O: Baker CW: Co A 31 Mass Inf (Pvt) E/D: 5/62-5/65 LOS: 36 mos GAR: 1/11/1884 SP: 12/27/1889 DR: 10/25/1904 RE: 3/12/1912 Died: 8/8/1921 S: H
Schill, S.	N: Germany A: 43 O: Baker CW: Co F 31 Mass Inf (Pvt); Re-Enl?: Co A 31 Mass Inf (Pvt) E/D: 5/62-5/65 LOS: 36 mos GAR: 9/23/1886 D: 12/28/1888 S: H
Scholton, Charles	NOL/NFI S: DC
Schooley, Ellis L.	N: Penn A: 45 O: Carpenter CW: Co C 96 Ill Inf (Pvt) E/D: __/62-__/65 LOS: 36 mos GAR: 4/__/1884 SP: 6/30/1888 DR: 6/30/1891 RE: 12/4/1891 D: 12/4/1891 S: H
Schroeter, Charles	N: Germany A: 81 R: Retired CW: Co C 1 MO Cav (Pvt) E/D: 3/63-9/65 LOS: 30 mos GAR: 8/13/1918 on transfer from Post #130 Dept of New York Died: 1/27/1921 S: H
Schutte, Gerhard	N: Germany A: 66 O: Farmer R: Carlsbad, CA CW: Co E 3 Wis Inf (Pvt/1st Sgt) E/D: 4/61-7/65 LOS: 51 mos GAR: 5/25/1905 DR: 12/24/1918 S: H
Scofield, L.	N: New York A: 50 O: Hotel Keeper R: Ramona, CA CW: Co K 26 Iowa Inf (Pvt/Sgt) E/D: 8/62-5/64 due to disability LOS: 21 mos GAR: 5/8/1886 SP: 6/30/1888 DR: 6/30/1891 S: H
Seabold(t), Henry	N: Penn A: 64 O: Not stated CW: Co C 14 MD Inf (Corpl) E/D: 5/62-5/65 LOS: 36 mos GAR: 5/20/1886 SP: 6/30/1888 DR: 6/30/1891 RE: 6/14/1904 Died: 4/6/1913 S: H
Severy, Elisha	N: Conn A: 60 O: Stone Cutter CW: Co I 16 Conn Inf (Pvt) E/D: 8/62-2/63 due to disability LOS: 6 2/3 mos GAR: 12/23/1902 TR: 5/10/1904 S: H
Shaffer, Peter	N: Ohio A: 67 O: Liveryman CW: Co E 7 Kans Cav (Pvt) E/D: 8/61-9/65 LOS: 49 mos GAR: 5/8/1906 SP: 12/24/1912 Died: 12/27/1913 at Milo (?), MO S: H
Shall, Eugene E.	N: Ohio A: 49 O: Carpenter R: Oceanside, CA CW: Co H 177 Ohio Inf (Pvt) E/D: 8/64-6/65 LOS: 10 mos GAR: 10/8/1894 Died: "Died"--no date, Oceanside S: H
Sharp, William H.	N: Platt Co, MO A: 38 O: Farmer R: Bernardo (probably near present Rancho Bernardo, CA) CW: Co K 43 MO Inf (Pvt) E/D: 8/64-6/65 LOS: 10 1/2 mos GAR: 5/22/1884 DR: 3/28/1899 S: H
Shaw, A.C.	N: Dendmark, Ohio 1843 CW: Co C 85th Ohio ___ (Pvt) Term: 3 mos E/D: 5/62-__/62 Columbus, Ohio Re-Enl: Co B 5 Bat Cav (Pvt/Sgt) E/D: 7/63-2/64 Cincinnati, Ohio GAR: 10/13/1917 Died: "Dead" S: DC
Shea, Michael	N: Canada A: 56 O: Pension Attorney or Pension Agent CW: Co G 53 Ill Inf (Pvt) E/D: 4/64-7/65 LOS: 15 mos GAR: 2/12/1901 TR: 10/27/1912 S: H

Shelly, Thomas C.	N: Ohio A: 77 O: Rancher R: East San Diego CW: Co C 17 Ill Inf (Pvt) E/D: 5/61-5/64 Re-Enl?: Co H 15 Ill Inf (1st Lieut) E/D: 3/65-9/65 LOS: 3 yrs 5 mos GAR: 11/9/1920 TR: To Datus E. Coon Post--no date given S: H
Shelly, Thomas C.	N: Richmond, Jefferson Co, Ohio 12/27/43 CW: Co C 17 Ill Inf (Pvt) Term: 3 yrs E/D: 6/61-6/64 Springfield, IL Re-Enl: Co H 15 Ill Inf (1st Lieut) E/D: __/65-9/65 Fort Leavenworth, Kas GAR: 9/12/1925 on transfer from Heintzelman Post San Diego S: DC

Service record: Attended Monmouth College when he enlisted. Battles: Frederickstown, MO, Fort Donaldson, Shiloh, Seige of Corinth, Iuka (sp?), Hatchee, Siege of Vicksburg and others. Was in command of his Company at Grand Review, Washington, D.C. 5/24/65. When Sherman's Army discharged, his Brigade alone was sent across the plains to fight Indians. Returned to Ft. Leavenworth (still in command of his company) for discharge. Married Miss Mattie E. Bell at Orford, now Mouton, Iowa on 6/21/1869. |
Shepard, Charles T.	N: New York A: 70 O: Retired CW: Co E 17 Ill Cav (Pvt) E/D: 12/63-11/65 LOS: 23 mos GAR: 5/28/1918 S: H
Shepherd, A.C.	NOL/NFI S: DC
Shepherd, James	N: Kentucky 4/43 CW: Co G 3 KY Inf (Pvt) Term: 3 yrs E/D: 4/62-9/62 Smith's Plantation, LA due to disability. GAR: 9/8/1928 S: DC
Sherman, Frank M.	N: Mass A: 43 O: Laborer CW: Co I 34 Mass Inf (Pvt) E/D: 7/62-6/65 LOS: 34 2/3 mos GAR: 9/22/1887 TR: 1/26/1888 Died: 12/15/1903--is [grave] stone S:H
Shill, General	N: Ohio A: 66 O: Retired CW: Co D 11 Ohio Inf (Pvt) E/D: 6/61-6/64 LOS: 36 mos GAR: 9/12/1905 SP: 6/23/1908 Died: "Dead" S: H
Shindler, George	N: Germany CW: Co I 138 Ill Inf (Pvt) Term: 100 days E/D: 5/64-10/64 Springfield, Ill Re-Enl: Co A 156 Ill Inf (Pvt) E/D: 1/65-__/65 Memphis, TN GAR: 8/24/1912 DR: 7/14/1917 S: DC
Shock, William	N: Germany A: 43 O: Laborer CW: Co F 65 NY Inf (Pvt) E/D: 5/64-7/65 LOS: 14 mos GAR: 4/26/1888 TR: 6/28/1888 S: H
Shorton, William	N: New York A: 38 O: Painter CW: Co I 28 NY Inf (Drummer) E/D: 8/64-11/64 LOS: 3 mos GAR: 10/13/1887 SP: 3/26/1895 RE: 12/10/1895 T: 12/10/1895 S: H
Shultz, James F.	N: Illinois A: 45 O: Farmer R: Oneonta, CA CW: Co F 26 Ill Inf (Pvt) E/D: 2/64-7/65 LOS: 17 mos GAR: 9/9/1891 SP: 3/__/1893 DR: 3/28/1899 RE: 5/22/1900 Died: 10/20/1916 S: H
Shuyler, J.L.	N: Indiana A: 73 O: Retired CW: Co G 53 Ind Inf (Pvt) E/D: 1/62-7/65 LOS: 3 yrs GAR: 6/24/1919 Died: 6/23/1934 S: H
Sigman, Marcus	N: Easton, PA A: 43 O: Harness Maker CW: Co H 24 PA ___ (Pvt); Re-Enl?: Co H 15 US Inf (Pvt) E/D: 4/61-2/68 LOS: Not stated GAR: 10/21/1881 DR: "Dropped" S: H
Simmons, Clinton	N: New York A: 50 O: Laborer CW: Co K 123 Ohio Inf (Pvt) Re-Enl?: Co __ V R Corps (Pvt) E/D: 9/62-7/65 LOS: 33 mos GAR: 12/12/1893 TR: 4/24/1894 S: H
Simpson, Joseph	N: Missouri A: 48 O: Cook CW: Co G 79 Kans Col Inf (Pvt) E/D: 2/63-10/65 LOS: 32 mos GAR: 6/23/1896 SP: 9/28/1897 RE: 5/22/1900 Died: 11/5/1903 Soldier's Home S:H

Simpson, Jos. (Con't)	SAWTELLE: Died at Sawtelle Soldier's Home on 11/5/1903 and buried in "Branch USA" Sec 4, Row D, Grave 25 with tombstone inscription "Jos Simpson Co C(?) 79 US G I" (G in US G I hard to read) S: Los Angeles National Cemetery.
Sims, W.F.	N: Henry Co, KY A: 40 O: Farmer R: Cajon (probably the present El Cajon, CA) CW: Co F 99 Ind Inf (Pvt) E/D: 8/62-6/65 LOS: 34 mos GAR: 7/12/1883 S: H
Sisson, Elbert N.	N: New York 11/2/42 CW: Co H 2 Iowa Inf (Pvt) Term: 3 yrs E/D: 5/61-6/64 Mt Pulaski, TN GAR: 7/28/1917 Died 5/7/1923 A: 81 S: DC
Slade, Isaac	N: England A: 69 O: Retired CW: Co C 30 Wis Inf (Pvt/Drummer) E/D: 8/62-9/65 LOS: Not stated GAR: 6/25/1912 SP: 12/26/1916 RE: 9/24/1918 D: 9/24/1918 S: H
Slaughter, William	N: Canton, Ill, 1841 CW: Co F 67 Ill Inf (Pvt) Term: 3 mos E/D: 6/62-10/__ Chicago, Ill GAR: 4/11/1925 on transfer from John A. Martin Post Dept of Cal/Nev SP: 8/1926 S: DC
Sloane, Hampton P.	N: Ohio A: 81 O: Farmer R: Ramona, CA CW: Co C 74 Ill Inf (Capt) E/D: 8/62-4/63 due to disability LOS: 8 mos GAR: 7/25/1905 SP: 6/25/1907 S: H
Slusser, Abraham	N: Brookfield, Ohio CW: Co M 7th Ill Cav (Pvt) Term: 1 yr E/D: 3/65-11/65 GAR: 9/9/1911 on transfer from Phil Sheridan Post #4 Dept of Idaho. Died 11/28/1918 S: DC
Smart, James G.	N: New York A: 64 O: Retired CW: Co I 20 NY Cav (Corpl) E/D: 9/63-7/65 LOS: Not stated GAR: 5/28/1912 on transfer from Napa Post #192 Dept of Cal/Nev Past Commander Died: 12/11/1924 S: H
Smith, Ansel G.	N: New York A: 54 O: Carpenter CW: Co E 1 Mich Eng (Pvt) E/D: 8/61-10/64 LOS: 39 mos GAR: 5/24/1888 DR: 12/27/1889 DR: 6/30/1891 S: H
Smith, C.E.	N: Wisc A: 38 O: Laborer CW: Co F 46 Iowa Inf (Pvt) E/D: 6/64-9/64 LOS: 3 mos GAR: 7/8/1886 SP: 1/10/1889 DR: 3/28/1899 S: H
Smith, C.M.	NOL/NFI S: DC
Smith, D.M.	N: Indiana A: 37 O: Real Estate CW: Co F 7 Ind Inf (Pvt) E/D: 4/61-8/61 LOS: 4 mos GAR: 3/22/1888 SP: 1/10/1889 DR: 6/30/1891 S: H
Smith, Edward	N: New York A: 45 O: Furniture/Cabinet Maker CW: Co H 128 NY Inf (Musician) E/D: 7/62-7/65 LOS: 36 mos GAR: 4/25/1889 TR: 6/27/1889 RE: 5/27/1891 TR: 7/25/1893 S: H
Smith, Edward H.	N: Ohio A: 69 O: Clerk CW: Co B 16 Mich Inf (Sgt) Re-Enl: Co D 16 Mich Inf (Capt) E/D: 8/61-12/63 LOS: Not stated GAR: 9/13/1910 Died: 5/15/1916 S: H
Smith, Ernest L.	N: Ohio A: 76 O: Retired CW: Co G 29 Ohio Inf (Pvt) E/D: 9/61-11/62 due to disability LOS: 1 yr GAR: 11/9/1920 Died: 11/20/1926 S: H
Smith, Eugene E.	N: Illinois A: 71 O: Farmer CW: Co K 12 Kans Inf (Pvt) E/D: 8/62-6/65 LOS: Not stated GAR: 5/25/1915 on transfer from Montrose Post #38 Dept of Colo/Wyo Died: 1/7/1910 S: H
Smith, Frederick P.	N: New York City 1840 CW: Co K 8th NY Inf (Sgt) Term: 3 mos E/D: 5/62-9/62 New York City GAR: 12/12/1925 on transfer from Escondido Post #143 Died: 1/10/1929, Soldier's Home 1/10/1929 (GAR date of death is probably in error--it could be a date of burial--see below) S: DC

Smith, Fredr'k P.	SAWTELLE: Died 12/3/1928 at Soldier's Home and is buried in "Branch USA" Sec 59, Row D, Grave 8 with tombstone inscription "Sergt Fred'k P Smith Co K 8 NY S M Inf" S: Los Angeles National Cemetery
Smith, G.W.	N: Iowa A: 45 O: Real Estate CW: Co F 1 Iowa Inf (Pvt/Adj) E/D: 5/61-9/65 LOS: 52 mos GAR: 2/23/1888 TR: 1/9/1890 S: H
Smith, Henry F.	N: Maine A: 52 O: Bookkeeper Co E 10 ME Inf (Pvt/2nd Lieut) E/D: 5/61-5/63 LOS: 24 mos GAR: 9/9/1891 Died: 11/17/1922 S: H
Smith, Ichabod	N: Indiana A: 65 O: Farmer CW: Co C 89 Ind Inf (Sgt) E/D: 8/62-7/65 LOS: 33 mos GAR: 11/27/1906 Died: 8/13/1917 Buried: Haven, Kansas S: H
Smith, J. Bryant	N: New York A: 54 O: Bookkeeper CW: Co K 53 NY Inf (Pvt/Sgt) E/D: 11/61-3/62 due to disability LOS: 4 mos GAR: 3/26/1895 TR: 1/14/1896 S: H
Smith, Theron J.	N: New York A: 63 O: Real Estate CW: Co A 140 Ill Inf (Pvt) E/D: 3/64-12/64 LOS: 9 mos GAR: 9/24/1907 TR: 11/23/1909 S: H
Smith, Thomas B.	N: Ohio A: 72 O: Carpenter CW: Co D 78 Ill Inf (Pvt) Re-Enl?: Co G 1 US Eng (Sgt) E/D: 9/62-9/65 LOS: 37 mos GAR: 12/27/1904 TR: 1/14/1908 S: H
Smyth, Frank	N: Illinois A: 77 O: Retired CW: Co D 140 Ill Inf (Capt) E/D: 5/64-10/64 LOS: 100 days GAR: 6/14/1921 Died: 3/3/1931 S: H
Snider, Daniel S.	N: Perry Co, Ohio CW: Co H 90 Ohio Inf (Pvt/Com Sgt) Term: 3 yrs E/D: 8/62-6/65 Camp Helena, TN GAR: 9/26/1908 on transfer from from Geo. B. McClellan Post #76 Dept of Col/Wyo Died: 3/16/1916 A: 84 Buried: GAR (Mount Hope) S: DC Note: No record of the burial of Daniel S. Snider at Mount Hope Cemetery.
Snoderly, Emanual	N: Iowa A: 43 O: Farmer CW: Co K 4 MO Cav (Pvt) E/D: 5/62?-5/65 LOS: 36 mos GAR: 11/24/1887 TR: 2/28/1890 S: H
Southwell, Robert	N: England A: 64 O: Farmer CW: Co A 21 MO Inf (Pvt/Corpl) E/D: 11/62-2/65 LOS: Not stated GAR: 9/22/1908 SP: 12/24/1912 RE: 7/14/1914 TR: 7/14/1914 S: H
Southwick, Myron H.	N: Michigan A: 64 O: retired CW: Co H 8 Mich Inf (Pvt/Hosp.Steward) E/D: 2/64-7/65 LOS: Not stated GAR: 3/8/1910 Died: 7/7/1929 S: H
Spangler, Henry	N: Holmes Co, Ohio CW: Co G 21 Iowa ___ (Pvt) Term: 3 yrs Re-Enl: Co K 4th Vet Res Corps (Pvt) E/D: 8/62-8/65 Davenport, Iowa GAR: 2/14/1914 Died: 10/28/1925 A: 82/3/14 Buried: Soldier's Home S: DC SAWTELLE: No records for this veteran were found at Los Angeles National Cemetery. California Death Index indicated death in San Diego. Death certificate said death in San Diego; burial in San Gabriel Cemetery, San Gabriel, CA
Spates, John M.	N: Tenn A: 71 O: Janitor CW: Co A 115 Ill Inf (Pvt/Corpl) E/D: 8/62-6/65 LOS: Not stated GAR: 3/24/1914 on transfer from Trinidad Post #25 Dept of Col/Wyo TR: 1/26/1915 S: H
Spaulding, Edgar	N: New York A: 49 O: Musician CW: Co D 137 NY Inf (Drummer) E/D: 8/62-6/65 LOS: 33 mos GAR: 2/9/1888 SP: 9/26/1889 Died: 5/__/1894--no [grave] stone S: H

Spencer, James R.	N: Missouri A: 40 O: Carpenter CW: Co E 44 MO Inf (1st Sgt) E/D: 8/64-8/65 due to disability LOS: 12 mos GAR: 1/14/1884 SP: 6/28/1892 RE: 1/22/1894 TR: 6/23/1903 Died: "Died"--no [grave] stone S: H
Spencer, Myron T.	N: Madison Co, NY 2/17/44 CW: Co A 5 Mich Inf (Pvt/Corpl) Term: 3 yrs E/D: 8/61-9/62 due to disability Philadelphia, PA GAR: 12/25/1909 on transfer from Amboy Post #572 Dept of Illinois Died: 10/30/1925 S: DC
Sperry, W.L.	N: Ohio A: 48 O: Farmer CW: Co D 104 Ohio Inf (Pvt/Corpl) E/D: __/__-6/65 LOS: 34 mos GAR: 10/__/1887 DR: 3/28/1899 S: H
Spickert, Jacob	N: Germany A: 65 O: Shoe Maker CW: Co H 37 Ohio Inf (Pvt/Sgt) E/D: 8/61-1/63 due to disability LOS: 17 mos GAR: 7/22/1891 SP: 12/24/1912 DR: 12/24/1918 S: H
St. Clair, Hugh	N: Penn A: 70 O: Retired CW: Co A 28 Iowa Inf (Pvt/Corpl) E/D: 4/64-7/65 LOS: Not stated GAR: 12/13/1910 Died: 7/5/1923 S: H
Stacey, Arthur G.	N: Ohio A: 61 O: Publisher CW: Co E 46 Ind Inf (Pvt) Re-Enl?: Co __ 20 Ohio Batt (Pvt) E/D: 10/61-7/65 LOS: 45 mos GAR: 1/23/1906 Died: 1/7/1931 S: H
Stansberry, Charles H.	N: New York 1845 CW: Co C 28 Wis Inf (Pvt) Term: 3 yrs E/D: 8/62-4/63 due to disability Re-Enl: Co I 1 Minn Inf (Pvt) E/D: 4/65-7/65 GAR: 12/27/1919 Died: 3/1920 Soldier's Home S: DC
	SAWTELLE: Died 2/25/1920 at Sawtelle Soldier's Home and was buried in "Branch USA" Sec.40, Row A, Grave 8 with tombstone inscription "Corpl Chas H Stansbury Co 1 1 Minn Inf" S: Los Angeles National Cemetery
Starr, Henry P.	N: New York A: 50 O: Rancher CW: Co M 3 NY Cav (Pvt) Re-Enl?: Co A 22 NY Cav (Lieut) E/D: 8/62-8/65 LOS: 36 mos GAR: 12/13/1892 SP: 6/27/1907 Died: 5/11/1915 Buried: "Sent East" S: H
Steadman, William	N: England A: 55 O: Blacksmith CW: Co B 4 Iowa Cav (Pvt/Sgt) E/D: 9/61-10/62 due to disability LOS: 13 mos GAR: 6/28/1888 TR: 9/26/1889 S: H
Steinhour, William E.	N: Vermont A: 83 O: Retired R: East San Diego CW: Co F 1 Vt Inf (Pvt) E/D: 5/61-8/61 LOS: 3 mos GAR: 3/7/1921 SP: 12/26/1923 DR: 12/23/24 S: H
Stenger, W.H.	N: Ohio A: 36 O: Clergyman CW: Co A 178 Ohio Inf (Pvt) E/D: 9/64-6/65 LOS: 8 1/2 mos GAR: 6/25/1886 D: 5/28/1890 S: H
Stevens, E.L.	N: New York A: ;80 O: Retired CW: Co C 104 Ill Inf (Pvt) E/D: 8/62-__/65 LOS: 3 yrs GAR: 6/27/1922 Died: Reported died 1925 S: H
Stevens, L.W.	N: Michigan A: 40 O: Carpenter CW: US Navy (Seaman) E/D: __/63-__/64 LOS: 12 mos GAR: 6/27/1884 SP: 4/30/1890 RE: 12/10/1890 DR: 3/28/1899 S: H
Stewart, Perry	N: Rushville, Ind 1846 CW: Co E 66 Ill Inf (Pvt) Term: 3 yrs E/D: 2/64-7/65 Newport, RI GAR: 4/9/1921 on transfer from Appomattox Post #30 Dept of Cal/Nev S: DC
Stewart, Sylvester N.	N: Ohio A: 80 O: Retired CW: Co __ 18 Iowa Inf (Pvt); Promoted?: Co B 62 US C T (1st Lieut) E/D: 6/62-3/66 LOS: Not stated GAR: 11/13/1923 Died: 12/26/1923 S: H
Stewart, William M.	N: Penn A: 65 O: Farmer CW: Co B 85 PA Inf (Pvt) E/D: 9/61-11/64 LOR: 38 mos GAR: 8/11/1903 S: H Note: William M. Stewart is 49 in the 1880 census for San Diego; he is a comb. (combat?) merchant, and was born in Pennsylvania of Pennsylvania-born

Stewart, William M.	parents. He is married to "Mellie Stewart," who was 39, and born in Vermont. Her father was born in Ireland, and her mother was born in Scotland.
Stewins, Irenius D.	N: Illinois A: 67 O: Accountant CW: Co D 22 Ill Inf (Musician) E/D: 6/61-7/64 LOS: Not stated GAR: 8/27/1912 SP: 12/22/1914 DR: 12/24/1918 S: H
Stielberg, William	N: Germany A: 84 O: Retired R: East San Diego CW: Co A 28 Ohio Inf (Pvt/Corpl) E/D: 7/61-7/64 LOS: 3 yrs GAR: 10/9/1923 Died: 4/23/1927 S: H
Stockton, Charles A.	N: Ohio A: 60 O: Pension Agent CW: Co D 4 Ohio Inf (Pvt) E/D: 4/61-6/64 LOS: 39 mos GAR: 3/5/1890 TR: 10/24/1899 S: H
Stoddard, Silas E.	N: New York A: 77 O: Laborer CW: Co D 108 NY Inf (Pvt) E/D: 7/62-5/65 LOS: Not stated GAR: 6/24/1913 on transfer from O'Rourke Post #1 Dept of New York Died: 7/28/1915 S: H
Stone, A.B.	N: Penn A: 43 O: Carpenter CW: Co E 41 PA Vols (Pvt) E/D: 8/62-2/63 due to disability LOS: 6 mos GAR: 5/13/1886 SP: 1/10/1891 DR: 6/30/1891 S: H
Stone, William P.	N: Mass A: 55 O: Real Estate CW: Co I 1 Conn H A (Pvt) E/D: 5/61-5/64 LOS: 36 mos GAR: 1/24/1893 or 2/24/1893 Post Commander 1897 Died: 10/25/1915 S: H
Stonebraker, James A.	N: Belmont Co, Ohio 8/22/48 CW: Co K 82 Ohio Inf (Pvt) Term: 3 yrs E/D: 8/64-3/65 Ft Schuler, NY GAR: ? date on transfer from Henderson Post Dept of Iowa S: DC
Story, Hampton L.	N: Vermont A: 49 O: Manufacturer CW: Co C 12 VT __ (Pvt/Corpl) E/D: 8/62-7/63 LOS: 10 21/30 mos GAR: 4/23/1885 SP: 7/30/1888 RE: 12/10/1890 D: 12/10/1890 S:H

Note: Hampton Story had two wives. First was Ruth _____; the second was Adella _____, and there were children from both marriages. Adella Story was Hampton Story's wife during his San Diego days, and there are several San Diego Union newspaper articles about their social activities from 1882 to 1891 (parties, boat ownership of the "Della", trips to Los Angeles and San Francisco, and Mrs. Story's desire to purchase the Hubbell House at 7th and A Streets--(San Diego Union, September 10, 1889, column 1:4.) Finally, a San Diego Union article dated December 20, 1931 was titled: "Story Mansion Once Social Center." A note placed on the article by a staff member at San Diego Historical Society stated that [Hampton Story] "... also head of the firm Story, Blackmer and Schneider, dealers in pianos, organs, etc." Blackmer is probably Eli Blackmer, Civil War veteran of this study.

An article in the *Golden Era* magazine, October 1890, Vol. XXXIX, No. 9, stated that "H.L. Story was born on a New England farm in the town of Cambridge, Vt. in 1835. ... His ancestors on his father's side are of Puritan blood and came to this country in the May Flower. The family is not numerous but names some prominent individuals as Judge Story of the Supreme Court of the United States, and Story the sculptor now living in Rome, and W.F. Story who built up the Chicago Times--who was a near relative. On his mother's side there is an English family of Reeds who immigrated to New England in the early days."

The article goes on to discuss his migration to Illinois and Kansas, his Civil War service in the 12th Vermont regiment, his forming of Story & Camp, manufacturers of pianos and organs in Chicago, his purchase of the Peninsula in San Diego, his involvement in building the Hotel del Coronado, and other activities in San Diego.

Stout, James	N: Redding, PA 4/20/37 CW: Co B 1st US Cav (Pvt) Term: 5 yrs E/D: 11/60-6/64 Re-enl: Same company (rank unknown; no further information) GAR: 9/9/1916 Died 6/18/1918 Soldier's Home S: DC

Stout, James (Con't)	SAWTELLE: Died 6/2/1918 at Sawtelle Soldier's Home and is buried in "Branch USA" Sec.36, Row G, Grave 13 with tombstone inscription "Jas Stout Co B 1 U.S. Cav" S: Los Angeles National Cemetery
Strahle, Alphonso	N: Germany CW: Co E 12 Mich Inf (Pvt) Term: 1 yr E/D: 2/65-2/66 Camden, Arkansas GAR: 1/26/1900 TR: 3/10/1923 S: DC
Straw, Alonzo D.	N: New Hampshire A: 73 O: Shoe Maker CW: Co H 5 NH Inf (Pvt) E/D: 10/61-10/64 LOS: Not stated GAR: 2/11/1913 SP: 12/27/1921 RE: 7/25/1923 Died: 12/30/1923 (date of death hard to read) S: H
Strawbridge, J.B.	N: Penn A: 40 O: Carpenter CW: Co C 31 PA Inf (Pvt) E/D: 3/62-8/64 due to hernia LOS: 29 mos GAR: 3/10/1885 SP: 3/28/1889 DR: 6/30/1891 RE: 11/12/1894 TR: 11/12/1894 S: H NOTE: "Mary Strawbridge" is buried on GAR Hill Lot 8 (Mount Hope Cemetery) DOD/B: No further information
Strawbridge, John	NOL/NFI S: DC
Streeter, H.P.	N: Lowe, Canada (Chatham Province) A: 61 O: Merchant CW: Co H 11 Kans Cav (Pvt) E/D: _/64-9/65 LOS: 12 mos GAR: 12/22/1881 Died: 3/22/1883--no [grave] stone S: H
Streube, John	N: France CW: Co I 74 PA Inf (Pvt/Corpl) Term: 3 yrs E/D: 7/63-6/65 Grafton, West Virginia GAR: 4/13/1901 on transfer from Starking Post #52 Dept of Col/Nev Died: 9/3/1909 A: 90 Buried: "At sea by request" S: DC
Stuart, Alonzo B.	N: Maine 7/31/37 CW: Co I 11 Maine Inf (Pvt/Sgt) Term: 3 yrs E/D: 1/62-2/66 City Point GAR: 10/23/1915 on transfer from Burnside Post #188 Dept of Cal/Nev Died 9/27/1916 S: DC
Sunderland, John D.	N: Burlington, IA CW: Co C 1st Iowa Cav (Pvt) Term: 3 yrs E/D: 12/63-2/66 Austin, TX GAR: 10/14/1905 on transfer from D.C. Baker Post #8 Dept of Oregon TR: 8/12/1916 S: DC
Svenningson, John C.	N: Denmark A: 72 O: Blacksmith CW: Co I 1 NY Inf (1st Sgt) E/D: 4/61-5/63 LOS: Not stated GAR: 10/10/1911 on transfer from Unity Post #171 Dept of Cal/Nev Died: 11/16/1922 S: H
Swan, Thomas	N: Green Co, PA 2/8/42 CW: Co C 47 Ill Inf (Pvt/Corpl) Term: 3 yrs E/D: 8/61-9/64 Springfield, Ill GAR: 12/14/1914 on transfer from J.O. Hooker Post Dept of Cal/Nev S: DC
Sweetland, Seth	N: Maine A: 69 O: Laborer CW: Co E 3 Maine Inf (Pvt) E/D: 4/61-6/64 LOS: Not stated GAR: 12/27/1910 Died: 2/4/1929 S: H
Sweetman, Stephen	N: Ireland 1832 or 1833 CW: Co A 6 Mich Cav (Pvt) Term: 3 yrs E/D: 8/62-5/65 Detroit, Mich GAR: 1/14/1922 on transfer from Chris Myer Post Dept of Missouri Died: 5/26/1922 A: 90 Soldier's Home A: 90 S: DC SAWTELLE: No records of this veteran were found at Los Angeles National Cemetery. California Death Index indicates veteran died in Alameda County, CA
Tartt, Thomas M.	N: Ohio A: 42 O: Farmer CW: Co F 117 Ill Inf (Pvt) E/D: 9/62-8/65 LOS: 35 mos GAR: 10/28/1886 SP: 3/28/1889 DR: 6/30/1891 TR: 12/25/1900 S: H
Taylor, Charles Paxton	N: Delaware CW: Co E 2nd Del Inf (Pvt) Term: 3 yrs E/D: 7/61-12/63 Wilmington, Delaware due to disability GAR: 7/13/1912 SP: "Suspended" S: DC

Taylor, R.W.	N: England A: 46 O: Attorney CW: Co I 55 Ill Inf (Pvt) Re-enl?: Co D 3 Wis? Cav (Capt) E/D: 10/61-1/65 due to disability LOS: 39 mos GAR: No date stated SP: 12/28/1898 DR: 12/24/1918 S: H
Tengwall, Charles	N: Sweden A: 57 O: Farmer CW: US Navy (Masters Mate/Act'g Ensign) E/D: 9/63-8/65 LOS: 23 mos GAR: 12/23/1886 SP: 1/10/1889 DR: 6/30/1891 S: H
Terwilliger, C.H.	NOL/NFI S: DC
Theime, John F.	NOL/NFI S: DC
Thoman, John A.	N: Roisit, NY A: 43 O: Farmer CW: Co C 7 KY ___ (Pvt/Corpl) E/D: 7/62-5/65 LOS: 36 mos GAR: 6/16/1882 D: 1/25/1883 S: H
Thomas, Albert A.	N: Illinois A: 57 O: Conductor CW: Co G 44 Iowa Inf (Pvt/Corpl) E/D: 5/64-9/64 LOS: 3 1/3 mos GAR: 11/26/1901 Died: 9/22/1921 S: H
Thomas, John P.	N: Liverpool, England CW: Co F 24 Wis Inf (Pvt) Term: 3 yrs E/D: 8/62-9/63 with Surgeon's Certificate of Disability Louisville, KY GAR: 6/24/1911 Died: 8/11/1925 S: DC
Thomas, Thomas W.	N: England A: 71 O: Not stated CW: Co F 2 Ohio Inf (Pvt); Re-Enl?: Co C 5 Ohio Cav (Sgt) E/D: 4/61-11/65 LOS: Not stated GAR: 2/11/1913 on transfer from U.S.Grant Post #340 Dept of Ohio Died: 7/13/1926 S: H
Thompson, Archibald R.	N: New York A: 71 O: Carpenter CW: Co F 13 PA Cav (Pvt); Re-Enl?: US Signal Corps (Pvt 1st Class) E/D: 6/62-7/65 LOS: 37 mos GAR: 6/25/1907 SP: 12/24/1912 DR: 12/24/1918 S: H
Thompson, Charles D.	N: Canada A: 78 O: Retired CW: Co G 5 Wis Inf (Pvt) E/D: 5/61-7/64 LOS: 38 mos GAR: 10/8/1918 Died: 9/24/1931 S: H
Thompson, Frank	NOL/NFI S: DC
Thompson, Hiram P.	N: New York A: 62 O: Real Estate CW: Co H 49 NY Inf (Pvt/Com Sgt) E/D: 8/61-12/63 LOS: 52 1/2 mos GAR: 2/28/1905 (probably on transfer from G.H. Thomas Post #5 Dept of Illinois) Died: 7/1/1926 S: H
Thompson, J.J.	N: Warren Co, Ohio CW: Co A 146 OVI (Pvt) Term: 4 mos E/D: 5/64-9/64 Camp Dennison, Ohio GAR: 1/10/1914 on transfer from Granville Thurston Post #213 Dept of Ohio S: DC
Thornburg, Albert M.	N: North Carolina A: 50 O: Insurance Agent CW: Co B 8 Ind Inf (Pvt); Re-Enl?: Co __ 9 Ind Cav (Bugler) E/D: 4/61-5/65 LOS: 49 mos GAR: 3/27 or 5/27/1891 RE: 4/10/1900 TR: 4/10/1900 S: H
Tiffany, John F.	N: Conn A: 73 O: Carriage Maker CW: Co K 22 CT Inf (Pvt) E/D: 8/62-5/63 LOS: Not stated GAR: 5/24/1910 (probably on transfer from Dept of Massachusetts) Died: 4/30/1923 S: H
Tippett, Samuel D.	N: Maryland A: 68 O: Builder CW: Co B 2 MO Cav (Pvt/1st Lieut) E/D: 8/61-9/65 LOS: Not stated GAR: 12/10/1912 on transfer from U.S.Grant Post #28 Dept of Illinois TR: 12/26/1923 S: H
Titus, Anson	N: New York or New Hampshire A: 47 O: Mill Wright CW: Co E 3 Wis Inf (Pvt/Sgt) E/D: 11/61-11/64 LOS: 36 mos GAR: 5/22/1884 SP: 6/28/1892 DR: 3/28/1899 RE: 6/12/1900 SP: 5/28/1904 DR: 1/22/1907 S: H Buried: Sergt Anson Titus Co E 3 Wis Inf (official

Titus, Anson (Con't)	tombstone) Buried at La Vista Cemetery, National City, CA
Tomlin, George	N: England A: 52 O: Farmer CW: Co H 105 Ill Inf (Corpl) E/D: 8/62-10/64 due to disability LOS: 26 mos GAR: 11/27/1887 SP: 1/10/1889 DR: 6/30/1891 S:H
Toms, George O.	N: Maine A: 64 O: Farmer CW: Co E 71 Ohio Vols (2 Lieut/Capt) E/D: __/61-__/63 due to disability LOS: 24 mos GAR: 7/8/1886 SP: 4/30/1889 RE: 6/30/1890 D: 8/10/1898 S: H
Touhy, Martin	N: Ireland A: 52 O: Laborer CW: Co H 14 US Inf (Pvt) E/D: 12/64-12/67 LOS: 36 mos GAR: 10/22/1890 SP: 9/22/1896 RE: 3/14/1898 TR: 1/23/1900 S: H
Townsend, William E.	N: Penn A: 51 O: Rancher R: El Cajon and La Jolla, CA CW: Co I 2 W VA Cav (Pvt) E/D: 6/61-7/65 LOS: Not stated GAR: 2/27/1894 SP: 9/24/1895 DR: 3/28/1899 RE: 8/28/1900 SP: 10/25/1904 DR: 1/22/1907 RE: 6/27/1911 SP: 6/23/1914 DR: 12/24/1918 S: H
Trader, W.S.	N: Missouri A: 71 O: Clergyman CW: Co I 1 MO Cav (Pvt) E/D: 6/63-3/65 due to disability LOS: 21 mos GAR: 3/13/1917 on transfer from Post #53 Dept of Missouri Died: 7/8/1921 S: H
Traylor, Madison	Madison Traylor Co A 58 Ind Inf (official tombstone). Buried at La Vista Cemetery, National City, CA
Trego, Harrison	NOL/NFI S: DC
Triggs, John	N: England A: 79 O: Retired CW: Co G 96 Ill Inf (Pvt) E/D: 8/62-6/65 LOS: 34 mos GAR: 7/23/1918 on transfer from Post #5 Dept of Illinois. Died: 8/8/1918 Buried: Sent to Chicago S: H
Trogler, William A.	N: Penn A: 83 O: Retired CW: Co D 126 PA Inf (Pvt) E/D: 8/62-5/63 Re-Enl?: Co F 102 PA Inf (Pvt) E/D: __/64-8/65 LOS: 1 yr 9 mos GAR: 12/26/1922 Died: 12/16/1934 S: H
Trott, George F.	N: Boston, Mass 1845 CW: Co A 44th Mass Inf (Pvt) Term: 3 yrs E/D: 6/62-6/__ GAR: 9/11/1920 on transfer from Junction City Post #132 Dept of Kansas Died: Topeka, KA S: DC
Troxel, Joseph	N: Lebanon, PA A: 72 O: Merchant R: Coronado, CA CW: Co H 3 PA L A (Pvt) E/D: 10/62-7/65 LOS: 33 mos GAR: 7/13/1918 (dropped member from an Eastern post Died: 8/19/1933 S: H
Troxell, John P.	NOL/NFI S: DC
Tucker, James W.	N: Illinois A: 78 O: Retired CW: Co K 11 Ill Cav (Pvt) E/D: 11/61-9/65 LOS: 4 yrs GAR: 3/14/1922 Died: 12/30/1924 S: H
Tufs, Charles P.	N: New York A: 69 O: Retired CW: Co I 6 NY H A (Pvt/Sgt) E/D: 6/63-8/65 LOS: Not stated GAR: 6/13/1916 Died: 5/20/1922 S: H
Turner, David	B: Cambridge, Ohio 3/7/43 CW: Co D 42 OVI (Pvt) Term: 3 yrs E/D: 9/61-9/64 Columbus, Ohio GAR: 11/23/1929 Died 1/25/1930 S: DC
Tyson, William	N: Penn A: 72 O: Solicitor CW: Co I 53 PA Inf (Pvt) E/D: 9/61-6/65 LOS: 45 1/2 mos GAR: 4/23/1912 on transfer from Gen. George A. Custer Post #40 Dept of Illinois Died: 11/26/1922 S: H

Utt, Lee H.	N: Jersey Co, Ill A: 41 O: Horticulturist R: Pala, CA CW: Co B 1 MO Inf (Pvt); Promoted?: Co A 7 Kans Cav (Major) E/D: 4/61-9/65 LOS: 53 mos GAR: 2/9/1882 SP: 9/30/1883 Died: "Dead"--no [grave] stone S: H Note: No indication of where Lee Utt is buried. Sarah Utt died on 2/18/1928 at age 81, and was cremated at Greenwood Cemetery. She was buried at Mount Hope Cemetery on 8/19/1929, and is buried in Division 3 along with her daughter (?) Anita Lee Utt, who died on 4/30/1933, and who was buried on 9/14/1933.
Valentine, D.A.	N: Iowa A: 39 O: Paper Hanger CW: Co F 45 Iowa Vols (Pvt) E/D: 5/64-9/64 LOS: 4 mos GAR: 2/5/1885 SP: 1/10/1889 DR: 10/24/1904 S: H
Valentine, I.W.	N: Iowa A: 41 O: Paper Hanger CW: Co F 45 Iowa Vols (Pvt) E/D: 5/64-9/64 LOS: 4 mos GAR: 2/5/1885 SP: 4/30/1890 DR: 6/30/1891 RE: 10/22/1894 D: 10/22/1894 S:H
Van Scoten, M.L.	N: New Jersey A: 46 O: Tin Smith CW: Co I 31 NJ Inf (Sgt) E/D: 9/62-9/62? LOS: 9 mos GAR: 10/25/1888 SP: 4/30/1890 DR: 6/30/1891 RE: 11/22/1892 TR: 11/22/1892 S: H
Varnum, George M.	N: Washington, D.C. CW: Co __ Washington, D.C.? Volunteers (Surgeon) E/D: 2/63-11/63 due to resignation St Louis, MO GAR: 1/22/1896 TR: "Transferred" S: DC
Venters, George	N: Kentucky A: 75 O: Retired CW: Co D 36 Ohio Inf (Pvt) E/D: 10/61-11/62 due to wounds LOS: 2 yrs Re-Enl?: Co H 1 Ohio H A (Pvt) E/D: 7/63-7/65 LOS: 2 yrs GAR: 7/27/1920 Died: "31" (1931 date ?) S: H
Venters, Pleasant	N: Kentucky A: 78 O: Retired CW: Co I 5 KY Cav (Pvt) E/D: 5/64-8/65 LOS: 1 yr 3 mos GAR: 4/22/1924 Died: 5/31/1936 S: H
Vestal, W.L.	N: Indiana A: 48 O: Editor CW: Co A 7 Ind Inf (Pvt); Promoted: Co __ 53 Ind Inf (Colonel) E/D: 4/61-7/65 LOS: 38 2/3 mos GAR: 1884 TR: 12/27/1892 S:H
Vincent, J.W.	N: England CW: Co C 45 Ill Inf (1st Sgt/1st Lieut) Term: 3 yrs E/D: 9/62-6/65 Washington, D.C. GAR: 2/14/1903 TR: 4/10/1915 S: DC
Viney, William M.	N: Ohio A: 52 O: Minister CW: Co G 55 Mass Inf (Sgt) E/D: 6/63-9/65 LOS: 24 mos GAR: 1/23/1894 TR: 2/23/1897 S: H
Vredenberg, John L.	N: New York A: 81 O: Retired CW: Co F 17 NY Inf (Pvt) E/D: 4/61-4/63 LOS: 2 yrs GAR: 1/23/1923 Died: 12/25/1926 S: H
Wadlia, Andrew J.	N: Maine A: 55 O: Carpenter CW: Co G 3 NH Inf (Pvt/Capt) E/D: 8/61-2/65 LOS: 41? mos GAR: 2/12/1907 Died: "Dead" S: H
Walker, Leonard	N: Steuben Co, NY CW: Co K 13 NY Inf (Pvt) Term: 3 yrs E/D: 10/61-11/62 due to Surgeon's Certificate of Disability GAR: 1/14/1914 on transfer from Colorado Springs Post #22 Dept of Col/Wyo Died: 1/11/1922 A: 83 S: DC
Ward, Chaney	N: Ohio A: 75 O: Retired CW: Co G 22 Wis Inf (Pvt) E/D: 8/62-10/64 due to wounds LOS: 2 yrs GAR: 8/26/1919 Died: 11/15/1924 S: H
Ward, Curtis D.	NOL/NFI S: DC
Ward, Henry A.	N: Illinois A: 77 O: Merchant CW: Co A 72 Ill Inf (Corpl/2nd Lieut) E/D: 7/62-8/65 LOS: Not stated GAR: 4/23/1912 on transfer from Potter Post #17 Dept of Illinois Died: 2/30/1932 (hard to read date of death) S: H

Ward, James S.	N: New York A: 51 O: Real Estate CW: Co D 10 NY H A (2nd Lieut/1st Lieut) E/D: 8/62-5/65 due to disability LOS: 33 mos GAR: 4/9/1895 SP: 9/28/1897 or 9/27/1898 RE: 4/24/1900 TR: 8/9/1910 S: H
Ward, Samson L.	N: Indiana A: 34 O: Teacher CW: Co D 39 Ind Inf (Pvt/Sgt) E/D: 11/62-8/65 LOS: 33 or 38 mos GAR: 6/16/1882 SP: 9/26/1889 RE: 11/22/1898 Post Commander 1916 Died: 10/27/1927 S: H
Ward, Stephen I.	N: New York A: 80 O: Retired R: Encanto, CA CW: US Navy (Landsman) E/D: 8/64-5/65 LOS: 10 mos GAR: 5/8/1923 D: __/__/1933 S: H
Ward, Thomas S.	N: Ohio A: 68 O: Sadler CW: Co K 10 Ohio Inf (Pvt) Re-Enl?: Co __ 5 Ohio L A (Corpl) E/D: 4/61-7/65 LOS: 51 mos GAR: 5/23/1905 TR: 3/24/1908 S: H
Warden, M.W.	N: Louisville, KY 5/18/42 CW: Co D 2 Kans Cav (Pvt) Term: 3 yrs E/D: 4/61-9/64 Re-Enl: Co E 14 Kans Cav (Pvt) E/D: __/__ GAR: ? date on transfer from Grand Junction Post #55 Dept of Colorado DR: 2/27/1915 S: DC
Warne, Charles	N: New York A: 66 O: Carpenter R: Chula Vista, CA CW: Co H 3 Cal Inf (Pvt) E/D: 9/61-10/64 Re-Enl?: Co I 4 Cal Inf (Corpl) E/D: 2/65-11/65 LOS: 46 mos GAR: 5/10/1904 TR: 1/26/1909 GAR: 4/12/1910 Died: 1/28/1914 S: H
Warner, Robert T.	N: Conn A: 41 O: Lawyer CW: Co A 19 Wis ___ (Pvt) E/D: 12/61-4/65 LOS: 40 mos GAR: 6/11/1885 SP: 12/24/1918 S: H
Warren, Dillard	N: Ohio A: 41 O: Engineer CW: Co G 2 MO Cav (Pvt) E/D: 3/62-4/65 LOS: 3 1/2 yrs GAR: 5/13/1886 SP: 9/26/1889 DR: 6/30/1891 RE: 8/12/1898 D: 8/12/1898 S: H
Washburn, A. Judson	N: Maine A: 75 O: Farmer CW: Co D 11 RI Inf (Pvt) E/D: 10/62-7/63 LOS: 9 mos GAR: 1/13/1903 TR: 12/19/1906 S: H
Washington, Greenbery	N: Scott Co, KY 1845 CW: Co H 108 US Colored Troops (Pvt) Term: 3 yrs E/D: 7/64-3/66 Vicksburg, Miss GAR: 2/26/1921 on transfer from Wadsworth Post Dept of Montana DR: 9/24/1927 S: DC
Washington, Watkins	N: Not Stated A: 83 O: Retired CW: Co B 11 Ind Inf (Pvt) E/D: __/62-6/65 LOS: 3 yrs GAR: 8/10/1926 Died: 2/15/1932 Soldier's Home S: H
	SAWTELLE: No records for this veteran were found at Los Angeles National Cemetery, the Sawtelle Death Index, the California Death Index, or the County of San Diego.
Waterman, William A.	N: Mass A: 72 O: Clergyman R: La Mesa, CA CW: Co A 37 Mass Inf (Pvt/1st Lieut) E/D: 8/62-6/65 due to disability LOS: Not stated GAR: 6/25/1912 on transfer from George H. Thomas Post #5 Dept of Illinois Died: 1/14/1921 S: H
Watkins, G.C.	NOL/NFI S: DC
Watkins, Wm./Wilber F.	N: Ohio A: 46 O: Farmer CW: Co C 1 Ohio Inf (Pvt) E/D: 10/61-9/64 LOS: 36 mos GAR: 9/13/1892 TR: 10/8/1901 S: H (Also named Wilber F. Watkins in record; same dates for Wilber as for William F.)
Watson, Charles C.	N: Adrian, Michigan A: 42 O: Farmer R: Poway, CA CW: Co D 3 Iowa Inf (Corpl) E/D: 4/61-12/62 due to loss of right arm at Washatchie River, Miss LOS: 20 mos GAR: 12/22/1881 or 12/22/1884 SP: 9/28/1891 DR: 3/28/1899 RE: 11/9/1909 Died: 9/30/1911 S:H

Watson, John   N: Ohio 4/9/44 CW: Co A Independent Missouri ___ (Pvt) Term: 3 mos E/D: 5/61-10/61 Brookfield, MO Re-Enl: Co I 17 Iowa Inf (Pvt) E/D: 3/62-12/62 Jefferson Barracks, MO due to disability GAR: 5/9/1914 on transfer from McPherson Post Dept of Washington S: DC

Wattles, M. Richard   N: Illinois A: 72 O: Carpenter R: Teralta, CA CW: Co G 1 Minn Inf (Pvt) E/D: 4/61-1/63 due to disability LOS: Not stated GAR: 10/22/1912 on transfer from Green Lake Post # 112 Dept of Wash/Alaska Died: 3/2/1918 Buried: Soldier's Home S: H

SAWTELLE: Died 3/1/1918 at Sawtelle Soldier's Home and buried at "Branch ____", Sec.36, Row C, Grave 6 with tombstone inscription "R.M. Wattles Co G 1 Minn Inf" S: Los Angeles National Cemetery

Way, Francis B.   NOL/NFI S: DC

Way, Francis Burdett   N: New York A; 54 O: Carpenter CW: Co I 8 Mich Cav (Pvt) E/D: 9/62-9/65 LOS: 36 mos GAR: 11/12/1897 Died: 9/23/1905--is [grave] stone S: H

Weatherbee, Geo.M.   N: Mass A: 49 O: Mechanic CW: Co __ 1 Mass Inf (Musician) E/D: 5/61-6/65 LOS: 48 2/3 mos GAR: 7/__/1887 TR: 10/11/1890 Died: "Dead"--no date, no [grave] stone S:H First name George

Weatherby, Charles   N: New Jersey A: 62 O: Gardener CW: Co K 106 Ill Inf (Pvt) E/D: 8/62-7/65 LOS: 36 mos GAR: 7/24/1906 SP: 6/25/1907 DR: 12/24/1918 S: H

Weaver, Joseph L.   N: Penn A: 48 O: Merchant CW: Co C 31 Iowa Inf (Pvt/Corpl) E/D: 10/62-5/65 LOS: 31 mos GAR: 10/10/1893 SP: 9/24/1894 RE: 6/13/1899 TR: 6/13/1899 S: H

Weaver, Noah   NOL/NFI S: DC

Webber, George   N: Missouri A: 40 O: Soldier CW: Cavalry Troop (Trumpeter) E/D: 2/64-3/67 LOS: 36 mos GAR: 11/11/1891 SP: 9/28/1897 DR: 3/28/1899 RE: 5/12/1900 Post Commander 1896 Died: 1/22/1922 S: H

Webler, George A.   N: New York A: 59 O: Restaurant R: Oceanside, CA CW: Co E 39 Ill Inf (Pvt) E/D: 3/64-8/65 LOS: 17 1/2 mos TR: GAR: 2/25/1889 TR: 12/8/1908 GAR: 2/25/1909 GAR: 8/13/1912 SP: 12/26/1916 DR: 12/24/1918 S: H

Webster, Andrew B.   N: Park Co, Ind CW: Co I 1st Ind HA (Pvt) Term: 3 yrs E/D: 7/61-1/66 Baton Rouge, LA GAR: ? date on transfer from Walworth Post #93 Dept of Col/Wyo S: DC

Wells, James W.   N: Ohio A: 46 O: Carpenter CW: Co B 102 Ohio Inf (Pvt/Rgt Q.M.) E/D: 8/62-6/65 LOS: 35 mos GAR: 3/22/1888 SP: 12/28/1892 RE: 6/__/1898 SP: 6/25/1901 DR: 3/11/1902 RE: 3/11/1903 Died: 7/17/1910 S: H

Welsh, Elias R.   N: Ohio A: 74 O: Retired CW: Co I 67 Ohio Inf (Pvt/Corpl) E/D: 12/61-1/65 LOS: 3 yrs GAR: 7/22/1919 Died: 1/16/1932 or 1933 (last digit of date of death hard to read) S: H

Werth, F.A.   N: Germany A: 46 O: Minister CW: Co F 7 Mich Inf (Pvt) E/D: 4/64-7/65 LOS: 15 mos GAR: 1/24/1893 TR: 9/12/1893 S:H

Wescott, Lowrey   N: Penn A: 69 O: Salesman CW: Co H 22 Wis Inf (Pvt) E/D: 8/62-5/65 LOS: Not stated GAR: 4/9/1912 (probably on transfer from Staley Post #199 Dept of Nebraska Died: 5/8/1925 S: H

Wheaton, William H.	N: Maine 1835 CW: Co K 12 Maine Inf (Pvt/1st Sgt) Term: 3 yrs E/D: 11/62-1/__ Re-Enl: Co __ Vet Bat (1st Sgt) E/D: __/__-4/66 Madisonville GAR: 5/2/1924 on transfer from Joel A. Haycox Post Dept of Maine Died: 8/30/1931 at Soldier's Home Sawtelle, CA Buried: Oceanside, CA S: DC SAWTELLE: Records for this veteran were not found at Los Angeles National Cemetery S: Los Angeles National Cemetery
White, John C.	N: Illinois A: 43 O: Policeman CW: Co K 7 Cal Inf (Pvt) E/D: 1/65-10/5 LOS: 9 2/3 mos GAR: 3/22/1888 SP: 9/26/1889 DR: 6/30/1891 SP: 12/24/1901 DR: 1/22/1907 S: H
White, William I.	N: Ohio A: 76 O: Farmer CW: Co E 46 Ill Inf (Pvt) E/D: 12/63-6/65 LOS: Not stated GAR: 6/9/1908 SP: 6/28/1910 DR: 12/24/1918 S: H
White, William Othe	N: Adams Co, Ind CW: Co D 12th Ind Cav (Pvt) Term: 3 yrs E/D: 9/63-11/65 Vicksburg, Miss LOS: 2 yrs, 2 mos, 15 days GAR: 3/12/1927 on transfer from Pap Williams Post #28 Dept of Michigan S: DC
Whiteley, Clay	N: Ohio A: 76 O: Retired CW: Co K 152 Ohio Inf (Pvt) E/D: 5/64-9/64 LOS: 100 days GAR: 8/23/1921 TR: 6/26/1923 S: H
Whitman, Winfield S.	N: New Albany, Indiana A: 76 O: Retired R: Oakdale, LA CW: Co A 12 Ind Inf (Corpl/1st Sgt) E/D: 4/61-5/62 LOS: 13 mos Promoted?: Co I 66 Ind Inf (2nd Lieut/1st Lieut) E/D: 7/62-7/65 LOS: 36 mos GAR: 12/11/1917 Died: 2/14/1918 at Oakdale, LA S:H
Whitney, A.E.	N: Maine A: 66 O: Student CW: Co K 25 Maine Inf (Pvt) E/D: 9/62-7/63 LOS: Not stated GAR: 2/27/1912 Died: 5/15/1916 S: H
Whitney, Henry H.	N: New York A: 50 O: Engineer CW: Co H 106 NY Inf (Sgt) E/D: 7/62-6/65 LOS: 35 mos GAR: 5/24/1888 SP: 6/28/1892 DR: 3/28/1899 SP 12/24/1901 DR: 1/22/1907 S:H
Whitney, Willard J.	N: Wyoming, PA A: 50 O: Vineculturist R: Bernardo (probably present day Rancho Bernardo, CA CW: Co A 57 Penn ___ (Pvt/Sgt) E/D: 10/61-3/63 due to gun shot wounds in face LOS: 25 mos GAR: 6/22/1882 SP: 12/31/1883 Died: "Dead"--no [grave] stone S: H
Whitson, John	N: Indiana A; 50 O: Farmer CW: Co E 13 Iowa Inf (Pvt) E/D: 11/61-10/62 due to disability LOS: 11 mos GAR: 2/13/1894 SP: 9/24/1895 DR: 10/25/1904 S:H
Whittier, John F.	N: Maine A: 46 O: Expressman CW: Co F 26 Maine Inf (Pvt) E/D: 10/62-8/63 LOS: 10 mos GAR: 2/28/1889 SP: 12/27/1898 DR: 10/25/1904 S: H
Wickard, Phillip J.	N: Stark Co, Ohio 11/15/46 CW: Co G 189 Ohio Inf (Pvt) Term: Unstated E/D: 2/65-5/65 Huntsville, AL GAR: 3/9/1918 on transfer from Uncle Sam Post #177 Dept of Cal/Nev TR: 12/9/1922 S: DC
Wilber, Henry J.	NOL/NFI S: DC
Wilder, Nathaniel	N: Ohio A: 69 O: Stone Worker R: Oceanside, CA CW: Co A 29 Ohio Inf (Pvt) E/D: 8/61-7/65 LOS: Not stated GAR: 8/13/1912 SP: 6/27/1916 DR: 12/24/1918 S: H
Wilkins/Williams, Blair	N: Ohio A: 81 O: Retired CW: Co I 184 Ohio Inf (Pvt) E/D: 2/65-9/65 LOS: Not stated GAR: 2/14/1928 S: H (last name difficult to read in record)

Willey, George C.	N: New Hampshire CW: US Navy SS James Agar (Seaman/Pvt) Term: Unstated E/D: 12/61-__/__ Re-Enl: Co F 11 PA Cav (Pvt) E/D: 9/64-5/65 GAR: 1/11/1908 on transfer from Stevenson Post #46 Dept of Oklahoma S: DC
Williams, Abraham	N: Coles(?) Co, Ill A: 76 O: Retired CW: Co B 4 Minn Inf (Pvt) E/D: 9/61-9/64 LOS: 3 yrs GAR: 10/14/1919 Died: 5/10/1937 S: H
Williams, Albert J.	N: Ohio A: 82 O: Retired CW: Co C 3 Iowa Cav (Pvt) E/D: 2/64-8/66 LOS: Not stated GAR: 5/10/1927 S: H
Williams, George W.	N: New Market, NH A: 56 O: Tinsmith CW: Co O 25 Mass ____ (Pvt/Corpl) E/D: 9/61-___/65 LOS: 4 yrs GAR: 10/21/1881 D: 1/9/1883 S: H
Williamson, Jacob T.	N: Illinois A: 86 O: Retired CW: Co F 138 Ill Inf (Pvt) E/D: 5/64-9/64 LOS: 100 days GAR: 3/10/1924 Died: 4/16/1935 S: H
Willison, John W.	N: Ohio A: 65 O: Real Estate CW: Co G 1 Ohio H A (Pvt) E/D: 11/62-7/65 LOS: Not stated GAR: 2/1/1913 on transfer from John M. Palmer Post #102 Wash/Alaska TR: 1/26/1915 S: H
Wilson, Charles H.	N: New York A: 47 O: Insurance CW: Co B 106 NY Inf (Pvt/Corpl) E/D: 8/62-8/64 LOS: 25 mos GAR: 2/11/1891 SP: 9/24/1895 DR: 10/25/1904 S: H
Wilson, Frank	N: Denmark A: 68 O: Retired CW: USS Vandalia (Able Seaman) E/D: 3/65-2/68 LOS: 3 yrs GAR: 7/26/1921 Died: 7/7/1925 at Sawtelle S: H
	SAWTELLE: Died 7/7/1925 at Sawtelle Soldier's Home and is buried at "Service USN" Sec 25, Row M, Grave 15 with tombstone inscription "Frank Wilson Pennsy___ Seaman U.S. Navy July 7, 1921" S: Los Angeles National Cemetery.
Wilson, Robert I.	N: Ohio A: 69 O: Not stated CW: Co G 7 Ill Inf (Pvt) E/D: 2/65-6/65 LOS: Not stated GAR: 2/8/1916 SP: 12/22/1925 S: H
Wilson, William	N: Sweden A: 77 O: Sailer R: La Mesa, CA CW: Co D 4 Batt US Army (Pvt) E/D: 6/61-6/62 due to disability LOS: 11 1/2 mos GAR: 3/27/1917 on transfer from Post #372 Dept of Michigan Died: 4/1/1919 S: H
Winder, W.A.	N: Baltimore, MD A: 58 O: Physician CW: Co __ 3 US Arty (Capt) E/D: 8/48-6/66 due to resignation LOS: 18 yrs GAR: 5/24/1883 SP: 9/26/1889 DR: 6/30/1891 Died: "Dead"--no [grave] stone S: H
Withrow, Charles W.	N: Illinois A: 56 O: Farmer R: Poway, CA CW: Co K 30 Wis Inf (Pvt/Corpl) E/D: 8/62-7/66 due to disability LOS: 47 mos GAR: 5/9/1889 TR: 4/14/1892 SP: 12/27/1898 S:H
Witter, Charles	N: Germany A: 58 O: Laborer CW: Co G 195 PA Inf (Pvt) E/D: 2/65-8/65 LOS: 6 mos GAR: 4/23/1901 Died: 11/2/1903 Soldier's Home S: H
	SAWTELLE: Died on 11/2/1903 at Soldier's Home, Sawtelle, CA Buried: "Branch USA" Sec 4, Row D, Grave 23 with tombstone inscription "Chas Witter Co G 195 PA Inf" S: Los Angeles National Cemetery
Wolf, Addison C.	N: Washington, PA CW: Co D 11 PA Vet Reg (Pvt) Term: 3 yrs E/D: 8/64-7/65 Balls Cross Roads GAR: 8/14/1909 on transfer from Templeton Post #120 Dept of Pennsylvania Died: Pennsylvania, date unknown S: DC

Wolf, George	N: Germany A: 79 O: Retired R: National City, CA CW: Co __ 9 Ohio Inf (Band) E/D: __/61-__/62 LOS: Not stated GAR: 4/12/1921 S: H
Wolfe, Peter E.	N: Penn A: 54 O: Engineer CW: Co D 67 PA Inf (Pvt) E/D: 2/64-7/65 LOS: 17 mos GAR: 8/26/1902 SP: 3/22/1904 DR: 1/22/1907 S: H
Wood, Isaac	N: Indiana A: 77 O: Retired CW: Co F 144 Ind Inf (Corp) E/D: __/63-__/65 LOS: 2 yrs GAR: 6/26/1923 Died: 1/12/1937 S: H
Wood, Jeremiah G.	N: Winona Co, Minnesota CW: Co K 9 Minn Inf (Corpl) Term: 3 yrs E/D: 8/61-8/65 Enlisted at Minneapolis, MN LOS: 3 years GAR: 9/8/1928 Died: 4/26/1929 A: 89/8/2 Obit: Native of Vermont?; middle name "Garrish"; one child San Diego; one in Colton, CA and one in Polebridge, Montana, no wife listed. Buried: San Bernardino, CA S: DC
Wood, Nelson P.	N: New York A: 58 O: Carpenter CW: Co E 8 Wis Inf (Pvt) E/D: 10/61-__/64 LOS: 36 mos GAR: 3/26/1901 SP: 3/22/1904 DR: 1/22/1907 S: H
Woodard, John C.	N: Ohio A: 70 O: Contractor CW: Co C 93 Ohio Inf (Pvt) E/D: 6/61-__/64 due to wounds LOS: 46 mos GAR: 8/13/1903 SP: 1/28/1908 DR: 12/24/1918 S:H
Woodruff, J.D.	NOL/NFI S: DC
Woodward, W.D.	NOL/NFI S: DC
Work, Walter D.	N: Crawford Co, PA 2/6/44 CW: Co B 120 US Colored Inf (2nd Lieut) Term: 3 yrs E/D: 7/64-9/65 Louisville, KY GAR: 11/12/1927 on transfer from Strong Vincent Post Dept of PA Died: 6/22/1932 S: DC
Works, J.D.	N: Indiana A: 36 O: Lawyer CW: Co D 10 Ind Cav (Pvt) E/D: 12/63-8/65 LOS: 20 mos GAR: 10/24/1883 TR: "Transferred" S: H
Works, Lewis F.	N: Indiana A: 50 O: Dept. Recorder CW: Co E 50 Ind Inf (Pvt) E/D: 10/61-11/62 due to disability LOS: Not stated GAR: 7/9/1890 SP: 12/28/1892 RE: 2/28/1893 TR: 2/28/1893 S: H
Wright, Oliver	NOL/NFI S: DC
Yates, Elija N.	N: Indiana A: 70 O: Real Estate CW: Co C 71 Ind Inf (Pvt); Promoted?: Co __ 6th Ind Cav (Sgt/Major) E/D: __/62-__/65 LOS: Not stated GAR: 1/13/1914 SP: 12/23/1924 RE: 2/10/1925 TR: 2/10/1925 S: H
Yelton, William L.	N: Indiana A: 66 O: Retired CW: Co B 43 Ind Inf (Sgt/Capt) E/D: 4/61-6/65 LOS: 50 mos GAR: 10/14/1902 TR: 12/27/1904 S: H
York, Charles	N: Maine A: 37 O: Musician CW: Co B 2 ME Cav (Pvt) E/D: 12/63-12/65 LOS: 23 mos GAR: 2/9/1888 TR: 4/24/1891 S: H
Young, James A.	N: Ohio A: 43 O: Dentist CW: Co E 12 Ohio Cav (Sgt) E/D: 9/63-11/65 LOS: 26 mos GAR: 9/27/1888 TR: 12/11/1900 S: H
Young, Jeremiah F.	N: Penn A: 71 O: Retired CW: Co K 10 MO Cav (2nd Lieut/Capt) E/D: 8/62-6/65 LOS: Not stated GAR: 10/23/1906 probably on transfer from Col. Meuman Post #396 Dept of Missouri Died: 9/1/1913 S: H

Young, John F.	N: Illinois A: 72 O: Butcher R: San Ysidro, CA CW: Co K 1 Ohio Cav (Pvt/Corpl) E/D: 9/61-9/65 LOS: Not stated GAR: 2/26/1915 (probably on transfer from Riverside Post #118 Cal/Nev) TR: 12/14/1915 Died: 11/18/1919 S:H
Young, Robert	NOL/NFI S: DC
Young, Robert	N: Illinois A: 75 O: Retired CW: Co B 28 Ill Inf (Pvt/1st Lieut) E/D: 8/61-9/64 LOS: Not stated GAR: 4/13/1915 TR: 12/14/1915 S: H
Young, Rufus	N: Bellvill, Ontario, Canada 1846 CW: Co A 10 NY H A (Pvt) Term: 3 yrs E/D: 8/62-7/64 Watertown, NY GAR: 4/23/1921 on transfer from Baker Post Dept of Nebraska S: DC
Zimmers, Levi	N: Penn A: 69 O: Farmer CW: Co F 2 PA Cav (Pvt) E/D: 12/61-12/64 LOS: Not stated GAR: 10/14/1913 SP: 12/23/1924 DR: 6/23/1925 S: H

CHAPTER SIX: STATE OF FIRST ENLISTMENT OF CIVIL WAR VETERANS

The following is a "Unit List" containing the units that the Civil War veterans of this study first enlisted in, sorted by state and alphabetically by veteran's last name. Additional information includes the veteran's company, unit, and rank. If rank is unknown, a (?) will appear.

This list does not contain any of 74 "NOL/NFI" veterans included in Chapter Five. The units of these veterans were unknown, and nothing else was known about them other than they had at one time belonged to Datus Coon Post G.A.R. Also, if a veteran in this list is only cited as having "re-enl" (re-enlisted) in a particular state, that veteran initially enlisted in the Civil War from another state, and is now "re-enlisting" in the new state. Check the G.A.R. citation for the veteran in Chapter Four or Chapter Five to see his state of first enlistment and entire service record.

All states in this list are cited using standard state abbreviations. The following additional codes are used on this list:

Adj:	Adjutant	LA/HA:	Light Artillery/Heavy Artillery
Batt:	Battery	Lt:	Lieutenant
Bvt:	Brevet	Maj:	Major
Brig:	Brigadier	Mus'n:	Musician
Capt:	Captain	OVI:	Ohio Volunteer Infantry
Col:	Colonel	Pvt:	Private
Cpl:	Corporal	Regt:	Regiment
CSA:	Confed.States of America	Surg:	Surgeon
Eng'rs:	Engineers	USCT:	U.S. Colored Troops

ALABAMA UNITS--3 Veterans
Franklin, Robert C.   Co A 29 AL Inf (?)--CSA
Hughes, James D.   Co I 1 AL Inf (Pvt) (Re-enl)--CSA
Slocum, Milton L.   Co A 8 AL Cav (Pvt/Col)--CSA

ARKANSAS UNITS--2 Veterans
Hudson, John   Co A 54 AR Inf (Pvt)
Winchester, Lewis   Co H 1 AR Cav (Pvt/Sgt)

CALIFORNIA UNITS--50 Veterans
Bryant, Richard   Co A 4 CA Inf (?)
Camacho, Lorenzo   Co D 1 CA Native Cav (Sgt)
Campbell, B.P.   Co G 8 CA Inf (Pvt)
Carpenter, Stephen H.   Co E 7 CA ___ (Cpl)
Chard, James J.   Co G 4 Inf Cal Vols (1 Sgt)
Cleveland, Lewis C.   Co G 2 CA Cav (Pvt)
Coats, Henry   Co B 3 Regt CA Inf (Pvt)
Cowels, Frederick H.   Co H 3 CA Inf (Pvt)
Cowels, Frederick H.   Co H 6 CA Inf (Pvt) (Re-Enl?)
Deasdorff, William P.   Co C 7 CA Inf (Pvt)
Dickson, J.F.   Co K 2 CA Inf (Pvt)
Dorris, William A.   Co E 2 CA Vol (Pvt)
Emery, Herbert L.   Co C 4 CA Inf (Pvt)
Emery, J.S.   Co G 4 CA Inf (?)
Fitzpatrick, W.   Co F 1 CA ___ (Pvt)
Gardner, William H.   Co B 5 CA Inf (Pvt)
Goetze, William   Co M 2 CA Cav (Pvt)
Gragg, William H.   Co B 1 CA Cav Mountaineers (Pvt)
Green, John A.   Co A 8 CA Inf (Pvt)
Hall, H.I.   Co D 2 CA Cav (Sgt/Lt)
Hoffman, David B   Co __ 4 CA Inf (Lt/Asst Surg)

CALIFORNIA VETERANS (Con't)

Holt, D.H.	Co H 6 CA Inf (Sgt)
Howard, Henry A.	Co K 7 CA Inf (?)
Hurley, Cornelius G.	Co M 1 CA Cav (Cpl) ("Hearley")
Kelly, John L.	Co G 7 CA Inf (?)
Kenney, Robert D.	Co E 5 CA Inf (?)
King, Burley W.	Co B 2 CA Cav (Pvt)
Knowles, Amos P.	Co A 8 CA ___ (Lt)
Lewis, Charles W.	Co __ 7 CA Inf (Capt/Col)
Loomis, M.S.	Co B 5 CA Inf (Pvt)
McCauliff, Thomas M.	Co L 2 CA Cav (Pvt)
Moore, Alexander	Co G 2 CA Inf (?)
Mussey, Albert W.	Co E 2 CA Cav (Pvt)
Noble, John	Co D 5 CA Inf (Pvt/1st Sgt)
Nutt, Henry W.	Co A 2 CA Inf (?)
O'Neill, Patrick	Co D 2 CA Inf (?)
Ogden, Tully	Co C 2 CA Inf (Pvt)
Rainbow, James P.	Co E 1 CA Inf (Pvt/Cpl)
Rapeleye, A.W.	Co H 1 CA Cav (Farrier/Vet.Surg.)
Ross, Daniel	Co A 1 CA Cav (Pvt)
Salazar, Jose Maria	Co A 1 CA Cav (Pvt)
Shaw, Frank A.T.	Co H 7 CA Cav (Pvt)
Sherman, Matthew	Co G 4 CA Vol (1 Lt/QM)
Singleton, J.A.	Co D 5 CA Inf (?)
Smith, Samuel C.	Co F 4 CA Inf (Pvt)
Sullivan, John Cornwall	Co B 3 CA Cav (Pvt)
Tucker, Samuel F.	Co __ 2 Regt CA Cav (?)
Warne, Charles	Co H 3 CA Inf (Pvt)
Warne, Charles	Co I 4 CA Inf (Cpl) (Re-Enl?)
Weegar, Erastus H.	Co C 1 CA Vol Inf (Pvt)
Whipple, S.G.	Co __ 1st Batt Cal Mount'd RS (Lt.Col)
White, John C.	Co K 7 CA Inf (Pvt)

COLORADO UNITS--17 Veterans

Beach, Wade	Co D 1 Vet Batt CO Cav (Pvt) (Re-Enl?)
Brandis, William	Co E 1 CO Cav (Pvt/Bugler)
Crane, Luther K.	Co H 2 CO Cav (Pvt/Com Sgt)
Crane, Luther K.	Co F 2 CO Cav (Sgt) (Re-Enl?)
Detrick, Frank	Co K 3 CO Cav (Pvt)
Ferris, John C.	Co F 1 CO Cav (Pvt/Sgt)
Gilson, Sylvester	Co B 2 CO Cav (Pvt)
Gould, William H.	Co D 3 CO Cav (Pvt)
Hennion, Martin	Co S 3 CO Inf (Orderly)
Hennion, Martin	Co G 2 CO Cav (2nd Lieut) (Re-Enl?)
Keith, Alymer D.	Co G 2 CO Cav (Pvt/QM Sgt)
Leibey, Edward H.	Co E 2 CO Cav (Pvt/Cpl)
Mohr, Daniel	Co A 2 CO Cav (Pvt)
Morrow, Hugh P.	Co M 3 CO Cav (Pvt)
Nelson, George L.	Co A 2 CO Cav (?)
Putnam, George	Co E 2 CO Cav (Pvt)
Scidmore, G.B.	Co K 2 CO Cav (?) [or Co. N]
Ward, Peter	Co I 1 CO Cav (Pvt)
Weaver, Thomas F.	Co D 2 CO Vol Cav (?)
Weaver, Thomas F.	Co F 2 CO Cav (Pvt) (Re-Enl?)

CONNECTICUT UNITS--20 Veterans

Allen, Seth S.	Co G 25 CT Inf (Pvt)
Birmingham, Thomas	Co D 9 CT Inf (?)
Burr, Charles M.	Co E 19 CT Vol Inf (Pvt)
Burr, Charles M.	Co __ 2 CT H A (?) (Transfer)
Costello, Thomas	Co K 15 CT Inf (?) [or Co R]
Crook, George H.	Co H 23 CT Inf (Pvt)
Edwards, Nathan	Co D 1 CT H A (Pvt)
Forbes, David	Co C 1 CT Cav (Sgt)
Gaylord, Orvin N.	Co G 16 CT Vol Inf (Pvt)
Hefflin, Frederick	Co E 8 CT Inf (Pvt)
Holcomb, B.	Co L 1 CT Arty (Pvt)
Hunt, Ishabel	Co A 21 CT Inf (?)
Keeney, C.W.	Co H 16 CT Inf (Pvt)
Lyon, Edward	Co K 7 CT Cav (Pvt/Cpl)
Miller, Admiral N.	Co D 21 CT Inf (Pvt)
Moran, George E.	Co I 1 CT Art (Pvt)
Neisus, F.G.	Co G 7 CT Inf (Bugler)
Owens, John	Co L 2 CT H A (Pvt)
Severy, Elisha	Co I 16 CT Inf (Pvt)
Stone, William P.	Co I 1 CT H A (Pvt)
Tiffany, John F.	Co K 22 CT Inf (Pvt)

DELAWARE UNITS--4 Veterans

Boyd, David O.	Co K 1 DE Inf (Pvt/Sgt)
Collins, John T.	Co D 1 DE Inf (Pvt)
Davis, John H.	Co B 3 DE Inf (Pvt)
Taylor, Charles P.	Co E 2 DE Inf (Pvt)

DISTRICT OF COLUMBIA UNITS--3 Veterans

Hart, James	Co K 2 DC Vol Inf (Pvt)
McDowell, C.H.	Co G 2 DC Inf (Corpl)
Varnum, George M.	Co __ Washington?, DC Vols (Surg)

ILLINOIS UNITS--260 Veterans

Adams, Calvin J.	Co E 50 IL Inf (Pvt)
Archer, John R.	Co G 70 IL Inf (Sgt)
Atwood, Joseph R.	Co C 27 IL Inf (Corpl)
Avery, Henry J.	Co A 67 IL Inf (?)
Baker, James	Co F 113 IL Inf (Pvt)
Banks, Horatio	Co E 74 IL Inf (Pvt)
Barnes, Barton N.	Co G 22 IL Inf (?)
Barnum, Henry P.	Co C 96 IL Inf (Pvt/Cpl)
Battrum, Alexander	Co I 16 IL Inf (Pvt)
Baughman, Henry J.	Co C 10 IL Inf (Pvt)
Baughman, Samuel K.	Co C 10 IL Inf (Pvt/1 Lt)
Beach, Wade	Co G 18 IL Inf (Pvt)
Beamer, John	Co C 10 IL Inf (Pvt)
Beamer, Peter W.	Co K 16 IL Inf (Pvt/Sgt)
Beebe, Daniel L.	Co D 4 IL Cav (Pvt/Sgt)
Bell, John B.	Co C 144 IL Inf (Pvt)
Berry, Riley	Co B 133 IL Inf (Pvt)
Berry, Riley	Co G 149 IL Inf (Pvt) (Re-Enl)
Blake, Robert W.	Co G 39 IL Inf (Pvt)
Bogardus, Byron F.	Co __ 19 IL Inf (Mus'n)
Boyd, John B.	Co F 139 IL Inf (Pvt)

ILLINOIS VETERANS (Con't)

Brandt, Otto	Co A 72 IL Inf (Pvt)
Brewer, Joseph C./G.	Co __ 11 IL Cav R G S (Capt)
Bristinstine, Matthias	Co C 13 IL Cav (Pvt)
Bristinstine, Matthias	Co E 13 IL Cav (Pvt) (Re-Enl)
Browne, William S.	Chicago Mtd Batt (Pvt)
Browning, Thomas N.	Co F 62 IL Inf (Mus'n)
Bryan, Solon	Co E 4 IL Cav (Sgt)
Buck, Elijah	Co A 7 IL Inf (Pvt/Cpl)
Buck, Nathan	Co A 41 IL Inf (Pvt) (Re-Enl?)
Buck, Nathan	Co K 56 IL Inf (Pvt) (Re-Enl?)
Buckley, Joseph	Co H 89 IL Vol Inf (?)
Burch, Grenville L.	Co I 98 IL Inf (?)
Burkhard, Fred	Co F 140 IL Vol Inf (Pvt)
Butschli, Jacob	Co K 27 IL Inf (Pvt)
Calkins, Joel P.	Co G 2 IL Cav (Pvt)
Capsul, Lewis	Co __ Henshaw's IL Batt (Pvt) (Louis Capsel)
Chester, D.R.	Co G 88 IL Inf (2 Lt/Capt)
Chilcott, E.	Co B 129 IL Vol (2 Lt)
Childs, Benjamin F.	Co E 11 IL Cav (Pvt)
Christopher, William H.	Co C 7 IL Cav (Pvt/Sgt)
Clapp, E.S.	Co K 1 IL Art (Pvt)
Clark, J.C.	Co A 80 IL Vol Inf (Pvt)
Cleveland, James S.	Co E 146 IL Inf (Pvt)
Clevenger, Benj.C.	Co E 122 IL Inf (Cpl)
Cline, Joseph H.	Co A 26 IL Inf (Pvt)
Collins, Lewis R.	Co F 50 IL Inf (?)
Comstock, John	Co K 45 IL Inf (Pvt)
Conner, Samuel P.	Co F 18 IL Inf (Pvt/2 Lt)
Cook, Joseph	Co B 8 IL Inf (Pvt)
Coonwell, Robert	Co G 10 IL Inf (Pvt)
Coonwell, Robert	Co A 10 IL Inf (Pvt/1 Lt) (Re-Enl?)
Craig, George W.	Co E 132 IL Inf (Pvt/Sgt)
Cundall, Benjamin M.	Co D 53 IL Inf (Pvt)
Cushing, Allen D.	Co F 146 IL Inf (Pvt)
Cushman, Edmond S.	Co E 92 IL Inf (Cpl)
Darr, Milton B.	Co I 18 IL Inf (Pvt/Cpl)
Darrough, James W.	Co F 113 IL Inf (Pvt)
Davis, Josiah	Co G 8 IL Inf (?)
Davis, Wilber F.	Co B 45 IL Inf (Pvt)
Day, William G.	Co B 74 IL Inf (?)
Deakins, Henry C.	Co A 14 IL Inf (Pvt?)
Dissinger, David	Co H 16 IL Cav (Pvt)
Dixon, R.L.	Co K 56 IL Inf (Pvt)
Dodge, John G.	Co G 17 IL Inf (Pvt)
Dorey, Westly B.	Co __ 30 IL Inf (Mus'n)
Dort, Levi M.	Co E 84 IL Vol Inf (Pvt/Cpl)
Dougherty, Louis C.	Co B 59 IL Inf (Pvt/Cpl)
Dryden, James L.	Co C 36 IL Inf (Pvt)
Dumford, I.S.	Co K 99 IL Inf (?)
Dye, John W.	Co F 9 IL Inf (Pvt)
Eastman, Joseph	Co B 11 IL Cav (?)
Edgar, James A.	Co A 89 IL Inf (Pvt)
Edgar, James A.	Co B 59 IL Inf (Pvt) (Re-Enl)
Erickson, Mathias	Co D 7 IL Cav (Pvt/Chief Bugler)
Eubanks, J.J.	Co C 124 IL Inf (Pvt/Sgt)

ILLINOIS VETERANS (Con't)

Farrow, Stephen F.	Co D 3 IL Cav (Pvt)
Field, William B.	Co C 89 IL Inf (Pvt)
Field, William B.	Co F 59 IL ___ (?) (Re-Enl)
Fitzgerald, Edmond	Co K 53 IL Inf (Pvt/1 Lt)
Folks, John H.	Co F 26 IL Inf (Pvt/Capt)
Fonda, John G.	Co G 2 IL Inf (1 Lt/1st Post Surgeon)
Fonda, John G.	Co __ 12 IL Inf (Maj) (Promoted)
Fonda, John G.	Co __ 118 IL Inf (Lt Col/Col/Brvt Brig Gen) (Promoted)
Forker, Oliver H.P.	Co H 59 IL Inf (Pvt/Sgt)
Foster, Nehemiah D.	Co D 48 IL Inf (Corp)
Frank, Alonzo	Co E 89 IL Inf (Pvt/Cpl)
Frazell, Warren	Co E 10 IL Inf (Pvt)
French, Stephen	Co D 11 IL Vol Inf (Pvt) [or 111 IL Inf]
Froelich, Godfrey F.W.	Co D 10 IL Inf (Pvt)
Gardner, Horace	Co K 105 IL Inf (Pvt)
Gardner, Warren M.	Co B 151 IL Vol Inf (Pvt)
Garside, Joseph	Co B 83 IL Vol Inf (Pvt)
Gibson, Emory M.	Co G 105 IL Inf (Pvt)
Gilbert, Henry H.	Co C 66 IL Inf Western Sharpshooters (Pvt)
Gimelich, Christ	Co G 36 IL Inf (Pvt)
Gleason, Henry J.	Co G 72 IL Inf (Capt)
Goodspeed, Charles E.	Co D 74 IL Inf (Cpl)
Graham, Burton F.	Co I 1 IL Cav (Sgt)
Graham, Isaac A.	Co E 9 IL Cav (Sgt)
Gray, Joseph	Co I 96 IL Inf (Pvt)
Gray, William	Co I 22 IL Inf (?)
Green, Henry C.	Co D 127 IL Inf (Pvt)
Green, Henry C.	Co D 125 IL Inf (Pvt) (Re-Enl?)
Gregory, Star C.	Co A 105 IL Vol Inf (Pvt)
Gunn, John W.	Co I 14 IL ___ (Pvt)
Gunn, John W.	Co E 58 IL Inf (2 Lt) (Re-Enl)
Hall, William H.	Co E 58 IL Inf (?)
Hardy, Albert	Co K 100 IL Inf (Pvt)
Hargrave, William	Co F 141 IL Inf (Pvt)
Harmon, Ole O.	Co B 153 IL Inf (Pvt)
Harper, Joseph H.	Co I 117 IL Inf (Pvt/Sgt) (Re-Enl?)
Harvey, Rufus D./W.	Co B 1 IL L A (Pvt) (Re/Enl?)
Hefflin, William H.	Co D 95 IL Inf (Pvt/Sgt)
Henderson, Eliel F.	Co __ 101 IL Inf (Asst.Surg)
Henderson, William P.	Co I 17 IL Inf (Pvt)
Henderson, William P.	Co E 8 IL Inf (Pvt) (Re-Enl?)
Henneberry, Garrett J.	Co H 69 IL Inf (?)
Hesser, Wilber F.	Co C 124 IL Inf (Pvt)
Hill, Charles H.	Co H 23 IL Inf (Pvt)
Hill, John	Co H 2 IL Cav (Sgt)
Hinckley, Oscar S.	Co D 127 IL Inf (Pvt)
Hipwell, Richard J.	Co I 17 IL Cav (Pvt)
Hodge, Noah	Co C 124 IL Inf (Pvt)
Hoffman, W.E.	Co B 98 IL Inf (Pvt/Capt)
Hogeland, A.W.	Co I 47 IL Inf (Pvt/Cpl)
Holderness, William H.	Co K 8 IL Inf (Pvt)
Holman, Franklin	Co F 114 IL Inf (Pvt)
Hopkins, Ira K.	Co D 11 IL Cav (Pvt) [Hopkins/Hoskins, Ira K.]
Hopkins, Jerome	Co C 57 IL Inf (Drummer)
Hopkins, Jerome	Co I 113 IL Inf (Drummer/Prin.Mus'n) (Re-Enl)

ILLINOIS VETERANS (Con't)

Howell, William	Co F 52 IL Inf (Pvt)
Hughes, John H.	Co H 95 IL Inf (Pvt)
Hughes, Miles	Co I 10 IL Inf (Pvt)
Hulburd(t), Ebenezer W.	Co I 60 IL Inf (Pvt/2 Lt)
Humphrey, E.O.	Co I 102 Ill Inf (?)
Hunt, Cephas B.	Co I 112 IL Inf (Pvt/Sgt)
Jaggers, Thomas	Co D 8 IL Inf (Pvt)
Jaggers, Thomas	Co A 59 IL Inf (Pvt) (Re-Enl)
Jamison, Alexander	Co D 122 IL Inf (Re-Enl?)
Johnson, Edward	Co F 17 IL Inf (Pvt)
Johnston, John	Co D 9 IL Cav (Pvt/Sgt)
Jones, Henry H.	Co B 65 IL Inf (1 Lt)
Juvenal, Josiah	Co K 150 IL Inf (Pvt)
Kastner, Joseph	Co B 11 IL Cav (?)
Keldar, Abram	Co G 88 IL Inf (Pvt/Sgt)
King, John D.	Co A 33 IL Inf (Pvt)
King, William C.	Co B 125 IL Inf (Pvt/Corpl)
Knoles, Samuel S.	Co K 114 IL Vol Inf (Pvt/Sgt)
Kruger, Julius G.	Co I 24 IL Inf (Pvt)
Kurtz, Albert A.	Co K 143 IL Inf (Pvt)
Kurtz, Albert A.	Co F 149 Ill Inf (Drummer) (Re-Enl?)
Langdon, John W.	Co A 95 IL Inf (Pvt)
Langdon, Samuel J.	Co G 94 IL Inf (Pvt/Sgt)
Lashmit, W.E.	Co I 14 IL Inf (Pvt)
Little, William J.	Co B 2 IL Cav (Pvt) (Re-Enl)
Livingston, Frederick W.	Co A 14 IL Cav (Pvt/QM Sgt) (Re-Enl?)
Livingston, Frederick W.	Co __ 14 IL Cav (Asst Hosp Stwd) (Re-Enl?)
Long, Porter	Co A 8 IL Cav (Pvt)
Loudon, J.H.	Co M 11 IL Cav (Pvt)
Low, Francis M.	Co G 137 IL Inf (?)
Lyon, E.C.	Co E 2 IL Cav (Pvt)
Magee, Thomas L.	Co __ 51 IL Vol Inf (Asst Surg/1 Lt/Maj/Surg)
Mantania, James D.	Co 1 72 IL Inf (Corpl)
Martin, Nelson	Co E 12 IL Cav (Pvt)
Mathenia, William S.	Co D 64 IL Vol Inf (Pvt)
Matson, Albert	Co I 132 IL Inf (?)
Mattern, Henry J.	Co E 1 IL L A (?)
Maxwell, James F.	Co F 102 IL Vol Inf (Pvt)
McClelland, William T.	Co G 30 IL Inf (Pvt/Sgt)
McDonald, J. Wade	Co E 20 IL Inf (Pvt)
McIntosh, Henry C.	Co F 67 IL Inf (Pvt)
McIntosh, Henry C.	Co G 2 IL L A (Pvt) (Re-Enl?)
Meth, J. H.	Co D 97 IL Inf (Pvt)
Miles, John F.	Co __ 35 IL Inf (RQM)
Miller, Albert J.	Co A 11 IL Inf (Pvt)
Miller, Albert J.	Co B 25 IL Inf (?) (Re-Enl?) [or 26 Ill Inf]
Mitchell, J.H.	Co G 13 IL Cav (Pvt)
Mitchell, J.H.	Co _ 13 IL Inf (Regt QM Sgt) (Re-Enl?)
Mitchell, James P.	Co E 29 IL Inf (Sgt/Capt)
Moore, Alanson O.	Co F 95 IL Inf (Pvt/Sgt)
Moore, Francis T.	Co L 2 IL Cav (Pvt/Capt)
Morey, A.B.	Co E 124 IL Inf (?)
Morris, Samuel G.	Co G 1 IL Cav (Pvt)
Morris, Samuel G.	Co A 83 IL Inf (Pvt) (Re-Enl)
Morrison, David	Co B 129 IL Inf (?)

ILLINOIS VETERANS (Con't)

Moseley, William C.	Co A 75 IL Inf (Pvt/Cpl)
Munhall, Thomas T.	Co D 11 IL Cav (?)
Munhall, Thomas T.	Co B 11 IL Vol Cav (Pvt/Capt) (Promoted?)
Murdock, David H.	Co H 77 IL Inf (Corpl/Sgt)
Neer, Barton	Co H 46 IL Inf (Pvt)
Nelson, J. Martin	Co E 12 IL Inf (Pvt)
Newton, George A.	Co E 129 IL Inf (Pvt)
Ott, George K.	Co G 138 IL Inf (Sgt)
Ott, George K	Co A 156 IL Inf (Sgt) (Re-Enl)
Outcault, Lewis S.	Co F 26 IL Inf (Pvt) (or 86 IL Inf)
Packard, P.L.	Co D 154 IL Inf (Pvt/Cpl)
Palmateer, Charles D.	Co D 62 IL Inf (?)
Parish, Watson	Co G 39 IL Inf (Pvt/Cpl)
Parker, Dexter	Co F 105 IL Inf (Pvt)
Parker, George W.	Co H 126 IL Inf (Pvt/Lt/Adjt)
Parmenter, William P.	Co K 58 IL Inf (Pvt)
Partsch, Emil C.	Co G 82 IL Inf (Mus'n)
Patrick, Wellington	Co E 13 IL Cav (Pvt)
Pearce, Jacob	Co __ 151 IL Inf (Sgt)
Pickens, Frank	Co A 104 IL Inf (Cpl/1 Sgt)
Pierce, Sylvester L.	Co B 61 IL Inf (Pvt) (Re-Enl?)
Pitner, John L.	Co D 5 IL Cav (Pvt/Cpl)
Place, Samuel S.	Co A 2 IL Cav (?)
Pope, William W.	Co F 92 IL Mtd Inf (Pvt)
Potter, Milton M.	Co D 55 IL Inf (Pvt/2 M.Sgt)
Puterbaugh, George	Co F 8 IL Inf (Corp)
Puterbaugh, George	Co E 47 IL Inf (Capt) (Promoted?)
Rench, Lyman T.	Co K 77 IL Inf (?)
Riddle, James D.	Co C 69 IL Inf (?)
Riedelbauch, John	Co A 44 IL Inf (Pvt)
Riggs, Joseph	Co E 9 IL Cav (Pvt) (Re-Enl?)
Roberts, Samuel L.	Co C 75 IL Inf (Pvt)
Robertson, Simon	Co A 14 IL Cav (Pvt)
Root, Eleaser T.	Co I 65 IL Inf (Pvt)
Russell, Hiram W.	Co I 1 IL L A (Sgt)
Santee, Milton	Co A 13 IL Inf (Pvt)
Scherrer, Hieronimus	Co D 16 IL Cav (Pvt)
Schooley, Ellis L.	Co C 96 IL Inf (Pvt)
Schultz, James T.	Co F 26 IL Inf (Pvt)
Seabold(t), Gilbert L.	Co A 33 IL Inf (?)
Seidell, Charles W.	Co C 105 IL Inf (2 Sgt/1 Sgt)
Servoss, Freeman	Co C 52 IL Inf (Mus'n)
Shattuck, John	Batt A 3 IL L A (Pvt) (Re-Enl?)
Shay, William	Co K 23 IL Inf (?)
Shea, Michael	Co G 53 IL Inf (Pvt)
Shelly, Thomas C.	Co C 17 IL Inf (Pvt)
Shelly, Thomas C.	Co H 15 IL Inf (1 Lt) (Re-Enl?)
Shepard, Charles T.	Co E 17 IL Cav (Pvt)
Sherman, Edward	Co K 153 IL Inf (?)
Shindler, George	Co I 138 IL Inf (Pvt)
Shindler, George	Co A 156 IL Inf (Pvt) (Re-Enl)
Shultz, James F.	Co F 26 IL Inf (Pvt)
Simon(s), John	Co E 94 IL Inf (?)
Slaughter, William	Co F 67 IL Inf (Pvt)
Sloane, Hampton P.	Co C 74 IL Inf (Capt)

ILLINOIS VETERANS (Con't)

Slusser, Abraham	Co M 7 IL Cav (Pvt)
Smith, Charles F.	Co H 65 IL Inf (?)
Smith, Henry	Co E 10 IL Inf (?)
Smith, Theron J.	Co A 140 IL Inf (Pvt)
Smith, Thomas B.	Co D 78 IL Inf (Pvt)
Smyth, Frank	Co D 140 IL Inf (Capt)
Spates, John M.	Co A 115 IL Inf (Pvt/Cpl)
Stark, Nathaniel J.	Co C 150 IL Inf (Pvt)
Stevens, E.L.	Co C 104 IL Inf (Pvt)
Stewart, Perry	Co E 66 IL Inf (Pvt)
Stewins, Irenius D.	Co D 22 IL Inf (Mus'n)
Stover, Joseph W.	Co E 62 IL Inf (1 Lt)
Swan, Thomas	Co C 47 IL Inf (Pvt/Cpl)
Tartt, Thomas M.	Co F 117 IL Inf (Pvt)
Taylor, R.W.	Co I 55 IL Inf (Pvt)
Thompson, Samuel/Saul	Co I 132 IL Inf (Cpl)
Todd, Eugene	Co B 138 IL Inf (Pvt)
Todd, James	Co B 139 IL Inf (?)
Tomlin, George	Co H 105 IL Inf (Cpl)
Townsend, Daniel W.	Co I 15 IL Cav (Saddler)
Triggs, John	Co G 96 IL Inf (Pvt)
Tucker, James W.	Co K 11 IL Cav (Pvt)
Vincent, J.W.	Co C 45 IL Inf (1 Sgt/1 Lt)
Ward, Henry A.	Co A 72 IL Inf (Cpl/2 Lt)
Waugh, Samuel	Co B 14 IL Inf (Pvt)
Weatherby, Charles	Co K 106 IL Inf (Pvt)
Webler, George A.	Co E 39 IL Inf (Pvt)
Webster, Albert I.	Co E 113 IL Inf (Pvt)
Wells, Leonard B.	Co A 8 IL Inf (1 Sgt)
West, Joseph G.	Co K 9 IL Cav (?)
White, William I.	Co E 46 IL Inf (Pvt)
Wilkins, George A.	Co H 47 IL Vol (Capt)
Willey, John A.	Co G 67 IL Inf (Pvt)
Williamson, Jacob T.	Co F 138 IL Inf (Pvt)
Wilson, Robert I.	Co G 7 IL Inf (Pvt)
Winscott, James C.	Co A 50 IL Inf (Pvt)
Wood, Thomas E.	Co H 123 IL Inf (Capt)
Woodruff, George A.	Co H 113 IL Inf (Pvt/Sgt)
Wright, Henry Q.	Co I 11 IL Inf (Pvt)
Wright, Henry Q.	Co A 64 IL Inf (Pvt) (Re-enl?)
Wynn, Charles H.	Co I 35 IL Inf (Pvt)
Young, Robert	Co B 28 IL Inf (Pvt/1 Lt)
Young, Robert C.	Co E 84 IL Inf (Pvt)
Young, William A.	Co F 28 IL Inf (Pvt)

INDIANA UNITS--141 Veterans

Ackerman, Frank	Co M 17 IN Cav (Pvt)
Albee, Timothy M.	Co A 44 IN Inf (Pvt)
Albee, Timothy M.	Co C 152 IN Inf (Sgt) (Re-Enl?)
Alford, Robert	Co K 136 IN Inf (Pvt)
Alford, Robert	Co I? 152 IN Inf (Pvt) (Re-Enl?)
Alhoun, William H.	Co C 52 IN Inf (Pvt)
Allen, Charles W.	Co C 30 IN Inf (Pvt)
Arment, J.A.	Co H 140 IN Inf (Pvt)
Bailiff, Edward H.	Co F 148 IN Inf (Sgt)

INDIANA VETERANS (Con't)

Ball, Thomas P.	Co D 152 IN Inf (Pvt)
Bates, R.O.	Co H 9 IN? Cav (Pvt)
Bates, R.O.	Co A 129 IN ___ (?) (Re-Enl?)
Battroff, Martin P.	Co I 81 IN Inf (Pvt)
Bell, John R.	Co I 25 IN Inf (1 Lt/Capt)
Bennett, William H.	Co __ 21 Batt Ind Art (Pvt)
Billingsley, L.W.	Co I 7 IN Inf (Pvt)
Billingsley, L.W.	Co K 4 IN Cav (Cpl) (Re-Enl)
Black, Isaac	Co B 84 IN Vol Inf (Pvt/Cpl)
Brewington, James B.	Co A 7 IN Inf (Pvt)
Brooks, John B./P.	Co L 6 IN Cav (Cpl)
Brown, James D.	Co F 140 IN Inf (Corp)
Chapman, George B.	Co __ 9 IN Batt (Pvt)
Chapman, George B.	Co F 11 IN Cav (1 Lt)
Clark, Charles E.	Co L 1 IN Art (Pvt)
Clark, William A.	Co K 72 IN Inf (Pvt)
Colebaker, Samuel	Co __ 7 IN Batt (Pvt)
Conner, Samuel P.	Co C 124 IN Inf (Pvt/Capt) (Promoted?)
Corben, James G.	Co D 11 IN Inf (Pvt)
Coutant, Jacob B.	Co E 7 IN Inf (Pvt)
Coutant, Jacob B	Co A 7 IN Inf (Pvt) (Re-Enl)
Cox, Isaac S.	Co F 63 IN Inf (Cpl/Sgt)
Crittenden, Thomas T.	Co A 6 IN Inf (Capt)
Darkes, William W.	Co D 43 IN Inf (Pvt)
Davis, L. Murry	Co G 43 IN Inf (Pvt/2 Lt)
DeFord, Thomas J.	Co D 46 IN Inf (Sgt)
Denny, Eliza M.	Co F 81 IN Inf (Pvt)
Donaldson, Cyrus	Co H 63 IN Inf (Corpl)
Dunham, George B.	Co H 87 IN Inf (Pvt)
Dunn, W.T.	Co B 14 IN Inf (Pvt)
Dunn, W.T.	Co G 80 IN Inf (1 Lt) (Re-Enl?)
Edwards, John W.	Co F 14 IN Inf (Pvt)
Ellibee, Erastus T.	Co D 99 IN Inf (Pvt)
Evans, John H.	Co C 135 IN Inf (?)
Ewing, William E.	Co G 28 IN State Guard Inf (Pvt)
Ferris, Edmond	Co __ 8 IN Vol ___ (?)
Ferris, Edmond	Co __ 47 IN Vol ___ (?) (Re-Enl?)
Fesler, William H.	Co K 8 IN Inf (Pvt)
Finch, William W.	Co D 128 IN Vol Inf (Pvt/2 Lt)
Fitzgerald, Nathan W.	Co A 132 IN Inf (Pvt)
Flinn, Daniel L.	Co B 17 IN Inf (1 Sgt)
Fry, Edward J.	Co F 22 IN Inf (Pvt)
Garrett, James W.	Co __ 13 Batt IN L A (Pvt)
Green, Elias S.	Co H 117 IN Inf (Pvt)
Green, Elias S.	Co A 140 IN Vol Inf (Sgt) (Re-Enl?)
Green, J.N.	Co __ 19 IN Inf (Asst Surg)
Greenfield, John	Co K 48 IN Inf (Pvt)
Greenleaf, William C.	Co E 11 IN Inf (Pvt/Cpl)
Greenlee, James L.	Co G 37 IN Inf (Pvt)
Grinell, Calvin	Co D 33 IN Inf (Sgt)
Guy, Isaac J.C.	Co K 134 IN Inf (2 Lt)
Guy, Isaac J.C.	Co C 151 IN Inf (1 Lt/Act Adjt) (Re-Enl)
Hale, John A.	Co A 99 IN Inf (Pvt)
Hamilton, Martin D.	Co G 17 IN Vol __ (Pvt/1 Sgt)
Harris, Leander W.	Co B 3 IN Cav (?) [or Co G]

INDIANA VETERANS (Con't)

Haughn, Francis J.	Co A	124 IN Inf (Pvt)
Hazzard, George W.	Co B	134 IN Inf (Pvt)
Hilsher, Harmon	Co A	13 IN Cav (Pvt)
Hilscher, Herman	Co E	16 IN Mtd Inf (Pvt) (Re-Enl)
Hinckle, William S.	Co D	21 IN Inf (Lt/Capt) (Promoted?)
Hinckle, William S.	Co D	1 IN H A (Capt) (Promoted?)
Hodges, George W.	Co C	155 IN Inf (Pvt)
Hoffman, John S.	Co I	5 IN Cav (Pvt/Corpl)
Holmes, Philander	Co A	12 IN Cav (?)
Honeycutt, Daniel	Co H	50 IN Vol Inf (?)
Horrele, W.H.	Co B	27 IN Inf (Pvt)
Horst, Henry F.	Co A	16 IN Inf (Pvt)
Hubbard, Martin	Co L	7 IN Cav (Pvt)
Johns, James B.	Co G	43 IN Inf (Pvt/Sgt)
Johnson, Thomas G.	Co D	8 IN Inf (?) [or 9 Ind Inf]
Kelly, Abraham	Co C	118 IN Inf (Pvt)
Kelly, Abraham	Co K	23 IN Inf (Pvt) (Re-Enl)
Lane, M.W.	Co E	1 IN H A (Pvt)
Layton, Robert	Co D	40 IN Inf (Pvt)
Layton, Robert	Co A	3 IN Cav (Pvt) (Re-Enl)
Lewis, John	Co B	50 IN Inf (Pvt)
Lewis, John	Co B	52 IN Inf (Pvt) (Re-Enl?)
Light, Jacob J.	Co C	31 IN Inf (?) [or Co G]
Lindley, Charles	Co G	40 IN Inf (Pvt)
Lingenfelter, Alford	Co H	148 IN Inf (Pvt/Drummer)
Lingenfelter, Deliscus	Co D	68 IN Inf (Lt)
Lisher, O.B.	Co __	12 IN Inf (Band Leader)
Lockwood, Nathan S.	Co A	2 IN Inf (?) [or 2 IN Cav (Pvt)]
Lopshire, Adam J.	Co B	118 IN Inf (Pvt)
Lyman, James O.	Co A	9 IN Cav (Com Sgt)
Mathes, Z.C.	Co B	18 IN Inf (Pvt)
Maxwell, James H.	Co A	32 IN Inf (Pvt)
McClure, William P.	Co H	51 IN Inf (Pvt/Capt)
Meagher, John O.	Co I	129 IN Inf (Pvt)
Miller, Jacob L.	Co H	20 IN Inf (Pvt)
Miller, John G.C.	Co E	14 IN Inf (Lt)
Miller, William F.	Co F	17 IN Inf (Pvt/Cpl)
Milliron, Joseph C.	Co I	8 IN Inf (Pvt/Lt/Sgt)
Mills, Cleveland W.	Co K	10 IN Cav (Pvt/1 Sgt)
Mingus, Cyrus L.	Co G	130 IN Inf (?)
Moore, William H.	Co D	84 IN Inf (Pvt)
Morgan, James M.	Co D	17 IN Inf (?)
Newsome, Eli	Co A	120 IN Inf (Pvt/Cpl)
Northern, Walter B.	Co I	139 IN Vol Inf (Pvt)
Oliphant, John A.	Co A	124 IN Vol Inf (Pvt)
Owings, Luthur	Co D	33 IN Inf (Pvt)
Pendland, Alonzo	Co B	33 IN Inf (Pvt)
Perkins, Harrison	Co H	57 IN Inf (Cpl)
Pickett, Zedekiah	Co F	7 IN Inf (Pvt)
Pickett, Zedekiah	Co E	76 IN Inf (Pvt) Re/Enl?)
Pierce, Sylvester L.	Co B	98 IN Inf (Pvt)
Porter, Stephen	Co A	9 Indep Ind Inf (Sgt)
Powers, Marion	Co K	137 IN Inf (Sgt)
Pugh, Theophilus J.	Co I	7 IN Inf (Pvt)
Rafferty, E.G.	Co G	43 IN Inf (Pvt)

INDIANA VETERANS (Con't)

Read, John W.	Co A 87 IN Inf (Pvt)
Read, John W.	Co B 42 IN Inf (Pvt) (Re-Enl?)
Redfern, Alfred	Co K 91 IN Inf (?)
Richards, George W.	Co C 144 IN Inf (Pvt)
Ryan, John T.	Co __ 2 IN Batt (Pvt)
Sammis, Marsden H.	Co A 5 IN Cav (Pvt/Sgt)
Schaeffer, Jason	Co H 152 IN Inf (Pvt)
Schrader, Adolph	Co K 38 IN Inf (Pvt)
Sherman, Francis M.	Co I 9 IN Inf (Pvt/Cpl)
Shuyler, J.L.	Co G 53 IN Inf (Pvt)
Sloan, James L.	Co A 68 IN Inf (Pvt)
Sims, W.F.	Co F 99 IN Inf (Pvt)
Smith, D.M.	Co F 7 IN Inf (Pvt)
Smith, Ichabod	Co C 89 IN Inf (Sgt)
Smith, Peter C.	Co G 7 IN Inf (Pvt)
Sneer, Philetus E.	Co G 12 IN Cav (Pvt)
Snyder/Snider, Lorenzo	Co E 9 IN Inf (?)
Sprague, Joseph B.	Co K 15 IN Inf (Pvt/Sgt)
Stacey, Arthur G.	Co E 46 IN Inf (Pvt)
Stambaugh, William H.	Co A 49 IN Inf (Pvt) (or 149 IN Inf)
Talcott, Henry W.	Co __ 13 IN Inf (Mus'n)
Thornburg, Albert M.	Co B 8 IN Inf (Pvt)
Thornburg, Albert M	Co __ 9 IN Cav (Bugler) (Re-Enl?)
Tout, Henry C.	Co B 117 IN Inf (Pvt)
Traylor, Madison	Co A 58 Ind Inf (?)
Turner, Asbury	Co A 146 IN Inf (Pvt)
Vest, Authur E.	Co F 57 IN Inf (Pvt/Sgt)
Vestal, W.L.	Co A 7 IN Inf (Pvt)
Vestal, W.L.	Co __ 53 IN Inf (Col) (Promoted)
Ward, Samson L.	Co D 39 IN Inf (Pvt/Sgt)
Washington, Watkins	Co B 11 IN Inf (Pvt)
Webster, Andrew B.	Co I 1 IN H A (Pvt)
White, William Othe	Co D 12 IN Cav (Pvt)
Whitman, Winfield S.	Co A 12 IN Inf (Cpl/1 Sgt)
Whitman, Winfield S.	Co I 66 IN Inf (2 Lt/1 Lt) (Promoted?)
Wishmeyer, Frederick C.	Co H 1 IN Vol Inf (Cpl)
Wood, Isaac	Co F 144 IN Inf (Cpl)
Works, J.D.	Co D 10 IN Cav (Pvt)
Works, Lewis F.	Co E 50 IN Inf (Pvt)
Wroughton, William H.	Co D 49 IN Inf (Pvt/Cpl)
Yates, Elija N.	Co C 71 IN Inf (Pvt)
Yates, Elija N.	Co __ 6th IN Cav (Sgt/Maj) (Promoted?)
Yelton, William L.	Co B 43 IN Inf (Sgt/Capt)

IOWA UNITS--144 Veterans

Adair, Marion	Co _ 33 IA Inf (Pvt)
Alcorn, Robert A.	Co H 19 IA Inf (Cpl)
Allum, Leroy W.	Co C 22 IA Inf (Pvt/Color Sgt)
Allum, Thomas	Co C 22 IA Inf (Pvt)
Allum, Thomas	Co B 48 IA Inf (Lt) (also Capt?) (Promoted?)
Antrobus, John	Co I 6 IA Inf (Pvt)
Barnes, Rev. Henry B.	Co F 30 IA Inf (1st Sgt)
Barrick, William N.	Co B 38 IA Inf (Pvt)
Barrick, William N.	Co I 34 IA Inf (Pvt) (Re-Enl?)
Bennett, Gilbert P.	Co K 27 IA Inf (Sgt)

IOWA VETERANS (Con't)

Bennett, Jesse	Co E 3 IA Inf (Pvt)
Bentzel, Henry M.	Co A 6 IA Cav (?)
Blair, Samuel M.	Co I 7 IA Inf (Pvt)
Blakely, Joseph H.	Co D 11 IA Inf (Pvt)
Bowen, John W.	Co E 15 IA Inf (Pvt)
Bradley, Garrett R.	Co K 2 IA Cav (Pvt/Sgt)
Brimm, Boyd P.	Co F 4 IA Cav (Pvt/1 Lt)
Brobst, Albert M.	Co G 15 IA Inf (Pvt) ("Allert")
Brook, James F.	Co F 39 IA Inf (Pvt)
Brooks, John H.	Co B 38 IA Inf (1 Sgt)
Brouhard, George B.	Co B 2 IA Cav (Pvt)
Brownlee, Alex	Co B 3 IA Cav (Pvt)
Byers, John T.	Co L 8 IA Cav (Pvt)
Camp, Guy R.	Co E 2 IA Inf (Pvt)
Campbell, Milton K	Co B 5 IA Inf (Pvt)
Chapman, Joseph M.	Co __ 45 IA Vol ___ (?)
Chase, Thurston P.	Co G 35 IA Inf (Pvt)
Chrisman, Leonard	Co A 47 IA Inf (Pvt)
Clark, James S.	Co F 1 IA Inf (Pvt)
Clark, James S.	Co C 34 IA Inf (Pvt/Capt) (Promoted?)
Clarke, Frank	Co I 7 IA Inf (Pvt)
Coon, Datus E.	Co I 2 IA Cav (Capt)
Cooper, Jesse	Co K 3 IA Inf (Pvt/Sgt/1 Lt)
Cotton, John L.	Co D 31 IA Inf (Pvt)
Cotton, John L.	Co D 47 IA Inf (Pvt) (Re-Enl?)
Couchman, E.H.	Co C 18 IA Inf (Pvt)
Cravath, J.B.	Co B 32 IA Inf (Pvt)
Currier, Charles F.	Co O 29 IA Inf (Drummer) [or Co.D]
Curtis, David G.	Co I 26 IA Inf (Pvt)
Dibble, Edwin D.	Co K 45 IA Inf (Sgt)
Doig, John R.	Co C 19 IA Regt (?)
Doig, John R.	Co __ 2 IA Cav (Re-Enl?) (?)
Dostal, James C.	Co K 22 IA Inf (Pvt)
Easling, Henry L.	Co I 19 IA Inf (Corpl)
Edginton, Thomas J.	Co B 47 IA Vol Inf (Pvt)
Ellsworth, Chandler W.	Co E 1 IA Cav (Pvt)
Englehorn, John K.	Co E 9 IA Cav (Pvt)
Farley, Joseph	Co I 20 IA Inf (Pvt) (or 30 IA Inf)
Farnsworth, Robert N.	Co G 4 IA Inf (?)
Fletcher, Henry H.	Co G 3 IA Cav (Cpl)
Foote, Thomas J.	Co G 20 IA Inf (Pvt)
Frantz, Henry	Co H 15 IA Inf (Pvt/Cpl)
Gaffney, P.H.	Co K 20 IA Inf (Pvt/Sgt)
Gardner, Charles	Co I 37 IA Inf (Pvt)
Gaylord, Levi B.	Co C 44 IA Inf (?)
Gleason, Nathan B.	Co E 7 IA Cav (Pvt)
Haddock, Arthur H.M.	Co E 3 IA Inf (?)
Haines, Alfred	Co C 47 IA Inf (Pvt)
Harrigan, James	Co E 5 IA Inf (Pvt)
Hartley, James M.	Co D 44 IA Inf (Pvt)
Hartzell, Thomas B.	Co G 3 IA Cav (Cpl/Sgt)
Hayward, R.E.	Co D 4 IA ___ (Pvt)
Herrington, Beverly A.	Co H 10 IA Inf (Pvt)
Herrington, Beverly A.	Co D 24 IA Inf (Pvt) (Re-Enl?)
Hill, Edwin L.	Co A 4 IA Inf (Pvt/1 Lt)

IOWA VETERANS (Con't)

Hill, William F.	Co C 23 IA Inf (Pvt) (or Co G)
Hixon, D.W.	Co C 30 IA Inf (Pvt)
Hixon, George W.	Co I 8 IA Cav (Pvt/Cpl)
Hunt, Nathan	Co H 2 IA Cav (Pvt)
Jackson, Mason	Co C 26 IA Inf (Pvt/Cpl)
Jobes, Charles C.	Co E 1 IA Cav (Pvt)
Jones, David R.	Co G 39 IA Inf (Pvt)
Keltner, George F.	Co E 2 IA Inf (Pvt)
Key, Joseph F.	Co K 2 IA Cav (Mus'n)
Kilrain, John G.	Co B 26 IA Inf (Pvt)
Kincaid, Orlando D.	Co E 1 IA Cav (Pvt/Sgt)
Kingsland, Henry E.	Co F 35 IA Inf (?)
Laufer, Loammi	Co H 35 IA Inf (Cpl)
Laverty, Leander	Co A 48 IA Inf (Pvt)
Leheu, R.M.	Co G 11 IA Inf (Pvt)
Little, William J.	Co C 12 IA Inf (Pvt)
Manners, William A.	Co C 11 IA Inf (Pvt)
Marrs, David L.	Co B 48 IA Inf (Pvt)
Martin, Elihu G.	Co G 29 IA Inf (?)
Martin, John	Co A 8 IA Cav (Pvt/Sgt)
Mathis, Frederick B.	Co A 15 IA Inf (Pvt)
Maynard, Chauncey J.	Co C 31 IA Inf (Capt)
McClure, Joseph A.	Co B 8 IA Inf (Pvt)
McSurely, Anderson	Co G 3 IA Inf (Pvt)
Miller, Edwin H.	Co I 10 IA Inf (Pvt)
Miller, William K.	Co E 3 IA Cav (Pvt)
Mitchell, Ira	Co I 14 IA Inf (Cpl/Sgt)
Morrisy, Jessy M.	Co I 3 IA Cav (Pvt/Cpl)
Murphy, Charles H.	Co H 13 IA Inf (Pvt)
Neill, Dyas	Co H 1 IA Cav (Pvt)
Nesbitt, Everett G.	Co A 14 IA Inf (Pvt/Sgt)
Nichols, Absalom W.	Co F 3 IA Inf (Pvt)
Nichols, Absolom W.	Co F 3 IA Cav (Pvt) (Re-Enl?)
Nosler, James Mylan	Co D 2 IA Cav (?) (or Co O) [or Mylon]
Oviatt, William H.	Co C 6 IA Inf (Lt) [or Co G]
Patton, Morand D.	Co I 18 IA Inf (Pvt)
Paull, Benjamin B.	Co K 9 IA Cav (Pvt)
Paull, Charles M.	Co H 33 IA Inf (Pvt)
Pearson, M.R.	Co A 4 IA Inf (Pvt)
Pearson, Thomas J.	Co H 4 IA Inf (Pvt)
Piburn, Thomas B.	Co C 48 IA Inf (?)
Pickett, William T.	Co G 5 IA Cav (?) [or 6 IA Cav]
Porter, John	Co E 23 IA Inf (Pvt)
Porter, Watson B.	Co F 4 IA Cav (Capt)
Randall, Thomas J.	Co A 4 IA Inf (Pvt)
Reece, O.M.	Co E 5 IA Cav (Pvt)
Richmond, John	Co A 39 IA Inf (Pvt)
Rickard, Charles W.	Co G 24 IA Inf (Pvt)
Riddle, George H.	Co K 8 IA Cav (Pvt)
Roderick, Edward	Co E 5 IA Inf (Pvt)
Roderick, Edward	Co G 5 IA Cav (Corpl) (Re-Enl?)
Ross, R.H.	Co F 12 IA ___ (Pvt)
Ruff, Francis B.	Co D 21 IA Inf (Pvt)
Russell, John I.	Co A 1 IA Cav (Pvt/2 Lt)
Saum, Augustus B.	Co I 14 IA Inf (Pvt)

IOWA VETERANS (Con't)

Scofield, L.	Co K 26 IA Inf (Pvt/Sgt)
Shryock, Seymour	Co K 5 IA Inf (Pvt/Cpl)
Sisson, Elbert N.	Co H 2 IA Inf (Pvt)
Smith, C.E.	Co F 46 IA Inf (Pvt)
Smith, G.W.	Co F 1 IA Inf (Pvt/Adj)
Spangler, Henry	Co G 21 IA ___ (Pvt)
St.Clair, Hugh	Co A 28 IA Inf (Pvt/Cpl)
Steadman, William	Co B 4 IA Cav (Pvt/Sgt)
Stevens, Uzzial J.	Co M 3 IA Cav (Pvt/Cpl) [or Co N]
Stewart, Sylvester N.	Co ___ 18 IA Inf (Pvt)
Stiles, Alonzo R.	Co F 21 IA Inf (Pvt)
Stopher, Edgar A.	Co C 14 IA Inf (?)
Sunderland, John D.	Co C 1 IA Cav (Pvt)
Thomas, Albert A.	Co G 44 IA Inf (Pvt/Cpl)
Towers, Justus A.	Co F 7 IA Cav (?)
Tracy, James H.	Co B 2 IA Inf (Pvt)
Tracy, James H.	Co C 14 IA Inf (Pvt) (Re-Enl)
Valentine, D.A.	Co F 45 IA Vols (Pvt)
Valentine, I.W.	Co F 45 IA Vols (Pvt)
Walker, Fletcher J.	Co A 1 IA Cav (Pvt)
Watson, Charles C.	Co D 3 IA Inf (Cpl)
Watson, John	Co I 17 IA Inf (Pvt) (Re-Enl)
Watson, Joseph M.	Co H 2 IA Inf (Capt)
Watts, Peter	Co F 2 IA Inf (Pvt/Sgt)
Weaver, Joseph L.	Co C 31 IA Inf (Pvt/Cpl)
White, Asa G.	Co K 6 IA Cav (?)
Whitson, John	Co E 13 IA Inf (Pvt)
Williams, Albert J.	Co C 3 IA Cav (Pvt)
Wood, Augustus M.	Co A 44 IA Inf (Mus'n)
Worth, Jehoiada	Co D 4 IA Cav (Pvt)
Worth, John C.	Co D 4 IA Cav (Pvt) (or 41 IA Cav)
Wright, Philander D.	Co C 14 IA Inf (Pvt)
Wyatt, Charles C.	Co H 22 IA Inf (Pvt)

KANSAS UNITS--38 Veterans

Arnold, James M.	Co I 12 KA Inf (Sgt) (Re-enl?)
Ashton, John Q.	Co B 12 KA Inf (Pvt)
Ashton, John Q.	Co ___ 2 KA Col'd(?) ___ (QM Sgt) (Re-Enl?)
Booth, Oliver T.	Co E 2 KA Cav (Capt)
Bruner, Adam B.	Co A 22 KA State Militia (Pvt)
Clark, Newton A.	Co H 15 KA Cav (Pvt/QM Sgt)
Connell, Cornelius	Co G 7 KA Cav (?)
Elford, Peter	Co E 11 KA Mil Inf (?)
Heustis, Thomas B.	Co K 12 KA Inf (Pvt/Drummer)
Higgins, Robert W.	Co B 17 KA Inf (Cpl)
Hudgins, Amos E.	Co K 2 KA Inf (Pvt)
Hudgins, Amos E.	Co K 2 KA Cav (Pvt) (Re-Enl?)
Hunt, George W.	Co K 1 KA Mtd Inf (1 Lt)
Hutt, George W.	Co K 1 KA Inf (Pvt/1 Lt)
Hutt, George W.	Co E 17 KA Inf (1 Sergt) (Re-Enl)
Jilson, Fred E.	Co F 2 KA Vol Cav (Pvt)
Johnson, Curtis	Co E 6 KA ___ (Pvt)
Johnson, Curtis	Co E 15 KA ___ (Capt) (Promoted?)
Jones, Richard A.	Co F 11 KA Inf (Pvt) [or 11 KA Cav]
Kennedy, Charles	Co C 14 KA Cav (Pvt)

KANSAS VETERANS (Con't)

Kretsinger, David L.	Co A 10 KA Inf (Pvt)
Kurth, Andrew H.	Co I 1 KA Inf (Pvt)
Leaming, Edwin R.	Co F 16 KA Cav (?)
McGirl, Barney	Co __ 2 KA Inf (?)
Nichols, Wilmont D.	Co D 17 KA Inf (Pvt)
Oltman, Richard H.	Co F 6 KA ___ (Pvt)
Palmer, Ernest	Co A 5 KA Cav (Pvt)
Prescott, C.W.	Co L 16 KA Cav (Cpl)
Ramsey, Simmons	Co I 3 KA Inf (Pvt)
Ramsey, Simmons	Co E 10 KA Inf (Sgt) (Re-Enl?)
Rockwood, George	Co G 15 KA Cav (Pvt)
Schultheiss, Fred	Co I 1 KA Inf (Pvt)
Shaffer, Peter	Co E 7 KA Cav (Pvt)
Simpson, Joseph	Co G 79 KA Col Inf (Pvt)
Smith, Eugene E.	Co K 12 KA Inf (Pvt)
Smith, James A.	Co F 5 KA Cav (Pvt)
Smith, James A.	Co D 10 KA Inf (Sgt) (Re-Enl?)
Snyder, John H.	Co F 13 KA Inf (Pvt)
Strawn, James C.	Co C 9 KA Cav (Corpl)
Streeter, H.P.	Co H 11 KA Cav (Pvt)
Utt, Lee H.	Co A 7 KA Cav (Maj) (Promoted?)
Warden, M.W.	Co D 2 KA Cav (Pvt)
Warden, M.W.	Co E 14 KA Cav (Pvt) (Re-Enl)
Williams, Clarence J.	Co __ 2 KA Cav (Lt/QM)
Williams, Henry H.	Co __ 3 KA Inf (Maj)
Williams, Henry H.	Co __ 10 KA Inf (Maj)

KENTUCKY UNITS--11 Veterans

Boyette, William J.H.	Co D 14 KY Cav (Pvt)--CSA
Clark, Dillard H.	Co D 14 KY Cav (Pvt)
Conklin, Norman H.	Co D 2 KY Inf (Pvt)
Davidson, John M.	Co B 47 KY Inf (Pvt)
Lewis, William W.	Co B 24 KY Inf (Pvt)
Pfister, Adam	Co D 4 KY Cav (?)
Scarbrough, B.F.	Co A 12 KY Cav (Sgt)
Shepherd, James	Co G 3 KY Inf (Pvt)
Snead, William B.	Co E 14 KY Inf (Pvt)
Snead, William B.	Co A Batt 14 KY ___ (Pvt) (Re-Enl?)
Thoman, John A.	Co C 7 KY ___ (Pvt/Cpl)
Venters, Pleasant	Co I 5 KY Cav (Pvt)

MAINE UNITS--40 Veterans

Bragg, A.L.	Co A 6 ME Inf (Pvt)
Chase, Charles E.	Co L 31 ME Inf (Pvt)
Cummings, Wallace E.	Co H 10 ME Inf (Pvt) (or Co C)
Daily, Edwin V.	Co I 19 ME Inf (Pvt)
Eastman, Gilman E.	Co E 30 ME Inf (Pvt)
Eaton, Avery W.	Co H 26 ME Inf (Pvt)
Ellis, Alvin R.	Co B 19 ME Inf (Pvt/Cpl)
Fitch, Edwin P.	Co 1 1 ME Inf (Pvt/Sgt)
Fitzgerald, Thomas	Co F 19 ME Inf (Pvt/Cpl)
Fletcher, B.F.	Co A 16 ME ___ (Pvt)
Gilmore, Myron T.	Co B 15 ME Vol Inf (Pvt)
Gilpatrick, Jeremiah H.	Co F 1 ME L A (?)

MAINE VETERANS (Con't)

Gilpatrick, Jeremiah H.	Co __	6 ME L A (Pvt) (Re-Enl?)
Handy, John H.	Co __	9 ME Inf (Mus'n/Band)
Hanson, Parker W.	Co G	4 ME Inf (Pvt)
Haskell, John L.	Co A	5 ME Inf (Pvt/2 Sgt)
Hutchinson, G. O.	Co B	1 ME H A (?) [or Co D]
Jenness, Walter B.	Co H	1 ME Inf (Capt)
Jones, Danville P.	Co D	20 ME Inf (Pvt)
Jones, J.O.	Co K	2 ME Cav (Pvt)
Magoon, George A.	Co I	4 ME Batt L A (Pvt)
Magoon, George A.	Co _	4 ME Batt H A (Pvt/Cpl) (Re-Enl)
Mellus, Frances G.	Co C	4 ME Inf (Pvt)
Mellus, Frances G.	Co E	2 ME Cav (Pvt) (Re-Enl?)
Merrill, Augustus	Co A	7 ME Inf (Pvt/Maj)
Nickels, Edgar A.	Co C	11 ME Inf (Pvt/Capt)
Noble, Thomas P.	Co K	14 ME Inf (Cpl)
Paine, John O.W.	Co D	14 ME Inf (2 Lt)
Paine, John O.W.	Co E	14 ME Inf (Capt) (Promoted?)
Pease, John M.	Co H	25 ME Vol Inf (Pvt)
Reed, A.	Co C	23 ME Inf (Cpl)
Smith, Henry F.	Co E	10 ME Inf (Pvt/2 Lt)
Stuart, Alonzo B.	Co I	11 ME Inf (Pvt/Sgt)
Sweetland, Seth	Co E	3 ME Inf (Pvt)
Tinker, William H.	Co H	6 ME Inf (Pvt)
Webster, John O.	Co A	8 ME Inf (Pvt/Sgt)
Weston, Charles D.	Co F	28 ME Vol Inf (?)
Wheaton, William H.	Co K	12 ME Inf (Pvt/1 Sgt)
Whitney, A.E.	Co K	25 ME Inf (Pvt)
Whittier, John F.	Co F	26 ME Inf (Pvt)
Winslow, Charles C.	Co H	21 ME Inf (Pvt)
Woodman, Ezra E.	Co G	11 ME Inf (?)
Worthing, Ranford	Co M	1 ME H A (Pvt)
Worthing, Ranford	Co L	12 __ H A (2 Lt) (Promoted?)
York, Charles	Co B	2 ME Cav (Pvt)

MARYLAND UNITS--8 Veterans

Baer, N.	Co G	3 MD Inf (Pvt)
Baer, N.	Co A	3 MD Inf (Pvt) (Re-Enl?)
Davis, Edwin P.	Co B	2 MD Potomic Home Brigade (Pvt)
Eagle, J.O.	Co I	2 MD Inf (Pvt)
Gaches, William H.	Co G	1 MD Cav (?)
Lucy, Timothy J.	Co C	2 MD ___ (Pvt)
Moore, William Roby	Co K	19 MD Inf (Pvt)
Rouark, Nathan L.	Co D	1 MD Inf (Pvt)
Seabold(t), Henry	Co C	14 MD Inf (Cpl)

MASSACHUSETTS UNITS--68 Veterans

Allen, Horatio D.	Co A	23 MA Inf (Pvt/Cpl)
Barrett, William H.	Co I	20 MA ___ (Pvt)
Bassett, Edwin F.	Co H	29 MA Inf (Pvt)
Battles, Edgar C.	Co __	11 MA Inf (Pvt)
Bent, Judson	Co K	5 MA Inf (Pvt)
Bird, Frank	Co __	4 MA Batt (Pvt)
Blackmer, Eli T.	Co A	37 MA Inf (1 Lt)
Boodry, George O.	Co A	39 MA Inf (Pvt)
Burbeck, Lucius D.	Co E	4 MA Vol Inf (Cpl)

MASSACHUSETTS VETERANS (Con't)

Butler, Benjamin A.	Co I 55 MA Inf (Pvt)
Casey, Patricius H.	Co I 31 MA Inf (Pvt)
Coggswell, Thomas	Co B 50 MA Inf (Pvt)
Courtney, James	Co D 16 MA Inf (?)
Dame, Luther	Co C 11 MA Inf (Capt)
Davidson, Henry O.	Co A 46 MA Inf (Pvt)
Davidson, Henry O.	Co B 61 MA Inf (Pvt/Corpl) (Re-Enl?)
Day, Horace B.	Co __ 12 MA L A (Pvt)
Day, Joshua D.	Co H 12 MA Inf (Pvt)
Day, Joshua D.	Co C 39 MA Inf (Pvt/Cpl) (Re-Enl?)
Dennison, A.R.	Co D 27 MA Inf (Capt)
DeVoe, Joseph G.	Co B 50 MA Mil Inf (?)
Dill, Albert F.	Co E 43 MA Inf (Pvt)
Douay, Francis	Co C 31 MA Vol Reg (?)
Eaton, Benjamin	Co K 47 MA Inf (Pvt)
Eaton, Benjamin	Co L 56 MA Inf (Pvt) (Re-Enl?)
Fairbanks, Albert F.	Co D 43 MA Inf (Pvt)
Gilbert, John A.	Co C 25 MA Inf (Pvt)
Giles, Albert L.	Co G 32 MA Inf (Pvt/Sgt)
Guthrie, Roger C.	Co C 7 MA Inf (Wagoner)
Hamilton, James T.	Co E 43 MA Inf (Pvt)
Hanson, Parker W.	Co __ 7 MA H A (Pvt) (Re-Enl?)
Hardy, Daniel E.	Co H 5 MA Inf (?) [or 6 MA Inf]
Heath, James A.	Co K 35 MA Inf (Pvt)
Hodgkins, Emery	Co B 29 MA Inf (Pvt/Sgt)
Huntley, Matthew	Co A 2 MA Inf (Pvt/Cpl)
Kehoe, William	Co H 1 MA Cav (Pvt)
Kellend, Robert	Co K 34 MA Inf (Pvt)
Lawless, Stephen	Co C 11 MA Inf (Cpl)
Leonard, George D.	Co A 1 MA H A (Pvt)
Lewis, Charles H.	Co D 42 MA Inf (Pvt)
Loud, Charles A.	Co F 41 MA Inf (Pvt)
Meserve, William N.	Co __ 4 MA H A (Maj)
Mitchell, Reuben H.	Co E 1 Batt MA H A (Pvt)
Moore, Augustus H.	Co L 3 MA Inf (Pvt) [and Co H)
Moore, Augustus H.	Co F 47 MA Inf (Pvt) (Re-Enl?)
Moore, Patrick H.	Co E 15 MA Inf (Pvt)
Murdock, George L.	Co __ 34 MA Vol ___ (Capt)
Osgood, Isaac P.	Co B 32 MA Inf (Pvt)
Parker, William T.	Co I 52 MA Inf (Pvt/Sgt)
Pettengill, Amos	Co B 35 MA Inf (Corpl)
Phillips, Lionel D.	Co H 1 MA Inf (Pvt/Sgt)
Phillips, Lionel D.	Co E 61 MA Inf (Pvt/Sgt) (Re-Enl?)
Poland, Martin	Co A 10 MA Cav (Pvt) (Re-Enl?)
Pratt, C.W.	Co C 2 MA Cav (Pvt)
Richardson, Chas D.	Co C 30 MA Vol Inf (Pvt/QM Sgt) (or Co G)
Rose, George W.	Co L 33 MA Inf (Lt)
Rosswell, Edwin	Co H 2 MA H A (?)
Schill, S.	Co F 31 MA Inf (Pvt)
Schill, S.	Co A 31 MA Inf (Pvt) (Re-Enl?)
Shattuck, John E.	Co __ 4 MA Cav (?) (Re-Enl?)
Sherman, Frank M.	Co I 34 MA Inf (Pvt)
Stearns, Hiram A.	Co I 6 MA Mil Inf (?)
Sullivan, Marcus M.	Co G 1 MA Inf (Pvt)
Sullivan, Marcus M.	Co E 3 MA Cav (Com Sgt) (Re-Enl)

MASSACHUSETTS VETERANS (Con't)

Trott, George F.	Co A 44 MA Inf (Pvt)
Tucker, Samuel F.	Co __ 2 Regt MA Cav (?) (Re-Enl?)
Viney, William M.	Co G 55 MA Inf (Sgt)
Warner, Francis H.	Co __ 11 MA Batt (Pvt)
Waterman, William A.	Co A 37 MA Inf (Pvt/1 Lt)
Weatherbee, George M.	Co __ 1 MA Inf (Mus'n)
Wheeler, Lyman	Co I 25 MA Inf (Corpl/Sgt)
Wiley, George O.	Co B 34 MA Inf (?)
Willey, Norris M.	Co A 8 MA Inf (?)
Williams, Charles H.	Co K 13 MA Inf (Pvt)
Williams, George W.	Co O 25 MA ____ (Pvt/Cpl)

MICHIGAN UNITS--71 Veterans

Bailey, Clark C.	Co I 13 MI Inf (Pvt)
Barlow, Alfred	Co G 14 Mi Inf (?)
Beck, James M.	Co C 1 MI Eng'rs (Pvt/Sgt)
Bell, Harrison W.	Co M 1 MI Eng'rs (Pvt)
Bigelow, Lyman G.	Co D 10 MI Cav (Pvt)
Brown, Carleton L.	Co K 11 MI Cav (Pvt/Cpl)
Brown, Lyman	Co H 1 MI Eng'rs (Pvt)
Bryant, Elden S.	Co H 1 MI L A (Pvt)
Burton, Henry J.	Co D 1 MI L A (Pvt)
Cadman, James P.	Co I 11 MI Cav (2 Lt)
Cadman, James P.	Co I 8 MI Cav (Capt) (Promoted?)
Cahoon/Cahon, Charles	Co I 1 MI L A (Pvt)
Carpenter, Albert	Co F 4 MI Inf (Pvt)
Casey, Wilson	Co A 5 MI Cav (Pvt)
Chase, Charles M.	Co I 2 MI Inf (Pvt)
Chase, Samuel D.	Co H 1 MI Inf (Pvt)
Cole, W.I.	Co D 3 MI Inf (Pvt)
Coleman, Levi B.	Co G 4 MI Inf (?)
Collier, J.H.	Co L 4 MI Cav (Pvt)
Davis, William H.	Co A 11 MI Inf (?)
Dye, Bloomfield U.	Co E 1 MI Eng'rs (Pvt)
Earle, Francis S.	Co __ 4 MI Inf (Adj/Maj)
Emerson, George D.	Co L 1 MI Engr's (Capt)
Ewing, Edward	Co D 10 MI Cav (Pvt)
Fassett, Charles B.	Co D 6 MI Inf (2 Lt/Capt)
Ferdon, Charles M.	Co A 23 MI Inf (?)
Francis, William H.	Co B 2 MI Cav (Pvt)
Fuller, Andrew J.	Co I 5 MI Inf (Pvt)
Fuller, Andrew J.	Co F 9 MI Cav (2 Lt/1 Lt) (Promoted?)
Guilford, Andrew J.	Co F 11 MI Cav (Pvt/2 Lt)
Haney, Henry F.	Co K 6 MI Cav (Pvt)
Hicks, James V.	Co H 7 MI Cav (Pvt)
Hicks, John J.	Co H 7 MI Cav (Lt)-
Hobingnist, C.A.	Co I 16 MI Inf (Pvt)
Horton, George R.	Co I 3 MI Cav (Pvt)
Jenney, Royal A.	Co D 22 MI Inf (Pvt)
Kearney, Eli S.	Co G 21 MI Inf (Pvt)
Keeler, Ezra	Co B 22 MI Inf (Pvt/Sgt)
Knowles, John	Co K 1 MI Cav (Trumpeter/QM Sgt)
Lehman, Peter	Co I 9 MI Inf (Pvt)
Limebeck, George H.	Co E 30 MI Inf (Pvt)
Luce, Moses A.	Co E 4 MI Vol ___ (Pvt/Sgt)

MICHIGAN VETERANS (Con't)

Millichamp, Steph. W.	Co F	1 MI Cav (Pvt/Sgt/2 Lt)
Miner, H.W.	Co C	1 MI Engr's (Artificer)
Montney, Levi	Co F	16 MI Inf (Cpl)
Montney, Levi	Co L	18 MI Inf (Cpl) (Re-Enl?)
Moore, John C.	Co G	30 MI Inf (Pvt)
Nichols, Franklin P.	Co B	25 MI Inf (Pvt)
Nichols, Franklin P.	Co A	7 MI Cav (Lieut) (Re-Enl?)
Nichols, James G.B.	Co F	4 MI Cav (Pvt)
Olney, Eugene C.	Co G	30 MI Inf (Cpl)
Palmer, T.R.	Co C	13 MI Inf (Capt/Lt Col)
Perrin, William H.	Co H	25 MI Inf (Pvt)
Pierson, Ed. Aug.	Co C	1 MI L A (Pvt)
Rhodes, Ransom E.	Co E	9 MI Inf (Pvt)
Rice, Almeron F.	Co E	9 MI Inf (Pvt)
Roach, Henry	Co E	11 MI Vol Inf (Pvt)
Rowe, Josiah L.	Co K	2 MI Inf (?)
Rowley, Samuel B.	Co I	1 MI Inf (Pvt)
Smith, Ansel G.	Co E	1 MI Eng'rs (Pvt)
Smith, Edward H.	Co B	16 MI Inf (Sgt)
Smith, Edward H.	Co D	16 MI Inf (Capt) (Promoted?)
Smith, George H.	Co M	3 MI Cav (Pvt)
Southwick, Myron H.	Co H	8 MI Inf (Pvt/Hosp.Steward)
Spencer, Myron T.	Co A	5 MI Inf (Pvt/Cpl)
Stimson, Albert S.	Co A	28 MI Inf (Pvt)
Stone, George M.	Co A	2 MI Inf (Pvt)
Stone, George M.	Co G	1 MI Eng'rs (Artificer) (Re-Enl?)
Strahle, Alphonso	Co E	12 MI Inf (Pvt)
Sutherland, Thomas J.	Co L	1 MI Cav (?)
Sweetman, Stephen	Co A	6 MI Cav (Pvt)
Way, Francis Burdett	Co I	8 MI Cav (Pvt)
Werth, F.A.	Co F	7 MI Inf (Pvt)
Wilson, Hiram J.	Co B	18 MI Inf (?) [or Co D]
Woodward, Hiram P.	Co __	15 MI Vol Inf (2 Lt/Capt)
Woodward, Hiram P.	Co __	18 MI Vol Inf (Asst Surg)
Wyllis, Sidney A.	Co H	4 MI Inf (Cpl/Sgt)
Young, Edgar S.	Co G	14 MI Inf (?)

MINNESOTA UNITS—40 Veterans

Angier, Albert W.	Co I	1 MN Inf (Pvt) (or 3 MN Inf)
Arnold, E.M.	Co C	2 MN Inf (Pvt)
Barrett, Isaac S.	Co E	1 MN H A (Pvt)
Beck, Andrew	Co B	4 MN Inf (?)
Bell, Alonzo	Co F	Hatch's MN Cav (?)
Bohanan, Sylvester L.	Co E	Hatch's MN Cav (?)
Brayton, George	Co B	9 MN Inf (Pvt)
Brooks, John L.	Co M	2 MN Cav (?)
Brown, Charles A.	Co A	8 MN Inf (Pvt/Cpl)
Clark, Sheldon C.	Co I	2 MN Inf (Pvt)
Dauchey, Arthur H.	Co B	5 MN Inf (Pvt)
Doesser, Horace	Co F	4 MN Cav (Pvt)
Farris, J.M.	Co G	10 MN Inf (?)
Griswold, Benson	Co F	2 MN Cav (Pvt)
Harrington, David G.	Co C	1 MN Inf (Sgt)
Heath, James W./John W.	Co E	10 MN Inf (Pvt/Capt)
Hooker, J.B.	Co K	2 MN ___ (Pvt)

MINNESOTA VETERANS (Con't)

Hubbs, Charles L.	Co F	1 MN Inf (Pvt)
Huddleston, John	Co G	5 MN Vol Inf (Pvt/Wagoner)
Johnson, James A.	Co H	4 MN Inf (Pvt)
Keeney, Thomas B.	Co G	3 MN Vol Inf (Pvt)
Lamb, Morris H.	Co F	11 MN Inf (Pvt/Cpl)
Lane, Ansel S.	Co B	6 MN Inf (Pvt)
McKnight, Eugene V.	Co A	1 MN H A (Pvt/Sgt)
McPheeters, James H.	Co __	1 MN Batt (Pvt) (Re-Enl?)
Mogle, William	Co B	9 MN Inf (Pvt)
Mullaney, James	Co K	11 MN Inf (Pvt)
Nelson, Nelson E.	Co A	1 MN Vols (Sgt)
O'Brien, James	Co H	10 MN Inf (Pvt/Sgt)
Parker, Edwin A.	Co K	4 MN Inf (Pvt/Cpl)
Robinson, A.S.	Co A	7 MN Inf (Pvt/Cpl)
Schaler, Julius G.	Co E	5 MN Inf Vol (?)
Sly, George E.	Co A	4 MN Inf (Mus'n)
Stansberry, Chas H.	Co I	1 MN Inf (Pvt) (Re-Enl)
Stephen, Robert	Co A	1 MN Inf (?)
Tyler, Joseph H.	Co K	6 MN Inf (Pvt)
Wattles, M. Richard	Co G	1 MN Inf (Pvt)
Weaver, Charles S./W.	Co B	Brackett's Batt MN Cav (Pvt)
Williams, Abraham	Co B	4 MN Inf (Pvt)
Wood, Jeremiah G.	Co K	9 MN Inf (Cpl)

MISSISSIPPI UNITS--4 Veterans

Chenault, Leo O.		"Captain"--(enl.MS)--CSA
Fabian, Otto E.	Co B	Wirt Adams MS State Troops Cav (Pvt)--CSA
Haden, John F.	Co G	4 MS Cav (Pvt)--CSA
McQuinston, Thomas	Co C	1 MS Marine Brig (Pvt)

MISSOURI UNITS--70 Veterans

Alexander, W.F.	Co E	1 MO Cav (Pvt)
Andre, Zacheriah T.	Co B	2 MO L A (Pvt)
Arnold, Don J.	Co C	MO State Militia Mounted Inf (Pvt)
Arnold, Don J.	Co D	5 MO State Militia Cav (?) (Re-Enl)
Arnold, Don J.	Co C	5 MO Cav (Pvt) (Re-Enl)
Arnold, James M.	Co E	3 MO Cav (Sgt)
Bales, Dillon	Co B	51 MO Inf (Pvt)
Blanchard, George A.	Co B	1 MO Eng'rs (Artificer)
Boscher, Emil H.	Co A	__ MO L A (Pvt)
Bradley, Frances W.	Co A	44 MO Inf (Pvt)
Branson, James	Co C	42 MO Inf (Pvt)
Bray, John	Co H	1 MO Cav (Pvt)
Breedlove, R.D.	Co D	8 MO Cav (Corpl)
Brown, Max	Co H	1 MO Eng'rs (Pvt)
Casteel, Reubin S.	Co G	8 MO State Militia Cav (?)
Combe, Francis M.	Co __	6 MO Vol Inf (?)
Cordes, Charles S.	Co A	5 MO Cav (Pvt)
Cureton, David	Co A	32 MO Inf (Sgt/Maj)
Daley, Francis H.	Co B	9 MO Cav (Pvt)
Dana, William	Co G	27 MO Inf (Pvt)
Darling, Horace	Co C	24 MO Inf (Pvt)
Darling, Horace	Co G	21 MO Inf (?) (Re-Enl?)
Eagan, Michael I.	Co B	2 NE MO H G Inf (?)
Eagan, Michael I.	Co B	2 MO Inf (Pvt/Sgt) (Re-Enl?)

MISSOURI VETERANS (Con't)

Eagan, Michael I.	Co M 69 MO Cav ((Pvt) (Re-Enl?)
Evans, William V.	Co B 42 MO Inf (Pvt)
Ford, Daniel B.	Co B 1 Prov En MO Mil (?)
Froelich, Godfrey F.W.	Co H 10 MO Inf (Sgt) (Re-Enl?)
Geen, William	Co M 6 MO State Militia ___ (Pvt)
Geen, William	Co B 6 MO State Militia Cav (?)
Hopkins, L.C.	Co I 12 MO Cav (Pvt)
Hulburt, R.G.	Co C 12 MO Cav (Pvt)
Jacoby, Henry M.	Co G 42 MO Inf (Pvt/Sgt/Maj)
Jamison, Alexander	Co F 8 MO Inf (Pvt/Capt) (Re-Enl?)
Jewell, William O.	Co G 6 MO ___ (Pvt/1 Lt)
Judd, Alex	Co G 2 MO Cav (Pvt)
Keacht, Frederick	Co F 5 MO Cav (Pvt) [Co F consolidated with Co H, then Co D]
Kinsly, Samuel	Co F 10 MO? Inf (Pvt)
Kooken, John A.	Co E 1 MO ___ (Pvt) (Re-Enl?)
Kuttnauer, Isador	Co B 2 MO L A (Pvt)
Lewis, Charles	Co B 49 MO Inf (Pvt)
Loughrey, William	Co C 11 MO Cav (Pvt)
Majors, Archibald C.	Co B 43 MO Inf (Pvt)
Majors, Archibald C.	Co A 50 MO Inf (Pvt) (Re-Enl?)
McClerken, David W.	Co A 10 MO Inf (Pvt)
McClerken, David W.	Co C 10 MO Inf (Capt) (Re-Enl?)
McFarland, Schuler	Co A Hickory Co MO Home Guard (Pvt)
Mitchell Winfield L.	Co F 25 MO Inf (Pvt)
Murray, George L.	Co H 2 MO Art (W C A D) (?)
Nettlebeck, Herman	Co B 4 MO State Militia Cav (Sgt)
Nulton, O.D.	Co G 21 MO ___ (Mus'n)
Nulton, Sylvanus D.	Co G 21 MO Inf (Mus'n/Principal Mus'n)
Payton, William N.	Co I 26 MO Inf (Pvt)
Peer, James A.	Co E Benton Company MO Cadets (Pvt)
Powell, A.H.	Co __ 24 MO Inf (Chaplain)
Reames, Bartlett	Co A 7 MO Vol Inf (1 Lt)
Richmond, Jonathan E.	Co E 44 MO Inf (?)
Santee, Milton	Co __ 11 MO Cav (1 Lt) (Re-Enl?)
Schiller, Henry J.	Co G 1 MO Inf (Pvt)
Schroeter, Charles	Co C 1 MO Cav (Pvt)
Schudy/Schudey, John	Co __ 1 NE MO Inf (?)
Sharp, William H.	Co K 43 MO Inf (Pvt)
Snedecor, Isaac D.	Co A 1 MO Prov En Mil (?)
Snedecor, Isaac D.	Gov. Staff--MO (Maj) (Governor's Staff?)
Snoderly, Emanual	Co K 4 MO Cav (Pvt)
Southwell, Robert	Co A 21 MO Inf (Pvt/Cpl)
Spencer, James R.	Co E 44 MO Inf (1 Sgt)
Spencer, Jonathan R.	Co E 44 MO Inf (1 Sgt)
Sutemeier, Henry	Co C 4 MO Inf (Pvt/Cpl) (or 4 US R C MO Inf
Swetnam, James S.	Co A 2 MO Sharpshooters (Sgt)--CSA
Tippett, Samuel D.	Co B 2 MO Cav (Pvt/1 Lt)
Trader, W.S.	Co I 1 MO Cav (Pvt)
Utt, Lee H.	Co B 1 MO Inf (Pvt)
Warren, Dillard	Co G 2 MO Cav (Pvt)
Wasson, John	Co D 45 MO Inf; Co F, 50 MO Inf (Pvt) (Re-Enl?)
Watson, John	Co A Independent MO ___ (Pvt)
Whitlock, Sidney W.	Co K 2 MO State Militia Cav (?)
Winscott, James C.	Co B 33 MO Vol Inf (Pvt) (Re-Enl?)
Young, J.F.	Co K 10 MO Cav (Capt)

NEBRASKA UNITS--9 Veterans

Butschli, Jacob	Co A 1 NE ___ (?)
Carmichael, Jacob E.	Co A 1 NE Inf (Pvt)
Culp, John W.	Co M 2 NE Cav (Pvt)
Culp, John W.	Co G 1 NE Cav (Pvt) (Re-Enl?)
Dailey, Orin V.	Co E 1 NE Inf (Pvt)
Duling, John	Co G 1 NE Bat Cav (Pvt)
Hall, George P.	Co B 2 NE Inf (Pvt) [or 2 NE Cav]
Hall, George P.	Co D 2 NE Inf (Pvt) (Re-Enl?)
Holcomb, Herman	Co C 2 NE Cav (?)
Logan, John H.	Co B 2 NE Cav (Pvt)
Reed, Francis B.	Co I 1 NE Inf (Pvt)

NEVADA UNITS--5 Veterans

Brody, Paul E.	Co __ __ NV Medical Corps (Pvt)
Crombie, L.J.	Co C 1 NV Vol (Pvt)
Emery, H.U.	Co F 1 Batt NV Cav (Cpl)
Levings, John K.	Co D 1 NV Cav (Pvt)
Peterson, George	Co B 1 Batt NV Cav (?)

NEW HAMPSHIRE UNITS--17 Veterans

Blaisdell, S.(?) G.	Co F? 12 NH Inf (Pvt/Sgt)
Boutwell, William T.	Co B 13 NH Inf (Pvt)
Burns, Thomas J.	Co F 4 NH Inf (Pvt/Sgt)
Carlin, Patrick	Co I 10 NH Inf (?)
Diamond, Charles W.	Co E 2 NH Inf (Lieut)
Diamond, Ira K.	Co O 16 NH Inf (?)
Diamond, Levi W.	Co H 2 NH Inf (?)
Fortier, Zephraim	Co K 3 NH ___ (Pvt)
Gallager, Patrick	Co C 4 NH Inf (Pvt)
Gallagher, John	Co E 5 NH Inf (?)
Glidden, A.P.	Co G 1 NH Cav (Pvt)
Hood, Alan	Co C 16 NH Inf (Pvt)
Hood, Alan	Co B 1 NH Vol Cav (Corpl) (Re-Enl?)
Hurd, Warren H.	Co A 2 NH Inf (Pvt)
Johnson, J.J.	Co I 13 NH Inf (Pvt)
Noyes, Ira	Co G 12 NH Inf (Pvt)
Noyes, Ira	Co K 2 NH Inf (Pvt) (Re-Enl?)
Straw, Alonzo D.	Co H 5 NH Inf (Pvt)
Wadlia, Andrew J.	Co G 3 NH Inf (Pvt/Capt)

NEW JERSEY UNITS--15 Veterans

Baer, Charles J.	Co A Batt 1 NJ ___ (Pvt)
Cary, Charles A.	Co F 3 NJ Cav (Pvt/Sgt)
Cavileer, John C.	Co G 4 NJ Inf (Pvt)
Clark Edwin A.	Co K 1 NJ Inf (Pvt)
Comings, J.H.	Co I 15 NJ Inf (Pvt)
Fitzgerald, Charles R.	Co A 26 NJ Inf (Pvt)
Hall, Francis	Co A 1 NJ Inf (?)
Leonard, William	Co K 2 NJ Inf (Pvt)
Peirson, J. Lacy	Co D 5 NJ Inf (Pvt/2 Lt)
Peirson, J. Lacy	Co I 26 NJ Inf (Pvt/Capt) (Re-Enl?)
Probert, John	Co B 15 NJ Inf (Pvt)
Reintanz, O.J.	Co L 3 NJ Cav (Pvt/Sgt)

NEW JERSEY VETERANS (Con't)

Sherwood, James	Co F 10 NJ Inf (?)
Spileman, Edward B.	Co D 11 NJ Inf (Pvt)
Van Scoten, M.L.	Co I 31 NJ Inf (Sgt)
Webster, Calvin R.	Co __ 1 NJ L A (Batt B) (Artificer)

NEW YORK UNITS--171 Veterans

Ackley, Henry J.	Co D 194 NY ___ (Pvt)
Ainsley, G.W.	Co ? 25 N Y L A (Corpl)
Anthony, Charles E.	Co A 19 NY Inf (Pvt)
Anthony, Charles E.	Co __ 3 NY Art (Mus'n) (Re-Enl?)
Armstrong, Nelson	Co L 8 NY HA (Pvt/Corpl)
Auld, George	Co B 70 NY Inf (Pvt)
Austin, Henry C.	Co 1 14 NY H A (Pvt/Cpl)
Babcock, Edward A.	Co C 89 NY Vol Inf (1 Sgt)
Baker, Edward	Co F 12 NY Inf (Pvt)
Baker, Eldred	Co F 142 NY Inf (Pvt)
Barber, George	Co H 120 NY Inf (Mus'n)
Barkley, James T.	Co F 70 NY Inf (Pvt)
Barkley, James T.	Co E 70 NY Inf (2 Lt) (Promoted?)
Barnes, William H.	Co I 2 NY HA (Pvt)
Beardsley, John	Co I 179 NY Inf (Cpl)
Beck, Albert A.	Co B 157 NY Inf (Pvt)
Beebe, Milton E.	Co K 9 NY Cav (Pvt)
Bennett, DeForest P.	Co G 105 NY Inf (Cpl)
Bleeck, Oscar W.	Co A 104 NY Inf (Pvt)
Blodgett, Clark A.	Co C 185 NY Inf (Pvt)
Bogart, C.F.	Co I 109 NY Inf (Pvt/Cpl)
Booth, George H.	Co K 98 NY Inf (Pvt/1 Lt)
Bowman, John H.	Co I 20 NY Cav (Pvt)
Bradt, Jacob A.	Co G 2 NY Cav (Pvt)
Brinkman, Henry F.	Co H 4 NY Inf (Pvt)
Burk, Benjamin H.	Co A 89 NY Inf (Pvt)
Canfield, William J.	Co K 1 NY LA (Pvt/Lt/Adjt)
Carls, Frank	Co D 115 NY Inf (Pvt)
Carpinter, H.L.	Co F 4 NY H A (Pvt) (Promoted?)
Carpinter, H.L.	Co H 4 NY H A (Capt) (Re-Enl?)
Catlin, John	Co A 5 NY Cav (Bugler)
Center, Lewis W.	Co F 193 NY Inf (Sgt)
Chamberlin, Jacob	Co B 8 NY Cav (Cpl/1 Lt)
Coleman, John	Co A 3 NY Prov Cav (?) [or 8 NY Prov Cav]
College, James	Co C 146 NY Inf (Pvt)
Comings, J.H.	Co C 15 NY Inf (Brvt Maj) (Promoted?)
Cook, Augustus	Co D 3 NY Inf (Pvt/Sgt)
Crater, Cornelius	Co C 72 NY Inf (Pvt)
Crippen, George H.	Co __ Independent NY Batt (Pvt)
Cross, Harlow A.	Co G 26 NY Cav (Pvt)
Cunningham, Windsor T.	Co F 70 NY Inf (Pvt)
Cunningham, Windsor T.	Co A 86 NY Inf (Pvt) (Re-Enl?)
Dampf, Louis	Co D 7 NY Inf (Pvt)
Dannals, George M.	Co E 54 NY National Guard (Cpl)
Darling, Charles W.	Co E 32 NY Vol Inf (Major?)
Derbyshere, William H.	Co E 1 NY Eng'rs (Pvt/Artificer)
Eastman, H.D.	Co I 11 NY Cav (Pvt)
Eighmy, Philip H.	Co H 56 NY Vol Inf (Pvt)
Embler, James W.	Co G 1 NY L A (Pvt)

NEW YORK VETERANS (Con't)

Embler, James W.	Co C 147 NY Inf (1 Sgt) (Re-Enl)
Emmons, Ira J.	Co D 3 NY Cav (Pvt)
Evans, Philip H.	Co L 24 NY Cav (Pvt) (Re-Enl?)
Field, Putnam	Co I 10 NY Inf (Pvt)
Field, Putnam	Co C 10 NY Inf (Capt) (Promoted?)
Finley, Kellogg B.	Co G 8 NY H A (Pvt)
Finley, Kellogg B.	Co M 4 NY H A (QM Sgt) (Re-Enl?)
Fitzgerald, Robert V.	Co D 155 NY Inf (Pvt)
Foote, John W.	Co G 16 NY H A (Pvt/Sgt)
Fowler, Elijah P.	Co K 4 NY HA (Pvt/Cpl)
Fralich, Zachariah	Co L 9 NY H A (Pvt)
Fredericks, William M.	Co A 80 NY Inf (Pvt)
Ganoung, William H.	Co E 64 NY Inf (Pvt)
George, Henry W.	Co D 44 NY Inf (Pvt)
Gibbs, Artemus	Co K 1 NY Dragoons (?)
Gipson, John C.	Co __ 1 NY L A Batt C (Pvt/Sgt)
Goetsch, Ferdinand	Co E 69 NY Inf (Pvt)
Gomer, John H.	Co E 11 NY Inf (Pvt)
Gomer, John H.	Co H 1 NY Eng'rs (Cpl) (Re-Enl?)
Goodell, Maximillion	Co E 1 NY Cav (Pvt)
Goodspeed, John W.	Co D 136 NY Inf (Pvt/Sgt)
Granville, John H.	Co E 124 NY Inf (Pvt)
Granville, John H.	Co K 15 NY Cav (Pvt) (Re-Enl?)
Green, James	Co K 141 NY Inf (Pvt)
Green, William	Co D 140 NY Inf (?)
Griggs, John R.	Co H 76 NY Inf (Pvt)
Griggs, John R.	Co G 91 NY Inf (Pvt) (Re-Enl?)
Grinnell, William W.	Co E 97 NY Inf (?)
Grovesteen, James H.	Co H 8 NY State Militia (Pvt)
Grovesteen, James H.	Co G 174 NY Inf (Sgt) (Re-Enl)
Hahn, Joseph	Co I 7 NY Inf (Pvt)
Ham, Charles	Co D 1 NY LA (Pvt)
Hanna, John J.	Co K 148 NY Inf (Pvt)
Hanson, Martin	Co H 4 NY Cav (Pvt)
Harkins, Henry A.	Co B 35 NY Inf (Pvt)
Harkins, Henry A.	Co L 20? NY Cav (Sgt) (Re-Enl?)
Harris, Avril	Co A 89 NY Inf (Cpl)
Haskins, Alonzo	Co A 23 NY Cav (Pvt)
Hayes, Thomas	Co __ 18 NY Inf (Band)
Healey, Michael	Co D 10 NY Art (Pvt)
Himmell, Charles S.	Co F 25 NY Cav (Pvt) (Re-Enl)
Hogarty, M.J.	Co I 141 NY Inf (Pvt/1 Lt)
Hopkins, Eugene	Co H 14 NY H A (?)
Hover, Aaron S.	Co A 20 NY Militia? (Pvt)
Hughes, James W.	Co __ 59 NY Inf (Asst.Surg)
Hughes, James W.	Co __ 152 NY Inf (Surg) (Promoted)
Hull, Horace J.	Co M 50 NY Inf/Engr's (Artificer)
Hunt, William F.	Co E 22 NY Inf (?)
Huntington, C.	Co H 16 NY ___ (Pvt/Sgt)
Jenkins, Andrew J.	Co K 2 NY Cav (?)
Jenkins, Robert J.	Co E 64 NY Inf (Pvt)
Jenks, Park M.	Co B 109 NY Inf (Pvt)
Jones, Levi J.	Co A 179 NY Inf (Pvt)
King, George V.	Co G 13 NY ___ (Pvt)
Kinne, Orlando W.	Co G 14 NY Inf (Pvt)

NEW YORK VETERANS (Con't)

Lampman, Granville L.	Co G 184 NY Inf (?)
Lawrance, John C.	Co E 86 NY SVI (Pvt)
Lee, Charles P.	Co K 10 NY H A (Pvt)
Leslie, G.H.	Co D 4 NY H A (Sgt)
Lohr, N.	Co A 69 NY Inf (Pvt)
Louck, J.H.	Co D 2 NY LA (Pvt)
Mackey, Clarke D.	Co E 3 NY Inf (?)
Malloy, William	Co F 18 NY Inf (Pvt)
Mandeville, F.H.	Co K 23 NY Inf (Pvt)
Martin, Joseph	Co I 5 NY Art (Pvt) (or 5 NY H A)
Martin, Joseph	Co I 6 NY Art (Pvt) (Re-Enl) [or 6 NY H A]
McCarty, John	Co F 3 NY L A (?)
McFarland, Jesse	Co E 90 NY Inf (Pvt)
McFarland, Jesse	Co F 1 NY Vet. Corps (Pvt)
McIntosh, F.J.	Co B 10 NY Art (Pvt) (or 10 NY H A)
McNally, W.G.	Co C 21 NY Inf (Pvt)
Merriam, Gustavus F.	Co F 3 NY Art (1 Lt)
Merriam, Gustavus F.	Co __ 5 NY Art 3 Batt (Maj) (Promoted?)
Middleton, John	Co G 110 NY Inf (Pvt)
Middleton, John	Co B 184 NY Inf (Pvt) (Re-Enl?)
Mouter, John P.	Co G 13 NY Art (Pvt)
Nichols, Edmund	Co I 109 NY Inf (Pvt)
Norton, Daniel A.	Co G 125 NY Inf (Pvt)
Norton, Harry	Co B 23 NY Inf (Pvt)
Norton, Harry	Co G 1 NY Cav (Pvt) (Re-Enl?)
O'Farrell, William M.	Co I 26 NY Inf (Pvt)
Palmer, J.H.	Co I 26 NY Inf (Capt)
Pardo, Horace	Co C 123 NY Inf (Pvt)
Parker, Charles H.	Co G 1 NY Eng'rs (Pvt)
Parker, Edson O.	Co F 10 NY Art (Mus'n) (or 10 NY H A)
Peck, Hiram H.	Co L 16 NY H A (Pvt/Cpl)
Pells, James W.	Co C 156 NY Inf (Pvt)
Pells, James W.	Co G 156 NY Inf (Cpl) (Re-Enl?)
Pine, Albert B.	Co C 74 NY Inf (Pvt)
Pirnie, Alexander	Co K 3 NY L A (Pvt)
Pirnie, Alexander	Co __ 7 NY Batt L A (?)
Polhamus, Adelbert C.	Co F 9 NY Inf (Pvt) (aka Albert Howard)
Polhamus, Adelbert C.	Co D 192 NY Inf (Pvt/Sgt) (Re-Enl?) (aka Albert Howard)
Polhamus, Adelbert C.	Co __ 198 NY Inf (Sgt) (Re-Enl?) (aka Albert Howard)
Putnam, C.S.	Co E 106 NY Inf (Pvt)
Quackenbush, Chauncey	Co __ 11 NY Indep. Batt (Pvt)
Reid, Andrew D.	Co D 153 NY ___ (Pvt)
Reupsche, William	Co F 41 NY Inf (Pvt)
Reynolds, Hiram H.	Co K 148 NY Inf (Pvt)
Reynolds, Lewis D.	Co B 3 NY Cav (Pvt)
Richards, George J.	Co D 14 NY H A (Sgt)
Riley, William T.	Co D 86 NY Inf (Pvt)
Rodgers, Henry J.G	Co D 133 NY Inf (Pvt/Cpl)
Rose, John L.	Co L 14 NY Art (Pvt)
Rumpf, August	Co A 39 NY Inf (Pvt/2 Lt)
Sennett(ock), Judson L.	Co E 3 NY Art (Pvt) (also 3 NY L A; 3 NY H A)
Shock, William	Co F 65 NY Inf (Pvt)
Shorton, William	Co I 28 NY Inf (Drummer)
Skinner, Simon	Co D 50 NY Eng'rs (?)
Smart, James G.	Co I 20 NY Cav (Cpl)

NEW YORK VETERANS (Con't)

Smith, Edward	Co H 128 NY Inf (Mus'n)
Smith, Frederick P.	Co K 8 NY Inf (Sgt) (or 8 NY State Militia Inf)
Smith, J. Bryant	Co K 53 NY Inf (Pvt/Sgt)
Smith, Joseph H.	Co E 97 NY Vol Inf (Pvt/Capt)
Smith, Samuel W.	Co B 73 NY Inf (Pvt)
Snyder, Edward	Co G 178 NY Inf (Lt)
Spaulding, Edgar	Co D 137 NY Inf (Drummer)
Speers, Gustav/August	Co G 46 NY Inf (?)
Starr, Henry P.	Co M 3 NY Cav (Pvt)
Starr, Henry P.	Co A 22 NY Cav (Lt) (Re-Enl?)
Steele, Augustus F.	Co D 1 NY Dragoons (Pvt)
Stephens, Walter	Co D 169 NY Inf (Pvt)
Stewart, Thomas J.	Co D 28 NY Militia (QM Sgt)
Stoddard, Silas E.	Co D 108 NY Inf (Pvt)
Svenningson, John C.	Co I 1 NY Inf (1st Sgt)
Thompson, Hiram P.	Co H 49 NY Inf (Pvt/Com Sgt)
Thompson, James G.	Co K 4 NY H A (Pvt)
Tracy, J.E.	Co D 189 NY Inf (Sgt)
Tracy, John	Co K 5 NY H A (?)
Tufs, Charles P.	Co I 6 NY H A (Pvt/Sgt)
Tyrell, John	Co __ 4 NY L A (Pvt)
Unger, August	Co B 69 NY Inf (Pvt) [or Co D]
Van Ostrand, Jacob E.	Co B 56 NY N G (?)
Velbert, John	Co I 42 NY Tammany & 50 Inf (Pvt)
Vredenberg, John L.	Co F 17 NY Inf (Pvt)
Wade, Nelson W.	Co G 21 NY Inf (Pvt)
Walker, Leonard	Co K 13 NY Inf (Pvt)
Ward, James S.	Co D 10 NY H A (2 Lt/1 Lt)
Whitney, Henry H.	Co H 106 NY Inf (Sgt)
Williams, James	Co B 162 NY Inf (Sgt)
Williams, Morgan	Co K 1 NY Cav (Pvt/Sgt)
Wilson, Charles H.	Co B 106 NY Inf (Pvt/Corpl)
Woodruff, Joseph D.	Co I 61 NY Inf (Pvt)
Young, Rufus	Co A 10 NY H A (Pvt)

NORTH CAROLINA UNITS--1 Veteran

Patterson, James L.	Co D 25 NC Inf (Sgt/1 Sgt/2 Lt)--CSA

OHIO UNITS--183 Veterans

Abrahams, W.F.	Co F 84 OH Vol Inf (Pvt)
Adams, Frederick F.	Co B 43 OH Vol Inf (Sgt)
Babcock, Charles H.	Co F 43 OH Inf (Pvt)
Bahl, Perry W.	Co C 16 OVI (Pvt)
Bailey, G.W.	Co E 2 OH Cav (Pvt)
Bailey, G.W.	Co E 10 OH Cav (Sgt) (Re-enl?)
Baird, John R.	Co H 81 OH Inf (Pvt/Sgt)
Barton, R.H.	Co D 17 OH Inf (Pvt)
Barton, R.H.	Co B 1 OH Cav (2 M Sgt) (Re-Enl?)
Beam, Joseph C.	Co A 43 OH Vols (Pvt)
Belding, Sanford W.	Co __ 12 OH Independent Batt L A (Pvt)
Birdseye, Emos L.	Co B 123 OH Inf (?)
Blanchard, Oliver C.	Co A 179 OH __ (Cpl) (Re-Enl?)
Bogart, Elias F.	Co I 88 OH ___ (?)
Brenard, Frederick	Co I 3 OH Cav (Pvt/Capt)
Brown, J.H.	Co A 49 OH Inf (Pvt)

OHIO VETERANS (Con't)

Brown, John B.	Co G 49 OH Inf (Mus'n)
Brunner, Leo F.	Co __ __ OH L A (Pvt)
Burnap, Silas A.	Co F 18 OH Inf (Pvt)
Burnap, Silas A.	Co H 18 OH Inf (Pvt) (Re-Enl?)
Burnap, Silas A.	Co __ 7 OH L A (Capt) (Promoted?)
Burns, A.J.	Co H 42 OH Inf (Pvt)
Campbell, David	Co I 90 OH Inf (Pvt)
Carpenter, Charles D.	Co D 20 OVI (Sgt)
Casebeer, W.J.	Co I 1 OH Inf (Pvt)
Chatfield, James L.	Co D 10 OVI (Pvt/Sgt)
Coan, Henry C.	Co D 1 OH H A (Pvt)
Comer, Allen	Co D 17 OH Inf (Pvt)
Comer, Allen	Co A 58 OH Inf (Pvt) (Re-Enl)
Cone, William A.	Co B 53 OVI (Pvt)
Confer, John W.	Co E 93 OVI (Pvt); also 93 OH Inf (Sgt)
Cook, Henry	Co G 1 OH Inf (Pvt)
Cooper, Daniel C.	Co F 125 OVI (?)
Crockett, John	Co D 68 OH Inf (Pvt)
Curtis, Nathaniel A.	Co E 12 OH Vol Cav (Pvt)
Dakin, Horace E.	Co E 1 OH Inf (Pvt)
Dakin, Horace E.	Co F 124 OH Inf (Capt) (Re-Enl?)
Davis, George P.	Co B 125 OH Inf (Pvt) (also 125 OVI)
DeBurn, Eugene	Co E 80 OH Inf (Pvt)
DeShanaway, John	Co A 14 OVI (Pvt)
Desmont, Charles E.	Co A 23 OVI (Pvt) [Dermont?]
Duvall, William H.	Co H 6 OH Inf (Pvt)
Endly, C.F.	Co E 3 OH Cav (Pvt)
Erion, Jacob B.	Co A 4 OVI (Pvt)
Foote, Andrew J.B.	Co H 2 OH Inf (Pvt)
Fosnot, Hiram H.	Co C 24 OH Inf (Pvt)
Freede, Charles W.	Co C 68 OH Inf (Pvt)
Garwood, John F.	Co E 82 OH Inf (Cpl)
Garwood, John F.	Co E 83 OH Inf (Cpl) (Re-Enl)
George, _____	Co __ 80 OVI (?)
Gibbons, Homer W.	Co I 80 OH Inf (?)
Gillett, George A.	Batt E 1 OH L A (Pvt/Corpl)
Goodwin, Oliver R.	Co I 14 OH Inf (Pvt)
Graeter, Henry A.	Co C 16 OH Inf (Pvt)
Gregory, A.E.	Co D 25 OH Inf Batt (Pvt)
Gregory, A.E.	Co __ 12 OH Inf Batt (1 Lt) (Promoted?)
Grosvenor, Royal W.	Co C 94 OVI (Pvt)
Grovesteen, James H.	Co B 2 OH Inf (Pvt)
Hampson, Robert A.	Co D 1 OH Inf (1 Sgt) ("Rufus A. Hampson")
Harper, Joseph H.	Co I 89 OH Inf (Pvt)
Harris, Moses C.	Co C 77 OH Inf (Pvt)
Hathaway, Franklin	Co E 13 OH Inf (Mus'n)
Hathaway, Franklin	Co B 115 OH Vol Inf (Mus'n) (Re-Enl?)
Hathaway, Franklin	Co A 188 OH Inf (Mus'n) (Re-Enl?)
Hays, John	Co __ 46 OH Inf (?)
Hayward, William H.	Co A 1 OH L A (Pvt)
Heller, Moses	Co I 123 OH Inf (Pvt/Corp)
Hendershot, Lorenzo	Co K 174 OH Inf (Pvt) (or 174 OVI)
Herriman, Albert	Co D 41 OH Inf (Pvt)
Hiatt, Marvin	Co C 181 OH Inf (Pvt)
Hickox, L.M.	Co H 50 OH Inf (Pvt)

OHIO VETERANS (Con't)

Higbee, Elbert R.	Co C 125 OVI (Pvt)
Higbee, George	Co B 7 OVI (Pvt)
Higgens, M.L.	Co H 118 OH Inf (1 Lt)
Hills, Ralph H.	Co E 145 OH Inf (Pvt)
Holt, William J.	Co B 186 OH Inf (?)
Howell, Frank	Co K 1 OH V H A (Pvt)
Hutchison, Ezra P.	Co A 169 OH National Guard (Pvt)
Hutchison, George S.	Co H 102 OH Inf (Pvt/Corpl)
Imberie, James M.	Co __ 23 OH Inf (?)
James, William F.C.	Co E 63 OH ___ (Sgt)
Johns, Adam	Co F 13 OH Cav (?)
Johnson, Edward	Co C 4 OH Cav (Pvt/Sgt)
Johnson, John W.	Co D 2 OH Cav (Pvt)
Johnson, John W.	Co E 12 OH Cav (Lt/Capt) (Promoted?)
Johnson, Nathaniel S.	Co F 134 OH Inf (Lt)
Johnson, William	Co C 10 OH Inf (?) (or Co G)
Judd, Charles L.	Co E 1 OH L A (Sgt)
Kautz, George	Co B 140 OH Inf (Pvt)
Kelly, Eli C.	Co A 125 OH Inf (Pvt)
Kerr, John M.	Co F 25 OH Inf (Pvt) (Re-Enl?)
King, Albert J.	Co G 15 OH Inf (?)
Koehler, Edward	Co K 79 OVI (Pvt)
Kohuly, John	Co K 9 OH Cav (Pvt)
Kroff, Samuel W.	Co C 12 OH Inf (Pvt)
Kronskop, George W.	Co L 2 OH HA (Pvt)
Lakin, Cyrus B.	Co C 90 OH Inf (Mus'n)
Lamb, Harvey W.	Co C 125 OVI (?)
Lamme, Edwin H.	Co I 110 OH Inf (Pvt)
Leonard, Joseph	Co B 96 OH Inf (Capt/Maj)
Lowell, Marcus L.	Co F 101 OH Inf (Pvt)
Lyon, Theodore	Co G 1 OH Cav (Pvt)
MacDonald, Duncan H.	Co B 1 OH Cav (Pvt)
MacKinnon, Hector	Co A 12 OH Inf (Pvt)
Mallett, John	Co H 72 OH Inf (Pvt)
Martin, George M.	Co A 11 OH Inf (Pvt)
Maynard, Cloice S.	Co I 135 OH National Guard (Pvt)
Maynard, Cloice S.	Co D 64 OH Inf (Pvt) (Re-Enl)
McDuell, James H.	Co I 123 OH Inf (?)
McKenna, Augustine P.	Co G 61 OH Reg (Cpl)
McNally, W.G.	Co H 150 OH National Guard (Sgt) (Re-Enl?)
Michener, A.D.	Co C 49 OVI (Pvt)
Miner, Samuel G.	Co __ 9 OH Cav (Lt)
Minor, Mitchell A.	Co A 24 OH Inf (Pvt)
Moore, George M.	Co G 87 OH Inf (Pvt)
Moore, George M.	Co L 1 OH H A (Pvt) (Re-Enl?)
Morgan, Adam	Co A 9 OH Cav (Pvt)
Morse, Edward A.	Co B 23 OH Inf (Pvt) (or 23 OVI)
Nace, Uriah P.	Co B 81 OH Inf (Pvt)
Nagle, W.C.	Co I 193 OH Inf (Pvt/Sgt)
Neiberger, Samuel J.	Co I 44 OH Inf (Pvt)
Nesbitt, Jeremiah	Co G 162 OH Inf (Pvt)
Palmer, Isaac L.	Co A 36 OH Inf (Pvt)
Palmer, John D.	Co C 3 OH Inf (Pvt)
Palmer, John D.	Co C 182 OH Inf (Sgt) (Re-Enl?) [or Co G]
Payne, Erasmus	Co G 115 OH Inf (?)

OHIO VETERANS (Con't)

Peak, Jacob	Co G 34 OH Inf (Pvt/Mus'n)
Peer, James A.	Co K 20 OH Inf (?) (Re-enl)
Pfaff, George	Co H 24 OH Inf (? rank)
Pfister, Ferdinand	Co A 9 OH Inf (Pvt) (or 9 OVI)
Place, Daniel C.	Co D 2 OH H A (Pvt)
Pontious, Wilson	Co G 85 OH Inf (Pvt)
Potter, Daniel	Co G 179 OH Inf (1 Sgt)
Powers, Robert M.	Co M 2 OH H A (Pvt)
Purvis, George	Co B 51 OH Inf (Pvt)
Reed, James C.	Co A 13 OH Inf (Pvt) (or 13 OVI)
Rhoads, Abraham	Co F 63 OH Inf (Pvt/Sgt)
Richey, Jay H.	Co H 136 OH Inf (Pvt)
Roberts, Luzerne L.	Co L 6 OH Cav (Pvt)
Roberts, Luzerne L.	Co G 18 OH ___ (Pvt) (Re-Enl?)
Roberts, Joseph W.	Co C 97 OH Inf (Pvt)
Roberts, Joseph W.	Co L 97 OH Inf (Sgt) (Re-Enl?)
Robinson, George C.	Co B 7 OH Inf (Pvt/Cpl)
Roby, David B.	Co B 63 OH Inf (Pvt) (or 63 OVI)
Rodig, Charles H.	Co O 6 OH Cav (?)
Rogers, Eli	Co K 139 OH National Guard V I (Pvt)
Root, M.S.	Co K 103 OH Inf (Pvt/2 Lt)
Routson, John G.	Co C 104 OVI (Pvt)
Sackett, Charles H.	Co A 2 OH Inf (Pvt/Cpl)
Sammis, Marsden H.	Co B 178 OH Vol Inf (Sgt)
Saunders, Charles K.	Co G 15 OVI (?)
Scoby, Thomas H.	Co A 96 OH Inf (Pvt) [or 196 OH Inf]
Shall, Eugene E.	Co H 177 OH Inf (Pvt)
Shaw, A.C.	Co C 85 OH ___ (Pvt)
Sheldon, Richard H.	Co F 3 OH Cav (Pvt)
Sheldon, Richard H.	Co F 12 OH Cav (Pvt) (Re-Enl)
Shill, General	Co D 11 OH Inf (Pvt)
Simmons, Clinton	Co K 123 OH Inf (Pvt)
Sinks, John F.	Co __ 61 OH Inf (QM Sgt)
Smith, Ernest L.	Co G 29 OH Inf (Pvt)
Smith, Julius S.	Co B 141 OH Inf (Cpl) (or 141 OVI)
Snider, Daniel S.	Co H 90 OH Inf (Pvt/Com Sgt)
Sperry, W.L.	Co D 104 OH Inf (Pvt/Cpl)
Spickert, Jacob	Co H 37 OH Inf (Pvt/Sgt)
Stacey, Arthur G.	Co __ 20 OH Batt (Pvt) (Re-Enl?)
Statler, Sylvester	Co K 1 OH Inf (Pvt)
Stenger, W.H.	Co A 178 OH Inf (Pvt)
Stewart, E.B.	Co E 184 OH Inf (Pvt)
Stielberg, William	Co A 28 OH Inf (Pvt/Cpl)
Stockton, Charles A.	Co D 4 OH Inf (Pvt)
Stonebraker, J.A.	Co K 82 OH Inf (Pvt)
Stratton, Samuel S.	Co A 181 OH Inf (Sgt)
Teeters, Loftus	Co I 33 OH Inf (?)
Thomas, Thomas W.	Co F 2 OH Inf (Pvt)
Thomas, Thomas W.	Co C 5 OH Cav (Sgt) (Re-Enl?)
Thompson, J.J.	Co A 146 OVI (Pvt)
Tibbals, Joseph B.	Co B 146 OH Inf (?)
Tinker, Edgar C.	Co D 84 OVI (Pvt)
Tinker, Edgar C.	Co H 150 OVI (Pvt) (Re-Enl)
Toms, George O.	Co E 71 OH Vols (2 Lt/Capt)
Turner, David	Co D 42 OVI (Pvt)

OHIO VETERANS (Con't)

Underwood, Hugh	Co K 42 OH Inf (?)
VanDine, George B.	Co F 36 OH Inf (?)
Venters, George	Co D 36 OH Inf (Pvt)
Venters, George	Co H 1 OH H A (Pvt) (Re-Enl?)
Ward, Thomas S.	Co K 10 OH Inf (Pvt)
Ward, Thomas S.	Co __ 5 OH L A (Cpl) (Re-Enl?)
Warren, Jones K.	Co B 125 OH Inf (Pvt/Sgt)
Washington, S.W.	Co __ 1 HGO OH S.S. (Cpl) (Home Guard?)
Watkins, William F.	Co C 1 OH Inf (Pvt) [Wilber F.]
Wells, Homer L.	Co A 57 OH Inf (Pvt/1 Lt)
Wells, James W.	Co B 102 OH Inf (Pvt/Rgt Q.M.)
Welsh, Elias R.	Co I 67 OH Inf (Pvt/Cpl)
White, Nicander	Co D 8 OH Cav (Pvt) [or 8 OH Inf]
Whiteley, Clay	Co K 152 OH Inf (Pvt)
Wickard, Phillip J.	Co G 189 OH Inf (Pvt)
Wiggins, Francis C.	Co F 2 OH Cav (?)
Wilder, Nathaniel	Co A 29 OH Inf (Pvt)
Wilkins, Blair	Co I 184 OH Inf (Pvt) [Williams]
Willison, John W.	Co G 1 OH H A (Pvt)
Wolf, George	Co __ 9 OH Inf (Band)
Woodard, John C.	Co C 93 OH Inf (Pvt)
Young, James A.	Co E 12 OH Cav (Sgt)
Young, John F.	Co K 1 OH Cav (Pvt/Cpl)

OREGON UNITS--4 Veterans

Campbell, John T.	Co B 1 OR Inf (Pvt)
Carey, George H.	Co B 1 OR Inf 102nd Regt (?)
Clark, George	Co E 1 OR Cav (?) [aka Robert C. Clark]
Gracy, Robert A.	Co A 1 OR Cav (Pvt/Sgt)

PENNSYLVANIA UNITS--110 Veterans

Amick, Daniel B.	Co E 3 PA H A (Pvt)
Angstedt, Albert	Co B 205 PA Inf (Pvt)
Anthony, David R.	Co B 143 PA Inf (Pvt)
Baker, August Cesar	Co I 3 PA Cav (Pvt) (Re-Enl)
Bell, Samuel V.	Co B 10 PA R C (Pvt) (Reserve Corps?)
Bell, Samuel V.	Co B 159 PA Inf (Pvt) (Re-Enl?)
Birdsall, S.H.	Co K 150 PA Bucktails (Pvt)
Blankinhom, William F.	Co D? 27 PA Inf (Pvt)
Briggs, W.S.	Co K 14 PA Cav (Pvt)
Broughton, John B.	Co __ 2 PA LA (Pvt)
Brown, James	Co B 196 PA Inf (Pvt)
Burgess, William	Co E 203 PA Inf (Pvt)
Burke, C.M.	Co F 7 PA Cav (Pvt)
Camp, James H.	Co A 141 PA ___ (Pvt)
Campbell, George A.	Co I 1 PA Bucktails P R V C (?) (Reserve Vet or Vol Corps?)
Campbell, George A.	Co I 1 PA Inf Rifles (Pvt) (Re-Enl?)
Chalfant, Alfred	Co K 213 PA Inf (Pvt)
Clark, James S.	Co L 102 PA Inf (Sgt)
Cole, John C.	Co K 169 PA Inf (Sgt)
Daly, Francis	Co H 17 PA Inf (Pvt)
Daly, Francis	Co E 118 PA Inf (Cpl/Sgt) (Re-Enl)
Davis, I.R./J.R.	Co G 14 PA Cav (Pvt/Cpl)
Deash, Jacob N.	Co I 56 PA Inf (Pvt)
Dickson/Dixon, Geo.W.	Co D 131 PA Inf (Pvt) (Dixon)

PENNSYLVANIA VETERANS (Con't)

Dickson/Dixon, Geo.W.	Co B 131 PA Inf (Sgt) (Promoted?) (Dickson)	
Dixon, Henry G.	Co K 140 PA Inf (?)	
Donovan, J.W.	Co H 43 PA Inf (Pvt)	
Duffy, W.E.	Co F 48 PA Inf (?)	
Emiron, George W.	Co B 186 PA Inf (Pvt)	
Ewing, William E.	Co G 28 PA Inf (Pvt) (Re-Enl)	
Fell, Aurelius	Co G 10 PA Res Vol Corps (?)	
Fogarty, Patrick	Co A 7 PA Cav (?)	
Forest, Harry C.	Co C 196 PA Inf (Pvt)	
Forsythe, Thomas H.	Co A 147 PA Inf (?)	
Fox, Joseph	Co G 87 PA Inf (Pvt/Cpl)	
Frew, David W.	Co B 1 PA L A (Pvt)	
Frew, David W.	Co B 134 PA Inf (Sgt/2 Lt) (Re-Enl?)	
Fullerton, James S.	Co B 1 PA L A (Lt)	
Gangwer, Jess	Co E 28 PA Inf (Pvt/Cpl)	
Gates, William K.	Co I 55 PA Inf (Pvt)	
Gouchenaur, David	Co G 202 PA Inf (Capt) (Re-Enl?)	
Graham, Robert A.	Co A 90 PA Inf (Drummer)	
Griswold, Jesse	Co F 5 PA Cav (?)	
Hall, Joseph E.	Co I 148 PA Inf (Pvt)	
Hall, Joseph E.	Co __ 183 PA Inf (Adj) (Re-Enl?)	
Harlan, John	Co H 116 PA Inf (?)	
Herffendirfer, Jacob	Co B 203 PA Inf (Pvt)	
Hilscher, Herman	Co H 26 PA Reserves (Pvt) ("Harmon Hilsher")	
James, Charles P.	Co G 58 PA Inf (Sgt)	
Jones, Albert	Co C 8 PA Cav (Pvt)	
Jones, Alfred	Co E 16 PA Cav (Pvt)	
Kay, Thomas	Co F 29 PA Inf (Pvt)	
Kennedy, Nathaniel	Co H 149 PA Vols (Pvt)	
Kepler, Peter L.	Co I 150 PA Inf (Pvt)	
Knapp, John	Co I 97 PA Inf (Lt)	
Kooken, John A.	Co C 152 PA ___ (Pvt)	
Kooken, John A.	Co G 3 PA H A (?) (Re-Enl?)	
Lewes, Thomas D.	Co B 100 PA Inf (Pvt)	
Lohr, Henry	Co K 18 PA Cav (Cpl)	
Lohr, John	Co D 133 PA Inf (Pvt)	
Lohr, John	Co G 93 PA Inf (1 Lt) (Re-Enl?)	
Loring, William E.	Co E 141 PA Vol Inf (Pvt/Sgt)	
Lucas, Joseph H.	Co G 2 PA Vol (Pvt)	
Manning, Phillip	Co F 2 PA H A (?)	
McConnell, James E.	Co B 11 PA Cav (Pvt/Sgt)	
McConnell, James E.	Co B 4 PA Cav (Sgt) (Re-Enl?)	
McCoy, Thomas	Co D 114 PA Inf (Cpl)	McCrumb, John W. Co A 14 PA Cav (Sgt)
McDaniel, B.F.	Co D 81 PA Inf (Pvt)	
McDaniel, B.F.	Co __ 1 Batt PA L A (Pvt) (Re-Enl?)	
McGee, William J.	Co E 15 PA Inf (Pvt)	
Merritt, Thomas W.	Co G 11 PA Inf (?)	
Milford, David	Co A 6 PA H A (?)	
Miller, Joseph H.	Co H 2 PA Inf (Pvt)	
Miller, Joseph H.	Co E 57 PA Vet Vol (Pvt) (Re-Enl?)	
Morton, James A.	Co H 10 PA Inf (Pvt)	
Nevenhuisen, Wm.W.	Co H 111 PA Inf (?)	
Nichols, H.H.	Co G 46 PA Vols (Pvt)	
Noble, Patrick	Co E 11 PA Cav (Pvt)	
Ober, William	Co G 93 PA Inf (Pvt)	

PENNSYLVANIA VETERANS (Con't)

Ogle, John J.	Co K 3 PA H A (Pvt)
Painter, Samuel	Co F 7 PA Inf (Pvt/Cpl)
Palmanteer, David	Co K 69 PA Inf (?)
Perigo, William	Co A 151 PA ___ (Sgt)
Pierce, Maris	Co C 97 PA Inf (Pvt/Cpl)
Pollack, Samuel S.	Co D 14 PA Cav (1 Sgt/2 Lt)
Porter, John P.	Co B 58 PA Inf (Pvt)
Powell, John C.	Co E 8 PA Inf (Pvt/Sgt)
Quigley, George B.	Co D 13 PA Inf (Pvt)
Reed, John	Co B 1 PA L A (Pvt)
Reynolds, Joshua T.	Co F 9 PA Reserves (Pvt/Capt)
Ricksecker, Lucius E.	Co A 153 PA Inf (Cpl)
Robinson, Culbert B.	Co B 52 PA Inf (Pvt/Cpl)
Rose, Bowers L.	Co K 2 PA Inf (Pvt)
Rose, John	Co G 16 PA Cav (?)
Rose, John	Co M 16 PA Cav (Pvt) (Re-Enl?)
Rudrauff, William H.	Co K 19 PA Inf (Pvt)
Rudrauff, William H.	Co F 82 PA Inf (Pvt/2 Lt) (Re-Enl?)
Runk, Joseph B.	Co H 22 PA Cav (Pvt)
Sechrist, Jacob	Co K 7 PA Cav (?)
Sigman, Marcus	Co H 24 PA ___ (Pvt)
Smouse, Daniel F.	Co F 11 PA Res Inf (1 Sgt)
Spence, Samuel R.	Co A 62 PA Vol (?)
Stewart, Samuel W.	Co C 4 PA Cav (Pvt)
Stewart, William M.	Co B 85 PA Inf (Pvt)
Stone, A.B.	Co E 41 PA Vols (Pvt)
Strawbridge, John B.	Co C 31 PA Inf (Pvt)
Streube, John	Co I 74 PA Inf (Pvt/Cpl)
Thompson, Archibald R.	Co F 13 PA Cav (Pvt)
Trogler, William A.	Co D 126 PA Inf (Pvt)
Trogler, William A.	Co F 102 PA Inf (Pvt) (Re-Enl?)
Troxel, Joseph	Co H 3 PA L A (Pvt)
Tyson, William	Co I 53 PA Inf (Pvt)
Van Castle, Joseph	Co G 17 PA Cav (Pvt/Cpl)
Wearing, John	Co L 2 PA H A (Pvt/Color Bearer)
Wellington, Edwin W.	Co F 111 PA V Inf (?)
Wellington, Edwin W.	Co K 102 PA V Inf (?) (Re-Enl?) (or 162 PA V Inf)
Whitney, Willard J.	Co A 57 PA ___ (Pvt/Sgt)
Wilcox, David E.	Co F 76 PA Inf (Pvt)
Willey, George O.	Co F 11 PA Cav (Pvt) (Re-Enl)
Wilson, Alexander	Co H 78 PA Inf (Pvt)
Witter, Charles	Co G 195 PA Inf (Pvt)
Wolf, Addison C.	Co D 11 PA Vet Reg (Pvt)
Wolfe, Peter E.	Co D 67 PA Inf (Pvt)
Young, John A.	Co F 6 PA Cav (Pvt)
Young, John A.	Co E 88 PA Inf (Cpl) (Re-Enl?)
Zimmers, Levi	Co F 2 PA Cav (Pvt)

RHODE ISLAND UNITS--7 Veterans

Esleek, Issac A.	Co L 3 RI HA (Pvt) ("Esleck")
Haynes, George E.	Co D 5 RI Inf/H A (Pvt)
Hutchison, William N.	Co E 1 RI L A (Pvt/Sgt Major)
Mills, Charles A.	Co E 11 RI Inf (Pvt)
Poland, Martin	Co ___ 7 RI Cav (Pvt)
Warburton, Percival D.	Co H 9 RI Inf (Pvt)

RHODE ISLAND VETERANS (Con't)
Warburton, Percival D.	Co B 11 RI Inf (Pvt) (Re-Enl?)
Washburn, A. Judson	Co D 11 RI Inf (Pvt)

TENNESSEE UNITS--8 Veterans
Capps, Thomas J.	Co F 1 East TN Cav (Capt/Lt Col)
Capps, Thomas J.	Co __ 3 TN Cav (?) (Lt Col)
Davis, Charles S.	Co G 11 TN Cav (Bugler)
Holmes, Augustus	Co D 10 TN Cav (Pvt)
Holsinger, S.K.	Co D 13 East TN Cav (Pvt)
Holsinger, S.K.	Co D 1 East TN Cav (Pvt) (Re-Enl?)
Hopkins, Archibald	Co E 8 TN Cav (Corpl)
Hughes, James D.	Co __ John Morgan's Command, TN (?)--CSA
Hughes, James D.	Co A 5 TN Cav (?) (Re-Enl)--CSA
Roach, William H.	Co F 7 TN Cav (Pvt)--CSA
Smith, O. Cincinatus	Co C 10 TN Cav (Pvt)--CSA

TEXAS UNITS--4 Veterans
Asher, Bartlett	Co E 1 TX Inf (Pvt)
Maxwell, Wilton P.	Co C 4 TX Inf (Pvt/Maj?)--CSA
Orrick, Ephraim M.	Co _ TX Rangers/TX Scouts (Pvt)--CSA
Rice, Laban W.	Co D 1 TX State Cav (Pvt/Bugler)--CSA

UTAH UNITS--1 Veteran
Eardley, Josiah	Co B 1st UT ___ (Mus'n/Pvt)

VERMONT UNITS--17 Veterans
Barrett, John C.	Co G 1 VT Cav (?)
Chaney, O.F.	Co K 1 VT Cav (Cpl/Sgt)
Cook, Jacob L.	Co B 5 VT Inf (Pvt)
Goodrich, James M.	Co D 14 VT Inf (Pvt/Cpl)
Holabird, W.H.	Co C 12 VT Inf (Pvt)
Lockwood, Munson M.	Co F 5 VT Inf (Pvt/Sgt)
Morse, Nixon	Co D 3 VT Inf (Pvt)
Morse, Nixon	Co F 1 VT Cav (Pvt) (Re-Enl?)
Orcutt, Herman C.	Co C 6 VT Inf (Pvt) [or Co G]
Powers, Robert A.	Co B 13 VT Inf (?)
Rood, Vernon D.	Co H 2 VT Inf (Pvt)
Steinhour, William E.	Co F 1 VT Inf (Pvt)
Story, Hampton	Co C 12 VT __ (Pvt/Cpl)
Ward, G.G. (Geo.H.?)	Co 11 5 VT Inf (?)
Watson, Alexander G.	Co L 1 VT Cav (Pvt/Capt)
Webb, Charles A.	Co G 8 VT Vol Inf (Pvt)
Wells, Alpheno W.	Co H 9 VT Inf (?)
Wright, George P.	Co K 7 VT Inf (Pvt)
Wright, George P.	Co __ 7 VT Inf (Hosp Stwd) (Re-Enl?)

VIRGINIA UNITS--9 Veterans
Bowen, W.T.	Co B 4 VA Cav (Pvt)
Chenault, Leo O.	Co __ (enl. VA?) (Capt)
Davis, Stephen M.	Co F 5 VA Inf (Lt Col)--CSA
Edwards, Augustus	Co K 6 VA Inf (?)
French, James M.	Co __ 63 VA Inf (Maj/Col)--CSA
Gordon, Richard	Co A 55 VA Inf (?)--CSA
Kerr, John M.	Co D 1 VA Inf (Pvt)
Murdock, John P.	Co C 3 VA Inf (Cpl)

VIRGINIA VETERANS (Con't)
Savage, George B.   Co I   39 VA Inf (Pvt)--CSA
Savage, George B.   Co E   19 VA H A Batt (?) (Re-Enl)--CSA

WASHINGTON TERRITORY UNITS--2 Veterans
Haskins, William A.   Co H   1 WA Terr Inf (Pvt/Mus'n)
Rickit, H.V.   Co B   1 WA Terr (Pvt)

WEST VIRGINIA UNITS--11 Veterans
Baker, Oscar H.   Co L   1 WV Cav (Pvt)
Duffy, George M.   Co K   11 WV Inf (Pvt/Cpl)
Falkenstein, John   Co C   3 WV Cav (Sgt/QM Sgt)
Farrow, D.S.   Co G   2 WV Cav (Pvt)
Foote, Andrew J.B.   Co D   1 WV L A (Pvt) (Re-Enl?)
Jacobs, John W.   Co C   1 WV Inf (Pvt) [or Co G]
Jacobs, John W.   Co C   1 WV Art (Pvt/1 Lt) (Re-Enl?)
Menhennet, William. H.   Co D   1 WV Cav (Pvt/Cpl)
Murdock, John P.   Co C   3 WV Inf (Corpl) (or 3 VA Inf)
Slack, Andrew J.   Co A   7 WV Cav (?)
Townsend, William E.   Co I   2 WV Cav (Pvt)
Wilson, Silas   Co A   7 WV Inf (Pvt)

WISCONSIN UNITS--122 Veterans
Allen, Henry E.   Co A   1 WI Art. (Cpl) (Re-Enl)
Allen, Henry E.   Co K   2 WI Inf (Pvt)
Anderson, Mark B.   Co G   4 WI Cav (Pvt)
Bailey, Benjamin E.   Co A   36 WI Inf (Pvt)
Baxter, Albert B.   Co H   38 WI Inf (?)
Bill, Douglas G.   Co C   49 WI Inf (Pvt)
Bowers, William W.   Co I   1 WI Cav (Pvt/Sgt)
Bridges, Otis S.   Co __ 5 WI Bat LA (Cpl)
Brown, Benjamin W.   Co H   29 WI Inf (Pvt/Cpl)
Brunemer, James H.   Co H   7 WI Inf (Pvt/Cpl)
Budlong, David H.   Co C   33 WI Inf (Pvt)
Burk, William   Co D   13 WI Vol Inf (Pvt)
Butler, Robert H.   Co G   40 WI Vol Inf (Pvt)
Butler, Robert H.   Co H   49 WI Vol Inf (Pvt/Cpl) (Re-Enl?)
Callaghan, Patrick   Co H   20 WI Vol Inf (Pvt) (or 20 WI Inf)
Chapman, Joseph   Co C   48 WI Inf (?) (or Co G) (or 49 Wis Inf)
Chase, Charles M.   Co __ 7 WI Indep Batt (Pvt) (Re-Enl)
Colbert, Robert   Co H   14 WI Inf (Pvt)
Colby, Lloyd H.   Co B   6 WI Inf (Pvt/Sgt)
Coleman, Patrick   Co F   2 WI Inf (Pvt)
Cook, George H.   Co C   3 WI Inf (Cpl/Sgt)
Cooper, J.B.   Co __ 27 WI Inf (Asst Surg/Surg)
Corey, Albert W.   Co H   30 WI Inf (Pvt)
Couts, Seneca P.   Co E   13 WI Inf--(Pvt)
Craigo, Joseph M.   Co F   2 Regt WI Cav (?)
Craw, Frank W.   Co K   35 WI Inf (Pvt)
Curby, Augustus W.   Co K   14 Regt WI Inf (?)
Curby, William F.   Co K   33 WI Inf (Mus'n)
Curby, William F.   Co E   52 WI Inf (Mus'n) (Re-Enl)
Dann, Edward F.   Co D   28 WI Inf (Pvt)
Davis, Leonard F.   Co A   21 WI Inf (Pvt/Sgt)
Dolph, Franklin   Co __ 1 WI Cav (Lt)
Dorward, William H.   Co E   29 WI Inf (Pvt)

WISCONSIN VETERANS (Con't)

Dow, Francis I.	Co A 23 WI Inf (Pvt)
Downs, Nathan H.	Co G 11 WI Inf (Pvt/1 Lt)
Downs, Nathan H.	Co K 40 WI Inf (1 Lt) (Re-Enl)
Eggleston, H.J.	Co K 3 WI Inf (Pvt)
Ellis, Thomas G.	Co A 11 WI Inf (Pvt/Cpl)
Enoch, Charles	Co G 41 WI Inf (?)
Estay, Amos	Co B 21 WI Inf (Pvt)
Fay, William A.	Co G 32 WI Inf (Pvt)
Feathers, D.H.	Co C 31 WI Inf (Pvt)
Ferry, Charles H.	Co I 17 WI Inf (?)
Flamming, John	Co K 9 WI Inf (Pvt) [Flammang/Flammage]
Flamming, John	Co B 9 WI Inf (Pvt) (Re-Enl?) [Flammang/Flammage]
Foot, F.J.	Co __ 13 WI Inf (Chaplain)
Frees, Benjamin M.	Co H 38 WI Inf (Pvt/Capt)
George, Charles W.	Co H 11 WI Inf (Pvt)
Gilman, Benjamin W.	Co B 1 WI Inf (Pvt)
Gould, William P.	Co H 17 WI Inf (?)
Halversen, Soren	Co K 3 Regt WI Inf (?)
Harvey, Rufus D./W.	Co D 13 WI Inf (?) (Re-Enl?)
Hebbard, A.W.	Co E 28 WI Inf (1 Sgt/2 Lt)
Helms, Reuben	Co D 40 WI Inf (Pvt)
Himebaugh, Henry H.	Co E 40 WI Inf (Cpl)
Himebaugh, Henry H.	Co D 49 WI Inf (Recruiting 2 Lt/Asst Lt/1 Lt)
Hodge, William C.	Co I 22 WI Inf (Pvt/Cpl)
Hodges, John	Co I 28 WI Inf (Pvt)
Hoine, Samuel P.	Co M 2 WI Cav (?)
Holverson, Thomas	Co D 43 WI Inf (Pvt) ("Tostine Holverson")
Horder, George W.	Co H 31 WI Inf (Mus'n)
Hurd, George S.	Co E 1 WI H A (Pvt)
Hurd, Lavinus S.	Co C 11 WI Inf (Pvt/Sgt)
Irgens, John S.	Co K 15 WI Inf (?)
Jackson, Johiel	Co E 4 WI Cav (?)
Jackson, Herman	Co E 2 WI Inf (2 Lt)
Jackson, Herman	Co G 2 WI Inf (2 Lt) (Re-Enl?)
Jacobs, L.C.	Co B 36 WI Inf (Pvt/2 Lt)
Jerman, Thomas	Co B 17 WI Inf (Pvt)
Jones, Charles P.	Co D 5 WI Inf (Pvt)
Kidder, John W.	Co D 3 WI Inf (Pvt)
Klaus, Carl	Co B __ WI ___ (Pvt)
Large, Andrew T.	Co D 36 WI Inf (Pvt/Cpl)
Leatherman, George	Co I 47 WI Inf (Pvt)
Lince, Cornelius	Co C 44 WI Inf (Pvt)
Lindsey, Dennis	Co A 48 WI Inf (?)
Lynch, Thomas	Co K 1 WI Cav (Pvt/Com Sgt)
Malson, Nathan	Co B 2 WI Inf (?)
Marsh, George W.	Co __ 8 Batt WI Arty (Pvt/Sgt)
Marshall, William P.	Co K 30 WI Vol Inf (Pvt/Drum Maj/Band Master)
McDonald, Edward	Co H 1 WI Inf (Pvt)
McPheeters, James H.	Co E 16 WI Inf (Pvt)
Miner, August	Co G 17 WI Inf (?) ("August Mincur")
Moffatt, Henry G.	Co G 32 WI Inf (Pvt)
Moran, Edward H.	Co B 6 WI Inf (Pvt/Sgt)
Mosher, William H.	Co B 1 WI Inf (Pvt/1 Sgt)
Mulville, Martin	Co A 10 WI Inf (Pvt)
Noyce, William D.	Co A 39 WI Inf (Pvt)

WISCONSIN VETERANS (Con't)

Noyce, William D.	Co E 50 WI Inf (Pvt) (Re-Enl)
Olin, Dyer W.	Co I 50 WI ___ (Pvt)
Owen, George B.	Co E 3 WI Inf (?)
Owens, William T.	Co I 2 WI Cav (Pvt)
Parker, Stephen H.	Co B 2 WI Cav (Sgt)
Parks, Milton B.	Co I 28 WI Inf (Pvt)
Phelps, F.A.	Co E 3 WI Cav (Pvt)
Pillsbury, Cassius C.	Co F 39 WI Inf (1 Sgt)
Pool, Chester W.	Co D 40 WI Inf (Pvt)
Pratt, Charles E.	Co F 48 WI Inf (Sgt)
Riggs, Joseph	Co C 39 WI Inf (Pvt)
Roby, Rheuben T.	Co H 38 WI Inf (Pvt)
Rule, George A.	Co B 30 WI Inf (?)
Schutte, Gerhard	Co E 3 WI Inf (Pvt/1 Sgt)
Scruby, John	Co D 25 WI Vol Inf (?)
Seavy, James	Co D 19 WI Inf (?)
Shaughnessey, Wm M.	Co ___ 36 WI Inf (?)
Slade, Isaac	Co C 30 WI Inf (Pvt/Drummer)
Smith, Henry	Co B 51 WI Inf (?)
Smith, Richard	Co ___ 1 WI Cav (Chf Bugler)
Smout, Basil	Co K 23 WI Inf (Pvt/2 Lt)
Stansberry, Charles H.	Co C 28 WI Inf (Pvt)
Stephens, David	Co L 1 WI Art (Pvt) (or I WI H A)
Stevens, Edward R.	Co C 3 WI Cav (Capt)
Sunnocks, Melvin D.	Co D 40 WI Inf (Pvt)
Taft, Byron P.	Co F 10 Regt WI Inf (Pvt)
Tenny, Silas B.	Co C 3 WI Cav (Pvt)
Taylor, R.W.	Co D 3 WI? Cav (Capt)
Thieme, Charles B.	Co A 26 WI Inf (Pvt)
Thomas, John P.	Co F 24 WI Inf (Pvt)
Thompson, Charles D.	Co G 5 WI Inf (Pvt)
Titus, Anson	Co E 3 WI Inf (Pvt/Sgt)
Van Buskirk, Marshall	Co I 1 Regt WI Cav (?)
Veile, George C.	Co B 15 WI Inf (Pvt)
Veile, George C.	Co ___ 8 Batt WI L A (Cpl) (Re-Enl)
Ward, Chaney	Co G 22 WI Inf (Pvt)
Ward, Jerome L.	Co I 1 WI Cav (?)
Warner, Robert T.	Co A 19 WI ___ (Pvt)
Wescott, Lowrey	Co H 22 WI Inf (Pvt)
Wiard, Augustus J.	Co E 17 WI Inf (Pvt)
Withrow, Charles W.	Co K 30 WI Inf (Pvt/Cpl)
Wood, Calvin M.	Co I 19 WI Vol Inf (Ord Sgt/1 Lt)
Wood, Nelson P.	Co E 8 WI Inf (Pvt)

U.S. REGULARS--178 Veterans

Ackles, Willis	Co E 83 USCT (Pvt/Cpl)
Adams, George	USA (Post QM Sgt)
Adams, Stephen J.	Co D Marine Brigade (Pvt)
Allen, Andrew J.	US Army (?)
Arey, A.R.	SS Niphon (Ord.Seaman/Masters Mate)
Bailhache, William H.	Co ___ 1 US Vol (AQM)
Baird, Charles A.	Co B 19 US Inf (Cpl)
Baker, August Cesar	US Navy Ship Morse & Mystic (Carpenter's Mate)
Barrett, Michael	US Navy (Landsman)
Bell, G.V./G.U.	Co M 2 US Vol Engr's (Cpl)

U.S. REGULARS (Con't)

Berg, Anton	Co H 3 US Inf (?) (or 8 US Inf)
Bergman, Jacob	Co B 1 US Dragoons (Pvt)
Bigelow, Lyman G.	Co H 1 USCT (1 Lt) (Promoted?)
Billingsley, L.W.	Co K 14 USCT (2nd Lt) (Promoted?)
Billingsley, L.W.	Co A 44 USCT (Capt) (Promoted?)
Birdsall, S.H.	Co C 1 USCT (1 Lt/QM) (Promoted?)
Blanchard, Oliver C.	US Navy (Landsman)
Bolster, Robert	Co 1 3 US Art (?)
Bolting, Charles J.	US Navy (Ordinary Seaman/Petty Officer)
Brenner, George A.	US Cav 10 Regt (Chief Mus'n)
Britton, Thomas	US Army (Capt)
Brobst, Albert M.	Co I 63 USCT (1 Lt) (Promoted)
Brooks, John	Co H 10 US Cav (?) (Re-Enl?)
Broughton, George W.	US Navy (?)
Brown, Rodney D.	Str (Steamer?) U.S. Rhode Island (Master's Mate)
Bryan, William	USS North Carolina/USS Shomoken (Landsman/Seaman)
Buck, Nathan	Co B 4 US Art (Pvt)
Buckley, Michael	US Navy (3 GL Boy)
Budlong, David H.	Co __ 135 USCT (Lt Col) (Promoted?)
Bumpus, William B.	US Navy USS Kerrington/Ship North Carolina (Seaman)
Burnham, E.H.	Co B 3 US Arty (Pvt)
Burnham, E.H.	Co D 2 US Arty (Pvt)
Burns, A.J.	Co B 53 USCT (1 Lt) (Promoted?)
Burt, John P.	Co C 12 US Inf 2nd Batt (Pvt)
Caldwell, John G.	Co __ 23 US Inf (?)
Castle, William D.	US Navy (?)
Catlin, John	Co K 1 US Cav (Bugler) (Re-Enl?)
Charland, Maxim	U.S.S. Sabine (Landsman/Qtr Gunner)
Clark, John J.	USS Minnesota (Seaman)
Coleman, Ezekial	Co A 78 USCT (Lt)
Comings, L.B.	US Army (Medical Cadet)
Conklin, Norman H.	US Navy (Acting Ensign) (Re-Enl?)
Connor, James	Co M 2 US Art (Pvt)
Connors, John	Co B 4 US Art (Pvt)
Coon, Datus E.	US Col; Appointed by Lincoln Bvt Brig. Gen
Crater, Cornelius	Co E 14 US ___ (Sgt) (Re-Enl?)
Crittenden, Thomas T.	US Vols (Brig Gen) (Promoted)
Davis, Walker	Co K 65 USCI (Pvt)
Dayton, Richard	US Navy (Pvt)
Dennison, A.R.	Co __ 2 USCT (Maj) (Promoted?)
Dill, Albert F.	US Navy (Act. Ensign) (Re-Enl?)
Dillingham, John	US Navy (Acting Master)
Dodderidge, John H.	USS Great Western (Landsman)
Dodge, Richard V.	US Vols (Chaplin)
Dooley, Nate Edward	US Navy (?)
Duvall, William H.	Co E 5 US Art (Pvt) (Re-Enl?)
Earle, Francis S.	Army of the Potomic/General Army Corps (Asst Adj)
Easton, Orlando W.	Co H 47 USCT (Capt)
Edwards, John W.	Co A 4 US Inf (Pvt) (Re-Enl?)
Evans, Philip H.	Co C 14 US Inf (Pvt)
Fletcher, B.F.	US Navy (Seaman) (Re-enl?)
Folkin, Samuel J.	US Navy (Master Mate)
Folsum, Edward C.	Signal Corps (Pvt)
Freeborn, Fremont	Co A 15 US Inf 2 Batt (Pvt)
Freeman, Charles H.	US Navy–Ship Rhode Island (Landsman/Yeoman/Master's Mate)

U.S. REGULARS (Con't)

Glenn, James H.	Co F 3 US Vol Inf (Cpl)
Goodell, Maximilian	Co M 3 US Cav (Pvt) (Re-Enl)
Gould, Francis C.	U.S.S. Housatania (Landsman)
Grant, George W.	US Navy Steamer Chocure (Pay Steward/Pay Clerk)
Gregory, Hugh M.	US Navy (Acting Mate/Lt)
Grisswell, Robert H.	USA (Hosp Stewd)
Hallowell, Henry B.	USMC (Pvt)
Hamilton, Beverly	US Navy--USS Verlena (Landsman)
Hanretty, John	Co F 3 US Arty (Pvt)
Hanretty, John	Co P 3 US Arty (Pvt) (Re-Enl?)
Hayward, William H.	Co D 4 US Vet Vols (Pvt)
Hazzard, G.R.	Co 8 5 US Art (?)
Healey, Bernard	Co A 8 US Inf (Sgt)
Herrick, Amos P.	Co C 1 US Cav (Duty Sgt)
Higgins, William	Co B 5 US Inf (Pvt/Corpl Ordinance)
Himmell, Charles S.	US Navy (Landsman)
Hipwell, Richard J.	Co I 29 USCT (Lt) (Promoted?)
Hodge, Noah	Co __ 52 USCT (1 Lt) (Promoted?)
Hough, Charles W.	Co G 18 US Inf (Pvt)
Houston, John	Co B 3 US Inf (Pvt)
Hughes, James	USS Florida/Colorado/Lafayette (Ord Seaman/Seaman)
Hurd, Warren H.	Co B 23 USCT (Capt) (Promoted?) [or 28 USCT]
Iodine, Chief	US Navy S.S. Galena (Seaman)
Jackson, J.M.	US Navy--Monitor (Ensign)
Jackson, Thomas M.	Batt A 2 Regt US Col L A (Pvt)
Jackson, Thomas M.	Co M 9 US Cav (Pvt) (Re-Enl)
Johnsen, Peder	US Navy (Chf Bos'n Mate)
Johnson, William H.	Ship Colorado? (1st Class Apprentice/Ordinary Seaman)
Jones, James P.	US Navy/Gun Boat Sagamore (Fireman)
Jones, Samuel	Co I 8 US Inf (?)
Krebs, Augustus	Co K 3 US Inf (?)
Kretsinger, David L.	Co G 56 USCI (?) (Promoted?) (or 56 USCT)
Laws, William H.	Co F 20 USCT (Pvt)
Lilley, James	Co K 114 USCI (?)
Loud, Charles A.	Co G 88 USCT (2 Lt) (Promoted?)
Lucas, Joseph H.	US Signal Corps (Pvt) (Re-Enl)
Luckadoe, Joseph	Co H 4 U S Inf (Drummer/Pvt)
Luckett, Alexander	Co G 32 USCT (Pvt)
Lombardy, Frank K.	Co C 29 US Inf (Sgt) [or Co G]
Madden, Joseph	US Navy SS Nephron & Ohio (1st Class Boy)
Marshall, Edmund	Co D 118 USCT (Pvt)
Martin, Joseph	US Army (Hospital Steward)
Mate, W.B.	US Navy (Assistant Steward)
McCartin, Francis	USS Augusta (Landsman)
McCartin, Francis	USS Metacomet (Ordinary Seaman) (Re-Enl?)
McConville, Patrick H.	Co C 12 US Inf (Pvt) (or Co G)
McIntosh, Daniel	Co E 5 US Cav (Sgt)
McLaren, Benjamin F.	USS Pensacola (Landsman/Yeoman)
Mellus, Frances G.	U.S.S. Louisville (Seaman) (Re-Enl?)
Mendelson, Louis	Co M 4 US R C (Pvt)
Miller, Charles F.	Co F 6 US Cav (Pvt)
Miller, William F.	Co M 4 US Art (Pvt) (Re-Enl?)
Mitchell, Charles G./C.K.	Co D 18 US Inf (Pvt)
Mixter, Horace D.	Co A 2 US Sharpshooters (Pvt)
Montius, Augustus	US Navy (Engineer)

U.S. REGULARS (Con't)

Morris, Charles	Co D 2 US Troops (Pvt)
Moylan, Miles	Co C 2 US Drag (Pvt/1st Sgt)
Moylan, Mils	Co C 2 US Cav (1st Sgt/2 Lt) (Promoted?)
New, Edward	Co A 9 US Inf (?)
Nichols, George E.	US Navy (?)
Nickens, Samuel I.	US Navy USS Tuscarowa (Landsman)
O'Donnell, John F.	US Navy (Seaman)
O'Leary, Stephen	US Navy U.S.S. Glautus & Galatea (Landsman)
Otis, Elmer	USA (Col) (Retired Officer)
Palmer, Ernest	Co H 9 R 1st Army (?) (Re-Enl?)
Parsons, Benjamin F.	Co I 1 US Art (?)
Pennell, Robert J.	US Navy--US Mayflower (2nd Officer)
Phillips, Lionel D.	Co A 6 USCT (2 Lt/1 Lt) (Promoted?)
Picken, John	US Navy
Pierce, Charles O.	Co B 7 US Inf (Pvt)
Piher, William	Co __ 2 US Art--Luttons Bat (Sgt)
Price, Levi	Co G 11 U S Inf (Pvt/Ord Sgt)
Radford, Thomas	US Navy--U.S.S.Vesuvius (Seaman)
Remondino, Peter C.	US Vols (Medical Cadets)
Rice, Hosea B.	Co E 14 US Inf (Pvt)
Rice, John H.	US Navy (Act Ensign/Act Master)
Richardson, A. Tappen	USS Ohio (1st Class Fireman)
Rickit, H.V.	US Navy (Acting Ensign) [possible service]
Rimbach, Charles/Carl	Co A 3 US Arty (Artificer)
Roach, Henry	US Army 19th Inf (1st Sgt) (Re-Enl?)
Robinson, George	Co B 3 US Colored Inf (Pvt)
Robinson, George	Co H 9 US Cav (Pvt) (Re-Enl)
Ross, James	Co B 1 US Cav (?)
Russell, Enoch	Co C 12 US Inf (Pvt)
Scott, Winfield	USA (Chaplain)
Seidell, Charles W.	Co G 16 USCT (1 Lt/Capt) (Promoted?)
Shaw, Joseph M.	Co F 1 US Cav (?)
Sigman, Marcus	Co H 15 US Inf (Pvt) (Re-Enl?)
Simpson, John H.	Co I 5 US Inf (Sgt)
Smith, George H.	US Military Telegraph Corps (?)
Smith, Thomas B.	Co G 1 US Eng (Sgt) (Re-Enl?)
Stancliff, William H.	US Navy (Landsman/Ordinary Seaman)
Stevens, L.W.	US Navy (Seaman)
Stewart, Sylvester N.	Co B 62 USCT (1 Lt) (Promoted?)
Stewart, W.B.	US Navy (Mate, Asst)
Storey, William H.	US Signal Corps (?)
Stout, James	Co B 1 US Cav (Pvt)
Sweeney, Henry	Co H 2 US Dragoons (Pvt)
Sweeney, Henry	Co __ 4 US Cavalry (?) (Re-Enl?)
Sweeney, Henry	Co K 4 US Cav (Capt) (Re-Enl?)
Taylor, George O.	US Navy (?)
Tengwall, Charles	US Navy (Masters Mate/Act'g Ensign)
Thompson, Archibald	US Signal Corps (Pvt 1st Class) (Re-Enl?)
Tillman, Robert	Co A 127 US Colored Inf (Pvt)
Tinker, William H.	US Signal Corps (Sgt) (Re-Enl?)
Touhy, Martin	Co H 14 US Inf (Pvt)
Travers, Jones	US Navy (Quarter Gunner)
Turner, John C.	Co G 1 US Engineers (Artificer)
Tyrell, John D.	USS Kenawae (Seaman) (Re-Enl?)
Ward, Stephen I.	US Navy (Landsman)

U.S. REGULARS (Con't)

Washington, Greenberry	Co H 108 USCT (Pvt)
Webster, Francis E.	Co __ 10 US Inf (Sgt)
Welch, James	Co G 34 US V Inf (?)
Willey, George C.	US Navy SS James Agar (Seaman/Pvt)
Williams, Charles H.	Co __ 81 USCT (Mus'n)
Williams, Charles H.	Co __ 20 Brig Corps D'Afrique (Band)
Wilson, Frank	USS Vandalia (Able Seaman)
Wilson, William	Co D 4 Batt US Army (Pvt)
Winder, W.A.	Co __ 3 US Arty (Capt)
Wood, H.F.	US Navy (Capt)
Work, Walter D.	Co B 120 USCI (2 Lt)
Wright, Walter W.	Co C 12 US Inf (Pvt)
Young, John A.	USA (Sgt of Ord.)

VETERANS RESERVE CORPS UNITS--21 Veterans

Atwood, John R.	Co H VRC (Pvt)
Blake, Robert	Co H 2 U.S.V.V. (Pvt)
Blake, Robert	Co E __ U.S.V.V. Hancock's Corp (Pvt)
Boutwell, William T.	Co F 13 VRC (Pvt) (Re-Enl?)
Dale, John H.	Co F 10 VRC (Pvt)
Dye, John W.	Co __ 2 Batt VRC (Pvt) (Re-Enl?)
Giddings, J.R.B.	Co D 22 VRC (Corpl)
Grosvenor, Royal W.	Co B 15 VRC (?)
Haskell, John L.	Co B 8 Vet Inf (Pvt) (Re-Enl)
Hubbs, Charles L.	Co A 9 US V Vol (Pvt) (Re-Enl?)
Jones, Danville P.	Co A 6 VRC (Pvt) (Re-Enl?)
Kelly, Eli C.	Co B 15 VRC (Pvt) (Re-Enl?)
Moore, Alanson O.	Co E 4 VRC (Sgt) (Re-Enl?)
Riley, William T.	Co K 5 Hancock's Vet Vol (Pvt/Sgt) (Re-Enl?)
Rumph, August	Co D 1 US Vet Vols (1 Sgt)
Simmons, Clinton	Co __ _ VRC (Pvt) (Re-Enl?)
Spangler, Henry	Co K 4 VRC (Pvt) (Re-Enl?)
Spence, Samuel R.	Co __ 2 Batt Vet Reserves (Pvt/1st Sgt)
Spileman, Edward B.	Co H 2 VRC (Pvt) (Re-Enl?)
Wheaton, William H.	Co __ Vet Bat (1st Sgt) (Re-Enl)
Williams, L.A.	Co A 2 VRC (Corpl)
Wyatt, Charles C.	Co G _ VRC (Pvt)

UNKNOWN UNITS--54 Veterans

Veterans with unknown units: William T. Allen ("Major"), Elisha S. Babcock ("Union Army"), Absolom E. Barrow ("Confederate Vet"), Alexander Bell ("Confederate Plot--CSA"), George P.A. Brabason ("Capt"), Alexander N. Bradwell ("Confederate Vet"), Thomas E. Brink ("Civil War Veteran"), Charles Burgoyne ("CSA"), Charles W. Burnham ("Veteran of the Civil War"), Levi Chase ("Civil War Veteran"), Rubin Commo ("Captain"), Alonzo E. Dodson (Datus Coon G.A.R.), Horace Ellis ("Killed on Battlefield May 10, 1864 Aged 44 Years"), Marcus D. Faulk ("Confederate Plot" on his wife's burial card), William M. Fortesque ("Captain"), Peter Frasier ("GAR"), George Fry ("CSA"), Benjamin W. Gilman (Co B McCl Drag Pvt), David Gouchenaur ("Commisary Dept--Pvt"), J.S. Gray ("Captain"), William M. Green ("GAR"), Hugh G. Gwyn ("Major"), James Hewson ("Captain"), Jacob Hoeffle (Co __ __ Batt Art'ly--Capt. Pennington"), J.M. Leader ("Seaman"), William K. Logan ("Confederate Soldier--CSA"), George F. Lufbery ("Veteran of the Civil War"), Paris A. Magee ("Clara D"--Messenger Boy), Dr. Mahan (Datus Coon G.A.R.).

Henry Mahoney ("Ship Sybil--Seaman"), John H. Marshall ("Captain"), George Marston ("Colonel"), Thomas Matthews ("Captain"), William M. McCoy ("CSA"), Daniel McIntosh, ("Co __ Bat D 3rd Art") Swan A. Miller ("GAR"), John G. Moore ("Confederate Vet--Colonel"), J.A. Morrison (Datus Coon G.A.R.), David Hart Pivers ("Capt"), Ludlow Pruden ("Civil War Veteran"), John Reed ("Captain"), Chas F.W. Roneau "(S.S. Fredonia--Pvt/Seaman"), S.W. Roys ("Captain"), Arthur M. Sawtelle ("Charleston Navy Yard--Marine Engineer"), Thomas S. Sedgwick ("Colonel--A Soldier of the Civil War"), A.C. Shaw ("Co.B, 5 Bat Cav--Pvt/Sgt), Frederick A. Smith ("Civil War Veteran 1861-1865 1st Regt Co B"), George W. Smith ("Colonel--Confederate Vet"), S.G. Steele ("Captain--Seumere G. Steele"), John Van Arman ("Colonel"), Adolphus Ward, ("A member of 244 AOUW"), George Webber ("Cavalry Trumpeter, Heintzelman Post G.A.R.), Joshua K. Whims (Datus Coon G.A.R) and Aaron Wood, ("Confederate Veteran"--CSA).

CHAPTER SEVEN: SOURCE NOTES

INTRODUCTION

1. Stuart McConnell, *Glorious Contentment: The Grand Army of the Republic, 1865-1900*. (Chapel Hill & London: The University of North Carolina Press, 1992), 3.

2. Ibid, 3.

3. Ibid, 4.

4. Ibid

5. Ibid, 11.

6. Ibid.

CHAPTER I

1. Colonel George Ruhlen, "San Diego in the Civil War," *San Diego Historical Society Quarterly* VII (April 1961), 17.

2. Ibid.

3. Ibid.

4. Ibid, 17-18.

5. Leo P. Kibby, "California Soldiers in the Civil War," *California Historical Society Quarterly* XL (December 1961), 343.

6. Ibid, Ruhlen, 18, 20.

7. Ibid, Kibby, 345.

8. Ibid, 346.

9. Ibid, 346-347.

10. Brigadier General Richard H. Orton, Compiler, *Records of California Men in the War of the Rebellion, 1861-1867*. (Sacramento: State [Printing] Office, 1890), 5.

11. Ibid, Kibby, 346-347.

12. Robert W. Frazer, "Military Posts in San Diego," *The Journal of San Diego History* XX (July, 1974), 45.

13. Colonel George Rulen, "San Diego Barracks," *The Journal of San Diego History* XIII (April, 1967), 7. [This article has a map of where the barracks were located as well as a sketch of the placement of buildings in the barracks block.]

14. Ibid, Frazer, 45.

SOURCE NOTES (Con't)

15. Ed Scott, *San Diego County Soldier-Pioneers 1846-1866* (San Diego: County of San Diego Bicentennial Project, 1976), 125-126. [See also a biographical sketch on Samuel P.Heintzleman in *Dictionary of American Biography,* ed. by Allen Johnson and Dumas Malone (New York: Charles Scribner's Sons, 1960), 505-506; and Heintzelman, Samuel P., *Fifty Miles and a Fight: Major Samuel Peter Heintzleman's Journal of Texas and the Cortina War*, (Austin: Texas State Historical Association, 1998.]

16. Ibid.

17. Ibid, 126.

18. Ibid, Rulen, "San Diego Barracks," 7.

19. Ibid, Frazer, 46.

20. Ibid, Rulen, "San Diego Barracks," 9.

21. Ibid, 12.

22. Ibid, Scott, 101.

23. Ibid, p. 102.

24. Ibid, 107-108.

25. Ibid, 147.

26. Ibid, 149.

27. Ibid.

28. Ibid, 150.

29. Ibid, 151.

30. Ibid, 156.

31. Ibid, 151.

CHAPTER II

1. Laurie Bissell, "San Diego Cemeteries: A Brief Guide," *The Journal of San Diego History* XXVIII (Fall 1982), 270.

2. Fred Jay Rimbach, Jr, *A History of the Cemeteries in the City of San Diego, California.* (San Diego: Fred Jay Rimbach, Jr., 1949) (Manuscript available at California Room.)

3. Ibid, Bissell, 271.

4. John H. Sneed, "Records of Johnson-Saum and Knobel Mortuary Serving Since 1869," *Leaves and Saplings* (Undated). Publication of the San Diego Genealogical Society. (Available at San Diego Family History Center, 4195 Camino Del Rio South, San Diego, CA 92108).

5. Ibid, Bissell, 271.

SOURCE NOTES (Con't)

6. Ibid, 276.

7. Hillcrest-North Park Smart Shopper, "Tennis Courts to Replace Tombstones," April 9, 1970, p. 1. (A copy of this newspaper article in located in the "Cemeteries" vertical file in the California Room of the San Diego Public Library.)

8. Ibid, Bissell, 276.

9. Ibid, Hillcrest-North Park Smart Shopper.

10. R. Clinton Griffin, Compiler, in association with Sister Catherine Louise La Costa, CSJ, Sally West, Karna Webster and Georgia L. Callian, *Mission San Diego de Alcala Burials for Mission & Presidio 1775-1831; El Campo Santo 1849-1880; Mission Hills Catholic Cemetery (Old Cavalry) 1875-1969*. (San Diego: R. Clinton Griffin, 1997). (Copy at San Diego Historical Society Archives, Balboa Park).

11. Ibid, Rimbach, description of the meeting called to establish Mount Hope Cemetery, pages describing Mount Hope (or "Public") Cemetery. (Manuscript available at California Room.) NOTE: William Wallace Bowers (Civil War veteran of this study) attended this meeting.

12. Ibid, Bissell, 274.

13. Ibid, Rimbach, pages describing Mount Hope Cemetery.

14. Ibid, Rimbach.

15. Ibid, Rimbach.

16. Various compilers, *Mt. Hope Cemetery Burial Records 1869-1909*. (San Diego: San Diego Genealogical Society, 1998). (This publication can be purchased from the San Diego Genealogical Society. Their address is: 1050 Pioneer Way, Suite E, El Cajon, CA 92020.) The burial records are alphabetical by first letter of the surname, then chronological as individuals died. The book is not indexed.

17. Brae Canlen, San Diego Weekly Reader, "Tombstone Territory: The Business of Burial at Mount Hope Cemetery," April 7, 1988, p. 17.

18. Ibid, Rimbach, pages describing Greenwood Memorial Park and Mortuary.

19. Ibid, Rimbach.

20. Ibid, Bissell, 288.

21. Ibid, Rimbach, pages describing Holy Cross Cemetery.

22. Ibid, Bissell, 272.

23. Ibid.

24. Ibid, Rimbach, pages describing Post Cemetery, Fort Rosecrans.

25. Ibid, Bissell, 278.

26. Edward F. Adams, "The United States Soldiers' Home at Santa Monica," *The Overland Monthley* XII, Second Series (September 1888), 229. (Journal available at California Room, San Diego Public Library.)

SOURCE NOTES (Con't)

27. J.H. Griffes, Los Angeles Times, "The Soldiers' Home: How It Impresses a New Arrival," November 7, 1890, 3:1. An additional article on the Los Angeles Soldiers' Home appears in the Los Angeles Times on October 21, 1892, 6:3, "Soldier's Home: Where Nearly a Thousand Veterans Are Cared For," (Los Angeles Times microfilms for the years 1881-present are available at the Newspaper Room, San Diego Public Library).

CHAPTER III

1. Clarence Alan McGrew, *City of San Diego and San Diego County: The Birthplace of California*, Vol. 2 (Chicago and New York: The American Historical Society, 1922), 113.

2. Elizabeth C. MacPhail, *The Story of New San Diego and of its Founder Alonzo E. Horton*, Second Printing, Revised (San Diego: The San Diego Historical Society, 1989).

3. Ibid, 19.

4. Ibid, 53.

5. Richard Bigger, James D. Kitchen, Lyndon R. Musolf, Carolyn Quinn, *Metropolitan Coast: San Diego and Orange Counties, California*, (Los Angeles: University of California Los Angeles, Bureau of Governmental Research, 1958), 2-3.

6. Ibid, McGrew, 64-65.

7. Clare Crane, "Matthew Sherman: Pioneer San Diegan," *The Journal of San Diego History* XVIII (Fall 1972), 23.

8. Ibid, 23-24.

9. Elizabeth C. MacPhail, Ed., "Early Days in San Diego: The Memoirs of Augusta Barrett Sherman," *The Journal of San Diego History* XVIII (Fall 1972), 32. (See also an associated article in this journal volume by Rurik Kallis: "Matthew Sherman's First Home in New San Diego," 36-37. This Sherman home is still standing, though greatly remodeled, at 422 19th Street, San Diego).

10. Ibid, Crane, 24.

11. Ibid, Crane, 27. See also MacPhail, 26-27. (A footnote in this article notes that the journal *The Golden Era* (April 1887), 251) listed Civil War veteran A.T. Large of this study as the architect. This Sherman home is still standing, again greatly remodeled as the "Sherman Apartments," at 563 22nd Street, San Diego).

12. Obituaries for Matthew Sherman are available at the San Diego Historical Society Archives "Biographical File" under his name. He died July 5, 1898 and was buried in Division 3 at Mount Hope on July 7, 1898.

13. Obituaries for Augusta Barrett Sherman are available in the San Diego Historical Society Archives "Biographical File" under her name. She died January 5, 1913 and was buried in Division 3 at Mount Hope on January 7, 1913.

14. Samuel F. Black, *San Diego County, California: A Record of Settlement, Organization, Progress and Achievement*, Vol. I (Chicago: S.J. Clarke Publishing Company, 1913), 302 (Chapter XXXVIII, "Fraternal Bodies".)

15. Heintzelman Post #33 Collection, Box 3, "Military in San Diego," MS 365, San Diego Historical Society Archives.

16. Ibid, Black, 302-3.

SOURCE NOTES (Con't)

17. Ibid, 302-303. [See also Datus Coon Post #172 post ledger book, Box 6, "Military in San Diego," MS 365, San Diego Historical Society Archives.]

18. San Diego Union, "Gen. Coon Fatally Shot: Accidental Discharge of a Revolver in J.H. Grovesteen's Hand," December 17, 1893, 5:3.

19. San Diego Union, "General Coon's Funeral: Services to be Conducted by Heintzelman Post G.A.R.," December 18, 1893, 2:3. (Additional articles appeared in the San Diego Union as follows: "With Military Honors: Arrangements for the Funeral of Gen. Datus E. Coon," December 19, 1893, 5:3, and "A Hero Laid to Rest: Impressive Funeral Services of Gen. Datus E. Coon," December 20, 1893, 2:1).

20. San Diego Union, "Sunday in the Camp: Thousands of People Visit the Visitors on the Beach," August 4, 1890, 8:1.

21. Ibid, "Sunday at the Camp."

22. Ibid, "Sunday at the Camp."

23. San Diego Union, "Fort Union Fell: The Sham Battle Witnessed by Thousands," August 8, 1890, 8:1.

24. Ibid, "Fort Union Fell."

25. Ibid, "Fort Union Fell."

26. Ibid, McGrew.

27. Carl H. Heilbron, *History of San Diego County* (San Diego: The San Diego Press Club, 1936).

28. _____, *San Diego County, California: A Record of Settlement, Organization, Progress and Achievement*, Vol. 2 (Chicago: S.J. Clarke Publishing Company, 1913).

29. William E. Smythe, *History of San Diego 1542-1907*, (San Diego: The History Company, 1907).

30. Leland Ghent Stanford, *San Diego's Legal Lore & The Bar* (San Diego: San Diego County Bar Association Law Library Justice Foundation, 1968).

31. _____, *An Illustrated History of Southern California* (Chicago: The Lewis Publishing Company, 1890).

32. San Diego Historical Society, *San Diego County Pioneer Families: A Collection of Family Histories Compiled by Members and Friends of the San Diego Historical Society* (San Diego: San Diego Historical Society, 1977).

33. Don M. Stewart, *Frontier Port: A Chapter in San Diego's History* (Los Angeles: The Ward Ritchie Press, 1965).

34. Ibid, MacPhail, *The Story of New San Diego and of its Founder Alonzo E. Horton*.

35. Ibid, Ed Scott, *San Diego Soldier-Pioneers 1846-1866*.

36. _____, *The City and County of San Diego, Illlustrated and Containing Biographical Sketches of Prominent Men and Pioneers* (San Diego: Leberthon & Taylor, 1888.)

37. City of Chula Vista, *Chula Vista Heritage, 1911-1986* (Chula Vista: City of Chula Vista, 1986).

38. Eldonna P. Lay, *Valley of Opportunity: The History of El Cajon* (El Cajon: Eldonna P. Lay & Associates, 1987).

SOURCE NOTES (Con't)

39. Thomas Joseph Adema, *Our Hills and Valleys: A History of the Helix-Spring Valley Region* (San Diego: San Diego Historical Society, 1993).

40. San Diego Daily Transcript, series of articles on Moses A. Luce: 1/22/92--"The Civil War Comes to Life in a Journal"; 1/23/92--"Machine Gun Won't Defend Malvern Hill"; 1/24/92--"Underestimate the Valor of Union Army, and Die"; 1/27/92--"From a Promontory, a View of the Greatest Calvary Battle"; 1/28/92, "How Moses Luce Risked His Life to Save a Friend"; 1/30/92--"Moses Luce Gets a Wife and California Fever in 1870s"; 2/3/92--"Horton Plaza a Rough Place 120 Years Ago"; and 2/4/92--"San Diegans and Gen. [Harrison Gray] Otis Didn't Like Each Other."

41. Richard W. Crawford and other compilers, *A Guide to the Coroner's Inquests, 1853-1905, San Diego County* (San Diego: San Diego Historical Society, 1984).

42. Ibid, Scott, 151.

43. Ray Brandes, James R. Moriarty, Susan H. Carrico, *New Town, San Diego,* (San Diego: San Diego Science Foundation, 1985), 28. [This report was prepared for Centre City Development Corporation and is located in the stacks at James S. Copley Library, University of San Diego.]

44. Ibid.

45. Ibid, 39.

46. Ibid, Scott, 13.

47. Heintzelman, Samuel P., *Fifty Miles and a Fight: Major Samuel Peter Heintzleman's Journal of Texas and the Cortina War*, (Austin: Texas State Historical Association, 1998.], 55.

48. Ibid, 56.

49. Ibid, 57.

50. Ibid, MacPhail, *The Story of New San Diego and of its Founder Alonzo E. Horton*, 32.

51. For a biographical sketch of General William Starke Rosecrans, see Dumas Malone, ed., *Dictionary of American Biography*, Vol. VIII (New York: Charles Scribner's Sons, 1963), 163-164.

52. Ibid, MacPhail, 24.

53. Ibid, 30.

54. Ibid.

55. Ibid, 66-67.

56. Peter Arnold Ottaviano, *The Fever of Life: The Story of Peter Charles Remondino*, (San Diego: Peter Arnold Ottaviano, 1992), 4. Thesis submitted for Master of Arts in History. [Thesis is located in the James S. Copley library stacks, University of San Diego.]

57. Ibid, 5.

58. Ibid, 13.

59. Ibid, 23.

SOURCE NOTES (Con't)

60. Ibid, 26.

61. Ibid, 27.

62. Katherine Eitzen Carlin and Raymond Brandes, *Coronado: The Enchanted Island*, (Coronado: Mary and Tim Carlin; Coronado Historical Association, 1987), 18.

63. Ibid, 20.

64. Ibid.

65. Ibid, 23.

66. Ibid, 32.

67. Ibid, 34. [There is an article in the *Southern California Rancher*, August, 1944, called "Memories of Robert J. Pennell," by Frank G. Forward (San Diego Historical Society "Biographical Files"). Pennell is described as "...a person of dynamic energy ... endowed with a marvelous power of oratory and keen sense of humor ... unquestionably the greatest auctioneer and land salesman that ever operated in San Diego. ... Mr. Pennell was employed as the general auctioneer and handled the first auction of lots (for Coronado Beach Company) in October, 1886, and in subsequent auctions held during the years 1887-1889. [He was subsequently] appointed General Manager of ... Pacific Coast Land Bureau. ... One of the larger undertakings ... was the laying out ... and the auctioning of the huge Rancho El Cajon. This auction sale was handled by the redoutable Robert J. Pennell." He also sold land in La Jolla (as mentioned in Don A. Stewart's *Frontier Port: A Chapter in San Diego's History* (Footnote No. 33 above) and elsewhere in San Diego.]

68. Ibid, 35.

69. _____, "Grand Army of the Republic! Soldiers' Home. Grantville! San Diego County, Cal," advertisement in *The Golden Era: An Illustrated Monthly Magazine*, XXXVI (November, 1887), unnumbered page. (See also a two-page article on "Grantville" in this issue.)

70. Junipero Land and Water Company, *Grantville! San Diego County, California, Where the Grand Army of the Republic has a Soldiers' Home: A Descriptive Pamphlet of the Climate, Resources, Topography and Inducements to Settlers*, 10. (Pamphlet at San Diego Historical Society Archives).

71. Ibid, 9-10.

72. Ibid, 11.

73. Map of the location of the campus of the Soldier's Home in Grantville, from "Back to the Boom-Bust 1880's," Navaho News, April 18, 1994, p. 9.

74. Sophie Jaussaud Jackson, "Memories of Grantville, California," Allied Gardens Examiner, January 28, 1960, p. 1.

75. Ibid, "Back to the Boom-Bust 1880's", p. 9.

76. Ibid, McGrew, 185-186.

77. Ibid, Black, Vol. 2, 113-114.

78. Ibid, 291-292.

SOURCE NOTES (Con't)

79. Ibid, 301-302.

80. Ibid, 410, 413.

81. Levi Chase "Biographical File," San Diego Historical Society Archives.

82. Bertha Palmer Wohlers, *Follow the Light: The Palmer Family and the Savoy Theater* (San Diego: Tecolote Press, 1996).

83. Ibid.

84. San Diego Union, "Tenting Tonight on the Old Camp Ground--But There's Not a Heart Weary of Sunny San Diego," January 10, 1932, p. 1, Second Section.

85. San Diego Union, "2 Charter Members of Post Still Alive," October 29, 1933, 12:1.

86. San Diego Union, "Only Four Members of G.A.R. at Luncheon," June 1, 1937, 4:2.

87. San Diego Union, "4 S.D. Vets of Blue and Gray Will March at Gettysburg," June 5, 1938, p. 1.

88. Ibid.

89. Ibid.

90. San Diego Union, "Grand Army Veterans Honored at Luncheon," May 30, 1939, p. 1, Second Section.

91. San Diego Union, "The Past Meets the Present," May 30, 1937, B:1 (showing Arthur Vest holding likeness of himself taken during the Civil War--see photo on p. iv of this study)

92. San Diego Union, "Horace B. Day Will celebrate 90th Birthday Anniversary at Home Today," December 24, 1939, 5:2. (See also San Diego Union, "Horace B. Day, G.A.R. Veteran, Succumbs [yesterday] at 93," June 2, 1943, 11:3).

93. San Diego Sun, "He's 107" ...Hiram Reynolds just celebrated his birthday with a party...," March 11, 1936, 2:4. (See also the San Diego Sun, "Final Retreat: Ex-San Diego Veteran Passes at 107," January 30, 1937, 1:5).

94. San Diego Union, "Ordinance No. 229," September 7, 1893, 7:4.

95. San Diego Union, "Mortar for the G.A.R.: Will Occupy a Prominent Place Near the Soldiers' Graves," December 14, 1897, 5:2.

CHAPTER EIGHT: INDEX OF CIVIL WAR VETERANS AND THEIR WIVES

The index below contains a list of all of the Civil War veterans and their wives who are included in this book, and in several instances the index will also include the parents of some individuals. The page numbers referred to in this index are to the listings of the veterans and their families in Chapter 4 and Chapter 5 of this book. The index also includes the following additional information, where available:

State of Nativity
State of nativity citations appear directly after the names of the individuals in this index. For example, W.F. Abrahams, the first name on the index, was born in Steubensville, OH. At times the only available nativity citation for an individual will be "American", a designation used only on Mount Hope Cemetery records. All citations in the index use the standard abbreviations for states, presented below. City and town names are spelled out using the spelling found on each individual's tombstone, G.A.R., or other record.

State of First Enlistment
State of first enlistment citations, where available, have an "enl" notation, indicating an individual veteran's possible residence at the start of the Civil War. By comparing the state of first enlistment with the state or country of nativity, one can see migration patterns for the soldier and his family of origin from 1840-1860, for the locations often varied. "US" citations indicate a veteran enlisted in the U.S. Regular service; no state of first enlistment could be determined.

Location of a Veteran's Full Record
The index helps to locate an individual veteran's full record in this book. The page numbers in the index may seem oddly arranged. For example, the full record for W.F. Abrahams is found on p. 197 in the book, while the full record for Willis Ackles, the third name on the index, is found on p. 84. This is because the record for Abrahams is in Chapter 5, the list of veterans for whom no burial information could be found in San Diego. Abrahams may still be buried in San Diego, as some cemeteries did not allow full access to their records (see p. 197 for details). The record for Willis Ackles can be found in Chapter 4, where burial information was available. Since this is an all name index, names from the two chapters are combined, thus explaining the odd arrangement of page numbers. Some veterans may also be cited in Chapter 1 and Chapter 3 of this book, but those citations are not included in this index.

Citations with an (??)
Individuals with (??) after their names were individuals for whom no information about nativity or place of first enlistment was available in the sources searched. Most of these veterans are included in the Datus Coon Post G.A.R. intake records as "name only" entries. However, a (??) citation meant that a veteran was in San Diego on a certain date, although the date of entry into the Datus Coon post was not given. Research sources in Chapter 2 should be consulted for further information. Wives with (??) citations were wives whose nativity could not be determined.

State Abbreviations

AL Alabama	KY Kentucky	ND North Dakota
AK Alaska	LA Louisiana	OH Ohio
AZ Arizona	ME Maine	OK Oklahoma
AR Arkansas	MD Maryland	OR Oregon
CA California	MA Massachusetts	PA Pennsylvania
CO Colorado	MI Michigan	RI Rhode Island
CT Connecticut	MN Minnesota	SC South Carolina
DE Delaware	MS Mississippi	SD South Dakota
DC Dist. of Columbia	MO Missouri	TN Tennessee
FL Florida	MT Montana	TX Texas
GA Georgia	NE Nebraska	UT Utah
HI Hawaii	NV Nevada	VT Vermont
ID Idaho	NH New Hampshire	VA Virginia
IL Illinois	NJ New Jersey	WA Washington
IN Indiana	NM New Mexico	WV West Virginia
IA Iowa	NY New York	WI Wisconsin
KS Kansas	NC North Carolina	WY Wyoming

THE INDEX

Abrahams, W.F.--Steubensville, OH--(enl.OH)--197
Ackerman, Frank--France--(enl. IN)--197
Ackles, Willis--MO--(enl. US)--84
Ackley, Adelia (Mrs. Henry J.)--SC--84
Ackley, Henry J.--Steuben, NY--(enl. NY)--84
Adair, Marion--Columbus, OH--(enl. IA)--197
Adams, Calvin J.--MI--(enl. IL)--197
Adams, Frederick F.--OH--(enl. OH)--84
Adams, George--Canada--(enl. US)--84
Adams, Mary Virginia (Mrs. Frederick F.)--CA--84
Adams, Stephen J.--England--(enl. US)--197
Ainsley, G.W.--??--(enl. NV)--197
Albee, Timothy M.--CT--(enl. IN)--198
Alcorn, Robert A.--Beaver, PA--(enl. IA)--198
Alexander, W.F.--ME--(enl. MO)--198
Alford, Robert--IN--(enl. IN)--198
Alhoun, William H.--PA--(enl. IN)--198
Allen, Andrew J.--(enl. US)--84
Allen, Charles Warren--England/Greenville, OH--
    (enl. IN)--85
Allen, Henry E.--Buffalo, NY--(enl. WI)--198
Allen, Horatio D.--Salem, MA--(enl. MA)--198
Allen, John W.--??--198
Allen, Martha J. Ford (Mrs. Andrew J.)--??--84
Allen, Seth S.--CT--(enl. CT)--85
Allen, William--OH--(enl. ME)--198
Allen, William Tankerville--England--(enl. ?)--85
Allen, William W.--IA--(enl. IL)--198
Allum, Leroy W.--PA--(enl. IA)--198
Allum, Rebecca (Mrs. Thomas)--??--85
Allum, Thomas--PA--(enl. IA)--85
Amick, Daniel B.--Mifflin, PA--(enl. PA)--198
Anderson, Mark B.-Reading, PA--(enl. WI)--85
Anderson, William--(enl. NY)--85
Andre, Zacheriah Taylor--PA--(enl. MO)--198
Angier, Albert Warriner--NY--(enl. MN)--85
Angier, Josephine Sumner (Mrs. Albert W.)--??--85
Angstedt, Albert--Reading, PA--(enl. PA)--198
Angstedt, Louise (Mrs. Albert)--??--198
Anthony, Charles E.--Union Springs, NY--
    (enl. NY)--85
Anthony, David R.--PA--(enl. PA)--198
Anthony, Lucy M. or Leny (Mrs. Charles E.)
    --American--86
Antrobus, John C.--Decatur Co, IL--(enl. IA)--86
Antrobus, Margaret Jane (Mrs. John C.)--??--86
Archer, John R.--IN--(enl. IL)--198
Arey, A.R.--ME--(enl. US)--199
Arment, J.A.--Hagentown, IN--(enl. IN)--199
Armstrong, Nelson--Canada--(enl. NY)--199
Arnold, Don J.--OH--(enl. MO)--86
Arnold, E.M.--OH--(enl. MN)--199
Arnold, James M.--Hardy Co, VA--(enl. MO)--199
Asher, Bartlett--IN--(enl. TX)--86
Asher, Cynthia Ann (Mrs. Bartlett)--??--86

Ashton, J.M.--??--199
Ashton, John Quincy--PA--(enl. KS)--86
Ashton, Priscilla D. Hamlin (Mrs. John Q.)--??--86
Atwood, John R.--ME--(enl. VRC)--199
Atwood, Joseph R.--IL--(enl. IL)--86
Augenbaugh, W.L--??--199
Auld, George--Canada--(enl. NY)--199
Austin, Henry C.--DePeyster, NY--(enl. NY)--86
Austin, Julia A. (Mrs. Henry C.)--England--86
Averill, Charles W.--ME--(enl. ME)--199
Avery, Henry J.--(enl. IL)--86
Babcock, Charles H.--ME--(enl. OH)--199
Babcock, Edward A.--NY--(enl. NY)--86
Babcock, Elisha Spurr--Evansville, IN--(enl. ?)--87
Babcock, Fanny Irene (Mrs. Edward A.)--??--86
Babcock, Isabella Graham (Mrs. Elisha S.)--??--87
Bacon, David G.--American--(enl. IL)--87
Baer, Charles J.--Germany--(enl. NJ)--199
Baer, N.--Germany--(enl. MD)--199
Bahl, Clara Edith (Mrs. Perry W.)--??--87
Bahl, Perry William--Wooster, OH--(enl. OH)--87
Bailey, Benjamin E.--WI--(enl. WI)--199
Bailey, Clark Charles--NY--(enl. MI)--87
Bailey, G.W.--OH--(enl. OH)--199
Bailey, Lillie A. (Mrs. Clark Charles)--
    (Ontario, Canada)--87
Bailhache, Adaline A. Brayman or Ada (Mrs.
    William H.)--??--87
Bailhache, William Henry--Chillicothe, OH-(enl. US)-87
Bailiff, E.H./Edward H.--OH--(enl. IN)--199, 200
Baird, Charles A.--(enl. US)--87
Baird, John R.--OH--(enl. OH)--200
Baker, Abbie J. (Mrs. Oscar H.)--??--87
Baker, August Cesar--Belgium--(enl. US)--200
Baker, Edward--England--(enl. NY)--200
Baker, Eldred--NY--(enl. NY)--87
Baker, James--Bloomington, IL--(enl. IL)--200
Baker, Oscar Holmes--WV--(enl. WV)--87
Baldwin, C.W.--??--200
Bales, Dillon--MO--(enl. MO)--200
Ball, Thomas P.--OH--(enl. IN)--200
Banks, Alice F. (Mrs. Horatio) (later Craik)
    --??--88
Banks, Horatio--Canada--(enl. IL)--88
Barber, George--NY--(enl. NY)--200
Barkley, James T.--NY--(enl. NY)--200
Barlow, Alfred--American--(enl. MI)--88
Barnes, Barton N.--(enl. IL)--88
Barnes, Rev. Henry B.--White Oak, Estill Co,
    KY--(enl. IA)--200
Barnes, Ida L. (Mrs. Henry B.)--??--200
Barnes, William H.--NY--(enl. NY)--200
Barnum, Henry P.--Canada--(enl. IL)--200
Barrett, Isaac Stephens--Southport, PA--(enl.
    MN)--88

INDEX (Con't)

Barrett, J.J.--??--200
Barrett, John C.--(enl. VT)--88
Barrett, Louisa E. (Mrs. Isaac S.)--??--88
Barrett, Michael--NJ--(enl. US)--200
Barrett, William H.--Nantucket, MA--(enl. MA)--88
Barrick, William N.--OH--(enl. IA)--88
Barrow, Absolom E.--VA--(enl. Confederate)--88
Barrow, Emma (Mrs. Absolom E.)--VA--88
Barton, R.H.--OH--(enl. OH)--201
Bartwistle, James--??--201
Bassett, Edwin F.--MA--(enl. MA)--201
Bates, Daniel O.--NY--(enl. MI)--201
Bates, R.O.--OH--(enl. IN?)--201
Battles, Edgar C.--Lowell, MA--(enl. MA)--201
Battroff, Margaret E.--??--201
Battroff, Martin P.--Salem, MA--(enl. IN)--201
Battrum, Alexander--England--(enl. IL)--201
Baughman, Henry J.--IL--(enl. IL)--201
Baughman, Samuel K.--IL--(enl. IL)--201
Baxter, Albert Beverly--??--(enl. WI)--88
Baxter, Dana E. or Mandana E. (Mrs. Albert B.) --??--88
Beach, Wade--Fairfield, Wayne Co, IL--(enl. IL)--201
Beam, Joseph C.--PA--(enl. OH)--88
Beam, Margaret J. (Mrs. Joseph C.)--OH--88
Beamer, John--OH--(enl. IL)--89
Beamer, Julia Ann (Mrs. Peter W.)--??--89
Beamer, Mary E. (Mrs. John)--??--89
Beamer, Peter Walker--OH--(enl. IL)--89
Beardsley, John--Newfield, Thompson Co, NY--(enl. NY)--201
Beck, Albert A.--NY--(enl. NY)--201
Beck, Andrew--Germany--(enl. MN)--89
Beck, Emma J. (Mrs. James M.)--??--89
Beck, James Madison--NY--(enl. MI)--89
Beck, Sanford--??--201
Beebe, Daniel L.--NY--(enl. IL)--201
Beebe, Milton E.--NY--(enl. NY)--201
Belding, Lydia M. (Mrs. Sanford W.)--American--89
Belding, Sanford Whitfield--Greenwich, OH--(enl. OH)--89
Bell, Alexander--Canada--(enl. Confederate)--89
Bell, Alonzo--(enl. MN)--202
Bell, G.V./G.U.--(enl. US)--89
Bell, Harrison W.--Wayne Co, MI--(enl. MI)--202
Bell, John B.--Stanford, KY--(enl. IL)--202
Bell, John R.--IN--(enl. IN)--202
Bell, Margaret Phelan (Mrs. Alonzo)--MN? (dau. James & Catherine Phelan)--202
Bell, Mary (Mrs. Alexander)--LA--89
Bell, Samuel V.--PA--(enl. PA)--89
Bennett, Alma (Mrs. Gilbert P.)--??--90

Bennett, Annie B.Mulville (Mrs.DeForest)--??-90
Bennett, DeForest P.--Batavia, NY--(enl. NY)--90
Bennett, Eliza Ann (Mrs. Jesse)--??--90
Bennett, Gilbert P.--NY--(enl. IA)--90
Bennett, Jesse--Harlen Co, OH--(enl. IA)--90
Bennett, William H.--Kokomo, IN--(enl. IN)--202
Bent, Judson--MA--(enl. MA)--202
Bentzel, Carrie Victoria Lithgow/Kate E.? (later Binder?) (Mrs. Henry M.)--IL?--90
Bentzel, Henry M.--Dover, York Co, PA--(enl. IA)--90
Berg, Anton--Austria--(enl. US)--90
Bergman, Jacob--Germany--(enl. US)--202
Berry, Elizabeth (Mrs. Riley)--??--90
Berry, Riley--IL--(enl. IL)--90
Bigelow, Lyman G.--MI--(enl. MI)--202
Bill, Douglas G.--OH--(enl. WI)--202
Billingsley, L.W.--Putnam Co, IN--(enl. IN)--202
Bird, Frank--ME--(enl. MA)--202
Birdsall, S.H.--PA--(enl. PA)--202
Birdseye, E.L. (Enoch)--OH--(enl. OH)--91
Birdseye, Illa (Mrs. Emos) (later Knox)--OH--91
Birmingham, Thomas--(enl. CT)--91
Black, Edwin J.--NJ--(enl. CT)--91
Black, Eudora E. (Mrs. Isaac)--??--91
Black, Isaac--IN--(enl. IN)--91
Blackmer, Eli T.--New Braintree, MA --(enl. MA)--91
Blackmer, Louisa H. (Mrs. Eli T.)--NH--91
Blair, Samuel M.--Harden Co, OH--(enl. IA)--202
Blaisdell, S.G.--VT--(enl. NH)--203
Blake, Persis A. or Amanda Perris (Mrs. Robert W.)--VT--91
Blake, Robert Walter--England--(enl. IL)--91
Blakely, Joseph H.--OH--(enl. IA)--203
Blanchard, George A.--American--(enl. MO)--91
Blanchard, Margaret Jane (Mrs. George A.)--OH--91
Blanchard, Oliver C.--OH--(enl. OH)--203
Blankinhom, William F.--Germany--(enl. PA)--203
Bleeck/Bleak Oscar W.--Germany--(enl. NY)--203
Blodgett, Clark A.--NY--(enl. NY)--203
Bogardus, Byron Frank--NY--(enl. IL)--92
Bogardus, Kittie (Mrs. Byron F.)--??--92
Bogart, C.F.--NY--(enl. NY)--203
Bogart, Elias Fetheringale--OH--(enl. OH)--92
Bogart, Elizabeth Jane (Mrs. Elias F.)--??--92
Bohanan, Sylvester Lee--ME--(enl. MN)--92
Bolster, Robert--(enl. US)--92
Bolting, Charles J.--Portland, ME--(enl. US) --203
Boodry, Elizabeth (Mrs. George O.)--England--92
Boodry, George O.--MA--(enl. MA)--92
Booth, George H.--NY--(enl. NY)--203
Booth, Oliver T.--OH--(enl. KS)--92
Bortel, Peter--??--203
Boscher, Emil H.--Germany--(enl. MO)--92

INDEX (Con't)

Boscher, Ida (Mrs. Emil H.)--Germany--92
Botruff, M.F.--??--203
Boutwell, William T.--NH--(enl. NH)--203
Bowen, John W.--Wales--(enl. IA)--203
Bowen, W.T.--IN--(enl. VA)--203
Bowers, Lucy Horton (Mrs. William W.)--WI?--92
Bowers, William Wallace--NY--(enl. WI)--92
Bowman, John H.--NY--(enl. NY)--203
Boyd, David O.--PA--(enl. DE)--203
Boyd, John B.--Northumberland, PA--(enl. IL)--92
Boyette, Lucinda A. (Mrs. William J.H.)--??--93
Boyette, William James H.--(enl. KY)--93
Brabazon, George P.A.--Ireland--(enl. ??)--93
Brabazon, Rhoda Jane (Mrs. George P.A.)--Ireland--93
Bradley, Frances William--MO--(enl. MO)--93
Bradley, Garrett R.--OH--(enl. IA)--93
Bradt, Jacob A.--NY--(enl. NY)--203
Bradwell, Alexander N.--American--(enl. Confederate)--93
Bragg, A.L.--ME--(enl. ME)--204
Brandis, William--Germany--(enl. CO)--204
Brandley, Arnold--Switzerland--(enl. OH)--204
Brandt, Otto--Germany--(enl. IL)--204
Branson, James--Muncie, IN--(enl. MO)--204
Bray, John--Morgan Co, IN--(enl. MO)--204
Brayton, George--NY--(enl. MN)--93
Breedlove, R.D.--MO--(enl. MO)--204
Brenard, Frederick--Auburn, Crawford Co, OH--(enl. OH)--204
Brenner, George A.--Wertenberg, Germany--(enl. US)--93
Brenner, Mary E. (Mrs. George A.)--??--93
Brewer, Joseph C./G.--(enl. IL)--93
Brewington, James B.--IN--(enl. IN)--93
Bridges, Otis S.--ME--(enl. WI)--204
Briggs, W.S.--PA--(enl. PA)--204
Brimm, Boyd P.--England/Indiana--(enl. IA)--94
Brimm, Mary Hammond (Mrs. Boyd P.)--??--94
Brink, Thomas Edward--??--94
Brinkman, Henry F.--Germany--(enl. NY)--94
Bristinstine, Matthias--Mercer Co, OH--(enl.IL)--204
Britton, Katherine (Mrs. Thomas)--??--94
Britton, Thomas--England--(enl. US)--94
Brobst, Albert M.--Catarwissa, PA--(enl. IA)--204
Brody, Paul E.--(enl. NV)--94
Brook, James F.--(enl. IN)--204
Brooks, John B./P.--Franklin Co, IN--(enl. IN)--94
Brooks, John H.--York Co, PA--(enl. IA)--204
Brooks, John L.--(enl. MN)--94
Brooks, Lydia (Mrs. John L.)--??--94
Broughton, George W.--"on shipboard"--(enl. US)--94
Broughton, John B.--NY--(enl. PA)--205
Brouhard, George B.--Boone Co, IN--(enl. IA)--94

Brown, Atlanta (Mrs. George)--??--94
Brown, Benjamin W.--NY--(enl. WI)--205
Brown, Carleton L.--Edwardsburg, MI--(enl. MI)--205
Brown, Charles A.--ME--(enl. MN)--205
Brown, George--England--(enl. WI)--94
Brown, J.H.--Wyandot, OH--(enl. OH)--205
Brown, James Devoe--(enl. IN)--95
Brown, James Edwin--Ireland--(enl. PA)--95
Brown, John B.--Crawford Co, OH--(enl. OH)--95
Brown, Lyman--Wyoming Co, NY--(enl. MI)--205
Brown, Max--IL--(enl. MO)--205
Brown, Rodney D.--MA--(enl. US)--205
Browne, William S.--NY--(enl. IL)--205
Browning, Sarah Ann (Mrs. Thomas N.)--OH--95
Browning, Thomas Newton--Harrison Co, OH--(enl. IL)--95
Brownlee, Alex--IA--(enl. IA)--205
Brunemer, James H.--OH--(enl. WI)--205
Bruner, Adam B.--Woodville, IN--(enl. KS)--205
Brunner, Leo F.--France--(enl. OH)--205
Bryan, Mary Ellen (Mrs. Solon)--??--95
Bryan, Solon--OH--(enl. IL)--95
Bryan, William--Brantford, Canada--(enl. US)--205
Bryant, Elden S.--NY--(enl. MI)--95
Bryant, Nora Daley (Mrs. Richard)--??--95
Bryant, Richard--Ireland--(enl. CA)--95
Buck, Anna/Eliza Anna (Mrs. Nathan)--American--95
Buck, Elijah--NY--(enl. IL)--205
Buck, Nathan--NY--(enl. US/IL)--95
Buckley, Joseph--England--(enl. IL)--96
Buckley, Mary (Mrs. Joseph)--England--96
Buckley, Michael--(enl. US)--96
Budlong, David H.--NY--(enl. WI)--96
Budlong, Martha D. (Mrs. David H.) (later Gruell?)--??--96
Bumpus, Ella M. (Mrs. William B.)--??--96
Bumpus, William Bates--MA--(enl. US)--96
Burbeck, Lucius D.--East Canada--(enl. MA)--96
Burch, Grenville L.--(enl. IL)--96
Burgess, William--Bucks Co, PA--(enl. PA)--206
Burgoyne, Charles--VA--(enl. Confederate)--96
Burk, Benjamin H.--NY--(enl. NY)--96
Burk, Phoebe (Mrs. Benjamin H.)--??--96
Burk, William--Charlton, Saratoga Co, NY--(enl. WI)--206
Burke, C.M.--PA--(enl. PA)--206
Burkhard, Effie E. (Mrs. Fred)--??--96
Burkhard, Fred--Switzerland--(enl. IL)--96
Burnap, Silas A.--OH--(enl. OH)--206
Burnham, Charles W.--Routt Co, CO--??--97
Burnham, E.H.--NY--(enl. US)--206
Burns, A.J.--OH--(enl. OH)--206
Burns, Thomas J.--NH--(enl. NH)--206
Burr, Charles M.--Norfolk, CT--(enl. CT)--206

INDEX (Con't)

Burr, Lydia Barton (Mrs. Charles)--Milford, DE?--206
Burt, John P.--Franklinville, NY--(enl. US)--206
Burton, Henry J.--Charleston, NH--(enl. MI)--97
Butler, Benjamin A.--IN--(enl. MA)--97
Butler, Jennie Adele Ervin (Mrs. Robert H.) --??--97
Butler, Orpha (Mrs. Benjamin A.)--??--97
Butler, Robert Harris--Oakland, Jefferson Co, WI--(enl. WI)--97
Butschli, Jacob--Obeupp, Canton of Berne, Switzerland--(enl. NE/IL)--97
Byers, John T.--OH--(enl. IA)--206
Cadman, James P.--MI--(enl. MI)--206
Cahoon/Cahon, Charles--Portland, ME--(enl. MI)--97
Caldwell, John G.--IL--(enl. US)--97
Calkins, Anna Mary (Mrs. Joel P.)--??--97
Calkins, Joel P.--Hancock Co, IL--(enl. IL)--97
Callaghan, Patrick--Ireland--(enl. WI)--98
Camacho, Elena Valenzuela or Valencia (Mrs. Lorenzo)--??--98
Camacho (Comacho), Lorenzo--??--(enl. CA)--98
Camp, Guy R.--PA--(enl. IA)--206
Camp, James H.--Bradford Co, PA--(enl. PA)--207
Campbell, B.P.--MD--(enl. CA)--207
Campbell, David--OH--(enl. OH)--207
Campbell, George A.--NY--(enl. PA)--98
Campbell, John T.--Mt. Carmel, IL--(enl. OR)--98
Campbell, Milton K.--OH--(enl. IA)--207
Canfield, William J.--NY--(enl. NY)--207
Capps/Gapps, Augusta(tine) Skelley Kilborne (Mrs. Thomas J.)--??--98
Capps, Thomas J.--TN--(enl. TN)--98
Capsel/Capsul, Lewis--France--(enl. IL)--98
Carey, George W.--(enl OR)--98
Carlin, Patrick--NY--(enl. NH)--98
Carls, Frank--Providence, RI--(enl. NY)--207
Carmichael, Jacob Elson--IL--(enl. NE)--98
Carmichael, Sarah T. (Mrs. Jacob E.)--??--99
Carpenter, Albert--OH--(enl. MI)--207
Carpenter, Charles D.--(enl OH)--99
Carpenter, Maria H. or Hannah Maria (Mrs. Charles D.)--??--99
Carpenter, Stephen H.--Gennessee, NY--(enl. CA)--207
Carpinter, H.L.--NY--(enl. NY)--207
Carter, John H.--IL--(enl. IL)--207
Cary, Charles A.--NY--(enl. NJ)--207
Casebeer, W.J.--OH--(enl. OH)--207
Casey, Louise E.H. (Mrs. Patricius H.)--??--99
Casey, Patricius H.--Ireland--(enl. MA)--99
Casey, Wilson--West Canada--(enl. MI)--207
Casteel, Reubin S.--TN--(enl. MO)--99
Castle, William D.--MI--(enl. US)--99

Catlin, John--(enl NY)--99
Cavileer, John Charles--NJ--(enl. NJ)--99
Cavileer, Sarah (Mrs. John C.)--Scotland--99
Center, Lewis W.--NY--(enl. NY)--99
Chalfant, Alfred--Chester Co, PA--(enl. PA)--99
Chalfant, Josephine Stewart (Mrs. Alfred)--??--99
Chamberlin, Jacob--Addison, MI--(enl. NY)--207
Chaney, O.F.--NY--(enl. VT)--207
Chapman, Ella Ewing or Mary (Mrs. George B.)--American--100
Chapman, Fannie L. (Mrs. Joseph)--??--100
Chapman, George B.--IN--(enl. IN)--99
Chapman, Jennie (Mrs. Joseph M.) (later Barkley?)--??--100
Chapman, Joseph--(enl. WI)--100
Chapman, Joseph M.--(enl. IA)--100
Chard, James J.--Cleveland, OH--(enl. CA)--100
Charland, Maxim--NY--(enl. US)--207
Chase, Charles E.--ME--(enl. ME)--207
Chase, Charles M.--Canada/NY--(enl. MI)--100
Chase, Cornelia King (Mrs. Levi)--Morristown, NJ--208
Chase, Elizabeth Wheeler (Mrs. Levi)--??--208
Chase, Levi--ME--?? (son of Moses Chase, Mass. & Sarah Greenlaw, Canada--208
Chase, Samuel D.--MI--(enl. MI)--208
Chase, Sarah Ann (Mrs. Charles M.)--??--100
Chase, Thurston Purdy--Manchester, VT--(enl.IA)--100
Chatfield, James L.--Barton, OH--(enl. OH)--208
Chenault, Leo O.--VA--(enl. MS)--100
Chester, D.R.--OH--(enl. IL)--208
Chilcott, E.--PA--(enl. IL)--208
Childs, Benjamin F.--OH--(enl. IL)--208
Chrisman, Leonard--IN--(enl. IA)--208
Christopher, William Henry--Northfield, NY--(enl. IL)--100
Clapp, E.S.--Lawrence Co, NY--(enl. IL)--208
Clark, Charles E.--IN--(enl. IN)--208
Clark, Dillard H.--KY--(enl. KY)--208
Clark, Edwin A.--PA--(enl. NJ)--100
Clark, George (AKA Robert C. Clark)--NY--(enl. OR)--101
Clark, J.C.--IN--(enl. IL)--208
Clark, James S.--Johnson Co, IN--(enl. IA)--208
Clark, James S.--PA--(enl. PA)--208
Clark, John J.--NY--(enl. US)--208
Clark, Martha A. (Mrs. Edwin A.)--??--100
Clark, Newton Ambrose--PA--(enl. KS)--101
Clark, Sheldon C.--PA--(enl. MN)--209
Clark, William A.--IN--(enl. IN)--209
Clark, William L.--Boston, MA--(enl. MA)--101
Clarke, Frank--IL--(enl. IA)--209
Clemens, Carl--??--209
Cleveland, Charlotte Ann (Mrs. James S.)-OH--101

INDEX (Con't)

Cleveland, James S.--Hornellsville, NY--(enl. IL)--101
Cleveland, Lewis C.--Barron Co,IL--(enl.CA)--101
Clevenger, Benjamin C.--Macoupin, IL--(enl. IL)--101
Cline, Joseph Henry--IL--(enl. IL)--101
Cline, Luvica Jane (Mrs. Joseph H.)--??--101
Clothier, W.B.--??--209
Coan, Henry Clay--OH--(enl. OH)--101
Coats, Henry--England--(enl. CA)--209
Coffeen, Elizabeth E. (Mrs. Lewis/Louis)--NY--101
Coffeen, Lewis/Louis--??--101
Coffey, John--??--209
Coggswell, Thomas--NH--(enl. MA)--209
Colbert, Robert--NY--(enl. WI)--209
Colby, Lloyd H.--NH--(enl. WI)--209
Cole, John C.--(enl. PA)--102
Cole, W.I.--Canada--(enl. MI)--209
Colebaker, Samuel---Hagerstown, MD--(enl. IN)--102
Coleman, Delphine (Mrs. John)--??--102
Coleman, Mrs. Ezekial A.?--??--102
Coleman, Ezekial A.--American--(enl. US)--102
Coleman, John--Ireland--(enl. NY)--102
Coleman, Levi B.--NY--(enl. MI)--102
Coleman, Patrick--Ireland--(enl. WI)--209
College, James, Jr.--Northampton, England--(enl. NY)--102
College, Mary B. (Mrs. James)--??--102
Collier, J.H.--OH--(enl. MI)--209
Collins, John T.--VA--(enl. DE)--209
Collins, Lewis Rapalee--(enl. IL)--102
Collins, Margaret Bolles or Margaret Vesta (Mrs. Lewis R.)--??--102
Combe, Francis M.--(enl. MO)--102
Comer, Allen--Hutton Co, OH--(enl. OH)--209
Comings, J.H.--NJ--(enl. NJ)--209
Comings/Cummings, L.B.--American--(enl. US)--102
Comings, Mary T. (Mrs. L.B.)--American--102
Commo, Rubin--New Brunswick--(enl. ??)--102
Comstock, John--NY--(enl. IL)--102
Cone, William A.--Athens Co, OH--(enl. OH)--209
Confer, Della L. (Mrs. John W.)--??--103
Confer, John W.--Miamisburg, OH--(enl. OH)--103
Conklin,Myra Isabelle Reese(Mrs. Norman H.)--IN--103
Conklin, Norman Henry--Wyoming Co, PA--(enl. KY/US)--103
Connell, Cornelius--(enl. KS)--103
Conner, Samuel P.--Vernon Co, IN--(enl. IL)--210
Connor, James--Ireland--(enl. US)--210
Connors, John--Ireland--(enl. US)--210
Cook, Augustus--NY--(enl. NY)--210
Cook, George H.--MA--(enl. WI)--103

Cook, Henry--OH--(enl. OH)--103
Cook, Jacob L.--Wallingford, VT--(enl. VT)--210
Cook, Joseph--Austria--(enl. IL)--210
Cook, Mary D. (Mrs. Henry)--??--103
Coon, Datus E.--DeRuyter, Madison Co, NY--(enl. IA)--103
Coonwell, Robert--NY--(enl. IL)--210
Cooper, Anna B.(Mrs. Daniel C. (Noyes?)--??--103
Cooper, Catherine E. (Mrs. J.B.)--??--104
Cooper, Daniel C.--OH--(enl. OH)--103
Cooper, J.B.--PA--(enl. WI)--104
Cooper, Jesse--Leesburg, OH--(enl. IA)--210
Copeland, W.A.--??--210
Corben, James G.--OH--(enl. IN)--210
Cordes, Charles S.--St. Josephs, MO--(enl. MO)--210
Corey, Albert W.--WI--(enl. WI)--210
Costello, Mary (Mrs. Thomas)--??--104
Costello, Thomas--American--(enl. CT)--104
Cotton, Della Loretta (Mrs. John L.)--??--104
Cotton, John L.--IN--(enl. IA)--104
Couchman, E.H.--IN--(enl. IA)--210
Courtney, James--County Kerry, Ire.--(enl. MA)--104
Courtney, Julia (Mrs. James)--??--104
Coutant, Jacob Benson--NY--(enl. IN)--104
Coutant, Sarah E. (Mrs. Jacob B.)--??--104
Couts, Senaca P.--Boston, MA--(enl. WI)--211
Cowan, Allen--??--211
Cowels, Frederick H.--IL--(enl. CA)--211
Cox, Isaac S.--OH--(enl. IN)--211
Craig, George W.--IL--(enl. IL)--211
Craigo, Annie E. (Mrs. Joseph M.)--??--104
Craigo, Joseph M.--(enl. WI)--104
Crane, Luther Kent--MA--(enl. CO)--104
Crane, Mary A. (Mrs. Luther K.)--American--104
Crater, Cornelius--NY--(enl. NY)--211
Cravath, J.B.--PA--(enl. IA)--211
Craw, Frank W.--NY--(enl. WI)--211
Crippen, George Henry--Oswego, NY--(enl. NY)--104
Crippen, Melissa Charlotte (Mrs. Geo. H.)--??--104
Crittenden, Thomas T.--AL--(enl. IN)--211
Crockett, Ellen Shook (Mrs. John)--??--105
Crockett, John--OH--(enl. OH)--105
Croghan, Thomas--??--211
Crombie, L.J.--Scotland--(enl. NV)--211
Cromwell, Robert--NY--(enl. IL)--105
Crook, George H.--CT--(enl. CT)--211
Crosby, T.W.--??--211
Cross, Harlow A.--Champlain, NY--(enl. NY)--211
Crouch, George--??--211
Culp, John W.--IL--(enl. NE)--211
Cummings, Georgiana Louisa (Mrs. Wallace)--??--105
Cummings, Wallace E.--ME--(enl. ME)--105
Cundall, Benjamin M.--IL--(enl. IL)--212
Cunningham, Ida V. (Mrs. Windsor T.)--NY--105

INDEX (Con't)

Cunningham, Windsor T.--Albany, NY--(enl. NY)--105
Curby, Augustus W.--PA--(enl. WI)--105
Curby, Norma or Nora (Mrs. William F.)--??--105
Curby, William Franklin--Chester Co, PA--(enl. WI) --105
Cureton, David--(enl. MO)--105
Currier, Charles F.--American--(enl. IA)--105
Curtis, David G.--Oneida, NY--(enl. IA)--105
Curtis, Mary Ellen (Mrs. Nathaniel A.)--??--106
Curtis, Nathaniel A.--Allen Co, Ohio--(enl. OH)--106
Cushing, Allen D.--Aurora, IL--(enl. IL)--212
Cushman, Edmond S.--Ogle Co, IL--(enl. IL)--212
Dailey, Orin V.--New Brunswick--(enl. NE)--106
Daily, Edwin V.--Camden, ME--(enl. ME)--106
Daily/Dailey, Mary (Mrs. Edwin V.)--RI--106
Dakin, Horace E.--NY--(enl. OH)--212
Dale, John H.--NY--(enl. VRC)--212
Daley, Francis H.--PA--(enl. MO)--212
Daly, Francis--Philadelphia, PA--(enl. PA)--106
Dame, Luther--ME--(enl. MA)--212
Dampf, Louis--Germany--(enl. NY)--212
Dana, William--OH--(enl. MO)--212
Dann, Edward F.--Stanford, CT--(enl. WI)--212
Dannals, George M.--Rochester, NY--(enl. NY)--106
Dannals, Lucy L. (Mrs. George M.)--??--106
Darkes, William W.--IN--(enl. IN)--212
Darling, Charles W.--(enl. NY)--106
Darling, Horace--NY--(enl. MO)--106
Darling, Marcella Elizabeth Rolph (Mrs. Charles W.)--??--106
Darling, Mary E. (Mrs. Horace)--American--106
Darr, Milton B.--PA--(enl. IL)--106
Darr, Susan Elixa (Mrs. Milton B.)--??--106
Darrough, James W.--KY--(enl. IL)--212
Dauchey, Arthur H.--CT--(enl. MN)--213
Davidson (Davison), Hanna S. (Mrs. Henry O.) --??--107
Davidson (Davison), Henry O.--South Hadley, MA --(enl. MA)--107
Davidson, John M.--KY--(enl. KY)--107 and 213
Davis, Alice E. (Mrs. Stephen M.)--??--107
Davis, Charles S.--OH--(enl. TN)--213
Davis, Edwin P.--VA--(enl. MD)--213
Davis, Frances E. (Mrs. William H.)--??--108
Davis, George Perkins--Kinsman, OH--(enl. OH) --107
Davis, I.R./J.R.--Wales--(enl. PA)--213
Davis, John Henry--SC--(enl. DE)--107
Davis, Josiah--(enl.IL)--107
Davis, L. Murry--IN--(enl. IN)--107
Davis, Leonard F.--VT--(enl. WI)--213
Davis, Ruth C. (Mrs. George P.)--??--107
Davis, Sarah E. (Trimble) (Mrs. Leonard F.)--?? --213

Davis, Stephen Melvin--NY--(enl. VA)--107
Davis, Walker--Garrett Co, KY--(enl. US)--107
Davis, Wilber F.--Watertown, NY--(enl. IL)--213
Davis, William H.--(enl. MI)--108
Day, Horace B.--Newton, NH or Haverhill, MA--(enl. MA)--108
Day, Joshua Davis--MA--(enl. MA)--108
Day, Mary Elizabeth (Mrs. William G.)--??--108
Day, Mary Louise (Mrs. Joshua D.)--??--108
Day, Mary R. (Mrs. Horace B.)--??--108
Day, William G.--American--(enl. IL)--108
Dayton, Harriet (Mrs. Richard T.)--??--108
Dayton, Richard Thomas--East Cambridge, MA--(enl. US)--108
Deakins, Henry C.--IL--(enl. IL)--213
Deasdorff, William P.--Des Moines, IA--(enl. CA)--213
Deash, Jacob N.--PA--(enl. PA)--213
DeBurn, Eugene--Harrison Co, OH--(enl. OH)--108
DeBurn, Mamie Albee (Mrs. Eugene)--??--108
DeFord, Emma (Mrs. Thomas J.)--??--108
DeFord, Thomas J.--IN--(enl. IN)--108
Dennison, A.R.--ME--(enl. MA)--108
Denny, Eliza M.--IN--(enl. IN)--213
Derbyshere, William H.--Putnam Co, NY-(enl. NY)--213
DeShanaway, John--OH--(enl. OH)--109
Desmont/Dermont, Charles E.--Detroit, MI--(enl. OH) --213
Detrick, Frank--Prussia--(enl. CO)--213
Devoe, Joseph George--(enl. MA)--109
Diamond, Charles W., Ira K. & Levi W., sons of Ira & Lucy Diamond, Concord, NH, (enl. NH)--213, 214
Dibble, Belle M. (Mrs. Edwin D.)--??--109
Dibble, Edwin D.--MO--(enl. IA)--109
Dickens, Charles--??--214
Dickson/Dixon, George W.--PA--(enl. PA)--109
Dickson, J.F.--MA--(enl. CA)--109
Dickson, Mary Stearns (Mrs. J.F.)--American--109
Dill, Albert F.--MA--(enl. MA)--109
Dill, Isabelle Gay (Mrs. Albert F.)--??--109
Dillingham, Clara C. (Mrs. John)--??--109
Dillingham, John--MA--(enl. US)--109
Dissinger, David--Napuville, IL--(enl. IL)--214
Dixon, Henry G.--American--(enl. PA)--109
Dixon, R.L.--TN--(enl. IL)--214
Dodderidge, John H.--England--(enl. US)--214
Dodge, John G.--NH--(enl. IL)--214
Dodge, Richard Varick--Koskia, IL--(enl. US)--109
Dodge, Sarah E. (Mrs. Richard V.)--MD--110
Dodson, Alonzo E.--??--110
Dodson, Nannie J. (Mrs. Alonzo E.)--??--110
Doesser, Horace--NY--(enl. MN)--214
Doig, John R.--??--110
Doig, Nell E.--??--110
Dolph, Franklin--American--(enl. WI)--110

INDEX (Con't)

Donaldson, Cyrus--(enl. IN)--110
Donovan, J.W.--Oswego Co, NY--(enl. PA)--214
Donovan, M.--??--214
Dooley, Nate Edward--(enl. US)--110
Dooley, Patrick--Ireland--(enl. US)--110
Dorey, Westly B.--MO--(enl. IL)--214
Dorris, William A.--TN--(enl. CA)--214
Dort, Emma Jane Gabriel (Mrs. Levi M.)--??--110
Dort, Levi Morrison--Beechtown, Onion? Co, OH--(enl. IL)--110
Dorward, William H.--England--(enl. WI)--214
Dostal, James C.--Bohemia--(enl. IA)--214
Douay, Francis--VT--(enl. MA)--110
Dougherty, Louis C.--Westmoreland, PA--(enl. IL)--214
Douis, Walker--??--214
Dow, Francis I.--Wayne Co, PA--(enl. WI)--214
Downs, "Mother" (Mrs. Nathan)--??--214
Downs, Nathan H.--VT--(enl. WI)--214
Dryden, Francis Emily Hill (Mrs. James L.)--??--111
Dryden, James L.--Pigria, Miami Co, OH--(enl. IL)--110
Duffy, George M.--Belmont Co, OH--(enl. WV)--111
Duffy, W.E.--(enl. PA)--111
Duling, John--Coshocton Co, OH--(enl. NE)--215
Dumford, I.S.--American--(enl. IL)--111
Dunham, George B.--IN--(enl. IN)--215
Dunn, W.T.--IN--(enl. IN)--215
Duvall, Hansine O.G. (Mrs. William H.)--??--215
Duvall, William H.--AR--(enl. OH)--215
Dye, Bloomfield U.--MI--(enl. MI)--215
Dye, John W.--MI--(enl. IL)--215
Eagan, Michael I.--Newfoundland--(enl. MO)--111
Eagle, J.O.--MD--(enl. MD)--215
Eardley, Josiah--Derbyshire, England--(enl. UT)--215
Earle, Francis Sobieski--New York City--(enl. MI)--111
Earle, Harriet Frances Miller (Mrs. Francis S.)--Branford, CT--111
Easling, Henry L.--IA--(enl. IA)--215
Eastman, Gilman E.--York Co, ME--(enl. ME)--215
Eastman, H.D.--Manlius, NY--(enl. NY)--215
Eastman, Joseph--(enl. IL)--111
Easton, Martha Lee (Mrs. Orlando W.)--??--111
Easton, Orlando W.--(enl. US)--111
Eaton, Avery W.--ME--(enl. ME)--112
Eaton, Benjamin--MA--(enl. MA)--215
Eaton, Vianna (Mrs. Avery W.)--??--112
Edgar, James A.--Mumfordsville, Hunt Co, KY--(enl. IL)--215
Edginton, Mary Wykoff (Mrs. Thomas J.)--??--112
Edginton, Thomas Jefferson--OH--(enl. IA)--112
Edwards, Augustus--WV--(enl. VA)--112
Edwards, John W.--KY--(enl. IN)--215
Edwards, Nathan--CT--(enl. CT)--216
Eggleston, H.J.--England--(enl. WI)--216
Eighmy, Durinda Christina (Mrs. Philip H.)--??--112
Eighmy, Philip H.--Middletown, Delaware Co, NY--(enl. NY)--112
Elford, Peter--England--(enl. KS)--112
Ellibee, Erastus T.--Dayton, OH or Phillipsburg, OH--(enl. IN)--216
Elliot, Robert J.--??--216
Ellis, Alvin R.--ME--(enl. ME)--216
Ellis, Clara D. (Mrs. Thomas G.)--??--112
Ellis, Horace F.--??--112
Ellis, Thomas G.--England--(enl. WI)--112
Ellsworth, Chandler W.--NY--(enl. IA)--112
Ellsworth, Helen (Mrs. Chandler W.)--??--112
Elmer, Parmenus--Allegheny Co, NY--(enl. IL)--112
Elmer, Francis M. (Mrs. Parmenus)--??--113
Embler, James W.--Rome, NY--(enl. NY)--216
Emerson, George D.--American--(enl. MI)--113
Emery, H.U.--Rockland, ME--(enl. NV)--113
Emery, Herbert L.--Rockland, ME--(enl. CA)--113
Emery, J.S.--American--(enl. CA)--113
Emery, Lucy S. (Mrs. H.U.)--American--113
Emiron, George W.--PA--(enl. PA)--216
Emmons, Ira J.--NY--(enl. NY)--216
Endly, C.F.--OH--(enl. OH)--216
Engle, C.B.--??--216
Englehorn, John K.--Germany--(enl. IA)--216
Enoch, Charles--(enl. WI)--113
Erickson, Mathias--Sweden--(enl. IL)--216
Erion, Jacob B.--OH--(enl. OH)--113
Erwin, James--??--216
Esleek/Esleck, Isaac A.--Washington, D.C.--(enl. RI)--216
Estay, Amos--Canada--(enl. WI)--216
Eubanks, J.J.--TN--(enl. IL)--216
Evans, John H.--(enl. IN)--113
Evans, Marietta (Mrs. Philip H.)--??--113
Evans, Mary Barton (Mrs. John H.)--??--113
Evans, Philip H.--NY--(enl. US)--113
Evans, William V.--MO--(enl. MO)--216
Ewing, Edward--NY--(enl. MI)--217
Ewing, William E.--Goforth, KY--(enl. IN)--217
Fabian, Caroline Elizabeth (Mrs. Otto E.)--??--113
Fabian, Otto E.--Germany--(enl. MI)--113
Fairbanks, Albert F.--MA--(enl. MA)--114
Fairbanks, Martha (Mrs. Albert F.)--Sweden--114
Falkenstein, John--WV--(enl. WV)--217
Farley, Joseph--Gallatin Co, IL--(enl. IA)--114
Farnsworth, Rachel (Mrs. Robert N.)--??--114
Farnsworth, Robert N.--IN--(enl. IA)--114
Farris, J.M.--(enl. MN)--114
Farrow, D.S.--OH--(enl. WV)--217

INDEX (Con't)

Farrow, Elizabeth F. (Mrs. Stephen F.)--??--114
Farrow, Stephen French--IL--(enl. IL)--114
Fassett, Charles B.--Sanderson, MI--(enl. MI)--217
Faulk, Marcus D.--GA--(enl. Confederate)--114
Faulk, Margaret E. (Mrs. Marcus D.)--??--114
Fay, William A.--Grafton, MA--(enl. WI)--217
Feathers, D.H.--Canada--(enl. WI)--217
Fell, Aurelius--Orangeville, OH--(enl. PA)--114
Fell, Minnie L. (Mrs. Aurelius)--??--114
Ferdon, Charles M.--MI--(enl. MI)--114
Ferris, Arlene Marling or Adeline/Addie Clare (Mrs. Edmond)--??--115
Ferris, Edmond--OH--(enl. IN)--115
Ferris/Ferres, John Charles--Cohengo Forks, NY--(enl. CO)--115
Ferry, Charles H.--WI--(enl. WI)--115
Ferry, Susan A. (Mrs. Charles H.)--??--115
Fesler, William H.--IA--(enl. IN)--217
Field, Anna M. McGaffey or McGaffery (Mrs. Putnam)--Stansted, Quebec, Canada--115
Field, Putnam--Leverett, MA--(enl. NY)--115
Field, William B.--Chicago, IL--(enl. IL)--217
Finch, William W.--NY--(enl. IN)--115
Finley, Kellogg B.--NY--(enl. NY)--115
Finley, Louise Upton (Mrs. Kellogg B.)--??--115
Fitch, Edwin Peabody--Bridgeton, ME--(enl. ME)--115
Fitch, Elizabeth Powers (Mrs. Edwin P.)--??--115
Fitzgerald, Charles R.--NJ--(enl. NJ)--217
Fitzgerald, Edmond--Ireland--(enl. IL)--116
Fitzgerald, Nathan W.--Ripley Co, IN--(enl. IN)--217
Fitzgerald, Robert V.--NY--(enl. NY)--116
Fitzgerald, Thomas--Brewer, ME--(enl. ME)--116
Fitzpatrick, W.--Canada--(enl. CA)--217
Flamming/Flammang/Flammage, John--Belgium--(enl. WI)--116
Fletcher, B.F.--Troy, ME--(enl. ME)--217
Fletcher, Henry H.--NY--(enl. IA)--218
Flinn/Flynn, Daniel L.--(enl. IN)--116
Fogarty, Ellen (Mrs. Patrick)--??--116
Fogarty, Patrick--(enl. PA)--116
Folkin, Samuel J.--Montreal, Canada--(enl. US)--218
Folks, John H.--OH--(enl. IL)--218
Folsum, Edward C.--Gray, ME--(enl. US)--218
Fonda, John G.--NY--(enl. IL)--218
Foot, F.J.--CT--(enl. WI)--218
Foote, Andrew J.B.--OH--(enl. OH)--218
Foote, John Ward--Rushville, Yates Co, NY--(enl. NY)--116
Foote, Lenora (Mrs. John W.)--??--116
Foote, Thomas J.--England--(enl. IA)--218
Forbes, David--(enl. CT)--116
Ford, Daniel Boon--MO--(enl. MO)--116
Ford, Sarah Maria (Mrs. Daniel B.)--??--116

Forest, Harry Clay.--Philadelphia, PA--(enl. PA)--218
Forker, Oliver H.P.--Clinton, Beaver Co, PA--(enl. IL)--116
Forsythe, Thomas Hall--CT--(enl. PA)--117
Fortesque, Margaret Hook (Mrs. William M.)--??--117
Fortesque, William M.--??--117
Fortier, Zephraim--(enl. NH)--218
Fosnot, Hiram H.--PA--(enl. OH)--218
Foster, Nehemiah D.--ME--(enl. IL)--218
Fowler, Elijah P.--Rochester, NY--(enl. NY)--218
Fox, Joseph--PA--(enl. PA)--218
Fralich, Zachariah--Canada--(enl. NY)--117
Francis, William H.--MI--(enl. MI)--218
Frank, Almira (Mrs. Alonzo)--??--117
Frank, Alonzo--Troy, NY--(enl. IL)--117
Franklin, Robert Calvin--SC--(enl. AL)--117
Frantz, Henry--PA--(enl. IA)--219
Frasier, Peter--??--117
Frazell, Warren--Franklin Co, OH--(enl. IL)--219
Frazier, John A.--American--(enl. IN)--117
Fredericks, William M.--Denmark--(enl. NY)--219
Freeborn, Fremont--RI--(enl. US)--117
Freede, Charles William--OH--(enl. OH)--118
Freeman, Charles H.--Charlestown, MA--(enl. US)--118
Freeman, Rebecca C. (Mrs. Charles H.)--MA?--118
Freeman, William--??--219
Frees, Benjamin M.--ME--(enl. WI)--219
French, Alice/Margaret Alice (Mrs. Stephen)--??--118
French, James Milton--Giles Co, VA--(enl. VA)--118
French, Stephen--IL--(enl. IL)--118
Frew, David Webster or David F.--PA--(enl. PA)--118
Frew, Mary Jane (Mrs. David W./F.)--??--118
Friend, James Edward--American--(enl. ??)--118
Froelich, Godfrey F.W.--Germany--(enl. IL)--118
Fry, Edward J.--IL--(enl. IN)--219
Fry, George--England--(enl. Confederate/TX?)--118
Fuller, Andrew J.--MI--(enl. MI)--219
Fuller, Boyd--(enl. MA)--118
Fullerton, Amanda J. (Mrs. James S.)--PA--119
Fullerton, James S.--PA--(enl. PA)--119
Gaches, William Henry--(enl. MD)--119
Gaffney, P.H.--Ireland--(enl. IA)--219
Gallagher, John--(enl. NH)--119
Gallagher, Patrick--Ireland--(enl. NH)--219
Gangwer, Jesse--PA--(enl. PA)--119
Ganoung, William H.--NY--(enl. NY)--219
Gardner, Charles--ME--(enl. IA)--219
Gardner, Horace--PA--(enl. IL)--219
Gardner, Warren M.--IL?--(enl. IL)--119
Gardner, William H.--NY--(enl. CA)--119
Garrett, James W.--OH--(enl. IN)--219
Garside, Joseph--Yorkshire, England--(enl. IL)--119
Garside, Mary I. (Mrs. Joseph)--OH--119

INDEX (Con't)

Garwood, John F.--OH--(enl. OH)--219
Gates, William Klugh--PA--(enl. PA)--219
Gay, John--??--220
Gaylord, Levi B.--OH--(enl. IA)--119
Gaylord, Orvin N.--West Hartland, Hartford Co, CT --(enl. CT)--220
Geen, Anna Ida (Mrs. William)--??--119
Geen, William--MO--(enl. MO)--119
George, _____--(enl. OH)--119
George, Caroline Bigler (Mrs. Henry W.)--OH--120
George, Charles W.--Germany--(enl. WI)--220
George, Henry Wesley--Jay?, Essex Co, NY--(enl. NY)--120
Germain, O.--??--220
Gibbons, Homer W.--(enl. OH)--120
Gibbs, Artemus--(enl. NY)--120
Gibbs, Rosetta N. or Rose (Mrs. Artemus)--??--120
Gibson, Emory M.--NY--(enl. IL)--220
Giddings, J.R.B.--(enl. VRC)--120
Giffod, F.--??--220
Gilbert, Henry H.--Moudy Township, Genessee Co, MI--(enl. IL)--220
Gilbert, John A.--MA--(enl. MA)--220
Giles, Albert L.--NH--(enl. MA)--220
Gillett, George A.--Champlain, OH--(enl. OH)--120
Gilman, Benjamin W.--NY--(enl. WI)--220
Gilmore, Mary Parker (Mrs. Myron T.)--??--120
Gilmore, Myron Tyrrel--Dedham, ME--(enl. ME)--120
Gilpatrick, Jeremiah H.--ME--(enl. ME)--120
Gilpatrick, Leelah R. (Mrs. Jeremiah H.)--??--120
Gilson, Sylvester--NY--(enl. CO)--220
Gimelich, Christ--Germany--(enl. IL)--220
Gipson, John C.--Jefferson Co, NY--(enl. NY)--120
Gipson, Mary E. (Mrs. John C.)--??--121
Gleason, Fannie L./E. (Mrs. Henry J.)--??--121
Gleason, Henry J.--American--(enl. IL)--121
Gleason, Nathan B.--NY--(enl. IA)--220
Glenn, James H.--TN--(enl. US)--220
Glidden, A.P.--NH--(enl. NH)--220
Goetsch, Ferdinand--Prussia--(enl. NY)--220
Goetze, William--Germany--(enl. CA)--220
Gomer, John H.--NY--(enl. NY)--221
Goodell, Maximilian--CT--(enl. NY)--221
Goodrich, James M.--VT--(enl. VT)--221
Goodrich, V.R.--??--221
Goodspeed, Charles E.--NY--(enl. IL)--221
Goodspeed, John Willard--Perry, Wyoming Co, NY --(enl. NY)--121
Goodwin, Oliver R.--NY--(enl. OH)--221
Gordon, Richard--(enl. VA)--121
Gordon, Sallie L. (Mrs. Richard)--??--121
Gouchenaur, David--PA--(enl. PA)--221
Gould, Francis C.--Windham, ME--(enl. US)--221
Gould, William H.--PA--(enl. CO)--221

Gould, William P.--(enl. WI)--121
Gracy, Robert A.--Auburn, Lincoln Co, MO--(enl. OR) --221
Graeter, Henry A.--OH--(enl. OH)--221
Gragg, William H.--MA--(enl. CA)--221
Graham, Burton F.--IL--(enl. IL)--221
Graham, Isaac A.--OH--(enl. IL)--221
Graham, Robert A.--Ireland--(enl. PA)--221
Grant, George W.--Boston or Roxbury, MA--(enl. US)--121
Grant, Henry S.--??--221
Grant, Marie D. (Mrs. George W.)--American--121
Granville, Catherine or B.C. (Mrs. John H.)--??--121
Granville, John H.--England--(enl. NY)--121
Gray, Elizabeth M. (Mrs. William)--VA--122
Gray, J.S.--??--121
Gray, Joseph--IL--(enl. IL)--221
Gray, Mary J. Smith (Mrs. J.S.)--??--121
Gray, Robert A.--??--222
Gray, William--Scotland--(enl. IL)--122
Green, Alice K. (Mrs. William)--??--122
Green, Angeline A. or Angelina A. (Mrs. Henry C.) --??--122
Green, Antoinette M. (Mrs. William M.)--??--122
Green, Elias S.--IN--(enl. IN)--122
Green, Henry Clay--MI--(enl. IL)--122
Green, J.N.--Canada--(enl. IN)--222
Green, James--Ireland--(enl. NY)--222
Green, John A.--Central Falls, RI--(enl. CA)--222
Green, Lucy M. (Mrs. Elias S.)--??--122
Green, William--(enl. NY)--122
Green, William M.--NY--(enl. ?)--122
Greenfield, John--Muskingham Co, OH--(enl. IN)--222
Greenleaf, William Charles--OH--(enl. IN)--122
Greenlee, James L.--PA--(enl. IN)--222
Gregory, A.E.--OH--(enl. OH)--122
Gregory, Hugh M.--NY--(enl. US)--222
Gregory, Maria Marcia (Mrs. Starr C.)--??--122
Gregory, Starr Cozier--IL--(enl. IL)--122
Griggs, John R.--NY--(enl. NY)--122
Griggs, Mary A. (Mrs. John R.)--??--123
Grinell, Calvin--IN--(enl. IN)--222
Grinnell, Oliver C.--American--(enl. MI)--123
Grinnell, William W.--(enl. NY)--123
Grisswell, Robert H.--(enl. US)--123
Griswold, Alice (Mrs. Jesse)--??--123
Griswold, Benson--Troy, OH--(enl. MN)--222
Griswold, Jesse--PA--(enl. PA)--123
Grosvenor, Mary C. Stannard (Mrs. Royal)--??--123
Grosvenor, Royal W.--Shelby Co, OH--(enl. OH)--123
Grovesteen, James H.--NY--(enl. OH/NY)--222
Guilford, Andrew J.--OH--(enl. MI)--222
Gunn, John W.--Morgan Co, IL--(enl. IL)--222
Guthrie, Roger C.--ME--(enl. MA)--222

INDEX (Con't)

Guy, Isaac J.C.--Wayne Co, IN--(enl. IN)--223
Gwyn, Hugh Garvin--Ireland--(enl. TN)--123
Gwyn/Gwynne, Mary V. (Mrs. Hugh G.)--??--123
Haddock, Arthur H.M--American--(enl. IA)--123
Haden, John Franklin--Hernando, DeSoto Co, MS
 --(enl. MS)--123
Haden, Sarah Ophelia (Mrs. John F.)--??--124
Hahn, Joseph--Alsace, France--(enl. NY)--124
Haines, Alfred--PA--(enl. IA)--124
Haines, Flora Conklin (Mrs. Alfred)--??--124
Hale, John A.--Kennebeck, ME--(enl. IN)--124
Hale, Susan (Mrs. John A.)--??--124
Hall, Francis--(enl. NJ)--124
Hall, George P.--England--(enl. NE)--124
Hall, H.I.--PA--(enl. CA)--223
Hall, Harvy R.--??--223
Hall, Joseph E.--PA--(enl. PA)--223
Hall, Mary Elizabeth (Mrs. George P.)--??--124
Hall, William Henry--(enl. IL)--124
Hallowell, Henry B.--New York City--(enl. US)--223
Halversen, Mary Anna or Anna Marie (Mrs. Soren)
 --??--124
Halversen, Soren--(enl. WI)--124
Ham, Charles--Saratoga Co, NY--(enl. NY)--223
Hamilton, Beverly--WA (DC?)--(enl. US)--124
Hamilton, Fayette Lemon or Lemar (Mrs. Martin
 D.)--IN--125
Hamilton, James T.--MA--(enl. MA)--223
Hamilton, Martin Douglas--Jackson, IN--(enl. IN)
 --125
Hampson, Robert/Rufus A.--American--(enl. OH)--125
Handy, Emma J. (Mrs. John H.)--ME--125
Handy, John H.--ME--(enl. ME)--125
Haney, Henry F.--VT--(enl. MI)--223
Hanna, John J.--NY--(enl. NY)--223
Hanretty, John--Ireland--(enl. US)--223
Hanson, Martin--Denmark--(enl. NY)--125
Hanson, Parker W.--ME--(enl. ME)--223
Hardy, Albert--Meggs Co, OH--(enl. IL)--125
Hardy, Daniel Elson--MA--(enl. MA)--125
Hardy, Elizabeth H. (Mrs. Albert)--??--125
Hargrave, William--Canada--(enl. IL)--223
Harkins, Henry A.--NY--(enl. NY)--223
Harlan, John--American--(enl. PA)--125
Harlan, Mary Francis (Mrs. John)--??--125
Harmon, Laura (Mrs. Ole O.)--??--125
Harmon, Ole Oleson--Norway--(enl. IL)--125
Harper, Joseph H.--OH--(enl. OH)--125
Harper, Tamar Alice (Mrs. Joseph)--Amer.--126
Harrigan, James--East Bloomfield, Ontario Co,
 NY--(enl. IA)--126
Harrington, David G.--VT--(enl. MN)--223
Harris, Avril--(enl. NY)--126
Harris, Leander W.--American--(enl. IN)--126

Harris, Marietta (Mrs. Avril)--??--126
Harris, Moses Cox--(enl. OH)--126
Hart, James--VA--(enl. DC)--223
Hartley, James Monroe--Lee Co, IA--(enl. IA)--126
Hartley, Mary Jane Tibbetts (Mrs. James M.)--??--126
Hartzell, Letta E. (Mrs. Thomas B.)--??--126
Hartzell, Thomas B.--IA--(enl. IA)--126
Harvey, Rufus D./W.--(enl. IL/WI)--126
Haskell, John Lincoln--Norway, ME--(enl. ME)--126
Haskins, Alonzo--NY--(enl. NY)--223
Haskins, William A.--IL--(enl. Washington Territory)
 --127
Hathaway, Emma (Mrs. Franklin)--??--127
Hathaway, Franklin--OH--(enl. OH)--127
Haughn, Anna (Mrs. Francis J.)--??--224
Haughn, Francis J.--Fayette Co, IN--(enl. IN)--224
Hayes, Thomas--(enl. NY)--127
Haynes, Estella A. Smith (Mrs. George E.)--VT--127
Haynes, George E.--Wilmington, VT--(enl. RI)--127
Hays, John--(enl. OH)--127
Hayward, Marie A. (Mrs. William H.)--??--127
Hayward, R.E.--Clarksville, MO--(enl. IA)--224
Hayward, William H.--NY--(enl. OH)--127
Hazzard, Alice (Mrs. George W.)--MO--127
Hazzard, G.R.--(enl US)--127
Hazzard, George W.--Cambridge City, Wayne Co, IN
 --(enl. IN)--127
Healey, Bernard--Dublin, Ireland--(enl. US)--128
Healey, Margaret (Mrs. Bernard)--??--128
Healey, Michael--Ireland--(enl. NY)--224
Heath, Anna True (Mrs. James A.)--??--128
Heath, James A.--ME--(enl. MA)--128
Heath, James/John W.--NY--(enl. MN)--224
Hebbard, A.W.--ME--(enl. WI)--224
Hefflin/Hefflon, Frederick--CT--(enl. CT)--128
Hefflin, William H.--Canada--(enl. IL)--224
Hege, Jacob--??--224
Heller, Martha J. (Mrs. Moses)--??--128
Heller, Moses--OH--(enl. OH)--128
Helms, Reuben or Ruben E.--Monmouth, IL--(enl. WI)
 --224
Helpinstine, J.A.--??--224
Hendershot, Lorenzo--Layfayette, Monroe Co, NJ--
 (enl. OH)--128
Henderson, Anna Eliza (Mrs. William P.)--??--128
Henderson, Eliel F.--Fayette Co, PA--(enl. IL)--224
Henderson, William P.--IL--(enl. IL)--128
Henneberry, Garrett Joseph--(enl. IL)--128
Henneberry, Nora (Mrs. Garrett J.)--??--128
Hennion/Hinnion, Martin--NJ/NY--(enl. CO)--128
Hennion, Nannie J. (Mrs. Martin)--??--128
Herffendirfer, Jacob--PA--(enl. PA)--224
Herrick, Amos P.--Concord, NY--(enl. US)--129
Herrick, Arcella Stowe (Mrs. Amos P.)--NY--129

INDEX (Con't)

Herriman, Albert--IL--(enl. OH)--224
Herrington, Beverly A.--NY--(enl. IA)--224
Heustis, Thomas B.--IN--(enl. KA)--224
Hesser,Wilber F.-Louisa Court House, VA (enl.IL)--129
Hewson, James--Newark, NJ--(enl. ?)--129
Hewson, Tetuanuie A. Fanaue (Mrs. James)--Tahiti --129
Hiatt, Marvin--Rainsborough, OH--(enl. OH)--129
Hickox, L.M.--MI--(enl. OH)--224
Hicks, Emma L. (Mrs. James V.)--??--129
Hicks, James V.--NY--(enl. MI)--129
Hicks, John J.--NY--(enl. MI)--129
Higbee, Elbert R.--OH--(enl. OH)--129
Higbee, George--OH--(enl. OH)--225
Higbee, Hattie Goodman (Mrs. Elbert R.)--??--129
Higgens, M.L.--OH--(enl. OH)--225
Higgins, Robert Walter--(enl. KA)--129
Higgins, William--Ireland--(enl. US)--225
Hill, Ambrose--??--225
Hill, Charles H.--PA--(enl. IL)--225
Hill, Edwin L.--OH--(enl. IA)--225
Hill, John--Canada--(enl. IL)--225
Hill, Mary M. (Mrs. William F.)--??--130
Hill, William F.--(enl. IA)--130
Hillard, Lanson--NY--(enl. NY)--130
Hills, Ralph H.--Butler Co, OH--(enl. OH)--225
Hilsher, Harmon/Hilscher, Herman--New York City --(enl. IN)--225
Himebaugh/Himbaugh, Ada J. (Mrs. Henry H.)--?? --130
Himebaugh, Henry H.--Green Township, Erie Co, PA --(enl. WI)--130
Himmell, Charles S.--Zweybreiken, Bavaria--(enl. US)--130
Himmell, Susan H. (Mrs. Charles S.)--??--130
Hinchcliff, E.D.--??--225
Hinckle, Mary (Mrs. William S.)--??--130
Hinckle, William S.--IN--(enl. IN)--130
Hinckley, Oscar S.--MA--(enl. IL)--225
Hipwell, Richard J.--IL--(enl. IL)--225
Hixon, D.W.--Lowell, IA--(enl. IA)--225
Hixon, George W.--OH--(enl. IA)--225
Hobingnist, C.A.--Sweden--(enl. MI)--225
Hodge, Noah--IL--(enl. IL)--130
Hodge, Sarah W. Ashmun (Mrs. Noah)--Hudson, OH --130
Hodge, William C.--NY--(enl. WI)--225
Hodges, George W.--Logan's Port, IN--(enl. IN) --226
Hodges, John--Scriba or Scuba, NY--(enl. WI)--130
Hodgkins, Emery--Gloucester, MA--(enl. MA)--226
Hoeffle, Jacob--Germany--(enl. ??)--130
Hoffman, David Bancroft--NY--(enl. CA)--131
Hoffman, John S.--VA--(enl. IN)--226

Hoffman, Maria Delores Wilder y Machado (Mrs. David) (from Old Town SD family)--CA--131
Hoffman, W.E.--OH--(enl. IL)--226
Hogarty, M.J.--Ireland--(enl. NY)--226
Hogeland, A.W.--NY--(enl. IL)--226
Hoine, Orinda Estella (Mrs. Samuel P.)--??--131
Hoine, Samuel P.--(enl. WI)--131
Holabird, W.H.--VT--(enl. VT)--226
Holcomb, B.--Granby, CT--(enl. CT)--226
Holcomb, Herman--PA--(enl. NE)--131
Holcomb, Louisa or Nancy Louisa (Mrs. Herman)-- NY--131
Holderness, Leona B. (Mrs. William H.)--??--226
Holderness, William H.--Adams Co, OH--(enl. IL)--226
Holman, Franklin--Princeton, KY--(enl. IL)--131
Holmes, Augustus--GA--(enl. TN)--226
Holmes, Philander--(enl. IN)--131
Holsinger, S.K.--TN--(enl. TN)--226
Holt, D.H.--ME--(enl. CA)--226
Holt, William J.--(enl. OH)--131
Holtz, Fred--??--226
Holverson, Thomas or Tostine--WI--(enl. WI)--227
Honeycutt, Daniel--(enl. IN)--131
Honeycutt, Sarah Elizabeth (Mrs. Daniel)--??--131
Hood, Alan/Allen R.-Dearing, NH--(enl. NH)--131
Hood, Ellen R. (Mrs. Alan R.)--??--131
Hooker, J.B.--Brooklyn, NY--(enl. MN)--227
Hopkins, Archibald--(enl. TN)--131
Hopkins, Emma F. (Mrs. Eugene)--??--132
Hopkins, Eugene--(enl. NY)--132
Hopkins/Hoskins, Ira K.--Vicksburg, MS--(enl. IL)--227
Hopkins, Jerome--IA--(enl. IL)--227
Hopkins, L.C.--IN--(enl. MO)--227
Hopkins, Martha Ann (Mrs. Archibald)--NC--132
Horder, George W.--England--(enl. WI)--227
Horrele, W.H.--Davis Co, IN--(enl. IN)--227
Horst, Henry F.--OH--(enl. IN)--227
Horton, George R.--MI--(enl. MI)--132
Hoskin, O.F.--American--(enl. ??)--132
Hough, Charles Warren--NY--(enl. US)--132
Houston, John--Buffalo, NY--(enl. US)--132
Hover, Aaron S.--NY--(enl. NY)--132
Howard, Henry A.--(enl. CA)--132
Howell, Frank--OH--(enl. OH)--227
Howell, Lida (Mrs. William)--??--132
Howell, William--NY--(enl. IL)--132
Hubbard, Martin--IN--(enl. IN)--227
Hubbs, Charles L.--NY--(enl. MN)--227
Huddleston, John--NY--(enl. MN)--132
Huddleston, Salina Y. (Mrs. John)--??--132
Hudgins, Amos Edward--MO--(enl. KS)--133
Hudgins, Cynthia Ann (Mrs. Amos E.)--??--133
Hudson, John--MD--(enl. AR)--227
Huey, G.L.--American--(enl. KY)--133

INDEX (Con't)

Hughes, James--England--(enl. US)--227
Hughes, James Douglas--Jackson, MI--(enl. TN/AL)--133
Hughes, James W.--NY--(enl. NY)--133
Hughes, John Henry--IL--(enl. IL)--133
Hughes, Louisa (Nona) Roldham (Mrs. James Douglas)--CA--133
Hughes, Miles--IL--(enl. IL)--133
Hulburd(t), Ebenezer W.--VT--(enl. IL)--227
Hulburt, R.G.--MO--(enl. MO)--227
Hull, Horace J.--Athens, PA--(enl. NY)--133
Humphrey, Clara (Mrs. E.O.)--??--134
Humphrey, E.O.--(enl. IL)--134
Hunt, Annie W. (Mrs. Ishabel/Ashbel)--??--134
Hunt, Cephas B.--MA--(enl. IL)--227
Hunt, George W.--(enl. KA)--134
Hunt, Ida or Ada Ellen (Mrs. Nathan)--??--134
Hunt, Ishabel/Ashbel--(enl. CT)--134
Hunt, Nathan--OH--(enl. IA)--134
Hunt, William Foster--White Hall, NY--(enl. NY)--134
Huntington, C.--Chatauqua, NY--(enl. NY)--228
Huntley, Matthew--Trawbridge, England--(enl. MA)--228
Hurd, George S.--Wishauka, IN--(enl. WI)--134
Hurd, Lavinus S.--MI--(enl. WI)--228
Hurd, Mary Whitney (Mrs. George S.)--??--134
Hurd, Warren H.--NH--(enl. NH)--228
Hurley, Cornelius G.--IA--(enl. CA)--134
Hutchinson, G.O.--(enl. ME)--134
Hutchison, Catherine B. (Mrs. Ezra P.)--American--134
Hutchison, Ezra P.--OH--(enl. OH)--134
Hutchison, George S.--OH--(enl. OH)--134
Hutchison, Viola (Mrs. George S.)--??--135
Hutchison, William N.--VA--(enl. RI)--228
Hutt, George W.--New York City--(enl. KS)--228
Imberie, James M.--(enl. OH)--135
Imberie, Katherine R. (Mrs. James M.)--??--135
Ingraham, Andrew--Monroe Co, NY--(enl. NY)--135
Iodine, Chief--Oswego, NY--(enl. US)--228
Irgens, John S.--Norway--(enl. WI)--135
Irgens, Louisa or Louise P. (Mrs. John S.)--??--135
Jackson, Herman--IL--(enl. WI)--228
Jackson, J.M.--PA--(enl. US)--228
Jackson, Johiel--(enl. WI)--135
Jackson, Mason--Johnsonville, OH--(enl. IA)--228
Jackson, Rebecca Ann (Mrs. Joheil)--??--135
Jackson, Thomas Miller--Hanisonville, KY--(enl. US)--135
Jacobs, John W.--WV--(enl. WV)--228
Jacobs, L.C.--NY--(enl. WI)--228
Jacoby, Henry M.--IL--(enl. MO)--229
Jaggers, Thomas--IL--(enl. IL)--229
James, Charles P.--American--(enl. PA)--135
James, Frank/Francis--Canada--(enl. IN)--229
James, William F.C.--OH--(enl. OH)--229
Jamison, Alexander A.--Scotland--(enl. IL/OH)--135
Jenkins, Andrew J.--American--(enl. NY)--135
Jenkins, Robert J.--Ireland--(enl. NY)--229
Jenks, Augusta (Mrs. Park M.)--??--135
Jenks, Park M.--PA--(enl. NY)--135
Jenness, Walter B.--ME--(enl. ME)--135
Jenney, Royal A.--MI--(enl. MI)--229
Jerman, Thomas--Norway--(enl. WI)--229
Jewell, Emilia F. (Mrs. William S.)--Germany--136
Jewell, William S.--Philadelphia, PA--(enl. MO)--136
Jilson, Fred E.--Pautucket, MA--(enl. KS)--136
Jilson, Mary E. (Mrs. Fred E.)--??--136
Jobes, Charles Colic--OH--(enl. IA)--229
Johns, Adam--OH--(enl. OH)--136
Johns, Elizabeth (Mrs. Adam)--??--136
Johns, James B.--OH--(enl. IN)--229
Johnson, Curtis--St. Albans, VT--(enl. KS)--229
Johnson, Edward--MA--(enl. IL)--229
Johnson, Edward--OH--(enl. OH)--229
Johnson, J.J.--NH--(enl. NH)--229
Johnson, James A.--IN--(enl. MN)--229
Johnson, John W.--PA--(enl. OH)--229
Johnson, Nathaniel S.--VA--(enl. OH)--136
Johnson, Peder--(enl. US)--136
Johnson, Thomas G.--(enl. IN)--136
Johnson, William H.--NY--(enl. US)--229
Johnson, William M.A.--OH--(enl. OH)--136
Johnston, John--Sweden--(enl. IL)--229
Jones, Albert--PA--(enl. PA)--230
Jones, Alfred--PA--(enl. PA)--230
Jones, Charles P.--Bangor, ME--(enl. WI)--230
Jones, Danville P.--Solon, ME--(enl. ME)--136
Jones, David R.--North Wales--(enl. IA)--136
Jones, Henry Houston--IL--(enl. IL)--137
Jones, J.O.--ME--(enl. ME)--230
Jones, James P.--Madison, ME--(enl. US)--137
Jones, Levi J.--NY--(enl. NY)--230
Jones, Mary I. (Mrs. James P.)--ME--137
Jones, Richard A.--IN--(enl. KS)--137
Jones, Sadie M. (Mrs. Danville P.)--??--136
Jones, Samuel--England--(enl. US)--137
Jones, Sarah Effie (Mrs. David R.)--??--136
Judd, Alex--(enl. MO)--230
Judd, Charles L.--OH--(enl. OH)--137
Judd, Kate E. (Mrs. Charles L.)--??--137
Juvenal, Josiah--IL--(enl. IL)--230
Kastner, Joseph--(enl. IL)--137
Kautz, George--OH--(enl. OH)--230
Kay, Thomas--England--(enl. PA)--230
Keacht, Frederick--Germany--(enl. MO)--230

INDEX (Con't)

Kearney, Eli S.--New Brunswick--(enl. MI)--137
Kearney, Francis L. (Mrs. Eli S.)--??--137
Keeler, Ezra--MI--(enl. MI)--230
Keeney, C.W.--CT--(enl. CT)--230
Keeney, Esther Awilda (Mrs. Thomas B.)--??--137
Keeney, Thomas Benton--PA--(enl. MN)--137
Kehoe, William--Nova Scotia--(enl. MA)--230
Keith, Alymer D.--NY--(enl. CO)--137
Keith, Lizzie E. (Mrs. Alymer D.)--??--138
Keldar, Abram--Belisle, NY--(enl. IL)--138
Kellend, Robert--England--(enl. MA)--230
Kelly, Abraham--Henry Co, OH--(enl. IN)--138
Kelly, Anna M. or Annie Marie (Mrs. Abraham)--??--138
Kelly, Eli C.--PA--(enl. OH)--138
Kelly, John L.--American--(enl. CA)--138
Keltner, George Frances--Baltimore, MD--(enl. IA)--138
Kennedy, Charles--PA--(enl. KS)--231
Kennedy, Nathaniel--PA--(enl. PA)--138
Kennedy, Sarah (Mrs. Nathaniel)--American--138
Kenney, Anna M. (Mrs. Robert D.)--??--138
Kenney, Robert D.--American--(enl. CA)--138
Kepler, Peter L.--PA--(enl. PA)--231
Kerr, Emma (Mrs. John M.)--IN--139
Kerr, John M.--Jefferson Co, OH--(enl. VA/OH)--138
Key, Joseph F.--Virginia Grove, IA--(enl. IA)--231
Keyes, Hiram--(enl. KA)--231
Kidder, John W.--Manitowoc Co, WI--(enl. WI)--139
Kilrain, John G.--Canada--(enl. IA)--231
Kincaid, Orlando D.--Elk Co, PA--(enl. IA)--231
King, Albert J.--Poland--(enl. OH)--139
King, Alice C. (Mrs. William C.)--??--139
King, Burley W.--NY--(enl. CA)--231
King, George V.--NY--(enl. NY)--231
King, John D.--OH--(enl. IL)--231
King, Martha Elizabeth (Mrs. Albert J.)--??--139
King, William C.--OH--(enl. IL)--139
Kingsland, Henry Edmund--(enl. IA)--139
Kinne, Orlando W.--NY--(enl. NY)--231
Kinsly, Samuel--OH--(enl. MO?)--231
Klaus, Carl--Switzerland--(enl. WI)--231
Knapp, Christiana (Mrs. John)--??--139
Knapp, John--PA--(enl. PA)--139
Knoles, Lois B. (Mrs. Samuel S.)--??--139
Knoles, Samuel S.--IN--(enl. IL)--139
Knott, Peter--??--231
Knowles, Amos Pendleton-Northport,ME--(enl.CA)--139
Knowles, Anna (Mrs. Amos P.)--Germany--139
Knowles, John--MI--(enl. MI)--231
Koehler, Edward--Franklin Co, OH--(enl. OH)--231
Kohuly, John--Germany--(enl. OH)--231
Kooken, Anna Ewalt (Mrs. John A.)--??--139

Kooken, John A.--Johnstown, PA--(enl. PA)--139
Krebs, Augustus--Poland--(enl. US)--140
Kretsinger, David L.--IN--(enl. KS)--140
Kretsinger, Susan E. (Mrs. David L.)--??--140
Kroff, Carla Exuma/Exuna (Mrs. Samuel W.)--??--140
Kroff, Samuel W.--OH--(enl. OH)--140
Kronskop, George W.--Belfontaine, OH--(enl. OH)--231
Kruger, Julius G.--Germany--(enl. IL)--232
Kuhns, W.P.--??--232
Kurth, Andrew H.--Germany--(enl. KS)--140
Kurth, Susan (Mrs. Andrew H.)--American--140
Kurtz, Albert A.--OH--(enl. IL)--232
Kuttnauer, Isador--France--(enl. MO)--232
Lakin, Cyrus B.--Columbus, OH--(enl. OH)--232
Lamb, Bertha A. (Mrs. Henry)--??--140
Lamb, Harvey Willard--(enl. OH)--140
Lamb, Henry--American--(enl. IA)--140
Lamb, Morris H.--Madison Co, OH--(enl. MN)--232
Lamme, Edwin H.--OH--(enl. OH)--232
Lampman, Granville L.--(enl. NY)--140
Lane, Ansel S.--Old Town, ME--(enl. MN)--232
Lane, M.W.--IN--(enl. IN)--232
Langdon, Emily B. (Mrs. John W.)--London, England--140
Langdon, John W.--Racine, WI--(enl. IL)--140
Langdon, Samuel J.--OH--(enl. IL)--141
Large, Andrew T.--NJ/NY--(enl. WI)--141
Large, Sarah Ann (Mrs. Andrew T.)--MO--141
Lashmit, W.E.--NC--(enl. IL)--232
Laufer, Loammi--PA--(enl. IA)--232
Laverty, Leander--IN--(enl. IA)--232
Lawless, Stephen--Ireland--(enl. MA)--232
Lawrance, John C.--Tioga Co, NY--(enl. NY)--232
Laws, Rosetta (Mrs. William H.)--??--141
Laws, William Henry--PA--(enl. US)--141
Layton, Robert--Lafayette, IN--(enl. IN)--233
Leader, J.M.--PA--(enl. ?)--233
Leaming, Edwin R.--NJ--(enl. KS)--141
Leaming, Minerva L. (Mrs. Edwin R.)--??--141
Leatherman, George--Elgin, IN--(enl. WI)--233
Lee, Charles P.--Essex Co, NY--(enl. NY)--141
Leheu, R.M.--OH--(enl. IA)--233
Lehman, Peter--Germany--(enl. MI)--141
Leibey, Edward Hamilton--Miamisburg, OH--(enl. CO)--141
Leibey, Virgilla E. (Mrs. Edward H.)--NY--141
Leoinge, James--??--233
Leonard, George D.--VT--(enl. MA)--233
Leonard, Joseph--Amsterdam, Hol. (enl. OH)--141
Leonard, William--Baltimore, MD--(enl. NJ)--142
Leonard, William R.--OH--(enl. OH)--233
Leslie, G.H.--American--(enl. NY)--142
Levings, John K.--Canada--(enl. NV)--142
Lewes, Thomas D.--Jefferson Co, PA--(enl. PA)--233

INDEX (Con't)

Lewis, Charles--WI--(enl. MO)--233
Lewis, Charles H--East Hartford, CT--(enl. MA)--233
Lewis, Charles W.--(enl. CA)--142
Lewis, J.C.--PA--(enl. IL)--233
Lewis, John--IN--(enl. IN)--233
Lewis, William W.--KY--(enl. KY)--233
Light, Jacob J.--IN--(enl. IN)--142
Lilley, James--(enl. US)--142
Limebeck, Emma (Mrs. George H.)--??--142
Limebeck, George H.--NY--(enl. MI)--142
Lince, Cornelius--NY--(enl. WI)--142
Lince, Esther E. (Mrs. Cornelius)--NY--142
Lindley, Charles--Harrisburg, PA--(enl. IN)--233
Lindsey, Dennis--(enl. WI)--142
Lingenfelter, Alford--Carrelton, KY--(enl. IN)--233
Lingenfelter, Deliscus--KY--(enl. IN)--142
Lingenfelter, Elizabeth (Mrs. Deliscus)--American--142
Lisher, O.B.--OH--(enl. IN)--233
Little, William J.--RI--(enl. IA)--233
Livingston, Frederick W.--Jerico, Chittenden Co, VT--(enl. IL)--142
Livingston, Mary E. (Mrs. Frederick W.)--??--143
Lockwood, Ella D. (Mrs. Nathan S.)--??--143
Lockwood, Munson M.--St. Lawrence Co, NY--(enl. VT)--234
Lockwood, Nathan S.--Springfield, OH--(enl. IN)--143
Logan, John H.--KY--(enl. NE)--234
Logan, William King--(enl. Confederate)--143
Lohr, Hattie (Mrs. Henry)--??--143
Lohr, Henry--PA--(enl. PA)--143
Lohr, John--PA--(enl. PA)--234
Lohr, N.--NY--(enl. NY)--234
Lombardy, Elizabeth (Mrs. Frank K.)--??--143
Lombardy, Frank K.--(enl. US)--143
Long, Porter--MI--(enl. IL)--234
Loomis, Mrs. M.S.--??--143
Loomis, M.S.--MO--(enl. CA)--143
Loper, Newton--(enl. NY)--143
Lopshire, Adam Joseph--Allen Co, IN--(enl. IN)--234
Loring, Annie Cameron (Mrs. William E.)--??--143
Loring, William Edward--Newark Co, NY--(enl. PA)--143
Louck, James H.--NY--(enl. NY)--143
Loud, Charles A.--ME--(enl. MA)--144
Loud, Rhoda W. Tay (Mrs. Charles)--Medford, MA--144
Loudon, J.H.--IN--(enl. IL)--234
Loughrey, William--PA--(enl. MO)--234
Low, Francis M.--(enl. IL)--144
Lowell, Marcus L.--NY--(enl. OH)--234
Lucas, Joseph H.--Indiana Co, PA--(enl. PA)--234
Luce, Adelaide (Mrs. Moses)/dau. James & Olive Mantania below, NY?--144
Luce, Moses A.--Payson, IL--(enl. MI)--144
Luckadoe, Joseph--MD--(enl. US)--234
Luckett, Alexander--PA--(enl. US)--144
Luckett, Martha J. (Mrs. Alexander)--PA--144
Lucy, Timothy J.--Allegheny Co, PA--(enl. MD)--234
Lufbery, George F.--??--144
Lufbery, Martha Adeline Linn (Mrs. George)--??--144
Lundaker, Peter--??--234
Lyman, James O.--Andover, Ashtabula Co, OH--(enl. IN)--144
Lynch, Thomas--Coshocton, OH--(enl. WI)--234
Lyon, E.C.--IL--(enl. IL)--234
Lyon, Edward--Eastford, CT--(enl. CT)--234
Lyon, Theodore--PA--(enl. OH)--235
MacDonald, Duncan H.--NY--(enl. OH)--235
Mackey, Clarke D.--(enl. NY)--145
MacKinnon, Hector--Scotland--(enl. OH)--235
Madden, Joseph--Quincy, MA--(enl. US)--235
Magee, Elizabeth S. or Sarah Elizabeth (Mrs. Thomas L.)--??--145
Magee, Paris A.--OH--(enl. ?)--235
Magee, Thomas Lee--Guernsey Co, OH--(enl. IL)--145
Magoon, George A.--Harmony, ME--(enl. ME)--235
Mahan, Dr.--??--235
Mahoney, Henry--Ireland--(enl. ?)--235
Majors, Archibald C.--Adams Co, IL--(enl. MO)--145
Mallett, John--Cayahotz?, OH--(enl. OH)--235
Malloy, William--Ireland--(enl. NY)--235
Malson, Lizzie (Mrs. Nathan)--American--145
Malson, Nathan--American--(enl. WI)--145
Mandeville, F.H.--MD--(enl. NY)--235
Manners, William A.--PA--(enl. IA)--235
Manning, Barbara Ann (Mrs. Phillip)--??--145
Manning, Phillip--PA--(enl. PA)--145
Mantania, James D.--NY--(enl. IL)--145
Mantania, Olive B. (Mrs. James D.)--NY--145
Marrs, David L.--IN--(enl. IA)--145
Marrs, Mary M. (Mrs. David L.)--??--145
Marsh, George W.--NY--(enl. WI)--235
Marshall, Caroline F. (Mrs. William P.)--??--146
Marshall, Edmund--KY--(enl. US)--146
Marshall, Ellen M. (Mrs. John H.)--American--146
Marshall, John H.--ME--(enl. ?)--146
Marshall, Martha (Mrs. Edmund)--American--146
Marshall, William P.--IN--(enl. WI)--146
Marston, Etta L. (Mrs. George?)--??--146
Marston, George--NH--(enl. ?)--146
Martin, Elihu G.--OH--(enl. IA)--146
Martin, George M.--OH--(enl. OH)--235
Martin, John--IL--(enl. IA)--235
Martin, Joseph--Comowy, Austro/Hungary--(enl. NY)--146

INDEX (Con't)

Martin, Nelson--IL--(enl. IL)--235
Mate, W.B.--(enl. US)--146
Mathenia, William Samuel--Tuscarowa, OH--(enl. IL)--146
Mathes, Z.C.--IN--(enl. IN)--235
Mathis, Frederick B.--Taylorsville, KY--(enl. IA)--236
Matot, Edmund L.--Sudsbury, VT--(enl. VT)--146
Matot, Emma B. (Mrs. Edmund L.)--American--146
Matson, Albert E.--OH--(enl. IL)--147
Matson, Belle (Mrs. Albert E.)--??--147
Mattern, Henry J.--(enl. IL)--147
Mattern, Josephine W. or Josie (Mrs. Henry J.)--??--147
Matthews, Thomas--American--(enl. ?)--147
Maxwell, James F.--Knox Co, IL--(enl. IL)--236
Maxwell, James H.--MO--(enl. IN)--236
Maxwell, James T.--Canton, Fulton Co, IL--(enl. IL)--236
Maxwell, Wilton P.--Hamilton, OH--(enl. TX)--147
Maynard, Chauncey J.--NY--(enl. IA)--147
Maynard, Cloice S.--Marseilles, OH--(enl. OH)--147
Maynard, Cordelia B. (Mrs. Chauncey J.)--??--147
Maynard, Theodara E. or Theodora Estelle (Mrs. Cloice S.)--??--147
McCartin, Francis--NY--(enl. US)--236
McCarty, John--Canada--(enl. NY)--147
McCauliff, Thomas M.--Boston, MA--(enl. CA)--236
McClelland, Mattie A. (Mrs. William T.)--??--147
McClelland, William Thomas--PA--(enl. IL)--147
McClerken, David W.--IL--(enl. MO)--236
McClure, Joseph A.--OH--(enl. IA)--236
McClure, William P.--IN--(enl. IN)--236
McConnell, James E.--(enl. PA)--147
McConnell, Mary Louisa Ashton or Lula M. (Mrs. James E.)--American--148
McConville, Katherine (Mrs. Patrick H.)--??--148
McConville, Patrick Henry--New York City--(enl. US)--148
McCoy, Thomas--PA--(enl. PA)--236
McCoy, William Hill--VA--(enl. Confederate)--148
McCrumb, John W.--American--(enl. PA)--148
McDaniel, B.F.--PA--(enl. PA)--236
McDonald, Edward--NY--(enl. WI)--236
McDonald, Ann (Steffes) (Mrs. J. Wade)--??--148
McDonald, J. Wade--IL--(enl. IL)--148
McDowell, C.H.--NY--(enl. DC)--148
McDowell, Elizabeth (Mrs. C.H.)--??--148
McDuell, James H.--Washington, D.C.--(enl. OH)--148
McDuell, Norma/Nora Melvina (Mrs. James)--??--148
McFarland, Jesse--Colesville, Schenectady Co, NY--(enl. NY)--236
McFarland, Sarah (Mrs. Schuler)--??--236
McFarland, Schuler--MO--(enl. MO)--236

McGee, William J.--Pittsburg, PA--(enl. PA)--236
McGirl, Barney--County Leitrim, Ireland--(enl. KA)--148
McIntosh, Daniel--Scotland--(enl. US)--148
McIntosh, F.J.--NY--(enl. NY)--148
McIntosh, Henry Curtis--Elmira, NY--(enl. IL)--149
McIntosh, Mary Elizabeth Rhodes (Mrs. Henry C.)--??--149
McKenna, Augustine P.--Perry Co, OH--(enl. OH)--149
McKnight, Eugene V.-Mount Vernon, IL-(enl. MN)--236
McLaren, Benjamin F.--VT--(enl. US)--149
McLaren/McLeran, Martha M. (Mrs. Benjamin F.)--MA--149
McNally, W.G.--Ireland--(enl. NY)--237
McPheeters, Alpheus Leroy or Alphius--(enl. WI)--149
McPheeters, James H.--IL--(enl. WI)--237
McPheeters, Mary (Mrs. Alpheus L./Alphius)--??--149
McQuinston, Thomas--OH--(enl. MS)--237
McSurely, Anderson--Van Buren Co, IA--(enl. IA)--149
Meagher, John O.--St. John, New Brunswick--(enl. IN)--237
Means, Thomas Decater--(enl. IL)--149
Means, Viola (Mrs. Thomas D.)--??--149
Mellus, Frances G.--ME--(enl. ME)--149
Mellus, Mary Josephine (Mrs. Francis G.)--??--149
Mendelson, Louis--Russia--(enl. US)--237
Menhennet, William H.--England--(enl. WV)--237
Merriam, Gustavus F.--Leyden, NY--(enl. NY)--237
Merrill, Augustus--ME--(enl. ME)--237
Merritt, Alma C. (Mrs. Thomas W.)--??--149
Merritt, Thomas W.--(enl. PA)--149
Meserve, William N.--(enl. MA)--150
Meth, J.H.--PA--(enl. IL)--237
Meyer, Addie (Mrs. Christian Y.)--??--150
Meyer, Christian Y.--??--150
Michener, A.D.--Senaca Co, OH--(enl. OH)--237
Middleton, John--NY--(enl. NY)--237
Miles, John F.--IL--(enl. IL)--150
Milford, David--(enl. PA)--150
Milford, Jane (Mrs. David)--??--150
Miller, Admiral N.--RI--(enl. CT)--237
Miller, Albert Judson--Franklin Co, VT--(enl. IL)--150
Miller, Charles F.--Germany--(enl. US)--150
Miller, Eda M. (Mrs. Swan A.)--??--150
Miller, Edwin H.--OH--(enl. IA)--237
Miller, Jacob L.--IN--(enl. IN)--237
Miller, John G.C.--(enl. IN)--150
Miller, Joseph H.--PA--(enl. PA)--237
Miller, Lucretia (Mrs. Albert J.)--??--150
Miller, Swan A.--??--150
Miller, William F.--Germany--(enl. IN)--237
Miller, William Keith--IN--(enl. IA)--150
Millichamp, Julia A. (Mrs. Stephen W.)--??--151
Millichamp, Stephen W.--St. Claire, MI--(enl. MI)--150
Milliron, Fannie M. (Mrs. Joseph C.)--??--151

INDEX (Con't)

Milliron, Joseph C.--PA--(enl. IN)--151
Mills, Charles A.--RI--(enl. RI)--151
Mills, Cleveland W.--Morgenstown, OH--(enl. IN)--151
Mills, E.M. or Emma (Mrs.Charles A.)--??--151
Mills, Laura B. (Mrs. Cleveland W.)--??--151
Miner/Mincur, August--(enl. WI)--151
Miner, H.W.--Western OH--(enl. MI)--238
Miner, Samuel G.--OH--(enl. OH)--151
Mingus, Cyrus Luther--??--(enl. IN)--151
Mingus, Rebecca Viola Dille (Mrs. Cyrus L.)--??--151
Minor, Lucy G. (Mrs. Mitchell A.)--??--151
Minor, Mitchell A.--CT--(enl. OH)--151
Mitchell, Charles G./C.K.--Hillsboro Co, NH--(enl. US)--151
Mitchell, Ira--IN--(enl. IA)--238
Mitchell, J.H.--IL--(enl. IL)--238
Mitchell, James P.--TN--(enl. IL)--151
Mitchell, Matilda (Mrs. James P.)--??--152
Mitchell, Reuben H.--Nova Scotia--(enl. MA)--238
Mitchell, Winfield L.--IN--(enl. MO)--238
Mixter, Horace D.--Warren, MA--(enl. US)--238
Moffatt, Henry G.--VA--(enl. WI)--152
Mogle, William--OH--(enl. MN)--238
Mohr, Daniel--Ireland--(enl. CO)--238
Montius, Augustus--MA--(enl. US)--238
Montney, Levi--Jefferson Co Township, Clayton, NY--(enl. MI)--152
Moore, Alanson O.--Troy, Bradford Co, PA--(enl. IL/VRC)--152
Moore, Alexander--Ireland--(enl. CA)--152
Moore, Augustus H.--MA--(enl. MA)--238
Moore, Francis T.--IL--(enl. IL)--238
Moore, George M.--Louisburg, OH--(enl. OH)--238
Moore, John C.--MI--(enl. MI)--238
Moore, John Gollis--England--(enl. Confederate)--152
Moore, Patrick H.--MA--(enl. MA)--238
Moore, William H.--IN--(enl. IN)--238
Moore, William Roby--IN--(enl. MD)--238
Moran, Edward H.--VT--(enl. WI)--239
Moran, George E.--MA--(enl. CT)--239
Morey, A.B.--(enl. IL)--152
Morey, F.A.--??--239
Morgan, Adam--Muskingham Co, OH--(enl. OH)--239
Morgan, James M.--IN--(enl. IN)--152
Morris, Charles--Canada--(enl. US)--239
Morris, Samuel G.--Norwalk, OH--(enl. IL)--152
Morrison, David--(enl. IL)--153
Morrison, J.A.--??--239
Morrisy, Jessy M.--IN--(enl. IA)--239
Morrow, Hugh P.--Canada--(enl. CO)--239
Morse, Edward A.--PA--(enl. OH)--153

Morse, Nixon--VT--(enl. VT)--239
Morse, Rosetta E. (Mrs. Edward A.)--??--153
Morton, James Ami--NY--(enl. PA)--153
Moseley, William C.--England--(enl. IL)--239
Mosher/Moshier, William Henry--NY--(enl. WI)--153
Mouter, John P.--Sweden--(enl. NY)--239
Moylan, Miles--MA--(enl. US)--239
Muclish, Otto--??--239
Mullaney, James--Ireland--(enl. MN)--239
Mulville, Martin--Ireland--(enl. WI)--239
Munhall, Ella Grant (Mrs. Thomas T.)--??--153
Munhall, Thomas T.--OH--(enl. IL)--153
Murdock, Anna Frances Peck (Mrs. George)--RI--153
Murdock, David H.--OH--(enl. IL)--239
Murdock, George L.--(enl. MA)--153
Murdock, John Pierpont--VA--(enl. VA/WV)--153
Murphy, Charles H.--NY--(enl. IA)--153
Murphy, Nancy M. (Mrs. Charles H.)--??--153
Murray, George L.--MO--(enl. MO)--153
Murray, Minnie (Mrs. George L.)--??--153
Mussey, Albert W.--VT--(enl. CA)--240
Nace, Uriah P.--PA--(enl. OH)--240
Nagle, W.C.--Ireland--(enl. OH)--240
Neer, Barton--Kendall Co, IL--(enl. IL)--154
Neiberger, Samuel J.--OH--(enl. OH)--240
Neill, Dyas--Ireland--(enl. IA)--154
Neill, Elizabeth Augusta (Mrs. Dyas)--??--154
Neisus, F.G.--Prussia--(enl. CT)--240
Nelson, George L.--(enl. CO)--154
Nelson, J. Martin--IL--(enl. IL)--240
Nelson, Nelson Edward--(enl. MN)--154
Nesbitt, Everett G.--PA--(enl. IA)--240
Nesbitt, Jeremiah--OH--(enl. OH)--154
Nettlebeck, Herman--(enl. MO)--154
Nevenhuisen, William W.--PA--(enl. PA)--154
New, Edward--(enl.US)--154
Newsom(e), Eli--Bartholomew Co, IN--(enl. IN)--240
Newton, George A.--OH--(enl. IL)--240
Nichols, Absalom W.--VA--(enl. IA)--240
Nichols, Edmund--NY--(enl. NY)--240
Nichols, F.A.--??--240
Nichols, Franklin P.--NH--(enl. MI)--240
Nichols, George Ewing--WI--(enl. US)--154
Nichols, H.H.--NY--(enl. PA)--240
Nichols, James G.B.--NY--(enl. MI)--154
Nichols, Francis (Mrs. George E.)--??--154
Nichols, Sabra E. (Mrs. James G.B.)--American--154
Nichols, Wilmont D.--PA--(enl. KS)--240
Nickels, Edgar A.--ME--(enl. ME)--240
Nickens, Samuel I.--PA--(enl. US)--155
Noble, John--Chesterfield Co, VA--(enl. CA)--241
Noble, Patrick--Ireland--(enl. PA)--241
Noble, Thomas P.--ME--(enl. ME)--155
Northern, Walter B.--Lawrenceburg, IN--(enl. IN)--241

INDEX (Con't)

Norton, Daniel A.--ME--(enl. NY)--241
Norton, Harry--NY--(enl. NY)--241
Nosler, Esther L. (Mrs. James M.)--??--155
Nosler, James Mylan/Mylon--IN--(enl. IA)--155
Noyce, William D.--Hudson, NY--(enl. WI)--241
Noyes, Ira--NH--(enl. NH)--241
Nulton, O.D.--Morgan Co, OH--(enl. MO)--241
Nulton, Sylvanus D.--Morgan Co, OH--(enl. MO)--241
Nute, Charles N.--ME--(enl. DC)--155
Nute, Elizabeth (Mrs. Charles N.)--??--155
Nutt, Henry Walker--American--(enl. CA)--155
Ober, Cora (Mrs. William)--??--155
Ober, William--Somerset Co, PA--(enl. PA)--155
O'Brien, James--Kalamazoo, MI--(enl. MN)--241
O'Donnell, John F.--Ireland--(enl. US)--241
O'Farrell, Ellen G. or Ellen Cecelia (Mrs. William M.)--??--155
O'Farrell, William Morris--NY--(enl. NY)--155
O'Neill, Patrick--Co.Tyrone, Ireland--(enl. CA)--156
O'Neill, Lorenza Silvas y Machado--(Mrs. Patrick) (from Old Town SD family)--156
Ogden, Mina (Mrs. Tully)--??--156
Ogden, Tully--Norway--(enl. CA)--156
Ogle, Irene A. (Mrs. John J.)--??--156
Ogle, John Joseph--PA--(enl. PA)--156
O'Leary, Stephen--Ireland--(enl. US)--241
Olin, Alma (Mrs. Dyer W.)--??--156
Olin, Dyer W.--Maconogo(?), WI--(enl. WI)--156
Oliphant, Delphine C. (Mrs. John A.)--??--156
Oliphant, John A.--IN--(enl. IN)--156
Olney, Eugene C.--NY--(enl. MI)--241
Oltman, Richard H.--Bremen, Germany?--(enl. KS)--241
Oman, George B.--??--241
Orcutt, Eliza E. (Mrs. Herman C.)--VT--156
Orcutt, Herman C.--MA--(enl. VT)--156
Orrick, Emaline (Mrs. Ephraim/Ephream M.)--NC--156
Orrick/Ouick, Ephraim/Ephream M.--AR--(enl. TX)--156
Osgood, Isaac P.--Lowell, MA--(enl. MA)--242
Otis, Agnes (Mrs. Elmer)--??--157
Otis, Elmer--MA--(enl. US?)--157
Ott, George K.--Philadelphia, PA--(enl. IL)--242
Outcalt, Lewis A./S.--OH--(enl. IL)--157
Outcalt, Mary L. Whitmore (Mrs. Lewis A./S.)--OH--157
Oviatt, Augusta (Mrs. William H.)--??--157
Oviatt, William H.--OH--(enl. IA)--157
Owen, George B.--Tompkins Co, NY--(enl. WI)--242
Owens, John--England--(enl. CT)--242
Owens, William J./T.--Wales--(enl. WI)--157
Owings, Luther--IN--(enl. IN)--242

Packard, P.L.--Winnebago Co, IL--(enl. IL)--242
Paine, Jane Price/Jennie (Mrs. John O.W.)--MD--157
Paine, John O.W.--Chaleston?, ME--(enl. ME)--157
Painter, Samuel--PA--(enl. PA)--242
Palmateer, Charles Daniel--(enl. IL)--157
Palmanteer, David--??--(enl. PA)--242
Palmer, Ernest--OH--(enl. KS)--242
Palmer, Isaac Lassell--Marietta, OH--(enl. OH)--157
Palmer, J.H.--NY--(enl. NY)--242
Palmer, John Dresser--Washington Co, OH--(enl. OH)--158
Palmer, Lydia S. (Mrs. John D.)--OH--158
Palmer, M.J.--??--242
Palmer, Maria W. (Mrs. Isaac L.)--OH--157
Palmer, Mary Sophia (mother of Mrs. Ida Lillian Pirnie --see Pirnie below--??--161)
Palmer, T.R.--Herkimer Co, NY--(enl. MI)--242
Pardo, Horace--Whitehall, NY--(enl. NY)--242
Parish, Watson--TN--(enl. IL)--242
Parker, Charles H.--NY--(enl. NY)--242
Parker, Dexter--MA--(enl. IL)--242
Parker, Edson O.--NY--(enl. NY)--158
Parker, Edwin A.--VT--(enl. MN)--242
Parker, George H./W.--PA--(enl. IL)--158
Parker, Jane A. (Mrs. Edson O.)--American--158
Parker, Mary A. (Mrs. George W.)--American--158
Parker, Stephen H.--OH--(enl. WI)--243
Parker, William T.--MA--(enl. MA)--243
Parks, Milton B.--NY--(enl. WI)--243
Parmenter, William P.--IL--(enl. IL)--243
Parsons, Benjamin F.--VA--(enl. US)--158
Parsons, Francis Tenley or Talley (Mrs. Benjamin F.)--??--158
Partsch, Emil C.--TX--(enl. IL)--243
Patrick, Wellington--IL--(enl. IL)--243
Patterson, James Lloyd--Henderson Co, NC--(enl. NC)--158
Patton, Morand D.--Findley, Hancock Co, OH--(enl. IA)--158
Paull, Benjamin B.--IL--(enl. IA)--243
Paull, Charles M.--Kane Co, IL--(enl. IA)--158
Payne, Erasmus--American--(enl.OH)--159
Payton, William N.--Anderson Co, KY--(enl. MO)--243
Peak, Jacob--Lorraine, France--(enl. OH)--243
Pearce, Jacob--PA--(enl. IL)--159
Pearson, M.R.--Scott Co, KY--(enl. IA)--243
Pearson, Thomas J.--IN--(enl. IA)--243
Pease, John Melvin--Wilton, ME--(enl. ME)--243
Peck, Hiram H.--Henega? Falls, NY--(enl. NY)--159
Peck, Nellie E. or Mellie (Mrs. Hiram H.)--??--159
Peebles, L.R.--??--243
Peer, James A.--Putnam Co, OH--(enl. MO)--243
Peirson, J. Lacy--NY--(enl. NJ)--244
Pells, Francis A. (Mrs. James W.)--??--159

INDEX (Con't)

Pells, James William--NY--(enl. NY)--159
Pendland, Alonzo--Elkhart Co, IN--(enl. IN)--244
Pennell, Robert J.--NY--(enl. US)--159
Perigo, William--Susquehanna Co, PA--(enl. PA)--244
Perkins, Harrison--Greenbriar Co, WV--(enl. IN) --244
Perrin, William H.--England--(enl. MI)--244
Peterson, Bergette (Mrs. George)--??--159
Peterson, George--Norway--(enl. NV)--159
Pettingill, Amos--MA--(enl. MA)--159
Pettingill, Frances (Mrs. Amos)--American--159
Pettit, John Wycliffe--IL--(enl. WI)--159
Pettit, Mary (Mrs. John W.)--??--159
Petty, John W.--(enl. IL)--159
Pfaff, George--Germany--(enl. OH)--160
Pfister, Adam--Germany--(enl. KY)--160
Pfister, Ferdinand--Germany--(enl. OH)--160
Pfister, Frances (Mrs. Ferdinand)--??--160
Phelps, F.A.--WI--(enl. WI)--244
Phillips, Lionel D.--ME--(enl. MA)--244
Piburn, Mary E. (Mrs. Thomas B.)--??--160
Piburn, Thomas Benton--(enl. IA)--160
Picken, John--Scotland--(enl. US)--160
Pickens, Frank--IL--(enl. IL)--244
Pickett, Cynthia (Mrs. Zedekiah)--American--160
Pickett, William T.--American--(enl. IA)--160
Pickett, Zedekiah--IN--(enl. IN)--160
Pierce, Charles O.--Lowell, MA--(enl. US)--160
Pierce, Maris--PA--(enl. PA)--244
Pierce, Sarah J. (Mrs. Charles O.)--American--160
Pierce, Sylvester L.--Olney, Rockland Co, IL-- (enl. IN)--244
Pierson, Ed Aug--NY--(enl. MI)--244
Piher, Rachel Adair (Mrs. William)--MD--160
Piher, William--Scotland--(enl. US)--160
Pillsbury, Cassius C.--ME--(enl. WI)--244
Pine, Albert B.--NY--(enl. NY)--244
Pirnie, Alexander--Argill, Scotland--(enl. NY)--161
Pirnie, Ida Lillian Palmer (Mrs. Alexander)-- Webster Hill, Oneida Co, NY--161
Pirnie (Palmer, Mary Sophia (mother of Mrs. Ida Lillian Pirnie)--??--161
Pitner, John L.--IL--(enl. IL)--244
Pivers, David Hart--ME--(enl. ?)--161
Place, Daniel C.--OH--(enl. OH)--244
Place, Samuel S.--NY--(enl. IL)--161
Poland, Martin--MA--(enl. RI)--244
Polhamus, Adelbert C. (AKA Albert Howard)--29 Cannon St, New York City--(enl. NY)--161
Pollock, Emma (Mrs. Samuel S.)--KY--161
Pollock, Samuel S.--PA--(enl. PA)--161
Pontious, Wilson--OH--(enl. OH)--244
Pool, Chester W.--IN--(enl. WI)--245
Pope, Evaline Hendrix or Eva (Mrs. Wm.)--??--161

Pope, William W.--NY--(enl. IL)--161
Porter, John--Brown Co, OH--(enl. IA)--245
Porter, John P.--PA--(enl. PA)--161
Porter, Stephen--IN--(enl. IN)--245
Porter, Watson B.--IL--(enl. IA)--245
Potter, Daniel--OH--(enl. OH)--245
Potter, Milton M.--PA--(enl. IL)--161
Powell, A.H.--KY--(enl. MO)--162
Powell, John C.--PA--(enl. PA)--245
Powers, Anna E. (Mrs. Robert A.)--??--162
Powers, Marion--IN--(enl. IN)--162
Powers, Robert A.--VT--(enl. VT)--162
Powers, Robert M.--Alden, NY--(enl. OH)--245
Pratt, C.W.--MA--(enl. MA)--245
Pratt, Charles E.--WI--(enl. WI)--245
Prescott, C.W.--PA--(enl. KS)--245
Preston, Charles--??--245
Price, Levi--PA--(enl. US)--245
Probert, John--Patterson, NJ--(enl. NJ)--245
Pruden, Ludlow--American--(enl. ?)--162
Pugh, Theophilus J.--IN--(enl. IN)--162
Purvis, George--Scotland--(enl. OH)--245
Puterbaugh, Amy C. (Mrs. George)--??--162
Puterbaugh/Puterbough, Catherine H. (Mrs. George) --??--162
Puterbaugh, George--IL--(enl. IL)--162
Putnam, C.S.--NY--(enl. NY)--245
Putnam, George--MA--(enl. CO)--245
Quackenbush, Chauncey--NY--(enl. NY)--245
Quigley, George Beard--Warren Co, PA--(enl. PA) --162
Radford, Thomas--NY--(enl. US)--245
Rafferty, E.G.--Dearborn Co, IN--(enl. IN)--245
Rainbow, Augusta (Mrs. James P.M.) (later Lockwood)--??--162
Rainbow, James P.M.--Beaver Co, PA--(enl. CA)--162
Ramsey, Ada J. (Mrs. Simmons) (later Meehan?)-- ??--163
Ramsey, Simmons--IN--(enl. KS)--163
Randall, Thomas J.--MI--(enl. IA)--246
Rapeleye, A.W.--Fishkill, NY--(enl. CA)--246
Read, John W.--OH--(enl. IN)--246
Reames, Bartlett--(enl. MO)--163
Reames, Rebecca Boothman (Mrs. Bartlett)--??--163
Redfern, Alfred--(enl. IN)--163
Reece. O.M.--IA--(enl. IA)--246
Reed. A.--ME--(enl. ME)--246
Reed, Francis B.--OH--(enl. NE)--246
Reed, James C.--(Chillicote?, OH)--(enl.OH)--163
Reed, John--PA--(enl. PA)--246
Reed, John P.--ME--(enl. ?)--163
Reeder, T.W.--??--246
Reid, Andrew D.--Johnstown, NY--(enl. NY)--246
Reintanz, O.J.--Germany--(enl. NJ)--246

INDEX (Con't)

Remondino, Peter Charles--Italy--(enl. US)--163
Remondino, Sophia (Mrs. Peter C.)--France--163
Rench, Lyman T.--MD--(enl. IL)--163
Rench, Susan Agnes (Mrs. Lyman T.)--??--163
Reupsche, Dorothy (Mrs. William)--??--163
Reupsche, William--Germany--(enl. NY)--163
Reynolds, Amelia Maria (Mrs. Hiram H.)--??--164
Reynolds, Hiram H.--NY--(enl. NY)--163
Reynolds, Joshua Thomas--PA--(enl. PA)--164
Reynolds, Lewis D.--NY--(enl. NY)--164
Rhoads, Abraham--OH--(enl. OH)--246
Rhodes, Ransom E.--NY--(enl. MI)--246
Rice, Almeron F.--Newark, Wayne Co, NY--(enl. MI)--164
Rice, Hosea B.--Howard, NY--(enl. US)--246
Rice, John H.--Norway/ME--(enl. US)--164
Rice, Laban W.--TX--(enl. TX)--164
Richards, George J.--NY--(enl. NY)--164
Richards, George W.--Hamilton Co, OH--(enl. IN)--246
Richards, Hermina A. (Mrs. George J.)--??--164
Richardson, A. Tappen--MA--(enl. US)--246
Richardson, Charles D.--MA--(enl. MA)--164
Richardson, Sarah Titlon (Mrs. Chas.D.)--??--164
Richey, Flora Garvin (Mrs. Jay H.)--??--165
Richey, Jay Harvey--Maryville, OH--(enl. OH)--165
Richmond, John--IN--(enl. IA)--247
Richmond, Jonathan Edward--(enl. MO)--165
Richmond, Margaret A. (Mrs. Johnathan E.)--??--165
Rickard, Charles W.--OH--(enl. IA)--247
Rickit, H.V.--France--(enl. Washington Territory)--247
Ricksecker, Lucius Edgar--PA--(enl. PA)--165
Riddle, Catherine C. (Mrs. George H.)--??--165
Riddle, George Henry--PA--(enl. IA)--165
Riddle, James D.--(enl. IL)--165
Riedelbauch, John--Belvaria (Bavaria?)--(enl. IL)--247
Riggs, Joseph--England--(enl. WI)--247
Riley, Frances M. (Mrs. William T.)--??--165
Riley, William T.--Allegheny Co, NY--(enl. NY)--165
Rimbach, Charles/Carl--Germany--(enl. US)--247
Roach, Hattie Lee (Mrs. William H.)--??--165
Roach, Henry--England--(enl. MI)--165
Roach, Viola M. Carling (Mrs. Henry)--??--165
Roach, William Henry--Williams Co, TN--(enl. TN)--165
Roark, James A.--IL--(enl. IL)--166
Roberts, Joseph W.--OH--(enl. OH)--166
Roberts, Luzerne L.--OH--(enl. OH)--166
Roberts, Matilda (Mrs. Joseph W.)--OH--166
Roberts, Samuel L.--Lee Co, OH--(enl. IL)--247
Robertson, Simon--Monmouth, IL--(enl. IL)--247
Robinson, A.S.--Jefferson, PA--(enl. MN)--247

Robinson, Culbert Byron--PA--(enl. PA)--166
Robinson, George--Lancaster Co, PA--(enl. US)--247
Robinson, George Cromwell--England--(enl. OH)--166
Robinson, Melvin W.--Washington Co, OH--(enl. OH)--166
Roby, David B.--OH--(enl. OH)--166
Roby, Rheuben Theodore--OH--(enl. WI)--166
Rockwood, George--Kane Co, IL--(enl. KS)--247
Rockwood, Mary (Mrs. George)--??--247
Roderick, Edward--NY--(enl. IA)--247
Rodgers/Rogers, Ellen (Mrs. Henry J.G.)--England--167
Rodgers, Henry J.G.--NY--(enl. NY)--166
Rodig, Charles Herman--(enl. OH)--167
Rodig, Mary (Mrs. Charles H.)--??--167
Rogers, Eli--Seneca Co, OH--(enl. OH)--247
Rogers, Mary W. (Mrs. Eli)--??--247
Roneau, Charles F.W.--Hamburg, Germany--(enl. ?)--247
Rood, Vernon Dudley--VT--(enl. VT)--167
Root, Eleaser Talcut--Coventry, CT--(enl. IL)--167
Root, Francis E. (Mrs. Eleaser T.)--??--167
Root, M.S.--Medina, OH--(enl. OH)--247
Rose, Bowers L.--NY--(enl. PA)--248
Rose, Clara (Mrs. John)--??--167
Rose, George W.--American--(enl. MA)--167
Rose, John--PA--(enl. PA)--167
Rose, John L.--NY--(enl. NY)--248
Rosengarden, Moses--??--248
Ross, Daniel--Holland--(enl. CA)--248
Ross, James--(enl. US)--167
Ross, R.H.--NY--(enl. IA)--248
Rosswell, Edwin--(enl. MA)--167
Rouark, Nathan L.--MD--(enl. MD)--248
Routson, John G.--Columbiana Co, OH--(enl. OH)--248
Rowe, Charles Carroll--Guilford, NH--(enl. NH)--167
Rowe, Josiah Lemuel--MI--(enl. MI)--167
Rowley, Clara M. (Mrs. Samuel B.)--??--248
Rowley, Samuel B.--NY--(enl. MI)--248
Roys, S.W.--Pultneyville Wagner, England?--(enl. ??)--168
Rudrauff, William H.--PA--(enl. PA)--248
Ruff, Francis B.--Dearborn, MI--(enl. IA)--168
Ruff, Mary Ann Tiffin (Mrs. Francis B.)--England--168
Rule, Elizabeth A. (Mrs. George A.)--??--168
Rule, George A.--(enl. WI)--168
Rumpf, August--Germany--(enl. NY)--248
Runk, Joseph B.--PA--(enl. PA)--248
Russell, Enoch--IN--(enl. US)--248
Russell, Evaline (Mrs. Hiram W.)--??--168
Russell, Hiram W.--(enl. IL)--168
Russell, John I.--NY--(enl. IA)--168
Ryan, John T.--Ireland--(enl. IN)--248
Sackett, Charles H.--OH--(enl. OH)--248

INDEX (Con't)

Salazar, Jose Maria--Mexico--(enl. CA)--168
Sammis, Frances E. (Mrs. Marsden H.)--??--168
Sammis, Marsden H.--Westerville, OH--(enl. IN)--168
Sanborn, E.B.--ME--(enl. ME)--249
Santee, Milton--PA--(enl. IL)--249
Saum, Augustus B.--Homer, OH--(enl. IA)--168
Saum, Mary Emily (Mrs. Augustus B.)--??--168
Saunders, Charles K.--England--(enl. OH)--169
Savage, George B.--(enl. VA)--169
Sawtelle, Arthur M.--OH--(enl. ?)--249
Scarbrough, B.F.--American--(enl. KY)--169
Schaeffer, Jason--Tuscarora Co, OH--(enl. IN)--249
Schaler, Amalia (Mrs. Julius G.)--??--169
Schaler, Julius G.--(enl. MN)--169
Scherrer, Catherine (Mrs. Hieronimus)--??--169
Scherrer, Hieronimus--Germany--(enl. IL)--169
Schill, Charles--Germany--(enl. MA)--249
Schill, S.--Germany--(enl. MA)--249
Schiller, Henry J.--Prussia--(enl. MO)--169
Scholton, Charles--??--249
Schooley, Ellis L.--PA--(enl. IL)--249
Schrader, Adalia Layden (Mrs. Adolph)--American--169
Schrader, Adolph--Germany--(enl. IN)--169
Schroeter, Charles--Germany--(enl. MO)--249
Schudey/Shudy, John--PA--(enl. MO)--169
Schudey/Shudy, Leah (Mrs. John)--??--169
Schultheiss, Frederick L.--Germany--(enl. KA)--169
Schultheiss, Fredericka (Mrs. Frederick L.)--??--169
Schultz, Florence K. (Mrs. James T.)--??--170
Schultz, James T.--IL--(enl. IL)--170
Schutte, Gerhard--Germany--(enl. WI)--249
Scidmore, G.B.--(enl. CO)--170
Scoby/Scobey, Clara C. (Mrs. Thomas H.)--??--170
Scoby, Thomas Hertell--OH--(enl. OH)--170
Scofield, L.--NY--(enl. IA)--249
Scott, Helen Louise (Mrs. Winfield)--??--170
Scott, Winfield--MI--(enl. US)--170
Scruby, John--(enl. WI)--170
Seabold, Gilbert L.--IL--(enl. IL)--170
Seabold/Seabolt, Henry--PA--(enl. MD)--249
Seavy, Helen (Mrs. James)--??--170
Seavy, James--PA--(enl. WI)--170
Sechrist, Jacob--American--(enl. PA)--170
Sechrist, Lucy Enfield (Mrs. Jacob)--??--170
Sedgewick, Thomas Stewart--Zanesville, OH--(enl. ??)--170
Seidell, Charles W.--Germany--(enl. IL)--170
Sennock/Sennett Judson L.--NY--(enl. NY)--171
Servoss, Freeman--NY--(enl. IL)--171
Severy, Elisha--CT--(enl. CT)--249
Seymour, W.C.--American--(enl. US)--171
Shaffer, Peter--OH--(enl. KS)--249
Shall, Eugene E.--OH--(enl. OH)--249

Sharp, James L.--Richland, IN--(enl. IN)--171
Sharp, William H.--Platt Co, MO--(enl. MO)--249
Shattuck, John--Petersburg, IL--(enl. IL)--171
Shaughnessey/Shonessy, William M.--(enl. WI)--171
Shaw, A.C.--Dendmark?, OH--(enl. OH)--249
Shaw, Brigida M. (Mrs. Frank A.T.)--CA--171
Shaw, Frank A.T.--Philadelphia, PA--(enl. CA)--171
Shaw, Joseph M.--(enl. US)--171
Shay, William--(enl. IL)--171
Shea, Michael--Canada--(enl. IL)--249
Sheldon, Annie W. (Mrs. Richard H.)--England--172
Sheldon, Richard Henry--OH--(enl. OH)--172
Shelly, Mattie E. Bell (Mrs. Thomas C.)--Orford/Mouton, IA?--250
Shelly, Thomas C.--Richmond, Jefferson Co, OH--(enl. IL)--250
Shepard, Charles T.--NY--(enl. IL)--250
Shepherd, A.C.--??--250
Shepherd, James--KY--(enl. KY)--250
Sherman, Augusta J. Barrett (Mrs. Matthew)--ME--172
Sherman, Edward--(enl. IL)--172
Sherman, Francis M.--IN--(enl. IN)--172
Sherman, Frank M.--MA--(enl. MA)--250
Sherman, Jennie Dawley (Mrs. Francis M.)--American--172
Sherman, Matthew--Charlestown, MA--(enl. CA)--172
Sherwood, James--(enl. NJ)--172
Shill, General--OH--(enl. OH)--250
Shindler, George--Germany--(enl. IL)--250
Shock, William--Germany--(enl. NY)--250
Shorton, William--NY--(enl. NY)--250
Shryock, Mary Elizabeth (Mrs. Seymour)--??--172
Shryock, Seymour--IN--(enl. IA)--172
Shultz, James F.--IL--(enl. IL)--250
Shuyler, J.L.--IN--(enl. IN)--250
Sigman, Marcus--Easton, PA--(enl. PA)--250
Simmons, Clinton--NY--(enl. OH)--250
Simon(s), Johanna B. (Mrs. John)--Germany--172
Simon(s), John--Switzerland--(enl. IL)--172
Simpson, Anna Nancy (Mrs. John H.)--MO--172
Simpson, John H.--England--(enl. US)--172
Simpson, Joseph--MO--(enl. KS)--250
Sims, W.F.--Henry Co, KY--(enl. IN)--251
Singleton, J.A.--(enl. CA)--173
Sinks, Anna Elizabeth McKinney (Mrs. John)--??--173
Sinks, John F.--OH--(enl. OH)--173
Sisson, Elbert N.--NY--(enl. IA)--251
Skinner, Mary T. (Mrs. Simon)--??--173
Skinner, Simon--American--(enl. NY)--173
Slack, Andrew J.--American--(enl. WV)--173
Slade, Isaac--England--(enl. WI)--251
Slaughter, William--Canton, IL--(enl. IL)--251
Sloan, James L.--Fairfield, IN--(enl. IN)--173
Sloane, Hampton P.--OH--(enl. IL)--251

INDEX (Con't)

Slocum, Cella B. (Mrs. Milton L.)--MO--173
Slocum, Milton L--Charlotte Co, VT--(enl. AL)--173
Slusser, Abraham--Brookfield, OH--(enl. IL)--251
Sly, George Elliott--(enl. MN)--173
Smart, James G.--NY--(enl. NY)--251
Smith, Adelaide A. (Mrs. George H.)--??--174
Smith, Ana (Mrs. Henry)--??--174
Smith, Ansel G.--NY--(enl. MI)--251
Smith, C.E.--WI--(enl. IA)--251
Smith, C.M.--??--251
Smith, Charles F.--American--(enl. IL)--173
Smith, Charles F.--American--(enl. OH)--173
Smith, D.M.--IN--(enl. IN)--251
Smith, Edward--NY--(enl. NY)--251
Smith, Edward H.--OH--(enl. MI)--251
Smith, Eleanor M. (Mrs. Peter C.)--PA--175
Smith, Ernest L.--OH--(enl. OH)--251
Smith, Eugene E.--IL--(enl. KS)--251
Smith, Frederick A.--??--173
Smith, Frederick P.--New York City--(enl. NY)--251
Smith, G.C. or George W.--(enl. TN)--173
Smith, G.W.--IA--(enl. IA)--252
Smith, George H.--American--(enl. US)--174
Smith, George H.--NY--(enl. MI)--174
Smith, George William--(enl. Confedederate)--174
Smith, Harriet H. (Mrs. Charles F.)--??--173
Smith, Henry--(enl. IL)--174
Smith, Henry--(enl. WI)--174
Smith, Henry F.--ME--(enl. ME)--252
Smith, Ichabod--IN--(enl. IN)--252
Smith, J. Bryant--NY--(enl. NY)--252
Smith, James A.--IN--(enl. KS)--174
Smith, James K.--OH--(enl. IL)--174
Smith, Jeanette Fiske (Mrs. Joseph H.)--??--174
Smith, Joseph H.--Boston, MA--(enl. NY)--174
Smith, Julius S.--Athens, OH--(enl. OH)--175
Smith, Kittie Loree (Mrs. Samuel W.)--??--175
Smith, Martha (Mrs. Richard)--??--175
Smith, Mary Francis Brown (Mrs. George H.)--??--174
Smith, Mary W. (Mrs. Julius S.)--??--175
Smith. O. Cincinatus--Waverly, TN--(enl. TN)--175
Smith, Peter C.--IN--(enl. IN)--175
Smith, Priscilla A. (Mrs. James A.)--??--174
Smith, Richard--NY--(enl. WI)--175
Smith, Samuel C.--PA--(enl. CA)--175
Smith, Samuel W.--NY--(enl. NY)--175
Smith, Sarah C. (Mrs. George W.)--??--174
Smith, Theron J.--NY--(enl. IL)--252
Smith, Thomas B.--OH--(enl. IL)--252
Smouse, Daniel F.--(enl. PA)--175
Smouse, Lizzie Miller (Mrs. Daniel F.)--??--175
Smout, Basil--England--(enl. WI)--175
Smout, Emma L. (Mrs. Basil)--??--175
Smyth, Frank--IL--(enl. IL)--252

Snead/Smead, Della Margaret (Mrs. William B.) --??--176
Snead, William B.--Charlston?, Washington Co, VA--(enl. KY)--176
Snedecor, Isaac D.--MO--(enl. MO)--176
Sneer, Philetus E.--Richland Co, OH--(enl. IN)--176
Snider, Daniel S.--Perry Co, OH--(enl. OH)--252
Snoderly, Emanuel--IA--(enl. MO)--252
Snyder, Edward--Poland--(enl. NY)--176
Snyder, Jennie Whiteley (Mrs. John H.)--??--176
Snyder, John H.--OH--(enl. KS)--176
Snyder/Snider, Lorenzo--(enl. IN)--176
Snyder, Martha J. (Mrs. Lorenzo)--??--176
Snyder, Mary Stoddard (Mrs. Edward)--??--176
Southwell, Robert--England--(enl. MO)--252
Southwick, Myron H.--MI--(enl. MI)--252
Spangler, Henry--Holmes Co, OH--(enl. IA)--252
Spates, John M.--TN--(enl. IL)--252
Spaulding, Edgar--NY--(enl. NY)--252
Speers, Gustav(e)/August--Germany--(enl. NY)--176
Spence, Samuel R.--PA--(enl. PA/VRC)--176
Spence, Sarah (Mrs. Samuel R.)--OH--176
Spencer, James R.--MO--(enl. MO)--253
Spencer, Jonathan Richmond--MO--(enl. MO)--177
Spencer, Myron T.--Madison Co, NY--(enl. MI)--253
Spencer, Sarah Jane (Mrs. Jonathan R.)--OH--177
Sperry, W.L.--OH--(enl. OH)--253
Spickert, Jacob--Germany--(enl. OH)--253
Spileman, Edward Barnett--MA--(enl. NJ)--177
Sprague, Jennie (Mrs. Joseph B.)--??--177
Sprague, Joseph Benjamin--NJ--(enl. IN)--177
St.Clair, Hugh--PA--(enl. IA)--253
Stacey, Arthur G.--OH--(enl. IN)--253
Stambaugh/Stambough, Evaline (Mrs. William H.)--OH--177
Stambaugh/Stambough, William H.--OH--(enl. IN)--177
Stancliff, Florence (Mrs. William H.)--??--177
Stancliff, William Henry--McKean, Erie Co, PA--(enl. US)--177
Stansberry, Charles H.--NY--(enl. WI)--253
Stark, Elizabeth (Mrs. Nathaniel J.)--??--177
Stark, Nathaniel Jasper--IN--(enl. IL)--177
Starr, Henry P.--NY--(enl. NY)--253
Statler, M.E. (Mrs. Sylvester) (later Rogers)--OH--177
Statler, Sylvester--Miami Co, OH--(enl. OH)--177
Steadman, William--England--(enl. IA)--253
Stearns, Hiram Allen--MA--(enl. MA)--177
Stearns, Melissa Ann (Mrs. Hiram A.)--??--177
Steele, Augustus F.--NY--(enl. NY)--178
Steele, Julia C. (Mrs. Augustus F.)--??--178
Steele, Mary A. (Mrs. Seumere? G.)--ME--178
Steele, Seumere? G.--NY--??--178
Steinhour, William E.--VT--(enl. VT)--253
Stenger, W.H.--OH--(enl. OH)--253

INDEX (Con't)

Stephen, Robert--Scotland--(enl. MN)--178
Stephens, Catherine Elizabeth (Mrs. Walter)--??--178
Stephens, David--TN--(enl. WI)--178
Stephens, Mary Ellen (Mrs. David)--??--178
Stephens Walter--England--(enl. NY)--178
Stevens, E.L.--NY--(enl. IL)--253
Stevens, Edward R.--NY--(enl. WI)--178
Stevens, Esther (Mrs. Edward R.)--NY--178
Stevens, L.W.--MI--(enl. US)--253
Stevens, Uzzial J.--Knox Co, OH--(enl. IA)--178
Stewart, E.B.--MD--(enl. OH)--179
Stewart, Frances (Mrs. Samuel W.)--??--179
Stewart, Mellie--VT--253
Stewart, Perry--Rushville, IN--(enl. IL)--253
Stewart, Samuel W.--PA--(enl. PA)--179
Stewart, Sylvester N.--OH--(enl. IA)--253
Stewart, Thomas J.--NY--(enl. NY)--179
Stewart, W.B.--(enl. US)--179
Stewart, William M.--PA--(enl. PA)--253
Stewins, Irenius D.--IL--(enl. IL)--254
Stielberg, William--Germany--(enl. OH)--254
Stiles, Alonzo R.--Dubuque, IA--(enl. IA)--179
Stimson, Albert S.--Lawrence, MI--(enl. MI)--179
Stimson, Jessie Hall (Mrs. Albert S.)--??--179
Stockton, Charles A.--OH--(enl. OH)--254
Stoddard, Silas E.--NY--(enl. NY)--254
Stone, A.B.--PA--(enl. PA)--254
Stone, George M--MI--(enl. MI)--179
Stone, Susan Emma Farley (Mrs. George)--??--179
Stone, William P.--MA--(enl. CT)--254
Stonebraker, James A.--Belmont Co, OH--(enl. OH)--254
Stopher, Edgar A.--(enl. IA)--179
Stopher, Susie L. (Mrs. Edgar A.)--??--179
Storey, Clara Choate (Mrs. William H.)--CA--179
Storey, William Henry--NY--(enl. US)--179
Story, Adella (Mrs. Hampton L.)--??--254
Story, Hampton L.--VT--(enl. VT)--254
Story, Ruth (Mrs. Hampton L.)--??--254
Stout, James--Redding, PA--(enl. US)--254
Stover, Fannie M. (Mrs. Joseph W.)--??--180
Stover, Joseph W.--American--(enl. IL)--180
Strahle, Alphonso--Germany--(enl. MI)--255
Stratton, Samuel S.--OH--(enl. OH)--180
Straw, Alonzo D.--NH--(enl. NH)--255
Strawbridge, John B.--PA--(enl. PA)--255
Strawbridge, Mary (Mrs. John B.?)--??--255
Strawn, James C.--Delaware Co, IN--(enl. KS)--180
Strawn, Lida G. (Mrs. James C.)--??--180
Streeter, H.P.--Lowe, Chatham Province, Canada--(enl. KS)--255
Streube, John--France--(enl. PA)--255

Stuart, Alonzo B.--ME--(enl. ME)--255
Sullivan, John Cornwall--IL--(enl. CA)--180
Sullivan, Marcus M.--Boston, MA--(enl. MA)--180
Sullivan, Margaret(t) (Mrs. John C.)--??--180
Sullivan, Maude Belle (Mrs. Marcus M.)--??--180
Sunderland, John D.--Burlington, IA--(enl. IA)--255
Sunnocks, Eliza (Mrs. Melvin D.)--American--180
Sunnocks, Melvin D.--St. Lawrence Co, NY--(enl. WI)--180
Sutemeier, Henry--Germany--(enl. MO)--180
Sutemeier, Mary E. (Mrs. Henry)--??--180
Sutherland, Thomas J.--(enl. MI)--180
Svenningson, John C.--Denmark--(enl. NY)--255
Swan, Thomas--Green Co, PA--(enl. IL)--255
Sweeney, Agnes T. (Mrs. Henry)--??--181
Sweeney, Henry--Ireland--(enl. US)--181
Sweetland, Seth--ME--(enl. ME)--255
Sweetman, Stephen--Ireland--(enl. MI)--255
Swetnam, James S.--(enl.MO)--181
Taft, Byron Parker--Wetutown or Watertown?, WI--(enl. WI)--181
Taft, Sarah (Mrs. Byron P.)--??--181
Talcott, Emma Jane (Mrs. Henry W.)--IA--181
Talcott, Henry W.--IN--(enl. IN)--181
Tartt, Thomas M.--OH--(enl. IL)--255
Taylor, Charles Paxton--Delaware--(enl. DE)--255
Taylor, George O.--CT--(enl. US)--181
Taylor, R.W.--England--(enl. IL)--256
Teeters, Loftus--OH--(enl. OH)--181
Teeters, Rebecca (Mrs. Loftus)--??--181
Tengwall, Charles--Sweden--(enl. US)--256
Tenny, Silas B.--NY--(enl. WI)--181
Terwilliger, C.H.--??--256
Thieme, Charles B.--Germany--(enl. WI)--181
Thieme, John F.--??--256
Thieme, Theresa (Mrs. Charles B.)--??--181
Thoman, John A.--Roisit?, NY--(enl. KY)--256
Thomas, Albert A.--IL--(enl. IA)--256
Thomas, John P.--Liverpool, England--(enl. WI)--256
Thomas, Thomas W.--England--(enl. OH)--256
Thompson, Archibald R.--NY--(enl. PA)--256
Thompson, Charles D.--Canada--(enl. WI)--256
Thompson, Frank--??--256
Thompson, Hiram P.--NY--(enl. NY)--256
Thompson, J.J.--Warren Co, OH--(enl. OH)--256
Thompson, James Granville--Sandy Creek, NY--(enl. NY)--182
Thompson, Laura Elma (Mrs. James G.) (parents: Wm. & Caroline King DePoy of Ohio--??--182
Thompson, Samuel/Saul--Norway--(enl. IL)--182
Thornburg, Albert M.--NC--(enl. IN)--256
Tibbals, Joseph B./H.--American--(enl. OH)--182
Tibbals, Rena (Mrs. Joseph B./H.)--??--182
Tiffany, John F.--CT--(enl. CT)--256

INDEX (Con't)

Tillman, Robert--Fairfax, VA--(enl. US)--182
Tinker, Adelia J. Sholes (Mrs. Edgar C.)--??--182
Tinker, Edgar C.--Bedford, OH--(enl. OH)--182
Tinker, William H.--ME--(enl. ME)--182
Tippett, Samuel D.--MD--(enl. MO)--256
Titus, Anson--NY/NH--(enl. WI)--256
Todd, Eugene--NJ--(enl. IL)--183
Todd, Grace E. (Mrs. Eugene)--??--183
Todd, James--(enl. IL)--183
Tomlin, George--England--(enl. IL)--257
Toms, George O.--ME--(enl. OH)--257
Touhy, Martin--Ireland--(enl. US)--257
Tout, Henry Clay--Danville, IN--(enl. IN)--183
Tout, Neville S. Clay (Mrs. Henry C.)--??--183
Towers, Justus A.--(enl. IA)--183
Townsend, Daniel W.--American--(enl. IL)--183
Townsend, William E.--PA--(enl. WV)--257
Tracy, J.E.--NY--(enl. NY)--183
Tracy, James H.--MI--(enl. IA)--183
Tracy, John--Ireland--(enl. NY)--183
Trader, W.S.--MO--(enl. MO)--257
Traylor, Madison--??--(enl. IN)--257
Travers, Jones/Jonas--MA--(enl. US)--183
Trego, Harrison--??--257
Triggs, John--England--(enl. IL)--257
Trogler, William A.--PA--(enl. PA)--257
Trott, George F.--Boston, MA--(enl. MA)--257
Troxel, Joseph--Lebanon, PA--(enl. PA)--257
Troxell, John P.--??--257
Tucker, Emma R. (Mrs. Samuel F.)--??--183
Tucker, James W.--IL--(enl. IL)--257
Tucker, Samuel F.--(enl. MA)--183
Tufs, Charles P.--NY--(enl. NY)--257
Turner, Asbury--IN--(enl. IN)--184
Turner, David--Cambridge, OH--(enl. OH)--257
Turner, Hester S. (Mrs. John C.)--??--184
Turner, John Castle--Ireland--(enl. US)--184
Turner, Virginia A. (Mrs. Asbury)--??--184
Tyler, Joseph H.--NY--(enl. MN)--184
Tyler, Martha (Mrs. Joseph H.)--American--184
Tyrell, John D.--England--(enl. NY)--184
Tyrell, Julia D. Walker (Mrs. John D.)--ME--184
Tyson, William--PA--(enl. PA)--257
Underwood, Hugh--PA--(enl. OH)--184
Unger, August--Germany--(enl. NY)--184
Utt, Lee H.--Jersey Co, IL--(enl. MO)--258
Utt, Sarah M. Gunn--??--258
Valentine, D.A.--IA--(enl. IA)--258
Valentine, I.W.--IA--(enl. IA)--258
Van Arman, Amanda Convis (Mrs. John)--American--184
Van Arman, John--Plattsburg, NY--(enl. ?)--184
Van Buskirk, Emily (Mrs. Marshall)--??--184
Van Buskirk, Marshall--American--(enl. WI)--184

Van Castle, Jennie (Mrs. Joseph)--NY--185
Van Castle, Joseph--Germany/Belgium--(enl. PA)--184
Van Ostrand, J.E./Jacob--(enl. NY)--185
VanDine, George B.--(enl. OH)--185
Van Scoten, M.L.--NJ--(enl. NJ)--258
Varnum, Geo.M.--Washington, D.C.--(enl.DC)--258
Veile, George C.--Denmark--(enl. WI)--185
Velbert/Velvet, John--Germany--(enl. NY)--185
Venters, George--KY--(enl. OH)--258
Venters, Pleasant--KY--(enl. KY)--258
Vest, Ann (Mrs. Arthur E.)--??--185
Vest, Arthur E.--Cincinnati, OH--(enl. IN)--185
Vest, Roland (father of Arthur)--Franklin Co, VA--185
Vest, Edith Edwards (mother of Arthur)--Franklin Co, VA--185
Vestel, W.L.--IN--(enl. IN)--258
Vincent, J.W.--England--(enl. IL)--258
Viney, William M.--OH--(enl. MA)--258
Vredenberg, John L.--NY--(enl. NY)--258
Wade, Martha V. (Mrs. Nelson W.)--??--185
Wade, Nelson Walker--NY--(enl. NY)--185
Wadlia, Andrew J.--ME--(enl. NH)--258
Walker, Fletcher Jackson--OH--(enl. IA)--185
Walker, Leonard--Steuben Co, NY--(enl. NY)--258
Warburton, Eliza R. (Mrs. Percival D.)--??--186
Warburton, Percival D.--RI--(enl. RI)--186
Ward, Adolphus--Topeka, KA--(enl. A.O.U.W.?)--186
Ward, Chaney--OH--(enl. WI)--258
Ward, Curtis D.--??--258
Ward, Elizabeth (Mrs. Adolphus) (later Conklin?)--??--186
Ward, G.G. or George H?--(enl. VT)--186
Ward, Henry A.--IL--(enl. IL)--258
Ward, James S.--NY--(enl. NY)--259
Ward, Jerome L.--NY--(enl. WI)--186
Ward, Peter--Bellvue, IL--(enl. CO)--186
Ward, Samson L.--IN--(enl. IN)--259
Ward, Stephen I.--NY--(enl. US)--259
Ward, Thomas S.--OH--(enl. OH)--259
Warden, M.W.--Louisville, KY--(enl. KS)--259
Warne, Charles--NY--(enl. CA)--259
Warner, Elizabeth A. (Mrs. Francis H.)--??--186
Warner, Francis H.--MA--(enl. MA)--186
Warner, Robert T.--CT--(enl. WI)--259
Warren, Antoinette A. Peck (Mrs. Jones K.)--American--186
Warren, Dillard--OH--(enl. MO)--259
Warren, Jones K.--Canada--(enl. OH)--186
Washburn, A. Judson--ME--(enl. RI)--259
Washington, Greenbery--Scott Co, KY--(enl. US)--259
Washington, S.W.--(enl. OH)--186
Washington, Watkins--(enl. IN)--259
Wasson, Cynthia (Mrs. John)--??--186

INDEX (Con't)

Wasson, John--MO/IN--(enl. MO)--186
Waterman, William A.--MA--(enl. MA)--259
Watkins, G.C.--??--259
Watkins, William/Wilber F.--OH--(enl. OH)--259
Watson, Alexander G.--Burlington, VT--(enl. VT)--187
Watson, Charles C.--Adrian, MI--(enl. IA)--259
Watson, Delia Haskell (Mrs. Alexander G.)--
    American--187
Watson, Jennie B. (Mrs. Joseph M.)--??--187
Watson, John--OH--(enl. MO)--260
Watson, Joseph M.--(enl. IA)--187
Wattles, M. Richard--IL--(enl. MN)--260
Watts, Peter--Dundee, Scotland--(enl. IA)--187
Waugh, Samuel--PA--(enl. IL)--187
Waugh, Susan (Mrs. Samuel)--??--187
Way, Francis Burdett--NY--(enl. MI)--260
Wearing, Eleanor Jane (Mrs. John) (later Bray)
    --??--187
Wearing, John--Wayne Co, PA--(enl. PA)--187
Weatherbee, George M.--MA--(enl. MA)--260
Weatherby, Charles--NJ--(enl. IL)--260
Weaver, Charles S./W.--IL--(enl. MN)--187
Weaver, Emily J. or Emma J. (Mrs. Thomas F.)
    --??--187
Weaver, Joseph L.--PA--(enl. IA)--260
Weaver, Nettie (Mrs. Charles S./W.)--??--187
Weaver, Noah--??--260
Weaver, Thomas F.--OH--(enl. CO)--187
Webb, Charles Aden--Middlefield, MA--(enl. VT)
    --188
Webb, Flora (Mrs. Charles A.)--??--188
Webber, George--MO--(enl. ?)--260
Weber/Webber, Frances J.--NY--(enl. US)--188
Weber/Webber, Mary (Mrs. Francis J.)--??--188
Webler, George A.--NY--(enl. IL)--260
Webster, Albert I.--IL--(enl. IL)--188
Webster, Andrew B.--Park Co, IN--(enl. IN)--260
Webster, Anna Bartlett (Mrs. John O.)--??--188
Webster, Calvin R.--Newark, NJ--(enl. NJ)--188
Webster, Francis E.--(enl. US)--188
Webster, John O.--ME--(enl. ME)--188
Webster, Sylvia A. (Mrs. Albert I.)--??--188
Weeger, Erastus Henry--Williamsburg, Canada--
    (enl. CA)--188
Weegar, Mary Ann (Mrs. Erastus H.)--Troy,
    NY--188
Welch, James--(enl. US)--189
Wellington, Edwin W.--NY--(enl. PA)--189
Wellington, Mary E. (Mrs. Edwin W.)--
    American--189
Wells, Alpheno W.--American--(enl. VT)--189
Wells, Homer L.--IA--(enl. OH)--189
Wells, James W.--OH--(enl. OH)--260
Wells, Leonard Bates--(enl. IL)--189
Wells, Susan (Mrs. Leonard B.)--??--189
Welsh, Elias R.--OH--(enl. OH)--260
Werth, F.A.--Germany--(enl. MI)--260
Wescott, Lowrey--PA--(enl. WI)--260
West, Joseph G.--American--(enl. IL)--189
Weston, Charles D.--American--(enl. ME)--189
Weston, Mary (Mrs. Charles D.)--??--189
Wheaton, William H.--ME--(enl. ME)--261
Wheeler, Lyman--MA--(enl. MA)--189
Wheeler, Mary E. (Mrs. Lyman)--??--189
Whims, Joshua K.--PA--(enl. ?)--189
Whipple, Charles--NY--(enl. WI)--189
Whipple, Dotba (Mrs. Charles?)--??--190
Whipple, Georgia (Lord) (Mrs. S.G.)--??--190
Whipple, S.G./Stephen Girard?--RI--(enl. CA)--190
White, Asa G.--American--(enl. IA)--190
White, John C.--IL--(enl. CA)--261
White, Martha B. Keyes (Mrs. Asa G.)--American--190
White, Nicander--Highland Co, OH--(enl. OH)--190
White, William I.--OH--(enl. IL)--261
White, William Othe--Adams Co, IN--(enl. IN)--261
Whiteley, Clay--OH--(enl. OH)--261
Whitlock, Mina Elizabeth L. (Mrs. Sidney W.)--
    American--190
Whitlock, Sidney Winder--(enl. MO)--190
Whitman, Winfield S.--New Albany, IN--(enl. IN)--261
Whitney, A.E.--ME--(enl. ME)--261
Whitney, Henry H.--NY--(enl. NY)--261
Whitney, Willard J.--Wyoming, PA--(enl. PA)--261
Whitson, John--IN--(enl. IA)--261
Whittier, John F.--ME--(enl. ME)--261
Wiard, Augustus J.--PA--(enl. WI)--190
Wiard, Mary J. (Mrs. Augustus J.)--??--190
Wickard, Phillip J.--Stark Co, OH--(enl. OH)--261
Wiggins, Francis C.--(enl. OH)--190
Wiggins, Lucy J. (Mrs. Francis C.)--NY--190
Wilber, Henry J.--??--261
Wilcox, David Elias--Mt. Pleasant, Wayne Co, PA
    --(enl. PA)--190
Wilder, Nathaniel--OH--(enl. OH)--261
Wiley, Genevieve (Mrs. George O.)--??--191
Wiley, George O.--MA--(enl. MA)--191
Wilkins/Williams, Blair--OH--(enl. OH)--261
Wilkins, George A.--Ireland--(enl. IL)--191
Willey, George C.--NH--(enl. US)--262
Willey, John Alexander--Knox Co, IL--(enl. IL)--191
Willey, Norris M.--American--(enl. MA)--191
Williams, Abraham--Coles Co, IL--(enl. MN)--262
Williams, Albert J.--OH--(enl. IA)--262
Williams, Charles H.--NY--(enl. MA)--191
Williams, Clarence J.--NY--(enl. KS)--191
Williams, George W.--New Market, NH--(enl. MA)--262
Williams, Henry H.--NY--(enl. KS)--191
Williams, James--KY?--(enl. NY)--191

www.ingramcontent.com/pod-product-compliance
Lightning Source LLC
Chambersburg PA
CBHW080534300426
44111CB00017B/2716